PENGUIN

VISHNU PURANA

Bibek Debroy is a renowned economist, scholar and translator. He has worked in universities, research institutes, the industry and for the government. He has widely published books, papers and articles on economics. As a translator, he is best known for his magnificent rendition of the Mahabharata in ten volumes, the three-volume translation of the Valmiki Ramayana and additionally the *Harivamsha*, published to wide acclaim by Penguin Classics. He is also the author of *Sarama and Her Children*, which splices his interest in Hinduism with his love for dogs.

PRAISE FOR THE BHAGAVATA PURANA

'An exhaustive but accessible translation of a crucial mythological text'—*Indian Express*

'The beauty of recounting these stories lies in the manner in which the cosmic significance and the temporal implications are intermingled. Debroy's easy translation makes that experience even more sublime' —*Business Standard*

'The Puranas are 18 volumes with more than four lakh *shloka*s, and all in Sanskrit—the language of our ancestors and the sages, which only a few can speak and read today and only a handful have the mastery to translate. Bibek Debroy is one such master translator, who wears the twin title of economist and Sanskrit scholar, doing equal justice to both'—*Outlook*

PRAISE FOR THE MARKANDEYA PURANA

'[The] "Markandeya Purana" is a marvelous amalgam of mythology and metaphysics that unfolds a series of conversations in which sage

Markandeya is asked to answer some deeper questions raised by the events in the Mahabharata'—*The Indian Express*

'Bibek Debroy's translation of the Markandeya Purana presents the English reader with an opportunity to read the unabridged version in English. As he writes in the Introduction, *"But all said and done, there is no substitute to reading these texts in the original Sanskrit."* If you cannot read the original in Sanskrit, this is perhaps the next best thing'—Abhinav Agarwal

VISHNU PURANA

Translated by Bibek Debroy

PENGUIN BOOKS

An imprint of Penguin Random House

PENGUIN BOOKS

USA | Canada | UK | Ireland | Australia
New Zealand | India | South Africa | China | Singapore

Penguin Books is part of the Penguin Random House group of companies
whose addresses can be found at global.penguinrandomhouse.com

Published by Penguin Random House India Pvt. Ltd
4th Floor, Capital Tower 1, MG Road,
Gurugram 122 002, Haryana, India

Penguin
Random House
India

First published in Penguin Books by Penguin Random House India 2022

Translation copyright © Bibek Debroy 2022

10 9 8 7 6 5 4 3 2

The views and opinions expressed in this book are the author's own and the
facts are as reported by him which have been verified to the extent possible,
and the publishers are not in any way liable for the same.

ISBN 9780143456865

Typeset in Sabon by Manipal Technologies Limited, Manipal

Printed at Repro India Limited

www.penguin.co.in

MIX
Paper from
responsible sources
FSC® C047271

For Preeti and Sanjiv Goenka

Contents

Contents

Acknowledgements

The corpus of the Puranas is huge—in scope, coverage and size. The Mahabharata is believed to contain 100,000 *shloka*s. The Critical Edition of the Mahabharata, edited and published by the Bhandarkar Oriental Research Institute (Pune), doesn't have quite that many. But no matter, this gives us some idea of the size. To comprehend what 100,000 *shloka*s mean in a standard word count, the ten-volume unabridged translation I did of the Mahabharata amounts to a staggering 2.5 million words. After composing the Mahabharata, Krishna Dvaipayana Vedavyasa composed the eighteen Maha-Puranas, or major Puranas. So the belief goes. Collectively, these eighteen Puranas amount to 400,000 *shloka*s, translating into a disconcerting and daunting number of 10 million words.

After translating the Bhagavad Gita, the Mahabharata, the Harivamsha (160,00 words) and the Valmiki Ramayana (500,000 words), it was but natural to turn one's attention to translating the Puranas. (All these translations have been, and will be, published by Penguin India.) This is the formidable Purana Project. Treading the path of the Purana Project must not have been an intimidating one only for me. Penguin India must also have thought about it several times, before going ahead with the Purana translations. Most people have some idea about the Ramayana and the Mahabharata. But the

Puranas are typically rendered in such dumbed-down versions that the market must be created to find readers. And not all Puranas are as familiar as the Bhagavata Purana. However, Penguin India also believed in the Purana Project, which still stretches into some interminable horizon in the future, some fifteen years down the line. For both author (translator) and publisher, this is a long-term commitment. I am indebted to Penguin India for believing in the Project. In particular, Meru Gokhale, Ambar Sahil Chatterjee, Tarini Uppal and Rea Mukherjee have been exceptionally patient, persevering and encouraging. But for them, the Purana Project might not have taken off. These Purana translations have been brought alive by wonderful cover designs and illustrations. Thank you, Shamanthi Rajasingham. You are also part of the brand now.

The earlier Purana translations did well and were favourably received. The Bhagavata Purana (3 volumes, 500,000 words) was the first, followed by the Markandeya Purana (1 volume, 175,000 words). The pandemic affected most people and institutions adversely and publication schedules went for a toss. After a brief hiatus, publication resumed with the Brahma Purana (2 volumes, 390,000 words). This is the Vishnu Purana, in one volume, with 175,000 words. The Shiva Purana will follow. In any listing of major Puranas, the Vishnu Purana will find a prominent place. The first unabridged translation of any Purana in English was that of the Vishnu Purana, by Horace Hayman Wilson, in the second half of the 1860s (see also the Introduction to this volume). Along with the Bhagavad Gita and Bhagavata Purana, the Vishnu Purana has had a major role to play in the development of Vaishnava *dharma*. Yet, compared to the other Puranas, the Vishnu Purana is lean and thin, shorter in length. The other Puranas are like veritable encyclopaedias. The Vishnu Purana sticks to the core template of five subjects (described in the Introduction) that any Purana must cover and doesn't dilate and digress beyond. This was probably because this was one of the earlier Puranas, while in subsequent Puranas the originals were embellished.

In addition to the standard subjects, the Vishnu Purana recounts stories of Vishnu's ten *avatara*s, especially Krishna. Having visited so many temples to Vishnu, the Vishnu Purana almost chose itself as the next Purana to be translated. In *Pandava Gita* (also known as *Prapanna Gita*), there is an oft-quoted statement, attributed to Duryodhana. Part of this reads, केनापि देवेन हृदिस्थितेन यथा नियुक्तोऽस्मि तथा करोमि॥ 'There is a divinity who is established in my heart. I do whatever he engages me in.' Indeed. Any mention of Vishnu's *avatara*s reminds me of the poet Jayadeva's *Geeta Govindam*, *Dasavatara-stotram* and the *ashtapadi*s. Ever since this translation journey started in 2006, my wife, Suparna Banerjee Debroy, has been a constant source of support, ensuring the conducive and propitious environment for the work to continue unimpeded. Without her, the work of translation would have been impossible. A particular *ashtapadi* from the *Geeta Govindam* (number 19) is one of my favourites. Hence, for Suparna, त्वमसि मम भूषणं त्वमसि मम जीवनं त्वमसि मम भवजलधिरत्नम्। भवतु भवतीह मयि सततमनुरोधिनी तत्र मम हृदयमतियत्नम्॥

This translation of the Vishnu Purana is dedicated to our dear friends Preeti Goenka and Sanjiv Goenka. This is not only a tribute to this wonderful and extraordinary couple; it is also a tribute to the memory of RPG (Rama Prasad Goenka). Years ago, when I used to visit RPG in his Prithviraj Road house, I used to admire a beautiful image of Sarasvati. That Sarasvati statute has now moved to Kolkata and Preeti and Sanjiv take good care of it. In our own respective ways, we serve the same goddess.

Bibek Debroy
Delhi, March 2022

Introduction

The word 'Purana' means old, ancient. The Puranas are old texts, usually referred to in conjunction with Itihasa (the Ramayana and the Mahabharata).[1] Whether Itihasa originally meant only the Mahabharata, with the Ramayana being added to that expression later, is a proposition on which there has been some discussion. But that's not relevant for our purposes. In the Chandogya Upanishad, there is an instance of the sage Narada approaching the sage Sanatkumara for instruction. Asked about what he already knows, Narada says he knows Itihasa and Purana, the fifth *Veda*.[2] In other words, Itihasa–Purana possessed an elevated status. This by no means implies that the word 'Purana', as used in these two Upanishads and other texts too, is to be understood in the sense of the word being applied to a set of texts known as the Puranas today. The Valmiki Ramayana is believed to have been composed by Valmiki and the Mahabharata by Krishna Dvaipayana Vedavyasa. After composing the Mahabharata, Krishna Dvaipayana Vedavyasa is believed to have composed the Puranas. The use of the word 'composed' immediately indicates that Itihasa–Purana are *smriti* texts, with a human origin. They are not *shruti* texts,

[1] For example, *shloka*s 2.4.10, 4.1.2 and 4.5.11 of the Brihadaranyaka Upanishad use the two expressions together.
[2] Chandogya Upanishad, 7.1.2.

with a divine origin. Composition does not mean these texts were rendered into writing. Instead, there was a process of oral transmission, with inevitable noise in the transmission and distribution process. Writing came much later.

Pargiter's book on the Puranas is still one of the best introductions to this corpus.[3] To explain the composition and transmission process, one can do no better than to quote him.

> The Vayu and Padma Puranas tell us how ancient genealogies, tales and ballads were preserved, namely, by the *suta*s,[4] and they describe the *suta*'s duty . . . The Vayu, Brahmanda and Visnu give an account, how the original Purana came into existence . . . Those three Puranas say—Krsna Dvaipayana divided the single Veda into four and arranged them, and so was called Vyasa. He entrusted them to his four disciples, one to each, namely Paila, Vaisampayana, Jaimini and Sumantu. Then with tales, anecdotes, songs and lore that had come down from the ages he compiled a Purana, and taught it and the Itihasa to his fifth disciple, the *suta* Romaharshana or Lomaharshana . . . After that he composed the Mahabharata. The epic itself implies that the Purana preceded it . . . As explained above, the *suta*s had from remote times preserved the genealogies of gods, rishis and kings, and traditions and ballads about celebrated men, that is, exactly the material— tales, songs and ancient lore—out of which the Purana was constructed. Whether or not Vyasa composed the original Purana or superintended its compilation, is immaterial for the present purpose . . . After the original Purana was composed, by Vyasa as is said, his disciple Romaharshana taught it to his son Ugrasravas, and Ugrasravas the sauti

---

[3] *Ancient Indian Historical Tradition*, F. E. Pargiter, Oxford University Press, London, 1922.
[4] *Suta*s were bards, minstrels, raconteurs.

appears as the reciter in some of the present Puranas; and the sutas still retained the right to recite it for their livelihood. But, as stated above, Romaharshana taught it to his six disciples, at least five of whom were brahmans. It thus passed into the hands of brahmans, and their appropriation and development of it increased in the course of time, as the Purana grew into many Puranas, as Sanskrit learning became peculiarly the province of the brahmans, and as new and frankly sectarian Puranas were composed.

Pargiter cited reasons for his belief that the Mahabharata was composed before the original Purana, though that runs contrary to the popular perception about the Mahabharata having been composed before the Puranas. That popular and linear perception is too simplistic, since texts evolved in parallel, not necessarily sequentially.

In popular perception, Krishna Dvaipayana Vedavyasa composed the Mahabharata. He then composed the Puranas. Alternatively, he composed an original core Purana text, which has been lost, and others embellished it through additions. The adjective 'Purana', meaning old account or old text, became a proper noun, signifying a specific text. To be classified as a Purana, a text has to possess five attributes—*pancha lakshmana*. That is, five topics must be discussed: *sarga, pratisarga, vamsha, manvantara* and *vamshanucharita*. The clearest statement of this is in the Matsya Purana. Unlike the Ramayana and the Mahabharata, there is no Critical Edition of the Puranas.[5] Therefore, citing chapter and verse from a Purana text is somewhat more difficult, since verse, if not chapter, may

---

[5] The Critical Edition of the Valmiki Ramayana was brought out by the Baroda Oriental Institute, now part of Maharaja Sayajirao University of Baroda. The Critical Edition of the Mahabharata was brought out by the Bhandarkar Oriental Research Institute, Pune.

vary from text to text. With that caveat, the relevant *shloka* (verse) should be in the 53rd chapter of the Matysa Purana. *Sarga* means the original or primary creation. The converse of *sarga* is universal destruction, or *pralaya*. That period of *sarga* lasts for one of Brahma's days, known as *kalpa*. When Brahma sleeps, during his night, there is universal destruction.

In measuring time, there is the notion of a *yuga* (era) and there are four *yugas*: *satya yuga* (also known as *krita yuga*), *treta yuga*, *dvapara yuga* and *kali yuga*. *Satya yuga* lasts for 4,000 years, *treta yuga* for 3,000 years, *dvapara yuga* for 2,000 years and *kali yuga* for 1,000 years. However, all these are not human years. The gods have a different timescale and these are the years of the gods. As one progressively moves from *satya yuga* to *kali yuga*, *dharma* (virtue) declines. But at the end of *kali yuga*, the cycle begins afresh, with *satya yuga*. An entire cycle, from *satya yuga* to *kali yuga*, is known as a *mahayuga* (great era). However, a *mahayuga* is not just 10,000 years. There is a further complication. At the beginning and the end of every *yuga*, there are some additional years. These additional years are 400 for *satya yuga*, 300 for *treta yuga*, 200 for *dvapara yuga* and 100 for *kali yuga*. A *mahayuga* thus has 12,000 years, adding years both at the beginning and at the end. One thousand *mahayuga*s make up one *kalpa* (eon), a single day for Brahma. A *kalpa* is also divided into 14 *manvantara*s, a *manvantara* being a period during which a Manu presides and rules over creation. Therefore, there are 71.4 *mahayuga*s in a *manvantara*. Our present *kalpa* is known as the Shveta Varaha Kalpa. Within that, six Manus have come and gone. Their names are (1) Svayambhuva Manu, (2) Svarochisha Manu, (3) Uttama Manu, (4) Tapasa Manu, (5) Raivata Manu and (6) Chakshusha Manu. The present Manu is known as Vaivasvata Manu. Vivasvat, also written as Vivasvan, is the name of Surya, the sun god. Vaivasvata Manu has that name because he is Surya's son. Not only do Manus change from one *manvantara* to another, so do the gods, the ruler of the gods and the seven great sages, known as the *saptarshi*s (seven *rishi*s). Indra is a title of the ruler of the gods. It is not a proper name. The present Indra is Purandara. However, in a different *manvantara*, someone else will hold the title. In the present seventh *manvantara*, known as Vaivasvata *manvantara*, there will also be 71.4 *mahayuga*s. We are in the 28th of these. Since a different Vedavyasa performs that task of classifying and collating the *Veda*s in every *mahayuga*, Krishna Dvaipayana Vedavyasa is the 28th in that series. Just so that it is clear, Vedavyasa isn't a proper name. It is a title conferred on someone who collates and classifies the *Veda*s. There have been 27 who have held the title of Vedavyasa before him and he is the 28th. His proper name is Krishna Dvaipayana, Krishna because he was dark and Dvaipayana because he was born on an *dvipa* (island). This gives us an idea of what the topic of *manvantara* is about. This still leaves *pratisarga, vamsha* and *vamshanucharita*. The two famous dynasties/lineages were the *survya vamsha* (solar dynasty) and *chandra vamsha* (lunar dynasty), and all the famous kings belonged to one or other of these two. *Vamshanucharita* is about these lineages and the conduct of these kings. There were the gods and *rishi*s (sages) too, not always born through a process of physical procreation. Their lineages are described under the heading of *vamsha*. Finally, within that cycle of primary creation and destruction, there are smaller and secondary cycles of creation and destruction. That's the domain of *pratisarga*. In greater or lesser degree, all the Puranas cover these five topics, some more than the others. The Purana which strictly adheres to this five-topic classification is the Vishnu Purana.

There are Puranas and Puranas. Some are known as Sthala Puranas, describing the greatness and sanctity of a specific geographical place. Some are known as Upa-Puranas, minor Puranas. The listing of Upa-Puranas has regional variations and there is no countrywide consensus about the list of Upa-Puranas, though it is often accepted that there are 18.

The Puranas we have in mind are known as Maha-Puranas, major Puranas. Henceforth, when we use the word Puranas, we mean Maha-Puranas. There is consensus that there are 18 Maha-Puranas, though it is not obvious that this has been the number right from the beginning. The names are mentioned in several of these texts, including a *shloka* that follows the *shloka* cited from the Matsya Purana. Thus, the 18 Puranas are (1) Agni (15,400); (2) Bhagavata (18,000); (3) Brahma (10,000); (4) Brahmanda (12,000); (5) Brahmavaivarta (18,000); (6) Garuda (19,000); (7) Kurma (17,000); (8) Linga (11,000); (9) Markandeya (9,000); (10) Matsya (14,000); (11) Narada (25,000); (12) Padma (55,000); (13) Shiva (24,000); (14) Skanda (81,100); (15) Vamana (10,000); (16) Varaha (24,000); (17) Vayu (24,000); and (18) Vishnu (23,000).

A few additional points about this list. First, the Harivamsha is sometimes loosely described as a Purana, but strictly speaking, it is not one. It is more like an addendum to the Mahabharata. Second, Bhavishya (14,500) is sometimes mentioned with Vayu excised from the list. However, the Vayu Purana exhibits many more Purana characteristics than the Bhavishya Purana does. There are references to a Bhavishyat Purana that existed, but that may not necessarily be the Bhavishya Purana as we know it today. That's true of some other Puranas too. Texts have been completely restructured hundreds of years later. Third, it is not just a question of the Bhavishya Purana and Vayu Purana. In the lists given in some Puranas, Vayu is part of the 18, but Agni is left out. In some others, Narasimha and Vayu are included, but Brahmanda and Garuda are not. Fourth, when a list is given, the order also indicates some notion of priority or importance. Since that varies from text to text, our listing is simply alphabetical, according to the English alphabet. The numbers within brackets indicate the number of *shloka*s each of these Puranas has or is believed to have. The range is from 10,000 in Brahma to a mammoth 81,100 in Skanda. The aggregate is a colossal 409,500 *shloka*s. To convey a rough idea of the order of magnitude, the Mahabharata has, or is believed to have, 100,000 *shloka*s. It's a bit difficult to convey the word count of a *shloka* , especially because Sanskrit words have a slightly different structure than English words do. However, as a very crude approximation, one *shloka* is roughly 20 words. Thus, 100,000 *shloka*s account for 2 million words and 400,000 *shloka*s, four times the size of the Mahabharata, which comes to 8 million words. There is a reason for using the expression 'is believed to have', as opposed to 'has'. Rendering into writing is of later vintage, and the initial process was one of oral transmission. In the process, many texts have been lost, or are retained in imperfect condition. This is true of texts in general and is also specifically true of Itihasa and Puranas. The Critical Edition of the Mahabharata, mentioned earlier, no longer possesses 100,000 *shloka*s. Including the Harivamsha, there are around 80,000 *shloka*s. The Critical Edition of the Mahabharata has of course deliberately excised some *shloka*s. For the Puranas, there is no counterpart of Critical Editions. However, whichever edition of the Puranas one chooses, the number of *shloka*s in that specific Purana will be fewer than the numbers given above. Either those many *shloka*s did not originally exist, or they have been lost. This is the right place to mention that a reading of the Puranas assumes a basic degree of familiarity with the Valmiki Ramayana and the Mahabharata, more the latter than the former. Without that familiarity, one will often fail to fully appreciate the context. More than a passing familiarity with the Bhagavad Gita, strictly speaking a part of the Mahabharata, helps.[6]

---

[6] The Bhagavad Gita translation was published in 2006 and reprinted in 2019, the translation of the Critical Edition of the Mahabharata in 10 volumes between 2010 and 2014 (with a box set in 2015) and the translation of the Critical Edition of the Valmiki Ramayana in 2017. The translations are by Bibek Debroy, and in each case, the publisher is Penguin.

Other than the five attributes, the Puranas have a considerable amount of information on geography and even geological changes (changes in courses of rivers) and astronomy. Therefore, those five attributes shouldn't suggest the Puranas have nothing more. They do, and they have therefore been described as encyclopaedias. Bharatavarsha is vast and heterogeneous, and each Purana may very well have originated in one particular part of the country. Accordingly, within that broad compass of an overall geographical description, the extent of geographical information varies from Purana to Purana. Some are more familiar with one part of the country than with another. Though not explicitly mentioned in the five attributes, the Puranas are also about pursuing *dharma, artha, kama* and *moksha,* the four objectives of human existence, and about the four *varna*s and the four *ashrama*s. The general understanding and practise of *dharma* is based much more on the Puranas than on the *Veda*s. Culture, notions of law, rituals, architecture and iconography are based on the Puranas. There is beautiful poetry too.

Perhaps one should mention that there are two ways in which these 18 Puranas are classified. The trinity has Brahma as the creator, Vishnu as the preserver and Shiva as the destroyer. Therefore, Puranas where creation themes feature prominently are identified with Brahma (Brahma, Brahmanda, Brahmavaivarta, Markandeya). Puranas where Vishnu features prominently are identified as Vaishnava Puranas (Bhagavata, Garuda, Kurma, Matysa, Narada, Padma, Vamana, Varaha, Vishnu). Puranas where Shiva features prominently are identified as Shaiva Puranas (Agni, Linga, Shiva, Skanda, Vayu). While there is a grain of truth in this, Brahma, Vishnu and Shiva are all important and all three feature in every Purana. Therefore, beyond the relative superiority of Vishnu vis-à-vis Shiva, the taxonomy probably doesn't serve much purpose. The second classification is even

more tenuous and is based on the three *gunas* of *sattva* (purity),
rajas (passion) and *tamas* (ignorance). For example, the Uttara
Khanda of the Padma Purana has a few *shlokas* along these
lines, recited by Shiva to Parvati. With a caveat similar to the
one mentioned earlier, this should be in the 236th chapter of
Uttara Khanda. According to this, the Puranas characterized
by *sattva* are Bhagavata, Garuda, Narada, Padma, Varaha and
Vishnu. Those characterized by *rajas* are Bhavishya, Brahma,
Brahmanda, Brahmavaivarta, Markandeya and Vamana.
Those characterized by *tamas* are Agni, Kurma, Linga, Matysa,
Skanda and Shiva.

Within a specific Purana text, there are earlier sections, as
well as later ones. That makes it difficult to date a Purana,
except as a range. Across Purana texts, there are older Puranas,
as well as later ones. Extremely speculatively, the dating will
be something like the following: (1) Agni (800–1100 CE); (2)
Bhagavata (500–1000 CE); (3) Brahma (700–1500 CE); (4)
Brahmanda (400–600 CE); (5) Brahmavaivarta (700–1500 CE);
(6) Garuda (800–1100 CE); (7) Kurma (600–900 CE); (8) Linga
(500–1000 CE); (9) Markandeya (250–700 CE); (10) Matsya
(200–500 CE); (11) Narada (900–1600 CE); (12) Padma (400–
1600 CE); (13) Shiva (1000–1400 CE); (14) Skanda (600–1200
CE); (15) Vamana (450–900 CE); (16) Varaha (1000–1200 CE);
(17) Vayu (350–550 CE); (18) Vishnu (300 BCE to 450 CE); and
(19) Bhavishya (500–1900 CE). Reiterating once again that
there is no great precision in these ranges, by this reckoning, the
Vishnu Purana is the oldest and some parts of the Bhavishya
Purana are as recent as the 19th century.

As mentioned earlier, there is no Critical Edition for the
Puranas. Therefore, one has to choose a Sanskrit text one
is going to translate from. If one is going to translate all the
Puranas, it is preferable, though not essential, that one opts
for a common source for all the Purana texts. In all the Purana
translations, as a common source, I have used, and will use,

the ones brought out by Nag Publishers, with funding from the
Ministry of Human Resource Development. It is no different for
the Vishnu Purana.[7] To the best of my knowledge, other than
this translation, there are only two unabridged translations of
the Vishnu Purana in English, by Horace Hayman Wilson and
by Manmatha Nath Dutt.[8] Both these translations date back
to the second half of the 19th century. Of the two, Manmatha
Nath Dutt based his translation on the Wilson translation.
Indeed, the subtitle of Manmatha Nath Dutt's translation read,
'Based on Professor H. H. Wilson's translation'. Therefore, of
the two, the Wilson translation is the primary one. For its day
and age, and even now, the Wilson translation was remarkable.

In the second half of the 19th century, the contribution
of Calcutta and Bengal towards preserving the Itihasa–Purana
legacy was also remarkable. Consider the following works:
(1) Kaliprasanna Singha's unabridged translation of the
Mahabharata in Bengali; (2) The Sanskrit and unabridged
Bengali translation of the Burdwan edition of the Mahabharata;
(3) The unabridged Bengali translation of the Mahabharata,
published by Pratap Chandra Roy; (4) The unabridged English
translation of the Valmiki Ramayana by William Carey
and Joshua Marshman; (5) Hemachandra Bhattacharya's
unabridged translation of the Valmiki Ramayana in Bengali;
(6) Ganga Prasad Mukhopadhyay's verse translation of the
Valmiki Ramayana; (7) Panchanan Tarkaratna's Sanskrit
editions and Bengali translations of Valmiki Ramayana,
Adhyatma Ramayana and several Puranas; (8) Unabridged
translations of the Mahabharata in English by Kisari Mohan

[7] *The Visnumahapuranam*, Nag Publishers, Delhi, 1985.
[8] *The Vishnu Purana: A System of Hindu Mythology and
Tradition*, Horace Hayman Wilson, Trubner & Company, London,
1864-1870, five volumes and *Vishnu Purana, English Translation*,
Manmatha Nath Dutt, H. C. Dass, Calcutta, 1896.

Ganguli and Manmatha Nath Dutt; (9) the Asiatic Society's[9] Bibliotheca Indica Sanskrit editions of Agni Purana, Brihad Dharma Purana, Brihad Naradiya Purana, Kurma Purana, Varaha Purana and Vayu Purana; and (10) F. E. Pargiter's unabridged English translation of Markandeya Purana. Though Wilson's translation wasn't part of the Bibliotheca Indica corpus, it was part of the same broad tradition. Wilson's work was almost certainly the first unabridged translation of any Purana into English, and the scholarship was remarkable.

An act of research and scholarship still needs to be undertaken, cross-referencing names, genealogies and incidents across Itihasa and Purana texts. Often, when the same incident is narrated in different Purana texts, there are differences in nuances and details. Since ours is a translation, we have deliberately refrained from undertaking such an exercise. But the Horace Hayman Wilson translation did seek to do that.

For some Puranas, the range of possible dates of composition, as indicated earlier, is narrow. Agni, Brahmanda, Garuda, Kurma, Matsya, Varaha, Vayu and Vishnu are examples. There is consensus, though not unanimity that the Vishnu Purana dates to between 300 BCE and 450 CE. There are two respects in which the Vishnu Purana differs from any of the other Puranas. First, we earlier referred to the five attributes that define a Purana. The Vishnu Purana is the only Purana text that faithfully adheres to these five topics. Other Purana texts cover these five topics, but add plenty of additional material, of the kinds mentioned earlier. The Vishnu Purana is disciplined and essentially adheres to these five topics. Second, the usual Purana chain of verbal transmission is from Vedavyasa to Lomaharshana and Lomaharshana to the sages. The Vishnu Purana is narrated by the sage Parashara

[9] Asiatic Society went through several name changes, but it can simply be called Asiatic Society.

to the sage Maitreya. Tradition states that the Vishnu Purana has 23,000 *shloka*s. None of the manuscripts of the Vishnu Purana, available today, have that many *shloka*s. Nor do the available manuscripts, or the commentaries of Shridhara, Vishnuchitta and Ratnagarbha, suggest that any *shloka*s are missing. Depending on the manuscript, there will be between 6,000 and 7,000 *shloka*s. The text we have followed has 6,403 *shloka*s, spread over 126 chapters. The text of the Vishnu Purana is also divided into six *amsha*s (parts). The text of the Sanskrit Vishnu Purana we have followed is almost the same as the one followed by Wilson, but not always identical. There are differences, but none of these is major. However, a discerning reader, who compares the two translations, will find that we have differed from the Wilson translation in interpreting some verses and words.

R. C. Hazra's dissertation is still one of the best introductions to the Purana corpus, for all the Puranas and not just the Vishnu Purana.[10]

> This is one of the most important of the extant Puranas . . .
> Thus, the date of composition of the Visnu Purana falls
> between the end of the first and the middle of the fourth
> century A.D . . . Of all the extant Puranas, the Visnu has
> preserved the best text. Additions and alterations have
> been made in it much less freely than in the other Puranas.
> Consequently, the great majority of the verses quoted in the
> commentaries and Nibandhas[11] from the 'Visnu Purana' or
> 'Vaisnava' occur in the present Visnu and agree very closely
> in readings with those of the Purana . . . It was perhaps

[10] *Studies in the Puranic Records on Hindu Rites and Customs*, R. C. Hazra, University of Dacca, 1940. This has since been reprinted several times, by different publishers.

[11] Literally, essays.

the great fame and popularity of the Visnu Purana that encourages the composition of a spurious work of the same title and extent as those of the Visnu at a time earlier than the beginning of the twelfth century A.D. As no Manuscripts of this spurious work have been found as yet, it seems to have been lost.

One gets the idea, and it is obvious that the Vishnu Purana is one of the major Puranas.

A quote from Wilson's preface[12] will add to what has already been said.

The translation of the Vishnu Purana has been made from a collation of various manuscripts in my possession. I had three, whence I commenced the work; two in the Devanagari, and one in the Bengali, character. A fourth, from the West of India, was given to me by Major Jervis, when some progress had been made; and, in conducting the latter half of the translation through the press, I have compared it with three other copies in the library of the East India Company . . . In the notes which I have added to the translation, I have been desirous, chiefly, of comparing the statements of the text with those of other Puranas, and pointing out the circumstances in which they differ or agree; so as to render the present publication a sort of concordance to the whole; as it is not very probable that many of them will be published or translated.

As has been mentioned, there is no intention of converting this translation into anything resembling a concordance. True, very few Puranas have not been translated. But since they are being translated, a concordance is premature. Incidentally, Wilson

[12] Op. cit.

mentioned the commentaries of Shridhara Yati or Shridhara Swami, Ratnagarbha Bhattacharya and Chitsukha Yogi.[13]

In all Puranas, there are chapters that are almost verbatim reproductions of sections from the Mahabharata, Harivamsha and other Puranas. One should not deduce that a specific Purana text has copied from another, since these various texts might have had a common origin. That apart, even when the *shloka*s seem to be virtually identical, there are interesting changes in words and nuances.

In the translations of the Bhagavad Gita, the Mahabharata, the Harivamsha, the Valmiki Ramayana, the Bhagavata Purana and the Markandeya Purana,[14] we followed the principle of not using diacritical marks. The use of diacritical marks (effectively the international alphabet of Sanskrit transliteration) makes the pronunciation and rendering more accurate, but also tends to put off readers who are less academically inclined. Since diacritical marks are not being used, there exists the challenge of rendering Sanskrit names in English. Sanskrit is a phonetic language and we have used that principle as a basis. Applied consistently, this means that words are rendered in ways that may seem unfamiliar. Hence, Gautama will appear as Goutama here. This is true of proper names, and, in a few rare cases, of geographical names. The absence of diacritical marks causes some minor problems. How does one distinguish Vasudeva Krishna from Krishna's father, Vasudeva? Often, the context will make the difference clear. If not, we have included the son as 'Vaasudeva' and the father as 'Vasudeva'. The attempt has been to provide a word for word translation; so that if one were to hold up the Sanskrit text, there would be a perfect match. In the process, the English is not as smooth as it might have been,

[13] Vishnuchitta.

[14] *The Bhagavata Purana*, Volumes 1–3, Penguin Books, 2018. *The Markandeya Purana*, Penguin Books, 2019.

deliberately so. In this particular translation, we have also been pedantic, perhaps unnecessarily so. For example, the text refers to Parashara as both 'Shri Parashara' and 'Parashara' and refers to Maitreya as both 'Shri Maitreya' and 'Maitreya'. We have strictly adhered to whatever the text says, word for word. There was another minor issue one should flag. In most texts, chapters have headings. If chapters don't have headings, the colophon at the end of the chapter indicates what the heading or title of the chapter should be. The Vishnu Purana text has no such chapter headings before the chapter, or in the colophon. Therefore, the chapter headings we have given are subjective, based on the contents of that particular chapter.

The intention is to offer a translation, not an interpretation. That sounds like a simple principle to adopt, and for the most part, is easy to follow. However, there is a thin line dividing translation and interpretation. In some instances, it is impossible to translate without bringing in a little bit of interpretation. Inevitably, interpretation is subjective. We have tried to minimize the problem by (a) reducing interpretation; (b) relegating interpretation to footnotes; and (c) when there are alternative interpretations, pointing this out to the reader through those footnotes.

But all said and done, there is no substitute to reading these texts in the original Sanskrit. To the average person, the name of the Vishnu Purana may not be as familiar as that of the Bhagavata Purana or the Markandeya Purana, but it is an important Purana. Therefore, it is worth reading and translating.

Part I

Chapter 1(1) (Maitreya Questions Parashara)

Shri Suta[1] said, 'Oum! The supreme sage, Parashara, had completed his morning rites. Maitreya[2] prostrated himself before him and honouring him, asked him.'

Maitreya said, 'O *guru*! From you, in due order, I have studied all the *Veda*s and all the *Vedanga*s[3] and texts about *dharma*. O best among sages! Through your favours, others, even if they are generally those who hate me, will not say that I have not made efforts regarding the sacred texts. O one who knows about *dharma*! O immensely fortunate one! O *brahmana*! I now wish to know the truth about this universe: how it was, how it is and how it will be, what pervades the universe, and about mobile and immobile objects. What was it immersed in? How will it be destroyed? What are the dimensions of the elements? How did the gods and others originate? What is the location of the oceans and the mountains? O supreme among sages! What is the foundation of the earth, the sun and other things? What are their dimensions? What are the lineages

---

[1] *Suta*s were bards and raconteurs. Lomaharshana, also known as Romaharshana, means the body hair standing up. This may mean the *suta*'s body hair stands up. But it is usually taken to mean that his accounts made the body hair of listeners stand up. Lomaharshana was Vedavyasa's disciple and Vedavyasa taught him the Puranas. *Suta* is used as a proper name for Lomaharshana. In the process of transmission, when the sages conducted a sacrifice in Naimisha forest, Suta Lomaharshana was the one who recounted all the Puranas to them, though the Vishnu Purana is primarily in the form of a dialogue between Maitreya and Parashara.

[2] Maitreya was Parashara's disciple.

[3] *Vedanga* means a branch of the *Veda*s, and these were six kinds of learning that were essential to understand the *Veda*s—*shiksha* (phonetics), *kalpa* (rituals), *vyakarana* (grammar), *nirukta* (etymology), *chhanda* (metre) and *jyotisha* (astronomy).

of the gods and others? Who are the Manus? What are the
*manvantara*s? What are the *kalpa*s and how are the *kalpa*s
divided? How have the four *yuga*s been devised? What is the
nature of the end of a *kalpa*? What is the *dharma* of all the
*yuga*s? O great sage! What is the conduct of gods, *rishi*s and
lords of the earth? After Vyasa collated the *Veda*s, how were
they divided into branches? What is *dharma* for *brahmana*s
and others and for those who reside in different *ashrama*s?
O descendant of Vasishtha's lineage! I wish to hear the truth
about all this. O *brahmana*! O great sage! Be favourably
inclined towards me, so that through your favours, I get to
know everything that my mind desires.'

Shri Parashara replied, 'O Maitreya! O one who knows
about *dharma*! This is praiseworthy. You have reminded
me of what the illustrious Vasishtha, my father's father, had
said a long time ago. I heard that in ancient times, my father
had been devoured by a *rakshasa*, who had been egged on by
Vishvamitra.[4] O Maitreya! I was filled with unmatched rage
and started a sacrifice to destroy *rakshasa*s. In that sacrifice,
hundreds of roamers in the night[5] were reduced to ashes.
When the remaining *rakshasa*s were about to be destroyed,
my immensely fortunate grandfather, Vasishtha, spoke to
me. "O son![6] Enough of this anger. Conquer your rage. The
*rakshasa*s did not commit a crime. Your father's death was
ordained. It is fools who become angry. Those who are learned
do not. O son! Who kills? Through what is killing done?
Everyone enjoys the consequences of what he has himself

---

[4] The story is narrated in the Mahabharata. Vasishtha's son was
Shakti. Shakti cursed a king to become a *rakshasa*. In the form of a
rakshasa, the king (Kalmashapada) devoured Shakti.

[5] *Rakshasa*s roam around in the night.

[6] The word used is *tata*. This means son but is used for anyone
younger or junior.

done. O child! With a great deal of effort, men accumulate
a store of fame and austerities. Anger destroys these. In the
world hereafter, it prevents heaven and emancipation. O son!
Therefore, the supreme *rishi*s say that one must always avoid
anger. Do not come under its subjugation. Enough of burning
down the roamers in the night. They are distressed and have
not committed a crime. End this sacrifice. The virtuous have
the trait of forgiveness." Thus instructed by my great-souled
father,[7] I honoured his words and immediately stopped the
sacrifice. The illustrious Vasishtha, supreme among sages, was
pleased at this. At that time, Pulastya, Brahma's son, arrived at
the spot.[8] My grandfather offered him *arghya* and he accepted a
seat.[9] O Maitreya! Pulaha's immensely fortunate elder brother
spoke to me. Pulastya said, "Though there was great enmity,
you have listened to your senior's words and have resorted to
forgiveness now. Therefore, you will get to know all the sacred
texts. Though you were angry, you refrained from destroying
my offspring. O immensely fortunate one! Therefore, I will
bestow another great boon on you. O child! You will become
the creator of a Purana compilation.[10] You will comprehend
the supreme and true nature of the gods. O child! Whether
you are engaged in *pravritti* or *nivritti karma*,[11] through my
favours, your intelligence will be unblemished and without any
doubts." After this, the illustrious Vasishtha, my grandfather,

---

[7] The word used is again *tata*. This means father but is also used
for anyone older or senior. In addition, when Shakti died, Vasishtha
brought Parashara up, like his son.

[8] Pulastya was born through Brahma's mental powers. So was
Pulaha. Pulastya is also the ancestor of the *rakshasa*s.

[9] A guest is offer *padya* (water to wash the feet), *achamaniya*
(water to rinse the mouth), *arghya* (a gift) and *asana* (a seat).

[10] That is, Purana *samhita*.

[11] *Pravritti* is action with a desire for the fruits, whereas *nivritti* is
action without a desire for the fruits.

spoke to me. "Everything that Pulastya has said will happen."
This is what Vasishtha and the intelligent Pulastya said
earlier. Because of your questions, I have remembered it all.
O Maitreya! I will tell you everything that you have asked me
about. Hear accurately about the complete Purana *samhita*.
The universe originated from Vishnu and is established in him.
He is the cause behind its preservation and withdrawal. He is
the entire universe.'

Chapter 1(2) (Vishnu and Creation)

Shri Parashara said, 'He is without transformation. He is
pure. He is eternal. He is the *paramatman*. He is always
in a single form. He is Vishnu. He is the one who is victorious
over everyone. I prostrate myself before Hiranyagarbha,[12] Hari
and Shankara. He is the cause behind creation, preservation
and destruction. I bow down to Vasudeva, the one who makes
one cross over.[13] He is absolute, but he has many forms. I bow
down to the one who is both subtle and not subtle, the one who
is manifest and also unmanifest. He is Vishnu, the cause behind
emancipation. He is the cause behind the creation, preservation
and destruction of the universe. He pervades the universe. I
bow down to Vishnu, the *paramatman*, the cause. He is the
foundation of the universe. He is smaller than the smallest. He
is the one who should be worshipped. He is in all beings. He is
Achyuta Purushottama. His nature is *jnana*.[14] He is extremely
sparkling. He is the supreme objective. Though this is his true
nature, his form is also established in false insights. He is

[12] Brahma.
[13] The ocean of *samsara*.
[14] Knowledge.

Vishnu. He is the one who devours the universe. He is the lord behind creation and preservation. He is the one who should be worshipped. He is the lord of the universe. He is without birth. He is everlasting. He is without decay.'

'I will tell you what the illustrious grandfather, born from the lotus,[15] said earlier, when he was asked by Daksha and other supreme sages. On the banks of the Narmada, they repeated this to King Purukutsa. He told Sarasvata and Sarasvata told me. He is supreme. He is greater than the most supreme. He is the *paramatman*, established in his own *atman*. He cannot be indicated through form, complexion and other things. He is beyond any adjectives. He is devoid of decay. He is devoid of destruction. He is devoid of transformation and birth. He is the single cause. Who is capable of speaking about him? He is everywhere. Everything resides in him. That is the reason he is known, and read about, as Vasudeva.[16] He is the supreme *brahman*. He is eternal. He is without birth, without decline and without decay. He is always in a single form. He lacks in nothing. He is sparkling. Everything manifest and unmanifest exists in his form. He exists in the form of Purusha. He is established in the form of Kala. O *brahmana*! Purusha was the first form of the *brahman*. There were two other forms, manifest and unmanifest.[17] The form of Kala came next. He is superior to the forms of Pradhana, Purusha, the manifest[18] and Kala. The learned look on these as supreme forms of the pure Vishnu. In their respective portions, Pradhana, Purusha, the manifest and Kala are forms that are responsible for existence—creation, preservation and destruction. Vishnu is manifest. He is also unmanifest.

---

[15] That is, Brahma.
[16] Derived as someone who resides in (*vasati*) everything.
[17] Respectively, Prakriti and Pradhana.
[18] Prakriti.

He is Purusha and Kala. He plays like a child. Hear about his activities. Supreme *rishi*s speak of the unmanifest cause as Pradhana. Prakriti is subtle and has existence and non-existence[19] within it. It is without decay and has no other foundation. It is immeasurable. It is without decline. It is permanent. It is devoid of sound or touch and without form. It possesses the three *guna*s.[20] It is the origin of the universe. It is without a beginning. Everything that is created, dissolves into it. After the last destruction, everything was initially merged inside it. Those who are accomplished in what the *Veda*s say, those who are learned and controlled and know about the *brahman*, read about the origin of Pradhana in the following way. "There was no night or day. There was no sky or earth. There was no darkness or light. There was nothing else. There was only Pradhana, the *brahman* and Purusha. O *brahmana*! Those other two forms, Pradhana and Purusha, are Vishnu's own forms.[21] O *brahmana*! There is another form through which these two are connected or separated and that is known as Kala."[22] Everything manifest is established in Prakriti and the dissolution in which it is reabsorbed is known as *prakrita*.[23] O *brahmana*! The illustrious Kala is without a beginning and its end does not exist. The cycles of creation, preservation, destruction and restraint proceed intermittently.[24] There is equilibrium in the three *guna*s and

---

[19] Alternatively, cause and effect.

[20] *Sattva, rajas* and *tamas*.

[21] Vishnu being equated with the *brahman*.

[22] Kala is time. The quotation mark should end here, though that is not obvious.

[23] There are different levels of *pralaya* (dissolution). When the entire universe is dissolved into Prakriti, this is known as *prakrita pralaya*.

[24] Creation, preservation and destruction are attributes of Brahma's day, restraint refers to Brahma's night.

they exist separately in Purusha. O Maitreya! Kala whirls around, in the form of Vishnu. The *brahman* is superior to this. This is the *paramatman*, pervading the universe. This is Hari, who goes everywhere. He is the lord of all beings. He is the supreme lord who is in all *atman*s. Through his own will, he enters into Pradhana and Purusha. When the time for creation arrives, he agitates the permanent and the impermanent.[25] This is just like fragrance agitating the mind merely from its presence. In that way, Parameshvara[26] has no sense of ownership in doing anything. Purushottama, the *brahman*, is the one who agitates, and is also what is agitated. He is present in Pradhana, when it is contracted and when it is expanded.[27] In the process of expansion, Vishnu's own form is in the minutest of forms. The lord of all lords is in the forms of Brahma and the others. These are his manifest forms.'

'O sage! *Kshetrajna* is established in that equilibrium of the *guna*s.[28] O supreme among *brahmana*s! At the time of creation, there was a manifestation of these *guna*s. The great principle of Mahat[29] originated from Pradhana and is enveloped by the three, *sattva*, *rajas* and *tamas*.[30] Mahat was surrounded by the principle of Pradhana, like a seed is by its skin. From the principle of Mahat, originated the three kinds of *ahamkara*: *vaikarika*, *taijasa* and *tamasa*, responsible for

[25] Purusha is permanent, Pradhana is impermanent.
[26] The supreme lord.
[27] When contracted, there is equilibrium in the *guna*s. When expanded, there is disequilibrium.
[28] *Kshetra* (field) is the body. *Kshetrajna* is the one who knows the body, that is, the *atman*.
[29] Also known as *buddhi* (intellect).
[30] *Sattva* is the quality of purity, *rajas* is the quality of passion and *tamas* is the quality of darkness.

the elements.[31] O great sage! The three *guna*s are the cause
behind the subtle elements and the senses. Just as the manifest
Mahat was surrounded by Pradhana, Mahat was surrounded
by *ahamkara* and led to the creation of the *tanmatra* known
as sound.[32] When the *tanmatra* known as sound was created,
space, which has the attribute of sound, was created. Space
was pervaded by the *tanmatra* of sound. Thus energized, space
created the *tanmatra* of touch. The powerful wind resulted
from this, and it is held that the wind has the attribute of touch.
Space, with the *tanmatra* of sound, enveloped the *tanmatra* of
touch. Thus energized, wind created the *tanmatra* of form.
Form is said to be the attribute of light and this attribute of
form was thus created from the wind. The *tanmatra* of touch
and the *tanmatra* of form enveloped the wind. Thus energized,
light created the *tanmatra* of taste. Water, which is a store of
all the juices, was created from this. Water has the *tanmatra*
of taste and it was enveloped by the *tanmatra* of form. Thus
energized, water created the *tanmatra* of smell. It is held that
the quality of smell results from interaction between these. In
this way, the elements were based in their respective *tanmatra*s.
They are known by their *tanmatra*s. There was nothing but the
*tanmatra*s to distinguish them since they were undifferentiated.
They were not distinguished by characteristics of being serene,
terrible or confused. The *tanmatra*s of the elements were created
by *tamasa ahamkara*. Though the senses are *taijasa*, there are
ten *vaikarika* divinities who preside over these.[33] The mind is
the eleventh and these are said to be the *vaikarika* divinities.

[31] *Ahamkara* can imperfectly be translated as ego. *Vaikarika*
ahamkara is associated with *sattva*, *taijasa* with *rajas* and *tamasa* with
tamas.

[32] The *tanmatra*s are the subtle elements and senses.

[33] Presiding over ears, skins, eyes, tongue, nose, speech, hands,
feet, genital organs and anus.

O *brahmana*! The skin, the eyes, the nose, the tongue and the ears as the fifth were combined with intellect and led to the perception of sound and the others. O Maitreya! The anus, the genital organs, the hands, the feet and voice are said to lead to actions like excretion, generation, manipulation, movement and speaking. O *brahmana*! Space, air, fire,[34] water and earth progressively united with the attributes, sound and the others. They are said to be distinguished by the characteristics of being serene, terrible or confused. They possess their own separate kinds of powers. But until they were combined, they were incapable of creating subjects. With a view to creating, they approached each other. They interacted with each other and became dependent on each other. They united with each other and obtained all the signs of that specific union.'

'This happened when Purusha pervaded them and the unmanifest[35] showed its favours. Starting with Mahat and ending with the specific elements, an egg was created. Like a bubble in the water, it gradually increased in size. Created from the elements, this giant egg lay down in the water. In the form of Brahma, this was the natural and excellent abode of Vishnu. Though the lord of the universe has a form that is not manifest, he assumed a form that is manifest. It is Vishnu himself who was established in Brahma's form. Meru was the membrane that covered the embryo, and the great mountains were the outer skin of the embryo. The oceans were the fluid in the womb and the great-souled one[36] originated from this. O *brahmana*! Everything was inside this egg: mountains, *dvipas*,[37] oceans, stellar bodies, the aggregate of different worlds, gods, *asuras*, humans and the elements, water, air, fire, space and earth. The

[34] Synonymous with light.
[35] Prakriti.
[36] Brahma.
[37] Continents.

outside of this egg was covered by the ten characteristics, the
gross and the subtle elements. In addition, that expanse was
covered by Mahat. With Mahat, everything was also covered
by the unmanifest.[38] Indeed, that egg was covered by seven
forms of Prakriti.[39] This is like a coconut, with the seed inside
and a husk outside. Engaged in the creation of the universe,
Hari, the lord of the universe was himself there, assuming
rajas guna, in the form of Brahma. Across the *yuga*s, until the
kalpa ends, he creates and preserves. Vishnu possesses *sattva
guna* and his valour is immeasurable. At the end of the *kalpa*,
Janardana, in his form of Rudra, assumes *tamas guna*. O
Maitreya! In this extremely terrible form, he devours all beings.
Having devoured all beings and having converted the universe
into a single ocean, Parameshvara lies down, using the serpent
as a couch. When he wakes up, he assumes the form of Brahma
and creates again. To create, preserve and destroy, he assumes
the forms of Brahma, Vishnu and Shiva. Though these are the
designations, the illustrious Janardana is one. It is Vishnu who
himself creates. He is the one who preserves and protects. At
the time of destruction, the lord is himself the one who destroys
and withdraws. He is inside everything in the universe, earth,
water, fire, wind and space and all the senses. He is known as
Purusha. He is in the *atman*s of all beings. The universe is the
form of the one without decay. He is in all beings. He is the
cause behind creation, preservation and dissolution. He is what
is created. He is the creator. He is what is protected. He is the
protector. He assumes all the forms, Brahma and the others.
Vishnu is the greatest. He is the one who bestows boons. He is
the one who should be worshipped.'

[38] Prakriti.
[39] Corresponding to the seven principles mentioned earlier—the
five elements, Purusha and Mahat.

Chapter 1(3) (Units of Time)

Maitreya asked, 'Brahma is *nirguna*.[40] He is immeasurable. He is pure. His *atman* is without blemish. How can the agency of creation and other things be ascribed to him?'

Shri Parashara replied, 'All these powers and sentiments are unthinkable. They cannot be comprehended through knowledge. All these powers and sentiments, of creation and other things, exist in Brahma. This is like heat existing within fire, the best among those who scorch. Hear about how the illustrious Brahma, the grandfather of the worlds, known as the illustrious Narayana, went about the process of creation. Brahma is said to have been born. It should be known that this is how he always manifests himself. The measure of his own lifespan is said to be one hundred years. This is also known as *para* and half of that is spoken of as *parardha*. O unblemished one! I have already said that Kala is Vishnu's own form. O excellent one! Hear about how this is applied for his[41] duration and that of beings, mobile and immobile, the earth, the mountains, the oceans and everything else. O supreme among sages! Fifteen *nimeshas*[42] are a *kashtha*, thirty *kashtha*s are one *kala* and thirty *kala*s are said to be one *muhurta*. Thirty *muhurta*s are said to constitute a human day and night.[43] Thirty such days and nights constitute a month and there are two fortnights in a month. Six months amount to an *ayana* and there are two *ayana*s in a year, *dakshinayana* and

---

[40] Devoid of *gunas*.

[41] Brahma's.

[42] *Nimesha* is the time taken for the twinkling of the eye.

[43] Thus, a *muhurta* is a period of 48 minutes. It is usually said (not in this text) that 30 *kala*s are 1 *kshana* and 12 *kshana*s are 1 *muhurta*.

uttarayana.[44] *Dakshinayana* is night for *deva*s and *uttarayana* is their day. Twelve thousand divine years are described as *krita, treta* and the others. Hear from me about the division into the four *yuga*s. In due order, *krita* has four thousand, *treta* has three thousand, *dvapara* has two thousand and *kali* has one thousand divine years. Those who know about the ancient accounts have said this about the *yuga*s. However, that many hundreds of years precedes a *yuga* and is known as *sandhya*. There is an equal duration of *sandhyamsha* at the end of a *yuga*.[45] O excellent sage! The duration between a *sandhya* and a *sandhyamsha* is a *yuga*. An entire cycle of *krita*, *treta* and so on is known as a *mahayuga*. It consists of the four *yuga*s—*krita, treta, dvapara* and *kali*. O sage! One thousand such *mahayuga*s are spoken of as one of Brahma's days. O *brahmana*! In the course of one of Brahma's days, there are fourteen Manus. Hear about the consequences of this division of time. Within each *manvantara*,[46] the *saptarshi*s,[47] the gods, Shakra[48] and the kings who are Manu's sons are created and

---

[44] *Uttarayana* is the movement of the sun to the north of the equator, the period from the winter to the summer solstice. *Dakshinayana* is the movement of the sun to the south of the equator, the period from the summer to the winter solstice.

[45] *Sandhya/sandhyamsha* is the intervening period between one *yuga* and another. Usually, texts do not distinguish between *sandhya* and *sandhyamsha*. But here, *sandhya* is used for the preceding part and *sandhyamsha* for the succeeding part. *Krita yuga* thus has 400 years each as *sandhya* and *sandhyamsha*, *treta* has 300, *dvapara* has 200 and *kali* has 100. Hence, 2,000 years are added to 10,000.

[46] The period presided over by a Manu. There are 14 Manus in a *mahayuga* and 1,000 divided by 14 is 71.4.

[47] The *saptarshi*s are the seven great sages. The list varies, but the standard one is Marichi, Atri, Angira, Pulastya, Pulaha, Kratu and Vasishtha. In the sky, the *saptarshi*s are identified with the constellation of Ursa Major (Great Bear).

[48] That is, Indra.

destroyed. O excellent one! Compared to the measurement of
the four *yuga*s, there are more than seventy-one *manvantara*s,
the duration for a Manu, the gods and the others. O *brahmana*!
There are said to be more than 852,000 divine years in a
manvantara and more than 306,720,000 years of the mortals.[49]
O great sage! But this isn't complete since the aggregate is
a little more than this. O *brahmana*! Fourteen *manvantara*s
are said to be the duration of Brahma's day. When Brahma's
day ends, the dissolution known as *naimittika* takes place.
The three worlds, Bhuloka, Bhuvarloka and Svarloka, are
scorched.[50] Afflicted by the heat, the residents of Maharloka
leave for Janaloka. The three worlds become a single ocean.
When the three worlds have been withdrawn, Brahma, who is
Narayana's *atman*, sleeps on a couch that is the serpent. He is
the divinity, born from the lotus, whom the *yogi*s of Janaloka
meditate on. His night is of the same duration.[51] When this is
over, he creates again. Such is the duration of Brahma's year
and there are one hundred such years. The great-souled one's
lifespan is one hundred such years. O unblemished one! One
parardha of Brahma's life is over. At the end of this, there was
the great *kalpa* known as Padma.[52] O *brahmana*! The second
parardha is going on now and the first of the *kalpa*s is known
as Varaha *kalpa*.'

[49] 12,000 × 71 = 852,000. One day for the gods is 360 days for
humans. 852,000 × 360 = 306,720,000.
[50] *Bhuloka* is earth, *Svarloka* is heaven and *Bhuvarloka* is
the space in between the two. The seven worlds (*loka*s) above are
Bhuloka, Bhuvarloka, Svarloka, Maharloka, Satyaloka, Tapoloka
and Janaloka. The four upper worlds are not destroyed in the course
of *naimittika* dissolution.
[51] One thousand *mahayuga*s.
[52] *Kalpa* has multiple meanings. Here, it means one of Brahma's
days and therefore, a cycle of creation.

Chapter 1(4) (Varaha Saves the Earth)

Shri Maitreya said, 'O great sage! Please tell me how the illustrious Brahma, known as Narayana, created all beings at the beginning of the *kalpa*.'

Shri Parashara replied, 'The illustrious Brahma has Narayana in his *atman*. He is the divinity and lord who is Prajapati. Hear from me about how he created beings. At the end of the last *kalpa*, when night was over, the lord awoke. Brahma, full of *sattva*, saw that the worlds were empty. The supreme Narayana cannot be thought of. He is the supreme lord. He is the illustrious one who is without a beginning. In the form of Brahma, he created everything. That is the reason a *shloka* is cited about Narayana. In the form of Brahma, he is the imperishable divinity who created the universe. The waters are known as Naara because the waters are the offspring of Nara. Since they were his first *ayana*, he is spoken of as Narayana.[53] The entire universe was a single ocean of water and he discerned that the earth was submerged in the water. Inferring this, Prajapati wished to act so as to save it. He assumed another form, as he had done at the beginning of a *kalpa* earlier, assuming the forms of a fish, a tortoise and other things.[54] He assumed the form of Varaha. In this form, the *Veda*s, the sacrifices and the entire universe was inside him. He was established there, stable in his *atman*. He is in all *atman*s. He is Prajapati, the *paramatman*. Sanaka and the other siddhas had left for Janaloka and they praised him.[55] The one who holds up the earth, the one who holds up all *atman*s, entered

[53] That is, Naarayana. *Ayana* means motion or progress. Since he lay down in the water (*naara*), he is known as Naarayana.

[54] The Matsya and Kurma incarnations. Varaha is a boar.

[55] These were sages who were born through Brahma's mental powers: Sanaka, Sananda, Sanatana and Sanatkumara.

the water. The goddess Vasundhara had gone to the region of Patala.[56] She saw him and faithfully prostrated herself.'

'She bowed down and praised him. Shri Prithivi said, "O Pundarikaksha![57] O one who holds the conch shell, the *chakra* and the mace! Just as I have been raised up by you earlier, please raise me up from here now. O Janardana! I have been saved by you earlier. I am pervaded by you. This is true of all other beings too, the earth and all the other things. I bow down to the *paramatman*. I bow down to Purusha. You are Pradhana and you are the one who is manifest.[58] Kala is your form. I prostrate myself before you. You are the creator of all beings. You are the preserver and the destroyer. You are the lord of creation and everything else. You assume the forms of Brahma, Vishnu and Rudra. You are the one who devours everything and reduces the universe to a single ocean. O Govinda! You alone are the one left after that. You are the one the learned think about. No one knows the truth about your supreme nature. The residents of heaven worship your forms as an *avatara*.[59] Those who desire emancipation worship you as the supreme *brahman* and proceed towards emancipation. Without worshipping Vasudeva, who can obtain emancipation? Everything that can be grasped by the mind, everything that can be perceived by the eyes and other senses, everything that can be ascertained by the intellect—all these are your forms. I am nothing but you. I am held up by you. You have created me. I seek refuge with

---

[56] Just as there are seven upper worlds, there are seven nether worlds: Atala, Vitala, Sutala, Rasatala, Talatala, Mahatala and Patala. But Patala is also used as a general term for all nether regions. Vasundhara (the one who holds riches) and Prithivi are the earth's names.

[57] One with eyes like a lotus.

[58] Prakriti.

[59] Incarnation.

you. That is the reason the worlds refer to me as Madhavi.[60]
Victory to the one who is full of every kind of *jnana*. Victory
to the one who is steadfast. Victory to the one who does not
decay. Victory to the infinite one. Victory to the one who is
not manifest. Victory to the lord who is in everything that is
manifest. Victory to the one whose *atman* has cause and effect.
Victory to the one whose *atman* is the universe. O unblemished
one! Victory to the one who is the lord of sacrifices. You are
the sacrifice. You are *vashatkara*.[61] You are Omkara. You are
the sacrificial fire. You are the *Veda*s. You are the *Vedanga*s.
O Hari! You are the lord of sacrifices. You are the sun and
others, the planets, the stars and the *nakshatra*s.[62] You are the
universe. O Purushottama! You are everything that has form
and everything that does not have form. You are everything
that is seen and everything that is not seen. O Parameshvara!
You are everything that has been spoken about by me and
everything that has not been spoken about by me. You are
all that. I bow down to you. I prostrate myself before you. I
repeatedly bow down before you." In this way, Prithivi praised
Dharanidhara.'[63]

'The illustrious one emitted a deep and rumbling roar, like
the sound of Sama hymns. The eyes of the gigantic Varaha
were like blooming lotuses. His gigantic body was like Mount
Nila, with a complexion like that of lotus leaves. He held the
earth up on his own tusks and raised her up from Rasatala.
As he raised her up, the breath from his mouth raised drops
of water and cleaned the immensely radiant ones, Sanandana

[60] Madhava's consort.

[61] *Vashatkara* is the exclamation '*vashat*' made at the time of
offering an oblation. *Omkara* is the sound of Oum.

[62] A *nakshatra* is not a star. It can also be a constellation. There
are 27 (alternatively 28) *nakshatra*s.

[63] The one who holds up (*dhara*) the earth (*dharani*).

and the other faultless sages, who had resorted to Janaloka.
The tips of his hooves marked Rasatala and with a roar, the
waters rushed in there. The self-controlled *siddha*s resided in
Janaloka and the wind from his breathing scattered them in
all directions. His body consisted of the *Veda*s. As the giant
Varaha seized the earth and rose up from the water and shook
his body, beads of water clung onto his wet flanks and the
tips of his body hair. The sages praised him. The *yogi*s and
those who resided in Janaloka, Sanandana and the others,
were satisfied and filled with great delight. They lowered their
shoulders before Dharanidhara, the one with firm and steady
eyes. "Victory to Keshava, the supreme lord of all lords. He is
the lord who holds the mace, the conch shell, the sword and
the *chakra*. You alone are the lord who is the cause behind
creation, preservation and destruction. There is no other state
that is superior to you. The *Veda*s are your feet. Your tusks
are the sacrificial stake. Your teeth are the sacrificial offerings.
Your mouth is the sacrificial altar. Your tongue is the sacrificial
fire. Your body hair is the *darbha* grass.[64] O lord! You are the
embodiment of the sacrifice. Your eyes are day and night. All
the great-souled ones, Brahma and the others, find refuge in
your head. O divinity! Your mane consists of all the *sukta*s.
Your nostrils are all the oblations. Your snout is the sacrificial
ladle. Your rumbling roar is the sound of the Sama hymns.
Your body is the sacrificial pavilion. The joints in your body
are the sacrificial rites. O divinity! The rites of *purta* and *ishta*
dharma are your ears.[65] You are the eternal and illustrious one.
Please show me your favours. You are the one who has covered

---

[64] Sacred sacrificial grass, *kusha* grass.
[65] *Ishta* is a sacrifice performed with a desired objective. Therefore,
it is voluntary. *Purta* is an act of civic works and is often interpreted as
mandatory.

the earth in your stride.[66] You are the one who is creation, preservation and destruction. The universe is your form. In the universe, you are known as Parameshvara. You are the lord of the conscious and the unconscious. Be pleased with us. You are resplendent, with the entire circle of the earth spread out on your tusks. It is as if you have submerged yourself in a pond filled with lotuses and have taken away some lotus leaves mixed with mud. O one unmatched in powers! Your body covers the space between heaven and earth. O lord! For the welfare of the universe, you are blazing, capable of pervading the entire universe. O lord of the universe! You alone are the supreme objective. There is no one other than you. Everything mobile and immobile is pervaded by your greatness, everything that is seen and not seen and everything that has form and does not have form. Your form represents *jnana*. *Yogi*s who are confused in their *jnana* perceive you only as the universe. But those with intellect perceive that your true nature is *jnana*, and that this universe is nothing but that.[67] Submerged in a flood of delusion, they are whirled around in their false vision. Those who possess *jnana* have pure consciousness. O Parameshvara! They perceive that your form as the universe is nothing but *jnana*. O one who is everything. Be pleased. O one who is in all *atman*s, in the non-existent and in everything in the universe. O immeasurable one! O one with eyes like a lotus! May you save the earth. O illustrious one! You are spoken of as a store of *sattva*. O Govinda! O one with eyes like a lotus! O lord of existence! May you save the earth. O one with eyes like a lotus! For the welfare of the universe, may your inclinations turn towards creation. We prostrate ourselves before you." In this way, the *paramatman*, who was holding up the earth, was praised. He quickly raised up the earth and place her on that

---

[66] An allusion to the Vamana incarnation.

[67] That is, you are not just an object of perception.

giant mass of water. The earth floated on that flood of water,
like a giant boat. The earth was spread out on that expanse and
did not sink. The illustrious Parameshvara, the one without
a beginning, levelled the earth. He made the appropriate
divisions of mountains on earth. The mountains on earth
were just as they used to be during the earlier creation before
everything was consumed. He is invincible in his powers. He
is invisible in his wishes, and he created. He divided the earth
into seven *dvipa*s, as it used to be. He then devised the four
*loka*s, just as they used to be earlier.[68] In the form of Brahma,
the divinity was then enveloped in *rajas*. The illustrious Hari,
with four faces, performed the act of creation.[69] But engaged
in the task of creating what needs to be created, he[70] was only
an instrument. With all the power of creation, Pradhana is the
cause. He is spoken of as the instrument. There is nothing else[71]
that is required. An object is already imbibed with its own
powers and the best among scorchers[72] only brings them out.'

Chapter 1(5) (Specifics of Creation)

Shri Maitreya asked, 'O *brahmana*! How did the divinity
Brahma create *deva*s, *rishi*s, ancestors, *danava*s, humans,

---

[68] *Bhuloka, Bhuvarloka* and *Svarloka* were destroyed and had
to be created. Interpretations take the fourth to be Maharloka, but
Maharloka is not supposed to be destroyed. So, the fourth *loka*
probably means the nether regions.

[69] Brahma has four faces. To create, Brahma had to resort to
rajas.

[70] Brahma.

[71] Other than Pradhana.

[72] Referring to Brahma. That is, Brahma is only an instrument for
creation and brings out these powers.

inferior species, trees and the residents of earth, the sky and the water? What were the qualities, natures and forms of those who created? Please tell me everything.'

Shri Parashara replied, 'O Maitreya! I will tell you how the divinity, the lord of everything, created *deva*s and other things. Control yourself well and listen. Earlier, at the beginning of the *kalpa*, he was thinking about creation. A creation that started with ignorance appeared and it was full of darkness. Five entities appeared from that great-souled one and they are known as *tamas, moha, mahamoha, tamisra* and *andha-tamisra*.[73] The creation he thought of was based on five things: lack of understanding, an inward-looking tendency, lack of illumination, lack of feeling and lack of movement. Since immoveable entities were created first, this is known as *mukhya sarga*.[74] Seeing that this was futile, he embarked on another creation. As he meditated, this creation followed a crooked course. Since the nature was crooked, this is known as *tiryaka-srota*.[75] These became known as animals. They are generally full of *tamas* and are ignorant. They do not possess learning. They lack discrimination. They follow perverse paths. They suffer the misfortune of having intercourse with their mothers and other such things. They take ignorance to be proper knowledge. They are proud that they possess true knowledge. They suffer from egotism. Smeared by this ego, they are full of pride. Because of this, they are insolent about their own

[73] Respectively, darkness (of ignorance), delusion, great delusion, severe darkness and blinding and severe darkness. These are respectively interpreted as ignorance, selfishness, attachment, hatred and fear of suffering.

[74] Literally, first creation.

[75] Literally, with a crooked flow. *Tiryaka-srota* is interpreted as beings that draw their nourishment from inside the body.

bodies. They suffer from twenty-eight kinds of defects.[76] They only associate with their own kind. Taking this to be full of *tamas*, he meditated again. The third creation was full of *sattva* and the flow was upwards. This is known as *urddhva-srota*.[77] They experience a lot of happiness and delight. They are not covered, either inside or outside. They shine, both inside and outside. This is known as *urddhva-srota* creation. This third creation is known as that of *deva*s, and he was satisfied with it. However, Brahma wasn't completely satisfied with this creation. He knew that *mukhya sarga* and the other creations had not quite been successful. Therefore, he meditated, and this resulted in an excellent and successful creation. This is because the one who meditates is always successful in his resolution. This successful creation had a downward flow and appeared from what is not manifest. Since the flow is downwards, this creation is known as *arvak-srota*.[78] They possess plenty of radiance,[79] but *tamas* and *rajas* predominate. Therefore, they suffer a lot and are repeatedly urged to act. They possess internal and external knowledge, and this was a successful creation. O best among sages! I have thus told you about six creations. The first *sarga* was Mahat, also known as the one in which Brahma was created. The second *sarga* is known as *bhuta sarga*. The *tanmatra*s were created in this. The third *sarga* is known as *vaikarika*. The senses were created in this. These were *Prakrita sarga*s, preceded by the origin of intellect. The fourth was *mukhya sarga*, a primary creation said to

[76] This is interpreted as 28 kinds of animals, 6 with single hooves, 9 with cloven hooves and 13 with claws/nails.

[77] Literally, with an upward flow. *Urddhva-srota* is interpreted as beings that draw their nourishment from outside the body. *Deva*s obtain their food from outside the body.

[78] Literally, downward flow. This is interpreted as humans, because for humans, food flows downwards.

[79] Meaning knowledge.

consist of immobile objects. The fifth was *tiryaka-srota*, said to be for inferior species. The sixth was *urddhva-srota*, said to be the creation of *deva*s. After this, the seventh was *arvak-srota*, the creation of human beings. The eighth was *anugraha sarga*, possessing qualities of *sattva* and *tamas*. Three are said to be *Prakrita sarga*s, while five are *vaikrita sarga*s.[80] The ninth, *koumara sarga*,[81] has elements of both *prakrita* and *vaikrita*. I have thus told you about Prajapati's nine *sarga*s. They are both *prakrita* and *vaikrita* and are the causes behind the origin of the universe. The lord of the universe created them. What else do you want to hear?'

Shri Maitreya said, 'O sage! You have told me about the creation of *deva*s and others briefly. O supreme among the best sages! From you, I wish to hear about this in detail.'

Shri Parashara replied, 'It is known that created beings are withdrawn at the time of destruction. However, they are not freed from the bonds of their earlier *karma*. When Brahma creates the four kinds of beings[82] in a different state, they are bound by these. When the thought of creation enters Brahma's mind, he creates the four categories of gods, *asura*s, ancestors and humans. Desiring to create, he fixed himself in his own *atman*. When Prajapati fixed himself in his *atman* in this way, he was enveloped by *tamas*. When he desired to create, the *asura*s first originated from his thigh. He then cast aside the body that was made out of the *tanmatra* of *tamas*. O Maitreya! Night was born from the body he cast aside. Wishing to create, he assumed another body and was delighted. O *brahmana*!

---

[80] *Prakrita sarga*s originated from Pradhana. Brahma was responsible for the five *vaikrita sarga*s.

[81] The birth, through Brahma's mental powers, of Sanaka, Sananda, Sanatana, Sanatkumara and Rudra.

[82] Gods, humans, animals and inanimate objects. But it can also mean gods, *asura*s, ancestors and humans.

Thereupon, the gods originated from Brahma's mouth, and they were full of *sattva*. Day was born from the body he cast aside, and it is generally full of *sattva*. That is the reason *asura*s are stronger during the night and gods during the day. He assumed another body, full of the *tanmatra* of *sattva*. Since he thought of himself as a father, the ancestors originated.[83] After creating the ancestors, the lord cast aside this body and *sandhya*, the intervening period between day and night, was created from this. He then assumed another body, full of the *tanmatra* of *rajas*. O supreme among *brahmana*s! Humans, full of excessive *rajas*, originated from this. Prajapati swiftly cast aside this body and *jyotsna*, the period just before *sandhya*, originated from this.[84] O Maitreya! That is the reason humans are strong when *jyotsna* arrives. In a similar way, ancestors are strong at the time of *sandhya*. Thus, *jyotsna*, night, day and *sandhya* were created from four of the lord Brahma's bodies and they possess different combinations of the three *guna*s. Desiring to create, Brahma assumed another body that was full of the *tanmatra* of *rajas*. Kshudha[85] originated from this. In the darkness, the illustrious one created beings full of hunger. They were malformed and bearded. As soon as they were born, they rushed towards the lord. Some of them said, "Not like this. Let him be saved."[86] Those who said this became *rakshasa*s. Others said, "Let us eat." Because they wanted to eat, they became

---

[83] *Pitri*s are ancestors/manes, and the word means father. Although the text does not explicitly say so, the ancestors originated from Brahma's side.

[84] *Sandhya* normally refers to both dawn and dusk. *Jyotsna* means moonlight. But here, *jyotsna* clearly means dawn and *sandhya* means dusk.

[85] Hunger.

[86] Some of the beings wanted to devour Brahma. Some said, '*rakshyatam*', meaning 'Let him be saved.' The word *raksha* means to save.

yakshas.[87] Witnessing such a disagreeable event, the hair on
the creator's head dried up. Some of the hair fell down from his
head, but hair grew on his head again. Snakes were born from
the hair that had fallen down and they are also known as *ahis.*[88]
The creator of the universe became angry. Fierce *bhutas*[89] were
born from this rage. They were tawny in complexion and ate
flesh. As he meditated, *gandharvas*[90] were instantly born from
his body. O *brahmana*! They were born when they drank his
speech. Therefore, they are *gandharvas*. Having created these,
the illustrious Brahma easily created others by invoking his
energy. Birds were created from his lifespan, sheep from his
breast and goats from his mouth. Cattle were created from
Prajapati's stomach and sides. Horses, elephants, *sharabhas*,
gavayas, deer, camels, mules and species like ranku deer were
born from his feet.[91] Herbs, roots and fruits originated from his
body hair. O supreme among *brahmanas*! At the beginning of
the *kalpa*, Brahma created plants and herbs. At the beginning of
treta yuga, he properly used them for sacrifices. Cattle, goats,
humans, sheep, horses, mules and donkeys were classified
as village *pashus.*[92] Hear about the ones regarded as wild—

[87] The word *yaksha* means to devour. But this is a forced meaning.
Jaksha means to devour. *Yaksha* means to revere/sacrifice.

[88] *Sarpas* are snakes. It is derived from the word for creeping
along. The hair fell down from the head and crept along. *Ahi* also
means snake. Throughout this translation, we will use the word
'snake' for *sarpa* and the word 'serpent' for *naga. Nagas* are a semi-
divine species.

[89] *Bhutas* are malignant demons.

[90] Celestial singers and musicians. Etymologically, the word
gandharva is derived from the word for song or verse and drinking.

[91] A *sharabha* is a mythical eight-legged creature that feeds on
lions. However, the word also means a young elephant or a camel.
Gavaya is a kind of ox.

[92] *Pashu* implies domesticated (village) animal. But *pashu* means
more than just animal. It is a word used for a sacrificial animal.

predatory creatures, those with cloven hooves, elephants and
monkeys. The birds were the fifth.[93] Aquatic animals were
the sixth and reptiles the seventh. From the mouth towards
the east, he created *gayatri*, the hymns of the *Rig Veda*, *trivrit
sama*, *rathantara* and the *agnishtoma* sacrifice.[94] From the
mouth towards the south, he created the hymns of the *Yajur
Veda*, the *trishtubh* metre, the fifteen *stomas*, *brihat sama* and
uktha.[95] From the mouth towards the west, he created the
Sama Veda hymns, the *jagati* metre, the seventeen *stomas*,[96]
the *vairupa* hymn and the *atiratra* sacrifice. From the mouth
towards the north, he created the twenty-one *Atharva Veda*
texts, the *aptoryama* sacrifice, the *anushtubh* metre and the
vairaj mantra. Inferior and superior creatures were created from
his body. After having first created gods, *asuras*, ancestors and
humans, Prajapati, the grandfather, again resolved to create.[97]
He created *yakshas*, *pishachas*, *gandharvas*, large numbers of
apsaras, humans, *kinnaras*, *rakshasas*, birds, domestic animals,
wild animals, deer, *nagas*, those that decay and those that
do not, those that are mobile and those that are not.[98] The
illustrious Brahma, the original lord and creator, created all

[93] The count seems to be (1) *rakshasas* and *yakshas*; (2) herbs and
plants; (3) domestic animals; and (4) animals. It might also be that
humans are being counted, instead of *rakshasas* and *yakshas*.

[94] *Gayatri* is a metre, *trivrit sama* is a hymn from the *Rig Veda*
and *rathantara* is a hymn from the *Sama Veda*.

[95] *Stomas* are hymns sung in *soma* sacrifices, *brihat sama* is a
mantra and *ukthas* are hymns from *Sama Veda*.

[96] There is a repetition of *stoma*.

[97] The word 'again' is not inconsistent. It is being used with
respect to the last *kalpa*, not with respect to what has already been
created in this *kalpa*.

[98] A *pishacha* is a demon that lives on the flesh of others. A
kinnara or *kimpurusha* belongs to semi-divine species, companions
of Kubera. The text uses the word *uraga*, which is another word for
naga.

these. Depending on the *karma* that they had performed in the
earlier cycle of creation, they are thus born again and again.
Whatever appealed to them and was thought of is thus reaped
in this creation—violence, non-violence, mildness, cruelty,
preference for *dharma*, preference for *adharma*, preference for
truth, preference for falsehood. The lord himself created this
addiction to the senses in the diverse bodies of beings and their
conduct is a function of these propensities. With the sounds of
the *Veda*s as the beginning, he created gods and many other
names and forms of beings in this visible universe.[99] He gave
names to the *rishi*s and determined their appropriate tasks.
These are stated in the *Veda*s and other *shruti* texts. In different
seasons, many different kinds of signs are seen. So, different
kinds of signs are seen at the beginning of a *yuga*. In this way,
at the beginning of the *kalpa*, he undertakes many different
kinds of creation. He possesses the desire and the capacity to
create and is urged by that capacity to create.'

Chapter 1(6) (*Dharma* of the *Varnas*)

Shri Maitreya said, 'You have spoken about *arvak-srota* for
humans. O *brahmana*! Please tell me in detail about this.
How did Brahma create it? How did Prajapati create the *varna*s
and their qualities? What tasks were indicated for *brahmana*s
and others? Please tell me.'

Shri Parashara replied, 'O best among *brahmana*s! Earlier,
when Brahma meditated on the truth and wished to create,
beings were born from his mouth, and they were full of *sattva*.
Others originated from Brahma's chest, and they were full
of *rajas*. Those who were created from the thighs were full

[99] The text uses the word Prapancha, meaning the visible universe.

of *rajas* and *tamas*. O best among *brahmana*s! There were
other subjects who were created from Brahma's feet, and they
were full of *tamas*. O best among *brahmana*s! All the four
*varna*s were created in this way, *brahmana*s from the mouth,
*kshatriya*s from the chest, *vaishya*s from the thighs and *shudra*s
from the feet.[100] Brahma created all of them for the purpose of
sacrifices. O immensely fortunate one! The four *varna*s are
excellent instruments for sacrifices. When *deva*s are invoked
through sacrifices, they shower down rain on their subjects.
O one who knows about *dharma*! For the sake of welfare,
men who are always devoted to their own *dharma* perform
sacrifices and invoke them there. O sage! Through such pure
action, virtuous men proceed along virtuous paths. Such men
obtain heaven or emancipation. O *brahmana*! Such men reach
their desired destinations. Brahma thus created subjects in
these four *varna*s. O best among sages! They possessed proper
faith and good conduct. They resided wherever they willed
and did not suffer from any kind of impediment. They were
pure in their hearts. They were pure and without blemish in
their deeds. Since their minds were pure, Hari resided in their
pure hearts. With their pure *jnana*, they could see his state,
described as a *bilva* tree.[101] There is a portion of Hari that is
described as Kala. It is terrible. It was still feeble but removed
a little bit of substance and made them descend into sin.[102]
From darkness and avarice, the seed of *adharma* originated.

[100] This is mentioned in the *Purusha sukta*. *Purusha sukta*, also
found in *Shukla Yajur Veda* and *Atharva Veda*, is hymn 10.90 of *Rig
Veda*.

[101] A *bilva* tree is a wood-apple tree. Oddly, interpretations ignore
this word.

[102] *Dharma* has four feet in *satya/krita yuga*, three in *treta*, two
in *dvapara* and one in *kali*. As one goes down the *yuga*s, *dharma*
progressively declines. What was described earlier was *satya yuga*.
The onset of *treta yuga* is being described now.

O Maitreya! Among subjects, this led to attachment and
other things, impediments towards success. They could no
longer obtain the success they had easily obtained earlier.
They used to possess the eight kinds of success, *rasollasa* and
the others.[103] As sin gained in strength, these declined. The
subjects were afflicted by grief and suffered from the opposite
kinds of sentiments.[104] They therefore constructed places of
refuge above,[105] in mountains and in water. These artificial
fortifications were surrounded by moats, walls and other
things. As appropriate, they constructed houses and cities.
O immensely intelligent one! This was done to overcome
impediments like heat and cold. Having thus countered
cold and other things, the subjects next devised a means of
subsistence. They used their hands and cultivated seventeen
kinds of grain. These are said to be *vrihi, yava, godhuma, anu,
tila, priyangu, kovidara, koradusha, tinaka, masha, mudga,
mashura, nishpava, kulatthaka, adhaka, chanaka* and *shana.*[106]
O sage! Earlier, these plants grew near villages. O sage! From
the village and from the forest, there are fourteen kinds of
plants that can be used in sacrifices. O sage! These are said to
be *vrihi, yava, masha, godhuma, chanaka, tila, priyangu* as the
seventh, *kulatthaka* as the eighth, *shyamaka, nivara, jartila,*

---

[103] These are (1) *rasollasa* (spontaneous generation of juices
within the body, without external nutrients); (2) *tripti* (contentment);
(3) *dharma*; (4) *tulyata* (similarity among beings); (5) *vishoka* (lack
of grief); (6) devotion to austerities, meditation and the *paramatman*;
(7) an ability to go wherever one wills; and (8) an ability to sleep
wherever and whenever one wants.

[104] Heat and cold, joy and misery, and so on.

[105] In trees.

[106] Respectively paddy, barley, wheat, millet, sesamum, saffron,
camel's foot, *matar dal*, fennel, *urad dal, moong dal, masoor dal,*
corn, fine pulse, *arhar dal*, chickpea and hemp.

gavedhuka, *venuyava* and *markataka*.[107] These are said to be
fourteen plants from the village and from the forest. They are
excellent for undertaking sacrifices and they also originate
from sacrifices. They, along with sacrifices, are the supreme
reason behind subjects existing. The wise, who know about
sacrifices and cause and effect, know this. O supreme among
sages! From one day to another day, sacrifices used to be held
for the welfare of men and the destruction of their sins. O
great sage! However, there were some in whose minds Kala
created drops of sin. As this increased, they not only did not
wish to undertake sacrifices but they also criticized what the
*Veda*s said, all the rites of sacrifices stated in the *Veda*s and
the expansion that resulted from the *Veda*s. These revilers
of the *Veda*s were responsible for deviation from the path of
pravritti. They were evil-souled and wicked in conduct. They
resorted to crooked means. To ensure success, Prajapati had
ensured means of subsistence for subjects. He had established
norms, according to the place and according to the qualities.
The supreme upholder had laid down *dharma* and *adharma*
for *varna*s and *ashrama*s. For those who observed the proper
dharma, he had indicated worlds for all the *varna*s. The region
of Prajapatya is said to be for *brahmana*s who follow the rites,
the region of Aindra for *kshatriya*s who do not retreat from the
field of battle, the region of Maruta for *vaishya*s who follow
their own *dharma* and the region of Gandharva for *shudra*s
who practice servitude. There are eighty-eight thousand sages
who hold up their seed. That place is earmarked for those who
reside with their *guru*s.[108] The place of the *saptarshi*s is said

---

[107] The first nine are from the village and the last five are wild.
Shyamaka and *markataka* are kinds of grain, *nivara* is wild paddy,
jartila is wild sesamum, *gavedhuka* is a species of grass and *venuyava*
is the seed of cane.
[108] Those in *brahmacharya*.

to be for those who reside in the forest.[109] Prajapatya is for those who reside as householders.[110] The place named after Brahma is for those who have renounced.[111] There are *yogis* who are always solitary, meditating on the *brahman*. There is an immortal place for such *yogis*, who find satisfaction in their own *atmans*. The gods cannot see this supreme region. Having gone there, one does not return.[112] The sun, the moon and the planets do not circle there. This region is for those who meditate on the twelve *akshara*s.[113] For those who criticize the *Veda*s and cause impediments to sacrifices, there are the hells Tamisra, Andha-Tamisra, Maha-Rourava, Rourava, the terrible Asipatravana, Kalasutra and Avichika.[114] These are described as the regions for those who give up their own *dharma*.'

Chapter 1(7) (More on Creation)

Shri Parashara continued, 'As the intelligent one continued to meditate, mental subjects were born from his body, along with what they were supposed to do and how they were going to do it. All their *atmans* also originated from his body. I

[109] Those in *vanaprastha*.
[110] Those in *garhasthya*.
[111] Those in *sannyasa*. This is identified as Satyaloka.
[112] One does not return.
[113] *Oum! namo bhagavate vasudevaya.* There are twelve *askhara*s (syllables) in this *mantra*.
[114] Tamisra means darkness, Andha-Tamisra is blinding darkness, Rourava makes one scream, Maha-Rourava makes one scream loudly, Asipatravana has a forest where the leaves are like swords, Kalasutra means the strand of time/destiny and Avichika means a place where there are no waves. Chapter 2(6) has more details on these hells.

have described all this to you earlier. There were gods, ending
with immobile objects, established in the three *guna*s. In this
way, mobile and immobile beings were created. However,
their numbers did not increase. Therefore, the intelligent one
created other mental sons and they were just like him. Bhrigu,
Pulastya, Pulaha, Kratu, Angiras, Marichi, Daksha, Atri and
Vasishtha—these were the nine born through Brahma's mental
powers and their names have been enumerated in the Puranas.
He created Khyati, Bhuti, Sambhuti, Kshama, Priti, Sannati,
Urjja, Anasuya and Prasuti. Having created them, he bestowed
them as wives on these great-souled ones. The creator had
earlier created Sanandana and the others. But they were not
interested in the world and were indifferent towards creating
subjects. All of them possessed *jnana*. They were devoid of
attachment and devoid of envy. Brahma, the great-souled
creator of the worlds, saw that they were indifferent and was
filled with great rage. He was capable of burning down the
three worlds. O sage! From Brahma's rage, a blazing garland
of flames erupted and pervaded all the three worlds. Blazing
in rage, his forehead was furrowed. Rudra emerged from this,
and his radiance was like that of the mid-day sun. His form
was half male and half female. He was fierce, with a gigantic
body. Brahma said, "Divide yourself" and vanished. As told,
he divided himself into two parts—male and female. He again
divided the male segment into eleven parts.[115] Some of them
were amiable. Others were not amiable. Some of them were
serene. Others were not serene. The lord then divided the
female segment into many parts. They were like his own form.
Some were fair and some were dark.'

'O *brahmana*! After this, the lord Brahma first created
Svayambhuva Manu from his own self, so that he could rule
over the subjects. He was just like his own self. He created the

---

[115] There are eleven Rudras.

woman Shatarupa. Austerities cleansed her of all sins. The lord
and god, Svayambhuva Manu, accepted her as his wife. The
goddess Shatarupa had two sons, Priyavrata and Uttanapada.
O one who knows about *dharma*! She had two daughters,
known as Prasuti and Akuti. They possessed beauty, generosity
and all the qualities. Earlier, he bestowed Prasuti on Daksha
and Akuti on Ruchi. Prajapati Ruchi accepted her, and she
gave birth to Yajna and Dakshina.[116] O immensely fortunate
one! These twins became a couple and had sons. Through
Dakshina, Yajna had twelve sons. These were known as the
Yamas. They were *deva*s during Svayambhuva *manvantara*.[117]
Through Prasuti, Daksha had twenty-four daughters. Listen
to all their names. They were Shraddha, Lakshmi, Dhriti,
Tushti, Medha, Pushti, Kriya, Buddhi, Lajja, Vapus, Shanti,
Siddhi and Kirtti. The lord Dharma accepted these thirteen
of Daksha's daughters as wives. There were another eleven
daughters who were younger. They possessed excellent eyes.
They were Khyati, Sati, Sambhuti, Smriti, Priti, Kshama,
Santati, Anasuya, Urja, Svaha and Svadha. O supreme
among sages! These daughters, Khyati and the others, were
respectively accepted as wives by the sages Bhrigu, Bhava,
Marichi, Angiras, Pulastya, Pulaha, the supreme *rishi* Kratu,
Atri, Vasishtha, Vahni[118] and the ancestors. Dharma's sons
were Kama through Shraddha,[119] Darpa through Chala,[120]
Niyama through Dhriti,[121] Santosha through Tushti,[122] Lobha

---

[116] These are personified forms of *yajna* (sacrifice) and *dakshina*
(fee/donation given at the time of a sacrifice).

[117] *Deva*s change from one *manvantara* to another.

[118] The fire god, Agni.

[119] Shraddha means faith and Kama means desire.

[120] Lakshmi means prosperity and Darpa means pride. The text
uses the word Chala (one who moves and is fickle) for Lakshmi.

[121] Dhriti means fortitude and Niyama means norm/restraint.

[122] Tushti means satisfaction and Santosha means contentment.

through Pushti,[123] Shruta through Medha,[124] Danda, Naya and Vinaya through Kriya,[125] Bodha through Buddhi,[126] Vinaya through Lajja,[127] Vyavasaya through Vapus,[128] Kshema through Shanti,[129] Sukha through Siddhi[130] and Yashas through Kirtti.[131] Through Rati, Kama had a son named Harsha and he was Dharma's grandson.[132] Himsa was Adharma's wife. Through her, he had a son named Anrita and a daughter named Nikriti.[133] Maya and Vedana were born through them.[134] Maya and Vedana were twins. Maya gave birth to Mrityu,[135] who takes away living beings. Through Rourava, Vedana had her own son, Duhkha.[136] Mrityu's children were Vyadhi, Jara, Shoka, Trishna and Krodha.[137] Duhkha and all others are said to possess the attributes of *adharma*. They did not have any wives or sons. All of them held up their seed. O son of an excellent sage! These are Vishnu's terrible forms. They always act so as to become causes for the dissolution of

[123] Pushti means nourishment and Lobha means greed.

[124] Medha means intelligence and Shruta means what has been heard, that is, the *shruti* texts.

[125] Kriya means rites. Danda means punishment/the rod of punishment, Naya means policy and Vinaya means humility.

[126] Buddhi means intellect and Bodha means understanding.

[127] Lajja means modesty. There were two different sons named Vinaya.

[128] Vapus means body and Vyavasaya means exertion.

[129] Shanti means peace and Kshema means comfort.

[130] Siddhi means success and Sukha means happiness.

[131] Kirtti means deeds and Yashas means fame.

[132] Rati means pleasure/attachment and Harsha means delight.

[133] Adharma was Brahma's son. Himsa means violence. Anrita means falsehood and Nikriti means perverse deeds.

[134] Maya means illusion and Vedana means pain.

[135] Death.

[136] Unhappiness.

[137] Vyadhi means ailment, Jara means old age, Shoka means sorrow, Trishna means thirst and Krodha means anger.

the universe. O immensely fortunate one! However, Daksha, Marichi, Atri, Bhrigu and the others are lords of subjects. They are always the causes behind the creation of the three worlds. Manu's sons are *manava*s. They are lords of the earth and full of valour. All of them are brave and adhere to the proper path. They are responsible for preservation.'

Shri Maitreya said, 'O *brahmana*! Please tell me about the nature of *nitya*[138] creation, *nitya* preservation and *nitya* destruction.'

Shri Parashara replied, 'The illustrious Madhusudana's *atman* cannot be thought of. In these forms,[139] he is the one who causes constant creation, preservation and destruction. O *brahmana*! For all beings, there are four kinds of dissolution: *naimittika*, *prakritika*, *atyantika* and *nitya*. Brahma or *naimittika* occurs when the lord of the universe sleeps.[140] *Prakritika* dissolution occurs when everything manifest merges into the cosmic egg. It is said that when *yogis* use *jnana* to merge into the *paramatman*, that is *atyantika*. Night and day, the constant destruction of beings is known as *nitya*. The creation that originates from Prakriti is known as *prakritika*. Every day, beings are said to be destroyed. O supreme among sages! Every day, beings are also born. Those who are accomplished in the meanings of the Puranas speak of this as *nitya* creation. In this way, the illustrious one, the creator of beings, is in all bodies. Established in this way, Vishnu brings about creation, preservation and destruction. His capacity to create, preserve and destroy exists in all bodies. O Maitreya! Day and night, all the time, Vishnu circulates in these. O *brahmana*! Anyone who transcends his three great potencies, based on the three

---

[138] *Nitya* means constant.
[139] Of Prajapatis and Manus.
[140] That is, during Brahma's night.

*guna*s, goes to the supreme destination and does not have to return again.'

Chapter 1(8) (Rudra's Account)

Shri Parashara continued, 'O great sage! I have told you about Brahma's *tamas* creation. I will now tell you about Rudra's creation. Listen attentively. At the beginning of the *kalpa*, the lord meditated on having a son who would be like his own self. A son manifested himself and he was red and blue[141] in complexion. O best among *brahmana*s! As soon as he appeared, he started to cry in a melodious voice. As he wept, Brahma asked him, "Why are you crying?" "Give me a name," was the reply. Prajapati answered, "O divinity! Your name will be Rudra. Be patient and do not cry." Thus addressed, he created seven other parts and wept again. Thereupon, the lord gave him seven other names. The lord bestowed abodes, wives and sons on these eight. O *brahmana*! Prajapati said, "You are Bhava, Sharva, Ishana, Pashupati, Bhima, Ugra and Mahadeva." He gave them names and places to reside in. In due order, the abodes were the sun, water, the earth, the fire, the wind, space, an initiated *brahmana* and the moon. In due order, their names were Suvarchala, Usha,[142] Vikeshi, Shiva, Svaha, Disha, Diksha and Rohini. O best among *brahmana*s! These were the abodes, the sun and others. These were the names, Rudra and others. O immensely fortunate one! Those were said to be their wives. Now hear about their offspring. Their sons and descendants filled the world. In due order, the sons were Shanaishchara, Shukra, Lohitanga, Manojava,

---

[141] Nilalohita.
[142] In other texts, Usha is replaced by Uma.

Skanda, Sarga, Santana and Budha. In this way, Rudra obtained the unblemished Sati as his wife. He married the daughter of Prajapati Daksha. Because of her anger with Daksha, Sati gave up her own body.[143] O supreme among *brahmana*s! She became the daughter of Himavat and Mena. In this form as Uma, the illustrious Hara married her again. Bhrigu's wife, Khyati, gave birth to the divinities Dhatri and Vidhatri and to Shri, the wife of Narayana, the god of the gods.'

Shri Maitreya asked, 'It is heard that Shri originated when the milky ocean was churned for the sake of *amrita*. How can you say that she was born from Bhrigu and Khyati?'

Shri Parashara replied, 'Vishnu's Shri is the mother of the universe. She is eternal and does not perish. O best among *brahmana*s! Like Vishnu, she goes everywhere. Vishnu is meaning, she is speech. Hari is restraint and she is good policy. Vishnu is understanding and she is intellect. Vishnu is *dharma* and she is virtuous rites. Vishnu is the creator and she is creation. Hari is the one who holds up the earth and Shri is the earth. The illustrious one is contentment and Lakshmi is satisfaction. O Maitreya! She is eternal. The illustrious one is desire and Shri is the wish. He is the sacrifice, and she is the *dakshina*. Janardana is the sacrificial cake, and the goddess is the oblation of *ghee*. O sage! During a sacrifice, Madhusudana is the front part[144] and Lakshmi is the place where the women stay. Hari is the sacrificial stake and Lakshmi is the sacrificial altar. The illustrious one is the *kusha* grass and Shri is the kindling. The illustrious one's nature is in the *Sama* hymns and the one who is seated on the lotus[145] is the chanting of the hymns. Jagannatha Vasudeva is the sacrificial fire and Lakshmi

[143] This is the story of Daksha's sacrifice.
[144] Where the men reside. This front part represents Madhusudana. The rear, where women reside, represents Lakshmi.
[145] Lakshmi is seated on a lotus.

is *svaha*.[146] O supreme among *brahmanas*! The illustrious Shouri is Shankara, and Lakshmi is Gouri.[147] O Maitreya! Keshava is the sun and the one who is seated on the lotus is its radiance. Vishnu is the large number of ancestors and Padma,[148] the one who provides eternal nourishment, is Svadha. Vishnu, who exists in all *atmans*, is the wide expanse of the firmament and Shri is the sky. Shridhara is Shashanka[149] and the imperishable Shri is its radiance. Hari is the wind that blows everywhere in the universe and Lakshmi is fortitude. O *brahmana*! O great sage! Govinda is the ocean and Shri is the shore. Madhusudana is Indra of the gods and Lakshmi's nature is in Indrani.[150] The one who holds the *chakra* is Yama and the one who is seated on the lotus is Dhumarna.[151] The divinity Shridhara is himself the lord of riches[152] and Shri is prosperity. O immensely fortunate one! Keshava is himself Varuna and Lakshmi is Gouri. O Indra among *brahmanas*! Hari is the commander of the gods and Shri is Devasena.[153] O best among *brahmanas*! The one who holds the mace in his hand is stupefaction and Lakshmi is the strength. He is *nimesha* and she is *kashtha*. He is *muhurta* and she is *kala*. Hari, the lord of all the lords, is the lamp and Lakshmi is the light. Vishnu is spoken of as the tree and Shri, the mother of the universe, is in the form of a creeper. The

---

[146] *Svaha* is the utterance made when oblations are offered to the gods, *svadha* is the utterance made when oblations are offered to the ancestors.

[147] Shouri is Vishnu, Shankara is Shiva and Gouri is Uma.

[148] The one seated on a lotus, Lakshmi's name.

[149] Shridhara (the one who holds Shri) is Vishnu's name, Shashanka is the moon.

[150] Indra's consort, Shachi.

[151] Yama's wife.

[152] Kubera.

[153] The commander/general of the gods is Kumara/Skanda/Kartikeya and his wife is Devasana (literally, the army of the gods).

divinity who holds the *chakra* and the mace is the day and Shri
is the night. Vishnu, supreme among those who bestow boons,
is the groom and the one who resides in a clump of lotuses is
the bride. The illustrious one's nature is in male rivers, and she
is established in the form of female rivers. Pundarikaksha[154]
is the standard and the one who is seated on a lotus is the
flag. The supreme Narayana Jagannatha is greed and Lakshmi
is thirst. O Maitreya! Govinda is attachment and Lakshmi is
pleasure. What is the need to speak moret? It can be stated
briefly. The illustrious Hari is all those known as males among
*deva*s, inferior species and humans. Shri is all those known as
females. Other than these two, there is nothing else.'

Chapter 1(9) (Story of Lakshmi)

Shri Parashara said, 'O Maitreya! Now listen to what you
had asked me about. I have heard about Shri's account from
Marichi. Born from Shankara's portion, Durvasa wandered
around the earth. In the hands of a *vidyadhari*,[155] the *rishi* saw a
divine garland made out of *santanaka*[156] flowers. O *brahmana*!
Its fragrance spread everywhere in the forest and enchanted
those who roamed around in the forest. He was then observing
the vow of behaving like a lunatic.[157] He saw that beautiful
garland and asked the *vidyadhara*'s beautiful wife for it. The
slender-limbed *vidyadhara* maiden was asked for the garland.

[154] The one with eyes like a lotus, Vishnu's name.

[155] *Vidyadhara*s are semi-divine species. *Vidyadhari* is the
feminine.

[156] *Santanaka* is one of the five divine trees in Indra's garden.

[157] A vow where a *yogi* pretends to be mad before the external
world.

The large-eyed one lovingly prostrated herself before him and gave it to him. He was in the form of a lunatic. O Maitreya! Having obtained it, he placed it on his head. The *brahmana* continued to roam around the earth. At this time, he saw the god who is the lord of the three worlds,[158] Shachi's consort, advancing. He was astride Airavata and the other gods were with him. Intoxicated bees were buzzing around the garland. As he advanced, the sage, who was pretending to be a lunatic, took the garland from his head and flung it towards the king of the immortals. The king of the immortals seized it and placed it on Airavata's head, where it was as radiant as Jahnavi[159] on the summit of Kailasa. Because of musth, the elephant's eyes were blinded, and it was attracted by the smell. It seized the garland with its trunk and flung it down on the ground. O supreme among sages! The illustrious Durvasa was enraged at this. O Maitreya! He angrily addressed the king of the gods in these words. Durvasa said, "O Vasava![160] You are wicked. Because of your rise in prosperity, you have become insolent. This garland is Shri's abode, and you did not appreciate its greatness. Despite the favour shown, you did not speak to me. You did not prostrate yourself before me. With eyes dilated in delight, you did not place it on your own head. I gave you the garland, but you did not show sufficient respect to it. O foolish one! Therefore, your prosperity over the three worlds will be destroyed. O Shakra! It is evident that you think that I am just like other *brahmana*s. Hence, you have shown me the due respect. You have flung the garland I gave you down on the ground. Your prosperity over the three worlds will be destroyed. All mobile and immobile entities dread the arousal of Lakshmi's wrath. But because you take yourself to be the

---

[158] Indra. Airavata is Indra's elephant.
[159] Ganga.
[160] Indra.

king of the gods, in your pride, you have slighted her and me."
The great Indra swiftly descended from astride the elephant. He
sought to placate the sage Durvasa, who was without blemishes.
He prostrated himself before him and sought to please him.
However, the sage Durvasa, supreme among sages, addressed
the one with one thousand eyes in these words. Durvasa said,
"I do not have any compassion in my heart. Nor do I forgive
those who worship me. O Shakra! That may be true of other
sages, but I am Durvasa. Goutama and the others have granted
you this insolence in vain.[161] Know me to be Durvasa. There
is no substance of forgiveness in me. O Shakra! Vasishtha and
the others possess no substance. Since they praised you, you are
full of pride and have shown me disrespect. Who in the three
worlds is not filled with fear when they see my face with a
brow furrowed in rage and surrounded by matted and blazing
hair? O Shatakratu![162] What is the need to speak a lot? I will
not pardon you, regardless of whether you repeatedly entreat
me now that you face this hardship." Having said this, the
brahmana left.'

'O *brahmana*! The king of the gods again mounted
Airavata and returned to Amaravati.[163] Since then, Shakra and
the three worlds were bereft of Shri. O Maitreya! All the herbs
and plants decayed and died. There were no sacrifices and
ascetics no longer performed austerities. The minds of people
no longer turned towards the *dharma* of donations. All the
worlds were devoid of spirit. The senses were overwhelmed
by avarice. O supreme among *brahmana*s! Trifling objects
came to be desired. Wherever there is Lakshmi, there is spirit.
When there is spirit, the elements follow. When there is no

---

[161] Goutama's wife, Ahalya, was violated by Indra, but Goutama
forgave Indra.

[162] Indra, the one who performed one hundred sacrifices.

[163] Indra's capital.

Shri, how can there be spirit? Without spirit, how can there be
qualities? Without qualities, strength and valour do not exist
among men. In the absence of strength and valour, everything
was transgressed. If a famous person is transgressed in this
way, everything that is his is destroyed. In this way, devoid of
Shri, the three worlds lost their spirit. The *daitya*s and *danava*s
made efforts to raise an army against *deva*s.[164] *Daitya*s were
devoid of Shri and overwhelmed by greed. They did not possess
any spirit. Nevertheless, *deva*s were also without spirit, and
they started a battle against them. The *daitya*s defeated the
residents of heaven. With Hutashana[165] leading the way, Indra
and the others went and sought refuge with the immensely
fortunate grandfather. *Deva*s told him all that happened. At
this, Brahma spoke to the gods. "Seek refuge with the one who
is the lord of the superior and the inferior. Go to the one who
is the afflicter of *asura*s. There is nothing that causes him. But
he is the lord who is the cause behind creation, preservation
and destruction. He is the lord of Prajapatis. He is Ananta
Vishnu, the unvanquished one. He is Pradhana and Purusha.
He cannot be defeated. For all beings, he is the instrument,
and he is the task. He is the one who dispels grief. Prostrate
yourselves before Vishnu. He will determine what is best for
you." Brahma, the grandfather of the worlds, told all the gods
this. Along with them, he went to the northern shores of the
ocean of milk.'

'Along with all the residents of heaven, Brahma went there.
Along with them, in desirable and eloquent words, he praised

[164] Danu and Diti were both married to the sage Kashyapa. The
sons of Diti were *daitya*s and the sons of Danu were *danava*s. *Daitya*s
and *danava*s were cousins, though the words are sometimes used
synonymously. Kashyapa also married Aditi and Aditi's sons were
*aditya*s, *deva*s or *sura*s. *Asura*s are the antithesis of *sura*s and equated
with *daitya*s/*danava*s.

[165] Agni's name, the one who partakes of oblations.

Hari, the lord of all that is superior and inferior. Brahma said, "I bow down before the one who is everything. You are the lord of everything. You are infinite. You are without origin and without decay. You are the refuge of the worlds. You are the one who holds up the earth. You are self-illuminated. You cannot be divided. O Narayana! You are smaller than the smallest. You are also greater than the greatest. Everything is in you. Beginning with me, everything originated from you. You are the divinity who is in all beings. You are superior to everything that is supreme. You are the Purusha who is superior to the supreme. You assume your own form as the *paramatman. Yogis* who desire emancipation think of you as the cause behind emancipation. *Sattva* and the others do not exist in you. You are the lord who does not possess the *gunas* of Prakriti. You are pure. You are in everything that is pure. May that being now be pleased with us. Your pure potency cannot be perceived through *kala, kashtha, muhurta* and other things that make up the strands of time. May that Vishnu be pleased with us. He is spoken of as the supreme lord. He is pure and does not need aid from anyone. Vishnu is in the *atman*s of all those with bodies. May he show us his favours. He is the instrument, and he is the task. He is the cause behind all causes.[166] He is the cause, and he is the effect. May that Hari be pleased with us. He is the cause behind what should be done and what should not be done. He is himself what should be done and what should not be done. Cause and effect are in him. We prostrate ourselves before him. He is the cause behind the cause. He is the primary cause, and he is the secondary cause. We prostrate ourselves before that supreme lord. He is the enjoyer, and he is what is enjoyed. He is the creator,

---

[166] All these verses have complicated interpretations. It doesn't seem necessary to bring them in, since a simple translation is clear enough.

and he is what is created. The task and the agent are both
his nature. We bow down before that supreme destination.
He is pure. He is understanding. He is eternal. He is without
origin. He is without decay. He is imperishable. He is without
manifestation. He is without transformation. He is Vishnu,
the supreme destination. He is not gross. He is not subtle. He
cannot be perceived through any adjectives. He is always the
sparkling destination that is Vishnu. We prostrate ourselves
before him. The universe depends on him. But the energy of the
universe is only a millionth part of his potency. It is his nature
that is the supreme *brahman*. We prostrate ourselves before
the one without decay. Vishnu is the supreme destination. He
is the unthinkable. *Yogis* constantly make efforts to exhaust
their good and bad merits and see him in the sound of Omkara.
But the gods, the sages, I or Shankara do not know him. He is
the supreme lord. He is Vishnu, the supreme destination. His
potency exists in *deva*s and in the *atman*s of Brahma, Vishnu
and Shiva. He is what will happen, and he is what has never
happened earlier. He is Vishnu, the supreme destination. He is
the lord of everything. He is in the *atman*s of every being. He
is everything. He is Achyuta.[167] He is the refuge for everything.
O Vishnu! Be pleased with your devotees. Please show yourself
to us." The residents of heaven heard what Brahma said. They
prostrated themselves and said, "Be pleased with us. Show
yourself to us. You are the illustrious one and even Brahma
does not know you, the supreme destination. O Achyuta!
You are the refuge of the universe and everything merges into
you." When Brahma and the *deva*s finished speaking, all the
*devarshi*s,[168] with Brihaspati at the forefront, spoke. "You
are the one who should be worshipped. In a sacrifice, you
are the one who is worshipped first. You existed before our

[167] One who does not decay.
[168] Divine *rishi*s.

ancestors. You are the creator who created the universe. You are without adjectives. You are the illustrious one, the lord of everything that has occurred and will occur. You are the one without decay. You are the one who assumes the form of the sacrifice. Be pleased. We are prostrating ourselves before you. Show yourself to all of us. Brahma is with us. The three-eyed one[169] is with us and so are the Rudras. Pusha is here, along with all the Adityas. Pavaka[170] is here, along with all the other fires. The two Ashvins[171] are here. All the Vasus are here, along with large numbers of Maruts. The Sadhyas and the Vishvadevas are here. Indra of the gods, our lord, is also here. O protector! Suffering, we have prostrated ourselves before you. We have been vanquished by the *daitya* soldiers. All the large number of gods have come to you for refuge." In this way, the illustrious one, who holds the conch shell and the *chakra*, was praised. O Maitreya! The supreme lord showed himself to them. All the gods saw the one who holds the conch shell, the *chakra* and the mace. He was in a form that had never been seen. He was a mass of resplendent energy. He is the one who should be worshipped. Agitated, all of them closed their eyes and prostrated themselves before him. With the grandfather at the forefront, they praised Pundarikaksha. The gods said, "We bow down before you. We bow down before the one who cannot be defined. You are Brahma. You are the one who wields Pinaka.[172] You are Indra, Agni, Pavana,[173] Savita,[174] Yama, the Vasus, the Maruts, the Sadhyas and the large number of Vishvadevas. O divinity! The large number of

---

[169] Shiva.
[170] Agni's name, meaning the one who purifies.
[171] Physicians of the gods.
[172] Pinaka is the name of Shiva's bow.
[173] The wind god, Vayu.
[174] Surya.

gods have come before you. You are the creator of the universe. You are the one who goes everywhere. You are the sacrifice. You are *vashatkara*. You are Omkara. You are Prajapati. You are learning. You are what should be known. You are in all *atman*s. You pervade everything in the universe. Those who are afflicted seek refuge with you. O Vishnu! Vanquished by the *daitya*s, we have come before you. You are in all *atman*s. Show us your favours. Please use your energy to assure us. Until you do that, there will be affliction and delusion. We seek happiness from you. Until one seeks refuge with you, that does not happen. You are the one who destroys all sins. Your *atman* is full of bliss. Please show your favours to those who have sought refuge with you. O protector! Use your energy and your strength to assure all of us." In this way, they prostrated themselves and praised him.'

'The illustrious Hari, the creator of the universe who is without a beginning, cast a favourable glance towards them. He said, "O gods! I will do that which enhances your strength. O gods! I will tell you what needs to be done. Act accordingly. For the sake of *amrita*, along with the *daitya*s, bring all kinds of herbs and fling them into the ocean of milk. Do this along with all the *daitya*s and *danava*s. Make Mandara the churning rod and make Vasuki the rope for churning. O gods! For the sake of *amrita*, do the churning and I will be there as your aide. To obtain the help of the *daitya*s in this task, address them in words of conciliation. Tell them that they will obtain an equal share in the fruits and that when the ocean is churned, they will obtain an equal share in the *amrita*. O immortals! When you drink that, you will become strong. O gods! I will act so that the enemies of the gods do not obtain any *amrita*. They will merely have a share in the exertions." Thus addressed by the lord of the gods, all the gods made an alliance with the *asura*s and made efforts to obtain *amrita*. The *deva*s, *daitya*s and *danava*s brought many kinds of herbs. They hurled these into the ocean of milk, with waters that were as sparkling as autumn clouds. They made Mandara the churning rod and Vasuki the rope used for churning. O Maitreya! For the sake of *amrita*, they quickly started to churn. Krishna ensured that all the assembled gods held Vasuki's tail, while all the *daitya*s were stationed at his head. As a result of his breathing, flames issued from his mouth and struck by that poison, they lost all their energy. However, all the gods became infinitely energetic. The clouds were driven away by the breath that issued from his mouth. They were scattered towards the tail, showering down rain and comforting the gods. In the midst of the ocean of milk, the illustrious Hari stationed himself in the form of a tortoise.[175] O great sage! In the course of churning, as it was rotated, the mountain was placed on him. In other forms, the one who holds the *chakra* and the mace was present amidst the gods. He was also there amidst the *daitya*s, helping to tug the king of the *naga*s.[176] In another large form, Keshava was also present in the mountain that was being rotated. O Maitreya! He was also there in forms that the gods and the *asura*s could not see. Hari was there, to imbibe energy into the king of the *naga*s. In other forms, the lord was there, to enhance the energy of the gods.'

'When the gods and the *danava*s churned the ocean of milk, Surabhi,[177] the store of oblations, worshipped by the gods, arose first. O great sage! On seeing her, the minds of the gods and the *danava*s were agitated and they closed their eyes. They asked, "What is this?" The Siddhas in the firmament also wondered about this. The goddess Varuni[178] appeared. Her eyes rolled around in intoxication. From the whirlpool in the

[175] That is, Kurma.
[176] Vasuki.
[177] The celestial cow.
[178] The goddess of the liquor.

ocean of milk arose the *parijata* tree, the delight of celestial
women. It filled the world with its fragrance. O Maitreya! The
large number of *apsara*s arose from the ocean of milk. They
possessed beauty, generosity and all the qualities. This was
extremely wonderful. The one with the cool beams[179] arose and
was accepted by Maheshvara. The poison that arose from the
ocean of milk was accepted by the *naga*s. The god Dhanvantari
himself arose. He was clad in white garments, and he held a
radiant *kamandalu*[180] that was full of *amrita*. O Maitreya!
The minds of all the *daitya*s and *danava*s were assured at this.
Along with the sages, all of them were delighted at this.'

'The goddess Shri next arose from the water, holding a
lotus in her hand. Her beauty was dazzling, and she was seated
on a full-blown lotus. Full of delight, the *maharshi*s used Shri-
sukta to praise her.[181] With Vishvavasu leading the way, the
*gandharva*s sang in front of her. With Ghritachi leading the
way, large numbers of *apsara*s danced. The waters of Ganga
and other rivers arrived, so as to bathe her. The *diggaja*s[182]
took sparkling water in golden vessels and bathed the goddess,
who is the divinity of all the worlds. The ocean of milk
assumed a personified form and presented her with a garland
made out of lotuses that do not fade. Vishvakarma adorned
her with ornaments. She was adorned with divine garlands and
ornaments. She was bathed and adorned with these ornaments.
While all the gods looked on, she took her place on Hari's
chest. O Maitreya! The gods saw Lakshmi on Hari's chest and

[179] The moon.

[180] Water-pot.

[181] Shri *sukta* is not a part of the *Rig Veda* but is mentioned
in addition to the *Rig Veda*. These are the verses that begin 'Om
hiranyavarnam harinim suvarnarajatastrajam'.

[182] There are four elephants that dwell in the four directions.
These are known as *diggaja*s, an elephant (*gaja*) for each direction
(*dik*).

were filled with a great sense of satisfaction. But since Vishnu turned himself away from them, the *daitya*s were filled with great anxiety. O immensely fortunate one! Lakshmi abandoned them, with Viprachitti as their chief. The immensely valiant *daitya*s seized the *kamandalu*, full of excellent *amrita*, from Dhanvantari's hand. However, assuming a feminine form, Vishnu used his *maya* to confound them. The lord took it away from the *danava*s and gave it to the *deva*s. The large number of gods, Shakra and the others, drank the *amrita*. The *daitya*s raised their weapons and advanced against the residents of heaven. However, having drunk *amrita*, the *deva*s were strong and slaughtered the *daitya*s, who fled in different directions and entered Patala. The *deva*s were filled with joy and prostrated themselves before the one who holds the conch shell, *chakra* and mace. As was the case earlier, they began to rule over heaven. Surya regained his radiance and proceeded along his own course. O supreme among sages! The stellar bodies also proceeded along their own courses. The illustrious Vibhavasu[183] blazed in his extensive radiance. The minds of all beings turned towards *dharma*. O supreme among *brahmana*s! The three worlds were united with Shri again. Shakra, the best among the residents of heaven, reclaimed his prosperity. Having got his throne back, Shakra returned to heaven again.'

'Instated in the kingdom of heaven, he praised the goddess who is seated on a lotus. Indra said, "I bow down before the mother of all the worlds, who originated from a lotus. She is Shri, with eyes like a blossoming lotus. She reclines on Vishnu's chest. Her abode is the lotus. She is in a clump of lotuses. Her eyes are like the petals of lotuses. I worship the goddess whose face is like a lotus, the one who loves the stamen of a lotus. You are Siddhi. You are Svadha and Svaha. You are Sudha.[184]

[183] Agni.
[184] Nectar.

You are the one who purifies the worlds. You are Sandhya.
You are the night. You are radiance, prosperity and intellect.
You are Sarasvati.[185] O beautiful one! You are the knowledge
of sacrifices. You are the great knowledge. You are the secret
knowledge. You are the knowledge of the *atman*. You are
the goddess who bestows the fruit of emancipation. You are
reasoning. You are the three *Veda*s. You are the means of
subsistence. You are the policy of chastisement.[186] O goddess!
In forms that are amiable and not amiable, you are the one who
fills up the universe. The one who holds the mace is the lord
of the gods and *yogi*s meditate on him. His body pervades the
sacrifice. Other than you, who is capable of reclining on him?
All the three worlds were abandoned by you. They were almost
destroyed, but you have now made them fortunate again. O
immensely fortunate one! When you glance favourably towards
them, men always obtain wives, sons, houses, well-wishers,
grain, wealth and other things. O goddess! If men do not see
your favourable glances, it is extremely difficult for them to
obtain healthy bodies, prosperity, the destruction of enemies
and happiness. You are the mother of all the worlds, just as
Hari, the lord of the gods, is the father. O mother! You and
Vishnu pervade this universe, with its mobile and immobile
objects. O one who purifies everything! Do not forsake our
treasury, our cattle pens, our homes, our garments, our bodies
or our wives. O one who makes an abode on the chest of
Vishnu, my god! Do not forsake my sons, all my well-wishers,
my animals or my ornaments. O unblemished one! When you
forsake men, spirit, truth, purity, good conduct and other
qualities instantly abandon them. When you glance favourably
towards them, they instantly obtain good conduct and the
other qualities. Even if a man does not possess any qualities, his

[185] The goddess of speech.
[186] *Dandaniti.*

lineage obtains prosperity. O goddess! If you glance favourably towards a person, he becomes praiseworthy. He possesses the qualities and is blessed. He is born in a noble lineage and is intelligent. He becomes brave and valiant. O mother of the universe! O Vishnu's beloved! However, when you turn your face away from him, good conduct and his other qualities are transformed into a lack of qualities. Even the tongue of the creator[187] is incapable of describing your qualities. O goddess with eyes like a lotus! Show me your favours and never abandon me again." Shri was praised properly in this way. O brahmana! While all the beings were present and all the gods heard, the goddess spoke to Shatakratu. Shri said, "O lord of the god! O Hari![188] I am pleased with this stotram.[189] Ask for the boon you wish. I have come here to bestow a boon on you." Indra replied, "O goddess! O one who bestows boons! I am deserving of a boon, please do not abandon the three worlds. That is the supreme boon I ask for. O one who originated from the ocean! My second boon is that you should never forsake a person who satisfies you with this stotram." Shri replied, "O best among the gods! O Vasava! I will not abandon the three worlds. Since you have worshipped and satisfied me with this stotram, I bestow this boon on you. Morning and evening, if a man satisfies me with this stotram, I will not turn my face away from him." In ancient times, this is the boon the goddess bestowed on the king of the gods. O Maitreya! The immensely fortunate Shri was satisfied at being worshipped with this stotram.'

'However, Shri was first born as Bhrigu's daughter, through Khyati. Thereafter, when the gods and danavas made efforts to churn the ocean for amrita, she originated from the ocean again. In this way, when Janardana, the lord of the gods

---

[187] Brahma.

[188] Hari is also Indra's name.

[189] A hymn of praise.

and the master of the universe, assumes an *avatara*, Shri also
does so, as his aide. When Hari was born from Aditi,[190] she
again originated as Padma. When he was Bhargava Rama, she
was Dharani.[191] When he was Raghava, she was Sita. When he
was born as Krishna, she was Rukmini. She was his companion
in Vishnu's other *avatara*s too. When his form is divine, she
assumes a divine body. When his form is human, she too is
human. She assumes a body that is just like the body Vishnu
assumes. If a man reads or hears this account of Lakshmi's
birth, for three generations, Shri will not be dislodged from his
house. O sage! If a man reads this praise of Shri, Alakshmi,[192]
the store of dissension, will never reside with him. O *brahmana*!
I have thus told you what you asked me about—how Shri
originated from the ocean of milk and how she was formerly
born as Bhrigu's daughter. Her power is the cause behind the
expansion of all prosperity. Lakshmi's praise emanated from
Indra's mouth. If men read this every day, Alakshmi never
resides in their houses.'

Chapter 1(10) (Descendants of Daksha's Daughters)

Shri Maitreya said, 'O sage! You have told me everything
that I asked you about. Please tell me about the creation
that followed the creation of Bhrigu.'

Shri Parashara replied, 'Lakshmi was born through Bhrigu
and Khyati and married Vishnu. Two sons were also born to

[190] In the Vamana incarnation.
[191] Bhargava Rama is Parashurama, and this is an unusual
reference to Dharani as Parashurama's wife.
[192] The opposite of Lakshmi.

Bhrigu and Khyati, Dhatri and Vidhatri. They married Ayati
and Niyati, the daughters of the great-souled Meru. Through
their respective wives, Dhatri and Vidhatri each had a son,
Prana and Mrikandu. Markandeya was Mrikandu's son and
Markandeya's son was Vedashira. Hear about Prana's son.
Prana's son was Dyutimat and Dyutimat's son was Rajavat. O
immensely fortunate one! Bhrigu's lineage expanded in this way.
Marichi's wife, Sambhuti, gave birth to Pournamasa and the
great-souled one's sons were Viraja and Parvata. O *brahmana*!
I will recount his lineage when I speak about his son.[193] The
wife of Angiras, Smriti, gave birth to the daughters Sinivali,
Kuhu, Raka and Anumati.[194] Anasuya, Atri's wife, gave birth to
sons who were sinless: Soma, Durvasa and the *yogi* Dattatreya.
In an earlier birth, during Svayambhuva *manvantara*, Priti,
Pulastya's wife, had a son named Dattoli. He is now known
as Agastya. Kshama, the wife of Prajapati Pulaha, had three
sons, Kardama, Avarivat and Sahishnu. Kratu's wife, Santanti,
gave birth to sixty thousand sons who were the *valakhilyas*.
They were sages who held up their seed. They were merely
the length of a thumb and in their energy, they blazed like the
sun. Through Urjja, Vasishtha had seven sons: Raja, Gotra,
Urddhvabahu, Savana, Anagha, Sutapa and Shukra. These
were the sparkling *saptarshis*.[195] The proud Agni, was the
first among Brahma's sons. O *brahmana*! Through Svaha, he
had three sons who were extensive in their energy. They were
Pavaka, Pavamana and Shuchi, who drinks up water. They

[193] His lineage means Marichi's lineage and Parashara will
describe it when he speaks about Kashyapa, Marichi's son.
[194] Sinivali is the deity (and the day) for the day preceding the
night of the new moon, Kuhu is the deity (and the day) for the night
of the new moon, Raka is the deity (and the day) for the night of the
full moon and Anumati is the deity (and the day) for the 14th night of
shukla paksha.
[195] The list of *saptarshis* changes from one *manvantara* to another.

are said to have had forty-five sons. Along with the father,
Vahni,[196] and the three sons, there are thus said to be forty-
nine kinds of fires. O *brahmana*! I have described the ancestors
created by Brahma. There were Agnishvatta and Barhishad,
those who did not maintain the fire and those who maintained
the fire.[197] Through them, Svadha had the daughters known as
Mena and Dharini. O *brahmana*! Both of them were *yoginis*[198]
and knew about the *brahman*. All of them possessed excellent
jnana and the qualities. I have thus described the children of
Daksha's daughters to you. A person who faithfully remembers
this, will never suffer from lack of offspring.'

Chapter 1(11) (Story of Dhruva)

Shri Parashara said, 'Svayambhuva Manu had two sons,
Priyavrata and Uttanapada. They were immensely valiant
and knew about *dharma*. I have told you about them. Through
Suruchi, whom he loved, Uttanapada had a son named Uttama.
O *brahmana*! The father loved him a lot. O *brahmana*! The king
had another wife named Suniti. He did not love her that much
and she had a son named Dhruva. Dhruva saw Uttama, his
brother, seated on their father's lap, while he was seated on the
royal throne. He too wished to clamber up there. However, the
lord of the earth saw that Suruchi was present and he was full
of love for her. Therefore, he did not welcome the idea. Seeing

---

[196] Agni.

[197] *Barhi* is sacrificial grass like *kusha*. Barhishad means someone
who seats himself on *barhi* grass. The ancestors known as Barhishads
maintained the sacrificial fire. The ancestors known as Agnishvattas
did not maintain the sacrificial fire.

[198] *Yogini* is the feminine of *yogi*.

that her co-wife's son was eager to climb up there and that her own son was already seated there, Suruchi spoke these words. "O child! Why are you indulging in such a great, but futile, wish? You have been born from another woman's womb, while Uttama has been born from my womb. You cannot obtain this. Without any sense of discrimination, why are you desiring it? It is true that you are his son, but you have not been born from my womb. This royal throne, and everything else that a lord of the earth is entitled to, is appropriate for my son. Why are you suffering on account of this? Why do you vainly have such a lofty wish, as if you are my son? Don't you know that you have been born from Suniti?" Hearing what his mother[199] said, the child withdrew from his father. O *brahmana*! Full of anger, he went to his own mother's house. She saw that her son was angry and that his lips were quivering a bit. O Maitreya! Suniti picked him up on her own lap and spoke to him. "O child! Who has given you cause for anger? Who has shown you disrespect? Who does not know your father? O child! Who has committed a crime?" Thus addressed, he told his mother everything—how, in the king's presence, the extremely proud Suruchi had spoken to him. When her son told her this, she was miserable in her mind and sighed. Sighing, miserable and with agitated eyes, Suniti spoke the following words. Suniti said, "O son! Suruchi has spoken the truth. You are unfortunate. O child! Those who are not virtuous are addressed by their rivals in this way. O son! You should not be disturbed. Control your rage. This is because of what you did earlier. Who is capable of bestowing on you what you did not do earlier?[200] Therefore, you should not be miserable on account of those words. O son! A royal seat, a royal umbrella, the best of horses and the best of elephants are for those who are virtuous. Understanding this,

[199] That is, stepmother.
[200] It is the result of past *karma*.

be pacified. The king is bestowing these favours on Suruchi because she was virtuous in a former life. Others like me are devoid of virtue and are a wife only in name. Her son, Uttama, possesses a store of good merits. O Dhruva! You have been born as my son and your store of good merits is limited. O son! That is the reason you should not be miserable. O child! A man should be satisfied with whatever he has got. If you are exceedingly sorrowful at the words Suruchi has spoken, you should make efforts to accumulate good merits. That bestows every kind of fruit. Have good conduct. Have *dharma* in your soul. Be friendly and engaged in the welfare of beings. Prosperity flows even to those who are wounded, just as water flows downwards into a vessel." Dhruva replied, "O mother! You have spoken these words to pacify me. But my heart is shattered, and these words do not find a place there. I will make efforts to obtain a status that is superior to everything else, one that will be revered by the entire universe. Suruchi is loved by the king, and I have not been born from her womb. O mother! However, though I have been reared from your womb, witness my power. My brother, Uttama, has been reared from her womb. Let him obtain the royal throne my father bestows on him. O mother! I do not desire something that has been given to me by someone else. Through my own *karma*, I wish for a status that my father has not obtained." Dhruva told his mother this and left his home.'

'He left the city and went to a grove that was outside. Dhruva saw seven sages, who had already arrived there. They were seated on *kusha* grass, spread out over their upper garments and black antelope skin. The prince humbly bowed down before all of them. He prostrated himself and first greeted them in the proper way. He then spoke to them. Dhruva said, "O excellent ones! Know me to be the son of Uttanapada. I have been born from Suniti. Having lost all attachment, I have come before you." The *rishi*s replied, "You are a child, and you are the son of

a king. You are only four or five years of age. There is no reason
for you to lose all sense of attachment. As long as your father
is the lord of the earth, we cannot think of anything you do not
possess. O child! We do not see any reason why you should
be separated from what is desired. No signs of physical ailment
can be discerned in you. If there is a sense of non-attachment,
please tell us the reason for that." He told them what Suruchi
had said. Hearing this, the sages conversed among themselves.
"How wonderful is the great energy of a *kshatriya*. Though he is
a child, he cannot forgive. The words spoken by his stepmother
are creeping around in his heart. O son of a *kshatriya*! If you now
wish to pursue a path of non-attachment, if it so appeals to you,
we will tell you what must be done. O immensely radiant one!
Our task will be to help you. Therefore, tell us. We do notice
signs of non-attachment in you." Dhruva replied, "O excellent
brahmanas! I do not desire wealth. Nor do I desire a kingdom.
I only desire a place that no one has enjoyed earlier. That is
what I will do. O supreme sages! Please tell me properly how I
can obtain that, a station that is superior to all other stations."
Marichi said, "O son of a king! Without worshipping Govinda,
men do not obtain a best destination. Therefore, worship
Achyuta." Atri said, "He is Purusha, superior to the greatest.
When Janardana is pleased, one obtains a place that does not
decay. I have spoken the truth." Angiras said, "Everything flows
from Achyuta, whose *atman* is not manifest. If you desire the
foremost of places, worship Govinda." Pulastya said, "He is
the supreme *brahman*. He is the supreme refuge. He is superior
to Brahma. Worship Hari. You will then obtain emancipation,
which is so very difficult to obtain." Pulaha said, "He is the
supreme destination. Worshipping the lord of the universe, Indra
obtained the status of being Indra. O one excellent in vows! You
will obtain what you want if you worship Vishnu, the lord of
sacrifices." Kratu replied, "He is the being in the sacrifice. He
is the sacrifice. He is the lord of sacrifices. He is the supreme

being. If Janardana is satisfied, there is nothing that cannot be obtained." Vasishtha said, "If you worship Vishnu, you will obtain what is in your mind. O child! One obtains a station that is beyond the three worlds. What can be superior to that?" Dhruva replied, "I prostrated myself before you and you told me about the divinity I should worship and satisfy. You should now tell me about the *japa*[201] I should use when I perform the act of worshipping the great-souled one. O *maharshi*s! Please use your excellent mouths, show me your favours and tell me that." The *maharshi*s said, "O prince! You deserve to hear how men, who are supremely devoted to Vishnu, perform that act of worship. A man must first cast aside anything external that affects the mind. He must then unwaveringly and single-mindedly focus his mind on the refuge of the universe. He must immerse his *atman* in him. O son of a king! Now understand the *japa* that must be used. 'He is Hiranyagarbha. He is Purusha. He is Pradhana. His form is not manifest. Oum! I prostrate myself before Vasudeva. His own nature is pure *jnana*.'[202] In earlier times, your grandfather, the illustrious Svayambhuva Manu, used this *japa* to worship and satisfy Janardana. Thereafter, he obtained the success he wished for, which is extremely difficult for anyone in the three worlds to obtain. Hence, you should also satisfy Govinda by constantly performing this *japa*.'"

Chapter 1(12) (Dhruva Obtains Success)

Shri Parashara said, 'Hear the rest of it. The king's son prostrated himself before the *rishi*s and left that forest.

---

[201] *Japa* is the act of silently chanting a *mantra* and meditating.
[202] *Hiranyagarbhapurushapradhanavyaktarupine oum namo vasudevaya shuddhajnanasvarupine.*

O *brahmana*! He made up his mind to do whatever was
necessary to become successful. There was an extremely
desolate spot known as Madhu, along the banks of the
Yamuna. The *daitya* known as Madhu used to dwell there
earlier. Therefore, it is famous on earth as Madhuvana.
Shatrughna killed the *rakshasa* Lavana, Madhu's son, and
built the city known as Madhura[203] there. He performed
austerities in that tirtha that destroys all sins, in the presence
of Hari, the lord of the gods. Just as Marichi and the other
foremost sages had instructed him earlier, he fixed his entire
atman steadily on Vishnu, the lord of the gods, and on
nothing else. Single-minded in his focus, he meditated on
the illustrious Hari. O *brahmana*! He is in all beings and in
every kind of sentiment. O Maitreya! He immersed himself
in *yoga* and fixed his mind on Vishnu.'

'The earth, which holds all beings, was incapable of
bearing this burden. When he stood on his left foot, half of
the earth sank down under the burden. When he stood on his
right foot, the second half of the earth sank down under the
burden. When he stood on his toes, the entire earth suffered.
The entire earth, along with the mountains, quaked. The male
rivers, the female rivers and the oceans were greatly agitated.
O great sage! When they were agitated, the immortals were
greatly agitated. O Maitreya! The gods known as the Yamas
became extremely anxious. They consulted Indra and made
attempts to break the meditation. O great sage! Since they
were afflicted, along with Indra, the Kushmandas[204] assumed
many different forms and made great efforts. One assumed
the form of his mother, Suniti, and stood before him, weeping.

[203] That is, Mathura.

[204] Minor divinities, sometimes described as demons. They used
maya to assume different forms.

Fashioned out of *maya*, she addressed her son in these piteous words. "O son! Refrain from this extremely terrible act of making your body suffer. After a lot of hope and overcoming many impediments, I have obtained you. I am miserable and alone. You should not abandon me. I will be without a protector. O child! You cannot do this because of what my co-wife said. I have no refuge and you are my only refuge. You are only five years old. Why are you undertaking this terrible austerity? Withdraw your mind from this hardship. This kind of persistence is devoid of fruits. This is the time for you to play outside in a grove. After that, it is time for you to study. If you wish to perform austerities, that should be after you have enjoyed all the objects of pleasure. O son! You are a child, and this is the time for you to play. Do you wish to perform these austerities so as to destroy yourself? Your supreme *dharma* is love for me. The tasks to be undertaken depend on the age. Follow that. Refrain from this delusion and this *adharma*. O child! If you do not stop these austerities now, I will give up my life. If you do not cease, while you look on, I will give up my life." With anxious eyes, she lamented in this way. "O child! O child! Extremely terrible *rakshasa*s are appearing in the forest. They have raised their weapons and are advancing towards you." However, his mind was fixed on seeing Vishnu and he did not see her. She said this and left, but the *rakshasa*s manifested themselves. They raised fierce weapons. Their fierce faces had garlands of flames. They presented themselves before the prince and roared in fearful voices. Those roamers in the night released their blazing weapons and wandered around. Hundreds of jackals howled, and flames issued from their cruel mouths. They made efforts to terrify the child, who was steadfast in his *yoga*. "Kill him. Kill him. Slice him. Slice him. Devour him. Devour him." The roamers in the night said this. Assuming the faces of lions, camels and *makaras*,[205] they roared in many kinds of ways. To terrify the prince, those roamers in the right roared. There was the roaring of *rakshasa*s, the howling of jackals and those weapons. However, since his mind was fixed on Govinda, they were not perceived by his senses. His mind was constantly fixed on Vishnu, his *atman* was submerged in him. The son of the lord of the earth saw nothing else. After this, all the *maya* vanished. But the gods were still agitated and were anxious that they might be defeated.'[206]

'They went to Hari, the origin of the universe. He is without a beginning and without an end. He is the refuge one should seek. Those who torment themselves through austerities seek him as a refuge. The gods said, "O lord of the gods! O Jagannatha! O supreme lord! O Purushottama! O Janardana! We are terrified because of the austerities Uttanapada's son has undertaken. We have sought refuge with you, so that he refrains from his austerities. We do not know what he desires. Does he wish for the status of Shakra or Surya? Does he want the positions of the lord of riches, the lord of the waters, or Soma?[207] O lord! Therefore, show us your favours. Please uproot this stake from our hearts. Please make Uttanapada's son refrain from his austerities." The illustrious one replied, "He does not desire the status of Indra, Surya, Varuna or Kubera. O gods! I will grant him everything that he wishes for. O gods! Get rid of this anxiety and as you wish, return to your own abodes. I will make the child, whose mind is fixed on austerities, refrain." Thus addressed by the lord of the gods, the residents of heaven prostrated themselves before him.

[205] A *makara* is a mythical aquatic animal. It can loosely be translated as crocodile/shark.

[206] They didn't know what Dhruva wanted to achieve through his austerities. He might have wanted to oust them from heaven.

[207] Respectively, Kubera, Varuna and the moon god.

With Shatakratu leading the way, they returned to their own respective abodes.'

'The illustrious one, who is in all *atman*s, was satisfied at his intensity. Hari assumed a four-armed form and going to Dhruva, spoke to him. The illustrious one said, "O Uttanapada's son! O fortunate one! I am satisfied with your austerities. O one excellent in vows! I have come here to bestow a boon on you. Ask for a boon. Your mind is seeking what is beneficial and is indifferent towards external objects. It is immersed in me. I am pleased with you. Ask for an excellent boon." The child heard the words spoken by the lord of the gods. He opened his eyes and saw Hari, whom he had seen earlier, through his meditation. Achyuta held a conch shell, a *chakra*, a mace and a club. He wore a diadem. On seeing him, he lowered his head down on the ground. He was suddenly full of agitation and his body hair stood up. In his mind, Dhruva wondered about how he would praise the lord of the gods. What would he say in praise? Whose words of praise[208] should he use? When his intelligence was confused in this way, he sought refuge with the divinity himself.'

'Dhruva said, "O illustrious one! If you are greatly satisfied with my austerities, I wish to praise you. Please bestow that boon on me. Brahma and the others, those who know the *Veda*s, do not know your course. O divinity! How can a child like me have the capacity to praise you? O Parameshvara! My mind is full of devotion towards you. Please grant me the wisdom, so that I can present my praise before your feet." He joined his hands in salutation. O noble *brahmana*! Govinda, the lord of the universe, touched Uttanapada's son with the tip of the conch shell. The face of the king's son instantly turned pleasant. He prostrated himself and praised Achyuta, the one who upholds all beings. Dhruva said, "Earth, water, fire,

[208] Words of praise used by others.

wind, space, mind, intellect, the first element[209] and Prakriti
are his form. I bow down before him. He is pure. He is subtle
and pervades everything. He is the being who is superior to
Pradhana. They are his form. I bow down to Purusha, who
possesses the *guna*s in his *atman*. He is superior to all the
elements, smell and all the objects of the senses, intellect and
other things, Pradhana and Purusha. He is eternal. He is the
brahman. He is in the *atman*s of all beings. He is the lord of
the entire universe. O Parameshvara! I seek refuge in your pure
form. You are greater than the greatest. I bow down to your
form, known as Brahma. You are in all *atman*s. The *yogi*s think
about you. You are without transformation. You are Purusha,
with one thousand heads. You have one thousand eyes and
one thousand feet. You pervade everything on earth. You are
ten finger lengths beyond anything that can be touched.[210] O
Purushottama! You are everything that has happened and will
happen. Virat, Svarat, Samrat and Adhipurusha originated from
you.[211] Everything above and below the earth, and diagonally
across, is dependent on you. The entire universe originated in
you. Everything that will happen originates in you. Everything
in the universe originated in you and everything with form
ends in you. The sacrifice originated from you. So did all the
oblations, the mixture of milk and *ghee* and the two types of
animals.[212] The *Rig* and *Sama* hymns originated from you. The
metres were also born in that way. The *Yajur* hymns originated
from you. Horses, cattle and animals with teeth in both jaws,
or teeth in one jaw, originated from you. So did goats, sheep

[209] Interpreted as *ahamkara*.

[210] Simply meaning that you are beyond the senses.

[211] Virat, Svarat, Samrat and Adhipurusha are interpreted in
various ways. One possible interpretation is that Virat is the manifest
form of the universe, Svarat is Brahma, Samrat is the form of Prajapati
and Adhipurusha is Purusha.

[212] Domestic and wild.

and deer. *Brahmana*s were born from your mouth, *kshatriya*s
were born from your arms, *vaishya*s were born from your
thighs and *shudra*s were born from your feet. Your eyes are
the sun. The wind is your breath of life. The moon is your
mind. The breath of life in beings originated from your veins.
Fire was born from your mouth. Your navel stretches up to the
sky, your head stretches up to heaven. The directions are your
ears. The earth is your feet. Everything originated from you.
The great *nyagrodha* tree[213] exists in a small seed. Like that,
when it is withdrawn, the entire universe exists in you, in the
form of a seed. The seed becomes a sprout and a *nyagrodha*
results. It spreads in all directions. Like that, the entire universe
was created from you and dissolves in you. Because of the skin
and the leaves, a plantain cannot be seen. O lord! In that way,
nothing in the universe can be seen, other than in you. The
sensations of happiness and pain are all established in you. But
the causes of happiness, unhappiness and any mixed feelings
do not exist in you. You are devoid of *guna*s. You are one, but
you exist separately in beings. You are the cause of beings. I
prostrate myself before you. You are the cause of many kinds
of beings. You are in the *atman*s of all beings. I bow down
before you. You manifest yourself as Pradhana, Purusha, Virat,
Samrat and Svarat. In the form of the undecaying Purusha, you
are resplendent within the heart. You are in everything. You
are in all the elements. You are everything. Your own nature
exists in every kind of form. Everything flows from you. You
are in all *atman*s. I bow down before you. You alone exist in all
*atman*s. You are the lord of everything. You are established in
all beings. What can I possibly tell you? You know everything
that is in the heart. You are in all *atman*s. You are the lord of
all beings. All beings originated from you. Since you exist in
all beings, you know the wishes of all beings. O protector! Let

---

[213] The Indian fig tree.

my wishes be made successful by you. O lord of the universe! I have tormented myself through austerities. Since I have seen you, let those be successful."'

'The illustrious one replied, "O Dhruva! I have shown myself to you and have come here. Therefore, your tormenting yourself through austerities has become successful. O prince! The sight of me is never futile. O prince! Ask for a boon, whatever is in your mind. When I come into their line of vision, men obtain everything." Dhruva said, "O illustrious one! You are the lord of everything that has happened and will be. You are in the hearts of everyone. O *brahman*! How can the desire of my mind not be known to you? O lord of the gods! Nevertheless, I will tell you what I wish for in my heart. Perhaps I am not humble enough and this is extremely difficult to obtain. But when the creator of the entire universe is pleased, what is extremely difficult to obtain? It is through the fruits of your favours that Maghavan[214] enjoys the three worlds. My stepmother addressed me in haughty words. 'A person who has not been born from my womb is not worthy of the royal throne.' You are the foundation of the entire universe. O lord! Through your favours, I desire a station that will be superior to all the others, one that will not decay." The illustrious one replied, "You will obtain the station that you desire. O child! In a former life, I have been satisfied by you. Earlier, you were a *brahmana* who was always single-mindedly devoted to me. You always followed your own *dharma* and served your father and your mother. In the course of time, a prince became your friend. He was young and enjoyed all the excellent objects of pleasure. He had a dazzling and handsome form. Because of your association with him, you witnessed prosperity that was extremely difficult to obtain. Therefore, you had a wish that you might become a prince. Thus, according to your wishes,

[214] Indra.

you obtained the status of a prince. O Dhruva! You were born in Uttanapada's house, a status that is extremely difficult for others to obtain. This is Svayambhuva's lineage. O child! However, you sought something else and have thereby satisfied me. A man who worships me obtains emancipation, without any delay. O child! For someone whose mind is submerged in me, what purpose do heaven and other stations serve? There is a station that is beyond the three worlds. It is one that all the stars and planets resort to. O Dhruva! Through my favours, there is no doubt that this position will be yours.[215] O Dhruva! This is a region that is superior to Surya, Soma, Bhouma,[216] Soma's son,[217] Brihaspati,[218] the son of the fair sun,[219] and all the *nakshatra*s. O Dhruva! It is superior to all the *saptarshi*s and the gods on their *vimana*s. O Dhruva! I have given you a place that is above all of them. Some gods exist for four *yuga*s, some for a *manvantara*. The place that I have granted you will last for a *kalpa*. Your sparkling mother, Suniti, will be near you. She will become a small star on a *vimana* and will remain for that same duration. If a man controls himself and recounts this every morning and evening, he will obtain great merits." O immensely intelligent one! Earlier, in this way, Dhruva obtained a boon and an exalted station from Jagannatha Janardana, the lord of the gods. This is because he himself followed the *dharma* of serving his parents, because of the greatness of the twelve *akshara*s[220] and because of the power of austerities. On witnessing his proud prosperity and greatness, Ushanas,[221] the preceptor of the gods and the *asura*s, chanted a *shloka*. "How

[215] Dhruva became the Pole Star.
[216] Mars.
[217] Budha (Mercury).
[218] Jupiter.
[219] Shanaihshchara (Saturn) is Surya's son.
[220] *Oum! namo bhagavate vasudevaya.*
[221] Shukracharya.

wonderful are his austerities. How wonderful is his valour. How wonderful are the fruits of austerities. Because of these, Dhruva is placed ahead of the *saptarshis*. Dhruva's mother, Suniti, is also known under the name of Sunrita. Who on earth is capable of describing her greatness? She bore Dhruva, the refuge of the three worlds, in her womb and has obtained a supreme station. She obtained an excellent destination." If a person constantly chants the account of Dhruva's fame and ascent into the firmament, he is freed from all sins and attains greatness in the world of heaven. He is not dislodged from the position he obtains in heaven or on earth. He lives for a long time and possesses every kind of fortune.'

Chapter 1(13) (Story of Prithu)

Shri Parashara said, 'Dhruva's wife was Shambhu, and Dhruva's sons were Bhavya and Shishti. Through Succhaya, Shishti had five sons who were without blemishes: Ripu, Ripunjaya, Vipra, Vrikala and Vrikatejas. Through Brihati, Ripu's son was Chakshusha, and he possessed every kind of energy. Varuni, from Pushkarini, was the daughter of the great-souled Prajapati, Virana. Through her, Chakshusha had Chakshusha Manu as a son. Through Nadvala, the daughter of Prajapati Vairaja, supreme among ascetics, Manu[222] had ten immensely energetic sons: Kuru, Puru, Shatadyumna, Tapasvi, Satyavak, Shuchi, Agnishtoma, Atiratra and Sudyumna as the ninth. Nadvala's tenth son was the immensely energetic Abhimanyu. Through Agneyi, Kuru had six immensely radiant sons: Anga, Sumanas, Khyati, Kratu, Angiras and Shibi. Through Sunitha, Anga had a single son named Vena. For the

[222] Svayambhuva Manu.

sake of offspring, the *rishi*s kneaded his right hand.[223] O great
sage! When Vena's hand was kneaded, a great king named
Venya[224] was born. He is the one who is famous as Prithu.
Earlier, for the welfare of the subjects, he is the one who milked
the earth.'

Maitreya asked, 'O supreme among sages! What was the
reason for the supreme *rishi*s to knead Vena's hand, as a result
of which the immensely valiant Prithu was born?'

Shri Parashara replied, 'The one named Sunitha was
Mrityu's eldest daughter. She was given to Anga as a wife
and Vena was born from her. O Maitreya! Since he was
born as the son of Mrityu's daughter, he suffered from his
maternal grandfather's taint. As a result of this association,
he was born wicked. The supreme *rishi*s instated Vena in the
kingdom. He announced that he was the lord of the earth and
that throughout the earth, there would not be any sacrifices,
donations or offering of oblations. "I, the master, am the lord
of sacrifices. Who else can enjoy a sacrifice?" O Maitreya! The
*rishi*s approached the lord of the earth and first, honoured
him. They addressed him in placatory tones. The *rishi*s said,
"O king! O lord of the earth! Listen to the words we speak. To
prevent injury to the kingdom and to your own physical body,
and for the supreme benefit of the subjects, we should worship
Hari through a sacrifice that lasts for a long time. He is the
lord of the gods. He is the lord of all sacrifices. O fortunate
one! You will also have a share in the fruits. O king! Vishnu
will be pleased through a sacrifice. The sacrifice is his form.
He will then bestow everything that we, and you, desire. O

[223] The *brahmana*s killed Vena in their rage. Vena died without
having a son. So that there might be a king, the *brahmana*s kneaded
the dead body's right hand.

[224] The text sometimes uses the word Vainya. For the sake of
consistency, we have replaced it throughout as Venya.

king! If Hari, the lord of sacrifices, is worshipped through a sacrifice in the kingdom of a king, he bestows everything on the king." Vena replied, "Who is the one who is superior to me? Other than me, who is there to worship? Who is the one who is spoken of as Hari? Who is held to be the lord of sacrifices? Brahma, Janardana, Shambhu, Indra, Vayu, Yama, Ravi,[225] the one who partakes of oblations,[226] Varuna, Dhatri, Pusha, the earth, the maker of the night[227] and all the other gods who curse and show favours are present in the king's body. The king has all the gods in him. O *brahmana*s! Knowing this, I have issued instructions and please act accordingly. There should be no donations. There should be no sacrifices. There should be no oblations. It is held that the supreme *dharma* of women is to serve their husbands. O *brahmana*s! In that way, it is your *dharma* to follow my commands." The *rishi*s said, "O great king! So that *dharma* is not destroyed, please grant us permission. The entire universe is the consequence of oblations." Vena was told this by the supreme *rishi*s. Though he was repeatedly entreated, he did not grant them the permission. At this, all the sages were filled with anger and intolerance. They told each other, "He should be killed. The wicked one should be killed. Vishnu is the lord of all sacrifices. The lord is without a beginning and without an end. He has been reviled by a person who is wicked in conduct and is not fit to rule over the earth." Saying this, the large number of sages invoked *mantra*s on *kusha* grass and used this to kill him. However, because he had criticized the illustrious one who is without origin, he had already been slain. O *brahmana*! After this, the sages saw a dust arise in every direction. They asked the people, "What is this?" The people told them, "There are

---

[225] Surya.
[226] Agni.
[227] The moon.

thieves in the kingdom. In the kingdom, people are eager to seize the property of others. O best among sages! The great dust that you see has been raised by the great force with which thieves are rushing around, seizing the property of others."[228] Hence, all the sages consulted among themselves. The king didn't have any offspring and they kneaded his thigh for the sake of a son. When they kneaded his thigh, a man arose. He resembled a burnt stake of wood. He was extremely short. His mouth was small, and his nose was flat. Anxious, he asked the brahmanas, "What will I do?" They told him, "Nishida" and he became a nishada.[229] Since then, those descended from him reside in the Vindhya mountains. O tiger among sages! They are nishadas and show the signs of being engaged in wicked activities. But through this exit, wickedness was expelled from the king's body. The nishada ate up all the sin in Vena.'

'The brahmanas then kneaded his right arm. As they kneaded, the powerful Prithu Venya[230] was born. He was radiant and his body blazed, like Agni himself. The first bow, named Ajagava,[231] descended from the sky. Divine arrows and armour also fell down from the sky. When he was born, all the beings were delighted. Since a virtuous son had been born, Vena went to heaven. The extremely great-souled son saved him from the hell named put.[232] The ocean and the rivers brought all their jewels and waters and everything else required for his consecration and presented themselves. To consecrate

---

[228] Vena had died without leaving a son. Therefore, without a king, there was anarchy. The wicked were no longer punished and the virtuous no longer protected.

[229] Nishida means 'Sit'. Nishadas lived in the mountains and were hunters.

[230] Meaning Vena's son.

[231] Shiva's bow.

[232] The hell named put is for those who don't have sons. Since a son saves (trayate) from the hell named put, a son is known as putra.

Venya as the king, the illustrious grandfather arrived, along
with the gods, the descendants of Angiras[233] and all mobile and
immobile objects. From the mark of a *chakra* on his right hand,
the grandfather deduced that Prithu had been born as Vishnu's
portion and was filled with great satisfaction. The mark of
Vishnu's *chakra* on the hand is a sign of all *chakravartis*.[234] Even
the gods are incapable of restraining such a person's powers.
The powerful Prithu Venya was instated as a great king in the
kingdom. The immensely energetic one was consecrated in the
proper way by those who know about *dharma*. He delighted
the subjects, who had suffered on account of his father. Because
of this affection, he was named *rajan*.[235] When he travelled
through the ocean, the waters were stupefied.[236] The mountains
gave him a path. His standard was never impeded. Without
being tilled, the earth provided food that need not be cooked. As
soon as one thought about it, cooked food was available. Cows
yielded every kind of milk that was desired. There was honey
in every flower cup. As soon as he was born, the grandfather
performed an auspicious sacrifice. From the sacrifice that the
intelligent one performed on the very same day, *suta*s were
born as offspring.[237] From that same great sacrifice, the wise
*magadha*s were born. The excellent sages told the *suta*s and the
*magadha*s, "Praise the powerful king, Prithu Venya. That is a

[233] The various fires.
[234] *Chakravarti* is a universal emperor. The etymology suggested
here derives *chakravarti* from *chakra*. An alternative derivation
is that *chakravarti* is one whose wheel (*chakra*) travels unimpeded
throughout the earth.
[235] Etymologically, one who delights the subjects.
[236] And granted him passage.
[237] The *suta*s were charioteers, as well as raconteurs of tales.
*Magadha*s were minstrels and bards. So were *bandi*s. But *magadha*s
seem to have also composed, while *bandi*s sung the compositions of
others.

task that is appropriate for you and there is no other person
who is as worthy of praise." All of them joined their hands in
salutation and told the brahmanas, "We have just been born
and we do not know about the deeds the lord of the earth
has undertaken. We do not know about his qualities. Nor do
we know about this pervasive fame. What hymn will we use?
Please tell us about his deeds." The rishis replied, "Praise the
immensely strong Chakravarti for the deeds he will undertake.
Praise the king for the qualities he will possess." The king was
filled with great delight at these words of praise. "These words
praise my good qualities. My qualities must be similar to what
has been praised. From now on, my qualities and what has
been praised must be identical. I will control myself and do
whatever these words have said I will do. Whatever they have
described as avoidable, will be avoided by me." The king made
up his mind to do this. The intelligent one acted according
to whatever the hymn had described for Prithu Venya. The
words uttered in melodious voices by the sutas and magadhas
determined his appropriate future course of action. The sutas
and magadhas had spoken about the qualities in the following
way. "The lord of men is truthful in speech and generous in
donations. He adheres to his pledges. He is humble, friendly,
forgiving and valiant and punishes the wicked. He knows
about dharma. He is grateful, compassionate and pleasant in
speech. He shows respect to those who should be revered. He
performs sacrifices. He honours brahmanas and the virtuous.
In delivering justice, the king is impartial between friend and
enemy." He made up his mind that he would act in accordance
with these words. Accordingly, the lord of the earth ruled over
the earth. He performed many kinds of great sacrifices and
donated copious quantities of dakshina.'

'Suffering from hunger, the subjects approached the lord
of the earth. At the time when there was no king, the herbs
and plants had been destroyed. When they were asked about

the reason, they bowed down and told him. The subjects said, "O best among kings! When there was no king, the earth swallowed up all the herbs. O lord of subjects! All the subjects are being destroyed. The creator has identified you as the one who will protect the subjects and provide them with a means for subsistence. We are suffering from hunger. Please give the subjects the herbs and plants required to sustain their lives." At this, the king seized the divine Ajagava bow. Angrily, he affixed the divine arrows, so as to slay the earth. So that she would not be destroyed, the earth swiftly assumed the form of a cow. Terrified, the earth fled to Brahma's world and to all the other worlds. However, wherever the goddess, the sustainer of living beings, went, she saw that Venya was following her, with an upraised weapon. Therefore, the earth spoke to the valiant King Prithu. She was trembling and wished to save herself from those arrows. The earth said, "O Indra among men! Do you not see that you will commit a great sin if you kill a woman? O king! Why are you making efforts to kill me?" Prithu replied, "O evildoer! When one person's slaughter leads to peace for many, that kind of killing is virtuous." The earth said, "O best among kings! If you kill me to ensure the welfare of the subjects, who will support the subjects?" Prithu replied, "O earth! You have turned away from following my commands. If I use my arrows to kill you, I will support the subjects with the strength of my own *yoga*." Prostrating herself, the earth spoke to the king again. Her limbs were trembling, and she was filled with great alarm. The earth said, "If one uses the proper means, every kind of attempt is successful. Therefore, I will suggest a means. If you so wish, follow that. O lord of men! I have digested all the great herbs and plants. However, if you so wish, I will give them to you in the form of milk. O best among those who uphold *dharma*! Hence, for the welfare of the subjects, give me a calf and as a result of my affection, the milk will flow. In every direction, level the ground, so that the excellent seeds of herbs and plants flow in the form of my milk and there are seeds everywhere." The mountains had grown atop one another. At this, Venya used the extremity of his bow to uproot hundreds and thousands of mountains. In earlier cycles of creation, the surface of the earth wasn't level. He divided the earth into cities and villages and such divisions had not existed earlier. There had been no crops, agriculture and animal husbandry, nor routes for merchants. O Maitreya! Since Venya, all this became possible. O best among *brahmana*s! Wherever the ground became level, he arranged for the subjects to reside. Since all the herbs had been destroyed, the food for subjects used to be roots and fruits and they suffered from great hardships. He thought of the lord Svayambhuva Manu as a calf. Prithu, the lord of the earth, used his own hands to milk the earth. For the welfare of the subjects, he thus obtained all the different kinds of crops. O son![238] It is on the basis of this food that subjects constantly sustain themselves, even now. By granting life to the earth, Prithu became her father. Therefore, the one who sustains everything came to be known as Prithivi.[239] O sage! Using appropriate vessels, the gods, the sages, the *daitya*s, the *rakshasa*s, the mountains, the *gandharva*s, the *uraga*s, the *yaksha*s, the ancestors and the trees milked her. The vessel and the one who milked were specific to the category. The earth, and everything else, originated from Vishnu's feet. She became the mother, the nursemaid, the sustainer and the nourisher of all things. Such were the powers of Prithu, Vena's valiant son. Since he delighted men, the great king who was born became the first *rajan*. If a man chants the account of the birth of Prithu Venya, he does not have to suffer the consequences of any evil deed he commits. If men hear this excellent account about the

[238] The word used is *tata*.
[239] After Prithu. Prithivi is also known as Prithvi.

birth and power of Prithu, all their nightmares are pacified.
Men must constantly do this.'

Chapter 1(14) (Story of the Prachetas)

Shri Parashara said, 'Prithu had two sons named Antardhi
and Vadina[240] and they were knowledgeable about
dharma. Through Antardhi, his wife, Shikhandini, had a son
named Havirdhana. Agni's daughter was Dhishna. Through
Havirdhana, she had six sons: Prachinabarhi, Shukra, Gaya,
Krishna, Vraja and Ajina. O immensely fortunate one! The
illustrious Prachinabarhi was a great Prajapati and made the
subjects prosper, just as Havirdhana had. O sage! As long
as the immensely strong one remained on earth, *prachinagra
kusha* covered the surface of the earth.[241] That is the reason
he was known as Prachinabarhi. O immensely intelligent
one! After performing great austerities, the lord of the earth
obtained the ocean's daughter, Savarna, as a wife. Through
Savarna, the ocean's daughter, Prachinabarhi obtained ten
sons. All of them were known as Prachetas and they were
accomplished in *dhanurveda*.[242] All of them tormented
themselves through great austerities and observed the same
kind of *dharma*, immersed in the water of the ocean for ten
thousand years.'

[240] In other texts, this name is given as Palina.
[241] An auspicious sign. *Kusha* is sacred grass and *prachinagra* is
that kind of grass that always has its tips pointed towards the east.
Alternatively, Prachinabarhi performed so many sacrifices that the
earth was covered.
[242] *Dhanu* means bow and *veda* means knowledge. But *dhanurveda*
means the science of war.

Shri Maitreya said, 'O sage! You should tell me why the great-souled Prachetas performed austerities inside the waters of the ocean.'

Shri Parashara continued, 'Their father's mind was fixed on multiplying subjects, and he spoke to the Prachetas. Having been shown a great deal of respect, he had been appointed as Prajapati. Prachinabarhi said, "O sons! Brahma, the lord of the gods, has commanded me. He told me to multiply subjects. O sons! Therefore, to please me, you should single-mindedly try to multiply subjects. You should properly honour the words of a Prajapati and act accordingly." The sons of the king heard the words of their father and agreed. O sage! Having agreed, they again questioned their father. The Prachetas asked, "O father! How can we become capable of undertaking the task of multiplying subjects? You should explain everything about this task to us." The father replied, "Worship Vishnu, the one who bestows boons. There is no doubt that you will accomplish your desires. Other than approaching him, there is nothing else that a mortal can do. What else will I tell you? Hari is the lord of all beings. Therefore, for the purpose of multiplying subjects, worship Govinda, if you wish to be successful. Anyone who wishes for *dharma*, *artha*, *kama* and *moksha* must always worship the illustrious Purushuttoma, who is without a beginning. At the beginning of creation, Prajapati[243] worshipped him. Therefore, if you worship Achyuta, the subjects will be multiplied." Thus addressed by their father, the sons, the ten Prachetas, immersed themselves in the waters of the ocean. They controlled themselves and tormented themselves through austerities. O best among sages! For ten thousand years, they immersed their minds in Narayana, the lord of the universe, who is engaged in the welfare of the worlds. They remained there, single-mindedly focusing their minds on the divinity

[243] Meaning Brahma.

Hari. They praised the noble one, so as to obtain what they wished for. If a person praises him, he obtains his desire.'

Shri Maitreya said, 'While immersed in the waters of the ocean, the Prachetas used an extremely sacred hymn to praise Vishnu. You should describe it to me.'

Shri Parashara continued, 'O Maitreya! Earlier, immersed in the waters of the ocean and with their minds on Govinda, the Prachetas used a hymn to praise him. Listen to it. The Prachetas said, "You are the eternal one who is established in every kind of speech. We bow down before you. You are the supreme lord, the beginning and the end of the entire universe. You are the original illumination. There is no one who is your equal. You cannot be divided. You are infinite and without a limit. You are the origin of every being, mobile and immobile. You are without form, but your first form is said to be day, night and *sandhya*. You are the supreme lord. Kala is your *atman*. We prostrate ourselves before you. The nectar is your *atman*, and the gods and the ancestors survive on it every day. You are the seed of everything. We bow down before the one whose *atman* is Soma. Surya's fierce rays drive away the darkness and illuminate the sky. It is the cause behind heat, cold and rain. We bow down before the one whose *atman* is Surya. Through her solidity, the earth holds up the entire universe. She extends everywhere and sound and the other senses depend on her. We bow down before the one whose *atman* is the earth. Water is inside everything in the world and is the seed of all those with bodies. We bow down to the intelligent Hari, the lord. Water is his form. He is the mouth of all the gods when he partakes of *havya* and he is the mouth of the ancestors when he partakes of *kavya*.[244] I bow down to Vishnu, whose *atman* is Pavaka. In

[244] *Havya* is oblations offered to the gods and *kavya* is oblations offered to the ancestors.

the form of the five flows,[245] night and day, he makes efforts
in physical bodies. He is the illustrious one in the sky. I bow
down to the one whose *atman* is Vayu. The infinite and pure
is his form. I bow down to the one whose *atman* is space.
He is the association with all the senses. I bow down to the
intelligent Krishna, the excellent objective, whose form is in the
form of sound and the other objects of the senses. The senses
are his *atman* and receive the objects of the senses. He is the
perishable and the imperishable. I bow down to the intelligent
Hari, who is the root of *jnana*. He receives the perceptions of
the senses and conveys them to the *atman*. He is in the form of
what is inside.[246] I bow down to the one whose *atman* is in the
universe. He is the infinite one into whom the entire universe
is withdrawn. He is the place for dissolution. I bow down to
the one whose *dharma* is Prakriti. He is devoid of *guna*s and is
pure. However, those who are confounded perceive him in the
*guna*s. I bow down to the divinity Purushottama, who is his
own form. He is without transformation. He is without origin.
He is pure. He is devoid of *guna*s. He is without blemish. I
bow down to Vishnu, the supreme objective, who is beyond
Brahma. He is not tall or short. He is not heavy or light. He
is not dark or red. He is without attachment. He is without
shadow or body. He is not attached to those who have bodies.
He cannot be perceived through touch, smell or taste. He
is devoid of eyes or ears. He does not move. He is without
speech, hands and mind. He has no name or *gotra*. He is not
happiness or energy. He is without a cause. He is without fear
and without confusion. He is without injury and without sleep.

---

[245] The five flows of the breath of life: *prana, apana, samana,
udana* and *vyana*. *Prana* draws breath into the body, *apana* exhales
it. *Vyana* distributes it through the body and *samana* assimilates it.
Udana gives rise to sound.

[246] The *jivatman* (the *atman* in living beings).

He is without old age and without death. He is devoid of *rajas* and sound. He is the *amrita* that pervades everything. He is Vishnu, the supreme objective, who is cause and effect. He is Parameshvara. Though without *guna*s, he has a presence in all beings. We bow down before Vishnu, the supreme destination, who cannot be perceived through tongue or sight." In this way, focusing their intelligence, the Prachetas praised Vishnu. In the great ocean, they performed austerities for ten thousand years. Pleased with them, the illustrious Hari showed himself to them, inside the water. O sage! His complexion was like that of the petal of a blue lotus. The Prachetas saw him, astride the king of the birds.[247] Bent with the burden of devotion, they lowered their heads and prostrated themselves. The illustrious one told them, "Ask for the desired boon. I am pleased with you and my countenance is favourable. I have presented myself to bestow a boon on you." Prostrating themselves, the Prachetas replied to the one who bestows boons. "We have been instructed by our father to be the cause for the multiplication of subjects." Thus, the divinity bestowed the desired boon on them and quickly disappeared. They emerged from the water.'

Chapter 1(15) (Daksha and Marisha)

Shri Parashara said, 'When the Prachetas were engaged in these austerities, the earth was no longer protected and became covered with trees. Consequently, the subjects were destroyed. The trees rose up into the sky and the wind was incapable of blowing. For ten thousand years, the subjects found it impossible to move. Emerging from the water, all the Prachetas witnessed this and were angry. As a result of

[247] Garuda.

the rage, wind and fire issued from their mouths. That wind
uprooted and dried all the trees. The fire burnt them down.
In this way, the trees were destroyed. On discerning that the
trees were destroyed, but some branches were still left, King
Soma[248] approached and spoke to the Prajapatis.[249] He said,
"O kings! Restrain your anger and listen to my words. I will
arrange an alliance between you and those that rise up from
the earth.[250] This beautiful maiden is the daughter of the trees
and is full of jewels. Earlier, knowing about the future, I have
used my rays to rear her. She is named Marisha and she has
been fashioned from the trees. O immensely fortunate ones!
She will be your wife and will extend Dhruva's lineage. Using
half of your energy and half of my energy, she will give birth to
a learned son named Daksha Prajapati. Through your energy
and my energy, he will be like a fire generated from a fire and
will again multiply the subjects."'

'Soma continued, "Earlier, there was a sage named
Kandu and he was supreme among those who knew about
the *Veda*s. On the beautiful banks of Gomati, he tormented
himself through severe austerities. To distract him, Indra of
the gods spoke to Pramlocha, supreme among *apsara*s. He
employed the one with the beautiful smiles to distract the *rishi*.
Distracted, he resided with her for more than one hundred and
fifty years in the valley of Mandara. His mind was attached
to the material. O immensely fortunate one! After this, she
wished to return to heaven. She said, 'O *brahmana*! Please
show me a favourable glance and your favours. Please grant
me permission.' However, the sage's mind was still attached
to her, and he replied, 'O fortunate one! Please remain for
a few more days.' Thus addressed, she again remained with

---

[248] Soma is the lord of trees and herbs. Soma is the moon god.
[249] The Prachetas.
[250] The trees.

him for more than one hundred years. With the slender-limbed one, the great-souled one enjoyed material objects. She again said, 'O illustrious one! Please grant me permission to leave for the abode of the gods.' He again requested her to stay. The one with the beautiful face again remained for more than one hundred years. She again said, 'O *brahmana*! I will leave for heaven.' However, he was in love with the extremely beautiful one. Therefore, the sage told her, 'O one with excellent eyebrows! Do not remove yourself. It has been a short while. Remain for some more time. After that, you will be gone for a very long time.' The one with the beautiful hips sported with the *rishi* again. She remained for a little less than two hundred years. O immensely fortunate one! She again requested him about returning to the abode of the king of the gods. But he requested the slender-limbed one to stay. However, she was scared of being cursed by him. That apart, she felt kindness towards one who was kind. She would also have suffered a lot had she been separated from her love. Hence, she did not leave the sage. Day and night, the supreme *rishi* found pleasure with her. His mind was overwhelmed by Manmatha[251] and he found newer and newer forms of love. On one occasion, the sage was leaving his cottage in a hurry. As he was leaving, the auspicious one asked him, 'Where are you going?' He told her, 'O auspicious one! The day is coming to an end. I must complete my *sandhya* rites. Otherwise, the required tasks will be extinguished.' The one with the excellent teeth laughed and spoke to the great sage. 'O one who knows every kind of *dharma*! Is your day coming to an end now? O *brahmana*! The days of many years have passed. Why are you committing this amazing act of leaving? Please explain it to me.' The sage replied, 'O fortunate one! This morning, you came before me on the auspicious banks

---

[251] Kama, the god of love.

of the river. O slender-limbed one! I saw you and you came
to my hermitage. The day has ended now, and it is evening.
Why are you laughing at this? Please explain the nature of
your sentiment to me.' Pramlocha answered, 'O *brahmana*!
It is true that I came to you in the morning. But it is also
true that hundreds of years have passed since that time.' The
brahmana was astounded at this and asked the large-eyed one,
'O timid one! How much time has elapsed since the time I
started to sport with you?' Pramlocha replied, 'Nine hundred
and seven years, six months and three days.' The *rishi* said,
'O timid one! O auspicious one! Tell me the truth. Are you
jesting with me? I think that we have only spend one day
together.' Pramlocha answered, 'O *brahmana*! I will never
utter a falsehood in your presence. This is especially because
I follow your path and you have asked me.' O sons of a king!
Hearing her truthful words, the sage exclaimed, 'Shame!
Great shame on me!' He reprimanded himself a lot in this
way. The sage said, 'My austerities have been destroyed. The
store of my knowledge of the *brahman* has been destroyed.
Someone has devised this woman to confound me and destroy
my sense of discrimination. I had crossed the six waves[252] and
conquered my *atman*, getting to know the *brahman*. Someone
has taken away my intelligence. Shame on desire! It is like a
giant crocodile. I followed the vows responsible for getting
to know everything that is in the *Veda*s. But all that has been
taken away by attachment, which is a path to the aggregate of
hells.' In this way, the one who knew about *dharma* censured
himself. He approached the seated *apsara* and addressed her in
these words. 'O wicked one! Depart. You have accomplished
the task you wished to do. You made this effort because the
king of the gods had intentions of distracting me. Therefore,

[252] Interpreted as hunger, thirst, sorrow, confusion, decay and
death.

I will not use the fierce fire of rage to reduce you to ashes. The virtuous regard taking seven steps together as signifying friendship and I have dwelt with you and done that. What is your crime? Why should I be angry with you? It is indeed my sin that I wasn't able to conquer my senses. Nevertheless, to cause pleasure to Shakra, you extinguished my austerities. Therefore, shame on you. You created this contemptible and great delusion.' As long as the *brahmana rishi* spoke to her in this way, the slender-waisted one remained there. There were beads of perspiration all over her body and she quaked. She trembled like a creeper that has just been cut off from the main trunk. The supreme sage angrily told her, 'Go! Leave!' Thus reprimanded, she emerged from that hermitage. She travelled through the air and wiped off her sweat with the branches of trees. In this way, the maiden travelled from one tree to another tree, wiping away the beads of perspiration from her body with the red tips of branches. The *rishi* had impregnated her womb. In the form of sweat, this emerged from her body through the pores in her limbs. The trees collected her sweat and the wind gathered it together in the form of one foetus. I nourished it with my rays, and it gradually grew. The foetus from the tops of trees became the one known as Marisha, beautiful in face. The trees will bestow her on you. Pacify your rage. Kandu's offspring originated from the trees. She is also my child and Vayu's. She is Pramlocha's daughter. The illustrious and excellent Kandu's austerities had decayed. O Maitreya![253] He went to Vishnu's temple, known by the name of Purushottama. There, with single-minded attention, he worshipped Hari. With an unwavering mind, he performed *japa* to the one who is beyond Brahma. O sons of a king! The great *yogi* raised his arms up and stood there."

[253] This is an inconsistency, since this is being related by Soma to the Prachetas.

'The Prachetas said, "O sage![254] We wish to hear the supreme hymn that Kandu used to perform *japa* and worship the divinity Keshava, who is beyond Brahma."'

'Soma replied, "Vishnu is beyond all boundaries. He is beyond everything that has a limit. He is greater than the greatest. The supreme truth is his form. He is beyond Brahma. He is beyond anything the senses can comprehend. His powers are beyond measurement. He is beyond all limits. He is the cause behind the cause. He is the reason behind the cause of the cause. In every kind of task, as the task and as the agent, he preserves everything. He is the lord Brahma. He is the *brahman* in all beings. He is Brahma, the lord of all beings. He is Achyuta. He is the *brahman* that does not decay. He is eternal and without origin. Vishnu is not subject to destruction or decay. He is not attached to anything. He is the *brahman*, without decay and without origin. The eternal Purushottama is like that. May my attachment and other sins be pacified." He performed this supreme *japa* and praised the one known as the supreme *brahman*. Having thus worshipped Keshava, he obtained supreme success. If a person constantly reads or hears this hymn, he is freed from desire and all other taints and obtains everything that he desires.[255] I will also tell you who Marisha used to be earlier. I will tell you about her praiseworthy acts, which are also beneficial for you. O excellent ones! Earlier, the immensely fortunate one was the wife of a king. Her husband died and she had no son. Therefore, she devotedly worshipped and satisfied Vishnu. Worshiped in this way, Vishnu showed himself to her and spoke to her. He said, "O auspicious one! Ask for a boon." She told him about her desire. "O illustrious

[254] Since the Prachetas are speaking to Soma, this too is an inconsistency.

[255] The text places this sentence within brackets. Therefore, it does not belong.

one! Though I am a child, I have become a widow. A birth like mine is in vain. O lord of the universe! I have been born as an unsuccessful and unfortunate person. From one birth to another birth, please let me have husbands who will be praised. Through your favours, let me have a son who will be a Prajapati. O Adhokshaja![256] Through your favours, let me be born, but not through a womb. Let me possess noble lineage, good conduct, youth, truthfulness, generosity, alacrity in action, undisputed spirit, servitude to elders, gratitude and beauty and let everyone find me handsome to behold." When she spoke to the lord of the gods in this way, Hrishikesha spoke to her. She was bent down in prostration. Parameshvara, the one who bestows boons, raised her up. The divinity answered, "In another life, you will have ten husbands. They will be immensely valiant and famous and extensive in their deeds. Your son will be extremely brave. He will be immensely strong and valiant. O beautiful one! You will have a son who will possess all the qualities of being a Prajapati. He will be the creator of a lineage that will spread over the entire universe. All three worlds will be populated by his descendants. You will not be born from a womb. You will be virtuous and will possess the qualities of beauty and generosity. Through my favours, you will cause delight in the minds of men." Saying this, the large-eyed divinity vanished. O sons of a king! She has been born as Marisha and will be your wife.'

Shri Parashara continued, 'At this, the Prachetas agreed to Soma's words. They withdrew their rage from the trees and following *dharma*, accepted Marisha as a wife. Through the ten Prachetas, Marisha gave birth to the immensely fortunate Daksha Prajapati, who, in an earlier life, had been Brahma's son. O extremely intelligent one! The immensely fortunate Daksha had sons, so that he could create subjects. There

[256] Vishnu's name.

were superior and inferior beings, bipeds and quadrupeds.
To follow Brahma's command about creation, this is what he
did. After this, through his mental powers, Daksha created
women. He bestowed ten of these daughters on Soma and
thirteen on Kashyapa. He bestowed twenty-seven[257] on the
moon, who marks out the passage of time. *Deva*s, *daitya*s,
*naga*s, cattle, birds, *gandharva*s, *apsara*s, *danava*s and others
were born in this way.[258] O Maitreya! Since then, offspring
have resulted from sexual intercourse. The earlier creation of
subjects is said to be one that resulted from resolution, sight
and touch.[259] This was done by ascetics, through success in
specific austerities.'

Shri Maitreya asked, 'I have heard that Daksha was formely
born from Brahma's right toe. O great sage! How could he
have been born as a son of the Prachetas? O *brahmana*! I have
a great doubt about this. He was Soma's maternal grandson.[260]
How did he become his father-in-law?'

Shri Parashara replied, 'For creatures, birth and destruction
are always perennial. *Rishi*s, who possess divine vision, are not
confused on this account. O supreme among sages! Daksha
and all the others are born in every *yuga* and again die in every
yuga. The learned are not confused on this account. O supreme
among *brahmana*s! Who is elder and who is younger is not
determined by who was born first. Austerities are supreme and
power is the determining factor.'

Maitreya said, 'O *brahmana*! Please describe to me in
detail the origin of *deva*s, *danava*s, *gandharva*s, *uraga*s and
*rakshasa*s.'

---

[257] The *nakshatra*s.
[258] From the daughters who were Kashyapa's wives.
[259] Through mental powers and without intercourse.
[260] Daksha was the son of Marisha, who was Soma's daughter.

Shri Parashara replied, 'Daksha had formerly been instructed by Svayambhu[261] to create subjects. O great sage! Listen to the way he went about creating offspring. Initially, Daksha created beings through his mental powers, such as *devas*, *rishis*, *gandharvas*, *asuras* and *pannagas*. But though he created them, the subjects did not multiply. For the sake of creation, Prajapati thought again. He wished to create many kinds of beings through the *dharma* of sexual intercourse. Virana Prajapati's daughter was Asikni, and he married her. This daughter had performed great austerities and was capable of holding up the worlds. Through Asikni, Virana's daughter, the valiant Prajapati Daksha had five thousand sons, for the purpose of creation. O *brahmana*! However, on seeing that they were ready to have offspring, *devarshi*[262] Narada, pleasant in speech, approached them and addressed them in these words. "O Haryashvas![263] O immensely valiant ones! It is evident that you are ready to have offspring. But why are you making efforts like these? Listen to my words. You are foolish. You do not know the top, the bottom, or the middle of the earth. How can you possibly create subjects? Where does the earth end? O foolish ones! Until you have seen everything, and your travels are unimpeded above, below and across, how can you possibly do this?" Hearing his words, they left in different directions. Like rivers that head for the ocean, they have still not returned. When the Haryashvas were destroyed, through Virana's daughter, the lord Daksha, the son of the Prachetas, had another one thousand sons. They were known as Shabalashvas and again desired to have offspring. O *brahmana*! However, Narada urged them with the words he had spoken earlier. They told each other, "What the great sage has said is right. There

---

[261] The one who created himself, Brahma.

[262] The celestial *rishi*.

[263] These sons were known as Haryashvas.

is no doubt that we must follow the footsteps of our brothers. We must create subjects only after we have determined the dimensions of the earth." Following the same path, they left in all the directions. Like rivers that head for the ocean, they have still not returned. O *brahmana*! Ever since then, a brother who sets out in search of a lost brother is swiftly destroyed. A learned person must never do something like this. Knowing that his sons had been destroyed, Daksha Prajapati was filled with rage. The immensely fortunate one cursed Narada.'[264]

'O Maitreya! The learned Prajapati desired to continue with creation. We have heard that, through Virana's daughter, he had sixty sons. He bestowed ten on Dharma, thirteen on Kashyapa, twenty-seven on Soma, four on Arishtanemi, two on Bahuputra, two on Angiras and two on Krishashva. Hear and learn about their names. Dharma's ten wives were Arundhati, Vasu, Jami, Langha, Bhanu, Marutvati, Sankalpa, Muhurta, Sadhya and Vishva. Hear about their offspring. Vishva gave birth to the Vishvadevas and Sadhya to the Sadhyas. Marutvati's sons were the Marutvats, and Vasu's sons are known as the Vasus. Bhanu's sons were the Bhanus, and the Muhurtas were born from Muhurta. Ghosha was the son of Langha, and Jami's daughter was Nagavithi. All entities on earth were born from Arundhati. From Sankalpaa was born Sankalpa, the resolution that is in the *atman* of everything. Nagavithi, Yami's daughter, gave birth to Vrishala. The divinities known as Vasus are full of life and proceed ahead of the stellar bodies. They are known as the eight Vasus, and I will speak about them in detail. The names of the Vasus are said to be Apa, Dhruva, Soma,[265] Dharma, Anila, Anala,[266] Pratyusha and Prabhasa. These are known as

---

[264] Mitigated a bit, the curse was that Narada would be born as Daksha's son.

[265] Not to be confused with the moon.

[266] The same as Agni.

the names of the Vasus. Apa's sons were Vaitandya, Shrama, Shranta and Dhvani. Dhruva's son was the illustrious Kala, who reckons time in the worlds. Soma's son was the illustrious Varcha and radiance results from him. Through Manohara, the sons of Dharma were Dravina, Hutahavyavaha, Shishira, Prana and Ravana. Shiva[267] was Anila's wife and her son was Manojava. Anila had two sons, the other was Avijnatagati. Agni's son, Kumara, was born in a clump of reeds. The descendants who followed him were Shakha, Vishakha and Naigameya. He is known as Kartikeya because he was the son of the Krittikas.[268] It is known that Pratyusha's son was the *rishi* named Devala. Devala had two sons who were forgiving and learned. Brihaspati's sister was a supreme lady who knew about the *brahman*. Her name was Yogasiddha, and she roamed around the entire earth, not attached to anything. She became the wife of Prabhasa, the eighth Vasu. The immensely fortunate Prajapati Vishvakarma was born from her. He is the creator of thousands of works of artisanship and is the architect of the gods. The supreme among artisans created all the ornaments of the gods and also all the divine *vimana*s. Humans earn subsistence through the great-souled one's art of craftsmanship. Ajaikapada, Ahirbudhnya and the valiant Rudra were born from Tvashta. The great ascetic, Vishvarupa, was also Tvashta's son. O great sage! The names of the eleven Rudras are said to be Hara, Bahurupa, Tryambaka, Aparajita, Vrishakapi, Shambhu, Kapardi, Raivata, Mrigavyadha, Sharva and Kapali.[269] They are famous as the lords of the worlds. One hundred infinitely energetic Rudras are also mentioned. Hear

[267] Shivaa.

[268] The Pleiades. Kartikeya/Kumara/Skanda was reared by the Krittikas. They adopted him as their son.

[269] These minor Rudras are not to be confused with the major Rudra, Shiva. There are eleven minor Rudras.

about the wives of Prajapati Kashyapa. O one who knows
about *dharma*! They were Aditi, Diti, Danu, Arishta, Surasa,
Khasa, Surabhi, Vinata, Tamra, Krodhavasha, Ira, Kadru and
Muni. Hear about their offspring. In the earlier *manvantara*,
there were twelve excellent and supreme *sura*s. They were
named the Tushitas. When the end of Chakshusha *manvantara*
approached, they assembled and spoke to each other. "O
gods! Come. Let us quickly enter Aditi's womb. When the
new *manvantara* presents itself, we will be born. That will be
best." During Chakshusha Manu's *manvantara*, all of them
said this. They have been born as the sons of Kashyapa and
Aditi, Daksha's daughter. Vishnu and Shakra have been born
again. The twelve infinitely energetic Adityas are said to be
Aryama, Dhatri, Tvashta, Pusha, Vivasvat, Savitar, Mitra,
Varuna, Amsha and Bhaga.[270] In Chakshusha *manvantara*, the
*sura*s were known as the Tushitas. In Vaivasvata *manvantara*,
they are known as the twelve Adityas. Soma's twenty-seven
wives have been mentioned and they were great in their vows.
All of them were *yogini*s and they are said to have given their
names to the *nakshatra*s. Their offspring blazed and were
infinitely energetic. Arishtanemi's wives had sixteen offspring.
The sons of the learned Bahuputra are said to be the four
Vidyutas.[271] The excellent Pratyangirasa hymns from the *Rig
Veda* are honoured by *brahmana rishi*s.[272] The sons of *devarshi*
Krishashva are said to be the weapons of the gods. In this
way, when one thousand *yuga*s are over, all of them are born
again, as they will. O son! There are thirty-three categories

[270] Twelve with Vishnu and Shakra included.

[271] *Vidyut* means lightning and there are believed to be four kinds
of lightning: tawny (with gusts of wind), red (during summer), yellow
(during the monsoon) and black (during famines).

[272] There are thirty-five such hymns. They were the descendants
of Angiras.

of gods.[273] They are also said to have origin and destruction. O Maitreya! Just as the sun rises and sets, from one *yuga* to another *yuga*, the gods are created and destroyed.'

'We have heard that from Kashyapa two sons were born to Diti, Hiranyakashipu and the invincible Hiranyaksha. She had a daughter named Simhika, who was married to Viprachitti. Their sons were immensely strong and were known as the Saimhikeyas. Hiranyakashipu had four sons who were famous for their energy: Anuhlada, Hlada, the intelligent Prahlada and the immensely valiant Samhlada. They extended the lineage of the *daitya*s. O immensely fortunate one! Among them, Prahlada was impartial in his outlook and supremely devoted. O *brahmana*! When the flames ignited by the Indra among the *daitya*s[274] enveloped all his limbs, he spoke to Janardana. O *brahmana*! Vasudeva was in his heart, and they could not burn him down. He was flung down from the summit of mountain into the great ocean and the earth trembled. However, though he was bound with ropes, he could still move. Many weapons brought down on him by the Indra among the *daitya*s could not mangle him. With his entire mind immersed in Achyuta, his body became as firm as a mountain. The lords of snakes were released on him, urged by the *daitya*. They were extremely energetic, and flames and poison issued from their mouths. But they could not destroy him. When his body was flung down from the mountain, he remembered Purushottama. Since he possessed the armour of remembering Vishnu, he did not give up his life. When he was flung down from the top by the lord of the *daitya*s, the earth welcomed the extremely intelligent one. The residents of heaven held him up. The Indra among the *daitya*s urged the wind to dry up his body. But since his mind

---

[273] Usually listed as twelve Adityas, eleven Rudras, eight Vasus and two Ashvins.
[274] Prahlada's father, Hiranyakashipu.

was in Madhusudana, it was instantly repulsed. The *diggajas*
were released against him by the Indra among the *daityas*. But
the outcome was that their pride was destroyed, and their tusks
were shattered. The priests of the king of the *daityas* invoked
evil portents against him. However, since his mind was already
immersed in Govinda, they could not destroy him. Shambara,
extremely well-versed in *maya*, released thousands of kinds of
maya against him. However, Krishna's *chakra* countered all
of these. The Indra of the *daityas* had his cooks administer
halahala poison.[275] But this could not harm or disturb him and
he digested it. He was impartial and looked upon all beings in
the universe in the same way. He possessed the quality of great
friendliness and looked upon others as his own self. He had
dharma in his soul and was a store of qualities like truthfulness
and valour. He was always a model for every kind of virtuous
person.'

Chapter 1(16) (Questions about
Prahlada's History)

Shri Maitreya said, 'You have spoken about the lineage of
the great-souled descendants of Manu and about the eternal
Vishnu, the cause behind this universe. O illustrious one! Please
tell me about Prahlada, the excellent *daitya*. Fire could not
burn him. Weapons could not pierce him. He did not give up
his life. When he fell down, the earth trembled. When he was
bound with ropes and flung down into the waters of the ocean,
he could still move around. He was controlled and moved his
limbs around. In those ancient times, though his body was flung

---

[275] A terrible and virulent poison.

down from a mountain, he did not die. You have spoken about
the intelligent one's wonderful greatness. O sage! Because of
his devotion towards Vishnu, his power was unmatched. I
wish to hear about the conduct of the one who blazed in his
energy. O sage! What was the reason why Diti's descendant
hurled those weapons towards him? Since he was devoted to
dharma, why was he flung into the ocean? Why was he struck
with boulders? Why did the giant *uragas* bite him? Why was
he flung down from the summit of a mountain? Why was he
thrown into the fire? Why did he use the tusks of the *diggajas*
to draw out marks on the ground? Why did the giant *asuras*
use the wind to dry him up? O sage! Why did the *guru* of the
*daitya*s invoke a *kritya*?[276] Why did Shambara use thousands
of different kinds of *maya*? Why did the *daitya* cooks make
him ingest *halahala* poison? Having ingested it, the intelligent
one was not destroyed, but merely digested it. O immensely
fortunate one! I wish to hear all this, about the conduct of
the great-souled Prahlada. They are marks of greatness. I am
not curious about the *daitya*s being unable to kill him. Who
is capable of bringing down a person who is single-mindedly
devoted to Vishnu? However, he was supremely devoted to
dharma and always worshipped Keshava. Moreover, he was
born in their own lineage. Why did the *daitya*s hate him,
something that is very difficult to do? He possessed *dharma*
in his soul. He was immensely fortunate. He was devoted to
Vishnu. He was without malice. Why did the *daitya*s strike
him? You should explain this to me. They struck a great-souled
one who did not belong to the adversary's side. He possessed
all the qualities. He was virtuous. Moreover, he was born on
their own side. O bull among sages! Therefore, you should tell

[276] A *kritya* is a female deity to whom sacrifices are offered for
destructive purposes.

me about all this. I wish to hear everything about the conduct
of the lord of the *daityas*.'[277]

Chapter 1(17) (Story of Prahlada)

Shri Parashara said, 'O Maitreya! Hear the complete account
of the intelligent one's conduct. The great-souled Prahlada
was always generous in his conduct. In ancient times, Diti's
descendant was the immensely valiant Hiranyakashipu. Insolent
because of a boon he had received from Brahma, he brought the
three worlds under his control. The great *asura* himself assumed
the status of Indra, Savitar, Vayu, Agni, the lord of the waters,
Soma, the lord of riches and Yama. The *asura* himself enjoyed
all the shares in sacrifices. O supreme among sages! The gods
abandoned heaven. All of them assumed human bodies and
roamed around the earth. He conquered the three worlds and
was insolent because of all the prosperity of the three worlds.
The *gandharva*s chanted his praise. He loved all the material
objects and enjoyed them. The great-souled Hiranyakashipu
was addicted to drinking and when he did this, all the *siddha*s,
*gandharva*s and *pannaga*s worshipped him. Others sang and
there were others who uttered sounds of "Victory". In front of
the king of the *daitya*s, the delighted *siddha*s did this. As the
asura happily drank liquor in the extremely beautiful palace
that was made out of crystal, the *apsara*s danced there.'

'He had an immensely fortunate son, known by the name
of Prahlada. When he was a child, he went to his *guru*'s house
and read the texts meant for children. On one occasion, with
his *guru*, the one with *dharma* in his soul went to his father,
the lord of the *daitya*s, when he was drinking. His father

[277] Meaning Prahlada, not Hiranyakashipu.

raised his son, who was prostrate at his feet. Hiranyakashipu
spoke to the infinitely energetic Prahlada. Hiranyakashipu
said, "O child! For some time, you have been instructed in all
the good sayings. Please tell me now the essence of the good
sayings[278] you have learnt." Prahlada replied, "O father! As
instructed by you, I will tell you the essence. Please listen. With
a controlled mind, this is what my heart is immersed in. He is
without a beginning, without a middle and without an end.
He is without origin. He is without increase or decrease. He
is the imperishable Achyuta. He is the cause behind all causes.
I prostrate myself before the one responsible for creation and
destruction." Hearing this, the eyes of the Indra among the
daityas turned red with rage. With quivering lips, he looked
towards the *guru* and spoke to him. Hiranyakashipu said, "O
brahma-bandhu![279] Why is he full of praise for an enemy? O
evil-minded one! Ignoring my command, you have taught the
child what is without substance." The *guru* replied, "O lord
of the *daityas*! You should not come under the subjugation
of this rage. What your son has said is not the result of
anything I have taught him." Hiranyakashipu responded,
"O Prahlada! O child! Who has taught you this? Please tell
me. Your *guru* has said that this is not something that he has
instructed you." Prahlada answered, "Vishnu is the instructor
of everyone in the universe and he is in the heart. O father!
Other than that *paramatman*, who else can be an instructor?"
Hiranyakashipu responded, "O extremely evil-minded one!
You are repeatedly speaking about Vishnu. Who is he? I am the
lord of the universe, and you are emphatically stating this in
front of me." Prahlada said, "He cannot be perceived through
sound.[280] He is the supreme objective that *yogis* meditate on.

---

[278] The text uses the word *subhashitam*.
[279] An inferior *brahmana*.
[280] That is, he cannot be described in words.

He is himself this entire universe, which flows from him. He
is Parameshvara Vishnu." Hiranyakashipu responded, "As
long as I exist, who else deserves to be called Parameshvara?
Neverthless, you are repeatedly saying this, as if you wish to
die." Prahlada said, "The *brahman* is Vishnu's form. O father!
He is not just in me, but in all beings, and in you. He is Dhatri
and Vidhatri. He is Parameshvara. Please be pacified. What
is the point of this rage?" Hiranyakashipu replied, "O evil-
minded one! Which great evildoer has entered your heart? With
this evil in your mind, you are uttering such wicked words."
Prahlada said, "Vishnu is not just in my heart. He traverses
all the worlds and is present in everything. O father! He goes
everywhere and urges the efforts of everyone—you, me and
all the others." Hiranyakashipu replied, "Take this evil one
away to his *guru*'s house. Who has goaded this evil-minded
one to praise my enemy?" Thus addressed, the *daitya*s again
took him to his *guru*'s house. Engaged in serving his *guru*, he
spent night and day in receiving learning. After a long period
of time had passed, the lord of the *asura*s summoned Prahlada
again and commanded him, "O son! Sing some chant."
Prahlada responded, "He is Pradhana and Purusha. He is the
cause behind everything mobile and immobile. May Vishnu be
pleased with us." Hiranyakashipu said, "This evil-souled one
should be killed. There is no point to his remaining alive. He is
causing harm to his own side. He is the worst of his lineage."[281]
Thus addressed, hundreds and thousands of *daitya*s seized
their large weapons and rushed towards him, so as to kill him.'

'Prahlada said, "O *daitya*s! Vishnu resides in me. By
that truth, the weapons you are attacking me with will fail."
Hundreds of *daitya*s repeatedly struck him with weapons.
But he did not feel the slightest bit of pain and his body was

---

[281] *Kulangara*, one who ruins his lineage. Literally, someone who
is like burning coal for the lineage.

as good as new. Hiranyakashipu said, "O evil-minded one! Refrain from praising an enemy. O extremely foolish one! I am granting you freedom from fear. Use your intelligence." Prahlada replied, "My mind is in the infinite one, who bestows freedom from fear. Where is there any fear in me? O father! When one remembers him, all fear on account of birth, old age and death goes away." Hiranyakashipu said, "O snakes! This one is evil in conduct and extremely evil-minded. Fill your mouths with garlands of flames and poison and destroy him." Thus addressed, the extremely poisonous snakes, Kuhaka, Takshaka and the others, bit him all over his body. However, his mind was immersed in Krishna. As he remembered that source of bliss, though the giant *uraga*s bit him all over his body, he felt no pain. The snakes said, "Our fangs have been shattered. Our jewels have broken.[282] Our hoods are scorched. Our hearts are trembling. We have not been able to pierce his skin, not even a little. O lord of the *daitya*s! Please command someone else to undertake this task." Hiranyakashipu said, "O *diggaja*s! Together, use your tusks to mangle and slay the one who has taken the side of the enemy. Though he was born from me, he is like a blazing fire in the forest." The *diggaja*s were like the summits of mountains. They flung the child down on the surface of the ground and struck him with their tusks. However, he remembered Govinda and those tusks struck against his chest and were shattered into thousands of fragments. He told his father, "The tusks of the cruel elephants were like the *vajra* at the tips. They have been shattered and that is not because of my strength. If a person's sentiments are such that he remembers Janardana, all his great hardships are destroyed." Hiranyakashipu said, "O *asura*s! Let the elephants go and let the fire burn him down. O wind! Kindle the fire and make it burn down this evildoer." The *danava*s piled a

---

[282] *Naga*s have jewels on their hoods.

huge heap of wood around the son of the Indra among the
*asura*s. Urged by their master, they tried to burn him down
with fire. Prahlada said, "O father! The fire and the wind are
unable to burn me down. In every direction, I see lotus flowers
spread out, with their cool faces." At this, the *brahmana*s who
were descendants of Bhargava spoke to the lord of the *daitya*s.
These were great-souled and eloquent priests, accomplished in
the *Sama Veda*.'

'The priests praised him and said, "O king! Restrain your
rage. He is a child and your own son. How can rage be successful
in the abode of the gods?" Hiranyakashipu's own priests spoke
to him in this way. "O king! We will instruct the child about
what is right, so that he is humble about the destruction of the
enemy. Childhood is the time for committing all kinds of errors
and you are the king of the *daitya*s. Therefore, you should not
exhibit this rage towards a child. If he does not listen to your
words and abandon Hari and if he does not come over to our
side, we will arrange for a *kritya* that will kill him. Please
refrain now." In this way, the priests requested the king of the
*daitya*s, and he instructed the *daitya*s to take his son out from
that mass of flames. The child resided in the house of his *guru*.'

'Whenever there was a gap in the *guru*'s instructions, he
taught the young *danava*s. Prahlada said, "O *daitya*s who
are the descendants of Diti! Hear from me about the supreme
truth. There is nothing else that is important. There is nothing
else to be coveted. O sons of lords among the *daitya*s! Every
being goes through birth and childhood and becomes a youth.
Every day, there is the onset of old age. Every being proceeds
towards death. This is evident and it will also happen to us. A
person who dies will be born again. It cannot but be otherwise.
This is stated in the *agama* texts.[283] But without a cause, there

---

[283] *Agama*s are texts other than the *Veda*s, such as the *tantra*
texts.

cannot be an origin. From the time of residence in the womb, if there are causes for rebirth, as long as there is existence, one must experience miseries. A person who is childish in his intelligence thinks that the pacification of hunger, thirst and cold is happiness. However, there is unhappiness again. If the limbs are extremely paralyzed, those who desire happiness try to exercise them. Those whose eyes are closed because they are confounded by *ajnana*,[284] take unhappiness to be happiness. This body is a great store of phlegm and all the others.[285] Where are qualities like beauty, grace, handsomeness, charm and others? The body is full of flesh, blood, pus, urine, excrement, sinews, fat and bones. A foolish person loves it and desires hell. When it is cold, the fire is agreeable. When one is thirsty, water is agreeable. When one is hungry, food is agreeable. A person uses these to find happiness. But in other situations, their opposites may give rise to happiness.[286] O sons of *daitya*s! A person who marries also provides for unhappiness in his heart. As long as a being acts because attachments provide pleasure to his mind, the stakes of sorrow and doubt are impaled in his heart. If a person has possessions in his house, wherever he goes, there are thoughts of destruction, fire and theft in his mind. Since birth, until the time of death, there are great hardships. When one dies, until one passes into a new womb, there are fierce hardships inflicted by Yama. If there is not the slightest bit of pleasure in the womb, you must also grant what I am saying—the entire universe is full of misery. There are many kinds of great misery in this ocean that is *samsara*. I am telling you the truth. Vishnu alone is the refuge. Since we

[284] Ignorance, the opposite of *jnana*.

[285] *Vata*, *pitta* and *kapha* can be loosely translated as wind, bile and phlegm. In *Ayurveda*, these are the three *dosha*s or humours in the body and they are always striving against each other.

[286] When it is cold, heat may be agreeable, and so on.

are children, we do not know that the *atman* in the body is
eternal. Old age, youth, birth and other things are the *dharma*
of the body, not of the *atman*. I am a child. Therefore, I think
that when I become a youth, it is best to exert myself. When
I become a youth, I think that when I attain old age, I will
do what is best for the *atman*. When I am old, I no longer
remember everything that I have done. I am evil-souled and no
longer capable of undertaking what should have been done.
In this way, a man always strives for his desires and his mind
is agitated. There is no one who is thirsty enough to proceed
towards the ultimate benefit. In childhood, one is addicted
to playing. In youth, one looks towards material objects.
Incapable and ignorant, one finds that old age has presented
itself. Therefore, even in childhood, one must be discriminating
and strive for what is beneficial. Hence, I have told you that
in childhood, youth and old age, one must not be attached to
physical sentiments. Since you know that is not false, for our
own pleasure, we should remember Vishnu. He is the one who
grants emancipation from this bondage. Why not make efforts
to remember him, since his memory brings pleasure? If one
remembers him night and day, sins are destroyed. He is present
in all beings and, night and day, one must love him a lot. The
entire universe is suffering from three kinds of hardships.[287]
What wise man will hate beings who are grieving? Even if
I am inferior in strength, I should be extremely delighted at
beings who are more fortunate than me.[288] The consequences
of hatred are injurious. Hence, if a person hates beings and
is bound in enmity towards them, the learned have said that
he is overwhelmed by pervasive confusion and needs to be
grieved over. O *daitya*s! I have thus described those who hold

[287] Relating to *adhidaivika* (destiny), *adhibhoutika* (nature) and
adhyatmika (one's own nature).
[288] I should not be envious.

a different kind of view. There are those who have successfully
risen above this. Hear briefly from me. Vishnu pervades
everything in this universe and every being. The discriminating
know that he should be seen as one's own self, without any
differentiation. Let us therefore set aside our *asura* sentiments
and make efforts so that we achieve *nivritti*. We can ourselves
achieve a state so that we do not suffer from any harm caused
by fire, the sun, the moon, the wind, Parjanya, Varuna, *siddhas*,
rakshasas, *yakshasa*, Indras among *daityas*, *uragas*, *kinnaras*,
humans or animals. We will not suffer from fever, ailments of
the eye and diseases of the stomach, spleen and liver. Hatred,
envy, attachment and avarice will be destroyed. We will not be
dragged away by any of these. Instead, we will proceed towards
what is sparkling. With Keshava in his heart, a man obtains
that which is without blemish. Do not get enmeshed in this
cycle of *samsara*, which is without substance. I am telling you
about supreme contentment. Therefore, all the *daityas* should
gather together. They should assemble and worship Achyuta.
When he is pleased, there is nothing that cannot be obtained.
The pursuit of *dharma*, *kama* and *artha* is trifling. If we resort
to the infinite, who is beyond Brahma, there is no doubt that
we will obtain great fruits."'

Chapter 1(18) (Hiranyakashipu's Attempts)

Shri Parashara said, 'The best of the *danavas* witnessed
this.[289] Out of fear, they went and informed the lord of the
daityas. He swiftly summoned his cooks and spoke to them.
Hiranyakashipu said, "O cooks! My evil-minded son is now
instructing other children about his wicked doctrines. Without

[289] Prahlada's *gurus* went and told Hiranyakashipu.

any delay, he should be killed. In every kind of food you give
him, mix *halahala* poison, so that he does not detect it. The
wicked one must be killed. There is no need to reflect about
this." They agreed. As instructed by the great-souled one's
father, they gave the great-souled Prahlada poison. Prahlada
was assured in his mind. He ate it and suffered from no adverse
effects. Since he remembered Ananta's name, the poison lost
all energy and was digested. Witnessing that the great poison
had been digested, the cooks were filled with fear. They went
to the lord of the *daitya*s. Prostrating themselves, they reported
this. The cooks said, "O king of the *daitya*s! We administered
extremely virulent poison to him. But along with the food,
your son, Prahlada, has digested it." Hiranyakashipu replied,
"O priests of the *daitya*s! Hurry. Immediately, make haste.
Without any delay, for his destruction, generate a *kritya*." The
priests went to Prahlada.'

'Full of humility, they first addressed him in conciliatory
tones. The priests said, "O one with a long life! You have
been born in Brahma's lineage, one that is famous in the
three worlds. You are the son of Hiranyakashipu, the king
of the *daitya*s. What need of gods? What need of Ananta?
Why do you need another refuge? Your father is that for all
the worlds and should be yours too. Abandoning him, you
have taken the side of an adversary. A father is praiseworthy.
Among all *guru*s, he is the supreme *guru*." Prahlada replied,
"O immensely fortunate ones! It is indeed true that Marichi's
great lineage is praised in all the three worlds. You have not
said what is false. Through his efforts, my father has become
the best in the entire universe. I understand that. It is true and
not false. You have said that the father is the supreme *guru*
among all *guru*s. There is not the slightest bit of confusion in
what you have said. There is no doubt that a father is a *guru*,
and one must make efforts to worship him. There is nothing I
contest, and my mind agrees with it. However, you have also

spoken about my being attached in this way to Ananta. Who
can say what is appropriate? This bit of what you have said
is without substance." Saying this, out of the respect due to
them, he was silent for a while. Then he laughed and spoke
again. "Why seek out Ananta? Those are laudable words. Why
Ananta? You are my praiseworthy *guru*s. If this does not cause
you any regret, hear about Ananta. *Dharma, artha, kama* and
moksha are spoken of as the objectives of human existence.[290]
What about the one from whom these four originate? What do
you have to say about him? Marichi, Daksha and the others
obtained *dharma* from Ananta. In this way, *artha* and *kama*
were obtained by others. There are those who have discerned
the truth through *jnana, dhyana* and *samadhi*.[291] With their
bonds destroyed, they have obtained emancipation with
the supreme being. Wealth, prosperity, greatness, learning,
offspring and deeds—there are many such divisions that can be
obtained. However, the single root for all these is the worship
of Hari. O *brahmana*s! He is the cause behind the fruits known
as *dharma, artha, kama* and emancipation. Therefore, how can
one ask, 'Why does one need Ananta?' What is the need to
speak a lot? You are my *guru*s. I am limited in my sense of
discrimination. It is not for me to decide whether what you
have said is right or wrong. What is the need to speak a lot
about this? He is the lord of the universe. He is the creator, the
preserver and the destroyer. He is established in the heart. He is
the one who enjoys what is to be enjoyed. He is the lord of the
universe. If I have spoken anything in my childishness, please
pardon me." The priests said, "O child! When you were about

---

[290] *Purushartha*s.
[291] *Yoga* has eight elements: *yama* (restraint), *niyama* (rituals),
asana (posture), *pranayama* (breathing), *pratyahara* (withdrawal),
dharana (retention), *dhyana* (meditation) and *samadhi* (liberation).
That's the reason the expression *ashtanga* (eight-formed) *yoga* is used.

to be burnt down in the fire, we protected you. We thought
you would no longer speak in this way. We did not know that
you lack in intelligence. O evil-minded one! Since, out of your
confusion, you did not accept our words and desist, we will
create a *kritya* that will destroy you." Prahlada replied, "Who
kills a being, and through what means? Who protects a being,
and through what means? Depending on whether he commits
virtuous or wicked deeds, a person protects or slays himself.
Everything originates from *karma*. *Karma* is the means whereby
the destination is determined. Therefore, one must make every
kind of effort to pursue virtuous *karma*." Addressed by him in
this way, the priests of the king of the *daitya*s became angry.'

'They created a *kritya* who blazed within a garland of
flames. Her form was flaming. She was extremely terrible and
approached, indenting the earth with her feet. She wielded an
excellent trident and swiftly struck him on the chest. The blazing
trident struck the child's heart and fell down on the ground,
shattered into a hundred pieces. If the illustrious Lord Hari
resides in a person's heart, even the *vajra* is shattered. What
need be said about a trident? The wicked *daitya* priests had
unleashed her against an innocent person. Therefore, the *kritya*
quickly turned against them and killed them. The immensely
intelligent one saw that they were being burnt down by the
kritya. He prayed to Krishna. Prahlada said, "O Krishna! O
Ananta! You pervade everything. The universe is your form.
O Janardana! You are the creator of the universe. Please save
these *brahmana*s from this *kritya*. This fire has been created
through the use of *mantra*s and is impossible to withstand.
You are in all beings. You pervade everything and are the *guru*
of the universe. O Vishnu! Therefore, let all these priests live.
Vishnu is everywhere and I do not harbor any inimical thoughts
towards them. Hence, considering this, I think the priests
should remain alive. I am not wicked. Those who approached
to kill me, those who administered poison to me, the fire, the

*diggaja*s that tried to crush me, and the snakes that bit me—I am impartial and have friendly sentiments towards all these. By that truth, let the priests of the *asura* king remain alive." When he said this and touched them, all of them became healthy. The *brahmana*s arose and spoke respectfully to him. The priests said, "May you have a long lifespan. May your strength and valour never face obstructions. O excellent child! May you have sons, grandsons, wealth and prosperity." O great sage! Having told him this, the priests went to the king of the *daitya*s and told him about everything that had happened.'

Chapter 1(19) (Prahlada's Story Continued)

Shri Parashara said, 'Hiranyakashipu heard that the *kritya* had been repulsed. He summoned his son and asked him about the reason for his power. Hiranyakashipu asked, "O Prahlada! What have you done to obtain these great powers? Are they the result of *mantra*s? Or have you naturally possessed them since birth?" The father asked Prahlada, the *asura* child. He prostrated himself at his father's feet and addressed him in these words. "O father! These are not due to *mantra*s. Nor are they a result of natural causes. If Achyuta is in a person's heart, such powers are perfectly ordinary. If a person looks towards others as if they are his own self and does not commit wicked deeds against them, all his wickedness vanishes, since the cause no longer exists. If a person causes suffering to others in thought, words and deeds, he creates a seed for a future birth in which he faces a lot that is inauspicious. I do not wish for anything evil. I do not do it. Nor do I speak it. I think of Keshava in all beings, just as he exists within my own self. Since my mind is pure throughout, how can there be physical or mental pain, caused by divine or natural causes, in me?

Those who are learned know that Hari exists in all beings. Therefore, it is their task to cherish all beings in this way." The Indra among the *daitya*s was standing atop his palace when he heard this. His face turned dark with rage, and he commanded the *daitya* servants.'

'Hiranyakashipu said, "From the top of this palace, hurl this evil-souled person one hundred *yojana*s away.[292] Let him fall down on the slope of the mountain and let his body be mangled against the rocks." All the *daitya*s and *danava*s flung the child away. Hurled from the top, he fell, but Hari was in his heart. Since he was full of devotion towards Keshava, the preserver of the universe, the earth, the mother of the universe, held him and embraced him. Hiranyakashipu saw that he was fine and that the bones of his body had not been shattered. He spoke to Shambara, supreme among those who knew about *maya*. Hiranyakashipu said, "We are incapable of killing this evil-minded child. You know about *maya*. Use that *maya* to kill him." Shambara replied, "O Indra among the *daitya*s! I will kill him. Behold the strength of my *maya*. Behold one thousand different kinds of *maya*. Behold a hundred crore." Shambara, the *asura*, unleashed his *maya* against Prahlada. The evil-minded one wished to kill someone who was impartial in outlook towards everyone. Prahlada composed himself and harboured no malice against Shambara. Full of friendliness, he remembered Madhusudana. For his protection, the illustrious one commanded the excellent Sudarshana *chakra* to go, blazing in a garland of flames. It arrived swiftly. For the sake of protecting the child, each and every one of Shambara's one thousand kinds of *maya* was countered. The Indra among the *daitya*s told Vayu, "Dry him up. Follow my instructions and swiftly destroy the evil-souled one." Thus instructed, the swift

[292] A *yojana* is a measure of distance, between eight and nine miles.

wind entered his body, so as to dry him up. That extremely harsh cold was difficult to withstand. Knowing that it had entered his body, the *daitya* child fixed the great-souled one, the one who holds up the earth, in his heart. Seated in the heart, Janardana angrily drank up the wind and the wind was destroyed. All the *maya* was destroyed and the wind was also destroyed.'

'The immensely intelligent one[293] returned to his *guru*'s house. From one day to another day, the preceptor instructed him about the good policy that yields fruits for a kingdom. The child learnt the principles that Ushanas had devised for kings. When the *guru* thought that he had humbly learnt all the principles of *niti shastra*,[294] he informed his father that he had been trained. The *acharya*[295] said, "O lord of the *daitya*s! Your son has learnt the texts of *niti shastra*. Prahlada now knows everything that Bhargava[296] propounded." Hiranyakashipu asked, "How should a king behave towards friends and enemies? O Prahlada! How should he act amidst the three kinds of people?[297] How should he treat ministers and advisers, those who are inside and those outside?[298] How should be employ spies amongst the citizens and amongst those he suspects? What are the norms for taking action and not taking action? How should forests and fortifications be extended? How should thorns be taken care of? O Prahlada! Please answer this accurately. That apart, tell me everything else that you have studied. I wish to know what is in your

---

[293] Prahlada.

[294] The texts on good policy.

[295] Both the *acharya* and the *upadhyaya* are teachers, but there is a hierarchy. An *upadhyaya* is just a teacher, whereas an *acharya* is a *guru*. The family priest is *purohita*.

[296] That is, Shukracharya/Ushanas.

[297] Friends, enemies and those who are neutral.

[298] Those inside the palace and those outside.

mind." Adorned with humility, he prostrated himself at his
father's feet. Prahlada joined his hands in salutation and spoke
to the Indra among the *daitya*s. Prahlada replied, "There is no
doubt that my *guru*s have instructed me about all this. I have
learnt them, but I do not agree with them. It has been said
that the four methods for making everyone a friend are *sama*,
dana, *danda* and *bheda*.[299] O father! But do not be angry. I do
not see anyone who is not a friend. O mighty-armed one! If
the objective does not exist, what is the need for a method? O
father! Jagannatha pervades the universe and is in the *atman*s
of all beings. Govinda is the *paramatman*. What does a friend
or enemy mean? The illustrious Vishnu exists in you, me and
in everyone else. That being the case, how is a friend different
from an enemy? There are many kinds of wicked things that
are explained in detail, but they are devoid of meaning. All such
enterprise results from ignorance. O father! One should strive
for what is beneficial. O father! One thinks this learning is due
to intelligence, but this so-called learning originates in *ajnana*.
O lord of the *asura*s! Does a child not take a firefly to be fire?
Tasks are those that do not bind. What emancipates is learning.
Even if accomplished easily, all other tasks and learning are
stuff devised by skilled artisans. That is the reason everything I
have learnt is without substance. O immensely fortunate one!
I will prostrate myself and tell you what the supreme essence
is. Listen. A man who does not think about the kingdom, or
about wealth, obtains benefit in this world and in the next one.
O immensely fortunate one! He then strives for greatness in
every possible way. The reason for a man's prosperity lies in
destiny and not in enterprise. O lord! Kingdoms and objects of
pleasure are bestowed on those who are dumb, those who have

---

[299] The traditional four means are *sama* (conciliation or
negotiation), *dana* (bribery), *danda* (punishment) and *bheda*
(dissension).

no discrimination, those who are not brave and those who do not know good policy. Hence, if one desires great benefit, one should focus on the sacred. If one desires *nirvana*,[300] one should be impartial in one's outlook. Gods, humans, animals, birds, trees and reptiles are Ananta's forms. Vishnu exists in different forms. One should know that everything in the universe, mobile and immobile, is nothing but that. Such a person sees that Vishnu, who assumes the form of the universe, exists in all these and in his own self. If one knows this, the illustrious Parameshvara, without a beginning, is pleased. When Achyuta is pleased, all hardships are destroyed." When he heard this, Hiranyakashipu angrily stood up from his excellent seat.'

'With his foot, he kicked his son in the chest. In his rage and intolerance, he seemed to blaze. He rubbed one hand with another. Desiring to kill him, he spoke. Hiranyakashipu said, "O Viprachitti! O Rahu! O Bali! Without any delay, firmly tie him with bonds of the *naga*s and hurl him into the great ocean. Otherwise, all the worlds and the *daitya*s and *danava*s will start to follow the views of this evil-souled and foolish one. Though he has been restrained several times, this wicked one continues to side with the enemy. He praises the wicked and causes harm. Therefore, kill him." The *daitya*s hurriedly tied him up in bonds of *naga*s. The servants obeyed the king and flung him into the water of the ocean. Though Prahlada had been rendered immobile, the great ocean started to move. It was agitated and giant waves arose in every direction. It seemed as if a giant flood of water would submerge the entire earth. O immensely intelligent one! Hiranyakashipu spoke to the *daitya*s. Hiranyakashipu said, "O *daitya*s! All of you hurl boulders into Varuna's abode, so that there is no gap in any direction and the evil-minded one is crushed under this. The fire did not burn him. Weapons did not pierce him. *Uraga*s

---

[300] The state of emancipation when everything is extinguished.

could not destroy him. The wind, poison or *kritya* could not destroy him. *Maya* did not harm him, nor the *diggaja*s. He survived being flung down. This child's mind is extremely wicked. There is no need for him to remain alive. Fling giant boulders into the water. Since the evil-minded one still retains his life, let him remain buried under these for one thousand years." The *daitya*s and *danava*s chose and dragged mountains and covered the great ocean for thousands of *yojana*s. In the ocean, the immensely intelligent one was covered under these mountains.'

'Since it was the time for daily rites, he fixed his mind on Achyuta. Prahlada said, "I bow down to Pundarikaksha. I bow down to Purushottama. I bow down to the one who is the *atman* of all the worlds. I bow down to the one with the fierce *chakra*. I bow down to the one whose form is in *brahmana*s and gods.[301] I bow down to the one who ensures the welfare of cattle and *brahmana*s. I bow down to the one who ensures the welfare of the universe. I bow down to Krishna. I bow down to Govinda. I bow down to him. I repeatedly bow down to him. In the form of Brahma, he creates the universe. He also protects in the form of the one who preserves. At the end of the *kalpa*, he assumes the form of Rudra. I bow down to the one who assumes the three forms. *Deva*s, *yaksha*s, *sura*s, *siddha*s, *naga*s, *gandharva*s, *kinnara*s, *pishacha*s, *rakshasa*s, humans, animals, birds, immobile objects, ants, reptiles, earth, water, fire, space, wind, sound, touch, taste, form, smell, the mind, the intellect, the *atman*, Kala, the *guna*s—you are the supreme truth in all these. O Achyuta! You are all these. You are knowledge and ignorance. You are truth and falsehood. You are poison and *amrita*. You are *pravritti* and *nivritti*. You are the rites

[301] This is a famous prayer: *namo brahmanyadevaya gobrahmanahitaya cha jagaddhitaya krishanya govindaya namonamh.*

mentioned in the *Vedas*. You enjoy all the *karma*. You are *karma* and the means. O Vishnu! You are everything. You are the fruits of all *karma*. You pervade me and other beings. O lord! You pervade all the worlds, and their qualities are indicative of your potency. The *yogis* think about you. Those who undertake sacrifices, sacrifice to you. You are the one who enjoys *havya* and *kavya*. Your own forms are there in the gods and the ancestors. Your form exists in Mahat. You are established in the universe. You exist in your subtle form in the universe. All your forms exist in differences within beings. In your extremely subtle form, you are in their *atmans*. You cannot be perceived through names and adjectives like subtle or gross. Your form is the *paramatman*. Your form cannot be thought of, in any possible way. I bow down to you. I prostrate myself before Purushottama. You are in all beings. You are in all their *atmans*. Resorting to *gunas*, you assume the form of supreme Shakti. I bow down to the eternal lord of the gods. You are beyond the perception of words, thoughts and adjectives. For those who know, you are enveloped in *jnana*. I worship that supreme lord. Oum! I always prostrate myself before the illustrious Vasudeva. Nothing other than you exists. In the entire universe, there is nothing other than you. I bow down to him. I prostrate myself before him. I bow down to the great-souled one. He has no name or form. He is one and can only be known by worshipping him. The residents of heaven worship his forms as *avataras*. But they do not see his supreme form. I bow down to the great-souled one. He is the only one who remains at the end. The lord sees everything, auspicious and inauspicious. He is a witness to everything in the universe. I prostrate myself before Parameshvara. I bow down to Vishnu. The universe is not distinct from him. The one who is the origin of the universe should be meditated upon. May the one without decay be pleased with me. He is in the warp and woof of the universe.[302] He is the imperishable one. He is without decay. He is the foundation for everything. May Hari be pleased with me. Oum! I bow down to Vishnu. I repeatedly prostrate myself before him. He is in everything. He is everything. He is the refuge for everything. Everything ends in him. He is Ananta and he exists inside me. Since he is in me, I am in everything. Everything is in me. Everything eternal is in me. I am also without decay and eternal. The *paramatman* finds a place in my *atman*. I am known as the *brahman*. I was there at the beginning, and I will be there at the end. I am the supreme being."'

Chapter 1(20) (The Narasimha Form)

S hri Parashara said, 'O *brahmana*! As he thought in this way, there was no difference between him and Vishnu. Deeply immersed in him, he took himself to be Achyuta. He forgot himself and did not know anything else. He thought, "I am Ananta, without decay. I am the *paramatman*." Because his thoughts were immersed in *yoga*, all his sins were gradually destroyed. Achyuta Vishnu, who is nothing but *jnana*, was established in his purified heart. Through the powers of his *yoga*, the *asura* Prahlada became full of Vishnu. O Maitreya! In an instant, the bonds of the *uraga*s were destroyed. Large numbers of crocodiles were whirling around, and they were quietened. The great ocean was pacified. The earth, along with its mountains, forests and groves, trembled. The *daitya*s had covered him under a mass of boulders. The immensely intelligent one swept them aside and emerged from the water.

---

[302] Literally, in the process of weaving, the long threads (*ota*) and the cross threads (*prota*).

When he saw the world again and saw the earth and the sky, Prahlada remembered himself and recollected who he was. The intelligent one again praised Purushottama, who is without a beginning. He single-mindedly controlled his words and thoughts and did this with a great deal of eagerness. Prahlada said, "Oum! I prostrate myself before the supreme truth. You are gross and subtle. You are perishable and imperishable. You are manifest and you are not manifest. You are beyond measurement. You are the lord of everything. You are without blemish. You are a store of *gunas*. You are the one who supports the *gunas*. You are *nirguna*. You are established in the *gunas*. You are embodied and you are not embodied. You are the one with the great form. You are the one with the subtle form. You are evident and you are not evident. Your forms are cruel and amiable. O Achyuta! You are learning and you are the absence of learning. Your forms are cause and effect. You are the cause of existence and non-existence. Your *atman* is in the eternal and the temporary in Prapancha. You are the sparkling one, beyond Prapancha. You are one and you are many. I bow down before you. You are Vasudeva, the original cause. You are gross and subtle. You are manifest and you are not manifest. You are in all beings. You are not in all beings. You are the universe. You are the cause of the universe. I prostrate myself before Purushottama." With all his senses, he thus praised the divinity.'

'The illustrious Hari appeared before him, clad in yellow garments. As soon as he saw this, he respectfully arose, his words faltering. O *brahmana*! He prostrated himself before Vishnu and spoke. Prahlada said, "O divinity! O one who removes all afflictions! O Keshava! Please show me your favours. O Achyuta! You have again purified me by showing yourself to me." The illustrious one replied, "Because of your unflinching devotion, I am pleased with you. O Prahlada! Ask for the desired boon from me." Prahlada said, "O Achyuta! As

I pass through thousands of births, may my devotion towards
you never decay. Those who have no sense of discrimination
love material objects. However, since I continue to remember
you, let these not distract my heart." The illustrious one replied,
"You will always possess devotion towards me. O Prahlada!
Now ask for another desired boon from me." Prahlada said,
"Since I was always tied in the bonds of praising you, I have
been hated. My father has committed sins. O divinity! Please
destroy those. Weapons have been brought down on my limbs.
A fire has been kindled and I have been flung into it. I have
been bitten by serpents. Poison has been mixed in my food. I
have been bound and flung into the ocean, with boulders piled
up above me. There are many other wicked deeds that my
father has committed. All of these sins have been committed
because I am devoted to you, O lord! Through your favours,
let my father instantly be freed from these." The illustrious one
replied, "O Prahlada! Through my favours, everything will be
exactly as you wish. O son of an *asura*! Ask for another boon
that I can bestow on you." Prahlada said, "O illustrious one!
Everything has been accomplished through the boon that you
have granted. Through your favours, my faith towards you
will be unwavering. You are the cause of the entire universe.
If a person is fixed in devotion towards you, he obtains
emancipation. *Dharma*, *artha* and *kama* are meaningless."
The illustrious one replied, "Since you are full of unwavering
devotion towards me, through my favours, you will achieve
nirvana." O Maitreya! Having said this, as he looked on,
Vishnu vanished.'

'He returned and worshipped his father's feet. His father
inhaled the fragrance of his head and crushed him in his
embrace. O *brahmana*! Eyes filled with tears, he exclaimed,
"O child! You are alive." Full of affection towards him, the
great *asura* lamented what he had done. The one who knew
about *dharma* served his *gurus* and his father. In his own form

of Narasimha,[303] Vishnu made his father ascend upwards.[304] O Maitreya! He became the king of the *daityas*. O *brahmana*! Having obtained the splendor of the kingdom, he performed purifying deeds. He obtained prosperity and a large number of sons and grandsons. But eventually, all his rights to good and bad deeds were extinguished. Devoted to the illustrious one, he achieved supreme *nirvana*. O Maitreya! Such were the powers of the immensely intelligent *daitya*, Prahlada. This is what you had asked me about. If a person hears about the conduct of the great-souled Prahlada, all his sins are instantly destroyed. O Maitreya! There is no doubt that if a man hears or reads about Prahlada's conduct, night and day, all his sins are destroyed. O brahmana! If he reads this account on the day of the full moon, the day of the new moon, *ashtami* or *dvadashi*,[305] he obtains the fruits of donating a cow. Just as Hari protected Prahlada from all calamities, he also protects a person who hears about Prahlada's conduct.'

Chapter 1(21) (*Daityas and Maruts*)

Shri Parashara said, 'Prahlada's sons were Ayushmat, Shibi and Bashkala. Virochana was also Prahlada's son and Virochana's son was Bali. O great sage! Bali had one hundred sons and the eldest was Bana. All of Hiranyaksha's sons were extremely strong—Jharjhara, Shakuni, Bhutasantapana,

[303] Half-man (*nara*), half-lion (*simha*), also referred to as Nrisimha.

[304] As Narasimha *avatara*, Vishnu actually killed Hiranyakashipu. But those details are omitted in this text.

[305] *Ashtami* is the eighth lunar day, *dvadashi* is the twelfth lunar day. *Pournamasi/Pournami* is the day of the full moon, *amavasya* is the day of the new moon.

Mahanabha, Mahabahu and Kalanabha. Danu's sons[306] were
Dvimurdha, Shambara, Ayomukha, Shankushira, Kapila,
Shankara, Ekachakra, Mahabahu, the immensely strong
Taraka, Svarbhanu, Vrishaparva, the immensely strong Puloma
and the valiant and famous Viprachitti. These were Danu's
sons. Svarbhanu's daughter was Prabha and Sharmishtha was
Vrishaparva's daughter. Vaishvanara's[307] excellent daughters
were Upadani, the famous Hayashiraa, Pulomaa and Kalaka.
Both these immensely fortunate daughters were married to
Marichi.[308] Their sons were sixty thousand supreme *danava*s,
known as Poulamas and Kalakeyas. These were said to
have been the sons of Marichi. There were others who were
extremely brave, fierce and cruel. Through Simhika, Viprachitti
had the sons Tryamsha, the powerful Shalya, the immensely
strong Nabha, Vatapi, Namuchi, Ilvala, Khasrima, Andhaka,
Naraka, Kalanabha, the immensely valiant Svarbhanu and
the great *asura*, Vakrayodhi. These best among *danava*s
extended Danu's lineage. They had hundreds and thousands
of sons and grandsons. The Nivatakavachas were born in
Prahlada *daitya*'s lineage. They were cleansed in their souls
and engaged in extremely great austerities. Tamra[309] is said to
have had six famous daughters: Shuki, Shyeni, Bhasi, Sugrivi,
Shuchi and Gridhrika. Shuki gave birth to parrots, owls
and crows. Sheyni gave birth to hawks, Bhasi gave birth to
kites and Gridhrika gave birth to vultures. Shuchi gave birth
to aquatic birds. Sugrivi gave birth to horses, camels and
donkeys. Tamra's lineage has thus been described. Vinata[310]

[306] The father was Kashyapa. These were *danava*s. The earlier
ones were *daitya*s.
[307] Vaishvanara has not been mentioned earlier. He was also a
danava.
[308] Meaning, Pulomaa and Kalaka.
[309] Kashyapa's wife.
[310] Vinata and Kadru were married to Kashyapa.

had two famous sons, Garuda and Aruna. Suparna[311] was
best among birds. He was fierce and ate serpents. Surasa
gave birth to one thousand immensely energetic snakes. O
brahmana! Those great-souled ones possessed many hoods
and travelled through the sky. Kadru had one thousand
strong and infinitely energetic sons. O *brahmana*! They too
possessed many heads and came under Suparna's subjugation.
The foremost among these were Shesha, Vasuki, Takshaka,
Shankha, Shveta, Mahapadma, Kambala, Ashvatara, the
naga Elapatra, Karkotaka and Dhananjaya. There were many
other Dandashukas,[312] with virulent poison. Know that all
of Krodhavasha's[313] lineage possessed sharp teeth. There
were birds on earth and aquatic birds and all of them fed
on flesh. Krodavasha also gave birth to extremely strong
*pishacha*s. Surabhi was the mother of cows and buffaloes,
Ira of trees, creepers, shrubs and all types of grass, Khasa of
*yaksha*s and *rakshasa*s, Muni of *apsara*s and Arishta of high-
spirited *gandharva*s.[314] Kashyapa's descendants, mobile and
immobile, have thus been described. They had hundreds and
thousands of sons and grandsons. O *brahmana*! This creation
took place during Svarochisha *manvantara*.'

'In Vaivasvata *manvantara*, a great sacrifice was performed
for Varuna. It is said that for the sake of generating offspring,
Brahma himself offered oblations. Earlier, he had created
seven *saptarshi*s through his mental powers. The grandfather
himself generated them as his sons now. O excellent one! There
were also the *gandharva*s, serpents, *deva*s and *danava*s. When

---

[311] Another name for Garuda.

[312] Venomous serpents.

[313] Also married to Kashyapa.

[314] Surabhi, Ira, Khasa, Muni and Arishta were Kashyapa's other
wives.

Diti's sons were destroyed,[315] she went and pleased Kashyapa.
Kashyapa, supreme among ascetics, was worshipped by her.
He offered to grant her a boon. She asked for the boon that she
might have a capable and infinitely energetic son who would
kill Indra. The excellent sage bestowed this boon on his wife.
Having granted her this fierce boon, Kashyapa spoke to her.
"You will give birth to a son who will kill Shakra only if you
bear the fetus for one hundred years, while remaining controlled,
extremely careful and pure." Having told the goddess this,
the sage Kashyapa departed. She nurtured the fetus, carefully
maintaining purity. Maghavan came to know that the fetus was
meant for his destruction. The lord of the immortals arrived,
full of humility and intending to serve her. The chastiser of
Paka[316] remained there, looking for a weakness. When a little
less than the one hundred years was over, he discerned the
deviation. Without washing her feet and purifying herself, Diti
lay down to sleep. While she was sleeping, the wielder of the
vajra penetrated through her side and shattered the embryo
into seven fragments. When the embryo was thus split by the
vajra, it cried in extremely sharp tones. Shakra repeatedly told
it, "Do not cry." Indra was enraged and using the vajra, he
sliced each of those seven fragments into seven fragments.
The gods known as the Maruts were created and they were
extremely swift. Because of what the illustrious one had said,
they came to be known as Maruts.[317] These forty-nine gods are
the aides of the wielder of the vajra.'

[315] In a battle with devas.
[316] Indra killed a demon named Paka.
[317] From 'ma ruda' ('do not cry'). The Maruts are sometimes
identified with the Rudras. They are also wind-gods and companions
of Indra. The number of Maruts varies and is sometimes given as 7 or
49.

Chapter 1(22) (Various Kingdoms)

Shri Parashara said, 'The *maharshi*s had earlier instated Prithu in the kingdom. In that way, in due order, the grandfather of the worlds bestowed other kingdoms. Brahma bestowed the kingdom of *nakshatra*s, planets, *brahmana*s, all the herbs and plants, sacrifices and austerities on Soma. Vaishravana[318] was given the kingdom of kings and Varuna of the waters. Vishnu became the lord of Adityas and Pavaka of Vasus. Daksha became the lord of Prajapatis and Vasava of Maruts. Prahlada was made lord over *daitya*s and *danava*s. Dharmaraja was consecrated in the kingdom of the ancestors. Airavata was made the lord over all magnificent elephants. Garuda became king of birds and Vasava of *deva*s. Ucchaihshrava became king of horses and Vrishabha of cattle. The lord bestowed the kingdom of all the animals on the lion. The undecaying one made Shesha the lord over Dandashukas. Himalaya was made the lord of immobile objects and the sage Kapila of sages. The tiger was made the lord over animals with nails and fangs. Plaksha was instated as the lord of *vanaspati*s.[319] In this way, for all species, the lord established the foremost. He progressively divided the kingdoms and then established the guardians of the directions. In every direction, Brahma set up Prajapatis. Sudhanvan, the son of Prajapati Vairaja, was instated as the king and guardian of the eastern direction. He instated the son of the great-souled Kardama Prajapati, named Shankhapada, as the king of the southern direction. He instated the great-souled Ketuman, the undecaying son of Rajas, as the king of the western direction. He instated the unassailable Hiranyaroma, the son of Prajapati

---

[318] Kubera. He was made the king of kings. Rajaraja (sovereign lord) is one of Kubera's names.

[319] Plaksha is the Indian fig tree. *Vanaspati* is any large forest tree. Specifically, it is a tree that has fruit, but no visible flowers.

Parjanya, as king of the northern direction. Even today, they follow *dharma* and as instructed, rule over the entire earth, with its *dvipa*s and habitations.'

'O excellent sage! All those engaged in this way, and other kings who possess prosperity, are established there because of the great-souled Vishnu. O *brahmana*! This is true of all lords of beings who have been there in the past and who will be there in the future. O supreme among *brahmana*s! All of them, over all beings, are portions of Vishnu. The lords of *deva*s; the lords of daityas; the protectors of *danava*s; the protectors of those who eat flesh; the lords of animals; the lords of birds; the lords of humans, *sarpa*s and *naga*s; the lords of trees, mountains and planets; and others in the past, the present and the future—all of them, over all beings, originate as portions of Vishnu. Without Hari, lord of everything, no one is capable of protecting and preserving. O immensely wise one! There is no one else. He is the creator who creates the universe. He is the eternal one who preserves and protects. As the destroyer, it is he who destroys. He is the one who resorts to *sattva*, *rajas* and so on. In his four forms, he is the one who creates. Established in four forms, he preserves. In his four forms, Janardana is the one who brings about destruction. In one portion, he manifests himself as Brahma. In another portion, he becomes Prajapatis, Marichi and the others. In a third portion, he is there as Kala. In his fourth portion, he is there in all beings.[320] In this way, resorting to *rajas guna*, in his four portions, he is engaged in creation. In one portion, Vishnu is engaged in protecting the world. His portion is there in the form of Manu and the others. Another portion is there in the form of Kala. Another portion

---

[320] The four forms of creation are Brahma, Prajapatis, Kala and all beings. The four forms of preservation are Vishnu, Manus, Kala and all beings. The four forms of destruction are Rudra, Agni, Kala and all beings.

is there in all beings and is engaged in preservation. Resorting
to *sattva guna*, Purushottama is established in the universe.
At the time of destruction, he resorts to *tamas guna*. The
illustrious one, without origin, has his own form in the form
of Rudra. Another portion is there, in original form, in Agni,
the fire of destruction. There is one portion in the form of Kala
and another portion in all beings. In this way, in four forms,
the great-souled one engages in destruction. O *brahmana*! For
all time, these are the divisions that are spoken about. For the
purpose of creation, Hari's potencies exist in the universe in the
form of Brahma, Daksha and the others, Kala and all beings. O
brahmana! For the purpose of preservation, Vishnu's potencies
exist in the form of Vishnu, Manu and the others, Kala and all
beings. For the purpose of destruction, Janardana's potencies
exist in the form of Rudra, the fire of destruction, Kala and all
beings. O *brahmana*! From the creation of the universe at the
beginning, through the middle, and ending with dissolution,
he acts in the form of Dhatri,[321] Marichi and the others and
all beings. At the original time of creation, Brahma creates.
Marichi and the others create subjects, and these subjects have
offspring all the time. O *brahmana*! But independent of Kala,
Brahma cannot bring about his act of creation. Nor can all the
Prajapatis, or all the beings. In this way, those four forms also
exist for preservation. O Maitreya! The divinity has four forms
for dissolution too. O *brahmana*! Everything that has been
created and all living beings that have originated all owe their
creation to Hari's body. O Maitreya! Everything mobile and
immobile, and every living creature that is destroyed, owe their
destruction to Janardana's terrible form as the destroyer. In
this way, he is the creator of the universe. In this way, he is the
one who protects the universe. The divinity Janardana is the
one who devours the entire universe. At the time of creation,

[321] The creator.

preservation and destruction, he exists in his three forms. He
resorts to the *gunas*. However, his supreme and great status
is devoid of *gunas*. That form is unmatched. Full of *jnana*, it
pervades. It can only be known by itself and not by anyone
else. The *paramatman*'s own nature has four forms.'

Shri Maitreya said, 'You have spoken about the supreme
state, when one merges into the *brahman*. Please tell me how it
can be said to have four forms.'

Shri Parashara replied, 'O Maitreya! For all objects, the
cause is spoken of as the means. For all objects, there is an
objective that one strives for. Desiring emancipation, yogis
use *pranayama* and other means. The objective is the supreme
brahman. If one attains that, one does not return. O sage! In
pursuit of emancipation, when *yogis* use *sadhana*[322] to achieve
jnana about discrimination, that is the first form of merging
into the *brahman*. O great sage! In pursuit of freedom from
hardships, when *yogis* use *sadhana* to achieve *vijnana* about
the *brahman*, that is the second form of merging into the
brahman.[323] The third form I have spoken about is when one
learns to differentiate between the objective and the means, and
one's *vijnana* is such that one has no sense of duality. O great
sage! The final form is when one rejects any remaining notions
of differentiation left by the first three kinds of knowledge. One
then realizes the nature of one's own *atman*. Vishnu is full of
jnana. He is beyond contemplation, beyond any adjectives used
by the mind. He is only pervasiveness, without an equal. He is
an object that is self-illuminated. His only sign is existence. He
is full of serenity and pure, without any fear. Logic cannot be
used to comprehend him. That *jnana* is a sign of the *brahman*.

[322] Meditation/worship to accomplish the objective.

[323] *Jnana* is knowledge obtained from texts and *gurus*, *vijnana* is
self-knowledge. But this distinction is not invariably the case, and the
two terms are often used synonymously.

O *brahmana*! When a yogi restrains all *ajnana* and attains dissolution, he is bereft of any seeds and is longer attracted by *samsara*. In this way, the supreme *brahman* is sparkling, eternal, pervasive and without decay. It is bereft of anything inferior. This is the supreme state, known as Vishnu. When a *yogi* attains this, he does not return again.[324] This supreme refuge is sacred. It is extremely sparkling and devoid of hardships. There are two forms of the *brahman*, embodied and disembodied. In perishable and imperishable forms, they exist in all beings. The imperishable part is the supreme *brahman*. The perishable part is this entire universe. When the fire burns in one place, it spreads illumination all around. In that way, the supreme *brahman*'s energy exists in the entire universe. O Maitreya! Depending on whether we are far or near,[325] the difference in the illumination may be more or less. The energy is like that. O *brahmana*! Brahma, Vishnu and Shiva are the most powerful forms of the *brahman*'s energy. O Maitreya! *Deva*s have less than that. Daksha and the others, lesser still. After that come humans, domestic animals, wild animals, birds and reptiles, ending with trees and creepers. Progressively, it becomes less and less. O supreme sage! In this way, the imperishable and eternal appears and disappears in this world, as if it is subject to birth and death. Vishnu is full of energy and is the supreme *brahman*'s own form. At the beginning of *yoga*, *yogi*s think of his embodied form. He exists as the seed and the method for embarking on that great *yoga*. O sage! Thereafter, when the mind is properly engaged, there is no need for this form. O immensely fortunate one! Hari is full of the *brahman*. He is supreme. In every direction, he is the supreme *brahman*'s energy. He is everywhere, in the warp and woof of the entire universe. O sage! He is existence and he is non-existence. He

---

[324] To *samsara*. He is not reborn.
[325] From the fire.

is the entire universe. Vishnu is the lord of everything. He is radiant in the perishable and the imperishable. He is Purusha and he is Prakriti. The weapons and the ornaments are his own form.'

Shri Maitreya said, 'The illustrious Vishnu is radiant in the entire universe and the weapons and ornaments are his own form. Please explain this to me.'

Shri Parashara replied, 'I prostrate myself before the powerful Vishnu, the Vishnu who cannot be measured. After doing this, I will tell you what Vasishtha told me. The illustrious Hari is radiant when he wears the *atman* of the universe. It is as if he is wearing the Koustubha jewel.[326] He is unsullied and without blemishes and *guna*s. Pradhana seeks a refuge in Ananta, in the place where he wears the Shrivatsa mark.[327] Intellect exists in Madhava in the form of his mace. The two forms, the senses and the objects of the senses, are the lord's *ahamkara*. The signs of these shine in the form of the conch shell and the Sharnga bow.[328] The mind is fickle and exceedingly fast, swifter than the wind. Vishnu holds this in his hand, in the form of the *chakra*. The wielder of the mace wears the Vaijayanti garland, made out of five jewels.[329] O *brahmana*! This is actually a garland of elements and is the aggregate of the five elements. Janardana holds all the senses of perception and action in the form of the arrows in his quiver. Achyuta possesses a radiant and extremely sparkling sword. This is learning, with the learning encased in a sheath of ignorance. O Maitreya! In this way, Purusha, Pradhana, intellect, *ahamkara*,

---

[326] Jewel worn by Vishnu.

[327] Literally, *shrivatsa* means the place where Shri (Lakshmi) resides. It is a twirl of curly hair on Vishnu's/Krishna's chest.

[328] Vishnu's bow, made out of horn.

[329] Pearl, ruby, sapphire, emerald and diamond. The Vaijayanti garland signifies victory.

the elements, the mind, all the senses, learning and ignorance—
all of these find a refuge in Hrishikesha. Though he is without
form, the weapons and ornaments are his own forms. For
the benefit of living beings, Hari resorts to his *maya* to be
radiant in these. The transformations, Pradhana, Purusha and
the entire universe are radiant in the form of Pundarikaksha
Parameshvara. O Maitreya! Learning and ignorance, existence
and non-existence—all these exist in the undecaying lord of
beings, Madhusudana. *Kala*, *kashtha*, *nimesha*, days, months,
seasons and years—all these measurements of time are the
illustrious and sinless Hari's undecaying forms. O supreme
among sages! The lord is the seven worlds, Bhuloka, Bhuvarloka,
Svarloka, Maharloka, Satyaloka, Tapoloka and Janaloka. All
these worlds are his form, each following the preceding one.
Hari is himself established there, as a store of every kind of
learning. He is established in many forms, as gods, humans,
animals and others. He is Ananta, the lord of everything. He
has an embodied form, and he has a disembodied form. The
great-souled Vishnu assumes the form of sound and exists as
the *Rig Veda*, the *Yajur Veda*, the *Sama Veda*, the *Atharva
Veda*, Itihasa, the minor *Vedas*, *Vedanta*, everything that has
been stated by Manu and the others, all the sacred texts and
accounts, *anuvakas*,[330] *kavya*,[331] *alapa*[332] and everything else
that is sung. There is nothing here or elsewhere, embodied
or disembodied, that does not have him. Every kind of object
is his form. I am Hari. Everything is Janardana. Cause and
effect have their origin in him. If a person's mind is like this,
he does not have to be born in *samsara* again. He does not
have to face the opposite pairs of sentiments. O *brahmana*! I
have accurately described the first part of this Purana to you.

[330] Subdivisions of the *Vedas*.
[331] Poetry.
[332] Narration.

If one listens to this, one is freed from all sins. O Maitreya! A
man who listens to it obtains the same fruits that are obtained
by bathing in Pushkara in the month of Karttika[333] for twelve
years. O sage! If a man listens to this, *deva*s and others bestow
on him the boon that he will become a *devarshi*, an ancestor, a
gandharva, a *yaksha* and so on.'

This ends Part I.

---

[333] October–November.

Part II

Chapter 2(1) (Priyavrata's Descendants)

Maitreya said, 'O illustrious one! O *guru*! You have completely described everything that I had asked you about the creation of the universe. O supreme sage! But there is a bit about the creation of the universe that I wish to hear again. You said that Svayambhuva had two sons, Priyavrata and Uttanapada, and you spoke about Uttanapada's son, Dhruva. O *brahmana*! However, you have not spoken about Priyavrata's sons. If you are so inclined, you should tell me about them.'

Shri Parasara replied, 'Priyavrata married Kardama's daughter.[334] Through her, he had two daughters, Samrat and Kukshi, and ten sons who were immensely wise, immensely valiant, humble and devoted to their father. Hear the names by which Priyavrata's sons were known: Agnidhra, Agnibahu, Vapushmat, Dyutimat, Medha, Medhatithi, Bhavya, Savana and Putra. The tenth son was Jyotishmat, and he made his name come true.[335] Priyavrata's sons were famous for their strength and valour. Medha, Agnibahu and Putra were three who were devoted to *yoga*. Those immensely fortunate ones remembered their past lives and their minds were not on the kingdom. O sage! Those sparkling ones observed the indicated rites in all the *tirthas*[336] all the time, not desiring the fruits. O supreme among sages! O Maitreya! Priyavrata divided the earth into seven *dvipas*[337] and gave these to his extremely great-souled sons. O immensely fortunate one! The father gave Agnidhra Jambudvipa. He next gave Medhatithi Plakshadvipa. He instated Vapushmat as the king in Shalmalidvipa. The lord made Jyotishmat the king of Kushadvipa. He instructed that Dyutimat should be the king of Krounchadvipa. Priyavrata made Bhavya the lord of Shakadvipa. The lord made Savana the lord of Pushkara. O supreme sage! Agnidhra was the lord of Jambudvipa, and he had nine sons who were the equals of Prajapati: Nabhi, Kimpurusha, Harivarsha, Ilavrita, Ramya, Hiranvat as the sixth, Kuru, Bhadrashva and King Ketumala, who sought to be virtuous. O *brahmana*! Hear about how he divided Jambudvipa. The father gave Nabhi the *varsha*[338]

---

[334] Other Puranas state that her name was Kamya.

[335] Jyotishmat means the shining one.

[336] Both *tirthas* and *kshetras* are sacred places of pilgrimage. However, *tirthas* are associated with water while *kshetras* are not.

[337] *Dvipa* means region or continent.

[338] *Varsha* is a subdivision of *dvipa*.

known as Hima, to the south.[339] He gave Kimpurusha the
varsha of Hemakuta. Harivarsha was given the third *varsha* of
Naishadha. Ilavrita was given the region which has Meru at the
centre. The father gave Ramya the *varsha* that is near Mount
Nila. The father gave Hiranvat the region that is to the north
of Shveta.[340] Kuru was given the *varsha* that is to the north
of Shringavat. He gave Bhadrashva the *varsha* that is to the
east of Meru. He gave Ketumala the *varsha* of Gandhamadana.
Thus, the lord of men gave these to his sons. The lord of the
earth instated his sons in those *varsha*s. O Maitreya! He then
went to the extremely sacred spot of Salagrama to perform
austerities. O great sage! In those eight *varsha*s, Kimpurusha
and the others, one is generally happy. Success can naturally
be obtained, without a great deal of effort. There are no
hardships and there is no fear of old age or death. There is
no notion of *dharma* or *adharma* and there is nothing that is
superior, medium or inferior. In those eight regions, there are
no circumstances associated with the *yuga*s.'[341]

'The great-souled Nabhi obtained the *varsha* known as Hima.
Through Merudevi, he had the immensely radiant Rishabha as a
son. Rishabha had one hundred sons and the eldest was Bharata.
He[342] ruled the kingdom according to his own *dharma* and as
instructed, performed many sacrifices. The lord of the earth then
instated his son, the brave Bharata. Having made up his mind to
follow the norms of *vanaprastha*, the immensely fortunate one
went to Pulaha's hermitage. As is proper, the lord of the earth
tormented himself through austerities there. He suffered through
these austerities and was so emaciated that he became a mass of
veins and skin. Naked, and with a pebble in his mouth, he then

[339] South of the Himalayas.
[340] The mountain Shveta. Likewise, for Shringavat.
[341] That is, *krita*, *treta*, *dvapara* and *kali* do not exist.
[342] Rishabha.

departed on the journey meant for heroes.[343] Since his father
gave Bharata the *varsha* before he left for the forest, the worlds
have spoken of it as Bharatavarsha thereafter.[344] Bharata had
a son named Sumati, who was extremely devoted to *dharma*.
Having ruled properly and performed the desired sacrifices, the
father bestowed the kingdom on him. Bharata, the lord of the
earth, bestowed all that prosperity on his son. O sage! Devoted
to the practice of *yoga*, he then gave up his life in Salagrama. He
was subsequently born as a *brahmana*, in an excellent family
of *yogis*. O Maitreya! I will describe his conduct to you again.
The energetic Sumati had Indradyumna as a son. His son was
Parameshthi and Parameshthi's son was Pratihara. Pratihara's
son was famous as Pratiharti. Pratiharti's son was Bhava and
Bhava's son was the lord Udgitha, whose son was Prastavi.
Prastavi's son was Prithu, Prithu's son was Nakta and Nakta's
son was Gaya. Gaya's son was Nara and Nara's son was
Virat. His son was the immensely valiant Dhimat. His son was
Mahanta and Mahanta's son was Manasyu. Manasyu's son was
Tvashta, Tvashta's son was Viraja and Viraja's son was Raja.
O sage! Raja's son was Shatajit. Shatajit had one hundred sons
and the foremost was Vishvagjyoti. In this way, the descendants
increased and ornamented Bharatavarsha, divided into nine
divisions. In ancient times, those born in this lineage enjoyed this
Bharatavarsha. Thus, Svayambhuva's[345] creation filled the world
and there was an aggregate of seventy-one of *krita*, *treta* and the
other *yugas*.[346] O sage! He[347] was the lord in the first *manvantara*
of *varaha kalpa*.'

[343] The journey meant for heroes is death. The pebble in the
mouth prevents eating and speaking.

[344] Earlier, it was named after Nabhi.

[345] Svayambhuva Manu's.

[346] One cycle of *krita*, *treta*, *dvapara* and *kali* is known as a
mahayuga and there are 71.4 *mahayugas* in one *manvantara*.

[347] Svayambhuva Manu.

Chapter 2(2) (Geography of the Earth)

Shri Maitreya said, 'O *brahmana*! O sage! You have spoken to me about Svayambhuva's creation. I wish to hear the truth about the entire globe of the earth, where it ends in the oceans, the *dvipa*s, the *varsha*s, the mountains, the forests, the rivers, the cities, the *deva*s and others. What are the dimensions of these? What are the foundations? What is the nature? Where are they established? O sage! You should tell me about this.'

Shri Parashara replied, 'O Maitreya! Listen. I will tell you briefly. Even if I speak for one hundred years, I will not be able to describe it in detail. O *brahmana*! The *dvipa*s are Jambu, Plaksha, Shalmali, Kusha, Krouncha, Shaka and Pushkara as the seventh. The seven *dvipa*s are respectively surrounded by seven oceans: Lavana, Ikshu, Sura, Sarpi, Dadhi, Dugdha and Jala.[348] Jambudvipa is located in the centre of all these. O Maitreya! And in its centre is the golden mountain of Meru. It extends upwards for eighty-four thousand *yojana*s. It penetrates into the earth for sixteen thousand. The circumference at the summit extends for thirty-two thousand and the base extends, in every direction, for sixteen thousand *yojana*s.[349] With the earth like a lotus, this mountain is like a pericarp. Himavat, Hemakut and Nishadha are to the south.[350] Nila, Shveta and Shringi are mountains to the north.[351] The two mountains in the centre are one hundred thousand *yojana*s long and their length

[348] These are oceans filled with salty water, sugar cane juice, liquor, *ghee*, curd, milk and fresh water.
[349] Meru is in the shape of an inverted cone.
[350] Of Meru.
[351] The word used in the text is *varsha parvata*. This means mountains that separate the *varsha*s.

progressively declines by ten thousand *yojana*s.[352] They are two thousand *yojana*s in height and this is also the breadth. Bharata is the first *varsha* and Kimpurusha is said to come after that. O *brahmana*! Harivarsha is the other one that is to the south of Meru. Ramyaka is the *varsha* to the north[353] and Hiranmaya comes after that. Just like Bharata,[354] Uttarakuru is to the north. O supreme among *brahmana*s! Each of these *varsha*s is nine thousand *yojana*s long.[355] So is Ilavrita and in its centre rises the golden mountain of Meru. O immensely fortunate one! Ilavrita extends for nine thousand *yojana*s on four sides of Meru and within it, there are four mountains that are like fortifications for Meru. Each of these is ten thousand *yojana*s high. Nine lakes can be seen, and they seem to be like hair on these mountains.[356] The mountain to the east[357] is named Mandara, that to the south Gandhamadana, that on the western flank Vipula and that on the north is said to be Suparshva. There are a *kadamba* tree, a *jambu* tree, a *pippala* tree and a *vata* tree.[358] Each of

[352] For instance, Hemakut is 90,000 *yojana*s long and the Himalayas (Himavat) 80,000 *yojana*s long. Shveta is 90,000 *yojana*s long and Shringi 80,000 *yojana*s long.

[353] North of Meru.

[354] Just like Bharata is to the south.

[355] Jambudvipa's diameter is 100,000 *yojana*s. Counting north to south, Meru's base is 16,000 *yojana*s. On both sides, north and south, Ilavrita *varsha* extends for 9,000 *yojana*s. 9,000 . . . 18,000 and 18,000 + 16,000 = 34,000. There are 6 more *varsha*s, each 9,000 *yojana*s. 9,000 . . . 54,000 and 34,000 + 54,000 = 88,000. There are 6 mountains, each 2,000 *yojana*s. 2,000 . . . 12,000 and 88,000 + 12,000 = 100,000.

[356] Though included in the text, this sentence doesn't seem to belong.

[357] Of Meru.

[358] *Kadamba* (a kind of flowering tree, *stephegyne parvifolia*) in Mandara, *jambu* (rose apple) in Gandhamadana, *pippala* (holy fig tree) in Vipula and *vata* (holy fig tree) in Suparshva.

these is eleven thousand *yojana*s in height and they are like
flags on these mountains. O great sage! The name Jambudvipa
is derived on account of the *jambu* tree. The *jambu* fruit is as
large as a gigantic elephant. It falls down everywhere on the
slope of the mountain and is shattered. From that juice flows
the river known as Jambunadi. Those who reside there drink
from this river and do not suffer from exhaustion, bad odour,
old age or decay of the senses. Having drunk this, people who
are born there are pure in their minds. When that juice, which
is like *amrita*, reaches the bank, it is dried up by the pleasant
breeze. This becomes the gold known as Jambunada, used as an
ornament by the *siddha*s. Bhadrashva is to the east of Meru and
Ketumala is to the west. O best among sages! Ilavrita is between
these two *varsha*s. The grove of Chaitraratha is to the east and
Gandhamadana is on the south. The grove of Vaibhraja is to the
west and the grove of Nandana is said to be on the north. There
are four lakes: Arunoda, Mahabhadra, Sitoda and Manasa.
The gods always enjoy them. Like filaments on Meru,[359] there
are mountains to the east and the main ones are Shitambha,
Kumunda, Kurari, Malyavat and Vaikanka. The mountains
which are like filaments to the south are Trikuta, Shishira,
Patanga, Ruchaka, Nishadha and others. The main mountains
which are like filaments to the west are Shikhivasa, Vaidurya,
Kapila, Gandhamadana and Jarudhi. The mountains that are
like filaments to the north are Shankhakuta, Rishabha, Hamsa,
Naga and Kalajangha. They extend like limbs from inside Meru
and are located around the region of the stomach. O Maitreya!
Brahma's great city is on Meru's summit. It is fourteen thousand
*yojana*s in size and is famous in heaven. In the eight directions
and sub-directions all around it, there exist the famous and
excellent cities of Indra and the other guardians of the worlds.
Originating from Vishnu's feet, Ganga floods the lunar disc and

---

[359] With Meru being compared to a lotus.

falls down from the sky in every direction of Brahma's city. Having descended, it flows in four directions. In due order, these are Sita, Alakananda, Chakshu and Bhadra. Towards the east, flowing from one mountain to another, Sita traverses the sky and enters the ocean in the *varsha* that is to the east, Bhadrashva. O great sage! In that way, Alakananda flows to the south, through Bharata, and dividing into seven rivers, merges into the ocean. Chakshu traverses the western mountain and passing through the entire region known as Ketumala *varsha*, flows into the western ocean. O great sage! Similarly, Bhadra goes beyond the northern mountain and traversing the Uttarakuru region, flows into the northern ocean. Like the pericarp of a lotus, Meru is between Nila and Nishadha[360] and between Malyavat and Gandhamadana.[361] Bharata, Ketumala, Bhadrashva and Kuru are like leaves on this lotus of the world, located outside the mountains that form the boundaries. Jathara and Hemakuta are the boundary-mountains that run from the north to the south, connecting Nila and Nishadha. Gandhamadana and Kailasa extend, eighty *yojana*s in breadth, from the east to the west. Nishadha[362] and Pariyatra are boundary-mountains to Meru's west, just as these exist towards the east. Trishringa and Jarudhi are boundary-mountains to the north. They extend from the east to the west, between the two oceans. O sage! I have thus spoken to you about the boundary-mountains. From Meru's stomach, a pair of these extend in each of the four directions. O sage! In all four of Meru's directions, there are also mountains that are like filaments. These are Shitanta and the others and they are extremely beautiful.'

[360] Respectively to the north and the south.
[361] Respectively to the west and the east.
[362] This is possibly a typo and the two Nishadhas cause confusion. This should probably be Rishabha.

'There are valleys between the mountains, frequented by *siddhas* and *charanas*.[363] Exceedingly beautiful groves and cities exist there. O excellent sage! There are wonderful abodes of Lakshmi, Vishnu, Agni, Surya and other *devas*, full of excellent *kinnaras*. Night and day, *gandharvas*, *yakshas*, *rakshasas*, *daityas* and *danavas* sport in the charming valleys of the mountains. O sage! Those who are devoted to *dharma* reside there and they are described as heavens on earth. Evildoers cannot go there, even after one hundred births. O *brahmana*! In Bhadrashva, the illustrious Vishnu exists in the form of Hayashira; in Ketumala, as Varaha; in Bharata, in the form of Kurma; in Kuru, Govinda Janardana exists in the form of Matsya; and everywhere, Hari, who is everything and can go everywhere, exists in the form of the universe. O Maitreya! He is in the *atman* of everything, and he holds up everything. O great sage! In eight *varshas*, Kimpurusha and the others, there is no grief or effort. There is no anxiety, hunger or fear. The subjects are healthy, with no reason to be scared. They are bereft of any kind of misery. The lifespan is fixed at ten or twelve thousand years. The god[364] does not shower down in these *varshas* since there is plenty of water in the ground. *Krita*, *treta* and the others have not been thought of in those places. In each of these *varshas*, there are seven *kulachalas*.[365] O supreme among *brahmanas*! Hundreds of rivers flow from these.'

Chapter 2(3) (Bharatavarsha)

Shri Parashara said, 'The *varsha* that is to the north of the ocean and south of the Himalayas is known by the name

[363] Divine singers and bards.
[364] Indra.
[365] A *kulachala* is a great mountain, but any great mountain is not a *kulachala*.

of Bharata and the subjects there are known as Bharati. O
great sage! It extends for nine thousand *yojanas*. This is *karma
bhumi*[366] for those who desire heaven or emancipation. The
seven *kulaparvatas*[367] here are Mahendra, Malaya, Sahya,
Shuktimat, Riksha, Vindhya and Pariyatra. From here, people
go to heaven. It is from here that they obtain emancipation. O
sage! It is also from here that men are born as inferior species
or go to hell. When the middle is over,[368] it is from here that
one goes to heaven or obtains *moksha*. Indeed, for mortals,
there is no other place that has been ordained as *karma
bhumi*. Hear about the nine subdivisions of Bharatavarsha:
Indradvipa, Kaseru, Tamraparna, Gabhastimat, Nagadvipa,
Soumya, Gandharva and Aruna.[369] Out of these, the ninth
dvipa is surrounded by the ocean. From the south to the north,
this *dvipa* extends for one thousand *yojanas*. The Kiratas live
to the east and the Yavanas to the west. In the middle region,
brahmanas, *kshatriyas*, *vaishyas* and *shudras* reside. They
perform sacrifices, fight, engage in trade and do other things
to ensure subsistence. Shatadru, Chandrabhaga and others
flow from the feet of the Himalayas. O sage! Others flow from
Pariyatra, Vedasmriti being the foremost. Narmada, Surasa
and other rivers flow from the Vindhyas. Tapi,[370] Payoshni[371]
and Nirvindhya[372] are the chief rivers that flow from Riksha.
Godavari, Bhimarathi,[373] Krishna, Venya and others rivers are
said to flow from the feet of Sahya. They dispel all fear of sin.

[366] Region where *karma* is performed, and its fruits enjoyed.
[367] The same as *kulachala*.
[368] A metaphor for life on earth.
[369] One seems to be missing. But the ninth subdivision is also
known as Bharata.
[370] Tapti.
[371] Identified with Purna, or part of Tapti.
[372] Speculatively identified as a tributary of Warda.
[373] The river Bhima.

Kritamala and Tamraparni are the foremost among those that
flow from Malaya. Trisama, Rishikulya and others are said to
be the ones that flow from Mahendra. Rishikulya,[374] Kumara
and others flow from the feet of Shuktimat. There are thousands
of rivers and minor rivers that are tributaries of these. The
Kurus and Panchalas are those who live in the central region.
There are those who reside in the east, such as the inhabitants
of Kamarupa. The Pundras, Kalingas and Magadhas dwell
everywhere in the south. Beyond these boundaries are those
from Sourashtra, Shuras, Abhiras, Arbudas, Karushas, Malavas,
those who live in Pariyatra, Souviras, Saindhavas, Hunas,
Shalvas, those who live in Kosala, Madraramas, Ambashthas,
Parasikas and others. They reside along the banks of the rivers
and always drink their waters. O immensely fortunate one!
Those people are happy and healthy. O great sage! The four
*yuga*s, *krita*, *treta*, *dvapara* and *kali*, exist in Bharatavarsha
and nowhere else. Sages torment themselves with austerities
here. The performers of sacrifices offer oblations. For the
sake of the world hereafter, people donate lovingly. It is in
Jambudvipa that sacrifices are always performed for Purusha,
who is embodied in sacrifices. Vishnu is worshipped through
sacrifices in this *dvipa* and nowhere else. O great sage! Within
Jambudvipa, Bharata is the best. It is here that one performs
karma. The other places are *bhoga bhumi*.[375] O excellent
one! After thousands and thousands of births, one sometimes
acquires enough good merits to be born as a human being
here. Therefore, the gods chant a song. "Those who are born
in this land of Bharata are blessed. That is because men who
are born here can obtain both heaven and emancipation. They
are better than the gods. One can resolve to undertake deeds
for the sake of the fruits. But these must be vested in Vishnu,

[374] Distinct from the earlier Rishikulya.
[375] Places of enjoyment.

the *paramatman*. When *karma* is exhausted, one obtains union with the infinite one. One obtains that unblemished end. We know that when the good merits that have granted us heaven have been exhausted, we will again be tied to *karma* and the bondage of the body. Blessed are those who are born as humans in Bharata. Indeed, those who are devoid of senses and intelligence, but are born here, are also blessed." O Maitreya! I have briefly described Jambudvipa and its nine *varsha*s to you. Its expanse is one hundred thousand *yojana*s. O Maitreya! On the outside of Jambudvipa, surrounding it for that expanse of one hundred thousand *yojana*s, the salty ocean exists like a girdle.'

Chapter 2(4) (Mountains and Rivers)

Shri Parashara said, 'Just as the *dvipa* known as Jambu is surrounded by a salty ocean. Plakshadvipa surrounds that salty ocean. The expanse of Jambudvipa is said to be one hundred thousand *yojana*s. O *brahmana*! Plakshadvipa is said to be double the size. The lord of Plakshadvipa, Medhatithi, had seven sons. The eldest was named Shantahaya and the others were Shishira, Sukhodaya, Ananda, Shiva, Kshemaka and Dhruva. All these seven were the lords of Plakshadvipa. Since they were the lords of Plakshadvipa, the *varsha*s of Plakshadvipa are named Shantahaya, Shishira, Sukhoda, Ananda, Shiva, Kshemaka and Dhruva. O supreme among sages! There are seven mountains that exist as boundaries of this region. Listen to their names. They are Gomeda, Chandra, Narada, Dundubhi, Somaka, Sumanas and Mount Vaibhraja as the seventh. Along with gods and *gandharva*s, the unblemished subjects always reside in these beautiful *varsha*s and in the mountains of these *varsha*s. Those habitations are sacred.

People die after a long period of time. They do not suffer from
physical or mental ailments and are happy all the time. There
are seven rivers in these *varsha*s, and they flow into the ocean.
I will tell you about their names. Hearing about them cleanses
all sins. They are Anutapta, Shikhi, Vipasha, Tridiva, Klama,
Amrita and Sukrita. These are the seven rivers. The chief
mountains and rivers have been mentioned to you. There are
thousands of minor mountains and rivers. The people in the
habitations drink the water from these rivers and are always
happy. O *brahmana*! All the rivers flow downwards, not a
single one flows upwards. O immensely intelligent one! The
divisions into *yuga*s do not exist in those seven regions. The
time is always like that in *treta yuga*. O *brahmana*! Beginning
with Plakshadvipa and ending with Shakadvipa, people live
for five thousand years and do not suffer from any disease.
Depending on the *varna* and the *ashrama*, there are four[376]
types of divisions of *dharma* there. There are four *varna*s too.
I will tell you about them. Listen. O supreme sage! Aryakas,
Kuraras, Vidishyas and Bhavinas are respectively *brahmana*s,
*kshatriya*s, *vaishya*s and *shudra*s. O supreme among
*brahmana*s! Right in the middle, there is an extremely large
plaksha tree that is as large as the *jambu* tree.[377] This results
in the name Plakshadvipa. Hari is the creator of everything in
the universe and the lord of everything. Aryakas and the other
*varna*s there worship the illustrious one in the form of Soma.
Plakshadvipa is surrounded by an ocean of sugar cane juice
that girdles it. This is of the same size as Plakshadvipa itself. O
Maitreya! I have thus spoken to you about Plakshadvipa.'

'I will now briefly tell you about Shalmala. Listen to
me again. The lord of Shalmala was the valiant Vapushmat.

---

[376] The text says five. That must be an error and we have corrected
it to four.
[377] The *jambu* tree in Jambudvipa.

O great sage! His sons were Shveta, Harita, Jimuta, Rohita, Vaidyuta, Manasa and Suprabha. There are seven *varsha*s named after them. Shalmaladvipa surrounds the ocean of sugar cane juice on every side and is twice the size of the ocean. It should be known that there are seven mountains there, which are the source of jewels. There are seven rivers that divide the *varsha*s. The mountains are Kumuda, Unnata, Balahaka as the third, Drona with great herbs as the fourth, Mount Kanka as the fifth, Mahisha as the sixth and Kakudma, supreme among mountains, as the seventh. Hear about the names of the rivers from me. They are Yoni, Toya, Vitrishna, Chandra, Mukta, Vimochani and Nivritti as the seventh. Remembering them pacifies all sins. The seven *varsha*s there are Shveta, Harita, Vaidyuta, Manasa, Jimuta, Rohita and the beautiful Suprabha. There are four *varna*s in those seven *varsha*s. O great sage! *Varna*s exist in Shalmala. They are distinct and Kapilas, Arunas, Pitas and Krishnas are respectively *brahmana*s, *kshatriya*s, *vaishya*s and *shudra*s. All of them worship the illustrious and undecaying Vishnu, who is in all *atman*s, in the form of Vayu. They worship him through the best of sacrifices, and he is present in those sacrifices. The gods reside near that extremely beautiful region. There is a giant *shalmali*[378] tree that gives the region its name. This *dvipa* is surrounded by an ocean of liquor on all sides and the size of this ocean is the same as Shalmala itself.'

'In every direction, that ocean of liquor is surrounded by Kushadvipa. Its dimensions are double the size of Shalmala. It was Jyotishmat in Kushadvipa.[379] Hear about his seven sons: Udbhida, Venumat, Vairatha, Lambana, Dhriti, Prabhakara and Kapila. The *varsha*s are named after them. Along with *daitya*s, *danava*s, gods, *gandharva*s, *yaksha*s, *kimpurusha*s and

[378] The silk cotton tree.
[379] As the lord.

others, humans reside there. There are four *varna*s, engaged in
their own activities. O great sage! In respective order, Damins,
Shushmins, Snehas and Mandehas are said to be *brahmana*s,
*kshatriya*s, *vaishya*s and *shudra*s. For the sake of protecting
their own rights of ownership in the decreed rites, they observe
them. In Kushadvipa, they worship Janardana in the form of
the *brahman*. They worship him and cast aside the strong sense
of ownership that exists in the fruits of the rites. O great sage!
In that *dvipa*, the seven mountains in the *varsha*s are Vidruma,
Hemashaila, Dyutimat, Pushpavat, Kusheshaya, Hari and
Mount Mandara as the seventh. There are seven rivers. In
due order, hear about their names: Dhutapapa, Shiva, Pavitra,
Sammati, Vidyutdambha, Mahi and Sarvapapahara. There are
thousands of other minor rivers and mountains. Kushadvipa
has a clump of *kusha* grass. This is said to be the reason for the
name. The *dvipa* is surrounded by an ocean of *ghee*, which is
the same size as the *dvipa* itself.'

'The ocean of *ghee* is surrounded by Krounchadvipa. O
immensely fortunate one! It has been heard that Krounchadvipa
is another great region. In expanse, its dimensions are double
the size of Kushadvipa. It is the great-souled Dyutimat[380]
in Krounchadvipa and the lord of the earth named the
*varsha*s after their names: Kushala, Mallaga, Ushna, Pivara,
Andhakaraka, Muni and Dundubhi. O sage! These were the
seven sons. O immensely intelligent one! There are extremely
beautiful mountains in these *varsha*s, frequented by gods and
*gandharva*s. I will name them. Listen. They are Krouncha,
Vamana, Andhakaraka as the third, Svahini, a mountain full
of jewels that resembles a horse as the fourth, Devavrit as the
fifth, Pundarikvan and the great mountain of Dundubhi. Each
is twice the size of the preceding one. Just as each *dvipa* is twice
the size of the preceding one, each beautiful mountain in a *varsha*

---

[380] As the lord.

is twice the size of the mountain in the preceding *varsha*. Along
with large numbers of gods, the subjects reside there, without
any fear. O great sage! Respectively, Pushkaras, Pushkalas,
Dhanyas and Tikhyas are *brahmanas*, *kshatriyas*, *vaishyas*
and *shudras*. O Maitreya! They drink the waters of the rivers.
Hear about those. There are hundreds of minor rivers that flow
downwards. But the seven main ones are Gouri, Kumudvati,
Sandhya, Ratri, Manojava, Kshanti and Pundarika. These are
the seven rivers in the *varshas*. There, the *varnas*, Pushkaras
and others, use sacrifices to worship the illustrious Janardana
in the form of Rudra and he is present at those sacrifices. In
every direction, Krounchadvipa is surrounded by an ocean of
curds that is exactly the same size as Krounchadvipa itself.'

'O great sage! The ocean of curd is surrounded by
Shakadvipa, which is twice the size of Krounchadvipa.
The extremely great-souled lord of Shakadvipa, Bhavya,
had seven sons and he gave them seven *varshas*. They were
Jalada, Kumara, Sukumara, Marichaka, Kusumoda, Moudaki
and Mahadruma as the seventh. The seven *varshas* were
respectively named after them. There are seven mountains
that divide the *varshas*. O *brahmana*! They are Udayagiri,
Jaladhara, Raivataka, Shyama, Ambikeya, Ramya and the
beautiful Kesari, supreme amoung mountains. There is a great
shaka tree[381] there, frequented by *siddhas* and *gandharvas*. If
one touches the breeze that blows through its leaves, one is
filled with great delight. There are sacred habitations there,
filled with the four *varnas*. Those great-souled ones reside
there, without any fear and without any disease. There are
extremely sacred rivers there and they cleanse all sins. They
are Sukumari, Kumari, Nalini, Dhenuka, Ikshu, Venuka and
Gabhasti as the seventh. O great sage! Other than these, there
are hundreds of other minor rivers. There are hundreds and

---

[381] The *shirisha* tree, a variey of acacia or mimosa.

thousands of mountains. Those who reside in Jalada and other places drink those waters and are happy. The habitations in the *varsha*s are populated by those who have returned from heaven to earth. *Dharma* does not suffer and there is no strife between them. In those seven regions, there is no violation of the ordinances. There are Vangas, Magadhas, Manasas and Mandagas. The Vangas are *brahmana*s, the Magadhas are *kshatriya*s, the Manasas are *vaishya*s and the Mandagas are *shudra*s. O sage! In Shakadvipa, Vishnu Hari exists in the form of Surya and is properly worshipped, following the prescribed rites, by those who have controlled their souls. O Maitreya! In every direction, Shakadvipa is girdled by an ocean of milk that has the same dimensions as Shakadvipa.'

'O *brahmana*! In every direction, that ocean of milk is surrounded by the region known as Pushkara and this *dvipa* is double the size of Shakadvipa. Savana was there in Pushkara[382] and his sons were Mahavira and Dhatuki. The two *varsha*s there are named after them and are known as Mahavira's region and Dhatuki's region. O immensely fortunate one! There is only one famous mountain in these *varsha*s, and it is known as Manasottara. It is right in the middle and is circular in shape, with an altitude of fifty thousand *yojana*s. In every direction, like a cylinder, its expanse is the same.[383] Pushkaradvipa is like a circle and stationed in the middle, the mountain divides it into two parts. The great mountain is located in the centre and each part is like a half-circle. Men live for ten thousand years there. They are free from disease and free from grief. They are devoid of attachment and hatred. O *brahmana*! There is no superior or inferior there, no one who is a killer and no one who is killed. There is no jealousy,

[382] He was the lord of Pushkaradvipa.
[383] This seems to indicate a radius of fifty thousand *yojana*s.

malice, fear, anger or avarice and the other vices. Mahavira's[384]
region is on the outside and ornaments Dhatuki's region. The
mountain of Manasottara is frequented by gods and *daitya*s.
In the region known as Pushkaradvipa, there is no notion of
truth or falsehood. In the region known as Pushkaradvipa,
there are no rivers or mountains.[385] Through destiny, all the
men there are identical in form. There is no notion of *varna*
or *ashrama* and no notion of rites of *dharma*. Concepts of the
three *Veda*s,[386] livelihood, punishment, policy and service do
not exist. O Maitreya! The two *varsha*s there are described as
heaven on earth. It is pleasant for everyone, all the time. Old
age and disease do not exist. O sage! This is what happens
in the Mahavira and Dhatuki parts of Pushkara. There is a
nyagrodha tree in Pushkaradvipa and it is Brahma's excellent
spot. Worshipped by the gods and the *asura*s, Brahma resides
there. Pushkara is surrounded by an ocean of sweet water. Its
expanse is exactly the same as that of Pushkara itself. Thus,
each of the seven *dvipa*s is surrounded by an ocean. Each
dvipa and each ocean is twice the size of the preceding one.
In each of the oceans, the volume of the liquid always remains
constant. Unlike water in a vessel when it is heated, the
volume never increases or decreases. Like that, when the moon
waxes, the volume of liquid in the oceans remains constant.
O supreme among sages! There is no increase or decrease in
the waters. O great sage! However, in both *shuklapaksha* and
krishnapaksha,[387] when the moon rises or sets, the waters in
the oceans are seen to increase and decrease by five hundred

[384] The text says Mahapita. It must be Mahavira.

[385] Obviously, other than Manasottara.

[386] The text only uses the word three, presumably meaning the
three *Veda*s.

[387] Respectively, the bright and dark lunar fortnights.

and ten *angula*s.[388] In Pushkaradvipa, food arrives on its own. The subjects always enjoy the six kinds of taste.'[389]

'A world is seen to exist around that ocean of sweet water, double the size of the ocean. The ground is golden and is devoid of all creatures. The mountain known as Lokaloka[390] exists there and it is ten thousand *yojana*s in expanse. The mountain is also that many *yojana*s high. Established there, the mountain is surrounded by darkness on every side. In every direction, that mountain is surrounded by terrible darkness. O great sage! Beyond this terrible mountain, the ground extends for fifty crores of *yojana*s, like the shell of an egg. Such is the earth, with its *dvipa*s, oceans and mountains. O Maitreya! It nurtures all beings and is superior in qualities. This is the foundation of everything and is the mother of the universe.'

Chapter 2(5) (Nether Regions)

Shri Parashara said, 'O *brahmana*! I have spoken about the expanse of the earth. Its height is said to be seventy thousand *yojana*s. O supreme among sages! Each of the nether regions is ten thousand *yojana*s below the preceding one. They are Atala, Vitala, Nitala, Gabhastimat, Talatala, Rasatala and Patala as the seventh. O Maitreya! The grounds there are respectively black, white, red, yellow, graveled, mountainous and golden. They are adorned with excellent mansions. O great sage! Hundreds of *danava*s, *daitya*s, giant *naga*s, and

---

[388] An *angula* is the length of a finger.
[389] Sweet, sour, salty, bitter, pungent and astringent.
[390] Lokaloka can be interpreted in various ways, places where there is light versus places where there is darkness, populated places versus uninhabited regions and so on.

their offspring, dwell there. From the nether regions, Narada
went to an assembly in heaven and said that for the residents
of heaven, the beautiful nether regions were more delightful
than the world of heaven. "The ornaments of the *naga*s in the
nether regions are made out of extremely radiant jewels. What
can possibly match this? The *daitya* and *danava* maidens are
extremely beautiful. Even an emancipated person is enchanted
in the nether regions. During the day, the sun's rays illuminate,
but do not scorch. During the night, the moon's beams
illuminate, but do not cause a chill. The serpents rejoice with
food, objects of pleasure and excellent drinks. The *danava*s
and others do not even realize how time passes. There are
beautiful groves and rivers, waterbodies filled with lotuses.
The sky resonates with the melodious calls of male cuckoos
and other birds. The ornaments, fragrances and unguents are
exceedingly beautiful. The sounds of *veena*s, flutes and drums
can be heard all the time. Other than this, there are extensive
objects of pleasure that the *danava*s enjoy. *Daitya*s, *uraga*s and
others who reside in the nether regions also enjoy them."[391] In
his *tamas* form, Vishnu exists below the nether regions. He is
known as Shesha and the *daitya*s and *danava*s are incapable of
describing his qualities. One reads about him as Ananta and is
worshipped by *siddha*s, gods and *devarshi*s. His one thousand
hoods are evident, decorated with a *svastika* mark and
sparkling ornaments. The jewels on his one thousand hoods
illuminate the directions. For the welfare of the universe, he
deprives the *asura*s of all their energy. He always wears a single
earring and his eyes roll around in intoxication. With a diadem
and a garland, he is as radiant as a mountain that is on fire. He
is attired in blue garments and is intoxicated. He is adorned
with a white necklace. The divine Ganga descends from Mount

---

[391] Though not clearly indicated, this seems to be the right place
to end Narada's quote.

Kailasa, and he is as lofty as that. The tip of his hand rests on
a plough and he holds an excellent and radiant mace. He is
worshipped by the handsome and embodied form of Varuna.
At the end of a *kalpa*, Rudra emerges from his mouth in the
form of Samkarshana, blazing like a fire with poisonous flames
to devour the three worlds. The resplendent form of Shesha
holds up the globe of the earth on his hoods. Shesha resides
in the nether regions and is worshipped by all the gods. Even
the gods are incapable of knowing, or describing, his valour,
powers, nature and form. The flames from the jewels on his
hoods turn the entire earth red. It[392] is like a garland of flowers
for him. Who can speak about his valour? His eyes rolling
around in intoxication, Ananta yawns and the earth, with
its mountains, waterbodies and forests, starts to tremble and
quake. The *gandharva*s, *apsara*s, *siddha*s, *kinnara*s, *uraga*s and
charanas do not know the extent of his qualities. He is Ananta,
the one without decay. The wives of the *naga*s use their hands
to apply yellow sandalwood paste on him. The wind from his
repeated breathing wafts this fragrance in all the directions.
In ancient times, Garga worshipped him and learnt the truth
about *jyotisha*. He thus understood everything about cause and
effect. That supreme serpent holds up the earth on his hoods.
He illuminates all the worlds, along with the gods, the *asura*s
and humans.'

Chapter 2(6) (Various *Naraka*s)

Parashara said, 'O *brahmana*! The *narakas*[393] are located
beneath the waters. The sinners are cast down there. O

[392] The earth.
[393] Hells.

great sage! Hear about them. They are Rourava, Shukara, Rodha, Tala, Vishasana, Mahajvala, Taptakumbha, Lavana, Vilohita, Rudhirambha, Vaitarani, Krimisha, Krimibhojana, Asipatravana, Krishna, Lalabhoksha, Daruna, Puyavaha, Papa, Vahnijvala, Adhahshira, Samdasha, Kalasutra, Tamas, Avichi, Shvabhojana, Apratishtha and the second Avichi.[394] Apart from these, there are other extremely terrible *naraka*s. Those regions of Yama are terrible and, because of weapons and fire, generate fear. Men who are engaged in sinful activities fall down there. If a man bears false witness, speaks with partiality or utters other kinds of falsehood, he goes to Rourava.[395] O supreme among sages! A person who kills a fetus, strangles someone by obstructing his breath or kills a cow goes to the *naraka* named Rodha.[396] His breathing is obstructed there. If a person drinks liquor, kills a *brahmana*, steals gold or associates with those who do these things, he goes to the hell Shukara.[397] If a person kills someone from the royal family, kills a *vaishya*, has intercourse with his *guru*'s wife, has intercourse with his sister or kills a king's servant, he goes to Taptakumbha.[398] If a person sells his faithful wife, is a jailor,[399] sells a maned animal[400] or abandons someone who is faithful to him, he falls into Taptaloha.[401] If

[394] Usually, twenty-eight hells are mentioned. That explains why the word Rodhastala has to be read as Rodha and Tala.

[395] Rourava is a hell where one suffers at the hands of fierce animals known as *rurus*.

[396] *Rodha* means obstruction.

[397] *Shukara* means pig. Shukara probably means a hell where people are so tortured that they squeal like pigs.

[398] The text says Taptakunda here, with the same meaning as Taptakumbha (heated pot/vessel).

[399] The reason for this being a crime is not clear.

[400] Interpreted as a horse.

[401] This hell has not been mentioned earlier. Taptaloha means heated iron, while Taptakumbha means heated pot. Since the pot can be filled with molten iron, the two hells can be identical.

a person has intercourse with his daughter or his daughter-in-law, he falls down into Mahajvala.[402] O *brahmana*! If the worst among men disrespects or reviles his *guru*, abuses the *Veda*s, sells the *Veda*s or has intercourse with someone he should not have intercourse with, he goes to Lavana.[403] A thief, or a person who violates a contract, falls down into Viloha.[404] A person who hates gods, *brahmana*s or ancestors or a person who spoils a jewel goes to Krimibhoksha.[405] A person who sacrifices in the wrong way goes to Krimisha.[406] The worst among men who has his food before ancestors, gods and guests goes to Lalabhaksha.[407] A person who makes excessively fierce arrows goes to Vedhaka.[408] If a person makes barbed arrows or makes swords and similar weapons, he goes to the extremely terrible *naraka* named Vishasana.[409] If a person receives gifts from a wicked person, he goes to the hell named Adhomukha.[410] If a person performs a sacrifice for someone who is not entitled to sacrifice, is a bad astrologer or constantly eats sweetmeats and food alone, he goes to Puyavaha.[411] O *brahmana*! If a *brahmana* sells lac, the extract of meat, sesamum or salt, he

[402] Literally, large blaze.

[403] Literally, salt.

[404] The same as Vilohita, full of iron.

[405] Where worms feed on the sinner, the same as Krimibhojana.

[406] Where worms lord over the sinner.

[407] Where the sinner feeds on saliva.

[408] Not mentioned earlier. An excessively fierce arrow probably means an arrow with poison at the tip, something generally condemned. Vedhaka probably means a place where the sinner is pierced or poisoned.

[409] Not mentioned earlier. A place where the sinner is slaughtered or set on fire.

[410] The same as Adhahshira, where the sinner is hung face downwards.

[411] A place where the sinner is borne along with pus.

too goes to the same hell.[412] O supreme among *brahmanas*! If a person keeps cats, cocks, goats, dogs, boars or birds, he goes to the same hell. If a *brahmana* earns a living as an actor, a fisherman, a pimp, a seller of poison, a spy, a buffalo-keeper or if he indulges in sexual intercourse on *parva* days,[413] he descends into Rudhirandha. This is also true of an arsonist, a slayer of friends, a person who performs a sacrifice in a village of astrologers and a seller of *soma*. If a man destroys honey or destroys a village, he goes to Vaitarani. If a person forces the drinking of semen, violates a contract, does not follow norms of purification or earns a living through deception, he goes to Krishna.[414] If a person cuts down a forest unnecessarily, he goes to Asipatravana.[415] O *brahmana*! Those who hunt sheep and deer fall into Vahnijvala.[416] O *brahmana*! Those who use a fire to cook what should not be cooked also go there.[417] If a person deviates from his vows or from his own *ashrama*, he falls in the middle of Samdasha.[418] If men are following *brahmacharya*, but discharge semen during the day or in their dreams or if they are taught by their sons, they descend into Shvabhojana.[419] There are hundreds and thousands of other *naraka*s. Evildoers are cooked there and face pain. In that way, there are thousands of other sins. Until the time in *naraka* is over, men suffer the consequences of these. Men who act against *varna* and *ashrama* in their deeds, thoughts or speech, descend into hell. With their

---

[412] Puyavaha.

[413] Special auspicious days. Rudhirandha means a place where one is blinded by blood.

[414] Literally, the dark place.

[415] A place where the leaves of trees and bushes are like swords.

[416] Literally, a net of fire.

[417] This is interpreted as potters since they apply fire to uncooked clay vessels. But such an interpretation isn't necessary.

[418] A place where the sinner is bitten.

[419] A place where the sinner is eaten by dogs.

heads hanging downwards, those in *naraka* can see the gods in heaven. The gods also see all the sinners in *naraka*, with their heads hanging downwards. In progressive order, the stages[420] are immobile objects, worms, aquatic creatures, birds, animals, ordinary men, men devoted to *dharma*, gods and those who attain *moksha*. Progressively, one thousand parts of the first amount to one part of the second.[421] O immensely fortunate one! Before attaining emancipation, everyone has to pass through these stages. After having been born one thousand times as one species, one moves on to the next stage. Until emancipation, everyone has to go through this. A being spends time in heaven or resides in hell.'

'Sinners who turn away from *prayashchitta*[422] go to hell. Atonement is proportionate to the sin that has been committed. The supreme *rishi*s have spoken about these, and they must be remembered. If the sin is major, the atonement is major. If the sin is minor, the atonement is also minor. O Maitreya! Svayambhu[423] and others have spoken about *prayashchitta*. Among many kinds of atonement are acts of austerities. However, among all these, remembering Krishna is the best. After committing a sin, if there is repentance in a man, the best atonement for him is to remember Hari. A man must remember Narayana in the morning, at night, at the time of the *sandhyas*[424] and at mid-day. All his sins will then be instantly destroyed. Through remembering Vishnu, all

---

[420] Of birth as these species and then moving upwards in subsequent births.

[421] This seems to mean that one thousand births as inferior species enables one to have a single birth in a species that is just above the inferior one.

[422] Atonement.

[423] Manu.

[424] *Sandhya* is dawn and dusk when night meets day and day meets night.

the store of hardships is destroyed. For such a person, even
the attainment of heaven is an impediment, and he proceeds
towards emancipation. O Maitreya! If a person's mind is set
on Vasudeva and he worships him through *japa* and oblations,
even a fruit like becoming Indra of the gods is an impediment.
What is there in going to the vault of heaven? It has the
quality of returning to *samsara* again. How can that compare
with *japa* towards Vasudeva, which is the excellent seed of
emancipation? O sage! Therefore, if a mortal man remembers
Vishnu night and day, he does not go to *naraka* and all his sins
are destroyed. That which causes delight to the mind is heaven.
Anything contrary is hell. O supreme among *brahmana*s! Good
deeds and wicked deeds are given the names of heaven and
hell. The same object can cause misery, as well as joy. It can
also give rise to anger. Therefore, there is no object that solely
gives rise to misery or to joy. Even if there is joy, there is misery
again. When the anger disappears, there is pleasure. Hence,
there is nothing that innately gives rise to misery or to joy.
The symptoms of misery and joy are consequences of the mind.
Jnana is the supreme *brahman*. *Jnana* destroys bondage. The
universe is formed out of *jnana*. *Jnana* is supreme. O Maitreya!
Jnana is the foundation of learning and ignorance. Therefore,
resort to *jnana*. I have thus spoken to you about the earth's
globe. O *brahmana*! I have also spoken to you about all the
nether regions, hells, oceans, mountains, *dvipa*s, *varsha*s and
rivers. I have spoken briefly about these. What else do you wish
to hear?'

Chapter 2(7) (Regions Above)

Maitreya said, 'O *brahmana*! You have told me everything
about the earth. O sage! I wish to hear about Bhuvarloka

and the other *loka*s and about the positions and dimensions of the planets.[425] O immensely fortunate one! Please tell me what I have asked you about.'

Shri Parashara replied, 'That which is illuminated by the rays of the sun and the beams of the moon, along with its oceans, rivers and mountains, is known as the earth. O *brahmana*! The size and circumference of the earth is the same as the size and circumference of the sky.[426] O Maitreya! The solar disc is at a distance of one hundred thousand *yojana*s from the earth. The lunar disc is at a distance of one hundred thousand *yojana*s from the sun. The entire circle of *nakshatra*s shines a full one hundred thousand *yojana*s away from the moon. O *brahmana*! Budha[427] is at a distance of two hundred thousand *yojana*s from the circle of *nakshatra*s. Ushanas[428] is stationed at a distance of two hundred thousand *yojana*s above Budha. Angaraka[429] is stationed at a distance of two hundred thousand *yojana*s from Ushanas. The preceptor of the gods[430] is stationed at a distance of two hundred thousand *yojana*s from Bhouma. Souri[431] is stationed at a distance of two hundred thousand *yojana*s above Brihaspati. O supreme among *brahmana*s! The circle of the *saptarshi*s is at a distance of one hundred thousand *yojana*s from Brihaspati. One hundred thousand *yojana*s from the *rishi*s is Dhruva, which is like a pivot for all the shining bodies. O great sage! I have briefly spoken about the three worlds. These are the places for sacrifices. These are the places for enjoying the fruits of sacrifices. Maharloka is one crore *yojana*s above Dhruva. Those destined to survive at the end of

---

[425] *Graha*s.
[426] We have translated *parimandala* as circumference.
[427] Mercury.
[428] Shukra or Venus.
[429] Mars. Bhouma is yet another name for Mars.
[430] Brihaspati or Jupiter.
[431] Saturn.

a *kalpa* reside in Maharloka. O Maitreya! Janaloka is two crore *yojana*s from Maharloka. Brahma's sons with unblemished minds, Sananda and the others,[432] live there. Tapoloka said to be is eight crore *yojana*s above Maharloka. The gods known as Vairajas, who are not consumed by the fire, live there. The radiant Satyaloka is forty-eight crore *yojana*s from Tapoloka. One is freed from death there and that place is also known as Brahma's world. If there is any place on earth where one can travel on one's feet, that region is said to be Bhuloka. I have spoken about it in detail. The region between the earth and the sun is frequented by *siddha*s and sages. O supreme among sages! This is the second region and is known as Bhuvarloka. The space between Dhruva and the sun is one million and four hundred thousand *yojana*s. Those who have thought about the location of the worlds have spoken of this as Svarloka. O Maitreya! One has read that these three worlds are created.[433] Janaloka, Tapoloka and Satyaloka are the three that have not been created.[434] Maharloka is said to be in between the created and the uncreated. At the end of a *kalpa*, it becomes empty, but is not destroyed. O Maitreya! I have spoken about the seven upper regions, Maharloka and the others. I have also spoken about the seven nether regions. These are the dimensions of the cosmic egg.'[435]

'This egg is surrounded by a shell, above, below and diagonally, just like the seed of a wood-apple is surrounded on all sides. O Maitreya! The egg is surrounded by water that is ten times in size. The water which surrounds it is in turn surrounded by fire on the outside. O Maitreya! The fire is surrounded by

[432] Sanaka, Sananda, Sanatana and Sanatkumara.
[433] Bhuloka, Bhuvarloka and Svarloka. Created afresh at the end of a *kalpa*.
[434] Not destroyed at the end of a *kalpa*.
[435] *Brahmanda*.

wind and the wind is surrounded by space. O best among sages! The space is surrounded by Mahat. O Maitreya! Each of these seven is such that it is ten times the preceding one.[436] Pradhana is established, surrounding Mahat. It is infinite and has no end. Its dimensions cannot be measured. It is infinite and cannot be subjected to any kind of measurement. O sage! This is supreme Prakriti, the cause behind creation. There are thousands and tens of thousands of such cosmic eggs. There are crores and hundreds of crores of such cosmic eggs. Fire is hidden inside wood and oil is hidden inside a seed of sesamum. Like that, Purusha is hidden inside Pradhana and pervades it. This is known as the conscious *atman*. Purusha and Pradhana are inside the *atman*s of all beings, but they are dependent. O immensely intelligent one! Vishnu's energy sustains them.[437] Their *dharma* is to come together. His energy is the reason behind their existing separately and coming together. O immensely intelligent one! At the time of creation, his energy is the cause of agitation. Just as the wind blows and chills every drop of water, Vishnu's energy is inside Pradhana and Purusha. O sage! A tree, with trunk, major branches and minor branches, grows out of an original seed and gives rise to other seeds. From those seeds, other trees grow, and they are said to possess the same characteristics, constituents and causes as the original. In this way, Mahat and the others evolve from what did not exist earlier. From this, specific elements of creation, gods and others, result. They have sons and those sons have other sons. The original tree does not suffer because another tree has grown from its seed. Like that, creatures do not suffer when other categories of creatures result from them. The mere presence of time may appear to be the visible cause behind the

---

[436] Since Pradhana is infinite, this actually means six: the cosmic egg, water, fire, wind, space and Mahat.

[437] Purusha and Prakriti/Pradhana.

original tree. In that way, the universe is a consequence of the illustrious Hari's presence. The root, the stalk, the sprout, the leaf, the stem, the bud, the flower, the milk, the husk, the rice, the chaff and the ear latently exist inside a seed of paddy. O supreme among sages! All the ingredients for growth already exist. In the same way, the bodies of gods and others already exist within their own *karma*. Growth results after coming into contact with Vishnu's energy. Vishnu is the supreme *brahman* and everything in the universe flows from him. The universe exists within him, and it is into him that it is dissolved. The *brahman* is the supreme refuge, the supreme state that is beyond cause and effect. The universe, with all its divisions and mobile and immobile objects, exists within him. He is the foundation of Prakriti. He is the manifested form of the universe. At the time of destruction, everything enters into him. He is the agent behind sacrifices. He is worshipped through sacrifices. He is the fruits of those sacrifices. He is the means for undertaking sacrifices. Other than Hari, what else exists? What is distinct from him?'

Chapter 2(8) (Surya and Other Bodies)

Shri Parashara said, 'O one excellent in vows! I have described the placement of *brahmanda* to you. Now hear from me about the placement and dimensions of Surya and the others. Bhaskara's[438] chariot is nine thousand *yojana*s long. O supreme among sages! The pole of the chariot is twice as long. The axle of the chariot is one and a half crores and seven hundred thousand *yojana*s long. The axle has a wheel

---

[438] Bhaskara is one of Surya's names.

with three naves, five spokes and six segments of the rim.[439]
All of these are based on *samvatsara,* and this constitutes
the entire wheel of time. Hear about the names of the seven
horses which are the metres. Gayatri, Brihati, Ushnik, Jagati,
Trishtubh, Anushtubh, and Pankti—these metres are Ravi's
horses.[440] O immensely intelligent one! Vivasvat's chariot has
a second axle, which is forty-five thousand and five hundred
*yojana*s long. The two halves of the shaft are as long as the two
axles.[441] The short axle and shaft are attached to Dhruva. With
the longer axle, the wheel rests on Mount Manasa. Vasava's
city is to the east of Mount Manasottara. Yama's city is to
the south, while Varuna's city is to the west. Soma's city is
to the north. Hear about their names from me. Shakra's city
is Vasvoukasara, Yama's is Samyamani, the city of the lord
of the waters is Sukha and Soma's is Vibhavari. O Maitreya!
The illustrious Bhanu[442] moves, like a swift arrow, on his
southern course, with the *nakshatra*s attached to his wheel.
The illustrious Ravi is responsible for the difference between
day and night. *Devayana*[443] is the supreme path, resorted to
by *yogi*s who have destroyed their miseries. O Maitreya! All
the time, when Ravi shines on a *dvipa* at midday, on a *dvipa*

[439] The six segments of the rim are the six seasons. The three
naves are interpreted as periods of four months each, or as divisions of
the day (morning, midday and night). The five spokes are *samvatsara,
parivatsara, idavatsara, anuvatsara* and *vatsara. Samvatsara* is the
solar year, *anuvatsara* is the lunar year, *parivatsara* seems to have been
calculated on the basis of Jupiter's orbit and *vatsara* was calculated on
the basis of the *nakshatra*s. Since *idavatsara* occurred once every five
years, it probably had an intercalary month.

[440] The seven Vedic metres. Ravi is Surya's name, as is Vivasvat.

[441] There is a long axle/shaft and a short axle/shaft. It is similar to
an oil press.

[442] Surya.

[443] The path of the gods.

that is at the opposite end, it will be the middle of the night. O
brahmana! Rising and setting occur all the time and the points
are at the opposite ends of the directions. When the sun is
seen, it is said that he rises. When the sun disappears, it is said
that Ravi has set. But Arka[444] never actually rises or sets. The
descriptions of rising and setting are merely based on whether
Ravi is seen or unseen. For the cities of Shakra and the others,
when at midday, the sun is placed above one of these cities, his
light touches three cities and two intermediate points. When
the sun is above an intermediate point, his light touches two
cities and three intermediate points. From the time of rise until
midday, the intensity of Ravi's rays increases. After this, the
intensity of the rays decreases, until the sun sets. The eastern
and western directions are so named because of the rising and
the setting. Just as the sun shines at the front, he shines at the
back and on the sides. The only exception is atop Mount Meru,
the mountain of the immortals, where Brahma's assembly hall
is located. The radiance from Brahma's assembly hall repels
Arka's rays. The illumination is repelled and retreats. Staring
with Meru, all the other *dvipa*s and *varsha*s always have day
and night. However, to the north of Meru, it is always night.[445]
At night, when Bhaskara has set, his radiance enters the fire.
That is the reason a fire is seen from a greater distance at
night. O *brahmana*! During the day, some of the fire's radiance
enters Bhanu. With the addition of the fire's radiance, Surya is
extremely radiant during the day. Bhaskara and Agni possess
their respective energy and radiance. In this way, during night
and day, they reinforce each other and take away from each
other. Whether Bhaskara is in the northern hemisphere or the
southern hemisphere, during night and day, depending on

---

[444] Surya.
[445] Since the sun revolves around Meru, this north is a relative
position.

whether there is darkness or there is light, his radiance enters the water and is cooled. Therefore, since night has entered it, the water looks dark by day. When Bhaskara sets, his radiance enters water. Therefore, water looks fair by night, the radiance of day having entered it.'

'When Divakara[446] proceeds to the middle of Pushkara, in the course of a *muhurta*, he traverses one thirtieth of the earth's circumference. O *brahmana*! Whirling around like a potter's wheel, Divakara divides the earth into night and day. As *uttarayana* starts, Bhaskara moves into Makara.[447] O *brahmana*! He then moves to Kumba and then to Mina, moving on from one *rashi* into the next *rashi*.[448] After passing through these three, he reaches the *vishuva* point.[449] At this time, Savita makes night and day equal. After this, the night becomes shorter, and the day becomes longer. When the sun reaches the end of Mithuna,[450] the reverse movement starts. When he reaches Karkataka,[451] *dakshinayana* commences. Just as the circumference of a potter's wheel moves speedily, Surya swiftly proceeds along his southern course. With the speed of the wind, he travels over a great deal of ground in a short span of time. O *brahmana*! At the time

---

[446] Surya's name, the maker of the day.

[447] Capricorn.

[448] Kumba is Aquarius and Mina is Pisces. *Rashi* is a sign of the zodiac.

[449] In this context, the first point of Aries, the vernal equinox. *Vishuva* refers to both the first point of Aries and the first point of Libra (the autumnal equinox). *Sankranti* is the movement of the sun from one sign of the zodiac (*rashi*) to another. Thus, there are twelve of these. The entry of Surya into Capricorn (Makara), with the movement from *dakshinayana* to *uttarayana*, is known as *makara sankranti*, while its entry into Cancer, with the movement from *uttarayana* to *dakshinayana*, is known as *karka sankranti*. The entry into Aries (Mesha) and Libra (Tula) is known as *vishuva sankranti*.

[450] Gemini.

[451] Cancer, also known as Karkataka.

of *dakshinayana*, over twelve *muhurta*s, he travels over thirteen
and a half *nakshatra*s during the day. Over eighteen *muhurta*s,
he travels over the same number of *nakshatra*s during the night.
The centre of a potter's wheel moves slowly. Like that, when
the sun is on his northern course, he moves relatively slowly. He
covers a lesser amount of ground over a longer span of time. At
the end of *uttarayana*, since the speed is slow, the day consists
of eighteen *muhurta*s and Ravi traverses thirteen and a half
*nakshatra*s in the course of the day. In the course of the night,
he traverses the same number of *nakshatra*s in twelve *muhurta*s.
When a potter's wheel rotates, the lump of clay in the centre of
the wheel moves relatively slowly. O Maitreya! Like the centre
of a potter's wheel, Dhruva, at the centre, turns. But it moves
slowly. The length of day and night depends on the speed at
which Surya moves between the two end points of the horizon.
During the *ayana* when he moves fast during the day, he moves
slowly at night. When he moves slowly during the day, he moves
fast at night. However, the distance measured out by Divakara's
progress remains the same. O *brahmana*! Across night and day,
he has to pass through all the *rashi*s. He passes through six *rashi*s
during the day and the other six *rashi*s at night. Whether the day
is long or short, depends on the *rashi*s travelled. Whether the
night is long or short, depends on the *rashi*s travelled. Whether
the day is long or short, depends on the distance that has been
travelled. At the time of the northern course, he moves swiftly at
night and slowly during the day. During *dakshinayana*, Vivasvat
does the opposite. The period known as Usha is part of night
and Vyushti is said to be part of day.[452] The period between
Usha and Vyushti[453] is spoken of as *sandhya*. When *sandhya*

---

[452] Usha is not quite dawn; it is the period before the sun rises. In
calculations, it is included as part of the night. Similarly, Vyushti is
not quite dusk. It is the period before the sun sets.
[453] With these two words interpreted as night and day.

arrives, the extremely horrible, fierce and awful *rakshasa*s, known as Mandehas, seek to devour Surya. O Maitreya! This is because of the curse Prajapati[454] invoked on them. With bodies that would not be destroyed, they would die from one day to another day.[455] Therefore, there is this extremely terrible clash between them and Surya. O great sage! That is the reason excellent *brahmana*s pronounce Omkara, invoke the *gayatri mantra* on water and sprinkle the water at this time. With water that has the essence of the *vajra*, those sinners are scorched by this. At the time of *agnihotra*,[456] the first oblations are offered with a *mantra*. "The radiant Surya has one thousand rays. Throughout the year, Bhaskara provides radiance." Omkara is the illustrious Vishnu, the lord of speech, and the three reside in him.[457] Hence, when it is pronounced, the *rakshasa*s are destroyed. Surya is Vishnu's supreme portion and inside, he is a flood of radiance. This essence is supremely stimulated through the utterance of Omkara. With the radiance energized in this way, this blaze becomes the reason for the burning down of all the *rakshasa*s. Therefore, one must never transgress this worship at the time of the *sandhya* rites. If a person does not perform this worship at the time of *sandhya*, he slays Surya. Thus, protected by the *brahmana*s, the illustrious one progresses, and along with the *valakhilya*s,[458] is ready to protect the entire world.'

'Fifteen *nimesha*s[459] make up one *kashtha* and thirty *kashtha*s make up one *kala*. Thirty *kala*s constitute a

---

[454] Brahma.

[455] They would be revived at night.

[456] Oblations offered into a fire.

[457] Interpreted both as the three *Veda*s and as Brahma, Vishnu and Shiva.

[458] The *valakhilya rishi*s accompany the sun's chariot.

[459] The twinkling of an eye.

muhurta. Thirty *muhurta*s make up a day and night.[460] I have told you how the day can progressively be longer or shorter. But the two *sandhyas*[461] are not said to be subject to increase or decrease. Their duration is one *muhurta* each. From the time a line can be drawn across the solar disc[462] till the expiry of three *muhurta*s, that time interval is called *pratah*.[463] It amounts to one-fifth of the day. The next time interval, three *muhurta*s from the end of *pratah*, is *sangava*.[464] The next time interval, three *muhurta*s from the end of *sangava*, is *madhyahna*.[465] The learned speak of the next time interval, three *muhurta*s from the end of *madhyahna* as *aparahna*.[466] The next time interval, three *muhurta*s from the end of *aparahna*, is *sayahna*.[467] The fifteen *muhurta*s of the day are thus divided into groups of three *muhurta*s each. However, the day is said to consist of fifteen *muhurta*s only at the time of *vishuva*. Otherwise, depending on whether it is *uttarayana* or *dakshinayana*, it increases or decreases. The day devours up the night, or the night devours up the day. *Vishuva* occurs in the middle of spring and autumn, when Bhanu enters Mesha or Tula. Night and day are equal then. When Bhanu enters Karkataka, *dakshinayana* starts. When Divakara enters Makara, *uttarayana* commences. I have spoken about thirty *muhurta*s constituting day and night. O *brahmana*! Such fifteen days and nights are known as a

---

[460] Therefore, a *muhurta* is firty-eight minutes.

[461] Morning and evening.

[462] When half the solar disc becomes visible at sunrise.

[463] *Pratah* means morning. It thus lasts for two hours and twenty-four minutes.

[464] Forenoon.

[465] Midday.

[466] Afternoon.

[467] Evening.

paksha.[468] Two *paksha*s are known as a month and two solar
months constitute a *ritu*.[469] Three *ritu*s make up an *ayana* and
two *ayana*s are known as a *varsha*.[470] *Samvatsara* and the
others[471] are based on four different kinds of months. For all
determinations of time, a *yuga* is also spoken about.[472] The
four types of years are *samvatsara* as the first, *parivatsara*
as the second, *idavatsara* as the third and *anuvatsara* as the
fourth. The fifth is *vatsara* and such a reckoning of time is
known as *yuga*.'

'The mountain that is to the north of Shveta is famous as
Shringavat. O Maitreya! It is known as Shringavat because it
has three peaks, to the north, to the south and in the centre.[473]
In spring and autumn, Bhanu reaches the one in the middle.
O Maitreya! This is known as *vishuva* because the sun enters
Mesha and Tula. At that time, the dispeller of darkness makes
day and night equal. Both are then said to be equal to fifteen
*muhurta*s. O sage! When the sun is in the first part of Krittika
and the moon is in the fourth part of Vishakha, or when Surya
is in the third part of Vishakha and the moon is on Krittika's
head, and it also happens to be *vishuva*, there is no doubt that

---

[468] Lunar fortnight.

[469] Season.

[470] *Ayana* is a six-month period and *varsha* is a year.

[471] *Samvatsara* is the solar year, *anuvatsara* is the lunar year,
parivatsara seems to have been calculated on the basis of Jupiter's
orbit and *vatsara* was calculated on the basis of the *nakshatra*s.
Three types of months are: (i) solar month, thirty days of sunrise and
sunset; (ii) lunar month, thirty days of *tithi*s (lunar days); and (iii) a
nakshatra-based month, time taken by the moon to transit twenty-
eight *nakshatra*s. The fourth might either be the time taken by the sun
to pass through one *rashi*, or one based on Jupiter's orbit.

[472] Not to be confused with the other notion of *yuga*.

[473] *Shringa* means peak.

this time is sacred.[474] At that time, one must control oneself and
donate what must be given to gods, ancestors and *brahmana*s.
Such donations generate happiness. If one donates at the
time of *vishuva*, all the necessary tasks are completed. Before
making donations, one should know the day, the night, the
fortnight, the *kala*, the *kashtha*, the *kshana* and whether it is
pournamasi, amavasya, sinivali, kuhu or *anumati*.[475] The sun
is in *uttarayana* in the months of Tapas, Tapasya, Madhu,
Madhava, Shukra and Shuchi.[476] The sun is in *dakshinayana*
in the months of Nabhas, Nabhasya, Isha, Urja, Sahas and
Sahasya.'[477]

'Earlier, I have spoken to you about Mount Lokaloka. The
four guardians of the worlds, excellent in their vows, reside
there. O *brahmana*! They are Sudhama and Shankhapada,
both sons of Kardama, Hiranyaroma and Ketumat as the
fourth. They are devoid of the opposite pairs of sentiments.
There are without pride and without lassitude. They have no

---

[474] There are twenty-seven *nakshatra*s (asterisms), twenty-eight
with Abhijit added. *Nakshatra*s are not necessarily stars, they can
be constellations too. The order in the list often varies, perhaps a
reflection of precession of the equinoxes. If one begins with Krittika,
the standard list is Krittika, Rohini, Mrigashira, Ardra, Punarvasu,
Pushya, Ashlesha, Magha, Purva Phalguni, Uttara Phalguni, Hasta,
Chitra, Svati, Vishakha, Anuradha, Jyeshtha, Mula, Purva Ashadha,
Uttara Ashadha, Abhijit, Shravana, Dhanishtha, Shatabhisha, Purva
Bhadrapada, Uttara Bhadrapada, Revati, Ashvini and Bharani.

[475] *Sinivali* is the day preceding the night of the new moon, *kuhu*
is the night of the new moon, and *anumati* is the fourteenth night of
shukla paksha.

[476] Respectively, Magha, Phalguna, Chaitra, Vaishakha, Jyaishtha
and Ashada. The names mentioned in the text are the older names of
these months.

[477] Respectively, Shravana, Bhadrapada, Ashvina, Karttika,
Agrahayana and Pousha. The names mentioned in the text are the
older names of these months.

possessions. They are there, in the four directions of Lokaloka, as the guardians of the worlds. To the north of Agastya and to the south of the Ajavithi, is the path known as *pitriyana*. This is outside Vaishvanara's path.[478] The great-souled *rishi*s who perform *agnihotra* sacrifices reside there. They are the officiating priests who perform these sacrifices, before Brahma created beings.[479] There are located along the southern path, undertaking such sacrifices between one *yuga* and another *yuga*, before Brahma establishes the worlds again. They perform austerities and preserves the ordinances of the *shruti* texts. Those who were born earlier, are born later. Those who were born later, are born earlier.[480] In this way, they continue and remain there, firm in their vows. As long as the moon and the stars exist, they remain there, beyond Savita's southern course. The region that is to the north of Savita's course, to the north of Nagavithi[481] and to the south of the *saptarshi*s is known as *devayana*. The sparkling *siddha*s, who are *brahmachari*s, reside there. They have conquered death and therefore, do not desire offspring. These are eighty-eight thousand sages who hold up their seed. They remain there until the onset of the deluge, north of the sun's course. They are devoid of avarice and have given up sexual intercourse. They lack desires and hatred and have given up activities to propagate beings. Since they have comprehended the nature of the objects of the senses, they have given up desire. Because of this reason, they have

[478] The reference is astronomical. Agastya is the star Canopus. Ajavithi means the three *nakshatra*s that indicate *dakshinayana*: Mula, Purvashada and Uttarashada. In this context, Vaishvanara means the sun. This region is beyond the sun's path through the sky.

[479] These verses are difficult to understand, and some liberties have been taken with the text.

[480] Across successive births, a father becomes a son, and a son becomes a father.

[481] The *nakshatra*s Ashvini, Bharani and Krittika.

tasted immortality. Immortality means existence until the onset of the deluge. Existence for the duration of the three worlds is said to be freedom from death. O *brahmana*! The fruits of good deeds like horse sacrifices and bad deeds like killing a *brahmana* last till the onset of the deluge. O Maitreya! At that time, everything that exists in the region between the earth and Dhruva is destroyed.'

'There is a third[482] radiant layer in the firmament, between the *saptarshi*s and Dhruva. This is Vishnu's divine position. O *brahmana*! This is the supreme place for ascetics who have controlled themselves. They have cleansed the mire of sins and have exhausted their good and bad deeds. They have exhausted all the reasons for good and bad deeds. Having gone to Vishnu's supreme position, one does not grieve. Dharma, Dhruva and other witnesses of the worlds reside there. In that supreme position, with their minds immersed in *yoga*, they possess the same powers as Vishnu. O Maitreya! Vishnus's supreme position is in the warp and woof of everything, mobile and immobile, that exists in the universe and everything that will be. If a *yogi*'s *atman* is immersed in the *jnana* that confers discrimination, he can see that Vishnu's supreme position is like an eye in the firmament. Dhruva himself is established there, like a pivot. O *brahmana*! All the stellar bodies are dependent on Dhruva and the clouds depend on the stellar bodies. When the clouds come together, there is rain. O great sage! When rain is created, there is nourishment. Gods and all the others welcome it. The gods are those who partake of sacrificial oblations. Nourished by these oblations, they cause rain to shower down again, and this ensures the preservation of beings. Such is the nature of the sparkling third layer that

---

[482] The first and the second are not clearly mentioned. The first is probably the three worlds of earth, the sky and heaven, while the second is that of the *rishi*s.

belongs to Vishnu. It is a foundation for the three worlds and
is the cause of rain.'

'O *brahmana*! The river that destroys all sins flows from
there. Her waters are fragrant with the unguents of divine
maidens who have bathed in her. Her radiant flow originates
from the nail of the big toe on Vishnu's left foot. Full of devotion,
night and day, Dhruva holds her on his head. The *saptarshi*s
are there, devoted to *pranayama*. They weave the garlands of
her waves into their matted hair. Aided by the wind, her flow
then floods the lunar disc, with its beauty enhanced because of
this. Emerging from the lunar disc, she then descends on Meru's
summit. To purify the world, she flows in four directions as Sita,
Alakananda, Chakshu and Bhadra. It is a single flow, divided
into four, according to the direction in which she proceeds.
The flow towards the south in known as Alakananda. For
more than one hundred years, Sharva[483] lovingly bore her on
his head. When she emerged from Shambhu's matted hair, she
was brought down from heaven and flooded the mass of bones
of Sagara's wicked descendants.[484] If one bathes in her waters,
all sins are instantly destroyed. O Maitreya! One immediately
obtains good merits that have never been obtained before. O
Maitreya! If one faithfully offers her water in water-rites to
ancestors for one hundred years, they obtain a satisfaction that
is extremely difficult to obtain. Purushottama is the lord of
sacrifices. *Brahmana*s and kings who worship him through
great sacrifices obtain supreme success. Ascetics who bathe in
these waters have their sins cleansed. With their minds fixed on
Keshava, they achieve excellent *nirvana*. This purifying flow
has been heard about. It is desired. It has been seen. It has been
touched. When beings bathe in it, they are purified. Even at
a distance of one hundred *yojana*s from it, if people exclaim,

---

[483] Shiva.
[484] She was brought down by Bhagiratha.

"Ganga! O Ganga!" the sins they have committed in three
births are destroyed. For the purpose of purifying the three
worlds and the universe, she originates from a certain spot.
This is the third supreme layer, the illustrious one's abode.'

Chapter 2(9) (Rain and Narayana)

Shri Parashara said, 'The illustrious lord's form, with all the
stars in it, is in the form of a *shishumara*.[485] This is Hari's
form in the firmament and Dhruva is located on the tail. As
Dhruva revolves, it makes the moon, the sun and the planets
to revolve around it. The *nakshatras* also revolve, in a circle.
The sun, the moon, the stars and the *nakshatras* seem to be
bound to Dhruva by bonds in the sky. Narayana's form in the
firmament, in the form of the radiant bodies, has been spoken
of. This is *shishumara*. He is himself located in the heart and he
sustains all of these. Uttanapada's son worshipped the lord of
the universe. Therefore, he became the star Dhruva, located on
shishumara's tail. Janardana, who controls everything, is the
support for *shishumara*. Dhruva is supported by *shishumara*
and Bhanu is supported by Dhruva. The sun is the support for
the entire world, with *devas*, *asuras* and humans. O *brahmana*!
Listen attentively to what has been ordained for it. For eight
months, Vivasvat sucks up the juices from the water. He
showers it down as rain, which leads to food. Food nourishes
the entire world. Vivasvat's sharp rays suck up water from the
entire world. This is then used to nourish Soma. Using hollow
arteries made out of air, the moon flings these on clouds, which
are the embodied forms of smoke, fire and wind. Since the

[485] Dolphin/porpoise.

water inside them is dispersed, clouds are known as *abhra*.[486]
O Maitreya! However, at the right time, urged by the wind,
the water in the clouds becomes clean and sparkling. O sage!
Savita sucks up water from four kinds of entities: rivers, oceans,
the earth and living bodies. The one with the rays receives the
water from the Ganga that is in the firmament.[487] Without any
clouds, he uses his rays to instantly fling this down on earth.
O supreme among *brahmanas*! Those who are touched by this,
are immediately cleansed of their mire of sins. Such mortals
do not go to hell, and this is known as a divine bath. When
the sun can be seen, there is water that falls down from the
firmament, without any clouds being present. This is water
from *akashaganga*, and Ravi uses his rays to fling this down.
However, when Krittika and the other odd *nakshatras* are in
the firmament, even when Arka can be seen, the water that
falls down is scattered by the *diggajas*, though it is water from
the heavenly Ganga. It is only when even *nakshatras* are in the
firmament that water which falls down from the sky is scattered
by Surya's rays. But both are extremely sacred and dispel the
fear of sin from men. O great sage! The water from *akashaganga*
is a divine bath. O *brahmana*! The water that descends from
the clouds nourishes all herbs and plants and living beings.
For the sake of life, it is like *amrita*. All the large numbers of
plants and trees obtain supreme nourishment because of this.
O *brahmana*! The consequence is success in the ripening of
crops and subjects are born. Therefore, men who possess the
insight of the sacred texts undertake the mentioned sacrifices.
They constantly nourish and worship *devas* with these. In this
way, sacrifices, the Vedas, the *varnas*, *brahmanas* being the
foremost, all the abodes of the gods and all the different kinds

---

[486] *Bhramsha* means to fall down, drop or lose. The word *abhra*
(cloud) is a negation of this.

[487] Ganga's flow in the sky, *akashaganga*, the Milky Way.

of beings are supported by rain and the food that results from
this. O supreme among sages! But rain results from Savita. O
supreme among the best of sages! In turn, Dhruva is Savita's
support. Dhruva's support is *shishumara*, which is nothing but
Narayana's *atman*. Narayana is located in *shishumara*'s heart.
The radiant and eternal one is the original cause behind all
beings.'

Chapter 2(10) (Twelve Adityas)

Shri Parashara said, 'Between the two points of ascent and
descent,[488] during the course of the year, Bhanu travels
through one hundred and eighty degrees.[489] *Devas* known as
Adityas, *rishis*, *gandharvas*, *apsaras*, *gramanis*, *sarpas* and
rakshasas ride on his chariot.[490] In the month of Chaitra or
Madhu,[491] the seven are Dhatri as Aditya, Pulastya as *rishi*,
Tumburu as *gandharva*, Kratusthala as *apsara*, Rathabhrit as
gramani, Vasuki as *sarpa* and Heti as *rakshasa* as the seventh.
O Maitreya! These are the seven on Bhanu's chariot. In the
month of Madhava, the seven on Ravi's chariot are Aryama as

[488] *Uttarayana* and *dakshinayana*.

[489] *Mandala* has been translated as degree. This means 180
degrees during the ascent and 180 degrees during the descent, adding
up to 360.

[490] One set every month. *Gramani* means leader. In this context,
the word is interpreted as *yaksha*.

[491] Chaitra (Madhu) is March–April, Vaishakha (Madhava) is
April–May, Jyeshtha (Shuchi) is May–June, Ashadha (Shukra) is June–
July, Shravana (Nabhas) is July–August, Proushtha (Proshthapada
or Bhadrapada) is August-September, Ashvayuja (Ashvina) is
September–October, Karttika is October–November, Margashirsha
(Agrahayana) is November–December, Pousha is December–January,
Magha is January–February and Phalguna is February–March.

Aditya, Pulaha as *rishi*, Narada as *gandharva*, Punjikasthala as
apsara, Rathouja as *gramani*, Kacchavira as *sarpa* and Praheti
as *rakshasa*. They always reside there in Madhava. Hear about
the names of the ones in Shuchi. O Maitreya! The ones who
reside are Mitra as Aditya, Atri as *rishi*, Haha as *gandharva*,
Menaka as *apsara*, Rathasvana as *gramani*, Takshaka as *sarpa*
and Pourusheya as *rakshasa*. The ones who reside in Shukra
or Ashadha are Varuna as Aditya, Vasishtha as *rishi*, Huhu
as *gandharva*, Sahajanya as *apsara*, Rathachitra as *gramani*,
Rambha as *sarpa* and Ratha as *rakshasa*. The seven who
reside with Arka in Nabhas are Indra as Aditya, Angiras as
rishi, Vishvavasu as *gandharva*, Pramlocha as *apsara*, Srota
as *gramani* and Elapatra as *sarpa*.[492] In Bhadrapada, they are
Vivasvat as Aditya, Bhrigu as *rishi*, Ugrasena as *gandharva*,
Anumlocha as *apsara*, Apurana as *gramani*, Shankhapala as
sarpa and Vyaghra as *rakshasa*. The ones who reside with Ravi
in Ashvayuja are Pusha as Aditya, Goutama as *rishi*, Suruchi
as *gandharva*, Ghritachi as *apsara*, Sushena as *gramani*,
Dhananjaya as *sarpa* and Vata as *rakshasa*. Those who reside in
Karttika are Parjanya as Aditya, Bharadvaja as *rishi*, Visvavasu
as *gandharva*, Vishvachi as *apsara*, Senajit as *gramani*, Airavata
as *sarpa* and Chapa as *rakshasa*. The ones who possess those
rights in Margashirsha are Amsha as Aditya, Kashyapa as
rishi, Chitrasena as *gandharva*, Urvashi as *apsara*, Tarkshya
as *gramani*, Mahapadma as *sarpa* and Vidyut as *rakshasa*. In
the month of Pousha, the seven who reside in the solar disc
are Bhaga as Aditya, Kratu as *rishi*, Urnayu as *gandharva*,
Purvachitti as *apsara*, Arishtanemi as *gramani*, Karkotaka as
sarpa and Sphurja as *rakshasa*. O *brahmana*! They possess
the rights for illuminating the world. O Maitreya! The seven
who reside with Bhaskara in the month of Magha are Tvashta

---

[492] The *rakshasa*'s name is missing. Alternatively, both *sarpa* and
rakshasa are known as Elapatra.

as Aditya, Jamadagni as *rishi*, Dhritarashtra as *gandharva*,
Tilottama as *apsara*, Ritajit as *gramani*, Kambala as *sarpa* and
Brahmapeta as *rakshasa*. Finally, hear about the ones who
reside with Surya in Phalguna. O great sage! They are Vishnu
as Aditya, Vishvamitra as *rishi*, Suryavarcha as *gandharva*,
Rambha as *apsara*, Satyajit as *gramani*, Ashvatara as *sarpa* and
Yajnapeta as *rakshasa*. O Maitreya! O *brahmana*! In this way,
energized by Vishnu's energy, every month, these seven reside
in the solar disc. The sages praise Surya. The *gandharva*s sing
in front of him. The *apsara*s dance. The roamers in the night
follow Surya. The *pannaga*s bear him and the *yaksha*s gather
the reins together. The *valakhilya*s assemble around him. O
supreme among sages! In this way, those seven are there in
the solar disc. When their own time arrives, they are the cause
behind cold, heat and the showering down of rain.'

Chapter 2(11) (Duties of the Sun)

Maitreya asked, 'O illustrious one! You have told me
about the seven categories in Ravi's disc. I have also
heard that they are responsible for heat and cold. O *guru*! You
have also told me about the conduct of *gandharva*s, *uraga*s,
*apsara*s, *rishi*s, *valakhilya*s, *rakshasa*s and *yaksha*s on Bhanu's
chariot, energized by Vishnu's powers within them. O sage!
However, you have not told be about Aditya's[493] task. If those
seven categories shower down rain, heat and cold, why is it
said that Ravi is responsible for rains? What does Surya do?
If those seven categories perform the tasks, why do people say
that Vivasvat rises, attains a midpoint and sets?'

[493] Surya's.

Parashara replied, 'O Maitreya! Hear the answer to what you have asked me about. Though those seven categories exist, Ravi alone is the most important and superior to them. All powers exist in the supreme Vishnu. The *Rig, Yajur* and *Sama Veda*s are in him. He is in these three. He is the one who scorches the universe and destroys it. Vishnu is established there, for the protection and preservation of the universe. O *brahmana*! The *Rig, Yajur* and *Sama Veda*s are established inside Savita. Ravi appears from one month to another month. But he is nothing but Vishnu's three-fold and supreme powers, which are established in him. The hymns of the *Rig Veda* praise him in the forenoon, the hymns of the *Yajur Veda* at midday. The great *rathantara* and other hymns from the *Sama Veda* praise Ravi when the day draws to a close. These three, known as *Rig, Yajur* and *Sama*, are Vishnu's limbs. It is Vishnu's energy which always exists in Aditya and undertakes everything. Vishnu's three-fold energy does not exist in Ravi alone. Brahma, Purusha[494] and Rudra also have this three-fold energy in them. At the time of creation, the *Rig* energy is present in Brahma. The *Yajur* energy is in Vishnu and Rudra is full of the *Sama* energy. That is the reason the utterance of this sound purifies.[495] Vishnu's energy has all three and is based on *sattva*. It is this energy that exists in the sun and in the seven categories. Because this energy exists, the sun uses its rays to radiate. It conveys the darkness that pervades the entire world towards destruction. Hence, the sages praise him and the *gandharva*s sing in front of him. The *apsara*s dance and the roamers in the night follow him. The *pannaga*s bear him and the *yaksha*s gather the reins together. The *valakhilya*s assemble around him. Vishnu's energy does not rise or set. Vishnu's energy

[494] In this context, Purusha is interpreted as Vishnu, as part of the trinity.

[495] This must mean 'OUM', O standing for Brahma, U for Vishnu and M for Shiva.

exists in the seven categories and in the sun. But the undecaying Vishnu is distinct from them. This is just like a person who approaches a mirror and sees his own image reflected inside it. O *brahmana*! Like that, Vishnu's energy exists in the sun from one month to another month. But it is also distinct.[496] O *brahmana*! The lord Surya always revolves, satisfying ancestors, gods and humans. The moon is nourished by the sun's *sushumna* rays.[497] In *krishna paksha*, the immortals perpetually drink this nectar. O *brahmana*! When *krishna paksha* comes to an end, the ancestors drink the remaining two portions from Soma. Thus, Bhaskara satisfies them. Using his rays, Ravi sucks up juices from the earth. For the sake of sustaining beings and enhancement of crops, he releases these. In this way, the illustrious Ravi pleases all beings. Gods, ancestors, humans and others are satisfied. Gods are satisfied for a fortnight and the ancestors for a month.[498] Arka constantly bestows satisfaction on mortals.'

Chapter 2(12) (The Moon and Planets)

Shri Parashara said, 'Soma's chariot has three wheels and is yoked to ten horses that are as white as the *kunda* flower.[499]

---

[496] The energy in the sun is like the image in the mirror.

[497] The sun has one thousand rays. Seven of these are the most important. The list varies. But out of these seven important rays, one is *sushumna*.

[498] This implies the gods drink once every *paksha* and the ancestors drink once every month. But before this, the text has not suggested that. What is probably intended is something like the following. Both the gods and the ancestors drink when the moon wanes, that is, during *krishna paksha*. The gods drink for the first fourteen lunar days. The ancestors drink the two remaining portions, out of sixteen, on the last day of *krishna paksha*.

[499] Jasmine.

They are on the left and on the right. It moves swiftly through the *nakshatra*s, with Dhruva providing the support. As is the case with the sun, the rays progressively wax and wane. Just as in the case of the sun, it is yoked to well-trained horses. O best among sages! They originated from the water of the ocean and last for an entire *kalpa*. When the gods drink, Soma wanes. O Maitreya! Using one of its rays, the radiant Bhaskara reinforces one digit.[500] Progressively, the gods drink from the maker of the night.[501] Every day, proportionately, Bhaskara, the one who steals water, fills it up. In the course of half a month, Soma is thus filled with the nectar of *amrita*. O Maitreya! The gods drink this store of nectar and become immortal. Thirty-three thousand, thirty-three hundred and thirty-three *deva*s drink from the moon. When only two digits remain, the moon enters the solar orbit. It resides in the ray known as *ama*.[502] Therefore, this day is described as *amavasya*. Initially, for a day and a night, the moon enters water. After this, it progressively goes to plants and trees. Thereafter, it resides in the sun. If a person cuts down a branch when the maker of the night resides in plants and trees, or if he throws down a leaf, he is guilty of the sin of killing a *brahmana*. Out of Soma's fifteen parts, when only a single digit remains, the ancestors approach it in the afternoon. They drink up the two sacred digits that still remain. O sage! On the day of Amavasya, the ancestors drink up the sacred nectar that exists in the form of *amrita* in the moon's rays. The ancestors are satisfied and, no longer anxious, withdraw for an entire month. The ancestors are of three kinds: Soumyas,

---

[500] The moon has sixteen digits (*kala*s).

[501] The moon.

[502] The word *ama* has several meanings: day of the new moon, day when there is a conjunction between the sun and the moon, the moon's sixteenth digit. *Vasya* is derived from the word for residing.

Barhishads and Agnishvattas.[503] Just as the ancestors drink
during *krishna paksha*, the gods drink during *shukla paksha*.[504]
Plants and trees are nourished with the cool particles that are
full of *amrita*. As plants and trees grow, they sustain humans,
animals and insects. The radiance of those cool beams also
delights them.'

'The chariot of Chandra's son is made out of wind and fire.
It is also yoked to eight tawny horses that are as swift as the
wind.[505] Shukra's[506] giant chariot has a bumper, a seat, all the
equipment and a flag. It is yoked to horses that originated on
earth. Bhoumya's[507] large and splendid chariot is made out of
gold. It is yoked to eight red horses that originated from the fire.
They have the complexions of rubies. Brihaspati[508] is on a golden
chariot, yoked to eight pale horses. Over the course of a year,
it travels from one *rashi* to another *rashi*. Shanaihshchara[509] is
astride a chariot yoked to speckled horses that originate from
space. The chariot moves slowly and gradually. Svarbhanu[510]
is astride a grey chariot that is yoked to eight horses with the
complexion of a bee. O Maitreya! Once they have been yoked
properly, they constantly draw the chariot. Depending on the
day, Rahu moves from Aditya to Soma. Depending on the solar
day, it again moves from Soma to Aditya. Ketu's chariot has
eight horses that are as fleet as swans. Their complexions are
like the smoke of burning straw and as red as lac. I have thus

---

[503] Soumyas are also identified with years, Agnishvattas with
seasons and Barhishads with months.

[504] There is an inconsistency with what has been said earlier.

[505] Chandra's son is Budha (Mercury).

[506] Venus.

[507] Mars.

[508] Jupiter.

[509] Saturn. The word Shanaihshchara means one who moves
slowly.

[510] Rahu.

told you about the nine chariots of the planets.[511] O immensely
fortunate one! All of them are attached to Dhruva by bonds
made out of air. The discs of planets, *nakshatra*s and stars
are attached to Dhruva. O Maitreya! Tied by bonds of air,
they revolve in their designated places. Wherever stars exist,
the bonds of air also exist. All of them are bound to Dhruva.
They revolve around him and also make him revolve. This is
just like oil being squeezed in an oil press. The wheel moves
and makes the spindle also move. Tied by bonds of air, all the
stellar bodies revolve. This is just like a wheel of fire, driven by
a wheel of wind. The wind that bears along the stellar bodies
is known as *pravaha*.'

'I have spoken about *shishumara*. Dhruva is there. O
supreme among sages! Hear about its placement. If one sees it
at night, one is freed from all sins committed during the day.
If one looks at it, one lives for more years than there are stars
in *shishumara*. Uttanapada is known as its upper jaw, sacrifice
is the lower jaw. Dharma is known to be located on its head
and Narayana is in the heart. The two Ashvins are in the two
front feet and Varuna and Aryama are in the two hind feet.
Samvatsara is the penis and Mitra is the anus. Agni, Mahendra,
Kashyapa and Dhruva are located on the tail. These four stars
in *shishumara* never set. Such is the location of the earth,
the stellar bodies, the *dvipa*s, the oceans, the mountains, the
*varsha*s and the rivers. I have also described those who reside
in them. I have described their nature. But briefly, hear about it
again. O *brahmana*! The waters are Vishnu's body. The earth,
which is in the shape of a lotus, was produced, along with its
mountains and oceans, from the water. The stellar bodies are
Vishnu. The worlds are Vishnu. The forests, mountains and
directions are Vishnu. O noble *brahmana*! He is rivers and
oceans, everything that exists and everything that does not

[511] Including the moon.

exist. Jnana is the illustrious one's form. Though he exists in objects, he is disembodied. Therefore, you must know that mountains, oceans, the earth and all the other differences represent deficiencies in understanding. When one's own form is pure, when all one's *karma* and taints have been exhausted, one obtains *jnana*. That is when one's resolutions become successful, not through objects and differences among objects. What is there in objects? Where is the one who is without a beginning, without a middle and without an end? He is the one who constantly exists in a single form. O *brahmana*! If something is subject to transformation, it cannot have any substance. Therefore, there is no truth in it. A large pot is fashioned out of earth. It is then splintered into shards. The shards are crushed and become particles of dust. A person's own *karma* clouds his *atman*, and he does not perceive what is certain. Tell me, what exists in an object? O *brahmana*! Therefore, there is nothing other than *vijnana*. There is nothing that can be derived from objects. *Vijnana* is one. But because differences in one's own *karma* lead to differences in consciousness, it appears in different forms. *Jnana* is pure, sparkling, without grief, devoid of greed and bereft of any sense of attachment. It is one. It is supreme and always exists. It is nothing other than Vasudeva, the supreme lord. I have spoken to you about true sentiments, about *jnana* which is true and about everything else which is false. However, I have also told you about the conduct of beings who find refuge in the worlds. Sacrifices, sacrificial animals, sacrificial fires, officiating priests, *soma*, gods, the desire for heaven, different kinds of *karma* and their paths, their fruits and objects of pleasure have also been described. I have told you everything about the worlds. Those who are under the subjugation of *karma* go there. But one should know about the form of the eternal, immutable and constant one. One should act so as to enter that Vasudeva.'

Chapter 2(13) (Bharata's Story)

Maitreya said, 'O illustrious one! You have indeed properly answered everything that I asked you about—the earth, oceans, mountains, rivers, placement of planets and the placement of the three worlds, supported by Vishnu. You have also spoken about the importance of *jnana* and the supreme objective. You spoke about Bharata, lord of the earth. I wish to hear about his conduct, and you should describe it to me. Bharata, lord of the earth, resided in Salagrama. He immersed himself in *yoga*, with his mind only fixed on Vasudeva. As a consequence of the power of that sacred region, he constantly meditated on Hari. Why did he not obtain emancipation and why was he again born as a *brahmana*? When he was reduced to the state of being a *brahmana*, what did the extremely great-souled one do? O best among sages! You should tell me everything about Bharata.'

Shri Parashara replied, 'O Maitreya! The immensely fortunate one, lord of the earth, resided in Salagrama for a long period of time, with his mind fixed on the illustrious one and on nothing else. He resorted to non-violence. He possessed all the qualities. He was supreme among those who possessed qualities. He achieved the supreme objective of control over his mind. King Bharata only pronounced Hari's name. "I prostrate myself before the lord of sacrifices, Achyuta, Govinda, Madhava, Ananta, Keshava, Krishna, Vishnu, Hrishikesha, Vasudeva." O Maitreya! He did not utter anything else, not even in his dreams. He thought of nothing, other than the meanings of these names. Collecting kindling, flowers and *kusha* grass, he performed rites for the divinity. He performed no other rites. He was devoid of attachment, immersed in *yoga* and austerities. For the sake of his ablutions, he once went to

Mahanadi.[512] He had his bath and performed the other rites.
O *brahmana*! At that time, a doe emerged from the forest and
came to the bank of the river. She was thirsty and wished to
drink water. She was pregnant and about to give birth. When
she had almost finished drinking water, a lion's loud roar was
heard, terrifying for all creatures. Overwhelmed with fear, she
jumped from the river onto the bank. However, since it was too
high, she fell into the river and miscarried. She was confounded
and submerged in the tumultuous waves. The king seized the
fawn delivered as a result of the miscarriage. O Maitreya! As a
result of the miscarriage and the progressive exertions she had
made, the doe fell down and died. The ascetic king saw the
distressed doe. He gathered up the fawn and returned to his
own hermitage. Every day, the king nurtured the fawn. O sage!
He nourished it and it grew. In search of grass, it would stray
up to the end of the hermitage. Having gone to desolate and
distant parts, when it was scared of tigers, it would rush back
again. Even when it went far away in the morning, it would
again return to the hermitage in the evening, to Bharata's
cottage in the hermitage. O *brahmana*! Whether the deer was
near or far, his mind was attached to it, and he could not think
of anything else. He had cast aside his kingdom and sons.
He had freed himself from all his relatives. Nevertheless, he
now possessed a sense of ownership in the fawn. "Has it been
devoured by wolves or tigers? Has a lion brought it down?" If
a long time elapsed since its departure, these were his thoughts.
"This earth is marked by impressions of its hooves. What has
become of the fawn, which brings delight to me? With the tips
of its horns, it rubs against my arms. When it returns safe from
the forest, I am filled with joy. With its budding teeth, it has
nibbled at these tufts of *kusha* grass, and they resemble the

[512] We have translated this as a proper name, but Mahanadi might
simply mean a great river.

shaven heads of *brahmana*s chanting from the *Sama Veda*."
When it was away for a long time, these were the sage's
thoughts. When the deer was next to him, his happy face was
full of joy. Since nothing else was in his mind, his meditation
was disturbed. This was despite the king having abandoned
his kingdom, objects of pleasure and relatives. The restless
deer went far and near and his mind also became restless. The
king lost his steadfastness. A long period of time passed. In the
course of time, the king died, gazing at the deer with tears in
his eyes, like a father towards a son. As he gave up his life, his
thoughts were on the deer.'

'O Maitreya! His mind was only on it, and he thought
of nothing else. Since his thoughts were like that, destiny
reduced him to such a state. He was born in the great forest
of Jambumarga, as a deer that remembered its past life. O
supreme among *brahmana*s! Since he remembered his past
life, he was not interested in *samsara*. He left his mother and
went to Salagrama again. He sustained himself on dry grass
and leaves. He sought to free himself from the *karma* that
had led to his becoming a deer. Therefore, when he gave up
his body, he was reborn as a *brahmana* who remembered his
past life. He was born in a pure and noble family of *yogis*
who followed good conduct. He possessed every kind of
knowledge and knew the truth about every sacred text. O
Maitreya! He perceived the *atman* as distinct from Prakriti.
O great sage! Since he possessed knowledge about the *atman*,
he perceived no difference between him and the gods and all
other beings. He did not read the sacred texts, as instructed
by his preceptor. He did not go through the sacred thread
ceremony. He saw nothing in the rituals. He did not accept
the sacred texts. Even when people spoke a lot to him, he said
little in reply and that too was incoherent. His speech did not
possess the quality of being polished. His words were like
those uttered by vulgar people. His body was unclean. He was

clad in faded garments. Saliva could be seen between his teeth. All the citizens abused him. For those who pursue *yoga*, regard shown by others causes great damage. A *yogi* obtains success in *yoga* when people dishonour him. In this way, a *yogi* must follow the virtuous path of *dharma*. He must not contest people who show his disrespect. Instead, he must avoid any association with them. The immensely intelligent one followed Hiranyagarbha's[513] words. He knew the nature of the *atman*, though people took him to be Jada.[514] He subsisted on gruel, shreds of plants, wild fruits and fragments of grain. He ate whatever little he got. When he was given, he ate a lot. He did not follow norms about what should be eaten when. When his father died, his brother, nephews and relatives made him work in the fields and nourished him with inferior food. His body was stout, but his acts were like those of an idiot. He bore burdens for everyone and was given food in return for carrying loads.'

'The king of Souvira's *kshatta*[515] saw that he had the appearance of a *brahmana* but had not been through any of the *samskaras*.[516] He thought he could be employed, like an animal. Mahakali got to know that the lord of *yoga* had been

---

[513] Brahma's.

[514] *Jada* means foolish and stupid, an idiot. Thus, he was known as Jada Bharata.

[515] Attendant/charioteer.

[516] There are thirteen *samskaras* or sacraments. The list varies a bit. But one list is *vivaha* (marriage), *garbhalambhana* (conception), *pumshavana* (engendering a male child), *simantonnayana* (parting the hair, performed in the 4th month of pregnancy), *jatakarma* (birth rites), *namakarana* (naming), *chudakarma* (tonsure), *annaprashana* (first solid food), *keshanta* (first shaving of the head), *upanayana* (sacred thread), *vidyarambha* (commencement of studies), *samavartana* (graduation) and *antyeshti* (funeral rites).

employed in this way.[517] When night arrived, as is ordained for
someone who is to be slaughtered, she seized her sharp sword.
In the middle of the night, she seized the *kshatta*, who was cruel
in his deeds. She sliced off the base of his throat and along with
her companions, drank the copious flow of blood. The great-
souled king of Souvira was about to leave. People who could
be employed without wages were being sought. The great-
souled one resembled a fire shrouded in ashes. With that kind
of appearance, he was taken to be one who could be employed
without wages. The king of Souvira's *kshatta* assumed that he
could be thus employed, without payment.'

'O *brahmana*! Astride his palanquin, the king made up his
mind to leave. He was going to go to the banks of Ikshumati,
where Kapila's excellent hermitage was located. What is best
in this *samsara*, where men generally face misery? He wished
to ask the great sage known as Kapila, who knew about the
dharma of *moksha*, the answer to this question. Urged by the
words of the *kshatta*, men had been rounded up to carry the
palanquin. Among all the others who had been rounded up to
bear the burden without payment of wages, was the *brahmana*
who possessed every kind of knowledge. He remembered his
past lives and bore the burden so as to destroy those sins. The
best among intelligent ones stumbled along like an animal,
without looking. The other bearers proceeded fast. The king
noticed that the palanquin was being carried in uneven fashion.
"What is this?" he asked. "Please keep pace with each other."
When the king said this many times, the other palanquin-
bearers responded, "This one is moving slowly." The king
said, "Are you tired? You have only carried the palanquin
for a short distance. Can't you take some exertion? I can see

[517] These sudden verses about Mahakali do not fit at all. Mahakali
killed the *kshatta* later, in the night. This incident happened after the
kshatta had employed Bharata.

that you are quite stout." The *brahmana* replied, "I am not
stout, nor am I carrying your palanquin. O lord of the earth! I
am not exhausted, nor am I incapable of exertion." The king
said, "I can see that you are stout and that you are bearing
this palanquin. For all those with bodies, the carrying of a
load causes exhaustion." The *brahmana* replied, "O lord of
the earth! Please tell me what you have seen of me. Strong or
weak are adjectives that can be used later. The assertions that
you are astride this palanquin and that it is being borne by
me are false. Listen to my words. The feet are placed on the
ground and the legs rest on the feet. The thighs are based on
the legs and provide a foundation for the stomach. The chest
finds support in the stomach and the arms and the shoulders
rest on the chest. The palanquin rests on my shoulders. How is
that a burden for me? There is a body that can be seen astride
the palanquin. The words 'you' and 'I' are used because of that
reason and not otherwise. O lord of the earth! 'You', 'I' and
everything else is made out of the elements. All this is because
the elements follow the flow of *guna*s. *Sattva* and the other
*guna*s follow *karma*. O lord of the earth! Because of ignorance,
all beings are subject to the accumulation of *karma*. The *atman*
is pure and without decay. It is serene and devoid of *guna*s. It
is beyond Prakriti. In all those with bodies, it is the only one
that does not increase or decrease. O king! It is not enhanced or
diminished. That being the case, how could you have said that
'I' am stout? The palanquin rests on the shoulders, which rest on
the stomach and other things, the waist, the thighs, the feet and
the ground. Therefore, the burden is borne equally by you and
me.[518] O lord of the earth! This is true of all other beings, not
just those who are astride palanquins. Mountains, trees, houses
and the earth have the same origin.[519] O king! When men seem

---

[518] In the sense that 'you' and 'I' are not physical bodies.
[519] They result from the elements.

to be different, that is because of Prakriti. O king! How does
the question of me exerting, or not exerting, myself arise? The
substance in the palanquin is made out of the elements. Even
though we have developed differently, you, I and everything
else are made out of the same elements." O *brahmana*! Having
said this, he continued to bear the palanquin, but was silent.'

'Quickly, the king descended and clasped his feet. The king
said, "O *brahmana*! Let go of this palanquin and show me
your favours. Please tell me. Who are you, present here in the
form of a degraded person? Why have you come here? You
must be the instrument for something. O learned one! Please
tell me everything. Please do me this service." The *brahmana*
replied, "Please listen. I am incapable of telling you who I am.
All arrivals at a place are for the sake of enjoyment. The body
is generated for the sake of enjoying pleasure and pain. A living
being desires to assume a body for the sake of enjoying the
fruits of *dharma* and *adharma*. O protector of the earth! For all
beings everywhere, *dharma* and *adharma* are the sole reasons.
Why are you then asking me about the reason?" The king said,
"There is no doubt that *dharma* and *adharma* are the cause
behind all action. The enjoyment of their fruits is the reason
for moving from one body to another body. But you have also
told me that you are incapable of telling me who you are. I
wish to hear the reason how this has come about. O *brahmana*!
How can a person declare that he does not know who he is?
O *brahmana*! There can be no sin in using the word 'I'." The
brahmana replied, "Indeed, there is nothing wrong in using the
word 'I' for one's own self. However, if one knows about the
nature of the *atman*, the use of that word for something that
is not the *atman* can give rise to confusion. O king! With the
help of the teeth, the lips and the palate, the tongue utters 'I'.
All of these are responsible for the articulation of speech. These
being the causes, it will be inaccurate that speech constitutes
one's own self. That is the reason words like 'stout' should

also not be used. A man possesses a separate lump of a body.
The head and the feet are its signs. O king! How can I possibly
use the word 'I' for this? O excellent king! If something exists
here, but not anywhere else, I can use the word 'I' for what
is here and 'that' for what is somewhere else. However, the
same *atman* exists equally in all bodies. That being the case,
words like 'I' and 'you' have no use. Who are you? You are
a king. This is a palanquin. These are bearers. These are the
attendants. However, it is not correct to say that any of these
companions belong to you. The palanquin that you ride is
made out of wood from a tree. O king! Will this palanquin be
called wood or a tree? People will not say that the great king is
seated astride a tree. Nor, when you are seated on a palanquin,
will they say that you are seated on wood. This is despite the
palanquin being constructed out of an aggregation of wood.
O best among kings! But you decide, what is the difference
between the palanquin and wood? In that way, differentiate
between the separate spokes in your umbrella. When does it
become an umbrella? Apply the same logic to you and me. A
man, a woman, a cow, a goat, a horse, an elephant, a bird, a
tree—people apply all these different names to bodies because
of their *karma*. O lord of the earth! A person is not a man,
a *deva*, an animal or a tree. *Karma* is responsible for these
differences in bodies and forms. In this world, the appellation
of king or servant of a king does not apply to the *atman*. This
is other than the king. All such appellations are the construct of
our imaginations alone. O king! With the passage of time, and
as a consequence of that, is there any object that is not subject
to a different appellation? You are the king of all the worlds.
You are the father of your son. You are the enemy of your
enemies. You are the husband of your wife. You are the father
of your sons. You are the lord of the earth. What will I address
you as? Are you this head? Are you the throat or the stomach?
Are you the feet or other things? O lord of the earth! Are you

these or something else? Is your existence distinct from all these limbs? O lord of the earth! Who am 'I'? Be accomplished and think about this. O king! That being the case and the truth, how can I separately determine and address myself as 'I'?"'

Chapter 2(14) (Bharata's Teachings)

Shri Parashara continued, 'The king heard these words, which were full of deep meaning. He humbly bowed down and spoke to the *brahmana*. The king said, "O illustrious one! The words that you have spoken are full of deep meaning. However, after hearing them, my mind is in a great whirl. O *brahmana*! This is based on the *vijnana* of discrimination. You have instructed me about Mahat, which is beyond Prakriti and exists in all beings. 'I am not bearing the palanquin. The palanquin does not rest on me. I am other than the body, which is holding up this palanquin. Goaded by *karma*, it is the flow of *guna*s that urges action in beings. Since this is the result of the flow of *guna*s, who am I?' This is what you have told me. O one who knows about the supreme truth! These words have entered through my ears. My mind wants to know about the supreme truth but is bewildered. O *brahmana*! Earlier, I was ready to go to the immensely fortunate *rishi*, Kapila, to ask him about what is best. But meanwhile, you have addressed me in these words. Please instruct me. In search of the supreme truth, my mind turns towards you. O *brahmana*! The illustrious Kapila *rishi* is Vishnu's portion, who has arrived to destroy delusion from the world. There is no doubt that the illustrious one has our welfare in mind. Therefore, he has manifested himself here, in the form of what you have said. O *brahmana*! I have prostrated myself before you. Please tell me what is most beneficial. You are like an ocean, with its waters

and waves consisting of all *vijnana*." The *brahmana* replied,
"O lord of the earth! You asked me about what is best. You
did not ask me about the supreme truth. O lord of the earth!
There are many things that can be called 'best' or 'the supreme
truth'. O king! Worshipping the gods, desiring wealth and
riches, wanting sons or a kingdom is also the 'best'. Rites and
sacrifices are also the 'best'. Their fruits are a sign of this.
But the 'best' among all these is one where the fruits are not
asked for. O lord of the earth! For those immersed in *yoga*,
meditating constantly on the *atman* is the 'best'. However,
among all these different kinds of 'best', the true 'best' is
union with the *paramatman*. There are many hundreds and
thousands of 'best'. But these do not represent the supreme
truth. Listen to me. Wealth cannot be the supreme objective
since it is given up for the sake of *dharma*. Why is one of its
characteristics that of it being expended in pursuit of *kama*? O
lord of men! Since the son gives birth to another, how can he
be a supreme objective? Is the supreme objective one's son, the
father? Or is the supreme objective the other one, the one born
from the son? In this way, the supreme objective cannot be
found in the mobile and immobile objects of this world. When
an object is described as the supreme objective, there are many
different causes behind it. If the acquisition of a kingdom is
described as a supreme objective, that supreme objective may
sometimes exist and sometimes be non-existent.[520] If you
are of the view that the sacrificial rites of the *Rig*, *Yajur* and
*Sama Veda*s represent the supreme objective, then listen to
my words. O king! Any act undertaken with earthly objects
assumes the trait of the cause. Since it follows the cause, it
also has the nature of clay.[521] In this way, objects like kindling,

---

[520] Since a kingdom is temporary.

[521] Implying that the fruits are not permanent. Like clay, they do
not last.

ghee, kusha grass and other things are perishable. Any rites undertaken with them will also lead to perishable results. The wise seek to obtain the supreme objective that is indestructible. There is no doubt that if the material used is perishable, the object attained will also be perishable. If you hold the view that performing tasks without desiring fruits is the supreme objective, you must understand that these are means to attain liberation. The means cannot be the supreme objective. O lord of the earth! Meditation on the atman is spoken of as the supreme objective. But this implies difference between this and that.[522] The supreme objective cannot create differences. Union between the jivatman and the paramatman is spoken of as the supreme objective. But this is also false. Two different objects cannot become one.[523] Therefore, there is no doubt that there are many things that are the 'best'. O lord of the earth! I will briefly tell you about the supreme truth. Listen. There is a single one who pervades everything equally. It is pure and devoid of gunas. It is beyond Prakriti. It is devoid of birth and old age. The undecaying atman is without a beginning and goes everywhere. The lord is full of supreme jnana and cannot be described through existence, names and jatis.[524] O lord of the earth! He cannot be united through yoga. But nor is it the case that he cannot be united. The supreme objective is the vijnana that what exists in one's own body also exists in the body of others. A person with insight understands the nature of this duality. The same air passes through the different holes of a flute and produces the different notes known as shadaja

[522] Interpreted as a difference between the body and the jivatman. But the jivatman and the paramatman is also possible.

[523] If the jivatman and the paramatman are the same, the talk of union between them is meaningless. If they are different, they can never become one.

[524] Jati is class, as in genus.

and the others.[525] Similarly, there is no differentiation in the
paramatman. Its nature is one, without any differences. The
perceived differences are the outcome of external action. When
differences, like *deva*s and others, are destroyed, the covering
ceases to exist."'

Chapter 2(15) (Ribhu and Nidagha)

Shri Parashara said, 'The lord of the earth was silent and
immersed in thought. The *brahmana* told him an account
about the nature of what is inside.'

'The *brahmana* said, "O tiger among kings! Listen to what
was chanted by Ribhu in ancient times. The great-souled one
wished to develop understanding in Nidagha. Parameshthi
Brahma had a son named Ribhu. O lord of the earth! Ever
since birth, he was virtuous and knew about the truth. In those
ancient times, his disciple was Nidagha, Pulastya's son. Full of
great affection, he bestowed all the different kinds of *vijnana*
on him. O lord of men! Ribhu had no doubt that once Nidagha
had obtained knowledge, he would no longer have any sense
of duality. On the banks of the Devika, there was a city known
by the name of Viranagara. It was prosperous and extremely
beautiful. Pulastya lived there, in a charming grove that was on
the outskirts. O supreme among kings! In those ancient times,
Ribhu had a disciple named Nidagha and he knew about *yoga*.
He resided in that city for one thousand divine years. After this,
Ribhu went to visit his disciple, Nidagha. A sacrifice to the
Vishvadevas was going on and as it was about to end, he stood

---

[525] The seven *svara*s (notes) are *shadaja, rishabha, gandhara,
madhyama, panchama, dhaivata* and *nishada*.

near the gate. He[526] noticed him standing there. He took some *arghya* and made him enter his house. When he had washed his hands and feet and had accepted a seat, the best among *brahmana*s lovingly asked him to eat. Ribhu said, 'O noble *brahmana*! What food, capable of being eaten, exists in your house? Please tell me. I have never been fond of inferior food.' Nidagha replied, '*Saktu*, food made out of barley, *vataka*s and *apupa*s exist in my house.[527] O best among *brahmana*s! As you wish, eat whatever pleases you.' Ribhu said, 'For brahmanas, this is inferior food. Give me sweet rice, *payasam* made out barley, mixed with *phanita*.'[528] Nidagha responded, 'O housewife! Use what is best in the house to prepare sweet food for him to enjoy.' His wife was thus instructed to prepare sweet food for the *brahmana*. Honouring her husband's words, she prepared it. O protector of the earth! She placed this sweet food before the great sage. While he ate, Nidagha stood humbly before him. When he had finished, Nidagha spoke. Nidagha said, 'O *brahmana*! Are you greatly satisfied with the food? Are you content? Did the food you ate bring you mental pleasure? O *brahmana*! Where do you live now? Where are you going? Why have you come here? O *brahmana*! You should tell me this.' Ribhu replied, 'O *brahmana*! When a hungry man has eaten food, he must be satisfied. Why are you asking me if my hunger has been satisfied? When something made out of earth is scorched by the fire,[529] hunger is flung out as a consequence. When the water has been exhausted, thirst is generated in men. O *brahmana*! Hunger and thirst belong to the body. I have

---

[526] Nidagha.

[527] *Saktu* is pounded ground meal, colloquially known as *sattu*, *vataka* is a small cake, *apupa* is a sweet cake.

[528] *Payasam* is a dish made out sweetened milk and rice, *phanita* means molasses.

[529] The body is scorched by the digestive fire.

no sense of ownership in them. When hunger results from a
deficiency, I must always act so as to satisfy it. O *brahmana*!
However, the welfare and satisfaction of the mind have to do
with the *dharma* of consciousness. A man is not concerned with
them.[530] Therefore, you should ask about the consciousness.
You asked me where live. You also asked me where I am going.
Your third question was where I have come from. Listen to my
words. The *atman* goes everywhere. It pervades everything. It
is like space. Whence have I come? Where am I? Where will I
go? Do such questions make sense? I do not go. I do not come.
There is not a single place where I reside. You are not different
from someone else. Nor is someone else different from you.
Nor are they different from me. No doubt you have a question
about sweet food versus food that is not sweet. If you ask
me, what will I say? O supreme among *brahmanas*! Listen.
When one is eating, what is sweet and what is not sweet? If
sweet food causes anxiety, it is no longer sweet. Food that is
not sweet becomes sweet when sweetness causes anxiety to
a person. What food is pleasing at the beginning, the middle
and the end?[531] A house made of earth becomes stable when
more mud is plastered on it. In this way, the body is made out
of earth and the earth is made out of atoms.[532] Barley, wheat,
mudga,[533] *ghee*, oil, milk, curd, molasses, fruit and other things
are made out of atoms of the earth. In thinking about food
that is sweet and food that is not sweet, this is what you must
understand. Your task is to have this parity in your mind. This
equilibrium is the path to emancipation.' O king! Having heard

[530] Hunger and thirst.

[531] At the beginning of a meal, food may seem to be sweet. When
one has eaten some of it, it seems less sweet. When one has eaten too
much, it no longer seems sweet.

[532] We have translated *paramanu* as atom.

[533] *Moong dal.*

these words about the supreme truth, Nidagha prostrated himself before the immensely fortunate one and addressed him in these words. 'O *brahmana*! For the sake of my welfare, please show me your favours. Please tell me the truth about who has come here.[534] Hearing your words, all my delusion has been destroyed.' Ribhu replied, 'O *brahmana*! I am Ribhu, your preceptor. I have come here to impart wisdom to you. Now that I have told you about the supreme truth, I shall leave. Know that in this entire world, there are no differences. All this is one and the *paramatman*'s nature is known by the name of Vasudeva.' Thus addressed, Nidagha prostrated himself before him. Ribhu was worshipped with great devotion and left as he willed."'

Chapter 2(16) (Ribhu and Nidagha Concluded)

'The *brahmana* continued, "O lord of men! After one thousand years had passed, Ribhu again went to that city, to impart knowledge to Nidagha. The sage saw a king entering the city, surrounded by a large army. He also saw the immensely fortunate Nidagha standing outside the city, some distance away, so as to avoid contact with the people. His throat was parched, and he was hungry. He had collected kindling and *kusha* grass from the forest. On seeing him, Ribhu approached and greeted him.[535] He asked, 'O *brahmana*! Why are you standing here, alone?' Nidagha replied, 'O *brahmana*! Since the king is entering the beautiful

---

[534] There was no reason for Nidagha not to recognize Ribhu. Therefore, Ribhu must have appeared in the disguise of an ordinary *brahmana*.

[535] In disguise again.

city, there is a great assembly of people. Therefore, I am
standing here.' Ribhu asked, 'Tell me, who is the king? Who
are the other people? O best among *brahmana*s! It is my view
that you are accomplished in this matter.' Nidagha replied,
'There is one who is astride that crazy and mighty elephant,
as large as the summit of a mountain. He is the king. The
others are his attendants.' Ribhu said, 'You have shown me
the king and the elephant together. You have not described
any specific signs whereby I can distinguish between them. O
immensely fortunate one! Therefore, tell me what is specific
to each of them. I wish to know which one is the elephant
and who is the king.' Nidagha replied, 'O *brahmana*! The
elephant is the one who is below, and the king is the one who
is above. O *brahmana*! Who does not know the difference
between the mount and the one who is borne?' Ribhu replied,
'O *brahmana*! I know that, but please explain it to me. What
does the word below mean and what is above?' As soon as he
said this, Nidagha suddenly leapt up onto Ribhu's shoulders
and said, 'Hear the answer to the question you have asked me.
I am above, like the king. You are below, like the elephant.
O *brahmana*! To make you understand, I have demonstrated
with the use of this example.' Ribhu replied, 'O best among
*brahmana*s! You are like the king, and I am like the elephant.
But please tell me, which one is you and which one is me?'
Thus addressed, Nidagha swiftly clasped his feet and said, 'O
illustrious one! You are certainly my preceptor, Ribhu. There
is no one else with as clean and as polished a mind as my
acharya. Hence, I think that I have obtained my *guru*.' Ribhu
replied, 'I am indeed your *guru*, named Ribhu. Earlier, you
served me. O Nidagha! Out of affection towards you, I have
come here, so as to instruct you. O immensely intelligent one!
Therefore, I have instructed you briefly. The essence of the
supreme truth is that there is no duality in anything.' Having

said this, Ribhu, Nidagha's learned *guru*, went away. He[536] saw
his own *atman* inside all beings, without any differentiation.
The *brahmana* thus merged into the supreme *brahman* and
obtained supreme emancipation. O one who knows about
dharma! You must also treat friends and enemies equally. O
lord of the earth! You should know that your own atman is in
all beings that have been created on earth. Differences of white
and blue can be seen in the sky. It is one. But faulty vision
makes the undifferentiated one appear as one with differences.
Everything that exists is one and there is nothing other than
Achyuta. I am he. You are he. Everything is a form of his
atman. Hence, cast aside this delusion about differentiation.'"

Shri Parashara concluded, 'Thus, the king obtained insight
about the supreme truth and cast aside all differentiation. Since
he[537] remembered his earlier lives, he obtained understanding
and was freed from any future births. This is the substance of
the conversation between Bharata and the Indra among men.
If a person listens to this devotedly, his intelligence becomes
sparkling. There is no delusion in him, and he deserves to be
liberated from *samsara*.'

This ends Part II.

[536] Nidagha.
[537] Bharata.

Part III

Chapter 3(1) (Manus and *Manvantaras*)

Maitreya said, 'The *guru* has spoken about the earth, the positions of the oceans and the mountains and the positions of Surya and other stellar bodies in great detail. The creation of *devas* and *rishis* has also been described. So has the origin of the four *varnas* and inferior species. You have described the conduct of Dhruva and Prahlada in detail. I desire to hear, in due order, about all the *manvantaras*, about the lords of the *manvantaras* and about Shakra, foremost among *devas*. O *guru*! I desire to hear about this. Please tell me.'

197

Shri Parashara replied, 'There are *manvantara*s of the past and those of the future. In due order, I will tell you about them properly. Svayambhuva Manu was the first. Svarochisha came after him. Uttama, Tamasa, Raivata and Chakshusha followed. These were the six Manus of the past. The current one is Vaivasvata, Ravi's son. This seventh one is going on now. I have already told you about Svayambhuva, at the beginning of the *kalpa*. I have also accurately described to you the *deva*s and *saptarshi*s of that period. I will next properly tell you about Svarochisha Manu who followed, about the lords of the *manvantara*, *deva*s, *rishi*s and their sons. During Svarochisha *manvantara*, *deva*s were Paravatas and Tushitas. O Maitreya! The immensely strong Vipashchit was Indra of the gods. The *saptarshi*s were Urjja, Stambha, Prana, Vata, Prishabha, Niraya and Pariva. Chaitra, Kimpurusha and others were the sons of Svarochisha. After this second one, hear about Uttama *manvantara*. O *brahmana*! In this third *manvantara*, the Manu was Uttama. O Maitreya! The Indra of the gods was named Sushanti. *Deva*s were[538] Sudhamans, Satyas, Japas, Pratardanas and Vashavartis. Within each of these five categories, there are said to have been twelve.[539] Vasishtha's sons were the seven *saptarshi*s. Uttama Manu's sons were Aja, Parashu, Dipta and others. In Tamasa *manvantara*, *deva*s were Suparas, Haris, Satyas[540] and Sudhis. There were twenty-seven within each of these categories. Shibi was the Indra, and his trait was that he performed one hundred sacrifices. Hear about the names of the ones who were *saptarshi*s. They were Jyotirdhama, Prithu, Katya, Chaitra, Agni, Dhanaka and Pivara. These were the seven *rishi*s in that *manvantara*. The sons of Tamasa were

---

[538] The text says sons of Indra. This is clearly a mistake.
[539] Twelve divinities.
[540] A different set of Satyas.

Nara, Khyati, Keturupa, Janujangha and others. They were
extremely strong kings. O Maitreya! The fifth *manvantara*
was known after the name of Raivata Manu. Vibhu was
Indra then. Hear about the names of *deva*s during that
manvantara. They were Amitabhas, Bhutarayas, Vaikunthas
and Suptamedhasas. There were fourteen categories of *deva*s
and there were fourteen divinities within each category. O
brahmana! During that *manvantara*, the *saptarshi*s were
Hiranyaroma, Vedashri, Urdhvabahu, Vedabahu, Sudhama,
Parjanya and Mahamuni. O supreme among sages! The
sons[541] were Balabandhu, Sambhavya, Satyaka and others.
They were immensely valiant kings. Svarochisha, Uttama,
Tamasa and Raivata—these four Manus are said to have
been descended from Priyavrata. The royal sage, Priyavrata,
performed austerities and worshipped Vishnu. He thereby
obtained the boon that these lords of *manvantara*s would
be born from his lineage. During the sixth *manvantara*, the
Manu was known as Chakshusha. Manojava was Indra.
Now hear from me about *deva*s. The residents of heaven
were Apyas, Prasutas, Bhavyas, Prithugas and the immensely
generous Lakhas. There were eight divinities within each
of these five categories. The seven *rishi*s were Sumedha,
Viraja, Havishmat, Uttama, Madhu, Atinama and Sahishnu.
Chakshusha Manu's prominent sons were Uru, Puru and
Shatadyumna. They were extremely strong and were lords of
the earth. O *brahmana*! Vivasvat's[542] son was the immensely
radiant Shraddhadeva. The intelligent one is the Manu during
the current seventh *manvantara*.[543] O great sage! *Deva*s
now are Adityas, Vasus, Rudras and others. O Maitreya!
Purandara is the lord of the gods. The seven *saptarshi*s

---

[541] Of Raivata.

[542] Surya's.

[543] Hence, is it known as Vaivasvata *manvantara*.

are Vasishtha, Kashyapa, Atri, Jamadagni, Goutama,
Vishvamitra and Bharadvaja. Vaivasvata Manu had nine sons
who were extremely devoted to *dharma*: Ikshvaku, Nriga,
Dhrishta, Sharyati, the famous Narishyanta, Nabhagorishta,
Karusha, Prishadhra and Sumahat, famous in the worlds.
Vishnu's unmatched potency, established in *sattva*, was there
in the form of a divinity, during all the *manvantara*s. In the
first Svayambhuva *manvantara*, that divinity, born from his
portion, was Yajna. He was the son of Akuti, born through
mental powers. When Svarochisha *manvantara* arrived,
that divinity was born again, along with the Tushitas. He
was Ajita, the son of Tushitaa. In Uttama *manvantara*, that
divinity, who was Tushita earlier, was born again, along with
the excellent gods known as Satyas. His name was Satya, and
he was the son of Satyaa. When Tamasa *manvantara* arrived,
he was born again, along with the Haris. He was Hari and
he was the son of Haree. In Raivata *manvantara*, the divinity
who was Hari earlier, was born, along with the Raivatas.
His name was Sambhuta, and he was born from Sambhuti,
through mental powers. In Chakshusha *manvantara*, the
divinity was born, along with the gods known as Vaikunthas.
Purushottama's name was Vaikuntha, and he was the son of
Vikuntha. O *brahmana*! Vaivasvata *manvantara* has arrived
now. Vishnu has been born as Vamana, the son of Kashyapa
and Aditi. In three strides, the great-souled one won over all
the worlds and bestowed the three worlds, bereft of thorns,
on Purandara. O *brahmana*! These were the seven forms
through which subjects were protected, and prospered, during
the seven *manvantara*s. This entire universe is permeated by
the great-souled one's potency. Because of the verbal root
"*vish*", meaning "to enter", he is spoken of as Vishnu. All
*deva*s, Manus, all *saptarshi*s, Manu's sons, Indra and all the
residents of heaven are portions of Vishnu's infinite potency.'

Chapter 3(2) (Future *Manvantaras*)

Maitreya said, 'You have spoken to me about seven *manvantaras*. O *brahmana rishi*! You should tell me about the future ones.'

Shri Parashara replied, 'Surya's wife was Samjna. She was Vishvakarma's daughter. O sage! She had three children: Manu,[544] Yama and Yami. She was unable to tolerate her husband's energy. To serve her husband, she engaged Chhaya.[545] She herself retired to the forest, so as to perform austerities. Taking Chhaya to be Samjna, Arka[546] had three children through her: Shanaishchara,[547] Manu[548] and Tapati. When she was angry with Yama, Samjna's son, Chhaya cursed him. It thus became clear to Surya and Yama that Yama was the son of another. She also told Vivasvat that Samjna was in the forest. Through his insight of meditation, he saw that she was engaged in austerities, in the form of a mare. Assuming the form of a horse, through her, he had the two gods, the Ashvins, as sons. Revanta was also born through Bhaskara's[549] flow of semen. The illustrious Ravi brought Samjna back to his own abode. Vishvakarma arranged for his energy to be reduced. He placed Surya on his wheel and pared off some of his energy. In this way, he reduced the undecaying energy to one eighth of what it used to be. O supreme among sages! Vishvakarma pared off Vaishnava

---

[544] Vaivasvata Manu.

[545] *Chhaya* means shadow. Samjna constructed Chhaya in her own image.

[546] Surya.

[547] Saturn.

[548] Savarni Manu.

[549] Surya's. Ravi is also one of Surya's names.

energy.[550] Blazing, it fell down on the ground. Using all this energy, Tvashta Vishvakarma constructed Vishnu's *chakra*, Sharva's trident, Dhanada's palanquin, Guha's spear and all the other weapons of the gods.[551] Chhaya had a son who is spoken of as the second Manu. Since he possessed the same complexion as his elder brother, he was known as Savarni.[552] His *manvantara*, the eighth, is spoken of as Savarni *manvantara*. O immensely fortunate one! Listen. I will tell you what will happen then. O Maitreya! When Savarni is the Manu, the gods will be Sutapas, Amitabhas and Mukhyas. Within each of these categories, there are said to be twenty-seven *deva*s. O excellent sage! I will tell you about the future *saptarshi*s: Diptimat, Galava, Rama, Kripa, Droni, my son, Vyasa and Rishyashringa as the seventh. Through Vishnu's favours, the unblemished Bali, Virochana's son, has gone to Patala. He will be the Indra then. The sons of Savarni Manu will be Viraja, Arvarivat, Nirmoka and others and they will be the lords of men. O sage! The ninth Manu will be Daksha-Savarni. There will be three categories of *deva*s: Paras, Marichigarbhas and Sudharmas. Each of these categories will have twelve divinities. O *brahmana*! The immensely valiant Adbhuta will be their Indra. The great *rishi*s will be Savana, Dyutimat, Bhavya, Vasu, Medhatithi, Jyotishmat and Satya as the seventh. Daksha-Savarni's sons will be Dhritaketu, Diptiketu, Panchahasta, Niramaya, Prithushrava and others. O sage! The tenth Manu will be Brahma-Savarni. The gods will be Sudhamas, Vishuddhas and Shatasamkhyas. Their Indra will be the immensely strong Shanti. Hear about the

[550] The energy in the sun was Vishnu's.
[551] Sharva is Shiva, Dhanada is Kubera and Guha is Kumara/Kartikeya.
[552] The elder brother is Vaivasvata Manu. *Savarna* means with the same complexion.

ones who will be saptarshis: Havishmat, Sukrita, Satya, Tapomurti, Nabhaga, Apratimouja and Satyaketu. Brahma-Savarni's ten sons will be Sukshetra, Uttamouja, Bhurishena and others. They will protect the earth. The eleventh Manu will be Dharma-Savarni. The chief *deva*s will be Vihangamas, Kamagamas, Nirvanas and Rishis. There will be thirty divinities within each of these categories. The Indra will be Prisha. The *saptarshi*s will be Nihsvara, Agniteja, Vapushmat, Ghrini, Aruni, Havishmat and Anagha. Manu's sons, lords of the earth, will be Sarvatraga, Sudharma, Devanika and others. The twelfth Manu will be Rudra-Savarni, Rudra's son. Ritudhama will be the Indra then. Hear about the ones who will be gods: Haritas, Rohitas, Sumanasas, Sukarmas and Surapas. O *brahmana*! These will be *deva*s and within each category, there will be ten divinities. The seven *saptarshi*s will be Tapasvi, Sutapa, Tapomurti, Taporati, Tapodhriti, Dyuti and Tapodhana as the seventh. Hear about Manu's sons. They will be Devavat, Upadeva, Devashreshtha and others. They will be immensely valiant and will be great kings. O sage! The thirteenth Manu's name will be Ruchi. The immortals will be Sutramans, Sukarmans and Sudharmans. Within each category of *deva*s, there will be thirty-three divinities. The immensely valiant Divaspati will be their Indra. The *saptarshi*s will be Nirmoha, Tattvadarshi, Nishprakampa, Nirutsuka, Dhritimat, Avyaya and Sutapa as the seventh. Hear from me about his sons. They will be Chitrasena, Vichitra and others. They will be lords of the earth. O Maitreya! The fourteenth Manu will be Bhouma. Shuchi will be the Indra. Listen. There will be five categories of gods: Chakshushas, Pavitras, Kanishthas, Bhrajikas and Vachavriddhas. These will be *deva*s. Hear from me about the *saptarshi*s. They will be Agnibahu, Shuchi, Shukra, Magadha, Agnidhra, Yukta and Jita. Hear about Manu's sons. They will be Uru, Gambhira, Buddya and others. These sons of Manu will be kings. O tiger among sages! I have told you about the ones who will rule over the earth.'

'At the end of the four *yuga*s, the *Veda*s are submerged. To make them circulate again, the *saptarshi*s descend from heaven to earth. O *brahmana*! In every *krita yuga*, Manu creates the *smriti* texts. As long as the *manvantara* lasts, *deva*s enjoy their shares of sacrifices. In every *manvantara*, Manu has sons. They are their descendants who protect the earth. In every *manvantara*, Manu, the *saptarshi*s, *deva*s, Manu's sons who are lords of the earth and Shakra possess their rights. O brahmana! When fourteen *manvantara*s have elapsed, one thousand *mahayuga*s pass and the *kalpa* is said to be over. O excellent one! The night that follows[553] is of the same duration. The illustrious one is the lord who has created everything. He is the one who assumes Brahma's form. During the flood, he sleeps on Shesha, having devoured all the three worlds. O *brahmana*! In his own *maya*, Janardana is established in all beings. When he awakes, the illustrious one creates everything, just as it used to be earlier. His *atman* is without decay. From one *kalpa* to another *kalpa*, he resorts to the *guna* of *rajas*. O supreme among *brahmana*s! For the preservation of the world, his portion of *sattva* exists in the Manus, the kings, the Indras, *deva*s and the *saptarshi*s. In the four *yuga*s, Vishnu's attribute is that of preservation. O Maitreya! Hear about the way he arranges for conduct during the *yuga*s. In *krita yuga*, his own form exists in Kapila and the others. He is engaged in the welfare of all beings, and he is in the *atman*s of all beings. In this form, he bestows supreme *jnana*. In *treta yuga*, the *chakravarti* is the lord's own form. In this form, to protect the three worlds, he punishes the wicked. In *dvapara yuga*, the lord divides the single *Veda* into four *Veda*s and hundreds of branches, with innumerable divisions. Vedavyasa is his own

---

[553] Brahma's night.

form. When *kali yuga* is over, it is Hari's own form as Kalki. Thus, the lord establishes the wicked along the true path. In this way, the eternal one creates, preserves and destroys all the worlds. He is the one who enters all *atman*s and there is nothing superior to him. The great-souled one is the past, the present and the future of all beings. O *brahmana*! I have told you about his true nature. He is here and everywhere else. I have told you about all the *manvantara*s and about the lords of the *manvantara*s. What else will I tell you?'

Chapter 3(3) (Vedavyasa)

Maitreya said, 'I have learnt from you about the truth behind the entire universe. It is Vishnu. It originates from Vishnu. It dissolves into Vishnu. There is nothing else to be known. After this, I wish to hear about the great-souled ones who, assuming the form of Vedavyasa, classified the *Veda*s from one *yuga* to another *yuga*. O great sage! In different *yuga*s, who were the Vyasas? O illustrious one! Please tell me about that and the divisions and branches.'

Shri Parashara replied, 'O Maitreya! The *Veda*s are a tree that has thousands of divisions and branches. I am incapable of describing it in detail. Hear about it briefly. O great sage! For the welfare of the universe, in every *dvapara yuga*, it is Vishnu who assumes the form of Vyasa to divide the single *Veda* into many. He notices that human valour, energy and strength are limited. For the welfare of all beings, he therefore divides the *Veda*s. The lord who classifies the *Veda*s into different divisions is known as Vedavyasa.[554] However, he is the embodied form

---

[554] Literally, one who separates/distributes the *Veda*s.

of Madhu's enemy.[555] Hear from me about who has been Vyasa
in this *manvantara*. O sage! Within Vaivasvata *manvantara*, in
every *dvapara yuga*, twenty-eight *maharshi*s, the Vyasas, have
divided and classified the *Veda*s.[556] In the first *dvapara*, the
classification was done by Svayambhu[557] himself. In the second
dvapara, Prajapati[558] was Vedavyasa. In the third, it was
Ushanas and in the fourth, it was Brihaspati. In the fifth, Savita
was Vyasa. In the sixth, it was the lord Mrityu. In the seventh,
it was Indra. In the eighth, it is said to have been Vasishtha. In
the ninth, it was Sarasvata. In the tenth, it is said to have been
Tridhama. In the eleventh, it was Tirshikha and in the twelfth,
it was Bharadvaja. In the thirteenth, it was Antariksha and in
the fourteenth, it was Varni. In the fifteenth, it was Trayyaruna
and in the sixteenth, it was Dhananjaya. In the seventeenth,
it was Ritunjaya and in the eighteenth, it is said to have been
Jaya. After this (the nineteenth), the Vyasa was Bharadvaja.
After Bharadvaja (in the twentieth), it was Goutama. After
Goutama (the twenty-first), the Vyasa was Uttara, also known
as Haryyatma. After Haryyatma (the twenty-second), it was
the sage Vajashrava. After that (the twenty-third), it was
Somashushkayana, also known as Trinabindu. After that (the
twenty-fourth), it was Riksha of the Bhargava lineage, also
known as Valmiki. O sage! After that (the twenty-fifth), my
father Shakti was Vyasa. After that (the twenty-sixth), it was I.
After me (the twenty-seventh), it was Jatukarna. After that (the
twenty-eighth), it was Krishna Dvaipayana. These were the
twenty-eight Vedavyasas of the past. In every *dvapara yuga*,
they divided the single *Veda* into four. O sage! In the next

---

[555] That is, Vishnu.
[556] Since twenty-eight *mahayuga*s of Vaivasvata *manvantara* have
elapsed.
[557] Brahma.
[558] That is, Manu.

dvapara yuga, when my son, Krishna Dvaipayana will cease to be Vedavyasa, Drouni will be Vedavyasa.'

'The eternal *brahman* is established in the *akshara* of Oum. The word *brahman* is used because its utterance signifies an increase.[559] Pranava[560] is always present when *bhur, bhuvah* and *svah* is uttered.[561] I bow down to the *brahman*. The *Rig, Yajur, Sama* and *Atharva Veda*s are inside it. It is known as the cause behind the creation and destruction of the universe. I bow down to the *brahman*. It is the extremely mysterious Mahat. It is fathomless. It cannot be crossed. It is without decay. It is the reservoir that is responsible for the delusion of the universe. To accomplish the *purushartha*s,[562] it manifests its own self in the form of *pravritti*. It is the destination for devoted ones who know about *samkhya*, serene in their *atman*s. It is immortal and not manifest. Such is the nature of the eternal *brahman*. Pradhana originates from within it. Its sound can be heard inside the heart. It cannot be divided. It is the origin and is without decay. It manifests itself in many ways. I always prostrate myself before that supreme *brahman*. I bow down. Its form is Vasudeva. The *paramatman* is his own form. Though the *brahman* cannot be divided, the lord divided it into three parts.[563] He cannot be divided. But those who are differentiated in their intelligence see him divided in all kinds of ways. He is in the *atman* of everything. The *Rig*, the *Sama* and the *Yajur* are

---

[559] There is a double meaning. The root word *brimh* means both roar and increase.

[560] Omkara.

[561] The first line of the *gayatri* (*savitri*) *mantra* is 'oum bhur bhuvah svah'.

[562] The objectives of human existence, *dharma, artha* and *kama*. *Moksha* is sometimes added to those three.

[563] Interpreted in various ways: the three *Veda*s, the three words in *gayatri mantra*, the three letters in Oum, Brahma, Vishnu and Shiva.

in him. The *Rig*, *Sama* and *Yajur* are in his *atman*. His *atman* is in all bodies. The *Veda*s are in him, and he himself acts so as to divide them into many different branches. He is the creator of those branches. The knowledge of all those different branches is his own form. The illustrious one is without attachment.'

Chapter 3(4) (The Work of Krishna Dvaipayana)

Shri Parashara said, 'In the beginning, the *Veda*s had four parts and numbered one hundred thousand.[564] From these, the ten kinds of sacrifices that satisfy all the objects of desire resulted.[565] In this *manvantara*, my son was the twenty-eighth Vyasa. The lord divided the single *Veda*, with four parts, into four divisions. Just as the intelligent Vedavyasa divided them, the *Veda*s had been divided by all the earlier Vedavyasas, including me. O supreme among *brahmana*s! Since then, the *Veda*s have had these different branches. They have been studied and nurtured in the four *yuga*s. Know Krishna Dvaipayana Vyasa to be the Lord Narayana. O Maitreya! On earth, who else could have composed the Mahabharata? O Maitreya! Hear accurately about the division my great-souled son did of the *Veda*s in this *dvapara yuga*. When he was urged by Brahma, Vyasa started to classify the *Veda*s. He accepted four, who were accomplished in the *Veda*s, as disciples. For studying the *Rig Veda*, the great sage accepted Paila. For the *Yajur Veda*, he

---

[564] *Shloka*s.
[565] The number of *yajna*s is not uniformly given as ten in various texts. A possible list of ten could be *bhuta-yajna*, *manushya-yajna*, *pitri-yajna*, *deva-yajna*, *brahma-yajna*, *darsha-yajna*, *pournamasa-yajna*, *agnihotra-yajna*, *soma-yajna* and *pashu-yajna*.

accepted the one named Vaishampayana. Jaimini was chosen
for the *Sama Veda*. The intelligent Vedavyasa accepted Sumantu
as the disciple and made him knowledgeable about the *Atharva
Veda*. The great sage accepted the immensely intelligent *suta*
named Romaharshana, as a disciple for the purpose of Itihasa
and Puranas. The *Yajur Veda* was one, but he divided it into
four parts. For the purpose of undertaking a sacrifice, the sage
arranged for four kinds of priests: the *adhvaryu* chanted hymns
from the *Yajur Veda*, the *hotri* chanted hymns from the *Rig
Veda*, the *udgatri* chanted hymns from the *Sama Veda* and the
brahmana chanted hymns from the *Atharva Veda*. Collecting
hymns known as Richas, the sage compiled the *Rig Veda*.
Collecting hymns known as Yajusas, he compiled the *Yajur
Veda* and collecting hymns known as Samans, he compiled
the *Sama Veda*. Through the *Atharva Veda*, the lord arranged
for all the rites for kings. O Maitreya! He also arranged for
where the *brahmana* should be placed. The *Veda*s were like
a single tree, but he divided them into four stems. Branches
resulted and the tree have a large grove. O *brahmana*! First,
Paila divided the tree known as the *Rig Veda*. He gave two
*samhita*s[566] to Indrapramiti and Bashkala. Bashkala divided his
samhita into four parts. The great sage bestowed these on his
disciples, Bodhya and others. O sage! Bodhya, Agnimadaka,
Yajnavalkya and Parashara accepted these branches, which
originated from the main stem. O Maitreya! Indrapramiti gave
his *samhita* to his great-souled son, Mandukeya, and made
him study it. In this way, it spread from disciple to sub-disciple
and from son to disciple. Vedamitra, or Shakalya, studied the
same *samhita*.[567] The immensely intelligent one divided this
into five *samhita*s and gave it to his disciples. O Maitreya!
Hear from me about the names of the five disciples. They were

[566] A *samhita* is a collection of *mantras*.
[567] Shakalya followed in the line of disciples from Mandukeya.

Mudgala, Gomukha, Vatsya, Shaliya and Sharira as the fifth.
O supreme among sages! Shakapurna devised three *samhita*s
and also added *nirukta* as a fourth. The great sage bestowed
the three *samhita*s on Krouncha, Vaitalika and Balaka. He
added *nirukta*, a *vedanga*, as the fourth to make a person
accomplished in the *Veda*s. O supreme among *brahmana*s!
In this way, secondary branches originated from primary
branches. O *brahmana*! Another Bashkala[568] devised three
*samhita*s and taught these to his disciples, Kalayani, Gargya
and Kathajapa as the third. I have thus told you about the main
*samhita*s that were circulated.'

Chapter 3(5) (Yajnavalkya's Story)

Shri Parashara said, 'The *Yajur Veda* has twenty-seven
branches. The great sage, named Vaishampayana, Vyasa's
disciple, gave this to his disciples and they accepted it, in the
due order. O *brahmana*! Among these, Yajnavalkya was the
son of Brahmarata. This disciple was extremely knowledgeable
about *dharma* and was always devoted to his preceptor. It had
earlier been decided that if a *rishi* did not go to an assembly held
on the great Meru, within a period of seven nights, he would
suffer from the sin of killing a *brahmana*. O *brahmana*! This
was the agreement a large number of sages had made earlier.
At that time, Vaishampayana was the only one who violated
this agreement. When he struck his sister's son with his foot,
the child died. He spoke to his disciples. "O disciples! To dispel
the sin of killing a *brahmana*, I must observe a vow. For my
sake, all of you must follow that vow. There is no need to think
about this." Yajnavalkya replied, "O illustrious one! How can I

---

[568] Not the one mentioned earlier.

follow a vow with these *brahmanas*? With a great deal of effort, they have accumulated limited amounts of energy." Enraged, the *guru* spoke to the great sage, Yajnavalkya. "O one who shows disrespect to *brahmanas*! Give up everything that you have learnt from me. You have said that the other bulls among *brahmanas* are devoid of energy. There is no point in having a disciple who does not follow my instructions." Yajnavalkya replied, "O *brahmana*! I spoke to you with devotion. But enough of what I have studied from you." Saying this, he vomited out the Yajusas, which were smeared with blood. The sage voluntarily returned to him that which he had learnt. O *brahmana*! Yajnavalkya gave up those Yajusas. Assuming the form of *tittiras*,[569] the other disciples swallowed this up and the text known as *taittiriya* resulted. They had been asked by their *guru* to follow the vow of dispelling the sin of killing a *brahmana*. O supreme among sages! Since they did this, they were known as Charanas.'[570]

'O Maitreya! Yajnavalkya devoted himself to *pranayama*. Desiring to get the Yajuas back, he controlled himself and praised Surya. Yajnavalkya said, "O infinitely energetic one! O Savita! O gate to emancipation! I prostrate myself before you. You are the reservoir of the three, the *Rig*, the *Yajur* and the *Sama*. I bow down to you. I bow down to the one whose form is Agni and Soma. Your *atman* is the cause behind the universe. O Bhaskara! O one with supreme energy! You are radiant with your *sushumna* rays. *Kala*, *kashtha*, *nimesha* and other measurements of time are your own *atman*. In the form of Vishnu, you are the one who should be meditated upon. The supreme *akshara*[571] is your form. Through your own rays, you make the large number of gods and the moon radiant. You are

---

[569] A *tittira* is a partridge.
[570] Literally, those who undertook/followed.
[571] Oum.

the one who satisfies the ancestors with *svadha* and *amrita*.
I prostrate myself before Tapana.[572] You are the creator of
the heat. You are the lord who nourishes with the cool drops
of rain. You are the three forms of time.[573] I prostrate myself
before Surya, the creator. O lord of the universe! You are the
one who dispels darkness from the universe. O divinity, who
holds everything up! O Vivasvat! I prostrate myself before
you. Until you rise, people cannot undertake virtuous rites
and the water cannot purify. O radiant divinity! I bow down
before you. When your rays touch the world, all the rituals
can be undertaken. Your *atman* is the reason for purification.
We bow down to the one whose *atman* is pure. We prostrate
ourselves before Savita, Surya, Bhaskara and Vivasvat. I bow
down to Aditya, who was the first to be born among *deva*s. I
prostrate myself. You are on a golden chariot and your flag
and horses are full of *amrita*. You are borne along, like the
eye of the worlds. I prostrate myself before you." In this way,
when he mentally praised, Ravi appeared before him in the
form of a horse and said, "Please ask what you desire." At this,
Yajnavalkya prostrated himself and told Divakara, "Please
give me Yajusas that my *guru* does not possess." Addressed
in this way, the illustrious Ravi gave him those Yajusas. These
were known as *ayatayama*[574] and his *guru* did not know them.
O supreme among *brahman*as! Since Surya bestowed them in
the form of a horse, *brahmana*s who study these Yajusas are
known as Vajins.[575] The Vajins, Kanva and other extremely
fortunate ones, studied fifteen branches of these texts, recited
by Yajnavalkya.'

[572] The one who heats/scorches, Surya's name.

[573] The past, the present and the future.

[574] Meaning, they were fresh.

[575] *Vajin* means horse. This is known as the *Vajasaneyi samhita*,
or *Shukla Yajur Veda*.

Chapter 3(6) (Details of Texts)

Shri Parashara said, 'O Maitreya! In due order, Jaimini, Vyasa's disciple, divided the branches of the *Sama Veda*. Hear about it from me. Jaimini's son was Sumantu and Sumantu's son was Sutva. Each of these immensely intelligent ones studied a single *samhita*. His son, Sukarma,[576] divided it into one thousand *samhita*s. O supreme among *brahmana*s! His two disciples, great in their vows, Hiranyanabha from Kosala and Poushpinji, accepted these. He[577] had five hundred disciples and they are known as those from the northern regions who chant the *Sama* hymns. There were excellent *brahmana*s who received the *samhita* from Hiranyanabha. The learned refer to them as those from the eastern region who chant the *Sama* hymns. Lokakshi, Oudhami, Kakshivat and Langali were Poushpinji's disciples. They divided the *samhita* into many parts. Hiranyanabha's disciple, the great sage known as Krita, taught twenty-four *samhita*s to his disciples. They also divided the *Sama Veda* into many branches.'

'I will now tell you about the collection known as the *Atharva Veda samhita*. The immensely radiant sage, Sumantu, taught the *Atharva Veda* to his disciple Kanbandha, who divided it into two parts. Having done this, he bestowed them on Devadarsha and Pathya. O supreme among *brahmana*s! Devadarsha's disciples were Medha, Brahmabali, Shoulkayani, Pippalada and others. O *brahmana*! Pathya had three disciples who created *samhita*s: Jabali, Kumudadi and Shounaka as the third. O *brahmana*! Shounaka divided it into two and gave one to Babhru. He gave the second *samhita* to the one

---

[576] This could mean either Sumantu's son or Sutva's son, probably the latter.

[577] Poushpinji.

known as Saindhava. Each of these two divisions, Saindhava
and Munjikesha,[578] was again divided into three. The different
divisions of the *Atharva Veda samhita* differ amongst each
other in five ways: what has been said about *nakshatra*s, Vedic
rituals, the rules for sacrifices, the Angiras hymns and hymns
for peace.'[579]

'He[580] was accomplished in the meaning of the Puranas
and composed a Purana *samhita*. It had accounts, sub-
accounts, chants and rules for purification. Vyasa had a famous
disciple, Suta Romaharshana. The immensely intelligent Vyasa
bestowed the Purana *samhita* on him. He[581] had six disciples:
Sumati, Agnivarcha, Mitrayu, Shamshapayana, Akritavrana
and Savarni as the sixth. These three, Kashyapa,[582] Savarni and
Shamshapayana composed *samhita*s of their own. There was
also Romaharshana's original *samhita*. O sage! All the four
*samhita*s will be found here.[583] The first among all the Puranas is
said to be Brahma Purana. Those who know about the Puranas
speak of eighteen Puranas: Brahma, Padma, Vishnu, Shiva,
Bhagavata, Narada, Markandeya as the seventh, Agni as the
eighth, Bhavishyat as the ninth, Brahmavaivarta as the tenth,
Linga as the eleventh, Varaha as the twelfth, Skanda as the
thirteenth, Vamana as the fourteenth, Kurma as the fifteenth,
Matysa, Garuda and Brahmanda. O great sage! These are the
eighteen Maha-Puranas. The sages also speak of Upapuranas.
All the Puranas describe *sarga, pratisarga, vamsha, manvantara*
and *vamshanucharita*. O Maitreya! The Purana I am describing

---

[578] This suggests Munjikesha is one of Babhru's names.

[579] These are convoluted *shloka*s and there has been some
interpretation in the translation. Angiras hymns are for defeating the
enemy, animate and inanimate.

[580] Vedavyasa.

[581] Romaharshana.

[582] Another name for Akritavrana.

[583] In the Vishnu Purana.

to you is known as Vishnu Purana. It comes after Padma Purana. O excellent one! It describes everything about *sarga*, *pratisarga*, *vamsha*, *manvantara* and the illustrious Vishnu. The four *Veda*s, the *Vedanga*s, *mimamsa*, *nyaya*, Puranas and *dharmashastra*—these are the fourteen kinds of knowledge.[584] With the addition of *ayurveda*, *dhanurveda*, *gandharvaveda* and *arthashastra*, there are eighteen kinds of knowledge.[585] It should also be known that depending on the nature, there are three types of *rishi*s: *brahmarshi*s are the first, *devarshi*s come after that, and there are also *rajarshi*s. I have thus told you about the branches, the sub-branches and the divisions, the creators of those branches and the reasons for the divisions. These branches and divisions are said to be applicable for specific *manvantara*s. O *brahmana*! However, Prajapati's[586] *shruti* texts are eternal. These are only modifications. O Maitreya! I have thus told you everything that you asked me about the *Veda*s. What else will I tell you?'

Chapter 3(7) (Vishnu and Yama)

Maitreya said, 'O *guru*! You have accurately answered everything that I asked you about. But I still wish to hear about one thing that you have not told me about. O great sage! In this cosmic egg,[587] there are seven *dvipa*s, the seven worlds and the nether regions. Everywhere, there are said to be beings gross and subtle, smaller and smaller still, and larger and larger

---

[584] There are six *Vedanga*s.

[585] *Ayurveda* is medicine, *gandharvaveda* is the art of music and dancing and *arthashastra* is political economy.

[586] Brahma's.

[587] *Brahmanda*.

still. O supreme sage! They exist everywhere, even in a space that is as small as one eighth of the length of a finger. Bound by the noose of *karma*, beings exist there. Indeed, all of them are under the subjugation of the illustrious Yama. Urged by him, when their lifespans are over, they undergo hardships. When those hardships are over, they are born as *deva*s and other species. As described in the sacred texts, beings are whirled around. I wish to hear how men are freed from Yama's control. Please tell me about that kind of *karma*.'

Shri Parashara replied, 'O sage! In this connection, the great-souled Nakula asked the grandfather a question. Hear from me what Bhishma told him.'

'Bhishma said, "O son! I had a *brahmana* friend who was from Kalinga. Earlier, when he came to me, he told me that he had asked the same question to a sage who knew about his past lives. 'Whatever he said, used to come true. Whatever the intelligent one said, used to happen.'[588] When I faithfully asked him, the *brahmana* told me. I have never seen the likes of what he told me about. Once, I asked the *brahmana* from Kalinga what you have asked me about and he remembered the sage's words. He told me about the supreme secret, related by the sage who remembered his past lives. This was about a conversation between Yama and his servants. I will tell you."'

'The person from Kalinga said, "Yama saw one of his attendants standing, with a noose in his hand. He whispered in his ear. 'Stay away from those who seek refuge with Madhusudana. I am the lord of all men, except those who are Vaishnavas.[589] To ensure good and bad in the worlds, the creator, who is worshipped by the immortals, appointed me as Yama. But Hari, who is his *guru*, is not under my control

---

[588] This seems to be what the *brahmana* friend told Bhishma, about the sage.

[589] A Vaishnava is Vishnu's devotee.

and is independent. Vishnu has the power to control even me. Gold is one. But it has different forms as bracelets, crowns and earrings. In that way, the pervasive Hari is one, though he has manifestations as gods, animals, humans and the like. When the wind raises drops of water from the earth, when the wind subsides, they fall down on the ground again. In that way, the eternal one taints gods, animals, humans and the like with *guna*s. If a mortal person pursues the supreme truth and prostrates himself before Hari's lotus feet, even the immortals respect him. A person who reaches him is freed from all the bonds of sin. Therefore, avoid such a person, just as one avoids a fire into which *ghee* has been poured.' With the noose in his hand, Yama's attendant heard Yama's words and replied to Dharmaraja. 'O lord! Please tell me what a devotee of Hari, who protects everyone, is like.' Yama said, 'He does not deviate from his own *varna* and *dharma*. He regards well-wishers, friends and adversaries as his own *atman*. He does not take, nor does he cause injury. His mind is always fixed on the superior. Such a person is Vishnu's devotee. The impurities of *kali yuga* do not pollute his *atman*. His intelligence is sparkling and is not sullied. His mind is on Janardana. Such a human should be known as Hari's devotee. Even if he sees a piece of gold in private, his intelligence is such that he regards it as a blade of grass, since it belongs to someone else. His intelligence is fixed on the illustrious one alone. Know that such a supreme man is Vishnu's devotee. His mind is as unblemished as a mountain made out of crystal. How can Vishnu be in the minds of men who suffer from envy and other vices? The scorching heat of the fire does not exist when there is a mass of cool and radiant beams.[590] His intelligence is sparkling and devoid of jealousy. His conduct is serene and pure. He is like a friend to all creatures. He always speaks pleasant and beneficial

---

[590] Meaning, the moon.

words. He is humble. Vasudeva always resides in his heart.
When the eternal one resides in a man's heart, in this world, he
always has an amiable form. He is compared to a young *sala*
tree, which has imbibed the beautiful juices from the earth.
Every day, he uses *yama* and *niyama* to cleanse himself and all
attachment has been cast aside from his mind. Insolence, pride
and jealousy have left him. O servant! Maintain your distance
from such humans. Hari is the one who wields the sword, the
conch shell and the mace, and his *atman* is immeasurable. The
illustrious one is without a beginning and without an end.
He is no different from the creator and the one who ordains.
When he is present in a person's heart, sin does not exist, like
darkness in the presence of the sun. Ananta does not exist
in the polluted mind of a person who steals someone else's
wealth, injures creatures, utters falsehoods, is cruel, panders
to the inauspicious and is difficult to control. Janardana never
exists in the mind of an inferior person who cannot tolerate
another person's prosperity, indulges in calumny, is polluted in
intelligence, acts in an injurious way towards virtuous people,
does not perform sacrifices and does not donate. If a person's
intelligence is such that he acts in a deceitful way towards great
well-wishers, relatives, wives, sons, children, fathers, mothers
and the retinue of servants and if he thirsts after wealth, his
actions are those of an inferior person. He is not a devotee. A
person who has inauspicious intelligence, is wicked in conduct,
whose mind is always attached, who always associates with the
ignoble and evildoers and who is always bound in the bondage
of sin is an animal, not a man. He is not Vasudeva's devotee.
Vasudeva is the supreme being. He is alone Parameshvara. He is
in everything and in me. If a person thinks unwaveringly in this
way, his heart is in Ananta. Avoid him and maintain a distance
from him. He is the lotus-eyed Vasudeva. He is Vishnu, the one
who holds up the earth. He is Achyuta, with the conch shell
and the *chakra* in his hand. He is the refuge of the world. O

servant! If a person thinks in this way, maintain your distance
from him. He is devoid of sins. The supreme being's *atman* is
immeasurable. If he resides in a person's mind, do not glance
towards him. He is outside the purview of your glance and
mine. The energy and strength of the *chakra* will repel us. Such
a person is meant for another world.' The divinity Dharmaraja,
Ravi's son, instructed his own servant in this way. O supreme
among the Kuru lineage! This is what he told me, and I have
restated it to you properly."'

'Shri Bhishma said, "O Nakula! This is what the extremely
great-souled *brahmana* from Kalinga had happily told me
earlier. I have faithfully reported it to you. Other than Vishnu,
there is no means of escape from this ocean of *samsara*. For
those who always seek a refuge in Keshava, Yama's hardships
and his servants, with nooses and staffs, are incapacitated."'

Shri Parashara concluded, 'O sage! I have thus properly
told you what Vaivasvata chanted. Through your question,
this is what you wished to hear.'

Chapter 3(8) (Ourva and Sagara)

Maitreya said, 'Please tell me how the illustrious Vishnu is
worshipped. How do men who are devoted to Govinda
worship him? What are the fruits obtained? O great sage! I
wish to hear this.'

Shri Parashara replied, 'What you have asked me was
asked by the great-souled Sagara to Ourva. Listen to the
answer. O supreme among sages! Sagara prostrated himself
before Bhargava Ourva and asked him about worshipping
Vishnu and about the fruits that resulted when men
worshipped Vishnu. Listen carefully to everything he said
when he was asked.'

'Ourva said, "A person who worships Vishnu obtains his wishes on earth, every possible desirable state in heaven and the excellent state of *nirvana*. When one worships Achyuta, one obtains the fruits one wishes for. O Indra among kings! Accordingly, one obtains a little, or a lot. O protector of the earth! You have asked me about how one worships Hari. I will tell you everything. Listen. If a man wishes to worship and satisfy Vishnu, the supreme being, there is no path other than that of following the *varna*s and the *ashrama*s. A person who undertakes sacrifices, sacrifices to him. O king! A person who engages in *japa*, performs *japa* for him. If one kills, one kills him, since Hari is in all beings. Thus, when a man observes good conduct and follows the *dharma* of his own *varna*, it is Janardana who is worshipped. O lord of the earth! *Brahmana*s, *kshatriya*s, *vaishya*s and *shudra*s must follow their own *dharma*. There is no other way to worship Vishnu. One must not indulge in slander, calumny and falsehood. Keshava is satisfied when one does not cause anxiety to others. O lord of the earth! When a man is not addicted to stealing another person's wife or possessions, or to causing violence to others, Keshava is satisfied with him. O Indra among men! When a man does not strike or kill beings, causing them injury, Keshava is satisfied with him. O lord of men! When a man is always ready to serve *deva*s, *brahmana*s and *guru*s, Govinda is satisfied with him. When a man acts towards all beings as he does towards himself or towards his son, desiring their welfare, Hari is always happy and satisfied with him. O king! When attachment and other taints are not seen in a person's mind and when his intelligence is pure, Vishnu is always satisfied with him. O supreme among sages! The way for a man to worship Vishnu is to adhere to the *varna*s and the *ashrama*s, as stated in the sacred texts. There is no other way."'

'Sagara said, "O noble *brahmana*! I wish to hear everything about the *dharma* of *varna*s and about the *dharma* of *ashrama*s. Please tell me about those."'

'Ourva replied, "In due order, I will tell you about the
dharma of *brahmana*s, *kshatriya*s, *vaishya*s and *shudra*s.
Listen attentively. A *brahmana* should donate, use sacrifices
to worship *deva*s, be engaged in studies and always perform
the rites with water and fire. For subsistence, he can officiate
at sacrifices of others and teach. A *brahmana* can accept gifts
through riches earned by legitimate means. A *brahmana* must
be engaged in the welfare of all beings and must never harm
anyone. The best wealth for a *brahmana* is friendliness towards
all beings. A *brahmana*'s intelligence must be such that he
regards another person's jewel as no different from a pebble.
It is recommended that he should have intercourse with his
wife at the right time. As he wishes, a *kshatriya* can donate to
*brahmana*s. A king[591] must undertake many kinds of sacrifices
and study. His best means of earning a living are through the
use of weapons and protecting the earth. But his first task is
thought to be that of protecting the earth. When lords of men
protect the earth, they accomplish their objective. Thereby,
a king obtains a share of the good merits in all the sacrifices
and other rites that are performed. A king must punish the
wicked and protect the virtuous. A person who acts according
to his own *varna*, obtains the desired worlds. O lord of men!
Brahma, the grandfather of the worlds, gave *vaishya*s animal
husbandry, trade and agriculture as means of subsistence.
Studying, sacrifices and donations are praised as their *dharma*.
They must undertake all the *nitya* and *naimittika* rites.[592] A
shudra earns his subsistence through wealth obtained by
serving *dvija*s,[593] through buying and selling or through wealth

---

[591] Meaning, a *kshatriya*.
[592] *Nitya karma* means daily rites and *naimittika karma* means
occasional rites. *Kamya karma* means rites undertaken with a specific
desire in mind.
[593] Here, *dvija* means the first three *varna*s.

earned through artisanship. He must not focus excessively on purification, but must serve his master, without any deception. He can undertake sacrifices without the use of *mantra*s and without *brahmana*s officiating at these. A *shudra* can donate through *paka yajna*s.[594] A *shudra* must perform all the rites required for ancestors. O lord of the earth! In general, the qualities for all the *varna*s are described as sustaining servants and others, receiving gifts, having intercourse with one's wife at the time of her season, compassion towards all beings, fortitude, lack of pride, truthfulness, purity, easy inclination towards everything auspicious, pleasant speech, desire to be friendly, lack of miserliness and lack of jealousy. In general, these are also the attributes for all the *ashrama*s. Hear about the quality of *dharma* for *brahmana*s and others when there is a calamity. At such times, it is said that a *brahmana* can follow the tasks of a *kshatriya* or the tasks of a *vaishya*. A *kshatriya* can follow the stated tasks of a *vaishya*. O lord of the earth! But to the extent possible, neither category should follow the tasks of a *shudra*. Even at such a time, one should not mix up tasks in this way. O king! I have thus described to you the *dharma* of *varna*s. I will now properly tell you about the *dharma* of *ashrama*s. Listen."'

Chapter 3(9) (The *Ashramas*)

'**O**urva continued, "When a child has been through the *upanayana* ceremony, he should devote himself to acquiring the *Veda*s. He should control himself and reside in the house of his *guru* in the form of a *brahmachari*. His

---

[594] In a *paka yajna*, food is cooked at home to perform the five sacrifices required of a householder.

task then is to observe all the rites of purification and serve his *guru*. Having made up his mind to receive the *Veda*s, he should observe the vows. O lord of the earth! At the time of the two *sandhya*s, he should control himself and honour the sun and the fire. He must then honour the *guru*. When his *guru* is standing, he must stand. When he walks, he must walk. When he sits, he must be seated below him. O best among kings! The disciple must never act against the *guru*. When he is asked, he must stand in front of him and study the *Veda*s, with his mind on nothing else. When his *guru* grants him permission, he must eat what has been obtained by asking for alms. He must bathe in water, in which, his preceptor has bathed earlier. At the right time, he must collect kindling, water and other things. When he has acquired the *Veda*s he was meant to acquire and has received his *guru*'s permission to leave, a wise person will enter the stage of *garhasthya*. He must obtain a wife in the prescribed manner. He must obtain wealth through his own tasks. O protector of the earth! To the best of his capacity, he must perform all the tasks required of a householder. He must perform the required sacrifices: worshipping the ancestors through water-rites, worshipping *deva*s through oblations, offering food to guests, honouring sages through studying, worshipping Prajapati through offspring and making offerings to living beings.[595] He must show love towards the entire world. Through his own deeds, a man conquers the worlds. After spending time as a householder, there are those who become mendicants, following *brahmacharya* and subsisting on what

---

[595] There are five daily sacrifices required to be performed by any householder: *brahma/rishi yajna* (studying), *deva yajna* (tending to the household fire), *pitri yajna* (water-rites for ancestors and having offspring), *bhuta yajna* (food offerings to living beings) and *manushya yajna* (feeding guests and others). The text states this slightly differently.

has been obtained through alms. O lord! Such *brahmana*s
roam around the entire world desiring to acquire the *Veda*s,
bathing at *tirtha*s and wishing to see the world. They do not
have a fixed residence and without having had any food,
arrive at a house in the evening. Like a parent, a householder
is the refuge for all such people. O king! He must welcome
them, give them gifts and address them with sweet words. He
must offer a bed, a seat and food to those who arrive at his
house. When a guest returns from a house without his wishes
having been met, he leaves his bad deeds with the householder.
When he leaves, he takes away the householder's good deeds.
In a virtuous person's house, disrespect, pride, insolence,
lamentation, insults and harsh words are not praised. If a
householder follows the supreme norms properly, he is freed
from all bondage and obtains excellent worlds. O king! When
he ages and has accomplished everything that is required of
a householder, he leaves for the forest.[596] He can entrust his
wife to the care of his sons or take her with him. He must
subsist on a diet of leaves, roots and fruits. He must let his hair,
beard and moustache grow and his hair must be matted. O
king! Every day, the sage must sleep on the ground. His upper
garment and his lower garment must be made out of hide,
kasha grass or *kusha* grass. O lord of men! Bathing thrice a
day is recommended for him. He must worship *deva*s and offer
oblations. He must welcome all those who come to him. O
lord of men! It is recommended that he should subsist through
begging and make offerings to other creatures. Smearing his
body and limbs with oil obtained from the forest is praised. O
Indra among kings! A sage who is in the stage of *vanaprastha*
will control himself and perform austerities, tolerating heat,
cold and the like. Like a fire, this will burn down all his sins
and he will conquer the eternal worlds. The learned speak of

[596] The stage of *vanaprastha*.

the fourth *ashrama* as that of a mendicant.[597] O king! I will tell
you about its nature. You should listen to this. O lord of men!
A man must proceed towards this fourth *ashrama* after giving
up all attachment towards sons, objects and wives and after
cleansing himself of all intolerance. O lord of the earth! He
must cast aside all attempts to pursue the three objectives of
human existence.[598] He must be impartial towards friends and
others. In his speech, thoughts and bodily action, he must be
friendly towards all creatures—those born from a womb, those
born from an egg and all the others. He must not engage in
any enmity. He must renounce all kinds of attachment. He will
not spend more than one night in a village and not more than
five nights in a city. He must reside such that there is affection
towards him and no hatred. For the sake of maintaining his
life, he should roam around, visiting the houses of different
*varna*s for alms. However, there is a recommended time for
this—when the householders have eaten and the fire has been
extinguished. Casting aside desire, anger, insolence, delusion,
avarice and other things, he must roam around, without any
sense of 'mine'. The sage must roam around such that he grants
all creatures freedom from fear. Nor does he suffer from fear
on account of any creature. Having imbibed the *agnihotra*
fire into his own body, he will use the fire within his body
to offer oblations into his own mouth.[599] Using this oblation,
this *brahmana* mendicant uses the fire within his consciousness
to obtain the worlds. This is said to be observance of the
ashrama of *moksha*, followed by those who have perfected
their intelligence, finding bliss in purification. Such a serene
dvija obtains a beneficial end in Brahma's world. He is like a
stellar body that does not die."'

[597] *Sannyasa*, the word used in the text is *bhikshu*.
[598] *Dharma, artha* and *kama*.
[599] In *samadhi*, he gives up his own life.

Chapter 3(10) (*Samskaras* and Marriage)

'Sagara said, "You have told me about the duties of the four *ashramas* and the four *varnas*. O supreme among *brahmanas*! I now wish to hear about the rites that a man should undergo. O best among the Bhrigus! Please tell me about all the *nitya*, *naimittika* and *kamya* rites for a man. It is my view that you know everything."'

'Ourva replied, "You have mentioned the *nitya* and *naimittika* rites that must be undergone. I will tell you about them. Please listen with an attentive mind. As soon as a son is born, a father must perform all the *jatakarma* and other rites, as well as a *shraddha*, because there has been *abhyudaya* for himself.[600] O lord of men! He must feed a pair of *brahmanas*, seated with their faces towards the east. In this way, he satisfies *devas* and ancestors. O lord of the earth! He must cheerfully offer *pindas* mixed with *badari* to *nandimukhas*, using *deva tirtha* or *prajapatya tirtha*.[601] He must circumambulate all the offerings. O lord of the earth! This must be done every time there is an increase in prosperity. On the tenth day, the father must give the son a name. The first part of the name must be that of a *deva*, the second part signifying a man, such as Sharma or Varma. Sharma is said to be appropriate for a *brahmana*, Varma for a *kshatriya*. Gupta is praised for a *vaishya* and Dasa for a *shudra*. The name must not be devoid of meaning. It should not use condemned or inappropriate

---

[600] *Shraddha* is performed, at the same time, for the ancestors. This type of *shraddha* is known as *abhyudaya shraddha* or *vriddhi shraddha*. It is not performed when someone has died, but whenever there is a rise (*abhyudaya*) or increase (*vriddhi*) in prosperity.

[601] *Pinda* is a funeral cake; *badari* is jujube; *nandimukhas* are a class of ancestors; *deva tirtha* is the tips of the fingers; and *prajapatya tirtha* is the base of the little finger.

words. The name should not be a condemned one or one that
gives rise to disgust. An even number of syllables must be used.
It should not be too long. It should not have too many short
syllables or too many long syllables. The name should be easy
to pronounce. It should not have 'Oum' in it. When he has
purified himself through the other *samskara*s, he will go to his
guru's abode. In the proper way, he must act so as to receive
knowledge. After having received the knowledge, he must give
the *guru* the *dakshina*[602] due to a *guru*. O lord of the earth! If
he wishes to become a householder, he will take a wife. On the
other hand, he may have made up his mind to spend his time as
a *brahmachari*. In that case, he will serve the *guru* and his sons.
Or he may wander around, wishing to be a *vaikhanasa*.[603] O
lord of men! One should act in accordance with the resolution
one has formerly made. When he marries, the wife should be
one-third his own age. She should not have too much hair
nor should she lack in hair. She should not be too dark nor
should she have a tawny complexion. He should not marry
someone who, from birth, has had an excess of a limb or is
lacking in a limb. She should not be impure, with body hair.
She should not be from a bad lineage or diseased. She should
not be wicked, one who uses evil words. She should not be one
who has inherited a diseased limb from her father or mother.
She should not have a beard nor should she resemble a man.
Her voice should not be indistinct or weak. But nor should her
voice be like that of a crow. A learned person will not marry
one who keeps her eyes closed or one whose eyes jut out. She
should not have hair on her legs or ankles that are thick. He
should not marry one whose cheeks dimple when she laughs.
Her skin should not be too rough. Her nails should not be
pale. Her eyes should not be red. A learned person will not

---

[602] The fee given after the completion of learning.
[603] One who subsists on wild grain.

marry one whose hands and feet are stout. She should not be a dwarf. She should not be excessively tall. Her eyebrows should not be joined together. A man should not marry one who has a cruel face, with gaps between her teeth. O king! Following the proper rites, a householder must marry one who is not related for five generations on the mother's side and seven generations on the father's side. It is held that there are eight forms of marriage: *brahma*, *daiva*, *arsha*, *prajapatya*, *asura*, *gandharva*, *rakshasa* and *paishacha*.[604] Of these, the *maharshi*s have spoken about what is *dharma* for each *varna*. When one accepts a wife, one should not follow any other mode. When the householder has obtained a wife, she will be his aide in following his own *dharma*. After having married, he obtains all the great and deep fruits.'"

Chapter 3(11) (*Sadacharas*)

'Sagara said, "O sage! I wish to hear what constitutes *sadachara*[605] for a householder, so that his status does not suffer in this world and in the next world."'

[604] In a *brahma* marriage, the father bestows an ornamented daughter on the groom. In the *daiva* form, the girl is bestowed on a priest, typically at the time of a sacrifice. In *arsha*, the father gave away his daughter after receiving a bride price, typically two cows. In *prajapatya*, husband and wife are instructed to follow *dharma* together. Usually, the bride is older than the groom in *brahma*. In *asura*, the bridegroom pays a bride price, significantly more than in the case of *arsha*. In *gandharva*, the groom and the bride fall in love and decide to marry. In *rakshasa*, the bride's family is defeated, and the bride is abducted, but not against her wishes. In *paishacha*, the bride is abducted against her wishes.

[605] Good conduct.

'Ourva replied, "O protector of the earth! Hear about the signs of *sadachara*. Through such *sadachara*, a man conquers the worlds. A *sadhu* is a person who has destroyed his taints. The word '*sat*' suggests the person is a *sadhu*. Their *achara*[606] is spoken of as *sadachara*. O lord of the earth! *Saptarshi*s, Manus and Prajapatis have spoken about those who follow *sadachara*. O king! A person must make up his mind to wake up at the time of *brahma muhurta*.[607] He must kindle his consciousness and think about *dharma* and *artha* and what does not conflict with these two. He must think about *kama*, as long as it does not conflict with the first two. He must consider what causes destruction, whether it is seen or unseen. He must be impartial vis-à-vis the three objectives. O king! If *artha* and *kama* are contrary to *dharma*, he must give them up. He must also avoid *dharma* if it causes misery and is hateful to the worlds. Having woken up at the right time, he must pass urine and excrement. Urine and excrement must be released on the ground, at a distance that is more than an arrow's flight from the habitation, towards the south-west direction. He must then wash his feet, but the remaining water should not be flung into the courtyard of the house. A wise person will never pass urine on his own shadow, the shadow of a tree or facing a cow, the sun, the fire or the wind. Nor will he do this before a *guru* or a *dvija*.[608] O bull among men! A wise person will not release urine or excrement in a field full of crops, in a pasture for cattle, in an assembly of people, on a road, in a river, at a *tirtha*, in water, on the banks of a river or in a cremation ground. O king!

[606] Conduct.

[607] A *muhurta* is a period of forty-eight minutes. *Brahma muhurta* is named after Brahma and is an auspicious time just before dawn, regarded as the last *muhurta* of the night. The precise hour depends on the time when the sun rises.

[608] In this context, one of the first three *varnas*.

During the day, a wise person releases himself while facing the north. At night, the direction is the reverse. If this is done, he does not suffer from hardships. He must cover his head and do this in a place where the ground is covered with grass. He must not take a long time and he must not say anything. To clean himself, he must not take earth from a termite hill or a rat's hole. Nor should he use earth or water left over after purifying or plastering the house. O king! He should not use earth that has minute living beings or that thrown up by the plough. Avoiding all such earth, he must complete all his acts of purification. O king! One handful is enough for the penis, three handfuls for the anus. The left hand must be cleaned ten times. Both hands must then be cleaned seven times each. Earth must be used to clean the feet. After having cleaned his limbs with earth, he must control himself and rinse his mouth with water that does not have any bubbles. When the feet have been cleaned, they must be cleaned yet again with water. He will drink water thrice and use it to wipe his face twice. He will use water to touch his head, the cavities in the head,[609] the forehead, the arms, the navel and the heart. After having rinsed his mouth, a man will dress his hair. He will stand before a mirror and use sandalwood and *durva* grass.[610] He will earn wealth through a means of livelihood that is appropriate for his own *varna*. O lord of the earth! He will devotedly perform sacrifices—*soma yajna*s, those with oblations and *paka yajna*s. Since these require riches, men should strive to earn wealth.''

'''For the sake of undertaking *nitya* rites, he should bathe near the banks of a male or female river, in the water of a natural waterbody, in a mountain waterfall or on the ground, with water drawn from a well. If water from the ground is not available, he can bathe with water kept at home. Having

[609] Eyes, ears, nostrils.
[610] Oil extracted from these.

bathed, he will wear clean clothes and worship *deva*s, *rishi*s and ancestors, controlling himself and using the *tirtha*s meant for them.[611] To please the *deva*s, three libations of water must be offered, and this is also the case for *rishi*s. O lord of the earth! He must offer water once to Prajapati and thrice to the ancestors. Using *pitri tirtha*, to please his paternal grandfather, paternal great-grandfather, maternal grandfather, maternal great-grandfather and father, he must control himself and offer water.[612] O king! As he wishes,[613] he can use *pitri tirtha* to offer libations to his mother,[614] his own mother, his mother's mother, his *guru*'s wife, his *guru*s, his maternal uncles and his friends. O lord of the earth! When he offers this voluntarily, he should utter the following *japa*. 'May *deva*s, *asura*s, *yaksha*s, *naga*s, *gandharva*s, *rakshasa*s, *pishacha*s, *guhyaka*s, *siddha*s, *kushmanda*s, animals, birds, aquatic creatures, those inside the ground, those in the air and everyone else be quickly satisfied with the water I have offered them.[615] There are those in *naraka*. May the water I have offered reduce their pain. There are relatives of relatives and there are those who were relatives in earlier births. May all those who desire libations from me be satisfied with this. There are those who are suffering from hunger and thirst, wherever they may be. May this libation of water and sesamum offered by me reduce their pain.' O king! I have described to you the water that is offered, as one wishes. When a man offers this, the entire world is satisfied.

[611] *Deva tirtha* has already been mentioned. *Pitri tirtha* is the region between the forefinger and the thumb. *Rishi tirtha* is the palm.

[612] The forefathers become ancestors/manes only beyond these three generations. Therefore, these three generations must be offered libations separately.

[613] This is optional. The others are mandatory.

[614] Allowing for the possibility of a stepmother.

[615] *Guhyaka*s are semi-divine species, companions of Kubera. *Kushmanda*s are a class of evil spirits.

O unblemished one! When the entire world is nourished, he obtains good merits. Therefore, full of faith, he should voluntarily offer this libation of water."'

"'Rinsing his mouth, he should then use the cup of his hands to offer water to Surya, using the following words. 'I prostrate myself before Vivasvat, the radiance of the *brahman* and Vishnu's energy. O Savita! You are the one who purifies the world. O Savita! You are the witness to all *karma*.' He should then worship the house and using water for *abhisheka*,[616] flowers, incese and other offerings, worship the god he desires. O king! After this, without any other rite, he must first used *agnihotra* to worship Brahma. After having offered it to Prajapati, he must in the due order, affectionately tender offerings to deities in his house, Kaashyapa and Anumati.[617] He can sprinkle the remainder of the oblations on the ground or in the air. He can sprinkle to Dhatri and Vidhatri, at the two sides of the door, and to Brahma, in the middle. O tiger among men! Now hear from me about the directions in the house. A wise person will then offer the remnants of the offerings to Indra, Dharmaraja, Varuna and Soma, in the four directions, the east and others.[618] A learned person will tender the offering to Dhanvantari in the north-eastern direction. He must next offer libations to all the Vishvadevas in all the directions, such as Vayu in the north-west.[619] The offerings for Brahma and

---

[616] *Abhisheka* is anointing and sprinkling the image with water.

[617] This is Kaashyapa, Kashyapa's son, meaning Aditya/Surya. Anumati is the fifteenth day of the lunar fortnight. Here, it means the moon.

[618] Indra to the east, Dharamaraja to the south, Varuna to the west and Soma to the north. Usually, Kubera is the guardian of the north.

[619] Ishana in the north-east, Agni in the south-east, Vayu in the north-west, Nirriti in the south-west, Brahma towards the zenith and Vishnu towards the nadir.

Bhanu must be flung in the air. O lord of men! Having offered it to the eight Vishvadevas, he will offer it to beings in the universe, the lords of the universe, ancestors and *yakshas*. As he wishes, a learned person will then control himself and place a little bit of food at a clean place on the ground, saying, 'I am offering this for *devas*, humans, animals, birds, *siddhas*, *yakshas*, *uragas*, large numbers of *daityas*, *pretas*, *pishachas*, trees, all those who desire food, ants, worms, insects, all those who are hungry and all those bound in the noose of *karma*.[620] Let them be satisfied with the food I have left. Let them be happy. There are those who have no father, mother or relative, no food or no means of cooking food. Let them be satisfied with the food I have left on the ground. Let them be content and happy. There is no difference between all creatures, this food, I and Vishnu. Therefore, for their satisfaction, I am offering this food, which is made out the bodies of creatures. All the large number of creatures, the fourteen categories of creatures,[621] may be present here. Let them be content and happy with the food I have offered.' Full of faith, a man must say this and offer the food. This is for the welfare of everyone on earth and the householder is a refuge for everyone. O lord of men! Food

[620] A *preta* is a ghost, the spirit of a dead person, or simply something evil. A *bhuta* has the same meaning. Strictly speaking, there are differences between *preta*, *bhuta* and *pishacha* (one who lives on flesh). A *preta* is the spirit (not necessarily evil) of a dead person before the funeral rites have been performed. A *bhuta* (not necessarily evil again) is the spirit of a dead person who has had a violent death and for whom, proper funeral rites have not been performed, and may not even be performed. A *pishacha* (necessarily evil) is often created deliberately through evil powers.

[621] *Siddhas*, *guhyakas*, *gandharvas*, *yakshas*, *rakshasas*, *pannagas*, *vidyadharas*, *pishachas*, humans, reptiles, monkeys, wild animals, domestic animals and birds.

must be scattered on the ground for dogs, *chandalas*,[622] birds, others who are outcasts and men who do not have sons. He should then remain in the courtyard of his house for as long as it takes to milk a cow, or more if he so wishes, to receive guests. When a guest arrives, he should receive him with words of welcome, offering him a seat and water to wash his feet. With devotion, he must be offered food. Thereafter, there must be pleasant conversation with him. When a guest leaves, the householder should address him with humble and affectionate words. Even if the guest happens to be of unknown name and lineage, from a different country, or a resident of no particular village, he must be honoured properly. A guest may be without possessions and relatives. His lineage and conduct may be unknown. If a person wishes to eat, without honouring and making such a guest eat, he heads downwards. A householder who possesses intelligence about Hiranyagarbha should not bother to ask about a guest's studies, *gotra*, conduct or lineage. O king! For the sake of the ancestors,[623] he should invite a *brahmana* who comes from the same region, so that his conduct and birth are known. He should be one who undertakes the five daily sacrifices. O lord of the earth! He should first offer cooked food to a learned *brahmana*. This is thought of as *hantakara*.[624] The third offering of alms must be

---

[622] One usually equates *chandala* with *shudra*, but there were eight different types of *shudra*s, though the listing varies. For instance, *vyadha* (hunter), *vyalagrahi* (those who eat snakes), *vagatita* (one with whom one does not speak), *chandala* (*brahmana* mother, *shudra* father) and so on.

[623] That is, at the time of a *shraddha* ceremony.

[624] *Hanta*, is an exclamation, which can roughly be translated as 'Oh!' *Hantakara* is the utterance of this exclamation and stands for an offering made to a guest. Interpretations say this *brahmana* must be given four mouthfuls of food and the mendicant must be given three mouthfuls. The text need not be construed in that way.

given to a wandering mendicant or a *brahmachari*. If a learned person is not constrained in adherence to the truth and if he possesses the requisite wealth, he may wish to give more. O king! But these four kinds of guests and mendicants are spoken about.[625] When they are worshipped, he is freed from sins. If a guest returns from a house with his wishes unsatisfied, when he departs, he takes away the householder's good merits and leaves his own bad merits instead. O lord of men! Dhatri, Prajapati, Shakra, Vahni[626] and Surya enter the form of the guest and enjoy the food. Therefore, a man must always make efforts to honour guests. If a man eats without guests having eaten, he only partakes of sin."

'"The householder must next ensure that the following are fed well-cooked food first, before he himself eats: a sister who lives with him, anyone miserable, a pregnant woman, the aged and children. Only an evildoer eats before such people have fed. When he dies, such a man goes to *naraka* and feeds on phlegm. If he eats without bathing, he feeds on filth.[627] A person who does not perform *japa*, feeds on pus and blood. A person who does not eat clean food, feeds on urine. A person who eats before children and others, feeds on excrement. A person who does not offer oblations, feeds on worms. A person who does not donate, feeds on poison. O Indra among kings! Therefore, hear how a householder should eat. If a man eats in this way, he is not bound in sin. O king! In this world, he obtains freedom from disease and extensive strength and intelligence. He obtains his wishes and peace, and adversaries cannot act against him. He must bathe in the proper way and offer oblations to *deva*s, *rishi*s and ancestors.

[625] The unknown *brahmana*, the known *brahmana*, the learned *brahmana* and the mendicant/*brahmachari*.

[626] Agni.

[627] After death, in hell. This applies to the ones that follow too.

When a householder eats, it is recommended that he should control himself and that he should be ornamented with jewels on his hands. O king! He must perform *japa*, offer oblations into the fire and be clad in fresh garments. He must first give to guests, *brahmana*s and seniors who reside with him. O lord of men! It is recommended that he should wear a garland and be decorated with auspicious fragrances. He should not be clad in only one piece of clothing. O lord of the earth! His hands and feet must not be wet. His face must be pleasant and happy. He should not eat with his face towards the sub-directions. A man must face the north or the east and his mind should not be distracted. The food must be healthy and wholesome, boiled in clean water. It should not have been acquired from a wicked person. It should not have been acquired in a condemned way. It should not have been cooked improperly. A householder should eat after giving to his devoted disciples and those who are hungry. It is recommended that a *brahmana* should eat from a clean vessel, without being angry. O lord of men! The vessel should not be placed on a stool or on a place that is inappropriate. He should not eat at the wrong place. The place where he eats should not be narrow. O king! Before eating, a man must pronounce *mantra*s and offer a little bit of food to the fire. The food must not be stale, with an exception made for fruits, roots, dry vegetables, *badari* and molasses. O lord of men! A man must never eat food from which the juices have been extracted. O lord of the earth! A discriminating man must never eat such that no remnants of the serving are left, with an exception being made for honey, water, curds, *ghee* and *saktu*. While eating, he must first attentively eat the food with sweet flavours. Food that is salty and sour must be eaten in the middle and bitter and pungent food at the end. If a man starts with fluids, eats solids in the middle and ends with liquids again, he is always strong and healthy. While eating, he should not condemn the food or use words to criticize it. For the sake of maintaining his breath of life, he should maintain great silence and only have five mouthfuls. After having eaten properly, he must face the north or the east and rinse his mouth. Rinsing his mouth again, he must wash his hands, up to the elbows. With a calm and serene mind, he must next be seated. A man must remember his desired *deva*s and say, 'May the element of fire, urged by the element of the wind, convert this food into the element of the earth. In the stomach, may the elements of space and water grant me happiness. With earth, water, fire and wind, may this food give me strength. May it be digested and bestow unmitigated happiness on me. May the food provide nourishment to *prana, apana, samana, udana* and *vyana*. May I have unmitigated happiness. May the Agasti fire and the Vadava fire digest all the food that I have eaten.[628] May the result be my happiness, so that there is no disease in my body. The illustrious Vishnu is the only one in the body and in all the senses in the body. Let this therefore not be futile. By that truth, let the outcome of all the food I have eaten be my freedom from disease. Vishnu is the one who ate this food. He is also the consequence. By that truth, let all the food I have eaten be digested.' Having said this, he should rub his stomach with his own hand. He can then easily and attentively undertake all the other tasks."'

"'He can then spend his day on such pleasures that are sanctioned by the sacred texts and are not contrary to the path of the virtuous. When *sandhya* arrives, he must control himself. O lord of the earth! When the *sandhya* at the end of the day arrives, a learned person must properly undertake the rites before the sun has set. At the time of the other *sandhya*, he must perform them before the sun rises. O lord of the earth! One should never deviate from the rites at the time of the two

[628] The Agasti fire is named after Agastya and Vadava is the subterranean fire. Here, both mean the digestive fire.

*sandhya*s. The only exception is when one is a *sutaka*, one is impure, one is confounded, one is afflicted or one is scared.[629] He should not sleep after the sun has risen. Nor should he sleep before the sun has set. Other than when he is suffering from a disease, if a man violates this, he must perform *prayashchitta*.[630] O lord of the earth! Therefore, every day, one should wake up before the sun rises. He should never sleep before the *sandhya* that comes at the end of the day. O king! If a person neglects the rites at the times of the eastern and western *sandhya*, he is evil-souled and goes to the *naraka* named *tamisra*. O lord of the earth! In the evening, along with his wife, let him take some food and render offerings to the Vishvadevas. Some food should be left for *shvapaka*s and others.[631] According to his capacity, a learned person should welcome any guest who arrives. He must honour him and greet him with words of welcome. O lord of the earth! He must offer him water to wash the feet, food and a bed. O king! If a guest arrives in the night and is refused, the sin a person reaps is eight times the sin reaped if a guest is refused during the day. O Indra among kings! Therefore, a man must make every effort to honour someone who arrives after sunset. When such a respected person is honoured, all the gods are worshipped. According to his own capacity, a man must offer him food, vegetables, water and a bed. If this is not possible, a spread on the ground will do. When it is evening and he has eaten, the householder will wash his feet and go to bed. O kind! It should clearly be made out of wood. It should not be too large nor should it be broken. It should not be

---

[629] *Sutaka* means one is impure because there has been a childbirth in the house. One can also be impure because there has been a death in the house. Affliction means suffering from a disease.

[630] A rite of atonement.

[631] *Shvapaka*s are sometimes equated with *chandala*s. *Shva* means dog and *paka* means to cook. Thus, *shvapaka* means someone who cooks dogs (eats dogs) or cooks for dogs (lives with dogs).

uneven or dirty. There should not be insects in the bed, and it should not be without a spread. O king! He should sleep with his head facing the east or the south. In this way, a man is always healthy. The opposite causes disease. O lord of the earth! When it is her season, a man must approach his wife, at a time when the *nakshatra*s are auspicious. Even nights[632] are the best. He should not approach a woman who has not bathed, is afflicted, has not had her periods, wishes to do harm, is angry, is frightened or is pregnant. He should not pay. She should not desire another. She should not be unwilling. She should not be someone else's wife. She should not be hungry nor should she have eaten a lot. He should himself possess these qualities. He should not be hungry. He should be cheerful, having bathed and ornamented himself with garlands and fragrances. A man must approach, full of desire and affection. O Indra among kings! A man must always avoid oil, meat and enjoyment with women on the fourteenth and eighth lunar days, on *parva* days and at the time of the sun's *sankranti*. Otherwise, when he dies, he will go to a *naraka* where he will feed on urine and excrement. A learned person will always show restraint on *parva* days. A man should follow the sacred texts, worship *deva*s and engage in *dhyana* and *japa*. He should not indulge in sexual intercourse with other species or use special herbs for this. O lord of the earth! Nor should he do this in the presence of *brahmana*s, *deva*s or *guru*s, in hermitages, *chaitya*s,[633] squares, banks, settlements of cows, crossroads, cremation grounds, in groves, or inside the water. O protector of the earth! If his mind turns towards intercourse on the mentioned *parva* days, or at the time of *sandhya*, he will suffer from a disease of the urinary tract. O king! Intercourse on *parva* days is condemned.

[632] Even lunar *tithi*s.
[633] The word *chaitya* has several meanings: sacrificial shed, temple, altar, sanctuary and a tree that grows along the road.

Indulging in it during the day leads to sin. For men, nor is it recommended inside water bodies, since this leads to disease. Even in thoughts, one must never approach another person's wife, not to speak of addressing her with intercourse in mind. In this world, this leads to a decrease in the lifespan. After death, he goes to *naraka*. For any man, addiction to another person's wife causes fear, both in this world and in the next world. Knowing this, a learned person will only approach his own wife, at the time of her season. As mentioned, this kind of desire is without falsehood and is devoid of taints."'

Chapter 3(12) (More on *Sadachara*)

'O urva said, "One should always worship *deva*s, cows, *brahmana*s, *siddha*s, the aged and *acharya*s. He should perform the rites for the two *sandhya*s and offer oblations into the fire. It is recommended that he should wear garments that are not torn and use the great herbs. A man should control himself and wear emeralds and other jewels. His hair should be clean and pleasant. He should wear perfumes and beautiful clothes. A man should always wear a garland made out of white flowers. He should not steal the possessions of others, nor say anything that is the least bit disagreeable. He should speak what is pleasant and not false. He should not talk about the faults of others. O bull among men! The idea of enmity towards women should not appeal to him. He should not mount a bad vehicle or seek refuge under a shadow near a bank.[634] A learned person will never be friendly with a person who is hated, fallen down, mad, one with many enemies, a person infested with insects,

---

[634] Probably because the tree casting the shadow might fall down on him.

a pimp, the husband of a courtesan, a liar, a spendthrift, a
slanderer or a fraud. He should not follow their path. O lord
of men! He should not bathe in a flow of water that has great
force. He should not enter a house that is on fire. He should
not climb to the top of a tree. He should not gnash his teeth or
pick his nose in public. Without covering his mouth, he should
not yawn or cough. A learned person will not laugh loudly or
pass wind loudly. He will not bite his nails, cut grass or etch on
the ground.[635] A discriminating person will not eat his beard or
pulverize a piece of stone.[636] O lord! Unless it is an auspicious
time, he will not look at stellar bodies. He will not look at the
sun at the time of rising or setting or at another person's wife,
when she is naked. He will not be disgusted at the smell of a
corpse since the smell of a corpse originates from the moon.
At night, he must always avoid crossroads, a *chaitya* tree, a
grove near a cremation ground and association with a wicked
woman. A learned person will not cross the shadow of a revered
person, a *deva*, a *brahmana* or a stellar body. He should not
pass through a forest alone. He should not reside in an empty
house. From a distance, he must avoid hair, bones, thorns, filth,
ashes from burnt offerings, chaff and earth that is wet because
someone has bathed in it. A learned person will not seek refuge
with any ignoble or deceitful person. He should not approach
a predatory beast. After waking up, he should not lie down
for a long time. A learned person will avoid excesses in staying
awake and sleeping. O lord of men! When it is time to exert
himself, he should not lie down on his bed. From a distance, a
wise person will avoid animals with tusks and horns. O Indra
among kings! He will avoid being exposed to fog, the easterly

[635] This probably means using the nails on the toes to scratch the
ground.
[636] As pointless exercises. The first presumably means biting the
beard.

wind or the sun's heat. A learned person will not bathe, sleep or rinse the mouth when he is naked. He should avoid rinsing his mouth or worshipping *deva*s when his hair is loose. While donning only a single garment, he should not offer oblations, worship *deva*s, perform rites, rinse his mouth or prostrate himself at the feet of *brahmana*s. He will never associate with those who are wicked in conduct and not his equal. For the virtuous, it is recommended *dharma* that this association should be for no more than half a *kshana*. A learned person will never oppose those who are superior or inferior. O king! Marriages and disputes must be between those who are equal in conduct. A wise person should not start a conflict. He should avoid an enmity that is dry.[637] A little bit of wealth can be tolerated. But wealth obtained through enmity must be avoided. After bathing, he must not wipe his limbs with a piece of cloth or with his hands. Without getting up from his bed, he should not shake his hair or rinse his mouth. While seated, he should not cross one leg over another or stretch out his feet towards someone revered. He should humbly be seated on a seat that is lower than that of a senior. He must never walk such that a temple to a *deva* or a crossroad is to his left. This is contrary. Auspicious and revered objects must always be to the right. A learned person will not pass urine or excrement in front of the moon, the fire, water, a respected person or against the wind. He will not pass urine while standing or pass urine alongside a road. Phlegm, urine, excrement and blood must never be crossed. Expectoration of phlegm is not recommended at the time of sacrifices, auspicious occasions, while performing *japa*, while offering oblations and at the time of eating. A learned person will not show disrespect to women nor trust them. A woman is noble and must never be reprimanded. A wise person, who follows good conduct, will not leave his house without first

---

[637] Over and done with.

honouring auspicious spots, jewels, flowers, *ghee* and revered
individuals. At the right time, he will offer oblations and show
his respect to crossroads. He must sustain virtuous and learned
individuals who are in distress. He must worship *deva*s and
*rishi*s in the proper way. He must offer *pinda*s to ancestors. If
a person is hospitable towards guests, he goes to the excellent
worlds. If a person controls himself and speaks moderately,
with agreeable and beneficial words, he obtains blissful and
inexhaustible worlds, attained by all beings and kings. Excellent
worlds are obtained by a believing[638] person who is intelligent,
modest, forgiving and humble and who honours learning, the
noble and the aged. A learned person will not study when it
thunders at the wrong time, on a *parva* day, when it is time for
an impurity, or at the time of eclipses. He will always pacify
rage. He will behave/act/conduct himself like a relative towards
everyone, without intolerance. He will comfort those who are
frightened. Such a virtuous person obtains the limited fruit of
heaven. As protection against rain and the sun, he will carry an
umbrella. When he walks around in the night, he will carry a
staff. If he desires to protect his body, he will always walk with
footwear on. When he walks, a learned person will not look
up, diagonally or a far distance away. When he walks, a man
should look at the ground, for a distance of two *yuga*s.[639] If he
controls himself and eliminates all the reasons for taints, there
is not the slightest bit of harm to *dharma*, *artha* and *kama*. A
wise person will always be devoted to good conduct. He will be
learned, humble and accomplished. He will be virtuous among
those who are wicked. Even if addressed harshly, he will reply
in agreeable words. His inner core will melt in friendliness.
Such a person holds emancipation in his hand. He is devoid

---

[638] *Astika.*

[639] Here, *yuga* means the length of a yoke, say the length of one
yard.

of desire, anger and greed. Lack of attachment is within his grasp. He bases himself on good conduct. People with such sentiments hold up the world. Therefore, a wise person will only speak the truth when it is agreeable to others. If the truth causes unhappiness to others, he will remain silent. However, if he thinks that agreeable words are not beneficial, he should not utter them. He should speak beneficial words, even if those are extremely disagreeable. An intelligent person is one who does what is good for beings, in thoughts, words and deeds, in this world and in the next one.'"

Chapter 3(13) (*Shraddha* Ceremonies)

'Ourva said, "When a son is born, it is recommended that a father should bathe, wearing his garment. After that, he should undertake *jatakarma* and *abhyudaya shraddha*. He should concentrate and have nothing else in his mind. He should properly worship both *deva*s and ancestors. In due order, he should honour and feed an even number of *brahmana*s, keeping them to his left.[640] O king! He should stand facing the east. Using the part of the body known as *deva tirtha*, he should offer a *pinda* made out of curds, *akshata*[641] and *badari*. O lord of the earth! He should satisfy the ancestors known as *nandimukha*s through a *shraddha*. A man should act so as to please them at every enhancement in prosperity—the marriage of a son or a daughter, entering a new house, the

---

[640] *Deva*s and ancestors are in the centre, and he circumambulates, keeping them to his right. As he circumambulates, *brahmana*s who are fed are seated on his left.

[641] This can mean grain of any kind. But it is specifically used for threshed and winnowed rice that has not been dehusked.

naming of a child, at the time of *chudakarma* and other rites, *simantonnayana* and when one beholds the face of a son.[642] A householder must always control himself and worship the category of ancestors known as *nandimukha*s. The aged have always spoken about worshipping the ancestors in the due order.'"

"'O lord of the earth! Now hear about the rites at the time of *pretakarma*.[643] The dead body must be bathed with auspicious water. When it has been bathed, it must be garlanded. It must be burned outside the village. Those who have done this, must bathe in a body of water, with their garments on. The relatives must stand in the water, with their faces towards the south. They must offer him water in the cups of their hands, uttering these words. 'This is for so and so, wherever you may be.' Along with the cattle, they must then enter the village.[644] When the *nakshatra*s are seen, they must perform the task of sleeping on a mat, spread on a slab of stone, or on the ground. O lord of the earth! Every day,[645] a *pinda* must be placed on the ground for the dead person. O bull among men! One should eat during the day, but one should not eat any meat. *Brahmana*s can be fed for as many days as one wishes. When large numbers of relatives eat, the dead person is satisfied. On the first, third, seventh and ninth days, the direct relatives must bathe and change their garments outside the house. They should offer a libation of water mixed with sesamum. O king! The ashes and bones must be collected on the fourth day. After this, the bodies of

[642] A newborn son.
[643] At the time of death.
[644] That is, in the evening.
[645] Until the *shraddha* ceremony is held.

those who have offered *pinda* can be touched.[646] They can participate in rites, as can *sahodaka*s. O king! Those known as *sapinda*s can sleep on beds, but they must refrain from use of unguents and flowers. After the ashes and bones have been collected, they must refrain from intercourse with women.[647] The dead person may be a child, someone who is in some other country, someone who has fallen down or a person who is a sage. In such cases, purification is instantaneous, and one can do what one wills. This is also true of those who have died by drowning, from a fire or through hanging. When a person dies, one should take food in the house of his relative for ten days. One should refrain from giving and receiving gifts, offering oblations and studying. For a *brahmana* and a *kshatriya*,[648] the duration of impurity is twelve days. It is half a month for a *vaishya*. It takes a *shudra* one month to get purified. On the first day after impurity is over, the closest relative should feed as many *brahmana*s as he wishes, but the number should be odd. Near the leftovers of the food that has been eaten, a *pinda* should be offered to the dead person, spread on *darbha* grass. After the *brahmana*s have eaten, depending on the *varna*, the mourner should touch water, a weapon, a goad or a staff. This leads to purification. After this, it is held that *brahmana*s and others can pursue the *dharma* of their own respective *varna*s. Through this,

---

[646] *Sapinda*s are those who can offer *pinda*s. There is a long list of those who are *sapinda*s, such as, in the absence of a son, a daughter, a daughter's son, a father, a mother, a brother, a brother's son and so on. From this point on, *sapinda*s become pure. *Sahodaka*s are those who can offer water. There is another such list of *sahodaka*s. For *sahodaka*s, the text uses the expression, 'those who offer libations of water'.

[647] Until the *shraddha* ceremony is held.

[648] The text uses the word *rajanya*, royalty. But this has been used in the sense of *kshatriya*.

a man can earn the subsistence indicated as *dharma* for his
category. It has been instructed as the supreme view that the
rites must be performed on the day of death.[649] However,
this must be done without invoking *deva*s. A *pinda* must be
offered to the dead person and *brahmana*s must be fed. The
person undertaking the rite will ask *brahmana*s if they have
been satisfied. When they say they have been satisfied, he will
cease, uttering the words, 'May so and so[650] obtain infinite
satisfaction.' It is said that this *dharma* of *ekoddishta*[651]
must be observed for one year. O Indra among kings! Hear
about the *sapindakarana* that must be done at this time.
Sapindakarana can be done at the end of twelve days, at the
end of six months, or at the end of one year. There will be
four vessels, filled with sesamum, fragrances and water. Three
of these are for the ancestors and one is for the *preta*.[652] Each
of these three vessels for the ancestors must be sprinkled with
some water from the *preta*'s vessel. O lord of the earth! At
this, the *preta* becomes one of the ancestors. In all the *dharma*
of *shraddha* ceremonies, when the ancestors are worshipped,
he is henceforth included with them. O king! Those who have
the right to perform the *sapindakarana* rite are the son, the
grandson, the great-grandson, the brother, the brother's son
or the son of someone else who is a *sapinda*. In their absence,
the son of a *sahodaka* will do or those connected through the
mother's side, either as *sapinda* or as *sahodaka*. O king! If
both families have become extinct, a woman can undertake
the rite. It can also be performed by a person who is *sapinda*
or *sahodaka* of the mother or father. The rite can also be

---

[649] On that day every month, for the duration of one year.
[650] Mentioning the dead person.
[651] A monthly rite continued for one year.
[652] The person who has died and has not yet become an ancestor.

performed by the member of a *sangha*[653] the dead person belonged to. If there are no relatives left, the king will have the *shraddha* ceremony performed. There are three kinds of funeral rites: those at the beginning, those in the middle and those at the end. There are three kinds of rites. Hear from me about their differences. The first rites are those when one touches things[654] at the end of ten days. Those in the middle are those known as *ekoddishta*, performed every month. O king! When the *preta* becomes one of the ancestors and *sapindakarana* rites are undertaken for the ancestors, those are spoken of as the final rites. The primary rites can also be performed by *sapinda*s and *sahodaka*s of the father or mother, members of a *sangha*, the king or a person who has inherited the dead person's wealth. O best among kings! The primary and final rites should be performed by the son, the daughter's son or their sons. The final rites, undertaken every year on the day the person died, can be performed by women. O king! Following the norms, they can also perform *ekoddishta*. O lord of the earth! O unblemished one! After this, hear about the final rites, about what are the norms for accurately undertaking them.'

Chapter 3(14) (More on *Shraddha*s)

'Ourva said, "For the sake of pleasing the entire world, one should faithfully undertake a *shraddha* for Brahma, Indra, Rudra, Nasatyas,[655] Surya, Agni, Vasus, Maruts,

---

[653] A collection of people who live together, a religious or social institution.

[654] Water, weapons and so on, as purification.

[655] The two Ashvins.

Vishvadevas, the large number of ancestors, birds, humans, animals, reptiles, large number of *rishi*s and all the others known as beings. O lord of men! Oblations must be offered to them every month, on the fifteenth day of *krishna paksha*,[656] the eighth day of *krishna paksha*[657] and at specific times one desires.[658] Hear about these from me. A *shraddha* must be performed when there is a special event or when a special *brahmana* has arrived. O protector of the earth! *Shraddha* must be performed when one knows there is *vyatipata*,[659] change of an *ayana*, *vishuva sankranti*, an eclipse of the sun or the moon, when the sun enters any *rashi*, when *nakshatra*s and planets suffer, when one sees a nightmare and when new crops have been harvested. As one wishes, *shraddhas*[660] should be performed at these times. In this way, the ancestors are satisfied for eight years when *shraddha*s are performed at the time of *amavasya*, when Maitra,[661] Vishakha or Svati are in the ascendant. If the ancestors are worshipped at the time of *amavasya* when the *nakshatra*s Pushya, Roudra[662] and Punarvasu are in the ascendant, they obtain satisfaction for twelve years. At the time of *amavasya*, when the *nakshatra*s

---

[656] Known as *darsha shraddha*. *Darsha* is the night of the new moon. But this also signifies that the moon will now wax.

[657] Known as *ashtaka shraddha*. *Ashtaka shraddha*s are typically performed during the months of Margashirsha (also known as Agrahayana), Pousha, Magha and Phalguna. Margashirsha is roughly mid-November to mid-December while Pousha is mid-December to mid-January. Magha is mid-January to mid-February and Phalguna is mid-February to mid-March.

[658] Known as *kamya shraddha*. *Kamya shraddha* is done for a specific purpose/desire.

[659] *Vyatipata* is an inauspicious period that lasts for almost twenty-four hours during every lunar month.

[660] *Kamya shraddhas*.

[661] Another name for Anuradha.

[662] Another name for Ardra.

Vasava, Ajaikapada and Varuna[663] are in the ascendant, if a man desires to please his ancestors, the satisfaction they obtain is extremely difficult for even *deva*s to get. O lord of the earth! At the time of *amavasya*, when these nakshatras are in the ascendant, these are the *shraddha*s that please the ancestors. Now hear about some others that Sanatkumara chanted about to the great-souled Aila,[664] when full of devotion towards the ancestors, he humbly asked. Sanatkumara replied, 'The third lunar day in the month of Vaishakha, the ninth lunar day in *shukla paksha* in the month of Karttika, the thirteenth lunar day in *krishna paksha* in the month of Nabhas[665] and the fifteenth lunar day in *krishna paksha* in the month of Magha. Those who know about the ancient accounts have said that these four days are sacred and mark the beginning of a *yuga*. On these days, when there is an eclipse of the sun or the moon, at the time of the three *ashtakas*[666] and at the start of an *ayana*, a man must control himself and offer water mixed with sesamum to the ancestors. The ancestors have revealed the secret that if a *shraddha* is performed at these times, they remain satisfied for one thousand years. O king! On the fifteenth lunar day in *krishna paksha* in the month of Magha, if the *nakshatra* Varuna happens to be in the ascendant, the satisfaction that the ancestors obtain is supreme and not a trifle. O protector of the earth! At the same time,[667] if Dhanishtha happens to be in the ascendant, food and water offered to the ancestors by men of their families satisfies them for ten thousand years. At a similar time, if Purva Bhadrapada happens to be in the ascendant, a

---

[663] Respectively, Dhanishtha, Purva Bhadrapada and Shatabhisha.

[664] Pururava.

[665] Shravana.

[666] There are four *ashtaka*s, so it is not obvious which three are meant, probably the ones in Margashirsha, Pousha and Phalguna.

[667] This seems to mean the fifteenth lunar day in *krishna paksha* in the month of Magha.

shraddha performed for the ancestors satisfies them for one thousand *yuga*s and they sleep in supreme contentment. After having lovingly worshipped the ancestors, if a man bathes in Ganga, Shatadru, Yamuna, Vipasha, Sarasvati or the Gomati in Naimisha, all his hardships are destroyed. The ancestors sing, "Our sons and others have again given us bliss and satisfaction by offering water to us at this auspicious *tirtha* at the end of *krishna paksha* in Magha." It is said that if the act is pure and is performed following the norms, at the right time, men obtain intelligence and wealth. It has been said that men who control themselves and devotedly undertake these rites are worthy recipients of everything auspicious. O lord of the earth! In this connection, there are *shloka*s sung by the ancestors. If you listen to these attentively, you will also obtain such benefits. "Our lineage, in which such an intelligent man has been born, is blessed. Without any deception, he has used his wealth to offer us *pinda*s. Let him obtain jewels, garments and all the objects of pleasure and let him be born in a noble lineage. At the right time, if a man faithfully feeds the best of *brahmana*s, according to his capacity, let him obtain prosperity. If he lacks the capacity to give them cooked food, let him give the best of *brahmana*s uncooked grain and a little bit of *dakshina*. If he is incapable of doing even that, he should prostrate himself before the best of *brahmana*s. He should take a few sesamum seeds on the tips of his fingers. Mixing the sesamum seed with water held in the cup of his hands, he should offer a libation to us and sprinkle this on the ground. Or he may gather as much of fodder as can be gathered in the course of a day and offer it to a cow. If he lacks means, but does this faithfully, it pleases us. If he lacks even this, he should go to a forest. He should raise his arms up to Surya and the guardians of the worlds and loudly state the following. 'I do not possess wealth and riches. I do not possess anything I can offer in a *shraddha* to my ancestors. Let them be satisfied with my raising my arms up towards the

path of the wind." Depending on what one possesses and what
one lacks, this is what the ancestors chanted about what needs
to be done. O lord of the earth! Anyone who acts accordingly
performs *shraddha*.'"

Chapter 3(15) (More on *Shraddha*s)

'Ourva said, "I will tell you about the qualities of
*brahmana*s to be fed at *shraddha*s. Listen to me.
He must be a person learned in *Trinachiketa*,[668] the three
*Madhu*s,[669] the three *Suparna*s,[670] and one who knows the six
*Vedanga*s. He must be learned in the *Veda*s. He must be a *yogi*,
accomplished in *Jyeshtha Sama*.[671] O king! The first invitees to
a *shraddha* are said to be the officiating priest, a sister's son,
a daughter' son, a son-in-law, a father-in-law, one devoted to
austerities, a person who follows the vows of the five fires,[672]
a disciple, a relation by marriage and a person who is devoted
to his father and mother. To satisfy the ancestors, a *brahmana*
has been thought of first, and then the others. The following
should never be invited to a *shraddha*: a *brahmana* who harms
his friends, has diseased nails, is a eunuch or has dark teeth, a
person who abuses a maiden, one who ignores the sacred fires
or the *Veda*s, a person who sells *soma*, a person who has been
accused, a thief, one who indulges in calumny, a person who
acts as an officiating priest for vulgar people, one who teaches

[668] *Trinachiketa* is a part of the *Yajur Veda*.
[669] The three verses in *Rig Veda* I.90.6–8.
[670] The *Yajur Veda* has three *mantra*s that are recited together,
and these are known as *trisuparna*.
[671] A *sukta* from the *Sama Veda*, typically recited at the time of a
shraddha.
[672] With four fires on four sides and the sun overhead.

servants, one who has been taught by a servant, the husband of a woman who has married before, a person who neglects his father and mother, one who nurtures the son of a *vrishala*,[673] the husband of a *vrishala* and one who is a priest at a temple. Let a wise person invite learned *brahmana*s and others on the first day and follow what they said on requirements for *deva*s and ancestors. Along with the *brahmana*s, let the person performing the *shraddha* refrain from anger and pleasures. These are great taints. Having fed *brahmana*s at a *shraddha* and having eaten himself, if a person engages in pleasures, he and his ancestors are immersed in a pit full of semen. The best of *brahmana*s, mentioned earlier, must be invited first. If a *brahmana* arrives without having been invited, he must also be fed. He must worship *brahmana*s who come to the house with water to wash the feet and other things. Once they have rinsed their mouths, holding sacred blades of grass in his hand, he must make them sit. For ancestors, an odd number of *brahmana*s must be invited. For *deva*s, an even number must be invited. However, for both ancestors and *deva*s, if he so wishes, it can be a single *brahmana*."'

"'Regardless of whether the *shraddha* is for the maternal grandfather or the Vishvadevas,[674] the principles are similar. Full of devotion, he must worship the Vishvadevas. For the maternal grandfather and Vishvadevas, when *brahmana*s are fed, they must be seated facing the east. For the father and the paternal ancestors, when they are fed, they must be seated facing the north. O king! Some say that the food cooked for a *shraddha* must be identical for the two sets of ancestors. Other *maharshi*s say they must be distinct. *Kusha*

[673] While this means *shudra*, it also means outcast.
[674] A *shraddha* for Vishvadevas is either a general *shraddha* or it covers both the maternal side and the paternal side.

is spread out for them[675] to be seated. Following the norms, they are then worshipped by giving them *arghya*. Taking their permission, a wise person then invokes *deva*s. A wise person who knows the rules will then offer barley mixed with water as an offering to *deva*s. Fragrances, garlands, incenses and lamps will be offered to them in the proper way. All the rites for the ancestors will be performed towards the right. Having obtained their permission,[676] double the quantity of *darbha* grass will be offered. A learned person must invoke the ancestors with *mantra*s. O king! To the right, he will render the *arghya* of water mixed with sesamum. O king! If a guest arrives at that time and desires food, with the permission of the *brahmana*s, he will feed him what he wishes. In different kinds of forms, *yogi*s do good deeds to men. They wander around the earth, their own forms remaining unknown. Therefore, a learned person will worship a guest who arrives at the time of a *shraddha*. O Indra among men! If a guest is not worshipped, he destroys the fruits of a *shraddha* rite. He will next offer food, without condiments or salt, into the fire. O bull among men! Taking the permission of the *brahmana*s, he will do this thrice. O king! The first oblation will be, 'To Agni, the bearer of oblations. Svaha.' The second will be, 'To Soma, revered by the ancestors. Svaha.' The third oblation will be, 'To Vaivasvata. Svaha.' What is left of the oblations must then be given to the *brahmana*s, in vessels. He must give then sweet food, which has been prepared well. Having given them the desired food he must address them in words that are not cruel. 'May you happily enjoy this.' Maintaining silence, they will attentively and happily enjoy the food. He must patiently and faithfully give them the food, without any anger. After this, he must chant *mantra*s that slay *rakshasa*s

[675] The *brahmana*s.
[676] Of the *brahmana*s.

and scatter sesamum seeds on the ground. He must next
meditate on his own ancesors. 'Along with these excellent
*brahmana*s, may my father, my grandfather and my great-
grandfather be satisfied. They are present in the bodies of
these *brahmana*s. Along with them, let them be satisfied
today. Let my father, grandfather and great-grandfather be
content. They have come here in these forms. Let them be
content with my libations today. Let my father, grandfather
and great-grandfather be content, satisfied with the *pinda* I
have laid down on the ground. Let my father, grandfather
and great-grandfather be content, satisfied with the libations
I have faithfully offered. Let my maternal grandfather,
his father and all his other ancestors be satisfied. Let the
Vishvadevas obtain supreme satisfaction. Let *yatudhanas*[677]
be destroyed. The lord Hari's *atman* is immeasurable. He is
the lord of sacrifices. May he enjoy the *havya* and *kavya* that
has been offered. In his presence, let all the *rakshasa*s and
*asura*s immediately leave this place.' When the *brahmana*s
have been satisfied, some food must be spread out on the
ground. Each of them must be given clean water to rinse
their mouths once. When they are extremely content, with all
their permission, some food must be laid out on the ground.
Controlling himself, he will properly place this *pinda*, mixed
with sesamum. Using *pitri tirtha*, he will offer them a libation
of water, joining both his hands together. Using *pitri tirtha*,
he will offer a *pinda* to his maternal grandfather. Near the
leftover food, he must offer the first *pinda* to his own father,
spread out on *darbha* grass, with the blades pointing south
and along with consecrated flowers and incense. The second
will be offered to the grandfather and the third to the great-
grandfather. Those who subsist on *lepa* are pleased when

[677] A class of demons.

he wipes his hand with the roots of the *darbha* grass.[678]
Similarly, he will worship *brahmana*s first, giving them water
to rinse their mouths. After this, he will offer a *pinda* to his
maternal grandfather, along with fragrances and garlands.
O lord of men! Attentive in his mind, he must first faithfully
offer the *pinda* to his paternal ancestors. According to
capacity, he will give *dakshina* to the *brahmana*s, who will
pronounce benedictions, uttering the words 'svadha'. After
giving them the *dakshina*, he will speak to the Vishvadevas.
'May the Vishvadevas be pleased with this.' The *brahmana*s
will agree to this and pronounce the required benedictions.
O lord of the earth! Thereafter, the paternal ancestors will
be granted permission to leave, followed by *deva*s.[679] That
is also said to be the order in which the maternal ancestors
and *deva*s are released. Beginning with the washing of the
feet, the rites for *deva*s and *brahmana*s involve, according to
one's capacity, feeding, donations and *visarjana*. *Visarjana*
must first be done for paternal ancestors and then for
maternal ancestors. The *visarjana* for *brahmana*s must be
done respectfully, with pleasant words. When they take his
permission and leave, he must accompany them all the way
up to the door. After this, a learned man will perform the
nitya rites for the Vishvadevas. He will worship them and
himself eat, along with his relatives and servants. In this
way, a learned person performs *shraddha* for his paternal
and maternal ancestors. When they are honoured through
a *shraddha*, the ancestors bestow everything that is desired.

---

[678] *Lepa* means wiping, in this case, the wiping of the hand
after *pinda*s have been offered. The right to *pinda* stops with the
third person in the lineage, the fourth is no longer entitled. Fourth
generation upwards becomes *lepabhuja*, surviving on *lepa*.

[679] *Visarjana* is sending away or dismissal, the end of the worship.
The beginning of the worship is *avahana* or invocation.

For a *shraddha*, three things are sacred: a daughter's son, a *brahmana*[680] and sesamum. Donation or the mention of silver is also propitious. O Indra among kings! Three things are not recommended in the course of a *shraddha*: anger, walking down a slope and hurrying. O king! The Vishvadevas, the paternal ancestors and the maternal ancestors all are nourished through a *shraddha* a man performs. The large number of ancestors are sustained by the moon. The moon is sustained through *yoga*. O protector of the earth! Therefore, at a *shraddha*, the presence of a *yogi* is praised. A *yogi* is placed ahead of one thousand *brahmana*s. O king! In this way, the person undertaking the rite makes everyone cross over and enjoys the objects of pleasure."'

Chapter 3(16) (The Permitted and the Condemned)

'Ourva said, "For *havishya* food,[681] ancestors are nourished for one month with fish, flesh of a hare, mongoose, pig, goat, *ena* deer, *ruru* antelope, *gavaya* and sheep or with products obtained from a cow. They are always satisfied for a month with the flesh of a rhinoceros.[682] O lord of men! The flesh of a rhinoceros, the herb known as *kalashaka* and honey is praised for such rites and gives them endless

---

[680] The word used is *kutapa*. So, it can also be translated as *kusha* grass. That will also fit.

[681] *Havishya* is food that can be offered as oblations. It is simple and has no seasoning. It is only eaten on special occasions, such as when a vow is being observed.

[682] *Vardhinasa*. Interpretations have taken this word to mean some kind of bird, but that isn't very convincing.

satisfaction. O lord of the earth! If a person goes to Gaya and performs *shraddha* there, his birth become successful, and his ancestors obtain satisfaction. O bull among men! *Prasatika*,[683] *nivara*,[684] the two types of *shyamaka*[685] and wild vegetables are fit to be offered at a *shraddha*. Also appropriate are barley, *priyangu*,[686] *mudga*, wheat, paddy, sesamum, *nishpava*,[687] *kovidara*[688]and mustard. O lord of men! When not cleaned, the first paddy of the season, *rajamasha*,[689] *anu*,[690] *masura*,[691] gourd, garlic, onion, *pindamulaka*,[692] *gandharaka*,[693] *karamva*[694] and salt thrown up from a salty desert must be avoided. The red extract from vegetables and direct use of salt should also be avoided. Their use in a *shraddha* is not recommended. O king! Water that has been collected at night, water that is so little that it will not satisfy a cow and water that stinks and is frothy is not appropriate for a *shraddha*. In *shraddha* rites, milk from animals with undivided hooves, camels, sheep, deer and buffaloes should be avoided. O bull among men! Gods and ancestors do not partake of food offered at a *shraddha* when it has been looked at by a eunuch, a person who has been cast out, a *chandala*, a heretic, a diseased person, a cock, a dog, a naked person,

---

[683] A kind of rice with small grains. The text says *prashantika*, which is a typo, and we have corrected it.

[684] Wild rice.

[685] A kind of grain. The two types are white and black.

[686] Saffron.

[687] Winnowed corn.

[688] Fruit of the Indian coral tree.

[689] Kind of bean, *chana*.

[690] Millet.

[691] *Masoor dal*.

[692] Carrot.

[693] Kind of plant, *Hedysarum alhagi*, the legume known as camelthorn.

[694] This should probably be *karanja*, a medicinal plant.

a village pig, a woman going through her season, a woman who has just given birth, an impure person or a bearer of corpses. Therefore, a *shraddha* must faithfully be performed in an enclosed space. To repel *yatudhanas*, sesamum should be sprinkled on the ground. O king! Food that has clippings of nails, hair or insects in it, food mixed with meat and food that is polluted must not be given. The food must be offered full of devotion, mentioning the names and *gotras* of the ancestors. It is this that becomes food for them. O lord of the earth! Earlier, a chant sung by the ancestors has been heard by Ikshvaku, Manu's son, in the grove of Kalapa. 'Let those who follow a virtuous path and those who lovingly offer a *pinda* to us in Gaya, be born in our lineage. Let those who offer us *payasam*, honey and *ghee* on the thirteenth lunar day during the monsoon,[695] when Magha is in the ascendant, be born in our lineage. When he marries a maiden who is a Gouri,[696] when he frees a black bull and when he performs a horse sacrifice, let him offer the appropriate *dakshina*.'"'

Chapter 3(17) (Praise of Vishnu)

Shri Parashara said, 'O Maitreya! In earlier times, this is what the illustrious Ourva told the great-souled Sagara, when he asked him about the complete nature of *sadachara*. O *brahmana*! I have told you everything about it. If one transgresses *sadachara*, one never obtains anything desirable.'

[695] The months of the rainy season, meaning Bhadrapada and Magha.

[696] A girl less than eight years of age, sometimes also defined as less than ten years of age.

Shri Maitreya asked, 'O illustrious one! I know about a eunuch, a person who has fallen and a woman in her season. But I wish to understand correctly what is meant by a naked person. Who is naked?[697] What kind of conducts leads to a man being described as naked? I wish that you should tell me about the true nature of being naked. O best among upholders of *dharma*! There is nothing that is unknown to you.'

Shri Parashara replied, 'O *brahmana*! The *varnas* are said to be covered in the three of *Rig Veda*, *Yajur Veda* and *Sama Veda*. In his delusion, if a *dvija* discards them, he is naked and is a sinner. O *brahmana*! These three are garments for all the *varnas*. If a person discards them, there is no doubt that he is naked. In this connection, hear what my grandfather, Vasishtha, who knew about *dharma*, told the great-souled Bhishma. I heard it from the great-souled one. O Maitreya! This concerns the question you asked me, about being naked. In ancient times, there was a battle between *devas* and *asuras* and it lasted for one hundred divine years. The *daityas*, with Hrada as their chief, defeated the *devas*. To worship Vishnu, they went to the northern shore of the milky ocean and tormented themselves through austerities. They chanted a hymn.'

'The *Devas* said, "For the sake of the worlds, we will utter these words to praise Lord Vishnu. May the illustrious Vishnu be pleased with us today. All beings originated from the great-souled one and it is into him that they will dissolve. Who is capable of praising the great Lord? You are beyond words. However, we are terrified, and our valour has been destroyed. We do not know your true nature. But we will use these words of praise to praise you. Everything is inside you—earth, water, fire, wind, space, Pradhana and Purusha. Everything is a manifestation of your body, though

[697] The word *nagna* means naked. But it also has a metaphorical sense and is used for a hypocrite or a mendicant.

you yourself are disembodied. Everything, from Brahma to a pillar, is you, though differences appear because of time and place. He is the lord who earlier emerged from the lotus in your navel. For the welfare of the universe, you assumed that form. I bow down to the one who has Brahma in his *atman*. Shakra, Arka, Rudra, the Vasus, the Ashvins, the Maruts, Soma and other differentiations, and even we, are your own form. I bow down before that divinity. O Govinda! Your form is also in the *daitya*s, who are generally full of insolence and lack understanding. They are devoid of fortitude and self-control. I prostrate myself before that form. Your form is in *yaksha*s, who do not possess the knowledge to comprehend your limitless energy. They are seduced by sounds and the like. I prostrate myself before that form. O Purushottama! Your form resides in roamers of the night.[698] They are terrible, cruel and full of *maya*. I prostrate myself before that form. O Janardana! Your form is known as that of *dharma*. This path of *dharma* is followed by those who reside in heaven. You are the fruits and the means of accomplishing that *dharma*. I prostrate myself before that form. Your form is known as that of the *siddha*s. They are generally full of delight because of their association with you. They can go wherever they wish. I prostrate myself before the one who has the *siddha*s in his *atman*. O Hari! There are the *naga*s, never satiated with objects of pleasure. They are cruel and do not follow the path of being forgiving. Their tongues are forked. I prostrate myself before the one who has the *naga*s in his *atman*. O one whose form pervades the universe! As a *rishi*, you are free from taints and sins. You possess knowledge and serenity. I prostrate myself before the one who has the *rishi*s in his *atman*. O Pundarikaksha! At the end of a *kalpa*, you are unrestrained and devour beings. I prostrate myself before the one who has

[698] *Nishachara*s (demons).

Kala in his *atman*. In your form as Rudra, you destroy all beings, *deva*s and others, and dance. I prostrate myself before the one who has Rudra in his *atman*. O Janardana! Driven by compassion, you undertake acts of *rajas*, assuming a human form. I prostrate myself before the one who has humans in his *atman*. Your *tamas* form, with the twenty-eight defects,[699] exists in all beings and makes them follow deviant paths. I prostrate myself before the one who controls them in this way. For the sake of preserving the universe, your form exists in the different limbs of a sacrifice. You are the six kinds of trees and others.[700] I prostrate myself before that foremost *atman*. It is your original form that is in everything—inferior species, humans, *deva*s, the sky, sound and other objects of the senses. I prostrate myself before the one who is in every *atman*. You are the *paratman*. Your form pervades Pradhana, *buddhi* and everything else, but you are also distinct. You are without parallel. I prostrate myself before the cause behind all causes. You do not possess complexions, like fair and the others. You do not possess form, like length and others. You do not possess denseness, like weight and others. You are beyond the perception of all adjectives. You are purer than the most pure. Only the supreme *rishi*s can perceive your form. O illustrious one! I bow down before you. You are in our bodies. You are in all other bodies. You are the one who should be praised. You are without decay. There is nothing beyond you. The *brahman* is your form. We bow down before you. You are without origin, and you are present in everything. You are

[699] This is interpreted as twenty-eight kinds of animals, six with single hooves, nine with cloven hooves and thirteen with claws/nails.

[700] There are six kinds of trees and plants: *agrabija* (those where flowers provide the seed), *mulaja* (those born from joints), *skandhaja* (those born from a trunk), *bijaruha* (those that sprout from a seed, like grain), *gulma* (creepers) and *trina* (grass).

the supreme destination. You are eternal. You are the refuge. You are the seed of everything. You are the Lord, without any blemishes. We bow down before that Vasudeva."'

Parashara continued, 'When they finished their hymn, the gods saw Parameshvara Hari. He was astride Garuda, with the conch shell, the *chakra* and the mace in his hand. All the gods prostrated themselves before him and spoke. "O protector! We seek refuge with you, so that we can be saved from the *daityas*. Please show us your favours. With Hrada as their chief, the *daityas* have robbed us of the three worlds and our shares in sacrifices. O Parameshvara! They have transgressed Brahma's rules. All of us have originated from your portion. Nevertheless, because of ignorance, we perceive the world to be differentiated. Every *varna* engages in its own *dharma* and follows the path indicated in the *Vedas*. We have also engaged in austerities, but we are incapable of destroying them. O illustrious one! Please pardon us. But please show all of us a means, whereby we can kill the *asuras*." Addressed in this way, from his body, the illustrious Vishnu produced an illusory form fashioned out of *maya*. He gave this to the excellent gods and spoke to them. "This is Mayamoha[701] and it will delude all the *daityas*. Thus, those who have deviated from the path of the *Vedas* will be destroyed. O *devas*! For the sake of preservation of creation, those who act contrary to the rights stated by Brahma should be destroyed by me. O gods! Leave. You need not be afraid. Mayamoha will proceed ahead of you. O gods! For the sake of your welfare, he will leave with you." Thus addressed, *devas* prostrated themselves and returned to wherever they had come from. Along with them, Mayamoha went to the place where the great *asuras* were.'

---

[701] *Maya* is illusion and *moha* is delusion.

Chapter 3(18) (Buddha and Heretics)

Shri Parashara said, 'O Maitreya! Mahaymoha went and
saw that the great *asuras* were engaged in austerities, along
the banks of the Narmada. O *brahmana*! He assumed the form
of a naked mendicant, with a shaven head and holding a bunch
of peacock feathers. Mayamoha addressed the *asuras* in gentle
words. Mayamoha said, "O lords of the *daityas*! Tell me. What
is the purpose of tormenting yourselves through austerities?
Through austerities, do you desire fruits in this world, or in the
next world?" The *asuras* replied, "O immensely intelligent one!
We are pursuing austerities for the sake of obtaining fruits in the
next world. That is the reason we have started them. Why are
you asking us?" Mayamoha said, "If you desire emancipation,
act in accordance with my words. You deserve to be told about
the *dharma* that is a door to emancipation. This is the *dharma*
of emancipation. There is nothing other than this or superior to
this. If you follow this, you will either go to heaven or obtain
emancipation. All of you are extremely strong. You deserve to
know about this *dharma*." In this way, Mayamoha persuaded
the *daityas* with many kinds of arguments and they abandoned
the path of the *Vedas*. Mayamoha told them many different
things, not just one. The same thing might lead to both *dharma*
and *adharma*, existence and non-existence, emancipation
and lack of emancipation, the supreme objective or not the
supreme objective. Therefore, what should be done and what
should not be done, is not at all clear. Since *dharma* dons many
kinds of garments, the *dharma* of those who go around naked
is unclear.[702] O *brahmana*! Taught in this way, the *daityas*
abandoned their own *dharma*. Mayamoha told them, "You
deserve to be taught about this great *dharma*." They thus came

---

[702] Mendicants.

to be known as Arhatas.[703] Mayamoha persuaded the *asura*s
to abandon the *dharma* of the three.[704] Immersed in this, they
taught others. Those whom they taught, taught others and so
on. Within a few days, most of the *daitya*s gave up the three.'

'Next, Mayamoha conquered his senses and donned red
clothing. He went to other *asura*s and addressed them in
gentle and sweet words. "O *asura*s! If you desire heaven, or
if you desire emancipation, then enough of killing animals.
Understand that this is wicked *dharma*. Understand that this
is all there is to *vijnana*. Comprehend my words. These are
in complete conformity with what the learned have said. This
world is without a foundation. Those who seek for a meaning
are bewildered by the wrong kind of knowledge. Excessive
attachment and similar sentiments make us whirl around in
this hardship of *samsara*." In this way, he told them, "Know."
They replied, "It has been known." and came to be known as
those who knew.[705] Mayamoha made the *daitya*s deviate from
their own *dharma*. He addressed them in many kinds of ways
and used diverse arguments. Wherever they were engaged in
following the *dharma* of the three, they were taught to deviate
from this and those who were taught, instructed others. O
Maitreya! In this way, the supreme *dharma* spoken about in
the *Veda*s and the *smriti* texts was given up. O *brahmana*!
There were many other different kinds of *pashanda*s.[706]
Mayamoha deluded the *daitya*s. Within a short space of time,
the *asura*s were confounded by Mayamoha. Thus deluded, all
of them gave up what is referred to as the path of the three. O

[703] '*Arhatha*' means 'You are worthy of'. Arhata is a term used for
a Buddhist or Jain mendicant. Subsequent *shloka*s allude to specific
Buddhist and Jain teachings.

[704] The three *Veda*s.

[705] In different grammatical forms, the words used for 'know' in
the text are based on the root *budh*. Thus, they became Bouddhas.

[706] Heretics.

brahmana! Some criticized the *Veda*s. Others criticized *deva*s. Others criticized the rites of sacrifices. Still others criticized *brahmana*s. They uttered the following words. "One should not follow a *dharma* that leads to violence. It is childishness to say that offering oblations into the fire will lead to fruits. How can Indra obtain the status of a *deva* by subsisting on oblations offered at sacrifices? It is better to save the wood. Animals that subsist on leaves are superior. If slaying an animal at a sacrifice leads to heaven, isn't it better for a person performing the sacrifice to kill his own father? If a person lives somewhere else, he might as well make the effort to eat food himself, instead of getting someone else at home to eat it for him.[707] Like that, how can food offered at a *shraddha* satisfy someone else?[708] Let if first be understood what drives faith in people. It is better to ignore those words. The words spoken by me are preferable. O *asura*s! Words of wisdom do not descend onto the ground from the sky. You should accept the words of reason spoken by me, not those spoken by others." In this way, Mayamoha addressed the *daitya*s in many different kinds of ways. They no longer found what was mentioned in the three as agreeable and thought these were futile. When the *daitya*s had thus deviated from the virtuous path, the immortals made great efforts to fight with them. O *brahmana*! Yet again, there was a battle between *deva*s and *asura*s. Since they acted contrary to the virtuous path, the *asura*s were slaughtered by *deva*s. O *brahmana*! The foremost armour is the following of one's own *dharma*. Formerly, they were protected by this. When it was destroyed, they were destroyed.'

'O Maitreya! Thus, people who have deviated from the path are naked. They have abandoned the covering provided

---

[707] To make the meaning clear, we have expanded the translation a bit.

[708] The ancestor.

by the three. When they criticized the *Veda*s in many kinds
of ways, this is what happened to the *asura*s, defeated by
*deva*s. There are four *ashramas*: *brahmacharya*, *garhasthya*,
vanaprastha and the fourth of becoming a mendicant.[709] There
is no fifth. O Maitreya! If a man in *garhasthya* gives up material
objects and does not proceed for *vanaprastha* or becoming a
mendicant, he is also wicked and naked. O *brahmana*! There
are *nitya* rites that have to be performed day and night. If one
does not perform these recommended tasks, even if one is
capable, one falls down for one day. O Maitreya! A man who
does not undertake these *nitya* rites for an entire fortnight, has
to make great efforts of *prayashchitta* to purify himself. If a
man does not undertake these rites for an entire year, he goes
to hell. Having looked at such a wicked person, one must look
at the sun. O immensely intelligent one! Having touched such a
wicked person, one must bathe with one's clothes on. However,
for the evildoer who performs the wicked act, no purification
has been spoken about. In this world, there is no evildoer as
great as a *brahmana* from whose house *deva*s, *rishi*s, ancestors
and beings leave, without being honoured. O *brahmana*! If a
person speaks, converses or laughs with one who is so wicked,
as to not having performed the rites for an entire year, he too
reaps an equal dose of sin. If the bodies of *deva*s and other suffer
in a person's house and they are made to sigh, they pollute his
house, his seats and his garments. Accordingly, if one eats in
such a person's house, sits on his seat or sleeps on his bed, one
instantly reaps the same degree of sin. If a person does not
honour *deva*s, ancestors, ancestors and creatures and himself
eats instead, he partakes of sin and there is no salvation for
him. *Brahmana*s and other *varna*s who turn their faces away
from their own *dharma* are known as those who are naked.
They are like those who engage in inferior deeds. O Maitreya!

[709] *Sannyasa*.

If a person has a connection with a place where the four *varna*s are mixed up, his good conduct suffers. If a man converses with someone who eats before honouring *rishi*s, *deva*s, ancestors, creatures and guests, he descends into hell. Those who discard the three are polluted and naked. Therefore, a wise person must always avoid conversation with them, contact with them and so on. A *shraddha* ceremony may be conducted carefully. But if such people look at it, *deva*s, ancestors and grandfathers are displeased.'

'It has been heard that, earlier, there was a king named Shatadhanu on earth. His wife was Shaivya, and she was devoted to *dharma*. The immensely fortunate one was devoted to her husband. She was truthful, pure and compassionate. She possessed all the auspicious signs. She was humble and knew about good policy. Along with her, the king worshipped Lord Janardana, lord of the gods. He faithfully immersed himself in great meditation, oblations, *japa*, donations and fasting. He worshipped him attentively every day, with nothing else in his mind. Once, along with his wife, the husband bathed in the waters of the Bhagirathi. O *brahmana*! It was the day of the full moon in Karttika. As he got up from the water, he saw a *pashanda* approaching. He was a friend of the *acharya* who taught the great-souled one archery. Because of respect due to him and because of friendliness, he conversed with him. However, his wife, the queen who was devoted to her husband, did not speak to him. Since she was fasting, when she saw him, she turned her glance away and looked at the sun. O supreme among *brahmana*s! Having returned, following the proper norms, the couple worshipped Vishnu and did everything that was needed for this. After a long period of time, having defeated his rivals, the king died. The queen followed him and ascended the funeral pyre of her husband, the king.'

'While fasting, the lord of the earth had conversed with a *pashanda*. Because of that sin, he was born as a dog. The auspicious one was born as the daughter of the king of Kashi, and she remembered her former birth. She was respected and possessed every kind of knowledge. She possessed all the auspicious signs. Her father wished to bestow her on a groom, but she restrained him. The king was thus restrained by her from any attempt to get her married off. With her divine insight, she saw that her own husband had been born as a dog. She went to the city known as Vidisha and saw him there, in that state. She saw her immensely fortunate husband, in the form of a dog. Following good conduct, the auspicious one placed the bridal garland around his neck. He ate the sweet food she gave him. However, he desired to act like his own species. Therefore, he played a lot and wagged his tail.[710] The maiden was ashamed at this and addressed him in agreeable words. She prostrated herself first and then spoke to her beloved, who had been born as inferior species. "O great king! Please remember why you have been reduced to flattering me in this way. After bathing at a *tirtha*, out of compassion and kindliness, you conversed with a *pashanda* and have been born as a dog. That is the reason you have been born as this inferior species. O lord! Don't you remember?" He was thus reminded by her about what he had done earlier. He thought for a long time and was filled with non-attachment, which is so very difficult to obtain. Distressed in his mind, he went outside the city.'

'He fell down and died there and was born as a jackal. Through her divine insight, she saw that he had been born a second time. Knowing this, she went to Mount Kolahala to see the jackal. She saw him there, born as a jackal, and spoke to him. The king's daughter, beautiful in her limbs, spoke to her husband. "O Indra among kings! Do you remember

[710] Strictly speaking, this is a mistranslation. The word used is *chatukara*, meaning, to indulge in flattery. For a dog, this is better translated as wagging the tail and rolling over on its stomach.

that I spoke to you when you had been born as a dog? That
happened because of what you had done earlier, engaging in
conversation with a *pashanda*." Because of what she said, the
supreme among truthful ones discerned the truth. He went to
a forest. He fasted there and gave up his body. This time, he
was born as a wolf. The unblemished one went and reminded
her husband about what had occurred earlier. "O immensely
fortunate one! You are not a wolf. You are King Shatadhanu.
Earlier, you were a dog, then a jackal. You have now become
a wolf." Reminded by her, he gave up his life and became a
vulture. The innocent and beautiful one reminded him again.
"O Indra among men! Enough of this behaving like a vulture.
Please remember. Because of the sin of conversing with a
pashanda, you have become a vulture." He remembered his
past lives and was born as a crow. Understanding this, the
slender-limbed one spoke to her husband again. "All the
kings used to offer you tribute earlier. O lord! You have
now become a crow that thrives on offerings scattered on the
ground."[711] In this way, he next became a crane. Remembering
what had happened earlier, the king gave up his life and was
born as a peacock. When he became a peacock, the auspicious
one adopted him. The maiden gave him food all the time—
food that was appropriate for his species. At that time, King
Janaka organized a huge horse sacrifice. At the *avabhritha*,[712]
the slender-limbed one bathed and bathed the peacock. She
reminded him of his birth as a jackal and other things and
the king understood. The extremely great-souled one gave
up his body and was born as Janaka's son. The father of the
slender-limbed one arranged for her marriage. Hence, the king

[711] There is a play on words. *Bali* means both tribute and offerings.
[712] *Avabhritha* is the most important final component of a
sacrifice, characterized by the taking of a bath.

organized a *svayamvara*.[713] The beautiful one continued to think of him as her husband. Therefore, when the *svayamvara* took place, she again chose him as her husband. Along with her, the prince enjoyed himself. When his father died, he ruled over the kingdom of Videha.[714] He performed a large number of sacrifices and donated to those who wanted things. He had sons and fought against his enemies. Following the rules, he enjoyed the kingdom and protected the earth. Following *dharma*, the king gave up his beloved life in a battle. The one with the auspicious eyes again ascended her husband's funeral pyre. As was the case earlier, she ascended the pyre and cheerfully followed him. Along with the princess, the lord of the earth obtained inexhaustible worlds, beyond Indra's world. O supreme among *brahmana*s! Such are the auspicious fruits obtained through purification. Such a couple is extremely rare. They obtained the unmatched and inexhaustible fruits of heaven.'

'O *brahmana*! I have thus spoken to you about taints associated with conversing with a *pashanda* and about the greatness of a horse sacrifice and *avabhritha*. Therefore, one should shun the sin of conversing with a *pashanda*, or seeing him, especially at the time of undertaking a rite or when one has consecrated oneself for a sacrifice. If the rites due to be performed by a householder are not performed for a month, an intelligent man must look at the sun for a month. O *brahmana*! What needs be said about a person who gives up the path of the three, is fed by a *pashanda* or is so wicked as to act against the words of the *Veda*s? Conversing with such a person, association with such a person and laughing with such

---

[713] *Svayamvara* is a ceremony where the maiden herself (*svayam*) chooses her husband (*vara*) from assembled suitors.

[714] Videha was King Janaka's kingdom. There were several kings named Janaka. This Janaka is not Sita's father.

a person are extremely terrible sins. One must avoid *pashanda*s and those who are wicked in conduct. One should not greet with words *pashanda*s, those who perform contrary deeds, those who are as hypocritical as cats, those who are deceitful, those who unnecessarily look for causes and those who are as hypocritical as cranes. One should avoid any association with such extremely wicked ones, even from a distance. Hence, one must shun *pashanda*s and those who are evil in conduct. These are known as those who are naked. When they see a *shraddha*, it is destroyed. If a man speaks with them, his good merits are destroyed for a day. These are *pashanda*s and wicked people. A learned person will not converse with them. If one converses with them, all the good merits obtained during the day are destroyed. There are men who wear matted hair, shave their heads, commit the sin of eating in vain,[715] are impure in every kind of way and perform wicked deeds. They are barred from offering water and *pinda*s to the ancestors. If a man converses with them, he goes to hell.'

This ends Part III

---

[715] Without having made offerings first.

Part IV

Chapter 4(1) (*Surya Vamsha* and *Chandra Vamsha*)

Maitreya said, 'O illustrious one! O *guru*! You have told me about the *nitya* and *naimmitika karma* a virtuous man must follow. You have also described to me the *dharma* of the *varna*s and the *dharma* of the *ashrama*s. I now wish to hear about the lineages of the kings. O *guru*! Please tell me about it.'

273

Shri Parashara replied, 'O Maitreya! Starting with Brahma, there have been many kings who have ornamented Manu's lineage. They have performed many sacrifices. They have been brave, valiant and patient. Hear about them. If one hears everything about their lineages, all one's sins are destroyed. O Maitreya! Hear about their account. At the beginning of the entire universe, there was the illustrious Vishnu, who is without a beginning. The *Rig*, *Yajur* and *Sama Veda*s were in him. Brahma was his embodied form. Within *brahmanda*, the illustrious Hiranyagarbha Brahma manifested himself first. Daksha Prajapati was born from Brahma's right thumb. His daughters were Diti and Aditi. Aditi's son was Vivasvat and Vivasvat's son was Vaivasvata Manu. Manu had ten sons: Ikshvaku, Nriga, Dhrishta, Sharyati, Narishyanta, Pramshu, Nabhaga, Dishta, Karusha and Prishadhra. Earlier, desiring a son, Manu had performed a sacrifice to Mitra and Varuna. However, since there was a deviation in the offering of oblations, a daughter named Ila resulted. O Maitreya! Through the favours of Mitra and Varuna, when shown to Manu, she became a son named Sudyumna. Again, because of Ishvara's rage, she turned into a woman.[716] She wandered around, near the hermitage of Budha, Soma's son. Budha fell in love with her and through her, Pururava was born. When he was born, the infinitely energetic and supreme *rishi*s performed a sacrifice to the illustrious one,[717] desiring that Ila should be restored to manhood, as Sudyumna. The *Rig*, *Yajur*, *Sama* and *Atharva Veda*s are in him. The mind is in him. *Jnana* is in him. There is nothing that is not in him. It is his own form that is the

---

[716] Shiva and Parvati were alone and anyone who entered that secluded place would become feminine. When Parvati interceded, the curse was made temporary. In this account, this was because of Vishnu's favours.

[717] Vishnu.

personified form of the sacrifice. Through that sacrifice, Ila again became Sudyumna. He had three sons, Utkala, Gaya and Vinata. However, since Sudyumna had been a woman earlier, he did not get a share in the kingdom. Urged by Vasishtha's words, his father bestowed on him the city named Pratishthana.[718] In turn, he gave it to Pururava.'

'All the other kshatriya sons were given different directions.[719] Manu's son, Prishadhra, happened to kill his guru's cow and because of this, became a shudra. The sons of Manu's son, Karusha, were the Kaarusha kshatriyas. They were immensely strong and valiant. Dishta's son, Nabhaga,[720] became a vaishya.[721] He had a son named Balandhana and his son was Vatsapriti, pervasive in his deeds. Vatsapriti's son was Pramshu.[722] Pramshu's son was Prajapati and Prajapati's son was Khanitra. Khanitra's son was Chakshusha and Chakshusha's son was the immensely valiant Vimsha. Vimsha's son was Vivimshaka and Vivimshaka's son was Khaninetra. Khaninetra's son was Ativibhuti and Ativibhuti's son was the immensely strong and valiant Karandhama. Karandhama's son was Avikshit and Avikshit had an immensely strong and valiant son named Marutta. Even now, a shloka is chanted about him. "On earth, there has never been a sacrifice like that of Marutta. At that extremely wonderful sacrifice, every object was made out of gold. Indra was intoxicated with soma juice and brahmanas with dakshina they received. The Maruts protected the sacrifice, and the residents of heaven were officiating priests." Chakravarti Marutta had a son

[718] Usually, but not invariably, identified as Paithan in Maharashtra.
[719] As shares of the ancestral kingdom.
[720] Clearly not the same as Manu's son, Nabhaga.
[721] Because he married a vaishya lady.
[722] Clearly a different Pramshu.

named Narishyanta. His son was Dama and Rajavardhana
was born as Dama's son. Rajavardhana's son was Suvriddhi
and Suvriddhi's son was Kevala. Kevala's son was Sudhriti
and Sudhriti's son was Nara. Nara's son was Chandra and
Chandra's son was Kevala.[723] Kevala's son was Bandhumat
and Bandhumat's son was Vegavat. Vegavat's son was Budha
and Budha's son was Trinavindu. Trinavindu had a daughter
named Ilavila. The beautiful *apsara* named Alambusa fell in love
with Trinavindu. Through him, she had a son named Vishala,
who constructed the city named Vishala.[724] Vishala's son was
Chandra and Chandra's son was Dhumraksha. Dhumraksha's
son was Srinjaya and Srinjaya's son was Sahadeva. Sahadeva
had a son named Krishashva. Krishashva's son was Somadatta,
who performed one hundred horse sacrifices. Somadatta's son
was Janamejaya and Janmejaya's son was Sumati. These were
the kings in the city of Vishala. In this connection, a *shloka*
is chanted. "Through Trinavindu's favours, all the kings who
ruled from Vishala had long lifespans. They were valiant, great-
souled and extremely devoted to *dharma*.'"

'Sharyati[725] had a daughter named Sukanya, who married
Chyavana. Chyavana had a son named Anarta, who was
extremely devoted to *dharma* and was descended from Sharyati.
Anarta had a son named Revata. He ruled over the dominion
known as Anarta and lived in the city known as Kushasthali.[726]
Revata had a son named Raivata, who was also known as
Kakudmi. He had *dharma* in his soul and was the eldest of
one hundred brothers. Raivata had a daughter named Revati.
Taking her with him, he went to the world of the illustrious
Brahma, who originated from a lotus, to ask him who he

---

[723] A second Kevala.
[724] Ujjayini is also known as Vishala.
[725] Vaivasvata Manu's son.
[726] Dvaravati or Dvaraka.

should bestow her on. At that time, in Brahma's presence, the *gandharvas* known as Haha and Huhu, and other divine *gandharvas*, were singing. As they sang in different tones and three accents,[727] Raivata stood there and listened. He thought that it was but one *muhurta*, but many *yugas* had actually passed. When the singing was over, Raivata prostrated himself before the illustrious one who originated from the lotus and asked him about an appropriate groom for his daughter. The illustrious one assured him and said, "Tell me. Who do you think is a worthy groom?" He prostrated himself again before the illustrious one and mentioned the desired grooms he had in mind. "O illustrious one! Among these, who do you think I should bestow my daughter on?" The illustrious one who originated from the lotus lowered his head a bit and smiled. He said, "The ones you have mentioned are no longer on earth now. Nor their sons or grandsons. Instead, their descendants are there, many generations down. As you listened to the *gandharvas* singing, many cycles of the four *yugas* have elapsed. Right now, the time of the twenty-eighth Manu is almost over and *kali yuga* is imminent. You should therefore wish to bestow this jewel among maidens on someone else. Time has passed by all your sons, friends, wives, ministers, servants, relatives, armies and treasuries." Anxious at hearing this, the king again prostrated himself before the illustrious one and asked, "O illustrious one! Since this is the state of affairs, who will I bestow her on?" He stood there, hands joined in salutation and shoulders lowered, before the illustrious one. The *guru* of all the worlds, who originated from a lotus, answered. Brahma said, "He is the creator of everything. He has no origin. We do not know about his beginning, middle or end. We do not know about Parameshvara's own nature, or his supreme form

---

[727] *Udatta* (acute accent, high pitch), *anudatta* (unstressed, low pitch) and *svarita* (high sounded pitch that falls).

and essence. He is Kala, with its components of *kala*, *muhurta* and others.[728] He is the cause behind all consequences. He is the embodied cause behind all birth and destruction. He has no name or form. He is eternal. It is because of Achyuta's favours that I have this form as the creator of beings and act accordingly. He is the supreme one, present in Rudra's rage. In the middle, for the sake of preservation, he is there as Purusha. The one without birth uses my form to create. In his own form of Purusha, he preserves. In the form of Rudra, he devours the universe. As Ananta, he holds everything up. In the form of Agni, he illuminates and cooks the world. In the form of the earth, he nourishes. In the form of Shakra and the others, he protects the world. In the form of Arka, he dispels darkness. In the form of the wind, he leads to enterprise. In the form of water and food, he provides satisfaction. In the form of space, for the sake of the existence of the entire universe, he provides all the required space. His *atman* is the creator and everything that is created. The divinity is the preserver and what is preserved. His *atman* is the destroyer and the universe which is destroyed. His *atman* does not decay, and he is separate from these three forms. The universe is in him. He is the universe. Svayambhu[729] is the origin of the universe, which finds a refuge in him. O king! He is the lord of all beings. A portion of Vishnu's powers has now descended on earth. O lord of the earth! Earlier, you used to possess a beautiful city, Kushasthali, which was like Amaravati. That is now known as Dvaraka. Keshava's portion is there, under the name of Baladeva. O Indra among men! Because of his *maya*, he is in the form of a man. You should bestow your daughter on him, as a wife. He is a worthy groom for your daughter. This jewel among women is equally an appropriate match for him." Having been thus addressed by

---

[728] Kaala and *kalaa* respectively.
[729] The one who creates himself. In this context, Vishnu.

the one who originated from the lotus, the lord of subjects returned to earth. He saw that men had become shorter. They were malformed and limited in energy. They were limited in valour and a sense of discrimination. The Indra among men, went to the city of Kushasthali and saw one who was different in form. This was the one who wielded the plough as a weapon. He wore a crystal around his neck, and it had the complexion of a mountain. His intelligence was unlimited. The one with the palm tree on his banner[730] saw that she was exceedingly tall. He used the tip of his plough to shorten her, and she instantly resembled other maidens. Following the prescribed norms of marriage, King Raivata bestowed his daughter, Revati, on him. Having bestowed his daughter, the king controlled his *atman* and went to the Himalayas to perform austerities.'

Chapter 4(2) (Other Descendants)

Shri Parashara said, 'When Raivata Kakudmi was away in Brahma's world, the *rakshasa*s known as Punyajanas destroyed his city of Kushasthali.[731] His one hundred brothers were terrified of the Punyajanas and fled in different directions. In different directions, their descendants became *kshatriya*s. Dhrishta's[732] sons became the *kshatriya*s known as Dharshtakas. Nabhaga had a son, also known as Nabhaga, and his son was Ambarisha. Ambarisha's son was Virupa and Virupa's son was Prishadashva. Prishadashva's son was

---

[730] Balarama has a palm tree on his banner.

[731] The word used is *punyajana*. *Saptajana* is a synonym. These were seven sages who were originally *rakshasa*s.

[732] The Dhrishta who was Vaivasvata Manu's son. The text says Vrishta. This is obviously incorrect, and we have amended it.

Rathitara. In this connection, there is a *shloka*. "Those born as *kshatriya*s in Rathitara's lineage are known as Angirasas. They were the best among *brahmana*s and *kshatriya*s." When Manu sneezed, Ikshvaku was born as his son, through his nose.[733] Ikshvaku had one hundred sons. The three who were the most important were known as Vikukshi, Nimi and Danda. He[734] had fifty sons, Shakuni being the foremost. They protected the region of Uttarapatha.[735] Another forty-eight were the kings in Dakshinapatha.[736] On the day of *ashtaka*,[737] Ikshvaku instructed Vikukshi, "For the sake of a *shraddha*, bring flesh that is appropriate." He agreed to this command. With a bow and arrow in his hand, he killed many deer in the forest. After this, Vikukshi was exhausted. Suffering from hunger, he killed a hare and ate it.[738] He brought the rest of the meat and gave it to his father. The preceptor of the lineage of Ikshvakus, Vasishtha, was requested to consecrate the meat. He said, "This meat is not fit to be offered. Since your evil-souled son has eaten a hare, the meat has been polluted." Because of the words spoken by the preceptor, Vikukshi came to be known as Shashada.[739] His father abandoned him. When his father died, Shashada followed *dharma* and ruled over the entire earth. Shashada had a son named Puranjaya.'

'Now, about something else. Earlier, in *treta yuga*, there was an extremely terrible battle between *deva*s and *asura*s. The immortals were defeated by the immensely strong *asura*s

---

[733] *Kshut* means to sneeze. Hence the name.

[734] Vikukshi.

[735] Literally, the northern road. The northern part of Jambudvipa.

[736] Literally, the southern road, the southern part.

[737] *Ashtaka* is the eighth lunar day, but during *krishna paksha*, the dark lunar fortnight.

[738] Since it had still not been offered at the *shraddha*, he should not have done this.

[739] One who has eaten a hare (*shasha*).

and started to worship the illustrious Vishnu. He is without
beginning and without an end. Narayana is the refuge of the
entire universe. He was pleased with *deva*s and said, "I know
about your wishes. Therefore, hear how it will come about.
There is a *rajarshi* named Puranjaya. He is Shashada's son,
and he is supreme among *kshatriya*s. In my portion, I will
myself descend in his body and slay all the *asura*s. Therefore,
for the sake of killing the *asura*s, engage Puranjaya." Hearing
his words, the immortals prostrated themselves before the
illustrious Vishnu and went to Puranjaya's presence. They
said, "O noble *kshatriya*! In the task of slaying our enemies,
we have come to you, desiring your help. That is the reason we
have come before you. You should not slight our affection."
Hearing this, Puranjaya replied, "Indra is the lord of the three
worlds. Let Shatakratu allow me to climb onto his shoulders.
I will then become your aide and fight with your enemies."
Hearing this, all *deva*s and Indra immediately agreed to this
wish. Shatakratu assumed the form of a bull and he seated
himself on its hump. The illustrious Achyuta is the *guru* of all
mobile and immobile objects and his energy pervaded him. In
the battle between *deva*s and *asura*s, he killed all the *asura*s.
Since he slaughtered the *daitya* army while he was seated on
the bull's hump, the king came to be known as Kakutstha.[740]
Kakutstha's son was Anenas and the son of Anenas was
Prithu. Prithu's son was Vrishtarashva, and his son was Ardra.
Ardra's son was Yuvanashva. Yuvanashva's son was Shavasta,
who constructed the city of Shavasti.[741] Shavasta's son was
Brihadashva and Brihadashva's son was Kuvalayashva. Filled

[740] *Kakud* means the hump of a bull. Kakutshtha is someone who
is seated on a hump.

[741] This is probably a typo. Other Puranas state this as Shravasta
and Shravasti. Shravasti is in UP, near Ayodhya, the capital of the
Kosala kingdom.

with Vishnu's energy, along with his twenty-one thousand sons, he surrounded and killed the *asura* named Dundu, who was harming *maharshi*s and causing impediments for them. He thus came to be known as Dundumara.[742] Because of the flames of fire that issued from Dundu's mouth, all his sons were destroyed. Only three were left: Dridhashva, Chandrashva and Kapilashva. Dridhashva's son was Haryashva and Haryashva's son was Nikumbha. Nikumbha's son was Amitashva and Amitashva's son was Krishashva. Krishashva's son was Prasenjit and Prasenjit's son was Yuvanashva.'

'Since he did not have any sons, Yuvanashva was distressed. He resided in a circle of hermitages of the sages. Driven by compassion towards him, the sages undertook a sacrifice for him so that he might have a son. When this was over, in the middle of the night, the sages placed a pot of water, filled with water over which *mantra*s had been pronounced, in the centre of the altar and went to sleep. While they slept, the lord of the earth felt extremely thirsty and entered the hermitage. Since the *rishi*s were asleep, he did not wake them up. He drank water from the pot, rendered powerful because of the *mantra*s. When they woke up, the *rishi*s asked, "Who has drunk the water purified with *mantra*s? Through this, King Yuvanashva's wife will give birth to an extremely strong and valiant son." Hearing this, the king replied, "In my ignorance, I have drunk it." Inside Yuvanashva's stomach, a fetus was conceived and gradually grew. When the time arrived, he used his right thumb to rip apart the king's side and emerged. The king died. When he was born, the sages asked, "Who will nurse him?" The king of the gods arrived and said, "I will nurse him." He thus came to have the name of Mandhata.[743] Indra

---

[742] The one who killed Dundu.

[743] He was known as Mandhata, from '*mam dhata*' meaning, 'Be suckled by me'.

placed his forefinger inside his mouth, and he drank from this. Nourished by this flow of *amrita*, he grew. Mandhata became a *chakravarti* and enjoyed the earth, with its seven *dvipas*. In this connection, there is a *shloka*. "The spot where the sun rises up to the spot where it sets, all this is said to be the dominion of Mandhata, Yuvanashva's son." Mandhata married Bindumati, Shashabindu's daughter. Through her, he had three sons, Purukutsa, Ambarisha and Muchukunda.'

'The lord of men also had fifty daughters. There was a *maharshi* named Soubhari, who was extremely learned in the hymns of the *Rig Veda*. At this time, he resided inside the water for twelve years. A lord of fish resided inside the water. His name was Sammada. He was large in size, and he had many offspring. He would swim around day and night, surrounded by his sons, sons of sons and sons of daughters, behind him, in front of him, along his sides and on top of his flanks, head and tail. The *rishi* saw how he was delighted when his offspring touched him and tugged at him in many kinds of ways and was distracted. Located inside the water, every day, Soubhari's concentration in meditation was disturbed. He saw the fish taking delight in his sons, sons of sons and daughters of sons. He thought, "How wonderful is someone like this. Though born as a different species, he is finding pleasure with his sons, sons of sons and sons of daughters. He has triggered a similar desire in me. I too wish to sport with my beloved sons in this way." He emerged from the water and made up his mind to search for a woman, so that he could have offspring. He went to King Mandhata. Hearing that he had come, the king immediately rose from his seat. He honoured him properly, with *arghya* and other things. When he had taken a seat, Soubhari spoke to the king. Soubhari said, "O Indra among men! Since I have made up my mind, please bestow one of your daughters on me. Please do not rebuff my affection. If someone asks something of a person belonging to the lineage

of Kakutstha, he does not leave refused. O Mandhata! There
are other kings on earth who have had daughters born to them.
You belong to the praised lineage of Ikshvaku, who are firm
in their vows. It is not their practice to refuse someone who
asks for something. O king! You have fifty daughters. Give
me one of them. I am scared that my request will be refused
by this supreme king and that I will be extremely miserable."
Hearing the *rishi*'s words, the king looked at his body. Because
of old age, the *rishi*'s body had decayed. On the other hand,
if he refused, he was scared that he might suffer on account
of a curse. Terrified, he remained in that state for some time,
his face cast downwards. Soubhari said, "O Indra among
kings! What are you thinking about? I have not spoken about
anything that is excessive. You should certainly bestow your
daughter on me. If you do so, there is nothing you will not be
able to accomplish." The king was scared that the illustrious
one would curse him. Therefore, he spoke humbly. The king
replied, "O illustrious one! It is the practice in our lineage
that a maiden makes her desired choice from among noble
grooms and the maiden is bestowed accordingly. O illustrious
one! Your desire is not yet known to my daughters. Until they
know, I do not know what I should do. That is the reason I
was thinking." Addressed by the king, the sage understood.
He thought, "This is a technique to refuse me. He is of the
view that I am an old man, with no appeal for women. Which
daughter will accept me?" He thought, "That being the case,
this is what I will do." Having thought, he replied to Mandhata.
"Since that is your recommended way, let a eunuch take me to
the inner quarters, where your daughters are. If any of your
daughters desire me, I will marry her. Otherwise, enough will
be enough. This will be ascribed to the large number of years
I have spent, and I will desist." Mandhata was scared that the
sage might curse him. Hence, he instructed a eunuch to take
him to the inner quarters, where the daughters were. When

he entered the inner quarters along with him, the illustrious one assumed a handsome form, surpassing all the *siddha*s and *gandharva*s. Entering the inner quarters, the eunuch spoke to the daughters. "Your father, the great king, has this instruction. This *brahmarshi* has come for a maiden. I have promised that if any of my daughters chooses the illustrious one, I will bestow her on him.[744] I will not act contrary to this." Hearing this, all the daughters were filled with love. They were like female elephants striving for the leader of the herd. Each said, "I will choose the *rishi*." Each told her sisters, "I have chosen him. He is not appropriate for you. Choose someone else. The creator has created him as my husband. I have also been created for him. Go away. Since I have chosen him first, I will accept him. Why are you creating an impediment?" A grave conflict arose amongst the daughters, as each said, "Mine. Mine." Out of their great love, the daughters fought with each other about the sage, whose deeds were unsullied. The person in charge of the inner quarters went and humbly reported to the king what had happened. Knowing this, the king exclaimed, "What is this? What will I do now? Why did I say that about the practice in my lineage?" Reluctantly, the king agreed that the *maharshi* should marry all his daughters. He married all the daughters and brought them to his hermitage.'

'Vishvakarma is the creator of all works of artisanship and is like the creator[745] himself. Having summoned him, he instructed him to construct a separate palace for each of the maidens. There were waterbodies, full of water, resonant with the sounds of swans, *karandava*s[746] and other aquatic birds. There were spaces, with excellent cushions, beds, garments

[744] The eunuch is conveying Mandhata's message.
[745] Brahma.
[746] A kind of duck.

and other objects. Tvashta,[747] the preceptor of every kind of
artisanship, did as he had been instructed. As instructed by
the supreme rishi, Soubhari, he used great *nidhi*s like *kunda* to
construct these residences.[748] There were supplies of excellent
food,[749] *lehya* and objects of pleasure, accompanied by servants.
With these inexhaustible supplies, the daughters of the king fed
and welcomed those who came.'

'On one occasion, the lord of the earth's heart was
attracted by love for his daughters. He wondered whether
they were happy or unhappy. Thinking this, he arrived at
the *maharshi*'s hermitage. He saw a garland of palaces made
out of crystals, as radiant as the rays of the sun. There were
enchanting groves and waterbodies. He entered one of these
palaces and embraced his daughter. He took his seat. Because
of his love and delight, there were drops of tears in his eyes.
The father asked the daughter, "O child! Are you happy here?
Is there the slightest bit of unhappiness? Does the *maharshi*
treat you with affection? Or do you remember the home with
me?" The daughter replied, "O father! Look at the enchanting
palace here. There are beautiful groves. There are waterbodies
with blossoming lotuses, resounding with the calls of swans
and other birds. There are food items, unguents, garments,
ornaments and objects of pleasure that are pleasing to the
mind. There are soft beds and seats. There is every kind of
affluence in my household. Therefore, why should I remember
my place of birth? Through your favours, I have obtained
everything that is wonderful. However, there is one reason for

[747] Vishvakarma.

[748] *Nidhi*s are Kubera's jewels and there are nine of these. The
usual list is Padma, Mahapadma, Shankha, Makara, Kacchapa,
Mukunda, Kunda, Nila and Kharba.

[749] The four types of food are those that are chewed (*charvya*),
sucked (*choshya* or *chushya*), licked (*lehya*) and drunk (*peya*).

me to be miserable. The *maharshi*, my husband, never leaves me. His great love is only for me. He does not approach any of my other sisters. I am therefore extremely sad on account of my sisters. There is nothing else." Having been told the reason for her misery, he went to a second palace. He embraced his daughter. Once he was seated, he asked about her welfare. She also told him that her palace possessed every kind of object of pleasure and happiness. However, she had only one reason for unhappiness. The *maharshi* was devoted only to her and neglected all her other sisters. In every palace that the king entered and asked his daughter, the daughter told him exactly this. Everyone told him this and he was content. But his heart was heavy with wonder. He approached the illustrious Soubhari, who was seated alone. He honoured him and said, "O illustrious one! I have witnessed the powers of your great *siddhi*.[750] I have not seen these kinds of powers in anyone else. O illustrious one! These are the fruits of your austerities." He worshipped the *rishi*. He spent some time with the noble *rishi*, enjoying the desired objects of pleasure.'

'He then returned to his own city. After some time, the princesses gave birth to one hundred and fifty sons. Every day, his[751] love for them increased and his heart was overwhelmed with a sense of "mine". "These are my descendants. Their conversation is charming. They will learn to walk. They will attain youth. They will marry and I will see their sons. Seeing these grandsons and their sons, every day, all my wishes will be met." In this way, as time passed, his desires also increased. He

---

[750] *Siddhi*s mean powers. Specifically, there are eight major *siddhi*s or powers. These are *anima* (becoming as small as one desires), *mahima* (as large as one desires), *laghima* (as light as one wants), *garima* (as heavy as one wants), *prapti* (obtaining what one wants), *prakamya* (travelling where one wants), *vashitvam* (powers to control creatures) and *ishitvam* (obtaining divine powers).

[751] Soubhari's, not Mandhata's.

thought, "What delusion is this! There is no end to my wishes. They only increase, even if there are ten thousand, or one hundred thousand years. When a present wish is satisfied, a new desire starts to sprout. They started to walk. They attained youth. They got wives. They had sons. I have seen the sons of my sons. Nevertheless, there is a new desire in my heart. When I saw their sons, another wish surfaced. When a present desire has been met, how does one prevent the germination of new wishes? I have now realized that, right up to death, there is no end to desires. If the mind is attached to desires, it can never be attached to the supreme objective. I dwelt inside the water, devoting myself to meditation. That fish was no friend of mine. Because of association with him, everything has been destroyed. The outcome of that association was my getting married. The consequence of marriage was these desires. There was misery because of the birth of one single body. But now, one hundred and fifty bodies have resulted. Having married the daughters of the king, because of their sons, the miseries have multiplied. Those sons will have sons and those sons will again have sons. They will marry. This extension of great misery is because of marriage and the root cause is the sense of 'mine'. Remaining submerged in water, I accumulated a store of austerities. That store of austerities was first destroyed by association with the fish and has been further destroyed by love for my sons. For mendicants who pursue the path of emancipation, non-attachment is the key. Attachment leads to many taints. A *yogi* who is limited in intelligence uses *yoga* to ascend but falls down because of attachment. I followed that path, but because my intelligence turned towards getting married, I have succumbed to desire. I will again strive to extinguish those sins, so that I do not suffer from the miseries people face. I will use austerities to worship Vishnu. He is the creator of everything. His form cannot be thought of. He is smaller than the smallest and larger than the largest. He is dark and fair. He is the lord

of the gods. He is the source of all energy. His form is manifest
in everything. The infinite one's action can be seen. My
consciousness will be unwaveringly devoted to Vishnu always,
so that my taints are destroyed, and I am not born again. He is
the sparkling refuge for all beings. He is the lord of everything.
He is the beginning, the middle and the end. There is nothing
other than him. Among all *gurus*, he is the supreme *guru*. I will
seek refuge with Vishnu." Thus, Soubhari fixed his *atman* in
the supreme *atman*. He gave up his sons, home, possessions
and everything else that was the result of prosperity. With all
his wives, he entered the forest. Every day, he observed the rites
followed by a *vaikhanasa*. Using these, he cleansed all his sins.
When his conduct had been cooked and matured in this way,
he ignited the fire in his mind and became a *bhikshu*. He offered
up all *karma* to the illustrious one. The supreme Ananta is the
supreme objective. He is beyond the dharma of beginning,
transformation and destruction. Having abandoned everything
identified with his own self, he became one with that Achyuta.
I have thus told you everything about Soubhari's conduct and
about his relationship with Mandhata's daughters. If a person
reads it, has it read, hears it, makes it heard, nurtures it, has it
nurtured, writes it, has it written, teaches it, studies it or has it
instructed, for six births, in thoughts, words and deeds, he will
not follow a deviant path. All causes contributing to a sense of
"mine" will be destroyed.'

Chapter 4(3) (Mandhata's Descendants)

Shri Parashara said, 'After this, one turns to Mandhata's
sons and descendants. Ambarisha was Mandhata's son and
Yuvanashva was the son of Ambarisha. His son was Harita and
the Angirasas known as the Haaritas were descended from him.

In Rasatala, there were *gandharva*s known as Mouneyas. Their
number was six crores. They defeated all the *naga* families,
stole all their main jewels and took away their lordship. The
*uraga*s were overwhelmed by the valour of the *gandharva*s.
They praised the illustrious one, the lord of all the gods. The
lotus-eyed one was sleeping on the waters. Hearing this, he
opened his eyes. When he woke up, they prostrated themselves
and said, "O illustrious one! Please grant us freedom from the
fear that has been caused by *gandharva*s. How can this fear
be pacified?" The illustrious Purushottama, who is without
a beginning, spoke to them. "Yuvanshva's son is Mandhata
and Mandhata's son is named Purukutsa. I will enter his body
and pacify all the wicked *gandharva*s." The illustrious one was
lying down on the water and they heard what he said. They
prostrated themselves before him and returned to the world
of the *naga*s again. The lord of the *pannaga*s asked Narmada
to bring Purukutsa. She brought him to Rasatala. When he
reached Rasatala, he was filled with the illustrious one's energy
and using that valour, he destroyed all the *gandharva*s. He then
returned to his own city again. All the lords of the *pannaga*s
bestowed a boon on Narmada. Whoever remembered her and
invoked her name, would never be scared on account of the
poison of snakes. In this connection, there is a *shloka*. "I bow
down to Narmada in the morning. I bow down to Narmada
in the night. O Narmada! I bow down to you. Please save me
from the poison of snakes." Whoever utters this day and night,
is never bitten by a snake when he enters a dark place. If he
remembers her when he happens to ingest poison, the poison
that he has consumed will not cause him any hardship. The
lords of the *uraga*s gave Purukutsa the boon that his lineage
would never be exterminated. Through Narmada, Purukutsa
had a son named Trasadasyu. Trasadasyu's son was Sambhuta.
Sambhuta's son was Anaranya, killed by Ravana when he was
engaged in his conquest. Anaranya's son was Prishadashva and

Prishadashva had a son named Haryashva. Haryashva's son was Hasta. Hasta's son was Sumanas and Tridhanva was the son of Sumanas. Tridhanva's son was Trayaruni. Trayaruni's son was Satyavrata, who obtained the name of Trishanku. He was reduced to the state of becoming a *chandala*.[752] There was a drought that lasted for twelve years. During this period, for the sake of nourishing Vishvamitra's wife and children, every day, he hung the flesh of deer on a *nyagrodha* tree that was on the banks of the Jahnavi, so that they would not have to receive it from a *chandala*. Satisfied at this, Vishvamitra made him ascend to heaven in his own physical body. Trishanku's son was Harishchandra and Harishchandra's son was Rohitashva. Rohitashva's son was Harita and Harita's son was Chanchu. Chanchu had two sons, Vijaya and Vasudeva. Vijaya's son was Ruruka and Ruruka's son was Vrika. Vrika's son was Bahu, who was defeated by Haihayas, Talajanghas and others. Along with his queens, he sought refuge in the forest.'

'When one of these wives conceived, a co-wife gave her poison. Because of this, the fetus remained in the womb for seven years. Having become old, Bahu died near Ourva's hermitage. Having made up her mind to follow him and die, his wife ascended his funeral pyre. However, Ourva knew about the three phases of time, the past, the present and the future. He emerged from his hermitage and told her, "Enough. This is not virtuous conduct. There is a *chakravarti* in your womb. He will be infinitely brave and valiant and will rule over the entire globe of the earth. He will perform more than one sacrifice. He will destroy the armies of adversaries. You should not be so rash as to do this." Addressed by him in this way, she refrained from her intention of dying. The illustrious

---

[752] The story is told in Harivamsha, among others. Having committed a crime, he was banished by his father and sought refuge with *chandala*s.

one brought her to his own hermitage. After a few days, she
gave birth to an energetic boy, along with some poison. Ourva
performed his *jatakarma* and other rites and gave him the
name of Sagara.[753] Bhargava Ourva performed his *upanayana*
and himself taught him the *Veda*s, the sacred texts and the use
of the *agneya* weapon. When his intelligence developed, he
spoke to his mother. "O mother! Why are we here? Who is
my father?" Asked by him, the mother told him everything.
At this, he became angry that his father's kingdom had been
seized and he pledged that he would kill the Haihayas and
Talajanghas. He killed almost all the Haihayas, Talajanghas,
Shakas, Yavanas, Kambojas, Paradas and Pahlavas.[754] The
remainder sought refuge with the *guru* of their lineages,
Vasishtha. Though they were still alive, they were as good as
dead. Therefore, Vasishtha spoke to Sagara. "O child! Enough.
Though they are alive, they are as good as dead and there is no
need to kill them. For the sake of fulfilling your pledge, I have
made them give up their own *dharma* as *dvija*s." Honouring
the *guru*'s words, he agreed, but made them change their garb.
He made the Yavanas shave their heads and the Shakas were
made to shave half their heads. The Paradas were made to wear
long hair and the Pahlavas[755] were made to sport beards. They
could no longer study, exclaim *vashatkara* or perform any of
the other rites of *kshatriya*s. Having been made to give up their
own dharma, they were abandoned by *brahmana*s and became
*mleccha*s.[756] Sagara returned to his own kingdom. He became
the undisputed *chakravarti* over the seven *dvipa*s and ruled
over the entire earth.'

[753] Sagara means along with *gara* (poison).
[754] The text says Paplavas, an obvious typo.
[755] Paplavas again.
[756] *Mleccha* can loosely be translated as barbarian but means
someone who does not speak Sanskrit.

Chapter 4(4) (Sagara's Descendants)

Shri Parashara said, 'Sagara had two wives, Sumati, the daughter of Kashyapa,[757] and Keshini, the daughter of the king of Vidarbha. Controlling himself properly, for the sake of offspring, along with them, he worshipped Ourva. He thus obtained a boon that one of them would have a single son who would carry the lineage forward, while the other one would have sixty thousand sons. They were left to choose whichever they wished. Thus addressed, Keshini chose the single son, while Sumati asked for sixty thousand. He[758] agreed. Within a few days, Keshini gave birth to a son named Asamanjas, who would carry the lineage forward. Sumati, Kashyapa's daughter's daughter, had sixty thousand sons. Asamanjas had a son named Amshumat. Since his childhood, Asamanjas was foolish and evil in conduct. His father thought that once he progressed beyond childhood, he would become extremely intelligent. However, even when he became older, this did not change. Because of his wickedness in conduct, his father abandoned him. The other sixty thousand sons also followed the conduct of Asamanjas. Since those sons of Sagara also followed the conduct of Asamanjas, sacrifices and the virtuous path were destroyed in the world. All the gods went to see the illustrious Kapila, who was born from Purushottama's lineage and was a reservoir of every kind of knowledge and was without any taints. They prostrated themselves and asked him. "O illustrious one! The other sons of Sagara have followed the conduct of Asamanjas. If this wicked conduct is followed, what will happen to the world?

---

[757] Kashyapa's daughter was Vinata and Sumati was Vinata's daughter.

[758] Ourva.

O illustrious one! For the sake of protecting the world,
which is suffering greatly, please assume an embodied form."
Hearing this, the illustrious one replied, "Within a few days,
they will be destroyed." Meanwhile, Sagara started a horse
sacrifice. Though his sons guarded the horse, someone stole
it and entered a hole in the earth. Asked to find the horse,
they followed the marks of its hooves. Each of them dug up
one *yojana*. The sons of the king saw the horse, wandering
around in Patala. The illustrious one, a store of austerities,
was seated, not far away. Full of energy, he was seated,
his head lowered. He resembled the sun, illuminated the
directions in an autumn sky that was without any clouds.
Having seen Kapila *rishi*, they took him to be the one who had
stolen the horse. They raised their weapons and said, "This
is the evil-souled one who has caused us harm and caused an
impediment in our sacrifice. He deserves to be killed. He is
the one who has stolen the horse." They rushed towards him.
The illustrious one cast his eyes around and looked at them.
The fire that arose from his own body burnt them down and
destroyed them. Sagara learnt that the army of his sons, sent
to follow the horse, had been consumed by the energy of
Kapila, the supreme *rishi*. He engaged Amshumat, the son of
Asamanjas, to bring the horse back. Following the path dug
up by the sons of Sagara, he approached Kapila. He faithfully
prostrated himself and praised him. The illustrious one said,
"O son! Take the horse and return to your grandfather. Ask
for a boon. Your grandson will bring Ganga down from
heaven to earth." Amshumat replied, "My uncles have been
destroyed by a *brahmana*'s staff,[759] though they brought the
affliction upon themselves. Please grant me the boon that
though they are undeserving of heaven, let them proceed to
heaven." Hearing this, the illustrious one said, "I have told

---

[759] *Brahmadanda*, meaning the curse.

you that your grandson will bring Ganga down from heaven to earth. When their bones and ashes touch that water, they will ascend to heaven. Those waters have emerged from the big toe in the illustrious Vishnu's feet and possess greatness. Even if a person involuntarily bathes in it, or involuntarily immersed himself in it, he goes to heaven. If a dead person's bones, skin, sinews, hair or anything else from the body touches the water, he is instantly conveyed to heaven, even if he happens to be a fallen person." Prostrating himself before the illustrious one, he took the horse and went to the place where his grandfather's sacrifice was being held. Having obtained the horse, Sagara completed the sacrifice. Sagara was pleased with his grandson and thought of him like a son.'

'Amshumat's son was Dilipa. Dilipa's son, Bhagiratha, brought down Ganga from heaven, which is why Ganga has the name of Bhagirathi. Bhagiratha's son was Suhotra and Suhotra's son was Shruta. Shruta's son was Nabhaga and Nabhaga's son was Ambarisha. Ambarisha's son was Sindhudvipa and Sindhudvipa's son was Ayutayu. Ayutayu's son was Rituparna, the one who taught Nala about playing with the dice. Rituparna's son was Sarvakama and Sarvakama's son was Sudasa. Sudasa's son was Soudasa, also named Mitrasaha. While roaming around in the forest on a hunt, he saw a couple of tigers. Because of them, all the deer had left the forest. He killed one of them with his arrow. While it was dying and giving up its breath of life, it assumed the form of an extremely terrible *rakshasa*, with a cruel face. The second said, "I will take revenge," and vanished. After some time had passed, Soudasa performed a sacrifice. When the sacrifice was over, the *acharya*, Vasishtha, left. Assuming Vasishtha's form, the surviving *rakshasa* arrived and said, "At the end of a sacrifice, human flesh must be given to me. Let it be cooked. I will return soon." Saying this, he left, and the king instructed accordingly. Assuming the form of a cook, the *rakshasa* now cooked some human flesh and offered it to the king, who placed the meat in a golden vessel and waited for Vasishtha to return. When Vasishtha returned, he offered it to him. Through his meditation, he got to know what this object was and thought, "Alas! Look at this king's wickedness in conduct. He has offered me this kind of meat. A man should not even look at this kind of flesh." His mind polluted by anger, he cursed the king. "Since you have given an ascetic like me food that should not be given to the likes of us, from now on, you will hanker after this kind of flesh." The king replied, "O illustrious one! You yourself asked me to do so." The sage exclaimed, "What? Did I ask you to do this?" He resorted to meditation yet again. Through his meditation, he discerned what had happened. Out of compassion, he said, "This will not be your food for ever, but for twelve years." Meanwhile, the king had taken up water in the cup of his right hand, so as to curse the sage back. But he thought, "The illustrious one is our *guru*. He is our *acharya* and is like the divinity of our lineage. He does not deserve to be cursed." His wife, Madayanti, also pacified him. What would be done with the water, with a curse invoked? Since the earth had to be protected, it could not be cast down on the earth. Flung up into the air, it would harm the clouds. Therefore, he sprinkled the water on his own feet. The water, based on rage, scorched and covered his feet, which became spotted. He thus came to obtain the name of Kalmashapada.[760] Because of Vasishtha's curse, every sixth time period,[761] he assumed the nature of a *rakshasa* and wandered around the earth, devouring many humans. On one such occasion, he saw a sage engaged in intercourse with his wife, when it was her season. Seeing the nature of that extremely terrible *rakshasa*, the couple was

---

[760] *Kalmasha* (spotted) *pada* (feet).

[761] With two meals a day, every sixth meal means every third day.

terrified and fled. However, he seized the *brahmana*. At this, the *brahmani*[762] entreated him in many ways. "Please show us your favours. O great king! You are the ornament of the Ikshvaku lineage. You are Mitrasaha, you are not a *rakshasa*. You know about the *dharma* of what pleases women. You should not kill my husband, who was trying to satisfy me." She lamented in many kinds of ways. However, he ignored this and ate the *brahmana*, the way a tiger devours an animal. The *brahmani* became extremely angry at this and cursed the king. "You devoured my husband when he had still not satisfied me. Therefore, you will also come by your death when you are engaged in an act of desire." Cursing him, she entered the fire. When the twelve years were over, he was freed from his curse. He desired to have intercourse with women again, but Madayanti reminded him. Therefore, he gave up all enjoyment with women.'

'Since the king was without a son, he sought Vasishtha's help and Madayanti conceived. She bore that fetus for seven years. After this, the queen struck her womb with a piece of stone.[763] A son was born, and he was therefore named Ashmaka.[764] Ashmaka's son was Mulaka. When *kshatriyas* were exterminated from the earth,[765] women stripped themselves naked, surrounding and protecting him. Mulaka's son was Dasharatha[766] and Dasharatha's son was Alivila. Alivila's son was Vishvasaha and Vishvasaha's son was Khatvanga. In the battle between *devas* and *asuras*, on behalf

---

[762] Feminine of *brahmana*.

[763] Since she had not delivered.

[764] *Ashman* means stone.

[765] By Parashurama. At that time, women saved Mulaka from destruction. Narikavacha means someone whose armour consisted of women. When all the *kshatriyas* were destroyed, a new line of *kshatriyas* was born through Mulaka. *Mulaka* means root.

[766] Not to be confused with Rama's father.

of *deva*s, he killed *asura*s. Since he did this, in heaven, *deva*s lovingly urged him to ask for a boon. He said, "I will certainly accept a boon, if you tell me what my lifespan will be." The gods replied, "Your lifespan is only one *muhurta*." On a *vimana* that possessed *laghima* and other qualities, his speed was unrestricted. He returned to the world of the mortals and said, "If I have loved *brahmana*s more than my own self, if I have never transgressed from observing my own *dharma*, and if I have seen all *deva*s, humans, animals, birds, trees and other things as no different from Achyuta, then, may I, without any faltering in my steps, merge into the illustrious one, whom the large number of sages remember." He thus obtained the illustrious one, whose form cannot be discerned, the infinite one who is the preceptor of all *deva*s. His *atman* is the only truth. He is the *paramatman*, known as Vasudeva. He merged into him and dissolved into him. In this connection, a *shloka* is heard. It was sung by *saptarshi*s in ancient times. "On earth, there will be no one who is Khatvanga's equal. He returned here from heaven when only a *muhurta* of his lifespan was left. Because of his intelligence and truth, he conquered the three worlds." Khatvanga's son was Dirghabahu and Dirghabahu's son was Raghu. Raghu's son was Aja and Aja's son was Dasharatha.'

'For the sake of the preservation of the world, the illustrious one, with the lotus in his navel, used his portions to become four of Dasharatha's sons: Rama, Lakshmana, Bharata and Shatrughna. While he was still a child, Rama went with Vishvamitra to protect his sacrifice and killed Tataka. At the sacrifice, he struck Maricha with his torrent of arrows and flung him into the ocean. He destroyed Subahu and others. By merely looking at Ahalya, he cleansed her of her sins. In Janaka's house, he easily shattered Maheshvara's bow. Sita was the daughter of King Janaka but was not born

from a womb. He obtained her as *viryashulka*.[767] Parashurama
was the one who destroyed all the *kshatriya*s. He was like a
meteor before the entire lineage of the Haihayas[768] and was
therefore proud of his valour and strength. However, Rama
humbled him. Obeying his father's command and oblivious of
any desire for the kingdom, along with his brother and wife,
he entered the forest. He killed Viradha, Khara, Dushana and
others, Kabandha and Vali. He bound the ocean, the store of
jewels, and destroyed the entire lineage of *rakshasa*s. He killed
Dashanana,[769] who had abducted his wife. To dispel the taint,
she entered the fire. The large number of *deva*s praised her
and said she was of good conduct and pure. He brought King
Janaka's daughter back to Ayodhya. O Maitreya! With all the
auspicious rites, he was consecrated as king there. Hear about
it briefly. I am not capable of describing it, even if I speak
for one hundred years. With blooming faces, Lakshmana,
Bharata, Shatrughna, Vibhishana, Sugriva, Angada, Jambavan,
Hanuman and others held umbrellas over his head and fanned
him with whisks, serving in attendance. Dasharatha's son
was praised by Brahma, Indra, Agni, Yama, Nirriti, Varuna,
Vayu, Kubera, Ishana and all the other immortals, Vasishtha,
Vamadeva, Valmiki, Markandeya, Vishvamitra, Bharadvaja,
Agastya and all the other supreme sages and by the hymns of
the *Rig Veda*, the *Yajur Veda* and the *Sama Veda*. There was
singing and dancing and the playing of all kinds of musical
instruments: *veena*s, flutes, drums, larger drums, kettledrums,
conch shells, trumpets and others. There were auspicious

[767] *Viryashulka* is a form of marriage when the maiden is offered
to the suitor who shows the most valour (*virya*), *shulka* meaning price.
[768] This is a reference to Parashurama killing Kartavirya Arjuna,
the king of the Haihayas.
[769] One with ten heads, Ravana.

pronouncements and benedictions. In the midst of all the kings
on earth, for the sake of protecting all the worlds, Dasharatha's
son was consecrated in the proper way. The Indra of Kosala was
an ornament in Raghu's lineage. He was loved by Janaki and
by his three brothers. Having ascended the throne, he ruled the
kingdom for eleven thousand years. Bharata left, to conquer the
dominion of the *gandharva*s, and killed three crore *gandharva*s.
Shatrughna killed the *rakshasa* named Lavana, Madhu's son,
who was extremely strong and powerful. Having done this, he
established Mathura. They were extremely strong and valiant.
They were brave and destroyed all the extremely wicked ones
in this world. Having accomplished the task of preservation,
Rama, Lakshmana, Bharata and Shatrughna again ascended to
heaven. The hearts of the people in Kosala's city and countryside
were devoted to the one who was born from the illustrious
one's portion. They too obtained that world. Rama was the one
who destroyed the extremely wicked. He had two sons, Lava
and Kusha. Lakshmana's sons were Angada and Chandraketu.
Bharata's sons were Taksha and Pushkala. Shatrughna's sons
were Subahu and Shurasena. Kusha's son was Atithi and
Atithi's son was Nishadha. Nishadha's son was Anala and
Anala's son was Nabhas. Pundarika was the son of Nabhas
and Pundarika's son was Kshemadhanva. Kshemadhanva's son
was Devanika. Devanika's son was Ahinaka and Ahinaka's
son was Ruru. Ruru's son was Pariyatraka and Pariyatraka's
son was Devala. Devala's son was Chala and Chala's son was
Ukta. Ukta's son was Vajranabha and Vajranabha's son was
Shankha. Shankha's son was Ushitashva and Ushitashva's
son was Vishvasaha. Vishvasaha's son was Hiranyanabha.
He was a great lord of *yoga* and learnt *yoga* after becoming
the disciple of Jaimini and Yajnavalkya. Hiranyanabha's
son was Pushya and Pushya's son was Dhruvasandhi.
Dhruvasandhi's son was Sudarshana and Sudarshana's son
was Agnivarna. Agnivarna's son was Shighraga, and he had a

son named Maru. Even now, resorting to *yoga*, Maru resides in Kalapagrama.[770] When the next *mahayuga* arrives, he will restore the vows of the *kshatriyas* of *surya vamsha*. Maru had a son named Prashushruka and Prashushruka's son was Susandhi. Susandhi's son was Amarsha, Amarsha's son was Sahasva and Sahasva's son was Vishvabhava. Vishvabhava's son was Brihadbala, who was killed by Abhimanyu, Arjuna's son, in the course of the Bharata battle. I have spoken about the main kings of the Ikshvaku lineage. If one hears about their conduct, one is freed from all sins.'

Chapter 4(5) (Kings of Mithila)

Shri Parashara said, 'Ikshvaku had a son named Nimi. He started a sacrifice that lasted for one thousand years and sought to engage Vasishtha as the *hotri*. Vasishtha told him, "I have already been engaged by Indra for a sacrifice that will last for five hundred years. When I complete that and return, I will become your officiating priest." The lord of the earth didn't say anything in reply. Vasishtha thought he had agreed and went away to complete the sacrifice of the lord of the immortals. During that period, he started the sacrifice with Goutama and others. When the sacrifice of the lord of the immortals was over, Vasishtha hurried back, to perform Nimi's sacrifice. He saw that ownership over the rites had been handed over to Goutama. The king was asleep then and

---

[770] The village (*grama*) of Kalapa has been speculatively located in various places, including near Badarikashrama. The last remaining kings of the solar and lunar dynasties are respectively Maru and Devapi. It is believed that they meditate and reside there, waiting for *kali yuga* to be over.

he cursed him. "You have refused me and have handed over ownership over the rites to Goutama. Therefore, you will cease to have a body."[771] When the lord of the earth woke up, he replied, "Without talking to me and without knowing, you have unleashed a curse on me while I was asleep. You are a wicked *guru*. Therefore, your body will fall down." Having cursed in this way, he gave up his body. When he was cursed in this way, Mitra and Varuna's energy entered Vasishtha. When they saw Urvashi, their semen fell down and Vasishtha obtained another body through them.[772] Nimi's body was preserved with extremely agreeable fragrances and oil. Cleaned in this way, there was not the least bit of taint in the corpse, and it was as if he had just died. When the sacrifice was completed, *deva*s arrived to receive their shares. The officiating priests said, "You should bestow a boon on the person who has performed the sacrifice." When *deva*s offered to, Nimi replied, "O illustrious ones! O ones who destroy the miseries of *samsara*! There is no misery as great as the separation of the mind from the body. I desire to reside in the eyes of people. I do not want to obtain a physical body again." Addressed in this way, *deva*s agreed, and he resided in the eyes of all creatures. That is how Nimi became *nimesha* in beings. The king was without a son and the sages were scared of there being no king. Therefore, they kneaded his body, like kindling. A son was born. Since he was born in this way, he came to have the name of Janaka.[773] Since his father was Videha, he was also known as Vaideha. Since he was produced through churning,[774] he was

---

[771] *Videha*, without a body.

[772] Agastya and Vasishtha were born in this way, through Mitra–Varuna.

[773] From *janana* (being born). Many kings in that lineage were known as Janaka and this should not be equated with Sita's father.

[774] *Manthana*. The root verb is *mathe*.

known as Mithi. Janaka's son was Udavasu and Udavasu's son
was Nandivardhana. Nandivardhana's son was Suketu and
Suketu's son was Devarata. Devarata's son was Brihaduktha
and Brihaduktha's son was Mahavirya. Mahavirya's son was
Sudhriti and Sudhriti's son was Dhrishtaketu. Dhrishtaketu's
son was Haryashva and Haryashva's son was Manu. Manu's
son was Pratika and Pratika's son was Kritaratha. Kritaratha's
son was Devamidha and Devamidha's son was Vibudha.
Vibudha's son was Mahadhriti and Mahadhriti's son was
Kritarata. Kritirata's son was Maharoma and Maharoma's
son was Svarnaroma. Svarnaroma's son was Hrasvaroma and
Hrasvaroma's son was Siradhvaja. To obtain a son, he ploughed
the ground, so that a sacrifice could be performed. A daughter
named Sita was born to him through the plough. Siradhvaja's
brother was Kushadhvaja, the lord of Kashi. Siradhvaja had a
son named Bhanumat and Bhanumat's son was Shatadyumna.
Shatadyumna's son was Shuchi and Shuchi had a son named
Urja. Urja's son was Shatadhvaja and Shatadhvaja's son was
Kriti. Kriti's son was Anjana and Anjana's son was Kurujit.
Kurujit's son was Arishtanemi and Arishtanemi's son was
Shrutayu. Shrutayu's son was Suparshva and Suparshva's son
was Srinjaya. Srinjaya's son was Kshemavi and Kshemavi's
son was Anenas. Bhoumaratha was the son of Anenas and
Bhoumaratha's son was Satyaratha. Satyaratha's son was
Upagu and Upagu's son was Upagupta. Upagupta's son was
Svagata and Svagata's son was Svananda. Svananda's son was
Suvarcha and Suvarcha's son was Suparshva. Suparshva's son
was Subhasha and Subhasha's son was Sushruta. Sushruta's
son was Jaya and Jaya's son was Vijaya. Vijaya's son was Rita
and Rita's son was Sunaya. Sunaya's son was Vitahavya and
Vitahavya's son was Dhriti. Dhriti's son was Bahulashva and
Bahulashva's son was Kriti. Janaka's lineage ended with Kriti.
These were those from Mithila. In general, these kings resorted
to knowledge of the *atman*.'

Chapter 4(6) (*Chandra Vamsha*)

Maitreya said, 'O illustrious one! You have described *surya vamsha* to me. I wish to hear about all the kings in *chandra vamsha*,[775] whose deeds are still talked about. Who were their children? O one with a pleasant face! O *brahmana*! If you wish to show me your favours, you should tell me about this.'

Shri Parashara replied, 'O tiger among sages! Hear about this lineage, famous for its energy. I will progressively describe the kings in Soma's lineage. In this lineage, there were those who were extremely strong, valiant, radiant and enterprising. They followed virtuous conduct and possessed supreme qualities. There were Nahusha, Yayati, Kartavirya Arjuna and others who ornamented it. I will tell you about them. Listen. The illustrious Narayana is the creator of the entire universe. Brahma, who was born from a lotus, originated from a lotus in his navel. Brahma's son was Atri and Atri's son was Soma. The illustrious one who originated from the lotus consecrated him as the lord of all the herbs, *dvija*s and *nakshatra*s. He performed a royal sacrifice and obtained excellent powers as a result of this. This, and the lordship, led to his being penetrated by insolence. As a result of this strength and insolence, he abducted Tara, the wife of Brihaspati, the *guru* of all *deva*s. Brihaspati entreated him in many ways. The illustrious Brahma urged. All the *devarshi*s also beseeched him. But he did not release her. Because of his enmity towards Brihaspati, Ushanas[776] sided with Chandra. The illustrious Rudra had obtained his learning from Angiras.[777] Therefore, he helped Brihaspati. Because of Ushanas, Jambha, Kumbha and all the other *daitya*s

---

[775] The word Soma is used for Chandra.
[776] Shukracharya.
[777] Brihaspati's bother.

and *danava*s made great efforts. Shakra and all the other *deva* soldiers helped Brihaspati. There was a great battle on account of Tara, and it came to be known as the Tarakamaya battle. Led by Rudra, *deva*s released divine weapons towards *asura*s. All the *danava*s released weapons directed at *deva*s. Heart agitated by this conflict between *deva*s and *asura*s, the world sought refuge with Brahma. The illustrious one, who was born from the lotus, made Ushanas, Shankara, *asura*s and *deva*s withdraw. Brihaspati got Tara back. Noticing that she was pregnant, Brihaspati said, "This is not mine. In my field, it is someone else's son. Enough of this. She should not continue to bear this outcome of rashness but should release it." She was devoted to her husband. When he said this, soon after her husband spoke those words, she released the fetus in a clump of grass. As soon as he was released, his extreme energy surpassed the energy of *deva*s. Noticing the child's great beauty, both Brihaspati and the moon desired to have him. To dispel the doubt that arose, *deva*s asked Tara. "O extremely fortunate one! Tell us the truth. Is this Brihaspati's son or Soma's?" Because of her modesty, Tara did not say anything. When she did not say anything, despite being asked several times by *deva*s, the boy got ready to curse her. He said, "Since you are not stating who my father is, you are wicked. I will punish you right now, so that from today, your shame becomes a false pretense and your words become crooked." At this, the illustrious grandfather restrained the boy and asked Tara himself. "O child! Please state whether this son is Soma's or Brihaspati's." Addressed in this way, she shamefully said, "He is Soma's." The illustrious lord of the *nakshatra*'s sparkling face was flooded with joy. He embraced the child and exclaimed, "O son! This is praiseworthy. You are wise." Hence, his named became Budha.'[778]

[778] *Budha* means wise/learned.

'You have already been told how he obtained Pururava
as a son, through Ila.[779] Pururava was extremely generous.
He was energetic and performed sacrifices. He was truthful in
speech and exceedingly handsome and spirited. When Urvashi
was cursed by Mitra and Varuna, she decided to dwell in
the world of humans and saw him. As soon as she saw him,
she lost her heart. She forgot all her honour and her desire
for the pleasures of heaven. With her mind on him alone, she
presented herself before him. He too saw that she was the most
beautiful woman in all the worlds. He saw her qualities of
beauty, delicacy, grace, gait, playfulness and smiles, and his
heart was also captivated by her. Since their hearts and eyes
were on no one else, there was no need for anything else. The
king boldly told her, "O one with the excellent eyebrows! I
desire you. Please show me your favours and love me back
in return." Somewhat shame-facedly, Urvashi replied, "I will,
provided you abide by my conditions. If you agree, I will tell
you what those are." He said, "Please tell me the conditions."
Thus asked, she spoke again. "I have these two rams,[780] which
are like my sons. They must always be next to my bed and must
never be taken away. You must never see me naked, and my
food will be only *ghee*." The lord of the earth agreed to these
conditions. For sixty-one years, the lord of the earth found
pleasure with her in Alaka, gardens like Chaitratha, where
there are clumps of lotuses and beautiful regions with Manasa
and other waterbodies. Every day, his attachment towards her
increased. Every day, Urvashi's love for him also increased and
she no longer felt any desire for residing in the world of the
immortals. However, without Urvashi, the *apsara*s, *siddha*s
and *gandharva*s no longer found the world of the gods to be
agreeable. Knowing about the agreement between Urvashi

[779] Chapter 4(1).
[780] This can also be translated as sheep.

and Pururava, the *gandharva*s appointed Vishvavasu. In the night, from near their bed, he stole one of the rams. As he was being taken away through the sky, Urvashi heard the sound. She exclaimed, "I am without a protector. Who has stolen my son? Who will I seek refuge with?" The king heard this. But since the queen would have seen him naked, he did not move. At this, the *gandharva*s stole the other ram and left. She heard the sound of it being taken away through the sky and again exclaimed in misery, "I am without a protector. I am the husband of a coward, who is no refuge." The king could not tolerate this. In the darkness, he seized his sword and rushed after them. "O wicked ones! Desist. You will be killed." The *gandharva*s created an extremely bright flash of lightning. In that light, Urvashi saw that the king was without a garment. In that very instant, the compact was violated. Abandoning the two rams, the *gandharva*s returned to the world of the gods. Cheerful in his mind, the king returned to his bed with the two rams. However, he could not see Urvashi. Unable to see her, he wandered around naked, as if he was mad. Finally, in Kurukshetra, in a lake full of lotuses, he saw Urvashi, sporting with four other *apsara*s. He was like one who was mad, and his mind was in a terrible whirl. He entreated her in many ways. "O wife! Stay. O deceiver! Stay."[781] Urvashi replied, "O great king! Do not strive in this way, without any sense of discrimination. There is a life inside me now. Leave this place. At the end of a year, I will come and hand over the son to you, staying with you for one night." Addressed in this way, he happily left for his own city. Urvashi told the other *apsara*s, "This is a supreme man. Till now, I have spent time residing with him. He attracted my mind and love." Thus addressed, the *apsara*s replied, "His beauty is praiseworthy. We would have

---

[781] Since his mind was in a whirl, his sentiments were mixed.

happily stayed with him forever." When the year was over, the king returned there. Urvashi handed over the son, Ayush.'

'Handing him over, she spent one night with him and conceived five sons.[782] She told the king, "Because of their affection towards me, all the gandharvas have decided to bestow a boon on you. Please ask for the boon." The king replied, "I have defeated all the enemies. All my senses are unimpeded, and I am capable. I possess relatives, unlimited strength and a treasury. There is nothing left for me, except that I should reside in the same world as Urvashi. I desire to spend my time with Urvashi." Hearing this, the gandharvas gave the king a vessel full of fire and said, "Take this fire and following the norms, divide it into three.[783] When you have done this, offer oblations properly and you will accomplish your desire of living in the same world as Urvashi. Your wishes will certainly be satisfied." Told this, he took up the vessel full of fire and left. He reached a forest and thought, "Alas! I have been extremely foolish. What did I do? I brought back the vessel full of fire, not Urvashi." Abandoning that vessel full of fire in the forest, he returned to his own city. Though half the night was over, he could not sleep and thought, "So that I could live in the same world as Urvashi, the gandharvas gave me a vessel full of fire. But I left it in the forest. I will now go there and get it back." Thinking this, he arose and went there, but the vessel full of fire could not be seen. In place of the vessel full of fire, he saw an ashvattha tree growing out of a shami tree.[784] He thought, "I left a vessel full of fire here, and now,

---

[782] The interpretation is that she and her four apsara friends spent one night with Pururava, thus leading to five sons.

[783] The three fires are garhapatya, ahavaniya and dakshinatya. Garhapatya is the fire that burns in households. Ahavaniya is used for invocations, dakshinatya is the fire that burns in a southern direction.

[784] Ashvattha is the holy fig tree, shami is a large tree believed to contain fire.

there is an *ashvattha* growing out of a *shami* tree. Thus, this is the form of the fire. I will take these to my city and make them *arani*.[785] I will use the fire that is generated to perform worship." In this way, he returned to his own city and made two pieces of *arani*, as many finger lengths long as there are *akshara*s in the *gayatri mantra*.[786] He then chanted the *gayatri mantra*. As he chanted it, the wood turned into *arani*. When he rubbed, fire issued. He divided it into the three recommended types and offered oblations, with the intended fruit of residing in the same world as Urvashi. Following the norms of offering oblations into the fire, he performed many kinds of sacrifices and reached the world of the *gandharva*s, where he was no longer separated from Urvashi. Fire was originally one. It was in this *manvantara* that it was divided into three by Aila.'

Chapter 4(7) (Pururava's Descendants)

Shri Parashara said, 'Pururava had six sons, known as Ayush, Dhimat, Amavasu, Vishvavasu, Shrutayu and Shatayu. Amavasu had a son named Bhima. Bhima's son was Kanchana, Kanchana's son was Suhotra and Suhotra's son was Jahnu. When Jahnu was performing a sacrifice, he noticed that the sacrificial arena was flooded by Ganga's waters. His eyes became red with

---

[785] *Arani* stands for the two churning sticks used to kindle a fire, by rubbing them against each other.

[786] The *gayatri mantra* has three lines, eight *akshara*s in each. There are thus twenty-four *akshara*s in the *gayatri mantra*. Each *arani* was twenty-four *anguli*s (length of a finger) long. An *anguli* can roughly be taken to be between half and three-fourth of an inch. Before chanting the *gayatri mantra*, it was just ordinary wood. Once the *gayatri mantra* was recited, the wood turned into *arani* and generated fire.

rage, and he meditated on the illustrious one, the supreme being
who is embodied in the sacrifice. Having immersed himself in
this way, he drank up the Ganga. To pacify him, *devas* and *rishi*s
made Ganga his daughter and got her back.[787] Jahnu had a son
named Sumantu. Sumantu's son was Ajaka and Ajaka's son was
Balakashva. Balakashva's son was Kusha. Kusha had four sons:
Kushamba, Kushanabha, Dhurtaraja and Vasu. Desiring a son
who would be like Shakra, Kushamba performed austerities.
Witnessing his fierce austerities, Indra thought, "There should
be no one else who is my equal in valour." Therefore, Indra
was born as his son, named Gadhi, or Koushika.[788] Gadhi had a
daughter named Satyavati. Bhargava Richika desired to marry
her. Gadhi did not wish to bestow her on an aged *brahmana* but
was also scared of his rage. As a bride price, he asked for one
thousand horses, as fleet as the wind, as radiant and white as
the moon in complexion, but with one black ear. At the place
known as Ashvatirtha,[789] the *rishi* obtained these one thousand
horses from Varuna and gave them to him. In this way, Richika
married the daughter. For the sake of a son, Richika gave her
some *charu*.[790] Requested by her, he also prepared some *charu*
for her mother, so that she might have a supreme *kshatriya* as a
son. "This *charu* is for you. This *charu* is for your mother. Each
is appropriate for the person." Saying this, he went to the forest.
When the time arrived to have the *charu*, Satyavati's mother
told her, "O daughter! Everyone wishes to see that her own son
possesses excellent qualities. No one desires a situation where a
daughter possesses greater qualities than her brother. Therefore,
you should give me the *charu* meant for you and you should take

[787] Hence, Ganga is known as Jahnavi.
[788] Koushika because he was descended from Kusha.
[789] The place of piligrimage (*tirtha*) of horses (*ashva*).
[790] An oblation of rice, barley and pulses, cooked in butter and milk.

the *charu* meant for me. My son will rule over the entire surface of the earth, whereas yours will perform rites." Accordingly, she gave her own *charu*, infused with a *brahmana*'s strength and valour, to her mother. When the *rishi* returned from the forest, he saw Satyvati. He said, "Alas! What is this wicked thing that you have done? It is evident that your body is full of great ferocity. There is no doubt that you have eaten the *charu* meant for your mother. This is not right. I infused her *charu* with all the traits of prosperity, valour, bravery, strength and wealth. Your *charu* was infused with all the traits of serenity, knowledge, forbearance and other qualities appropriate for a *brahmana*. You have done the opposite. Your son will now be extremely fierce, devoted to the wielding of weapons. He will follow the conduct of a *kshatriya*. On the other hand, her son will follow the conduct of a *brahmana* and will be inclined towards pacification." Hearing this, she prostrated herself and replied, "O illustrious one! I did this in my ignorance. Please be pacified. Let my son not be like that. If it must be like that, let my grandson be like that." The sage agreed that it would be that way. Thereafter, she gave birth to Jamadagni and her mother gave birth to Vishvamitra. Later, Satyavati became the river named Koushiki.[791] Jamadagni married Renuka, the daughter of Renu, born in the Ikshvaku lineage. Through her, Jamadagni's son was Parashurama, the destroyer of all the *kshatriya*s, born as a portion of the illustrious Narayana, the preceptor of all the worlds. Vishvamitra's son was Bhargava Shunahshepa. Since he was given by *deva*s, he got the name of Devarata.[792] Visvamitra also had other sons known as Madhuchchhanda, Dhananjaya,

---

[791] Koshi in Bihar.

[792] Devarata means, protected by the gods. Shunahshepa was born as the son of Ajigarta, in the Bhargava lineage. When he was being offered in a sacrifice, he prayed to *deva*s. The gods saved him and gave him to Vishvamitra, who adopted him.

Krita, Devashtaka, Kachchhapa and Hari. They established many lineages of Koushika *gotra* and married into families of other *rishi*s.'

Chapter 4(8) (Other Kings and Alarka)

Shri Parashara said, 'Pururava's eldest son, Ayush, married Rahu's daughter. Through her, he had five sons: Nahusha, Kshatravriddha, Rambha, Raji and Anenas as the fifth. Khastravriddha's son was Suhotra, who had three sons, Kashyapa, Kasha and Gritsamada. Gritsamada's son, Shounaka, established the system of the four *varna*s. Kasha's son was Kasheya, the king of Kashi. The king of that kingdom had Dirghatapa as a son. Dirghatapa's son was Dhanvantari. He knew about methods and was successful in every task he attempted. He possessed every kind of prosperity and every kind of knowledge. In the past, the illustrious Narayana had bestowed a boon on him. "You will be born in the *gotra* of the king of Kashi. You will compose the eight parts of *ayurveda* and obtain a share in sacrifices."[793] Dhanvantari's son was Ketumat and Ketumata's son was Bhimaratha. Bhimaratha's son was Divodasa and Divodasa's son was Pratardana. He defeated and destroyed all the enemies from the lineage of Bhadrashrenyas. Therefore, he was known as Shatrujit.[794] His son was Pritimat. Since his father often addressed this child

---

[793] Dhanvantari is also the physician of the gods, *ayurveda* is the art of medicine. The eight parts of *ayurveda* are *shalya* (extraction of external objects), *shalakya* (treatment of externally induced infections), *chikitsa* (treatment through medicines), *bhutavidya* (knowledge of the elements), *koumarabhritya* (pediatrics), *agada* (pharmacology), *rasayana* (use of chemicals) and *vajikarana* (use of aphrodisiacs).

[794] One who was victorious over enemies.

as "Vatsa",[795] he came to be known as Vatsa. Since he was
devoted to the truth, he came to be known as Ritadhvaja.[796]
Since he obtained a horse named Kuvalaya, he was famous
on earth as Kuvalayashva.[797] Vatsa had a son named Alarka.
Even today, a *shloka* is sung about him. "There has been no
one like Alarka. He was young and ruled over the earth for
sixty thousand and six hundred years." Alarka's son was
named Sannati and Sannati's son was Sunitha. Sunitha's son
was Suketu and Suketu's son was Dharmaketu. Dharmaketu's
son was Satyaketu and Satyaketu's son was Vibhu. Vibhu's son
was Suvibhu and Suvibhu's son was Sukumara. Sukumara's
son was Drishtaketu and Drishtaketu's son was Vitihotra.
Vitihotra's son was Bharga and Bharga's son was Bhargabhumi.
Bhargabhumi also propagated the *dharma* of the four *varna*s. I
have spoken about the kings of Kashi. Now hear about Raji's
descendants.'

Chapter 4(9) (Raji's Descendants)

Shri Parashara said, 'Raji had five hundred sons. They
possessed unmatched strength and valour. In the battle
between *deva*s and *asura*s, both sides were engaged in killing
each other. Both *deva*s and *asura*s approached Brahma and
asked, "O illustrious one! In our conflict, which side will be
victorious?" The illustrious one replied, "The side for which
Raji will wield his weapons is the side that will be victorious."
The *daitya*s approached him and solicited his help. Raji said,
"I will fight for your side, provided that after I have defeated

---

[795] *Vatsa* means child.
[796] One whose banner is the truth.
[797] One with a horse (*ashva*) named Kuvalaya.

the immortals, you make me Indra." Hearing this, they replied,
"We cannot promise something and act in a contrary way. Our
Indra is Prahlada, and we fight for him." Saying this, the *asuras*
departed. After this, *devas* came to the lord of the earth and
said the same thing. When he replied in the same way to *devas*,
they consented that he would become the Indra. Raji helped the
deva soldiers. Using many kinds of great weapons, he destroyed
the entire army of the great *asuras*. When the enemies had been
defeated, Indra of the gods kneaded Raji's feet and placed them
on his head. He said, "A person who provides food and saves
from fear is a father and you are like one to me. Since your
son is the Indra of the three worlds, you are greater than the
greatest." The king smiled and replied, "Such words of flattery
and affection should not be ignored even if they come from the
side of an enemy, not to speak of someone like you." Saying
this, he returned to his own city. Shatakratu remained Indra.
When Raji died, instigated by *rishi* Narada, Raji's sons asked
for the kingdom from Shatakratu, since what was the father's
now belonged to the sons. When Indra refused, the extremely
strong ones defeated him and themselves became Indra. After
a long period of time, Shatakratu, who had been deprived
of the three worlds and his share of sacrifices, privately met
Brihaspati and spoke to him. "To welcome me, you should
give me a *badari* fruit, or at least a little piece of *purodasha*."[798]
Brihaspati replied, "If you had spoken to me earlier and urged
me, I would have done something for you. Now I will act so that
you get back your position within a short period of time." Every
day, he used *abhichara*[799] and offered oblations so that their
intelligence would get confounded, and Shakra's energy would
increase. Because of this, their intelligence was confounded,
and they turned against *brahmanas*. They abandoned *dharma*

---

[798] Sacrificial oblation made out of ground rice.
[799] Magical *mantras* used for malevolent purposes.

and turned their faces away from the words of the *Vedas*. With
their conduct of *dharma* destroyed, they were killed by Indra.
Using the priest's energy, Shakra ascended to heaven. If a man
hears this account of Indra getting his own position back, he
never suffers from the hardship of losing his own status.'

'Rambha did not have a son.[800] Kshatravriddha's son was
Pratikshatra. Pratikshatra's son was Sanjaya and Sanjaya's
son was Jaya. Jaya's son was Vijaya and Vijaya's son was
Haryadhana. Haryadhana's son was Sahadeva and Sahadeva's
son was Adina. Adina's son was Jayatsena and Jayatsena's son
was Samkriti. Samkriti's son was Kshatradharma. This was
Kshatradvriddha's lineage. I will now tell you about Nahusha's
lineage.'

Chapter 4(10) (Nahusha's Descendants)

Shri Parashara said, 'Nahusha had six extremely strong
sons, known as Yati, Yayati, Samyati, Ayati, Viyati and
Kriti. Yati did not desire the kingdom and Yayati became the
king. He married Devayani, the daughter of Ushanas, and
Sharmishtha, the daughter of Vrishaparva. In this connection,
there is a *shloka* about his lineage. "Devayani gave birth to
Yadu and Turvasu. Sharmishtha, Vrishaparva's daughter,
gave birth to Druhyu, Anu and Puru."[801] After some time,
because of Kavya's curse, Yayati became old.[802] When Shukra

---

[800] The story goes back to the sons of Ayush.

[801] Though not clearly stated, this must be the end of the *shloka*.

[802] Kavya/Ushanas is Shukracharya, Devayani's father. As a result
of the quarrel between Devayani and Sharmishtha, Shukracharya
cursed Yayati, but allowed him to transfer the curse to someone else.
The story is recounted in the Mahabharata.

was placated, thanks to his words, he wished to transfer his old age. He spoke to his eldest son, Yadu. "O son! Ahead of time, your maternal grandfather's curse has inflicted this old age on me. Through his favours, I can transfer it to you. For one thousand years, let me satisfy myself with material objects. With your young age, I wish to enjoy material objects. You should not refuse me." Yadu did not wish to accept the old age. At this, his father cursed him. "Your offspring will not be worthy of the kingdom." After this, the lord of the earth asked Turvasu, Druhyu and Anu to accept the old age and give him their own youth. Each of them refused and were accordingly cursed. He then spoke to the youngest, Sharmishtha's son, Puru, whose intelligence was faultless. With a great deal of respect, he prostrated himself before his father, treating this as a generous and great favour. He accepted the old age and gave his father his own youth. With Puru's youth, as he willed, and appropriate to the time, he ruled over the kingdom, without violating *dharma*. He protected the subjects in the proper way.'

'At that time, he enjoyed himself with the divine maiden, Vishvachi.[803] Every day, he was maddened by desire and his mind was only on her. But every day, the more he enjoyed himself, the more his desire increased. Therefore, he sang some *shloka*s. "Desire is not pacified through enjoying. It increases, like the one with the black trail[804] fed through oblations. All the *vrihi*, barley, gold, animals and women are not sufficient. Hence, it is thirst alone that must be cast aside. If a man's sentiments are such that he does not act in a wicked way towards any creature and is impartial in attitude towards everyone, there is happiness for him in every direction. Though difficult to give up, thirst is evil in intelligence. Even if one ages, it does not age. If a wise man gives it up, he is flooded

[803] An *apsara*.
[804] Fire.

with happiness. As one ages, the hair turns grey. As one ages, the teeth fall out. But even when one ages, the desire for wealth and the desire for life does not age. My mind has been attached to objects of pleasure for a full thousand years. Nevertheless, every day, my thirst is kindled again. Therefore, I will give all this up and fix my mind on the *brahman*. Without the opposite pair of sentiments and without any sense of 'mine', I will roam around, along with animals." He gave Puru the youth and took back the old age. Instating Puru in the kingdom, he left for the forest, to perform austerities. He gave Turvasu the south-eastern direction, Druhyu the west, Yadu the south and Anu the north. They would rule over those regions as kings. However, he instated Puru as the lord of the entire earth and left for the forest.'

Chapter 4(11) (Yadu's Descendants)

Shri Parashara said, 'After this, I will tell you about the lineage of Yadu, Yayati's eldest son. The illustrious Vishnu is without a beginning and without an end. All humans, *siddhas*, *gandharvas*, *yakshas*, *rakshasas*, *guhyakas*, *kimpurushas*, *apsaras*, *uragas*, birds, *daityas*, *danavas*, *adityas*, Rudras, Vasus, Ashwins, Maruts and *devarshis*, who reside in different worlds and pursue *dharma*, *artha*, *kama* and *moksha*, always worship him to obtain fruits. His greatness cannot be encompassed. He is the one who descended in this lineage. In this connection, there is a *shloka*. "If a man hears about Yadu's lineage, he is freed from all sins. The supreme *brahman* assumed the form of a man and descended here, known as Krishna." Yadu had four sons, known as Sahasrajit, Kroshtu, Nala and Nahusha.[805]

---

[805] This is a different Nahusha.

Sahasrajit's son was Shatajit and Shatajit had three sons, Haihaya, Hehaya and Venuhaya. Haihaya's son was Dharma, Dharma's son was Dharmanetra, Dharmanetra's son was Kunti and Kunti's son was Sahajit. Sahajit's son was Mahishmat, the one who constructed the city of Mahishmati.[806] Mahishmat's son was Bhadrashrenya, Bhadrashrenya's son was Durdama and Durdama's son was Dhanaka. Dhanaka had four sons: Kritavirya, Kritagni, Kritadharma and Kritoujas.'

'Kritavirya had a son named Arjuna. He had one thousand arms and was the lord of the seven *dvipa*s. He worshipped the one known as Dattatreya, born in Atri's lineage as the illustrious one's portion. He thus obtained his desired boons: one thousand arms, the serving of the cause of *dharma*, the following of his own *dharma*, conquering the earth through battles, the observance of *dharma* in ruling, subjugation of all enemies and defeat at the hands of a person who was famous in all the worlds. He ruled over the earth, with all its *dvipa*s, exceedingly well. He performed ten thousand sacrifices. A *shloka* is chanted in this connection. "Indeed, no king will be able to traverse the path followed by Kartavirya[807] in sacrifices, donations, austerities, humility and learning." No object was ever destroyed in his kingdom. In this way, he ruled over the kingdom for eighty-five thousand years, with prosperity, strength and valour and without any disease. Ravana was insolent because of his strength, having defeated all *deva*s, *daitya*s and *gandharva*s. On one occasion, he arrived there, in an attempt to conquer Mahishmati. At the time, Arjuna was bathing and sporting in the waters of Narmada, distracted and intoxicated because he had drunk liquor. Nevertheless, he bound Ravana like an animal and imprisoned him in his own city. After eighty-five thousand years were over, the opportune

---

[806] Maheshwar.
[807] Kritavirya's son, hence Kartavirya.

time arrived and he was killed by Parashurama, born as the illustrious one's portion. Arjuna had five hundred sons. The five important ones were known as Shura, Shurasena, Vrishasena, Madhu and Jayadhvaja. Jayadhvaja's son was Talajangha. Talajangha's sons were known as the Talajanghaas. The eldest of these was Vitihotra and there was another one, Bharata. Bharata's son was Vrisha and Vrisha's son was Madhu. Madhu had one hundred sons, Vrishni and others. That is how the *gotra* known as Vrishnis came about. It is because of Madhu that the lineage is also named after Madhu. Because of Yadu, they are known as Yadavas.'

Chapter 4(12) (Kroshtu's Descendants)

Shri Parashara said, 'Kroshtu, Yadu's son, had a son named Dhvajinivat and his son was Svati. Svati's son was Rushanku and Rushanku's son was Chitraratha. Chitraratha's son was Shashabindu, who was a *chakravarti* and possessed the fourteen great jewels.[808] He had a hundred thousand wives and one million sons. There were six sons who were most important: Prithushrava, Prithukarma, Prithukirti, Prithuyasha, Prithujaya and Prithudana. Prithushrava's son was Prithutama and Prithutama's son was Ushanas, who performed one hundred horse sacrifices. Ushanas had a son named Shitapu. Shitapu's son was Rukmakavacha and Rukmakavacha's son was Paravrit. Paravrit had five sons, known as Rukmeshu, Prithu, Jyamagha, Valita and Harita.'

---

[808] Possessed by an emperor: a *chakra*, a chariot, a gem (*mani*), a sword, a shield, a jewel (*ratna*), a standard, a *nidhi*, a wife, a priest, a general, a charioteer, infantry and cavalry. But the list varies.

'Even now, a *shloka* is sung about Jyamagha. "Among
all those, dead, or those in the future, obedient to their wives,
the best was Jyamagha. This king was Shaivya's husband."
His wife was named Shaivya and she had no sons. Though he
wanted sons, he was so scared of her that he did not have any
other wife. On one occasion, with a large number of chariots,
horses and elephants, he fought in an extremely terrible and
tumultuous battle and defeated all those who fought on the
side of an enemy. That enemy fled in a certain direction,
abandoning his sons, wife, relatives, army, treasury and city.
When he fled, he saw a jewel among princesses. Her eyes were
rolling in fear and distressed and miserable, she was lamenting.
"O father! Save me. O brother! Save me. O mother!" On seeing
her, the king was filled with love for her, but he thought. "This
is fortunate. I do not have any children and I am the husband
of a woman who is barren. For the sake of offspring, no doubt
destiny has presented me with this jewel among maidens.
Therefore, I will marry her. But first, I will take her up on my
chariot and go to my own city. Thereafter, I will take Queen
Shaivya's permission and marry her." Thus, taking her up on
his chariot, he went to his own city. Along with all the citizens,
servants and relatives, Shaivya came to the gate of the city,
to see the victorious king. She saw the maiden on the king's
left. Her lips quivered a little in anger and she asked the king,
"Who have you taken up on your chariot? Her heart seems to
be very fickle." Since he was scared of her, he replied in words
that were spoken in a hurry, without reflection. "This is my
daughter-in-law." Shaivya answered, "I did not give birth to a
son, and you have no other wives. If she is your daughter-in-
law, where is your son?" Her words were polluted with jealousy
and anger. But he had a sense of discrimination. Out of fear, he
did not want to engage in further arguments. So. the lord of the
earth answered, "You will give birth to a son in the future, and
she will become his wife." Hearing the words spoken by her

husband, she smiled and agreed. Accordingly, the king entered
his house with her. This conversation happened at an extremely
auspicious *lagna*, *hora*, *amshaka* and *avayava*.[809] Shaivya's age
was such that she was no longer at an age when she could give
birth to a son. However, the conjunction was such that, within
a short period of time, she conceived. After some time, she
gave birth to a son. His father gave him the name of Vidarbha,
and he married the one referred to as a daughter-in-law. They
had Kratha and Koushika as sons. A third son, known as
Romapada, was born. Even today, he is studying with Narada,
to obtain *jnana* from him. Romapada's son was Babhru and
Babhru's son was Dhriti. Dhriti's son was Kaishika. Kaishika's
son was Chedi, and his descendants are the kings known as the
Chedis. Kratha was the son of the one referred to as daughter-
in-law and Kratha's son was Kunti. Kunti's son was Dhrishti
and Dhrishti's son was Nidhriti. Nidhriti's son was Dasharha
and Dasharha's son was Vyoma. Vyoma's son was Jimuta
and Jimuta's son was Vikriti. Vikriti's son was Bhimaratha
and Bhimaratha's son was Navaratha. Navaratha's son was
Dasharatha and Dasharatha's son was Shakuni. Shakuni's son
was Karambhi and Karambhi's son was Devarata. Devarata's
son was Devakshatra and Devakshatra's son was Madhu.
Madhu's son was Kumara. In Kumara's lineage, Anu was born
as Madhu's son and Anu's son was Purumitra, who became
a lord of the earth. Purumitra's son was Amshu and Amshu's
son was Satvata. Because of Satvata, they were known as the
Satvataas. O Maitreya! These were Jyamagha's descendants.

---

[809] These are astronomical/astrological terms. *Lagna* is the specific
rashi (zodiacal sign) which is on the horizon at that time. *Hora* loosely
means hour, but here, it means half of the *rashi*. A *rashi* is divided into
nine *amshaka*s and *avayava* is an even finer (one-twelfth) division of a
rashi.

Full of faith, if a man listens to this properly, he is freed from all his sins.'

Chapter 4(13) (Krishna and Syamantaka)

Shri Parashara said, 'Satvata had sons known as Bhajana, Bhajamana, Divya, Andhaka, Devavridha, Mahabhoja and Vrishni. Through one wife, Bhajamana's sons were Nimi, Krikana and Vrishni.[810] Through another wife, his three sons were Shatajit, Sahasrajit and Ayutajit. Devavridha's son was Babhru, and a *shloka* is chanted about him. "We have heard from far and have seen from a close distance that Babhru is the best among men and that Devavridha is an equal of *deva*s. Sixty-six followed Babhru, while six thousand and eight followed Devavridha, and all of these became immortal." Mahabhoja was extremely devoted to *dharma* and his descendants were Bhojas. Since they resided in the city of Mrittikavara, they were known as Marttikavaras. Vrishni had the sons Sumitra and Yudhajit. Sumitra's son was Anamitra and Anamitra's son was Nighna. Nighna's sons were Prasena and Satrajit.'

'Satrajit was a friend of the illustrious Aditya. On one occasion, along the shores of the ocean, Satrajit fixed his mind on Surya and praised him. To give him what he desired, the radiant one presented himself before him. However, Satrajit noticed that Surya's embodied figure wasn't very clear and said, "I have seen your figure in the sky, resembling a ball of fire. O illustrious one! You are now present in front of me. Please show me your favours, so that I am able to behold your specific form." Thus addressed, the illustrious Surya took off the supreme and great jewel, Syamantaka, from around his neck

[810] A different Vrishni.

and set it to one side. He immediately saw Aditya's form, short in stature, with a bright coppery complexion and slightly tawny eyes. Satrajit prostrated himself and praised him. The illustrious Aditya, the one with one thousand rays, told him, "Ask for your desired boon." He asked for the excellent jewel. Giving it to him, the lord of brilliance ascended into his own abode. Satrajit hung the sparkling jewel around his neck and became a mass of energy, like Surya himself. In that radiant form, he entered Dvaraka. The people who resided in Dvaraka saw him advancing. The original being, the illustrious Purushottama, had used his portion to assume a human form, so as to reduce the earth's burden. They went to him, prostrated themselves and said, "O illustrious one! There is no doubt that Aditya is coming here to see you." Thus addressed, the illustrious one replied, "This is not the illustrious Aditya. It is Satrajit. Aditya has given him the great jewel known as Syamantaka. That is the reason he is radiant as he is approaching. Do not be scared. Go and see him." Thus addressed, they went and saw him. Along with Syamantaka jewel, he entered his residence. Every day, that jewel exuded eight heaps of gold. Because of its powers, all calamities vanished from the kingdom—evil portents, lack of rain, predatory beasts, fire, famine and other kinds of fear. Achyuta desired that this divine jewel should belong to King Ugrasena. Though he was capable of seizing it, he did not do so, because it might create dissension among the various *gotra*s. However, Satrajit understood that Achyuta might ask him for the jewel. Hence, he gave his brother, Prasena, the jewel. The jewel had the property that if it was worn by a person who was pure, it would exude an infinite supply of gold. But if it was worn by a person who was not pure, it would lead to his being killed. Wearing Syamantaka around his neck, Prasena mounted his horse and went to the forest on a hunt. There, he was killed by a lion. The lion killed him and his horse. Holding the sparkling jewel in its mouth, it was about to leave. At that

time, it was seen by Jambavat, the lord of bears. Jambavat
killed the lion. Seizing the sparkling jewel, Jambavat entered
his own cave and gave it to his son, known by the name of
Sukumara, so that he could play.'

'Prasena did not return. The people of the Yadu lineage
whispered in each other's ears. "Krishna desired the jewel.
So as to get it, there is no doubt that he has done this." The
illustrious one got to know everything about the slander that
was being spread. Therefore, surrounded by all the Yadu
soldiers, he followed the trail left by Prasena's horse. They
saw the corpses of Prasena and the horse, slain by the lion.
Amidst all these people, when the lion's footsteps were seen, he
was cleansed of the slander. He followed the footsteps of the
lion and within a short while, came to the spot where the lion
had been killed by the lord of bears. Out of respect towards
the jewel, he now followed the bear's footsteps. He asked all
the Yadu soldiers to remain on the slopes of the mountain.
Following the footsteps, he entered the bear's cave. Having
entered inside, he heard Sukumara's nursemaid nursing him,
with these words. "The lion killed Prasena. Jambavat killed
the lion. O Sukumara! Don't cry. This is your Syamantaka."
Hearing this, so as to get Syamantaka back, he entered further
inside. He saw the child playing on the nursemaid's lap. He
saw Syamantaka in the nursemaid's hand, blazing in its energy.
The foremost being advanced, his eyes fixed on the desired
Syamantaka. Seeing him, the nursemaid screamed, "Save me!
Save me!" From further inside, Jambavat heard her afflicted
voice and rushed out, his heart full of intolerance. For twenty-
one days, there was an encounter between those two intolerant
ones. The Yadu soldiers remained there for seven or eight
days, waiting for him to emerge. Since he did not emerge, they
thought, "Madhu's enemy must certainly have perished inside
the cave. How can he possibly remain alive? It cannot take so
many days to defeat the enemy." Regretting this, they gave up

their wait and returning to Dvaraka, announced that Krishna
had been killed. At the right time, his relatives performed all the
required funeral rites. As they fought, the special and excellent
food offered in the *shraddha* vessels nourished Shri Krishna
and reinvigorated his strength and breath of life. Meanwhile,
day after day, the enemy was struck by the extremely heavy
blows inflicted by the preceptor of all beings. Those extremely
cruel blows made his entire body suffer. The lack of food made
him lose his strength. Defeated by the illustrious one, Jambavat
prostrated himself and said, "Gods, *asuras*, *gandharvas*,
yakshas, *rakshasas* and all the other beings are incapable of
defeating you. What need be said of those who appear in the
form of men, limited in valour? If this is true of those who are
human in form, what need be said of those who are born as
inferior species? There is no doubt that you are a portion of my
master, Rama. You must be a portion of Narayana, the refuge
of the entire universe." Thus addressed, the illustrious one told
him about what was going to happen, that the illustrious one
had descended for the sake of removing the entire burden of
the earth. As a token, he affectionately touched him with the
palm of his hand and removed all the pain he had suffered on
account of the encounter. He prostrated himself again. To seek
the favours of someone who had arrived in his house, as *arghya*,
he presented him with his daughter, named Jambavati. When
she was accepted, he prostrated himself and gave him the jewel
Syamantaka. Though he should not have accepted it, Achyuta
accepted the jewel out of love. Besides, he wanted to clear his
reputation. Along with Jambavati, he returned to Dvaraka.
When the illustrious one returned, all the residents of Dvaraka
were filled with great delight. As soon as they saw Krishna,
even those who were advanced in years seemed to become
young. Along with the women, all the Yadavas assembled
and exclaimed, "This is fortunate. This is good fortune." The
illustrious one told the assembly of Yadavas exactly what had

happened. He gave Syamantaka to Satrajit and cleansed himself
of the false accusation. Along with Jambavati, he entered his
inner quarters. Satrajit thought, "It is because of me that his
reputation has been tarnished." Scared, he bestowed his own
daughter, Satyabhama, on the illustrious one as a wife.'

'Earlier, foremost Yadavas like Akrura, Kritavarma and
Shatadhanva had sought her as a wife. When she was not
bestowed on them, they thought that they had been slighted.
They were bound in enmity towards Satrajit. The foremost
among them, Akrura and Kritavarma, told Shatadhanva, "This
evil-minded Satrajit has shown both us and you disrespect. We
sought his daughter, but he bestowed her on Krishna instead.
He has lived long enough. Why should you not kill him and
take away the jewel known as Syamantaka? As a result of this,
if Achyuta gets bound in enmity towards you, we will take your
side." Shatadhanva agreed to do this. At this time, the illustrious
one, who knew the supreme truth, got to know about the sons
of Pandu being burnt down in the house of lac.[811] To make
Duryodhana relax his efforts and to perform the rites for the
Parthas, he went to Varanavata. When he was gone and when
Satrajit was sleeping, Shatadhanva slew him and stole the jewel.
Full of rage towards her father's killer, Satyabhama mounted a
chariot and swiftly went to Varanavata. She told Krishna, "O
illustrious one! I will not forgive Shatadhanva. He has killed
my father and stolen the Syamantaka jewel. He is laughing at
you, the one whose radiance dispels darkness from the three
worlds. Reflecting on this, you should do what is necessary."
Internally, Krishna was always content. However, he had
been addressed by Satyabhama, whose eyes were coppery-red
with rage. Hence, he replied, "O Satya! It is true that he has
made me a subject of ridicule. I will not tolerate the evil-souled

[811] This story is from the Mahabharata. Krishna did not want
Duryodhana to know that the Pandavas had survived.

one. If birds have sought refuge and made a nest in someone else's tree, that tree must not be cut down. A person who does that should be killed. There is no need to utter these words of sorrow in front of me anymore." Having said this, with his companions, he returned to Dvaraka. In private, Vasudeva told Baladeva, "When he went to the forest on a hunt, Prasena was killed by a king of bears. Satrajit has now been killed by Shatadhanva. Since both of them have been killed, that jewel generally belongs to us. Arise. Ascend your chariot and make efforts to kill Shatadhanva." Baladeva, who had the same kind of wish, agreed and made efforts. Shatadhanva got to know. He approached Kritavarma and urged him to protect his flanks. Kritavarma replied, "Not I. I cannot indulge in enmity with Baladeva and Vasudeva." Thus addressed, he urged Akrura. Akrura said, "Not I. The three worlds tremble at the strides of the illustrious one. He makes the wives of the enemies of the gods become widows. With his *chakra*, he can repulse a strong circle of enemies. Who can withstand his *chakra*? The one who is worshipped by the entire universe is with the wielder of the plough. Even when his intoxicated eyes are closed, if he[812] glances at mighty enemy elephants, they are pacified. He dragged the earth with the tip of his plough and disfigured it.[813] The elephants of the immortals are incapable of fighting against them. What can I do? If you so wish, you should find refuge with someone else." Thus addressed, Shatadhanva replied, "Since you yourself understand that you are incapable of protecting me, take this jewel and keep it safely." Hearing this, he replied, "I will accept it provided that you do not tell anyone that I have taken it." When he agreed, Akrura accepted the jewel. Astride a speedy mare that could travel one hundred

---

[812] Baladeva.

[813] This story, about Baladeva changing the course of Yamuna, is recounted in Harivamsha.

*yojana*s in a single day, Shatadhanva fled. Baladeva and Vasudeva followed him, astride a chariot to which the four horses, Shaivya, Sugriva, Meghapushpa and Balahaka, were yoked. The mare bore him for a distance that measured one hundred *yojana*s. But then, in the forest around Mithila, it gave up its life. Abandoning it, Shatadhanva fled on foot. Krishna told Balabhadra, "Remain astride the chariot. I will follow that evildoer on foot and kill him. It is evident that the terrain here is not very good. Therefore, the horses will not be able to bear us across this stretch of ground." Thus addressed, Baladeva remained on the chariot. After following him along the ground for a distance of two *krosha*s,[814] from a distance, Krishna hurled his *chakra* and severed Shatadhanva's head. In many ways, he searched inside the garments on his body. He could not find the Syamantaka jewel. He returned on foot to Baladeva and said, "We have killed Shatadhanva in vain. We have not been able to find the great jewel known as Syamantaka, which is the essence of the entire universe." Hearing this, Baladeva became angry and told Vasudeva, "Shame on your greed for wealth. I no longer recognize my fraternal relationship with you. This is my path. You go wherever you want. I have nothing more to do with you, with Dvaraka or with all our relatives. Enough of your attempts to stand in front of me, taking false pledges." He reprimanded him in this way and refused to be placated. He went to the city of Videha. King Janaka welcomed him with *arghya* and he entered his house, remaining there. Vasudeva returned to Dvaraka. While Balabhara was in King Janaka's house, Duryodhana, Dhritarashtra's son, learnt from him how to fight with a club.'

'When a year was over, Babhru, Ugrasena and other Yadavas made up their minds that Krishna had not stolen the

[814] A *krosha* is a measure of distance, equal to one-fourth of a *yojana*. With a *yojana* taken as eight miles, a *krosha* is two miles.

jewel. They went to the city of Videha and persuading him, brought him back to Dvaraka. Using the gold that flowed out of the excellent jewel, Akrura constantly performed sacrifices, meditating on the illustrious one. "If one kills a *kshatriya* or a *vaishya* engaged in a sacrifice, that is as bad a sin as killing a *brahmana*." Consecrating himself with this armour, he was unharmed for sixty-two years.[815] Because of the powers of the jewel, there were no evil portents there, no famine, no epidemic and no death. When this period was over, the Bhojas, who belonged to Akrura's side, killed Shatrughna, the great-grandson of Satvata. Therefore, along with the Bhojas, Akrura fled from Dvaraka. From the day he left, there were evil portents there—famine, predatory beasts, lack of rain, epidemics and other calamities. The illustrious one, who has the enemy of serpents[816] on his flag, brought all the Yadavas together for consultations, Balabhadra and Ugrasena among them. "What is this? How can so many calamities occur?" As they discussed, an elder of the Yadu lineage, Andhaka by name, spoke. "Akrura's father is Shvaphalka. Famine, epidemics and drought do not occur in a place where he resides. When it did not rain in the king of Kashi's kingdom, Shvaphalka was taken there and at that very instant, it started to rain. The wife of the king of Kashi had conceived a jewel among daughters earlier. However, though the full period of pregnancy was over, the daughter did not emerge. Twelve years passed, but she did not emerge. The king of Kashi spoke to the daughter, who was still inside the womb. 'O daughter! Why are you not being born? Please emerge. I wish to see you. How long can your mother bear this hardship?' Thus addressed, the fetus replied, 'O father! Every day, if you give a cow to a *brahmana*, I think I will emerge at the end of three

---

[815] Akrura used this *mantra* like armour (*kavacha*).
[816] Garuda.

years. Indeed, I will certainly emerge from the womb then.'
Hearing this, every day, the king gave a *brahmana* a cow.
After the stipulated time, the daughter was born and her father
gave her the name of Gandini.[817] When Shvaphalka arrived in
his house and did him a good turn as *arghya*, he bestowed
the daughter, Gandini, on him. Through her, Akrura was
born as Shvaphalka's son. Therefore, he has been born from
a couple where both of them possess qualities. When he has
left, why should famine, epidemics and other calamities not
occur? Therefore, let him be brought back. When a person
possesses an excess of qualities, one should not search for
weaknesses." Hearing Andhaka's words, the elders of the
Yadu linage, Keshava, Ugrasena, Balabhadra and the other
Yadus, wished to forgive him his transgressions. They granted
Shvaphalka's son freedom from fear and brought him back to
their own city.'

'But Krishna wondered, "That Akrura has been born from
Shvaphalka and Gandini is not sufficient reason. Something
else with great powers must be a counter to drought,
famine, epidemics and other calamities. There is no doubt
that he possesses the great jewel known as Syamantaka. It
has been heard that it possesses this kind of power. He has
been continuously performing sacrifices. No one else is able
to perform such incessant sacrifices. However, though he
possesses limited means, he has constantly been performing
sacrifices." He made up his mind that there was no doubt that
he possessed the supreme jewel. Thinking of some other pretext,
he assembled all the Yadavas in his own house. When all the
Yadus were seated and the other reason had been first disposed
of, Janardana started conversing and jesting with Akrura. He

---

[817] From *gou* (cow) and *dina* (day). In declensions, *gam* is the
second case for cow.

said, "O Danapati![818] We know that Shatadhanva gave you the jewel Syamantaka, the essence of the entire universe. It brings great benefit to the kingdom and is with you. Since all of us enjoy the fruits of its powers, let it remain there. However, Balabhadra suspects me. Therefore, for our pleasure, please show it to us." Thus addressed by the illustrious Vasudeva, though he possessed the jewel, he thought in silence. "What should be done now? If I contradict him and say that I don't have it, they will search inside my garments and see the jewel. That great confrontation will not be pardoned." Thinking this, Akrura spoke to Narayana, the cause behind the origin of the entire universe. "O illustrious one! Shatadhanva did give the jewel Syamantaka to me. I waited. Perhaps the illustrious one will ask for it tomorrow, perhaps day after tomorrow. With a great deal of difficulty, I have kept it all this while. Because of these difficulties, I have not been able to enjoy any of these endless objects of pleasure. My mind has been anxious, and I have not known the least bit of happiness. Even though it does a lot of good to the kingdom, I am incapable of keeping it. You should not ask me to do so. Therefore, I am giving the Syamantaka jewel to you and you give it to whoever you wish." Saying this, he revealed a small golden box that had been secreted in the cloth tied around his stomach. He took out the Syamantaka jewel and showed it to the assembly of the Yadu lineage. As soon as it was taken out, its great beauty illuminated everything. Akrura said, "This is the jewel that Shatadhanva gave him. Let it be taken by whoever it belongs to." On seeing it, all the Yadavas were amazed and uttered words of praise. Seeing it, Balabhadra expressed a desire for it. "It generally belongs to Achyuta and me." Satyabhama also wanted it. "It is part of my father's property." Looking at

[818] Akrura was generous in giving gifts and was known as Danapati.

Bala and Satya, Krishna thought that he was like a cow caught
between the two wheels of a cart. In the presence of all the
Yadavas, he told Akrura, "To clear my reputation, I had this
jewel displayed among the Yadus. It does generally belong to
Balabhadra and me. It is also part of Satyabhama's father's
property. However, for the endless benefit of the kingdom, it
must always be kept by a person who possesses *brahmacharya*
and other qualities. It should never be kept by someone impure.
Since I have sixteen thousand wives, I am incapable of keeping
it. How can Satyabhama accept it? The noble Balabhadra will
not give up drinking liquor and pursuit of endless objects of
pleasure. O Danapati! Therefore, I, Balabhadra, Satya and all
the other Yadus are requesting you that you should keep it.
You alone are capable. Kept by you, it will do a lot of good
to the kingdom. For the sake of the kindom, please do not
refuse." Addressed in this way, Danapati agreed and accepted
that great jewel. Since then, Akrura publicly wore it around
his neck and he dazzled as he walked, like the sun with its
rays. If a person remembers this incident of the illustrious one
cleansing himself of the false accusation, he will never have to
suffer from the least bit of slander. All his senses will remain
intact, and he will be freed from all sins.'

Chapter 4(14) (Other Descendants and Shishupala)

Shri Parashara said, 'Anamitra's son was named Shini.
Shini's son was Satyaka and Satyaka's son was Satyaki, also
known by the name of Yuyudhana. Satyaki's son was Sanjaya,
Sanjaya's son was Kuni and Kuni's son was Yugandhara.
These were the Shaineyas. Vrishni was Anamitra's descendant.

Vrishni's son was Shvaphalka, whose power has been spoken
about. Shvaphalka had a younger brother named Chitraka.
Through Gandini, Shvaphalka's son was Akrura. The
other sons were known as Upamadgu, Mrida, Mridavishva,
Arimejaya, Giri, Kshatrapaksha, Shataghna, Arimardana,
Dharmadrik, Drishtadharma, Gandhamoja, Avaha and
Prativaha. He also had a daughter, known as Sutara. Akrura's
two sons were Devavat and Upadeva. Chitraka had many
sons; Prithu and Vriprithu were the important ones. Andhaka
had four sons, known as Kukura, Bhajamana, Shuchi and
Kambalabarhisha. Kukura's son was Dhrishta, Dhrishta's son
was Kapotaroma and Kapotaroma's son was Viloma. Viloma's
son was known as Anu, and he was Tumburu's[819] friend.
Anu's son was Anakadundubhi, Anakadundubhi's son was
Abhijit and Abhijit's son was Punarvasu. Punarvasu had a son
named Ahuka and a daughter named Ahuki. Ahuka had two
sons, Devaka and Ugrasena. Devaka had four sons, Devavat,
Upadeva, Sahadeva and Devarakshita. These had seven sisters,
Vrikadevaa, Upadevaa, Devarakshitaa, Shridevaa, Shantidevaa,
Sahadevaa and Devaki. Vasudeva[820] married all of them.
Ugrasena's sons were known as Kamsa, Nyagrodha, Sunaman,
Kahlva, Shanku, Subhumi, Rashtrapala, Yuddhatushti and
Tushtimat. Ugrasena's daughters were Kamsaa, Kamsavati,
Sutanu, Rashtrapali and Kahlvaa. Bhajamana had Viduratha
as a son. Viduratha's son was Shura, Shura's son was
Shami, Shami's son was Pratikshatra, Pratikshatra's son was
Svayambhoja and Svayambhoja's son was Hridika. Hridika's
sons were Kritavarma, Shatadhanu,[821] Devarha, Devagarbha
and others. Devagarbha's son was Shura and Shura's wife was
named Marisha.'

---

[819] A *gandharva*.
[820] Krishna's father.
[821] The same as Shatadhanva.

'Through her, he had ten sons and Vasudeva was the eldest. As soon as he was born, those with unimpeded vision saw that the illustrious one's portion would be born in his house and devas sounded their divine *anaka*s and *dundubhi*s.[822] Thus assured, he was given the name of Anakadundubhi. He had nine brothers, known as Devabhaga, Devashrava, Ashtaka, Kakuchakra, Vatsadharaka, Srinjaya, Shyama, Shamika and Gandusha. Vasudeva and the others had five sisters: Pritha, Shrutadevaa, Shrutakirti, Shrutashravaa and Rajadhidevi. Shura had a friend named Kunti.[823] Since he was without a son, following the proper norms, Shura gave him Pritha as a daughter. Pandu married her. Through Dharma, Anila and Indra, she gave birth to the three sons, Yudhishthira, Bhimasena and Arjuna. Earlier, when she was unmarried and was a maiden, through the illustrious Bhaskara, she gave birth to a son named Karna. Her co-wife was named Madri. Through Nasatya and Dasra,[824] she gave Pandu two sons, Nakula and Sahadeva. Shrutadevaa married Vriddhadharma, from the Karusha lineage. She gave birth to a giant *asura*, named Dantavakra. Shrutakirti married the king of Kekaya. She had five sons, Santardana and others. They were known as Kekayas. Through the king of Avanti, Rajadhidevi gave birth to Vinda and Anuvinda. Shrutashravaa married the king of Chedi, named Damaghosha. They obtained Shishupala as a son. In a former life, he used to be extensive in his valour. He was Hiranyakashipu, forefather of the *daitya*s. In his Narasimha form, the illustrious one, who is the preceptor of all the worlds, killed him. Subsequently, he became the one named Dashanana, infinite in his strength and valour and possessing all the qualities of prosperity and prowess. Through his powers, he conquered the three worlds and became their

---

[822] Respectively, large drums and kettledrums.
[823] That is, Kuntibhoja.
[824] The two Ashvins.

lord. He enjoyed all these for a long period of time. In his form of Raghava, the illustrious one killed him. Because of his good merits, he had obtained the fruit that his body would be brought down by the illustrious one. Subsequently, he became the one named Shishupala, the son of Damaghosha, the king of Chedi. The illustrious one, known as the one with eyes like a lotus, descended to remove the earth's burden. Shishupala's intelligence was such that he was once again bound in enmity towards him and acted accordingly. When he was killed by the illustrious one, he fixed his mind attentively on the *paramatman* and united with him. If the illustrious one is pleased, he bestows what is desired. If he is displeased and kills someone, he gives him a divine and unmatched position.'

Chapter 4(15) (Vasudeva's Descendants)

Maitreya said, 'Hiranyakashipu and Ravana were killed by Vishnu. The obtained objects of pleasure difficult for the immortals to get. But though they were killed by him, they were not dissolved into him. However, when Shishupala was killed, he united into eternal Hari. O one who upholds every kind of *dharma*! I wish to hear about this. I have intense curiosity. You should tell me this.'

Shri Parashara replied,[825] 'For the sake of killing the lord of the *daityas*, the cause behind the creation, preservation and destruction of the entire universe formerly assumed the Nrisimha form. However, since Hiranyakashipu did not know this was Vishnu, his mind was not immersed in him.

---

[825] This entire passage has a completely different sentence structure, with extended similes and metaphors, and is therefore, more difficult to translate.

He did originate from *sattva* and was thus born from what was exceedingly pure. But his intelligence was only driven by *rajas*. Thus, though he came by his death at Vishnu's hands, because of those sentiments, he did not obtain union with him. In his state as Dashanana, he obtained objects of pleasure and prosperity and a great deal of lordship over all the three worlds. However, his mind was not immersed in the illustrious one, who is without a beginning and without an end. Since he did not seek support in him, he did not dissolve into the supreme *brahman*. Thus, in his state as Dashanana, he came under the subjugation of Ananga[826] and his mind was attracted towards Janaki. He was killed by the illustrious one, in his form as Dasharathi.[827] However, though he saw that form, he did not realize this was Achyuta. Because of the attachment inside his heart, his intelligence was such that he took him to be only a man. The fruit of being killed by Achyuta was limited to being born as Shishupala in the lineage of the king of Chedi, one praised throughout that entire earth. He also obtained unlimited prosperity. As Shishupala, there were many reasons for the illustrious one's name to be brought to his attention. Across many births, the hatred towards Achyuta was constantly in his mind and at that time, was reinforced by the incessant hearing of his name. Though he continuously abused and criticized him, he had to constantly repeat his name. Because of these extremely firm sentiments of enmity, whether he was walking, eating, bathing or lying down, there was no other form in his mind except that of the one with eyes like the petals of blossoming lotuses, attired in bright yellow garments, with a sparkling diadem, armlets and bracelets, illuminating the directions with his extensive four-armed form, wielding a *chakra* and a mace. He pronounced his name and held that

---

[826] One without a body, the god of love, Kama.
[827] Dasharatha's son, Rama.

form in his heart, even though it was because of rage. This was also true at the time of his death, when the illustrious one raised his *chakra*, garlanded in rays and blazing in his own form of inexhaustible energy. Therefore, as he looked at the illustrious one, his hatred and other sentiments were destroyed, and he merged into the *brahman*. As his death was quickly brought about by the illustrious one's *chakra*, all his store of sins was burnt up. At that instant, he approached the illustrious one and dissolved into him. I have thus told you everything. If a person remembers the illustrious one's deeds, even if it is because of bonds of hatred, this bestows fruits that are difficult for all the gods, *asura*s and others to obtain. What need be said about a person whose mind is full of devotion?'

'Anakadundubhi Vasudeva had many wives: Pouravi, Rohini, Madira, Bhadra and Devaki being the foremost. Through Rohini, Anakadundubhi had the sons Balabhadra, Shatha, Sarana, Durmada and others. Baladeva[828] married Revati and had the sons Vishatha and Ulmuka. Sarana's sons were Arshti, Marshti, Shishu, Satya, Satyadhriti and others. Bhadrashva, Bhadrabahu, Durdama, Bhuta and others were born in Rohini's lineage. Madira's sons were Nanda, Upananda, Kritaka and others. Through Bhadra, the sons were Upanidhi, Gada and others. Vaishali[829] had only one son, Koushika. Through Devaki, Anakadundubhi had six sons, known as Kirtimat, Sushena, Udayu, Bhadrasena, Rijadasa and Bhadradeva. Kamsa killed them all. Subsequently, sent by the illustrious one, in the middle of the night, Yoganidra took away the seventh fetus and conveyed it to Rohini's womb. Since he was dragged away, he came to be known as Samkarshana.[830] The illustrious one is the foundation of the great tree that is

---

[828] The same as Balabhadra or Balarama.
[829] A wife not mentioned so far.
[830] Balarama's name. From *karshana* (dragging).

the universe. He cannot be comprehended by the minds of all
the gods, *asura*s, sages and people, be they of the past or the
future. The foremost ones, the one born from the lotus[831] and
Anala prostrated themselves before him and sought his favours,
so that he might remove the earth's burden. The illustrious
one is without a beginning, without a middle and without an
end. Vaasudeva descended in Devaki's womb. Because of his
favours, Yoganidra's powers increased and became extensive.
She took away the fetus and placed it in the womb of Yashoda,
Nandagopa's wife. When he was born, the sun, the moon and
the planets sparkled. Fear from predatory beasts and other things
was pacified. The entire universe was well. When the lotus-eyed
one was born, through him, there was *dharma*. As soon as he
was born, he made the entire universe turn towards the virtuous
path. When the illustrious one descended in the world of the
mortals, he had more than sixteen thousand and one hundred
wives. He had eight main wives: Rukmini, Satyabhama,
Jambavati, Charuhasini and others.[832] The illustrious one has
the universe as his form. He is without a beginning. Through
them, he had one hundred and eighty thousand sons. Thirteen
of them were important: Pradyumna, Charudeshna, Samba and
others. Pradyumna married Rukmavati, Rukmi's daughter and
through her, has a son named Aniruddha. Aniruddha married
Rukmi's granddaughter, named Subhadra. Through her, he had
a son named Vajra. Vajra's son was Pratibahu and Pratibahu's
son was Sucharu. In this way, the men of the Yadu lineage had
many hundreds and thousands of sons. Even in one hundred
years, one is incapable of enumerating them. Therefore, there
are *shloka*s about their conduct. "Three crore and eighty-eight
thousand *acharya*s are engaged in their homes to teach these

[831] Brahma.
[832] The number (and names) of Krishna's wives varies from text to
text.

sons. Who can count the numbers of the great-souled Yadavas? Where there is Ahuka,[833] there are seen to be tens of thousands and hundreds of thousands." In the battle between *deva*s and *asura*s, extremely strong *daitya*s were killed. They were born as humans and oppressed people. To exterminate them, *deva*s were born in the Yadu lineage. O *brahmana*! They descended in more than one hundred such families. Among these numbers, Vishnu was there as their lord. All the Yadavas followed his instructions and prospered. If a man constantly hears this account about the origin of the Vrishnis, he is freed from all his sins and obtains Vishnu's world.'

Chapter 4(16) (Turvasu's Descendants)

Shri Parashara said, 'I have told you everything about Yadu's lineage. Now hear about Turvasu's[834] lineage. Turvasu's son was Vahni and Vahni's son was Bharga. Bharga's son was Bhanu and Bhanu's son was Trayisanu. Trayisanu's son was Kardama and Kardama's son was Marutta. Marutta did not have offspring. Hence, he adopted Dushyanta, from Puru's lineage, as a son. In this way, because of Yayati's curse, this lineage had to find refuge in Puru's lineage.'

Chapter 4(17) (Druhyu's Descendants)

Shri Parashara said, 'Druhyu's son was Babhru and Babhru's son was Setu. Setu's son was named Arabdha. Arabdha's

---

[833] The king of the Yadavas, Ugrasena's father.
[834] The text says Durvasu. We have amended it to Turvasu.

son was Gandhara and Gandhara's son was Dharma. Dharma's son was Dhrita, Dhrita's son was Durdama and Durdama's son was Prachetas. Prachetas had one hundred sons. However, since they didn't follow *dharma*, they ruled over the many *mleccha*s in the northern direction.'

Chapter 4(18) (Anu's Descendants)

Shri Parashara said, 'Yayati's fourth son was Anu. He had three sons, known as Sabhanala, Chakshu and Parameshu. Sabhanala's son was Kalanala and Kalanala's son was Srinjaya. Srinjaya's son was Puranjaya and Puranjaya's son was Janamejaya. Janamejaya's son was Mahashala and Mahashala's son was Mahamana. Mahmana had two sons, Ushinara and Titikshu. Ushinara had five sons, known as Shibi, Nriga, Nava, Krimi and Varma. Shibi's four sons were Prishadarbha, Suvira, Kekaya and Madraka. Titikshu's son was Rushadratha. Rushadratha's son was Hema, Hema's son was Sutapa and Sutapa's son was Bali. In Bali's *kshetra*,[835] Dirghatama gave birth to the *kshatriya*s known as Anga, Vanga, Kalinga, Suhma and Poundra. Their descendants ruled[836] over the five kingdoms named after them. Anga's son was Pana, Pana's son was Diviratha and Diviratha's son was Dharmaratha. Dharmaratha's son was Chitraratha and Chitratha's son was known as Romapada. He was the one who was Dasharatha's[837] friend. Since Romapada didn't have a son, Dasharatha gave him his daughter, named Shanta, to be

---

[835] Through Bali's wife.

[836] Champa or Champapuri, the capital of the Anga kingdom, near Bhagalpur.

[837] Rama's father.

brought up as his daughter. Romapada's son was Chaturanga[838] and Chaturanga's son was Prithulaksha. Prithulaksha's son was Champa, who established the city of Champa. Champa had a son named Haryanga. Haryanga's son was Bhadraratha, Bhadraratha's son was Brihadratha, Brihadratha's son was Brihatkarma, Brihatkarma's son was Brihadbhanu, Brihadbhanu's son was Brihanmana and Brihanmana's son was Jayadratha. Jayadratha's wife had mixed parentage, one was a *brahmana* and the other was a *kshatriya*. Through her, Jayadratha had a son named Vijaya. Vijaya had a son named Dhriti. Dhriti's son was Dhritavrata, Dhritavrata's son was Satyakarma and Satyakarma's son was Atiratha. When he went to the Ganga, inside a basket, he found Karna, the son who had been cast away by Pritha.[839] Karna's son was Vrishasena. These were the ones from the Anga lineage. After this, you will hear about Puru's lineage.'

Chapter 4(19) (Puru's Lineage)

Shri Parashara said, 'Puru's son was Janamejaya, Janamejaya's son was Prachinvat, Prachinvat's son was Pravira, Pravira's son was Manasyu, Manasyu's son was Abhayada, Abhayada's son was Sudyu, Sudyu's son was Bahugata, Bahugata's son was Samyati, Samyati's son was Ahamyati and Ahamyati's son was Roudrashva. Roudrashva had ten sons, named Riteshu, Kaksheshu, Sthandileshu, Kriteshu, Jaleshu, Dharmeshu, Dhriteshu, Sthaleshu, Sannateshu and Vaneshu. Riteshu's son was Antinara and Antinara's sons were Sumati, Apratiratha and Dhruva. Apratiratha's son was Kanva and Kanva's son

---

[838] Obviously born after Shanta's adoption.
[839] Kunti.

was Medhatithi. The *brahmana*s known as Kanvayanas
were descended from Medhatithi. Apratiratha had another
son, Ailina. Ailina had four sons, Dushyanta and others.
Dushyanta's son was *chakravarty* Bharata. The *Deva*s chant
two *shloka*s about the reason for this name. "The mother
is the vessel. The father is the one through whom a son is
born. O Dushyanta! Nurture[840] this son and do not show
disrespect towards Shakuntala. O divinity among men! A son
born from a person's semen takes him away from Yama's
abode. Shakuntala has spoken the truth. You are the father
behind this conception." Through three wives, Bharata had
nine sons. However, the mothers feared that he would say,
"He does not look like me." and abandon them. Therefore,
the mothers killed those sons. Since his attempt to get a son
was unsuccessful, Bharata performed a *soma* sacrifice for the
Maruts. Utathya's wife was Mamata and through Brihaspati's
semen, she conceived Bharadvaja.[841] The Martus gave
Bharadvaja to Bharata as his son. A *shloka* is read about the
choice of this name. Brihaspati said, "O foolish lady! Nurture
this one, born from two fathers." She replied, "O Brihaspati!
You nurture this Bharadvaja." Saying this, both fathers left
and he came to be Bharadvaja.[842] Bharadvaja was also known
as Vitatha. Since Bharata's attempts to get a son were futile
and the Maruts gave him this son, that is how the son came
to have the name of Vitatha.[843] Vitatha's son was Manyu and
Manyu's sons were Brihatkshatra, Mahavirya, Nagara and

[840] Bharata was named from the root word for nurture (*bhara*).
[841] But Dirghatama kicked him out through the flank. Brihaspati
was Utathya's younger brother. Dirghatama was already in Mamata's
womb, conceived through Utathya. When Brihaspati had intercourse
with Mamata, she conceived Bharadvaja. Since there wasn't place for
two sons in the womb, Dirghatama kicked Bharadvaja out.
[842] From nurture (*bhara*) and born from two (*dvaja*).
[843] *Vitatha* means unsuccessful/futile.

Garga. Nagara's son was Sanskriti and Sanskriti's sons were
Gurupriti and Rantideva. Garga's son was Shini, and their
descendants are known as Gargyas and Shainyas. Though the
fathers were *kshatriyas*, they became *brahmanas*. Mahavirya
had a son named Durukshaya. He had three sons, Trayyaruni,
Pushkarina and Kapi. Of these three sons, the youngest became
a *brahmana*. Brihatkshatra's son was Suhotra and Suhotra's
son was Hastin. Hastin is the one who established the city of
Hastinapura. Hastin had three sons, Ajamidha, Dvijamidha
and Purumidha. Ajamidha's son was Kanva and Kanva's son
was Medhatithi. The *brahmanas* known as Kanvas descended
from him. Ajamidha's other son was Brihadishu. Brihadishu's
son was Brihaddhanu, Brihaddhanu's son was Brihatkarma,
Brihatkarma's son was Jayadratha and Jayadratha's son was
Vishvajit. Vishvajit's son was Senajit. Senajit's sons were
known as Ruchirashva, Kashya, Dridhahanu and Vatsahanu.
Ruchirashva's son was Prithusena, Prithusena's son was Para
and Para's son was Nila. Nila had one hundred sons. The
most important was Samara, the lord of Kampilya.[844] Samara
had three sons, Para, Supara and Sadashva. Supara's son was
Prithu, Prithu's son was Sukriti, Sukriti's son was Vibhraja
and Vibhraja's son was Anuha. Anuha married Kirti, Shuka's
daughter. Anuha's son was Brahmadatta and Brahmadatta's
son was Vishvaksena. Vishvaksena's son was Udaksena and
Udaksena's son was Bhallabha.'

'Dvijamidha had a son known as Yavinara. Yavinara's son
was Dhritimat, Dhritimat's son was Satyadhriti, Satyadhriti's
son was Dridhanemi, Dridhanemi's son was Suparshva,
Suparshva's son was Sumati and Sumati's son was Sannatimat.
Sannatimat's son was Krita, who studied *yoga* from
Hiranyanabha and composed twenty-four *Sama Veda samhitas*

---

[844] Kampilya was the capital of South Panchala and is today's
Aligarh.

for *brahmana*s from the east. Krita's son was Ugrayudha.
His prosperity destroyed the Nipas.[845] Ugrayudha's son was
Kshemya, Kshemya's son was Sudhira, Sudhira's son was
Ripunjaya and Ripunjaya's son was Bahuratha. These are the
Pouravas. Ajamidha had a wife named Nalini. Through her, he
had a son known as Nila. Nila's son was Shanti, Shanti's son
was Sushanti, Sushanti's son was Puranjaya, Puranjaya's son
was Riksha and Riksha's son was Haryashva. Haryashva had
five sons known as Mudgala, Srinjaya, Brihadishu, Yavinara
and Kampilya. The father said, "These five sons of mine
are capable of protecting the kingdom." Thus, they became
Panchalas.[846] Though the father Mudgala was a *kshatriya*, his
descendants became the Moudgalya *brahmana*s. Mudgala's son
was also Haryashva and this Haryashva had twins, Divodasa
and Ahalya.[847] Through Ahalya, Sharadvat had a son named
Shatananda. Shatananda had a son named Satyadhriti, who
knew about *dhanurveda*. When Satyadhriti saw the beautiful
apsara Urvashi, his semen fell down on a clump of reeds. This
divided into two and became two children, a son and a daughter.
When he went out on a hunt, Shantanu saw them and was filled
with compassion. They were known as Kripa and Kripi.[848]
The son was Kripa. The daughter was Kripi, Dronacharya's
wife and Ashvatthama's mother. Divodasa's son was Mitrayu,
Mitrayu's son was King Chyavana, Chyavana's son was Sudasa
and Sudasa's son was Soudasa, also known as Sahadeva.
Sahadeva's son was Somaka. Somaka had one hundred sons,
the eldest was Jantu and the youngest was Prishat. Prishat's
son was Drupada, Drupada's son was Dhrishtadyumna and
Dhrishtadyumna's son was Dhrishtaketu. Ajamidha had

---

[845] The kings known as the Nipas.
[846] From *pancha* (five).
[847] Respectively, a son and a daughter.
[848] From *kripa* (compassion).

another son, named Riksha. Riksha's son was Samvarana and Samvarana's son was Kuru. The *dharma kshetra* known as Kurukshetra was named after Kuru. Among Kuru's sons, the most important were Sudhanu, Jahnu and Parikshit. Sudhanu's son was Suhotra, Suhotra's son was Chyavana, Chyavana's son was Kritaka and Kritaka's son was Uparichara Vasu. Vasu had seven sons, Brihadratha, Pratyagra, Kushamba, Kuchela and Matsya being the most important. Brihadratha's son was Kushagra, Kushagra's son was Vrishabha, Vrishabha's son was Pushpavat, Pushpavat's son was Satyahita, Satyahita's son was Sudhanva and Sudhanva's son was Jantu. Brihadratha had another son, who was born in two parts. Since Jara[849] united these, he came to have the name of Jarasandha. Jarasandha's son was Sahadeva, Sahadeva's son was Somapa and Somapa's son was Shrutishrava. I have thus described to you the kings of Magadha.'[850]

Chapter 4(20) (Kuru's Lineage)

Shri Parashara said, 'Parikshit[851] had four sons, Janamejaya, Shrutasena, Ugrasena and Bhimasena. Jahnu's[852] son was Suratha and Suratha's son was Viduratha. Viduratha's son was Sarvabhouma, Sarvabhouma's son was Jayatsena, Jayatsena's son was Aradhita, Aradhita's son was Ayutayu and Ayutayu's son was Akrodhana. Akrodhana's son was Devatithi, while Riksha was another son. Riksha's son was Bhimasena, Bhimasena's son was Dilipa and Dilipa's son was

---

[849] A demoness. From Jara and *sandhi* (union).
[850] The dynasty descended from Brihadratha.
[851] Kuru's son.
[852] Kuru's son.

Pratipa. Pratipa had three sons, known as Devapi, Shantanu and Bahlika. When he was a child, Devapi entered the forst and Shantanu became the lord of the earth. A *shloka* about him is chanted on earth. "If he touches an old man with his hand, that person becomes young. Since all his deeds ensure peace first, he is known as Shantanu."[853] In Shantanu's kingdom, the divinity did not rain down for twelve years. The king saw that the entire kingdom would get destroyed. He asked *brahmana*s, "Why is the divinity not showering down on our kingdom? What is my crime?" The *brahmana*s told him, "By enjoying what belongs to your elder brother, you have become a *parivetta*."[854] The king asked them again, "What should be done by me now?" They answered again, "Until Devapi is brought down because of his taints, this kingdom rightfully belongs to him. Therefore, enough is enough. You should give it back to him." Ashmaravin was one of the foremost among the ministers. When he heard this, he sent some who spoke against the *Veda*s to the ascetic in the forest. The prince[855] was extremely upright in his intelligence. However, they turned his mind against the path of the *Veda*s and made him act accordingly. Meanwhile, King Shantanu was filled with sorrow and grief because of the words spoken by the *brahmana*s. Placing the *brahmana*s ahead of him, he went to the forest, to return the kingdom to his elder brother.

[853] From *shanti* (peace).

[854] A *parivetta* is someone who marries or accepts a share in a sacrifice before his elder brother. The story is recounted differently in different texts. Devapi had leprosy and was unworthy to succeed Pratipa. That is the reason he retired to the forest. Interpretations often suggest Devapi deviated from the norms. On the contrary, Devapi abided by the norms, and it is the ministers and *brahmana*s who deviated. When Devapi refused the kingdom, Indra, the god of rains, showered down.

[855] Devapi.

They reached the hermitage of Devapi, the son of a king. The *brahmanas* told him that, according to the words and norms of the *Veda*s, it was necessary that the kingdom must vest with the older brother. However, Devapi had been polluted by arguments that were against the *Veda*s and he refused them in many ways. At this, the *brahmana*s told Shantanu, "O king! Come away. Be tranquil. Enough of entreating him. The lack of rain is because of his wicked ways. The words of the *Veda*s have come down from time immemorial. But since he has argued against them, he is polluted and has fallen down. When the elder brother has fallen down, you are no longer a *parivetta*." Thus addressed, Shantanu returned to his own city and ruled over the kingdom. Though Devapi still existed, he had been polluted by uttering words that were against those of the *Veda*s. Despite the elder brother existing, the illustrious Parjanya showered down, and all the crops resulted.'

'Bahlika's son was Somadatta. Somadatta had three sons, known as Bhuri, Bhurishrava and Shalya. Through Jahnavi, the river of the immortals, Bhishma was born as Shantanu's son. He was extensive in his deeds and knew the purport of all the sacred texts. Through Satyavati, Shantanu had two sons, Chitrangada and Vichitravirya. While he was still a child, in a battle, Chitrangada was killed by a *gandharva*, also known as Chitrangada. Vichitravirya married Amba and Ambalika, the daughters of the king of Kashi. While he was pleasuring with them excessively, consumption took hold of him, and he died. Satyavati asked her son, Krishna Dvaipayana, to use *niyoga* and he did not go against his mother's wishes.[856] Accordingly, in Vichitravirya's *kshetra*, he had Dhritarashtra

---

[856] Before marrying Shantanu, Satyavati had Krishna Dvaipayana Vedavyasa as a son, the father being the sage Parashara. Under the *niyoga* system, in some situations, a man could have a son through his wife, but through another man.

and Pandu as sons. Through a maidservant who was sent, he
had Vidura as a son. Through Gandhari, Dhritarashtra had
one hundred sons, Duryodhana and Duhshasana being the
most important. While he went to the forest on a hunt, Pandu
was cursed by a *rishi* and was incapable of procreation. Five
sons were therefore born: Yudhishthira, Bhimasena and Arjuna
to Kunti through Dharma, Vayu and Shakra respectively, and
Nakula and Sahadeva to Madri through the two Ashvins.
Through Droupadi, they had five sons: Yudhishthira's son was
Prativindhya, Bhimasena's son was Shrutasena, Arjuna's son
was Shrutakirti, Nakula's son was Shatanika and Sahadeva's
son was Shrutakarma. The Pandavas also had other sons.
Through Youdheyi, Yudhishthira had Devaka as a son.
Through Hidimba, Bhimasena had Ghatotkacha as a son.
Through Kashi, Bhimasena had Sarvaga as a son. Through
Vijayi, Sahadeva had Suhotra as a son. Through Renumati,
Nakula had Niramitra as a son. Through Ulupi, the daughter
of the *naga*s, Arjuna had a son named Iravat. Through the
daughter of the king of Manipura, who was following the
dharma of a *putrika*,[857] Arjuna had a son named Babruvahana.
Through Subhadra, his son was Abhimanyu. Even as a child,
he was extremely strong and valiant and defeated all the enemy
charioteers. The fetus conceived in Uttara's womb through
Abhimanyu was destroyed when Ashvatthama unleashed his
brahmastra weapon and reduced it to ashes. The feet of the
illustrious one are worshipped by all the gods and *asura*s.
Because of his own wishes and reasons, he had assumed human
form. He again brought the fetus back to life and Parikshit
was born. He now follows *dharma* and rules over the entire
unrestricted globe of the earth.'

[857] In the absence of a son, a daughter who is brought up as a son
and heir.

Chapter 4(21) (Parikshit's Descendants)

Shri Parashara said, 'I will now describe to you the future
lords of the earth. The present lord of the earth, Parikshit,
will have four sons: Janamejaya, Shrutasena, Ugrasena and
Bhimasena. Janamejaya's son will be Shatanika. He will study
the *Vedas* under Yajnavalkya and the use of weapons under
Kripa. However, his mental inclinations will be such that
he will be detached from material objects and the kingdom.
Through Shounaka's instructions, he will become wise in
knowledge about the *atman* and obtain *nirvana*. Shatanika's
son will be Ashvamedhadatta and Ashvamedhadatta's son will
be Adhisimakrishna. Adhisimakrishna's son will be Nichaknu.
When Hastinapura is flooded by the Ganga, he is the one who
will establish Koushambi. His son will be Ushna, Ushna's son
will be Chitraratha and Chitraratha's son will be Shuchiratha.
Shuchiratha's son will be Vrishnimat, Vrishnimat's son will
be Sushena, Sushena's son will be Sunitha, Sunitha's son will
be Nripachakshu, Nripachakshu's son will be Sukhibala,
Sukhibala's son will be Pariplava, Pariplava's son will be
Sunaya and Sunaya's son will be Medhavin. Medhavin's son
will be Ripunjaya, Ripunjaya's son will be Tigma, Tigma's
son will be Brihadratha, Brihadratha's son will be Sudasa
and Sudasa's son will be Shatanika. Shatanika's son will
be Udayana, Udayana's son will be Ahinara, Ahinara's son
will be Dandapani, Dandapani's son will be Nimitta and
Nimitta's son will be Kshemaka. In this connection, there
is a *shloka*. "There was a lineage that *brahmarshis* cleansed
and *brahmanas* and *kshatriyas* originated from it. When
Kshemaka becomes the king of this lineage, *kali yuga* will
arrive."

Chapter 4(22) (Future Ikshvaku Kings)

Shri Parashara said, 'I will now describe the future kings of the Ikshvaku lineage. Brihadbala's son will be Brihatkshana, Brihatkshana's son will be Urukshaya, Urukshaya's son will be Vatsavyuha, Vatsvyuha's son will be Prativyoma, Prativyoma's son will be Divakara, Divakara's son will be Sahadeva, Sahadeva's son will be Brihadashva, Brihadashva's son will be Bhanuratha, Bhanuratha's son will be Supratika, Supratika's son will be Marudeva, Marudeva's son will be Sunakshatra, Sunakshatra's son will be Kinnara, Kinnara's son will be Antariksha, Antariksha's son will be Suparna, Suparna's son will be Amitrajit, Amitrajit's son will be Brihadraja, Brihadraja's son will be Dharmin, Dharmin's son will be Kritanjaya, Kritanjaya's son will be Rananjaya, Rananjaya's son will be Sanjaya, Sanjaya's son will be Shakya, Shakya's son will be Shuddhodana, Shuddhodana's son will be Rahula, Rahula's son will be Prasenjit, Prasenjit's son will be Kshudraka, Kshudraka's son will be Kundaka, Kundaka's son will be Suratha and Suratha's son will be Sumitra. These are those from the Ikshvaku and Brihadbala lineage. There is a *shloka* about this lineage. "The Ikshvaku lineage will end with Sumitra. When he becomes the king, *kali yuga* will arrive."'

Chapter 4(23) (Future Magadha Kings)

Shri Parashara said, 'I will now progressively tell you about the Brihadratha lineage of Magadha. There have been immensely strong and valiant ones in this lineage. Jarasandha was the most important. Jarasandha's son is Sahadeva, Sahadeva's son will be Somapi, Somapi's son will be

Shrutashrava, Shrutashrava's son will be Ayutayus, the son of Ayutayus will be Niramitra, Niramitra's son will be Sunetra, Sunetra's son will be Brihatkarma, Brihatkarma's son will be Senajit, Senajit's son will be Shrutanjaya, Shrutanjaya's son will be Vipra, Vipra will have a son named Shuchi, Shuchi's son will be Kshemya, Kshemya's son will be Suvrata, Suvrata's son will be Dharma, Dharma's son will be Sushrava, Sushrava's son will be Dridhasena, Dridhasena's son will be Subala, Subala's son will be Sunita, Sunita's son will be Satyajit, Satyajit's son will be Vishvajit and Vishvajit's son will be Ripunjaya. The kings of the Brihadratha lineage will rule for one thousand years.'

Chapter 4(24) (More on the Future)

Shri Parashara said, 'In the Brihadratha lineage, Ripunjaya will have an adviser named Munika. He will kill his master and instate his own son, named Pradyota. Pradyota's son will be named Balaka. Balaka's son will be Vishakhayupa, Vishakhayupa's son will be Janaka, Janaka's son will be Nandivardhana and Nandivardhana's son will be Nandi. In this way, the five Pradyotas will rule the earth for one hundred and thirty-eight years.'

'Shishunabha[858] will come after this. Shishunabha's son will be Kakavarna, Kakavarna's son will be Kshemadharma, Kshemadharma's son will be Kshatouja, Kshatouja's son will be Vidhisara, Vidhisara's son will be Ajatashatru, Ajatashatru's son will be Arbhaka, Arbhaka's son will be Udayana, Udayana's son will be Nandivardhana and Nandivardhana's son will be Mahanandi. These kings of the Shishunabha dynasty will rule the earth for three hundred and sixty-two years.'

---

[858] That is, Shishunaga.

'Through the womb of a *shudra* woman, Mahanandi will have a son named Mahapadma Nanda. He will be extremely avaricious and extremely strong. As a destroyer of all the *kshatriya*s, he will be like another Parashurama. After him, the *shudra* kings will start to rule. Mahapadma will enjoy the earth as a universal emperor, with his commands not violated anywhere. He will have eight sons, Sumalya and others. Following Mahapadma, they will enjoy the earth. Mahapadma and his sons will be lords of the earth for one hundred years. After this, the *brahmana* Koutilya will uproot these nine Nandas.'

'In their absence, the Mouryas[859] will enjoy the earth. Chandragupta will be born and Koutilya will instate him. Chandragupta's son will be Bindusara and Bindusara's son will be Ashokavardhana. Ashokavardhana's son will be Suyasha, Suyasha's son will be Dasharatha, Dasharatha's son will be Samyuta, Samyuta's son will be Shalishuka, Shalishuka's son will be Somasharma, Somasharma's son will be Shatadhanva and Shatadhanva's son will be named Brihadratha. In this way, the ten Mourya kings will rule for one hundred and thirty-seven years.'

'After this, the earth will be enjoyed by ten Shungas. Pushyamitra, the commander,[860] will kill his master and rule over the kingdom. Pushyamitra's son will be Agnimitra. Agnimitra's son will be Sujyeshtha, Sujyeshta's son will be Vasumitra, Vasumitra's son will be Apyundaka, Apyundaka's son will be Pulindaka, Pulindaka's son will be Ghoshavasu, Ghoshavasu's son will be Vajramitra, Vajramitra's son will be Bhagavata and Bhagavata's son will be Devabhuti. These Shungas will enjoy the earth for one hundred and twelve years.'

[859] Here, the text says Mourvyas.
[860] Of the last Mourya king.

'After this, the Kanvas will be kings. The Shunga king, Devabhuti will be addicted to vices. His adviser Kanva, also named Vasudeva, will kill him and enjoy the earth himself. Kanva's son will be Bhumitra, Bhumitra's son will be Narayana and Narayana's son will be Susharma. These four Kanvas will be kings for forty-five years.'

'The Kanva Susharma will be killed by his powerful servant, named Pucchaka, hailing from the Andhra region. He will enjoy the earth. After him, his brother, Krishna, will become lord of the earth. Krishna's son will be Shantakarni, Shantakarni's son will be Purnotsanga, Purnotsanga's son will be Shatakarni, Shatakarni's son will be Lambodara, Lambodara's son will be Pilaka, Pilaka's son will be Meghasvati, Megasvati's son will be Patumat, Patumat's son will be Arishtakarma, Arishtakarma's son will be Halahala, Halahala's son will be Palalaka, Palalaka's son will be Pulindasena, Pulindasena's son will be Sundara, Sundara's son will be Shatakarni, Shatakarni's son will be Shivasvati, Shivasvati's son will be Gomatiputra. Gomatiputra's son will be Alimat, Alimat's son will be Shantakarni, Shantakarni's son will be Shivashrita, Shivashrita's son will be Shivaskandha, Shivaskandha's son will be Yajnashri, Yajnashri's son will be Dviyajna, Dviyajna's son will be Chandrashri and Chandrashri's son will be Pulomapi. These thirty kings will enjoy the earth for four hundred and fifty-six years.'[861]

'After this, various servants of the Andhras will become kings, such as seven *abhira*s ten Gardabhinas, sixteen other kings,[862] eight Yavanas, fourteen Turushkas, thirteen Mundas and eleven Mounas. These lords of the earth will enjoy the

[861] The names of kings given number only twenty-five. But other Purana's have thirty names.

[862] Other Puranas mention these as Shakas.

earth for one thousand and ninety years.[863] Then, the eleven
Mounas will enjoy the earth for three hundred years.'

'When they are destroyed, the Kaikila Yavanas will sprinkle
their hair and become kings. Their lord will be Vindhyashakti.
Vindhyashakti's son will be Puranjaya, Puranjaya's son will
be Ramachandra, Ramachandra's son will be Dharmavarma,
Dharmavarma's son will be Vanga, Vanga's son will be
Nandana and Nandana's son will be Sunandi. Sunandi's
brother will be Shashukra and Shashukra's son will be Pravira.
They will be kings for one hundred and six years. After their
thirteen sons, there will be three Bahlikas.[864] After this, there
will be the Pushpamitras, the Patumitras, thirteen Kalashvas
and seven Andhras. There will be nine kings in Kosala, and
they will be Naishadhas. In Magadha, a person known as
Vishvasphatika will make other *varnas* kings. He will establish
kaivartas, *batus*, *pulindas* and *brahmanas* in the kingdom.[865]
All the *kshatriya* families will be exterminated. Nine Nagas
will rule over the city named Padmavati. Along the Ganga,
the Guptas and the Magadhas will rule in Prayaga and Gaya.
Devarakshita will rule over the Koshalas, Andhras and Pundras
from the city known as Tamralipta, located along the shores of
the ocean. The Guha kings will rule over Kalinga, Mahisha
and Mahendra. The Manidhanyaka lineage will rule over the
countries in Naishadha, Naimisha and Kalakoshaka. Those
known as Kanakas will enjoy the countries of Trairajya and
Mushika. *Shudras* and *abhiras* will rule over the countries in

---

[863] The next sentence suggests that this duration excludes the
eleven Mounas.

[864] These verses aren't clear at all and are subject to various
interpretations. Nor do they agree with the listings in other Puranas.

[865] *Kaivartas* are fishermen, while *pulindas* are mountainous
tribes. By *batu/vatu*, one might mean either a *brahmachari* or a foolish
person.

Sourashtra, Narmada and the desert regions. *Vratya-dvija*s,[866] *abhira*s, *shudra*s and others will enjoy the earth. The countries along the banks of the Sindhu, Davikorvi[867] and Chandrabhaga and the land of Kashmira will be ruled over by *vratya*s, *mleccha*s, *shudra*s and others.'

'All of these will rule over the earth at the same time. They will be limited in generosity and great in rage. On all occasions, they will be addicted to false *dharma*. They will kill women, children and cattle. They will be addicted to appropriating the property of others. They will be limited in substance and will generally be enveloped in darkness. With limited lifespans, they will rise and fall often. Their desires will be great, but their *dharma* will be limited. They will be avaricious. In these various countries, people will follow wicked conduct. Seeking refuge with the kings, they will follow the conduct of *mleccha*s. In this calamity, the subjects will be destroyed. Every day, little by little, faith, *dharma* and prosperity will diminish, and the world will be destroyed. Wealth alone will be the cause for respect. Desire will be the only cause for a relationship between a husband and wife. A woman will only be meant for enjoyment. Falsehood will determine the course of justice. Drops of elevation will determine the position on earth.[868] If a person wears a *brahmana*'s sacred thread, that will decide whether he is a *brahmana*. The possession of jewels and minerals will determine whether one is praiseworthy. Outward signs will identify an *ashrama*. Wrong policy will be the basis for all conduct. Weakness will also be the basis for all conduct.

[866] *Dvija*s who have been cast out of the *varna* system.

[867] The Devika river in Jammu.

[868] We have translated this sentence literally. This is not quite the sense in which it is interpreted. The interpretation is the following. Sacred spots on earth will not be determined on the basis of whether it is a *tirtha*, but on the basis of whether water is available, even if it is an elevated spot.

If a person fearlessly speaks a lot, that will become a sign of learning. Even if a person is not upright, it will be decided that he is virtuous. A simple bath will be regarded as sufficient for cleansing. If a person is generous, he will be deemed to follow *dharma*. Mutual acceptance will be tantamount to marriage. Wearing of good clothes will decide whether a person is worthy. Even if the water is some distance away, that will be regarded as visiting a *tirtha*. A cheat who wears good clothes will be regarded as great. In this way, there will be these and many other taints among all the *varna*s on earth. A person who is the strongest will become the king. Unable to tolerate these extremely avaricious kings, subjects will seek shelter in the valleys of mountains. They will have to subsist on honey, potherbs, roots, fruits, leaves and flowers as food. The only garments will be the barks of trees, leaves and tattered rags. Subjects will have to endure a great deal of wind, cold, heat and rain. There is no one who will live for more than twenty-three years. In this way, when it is *kali yuga*, all the people will decay.'

'The *dharma* of the *shruti* and *smriti* texts will be almost destroyed and submerged. The illustrious Vasudeva is the creator of everything in the universe, mobile and immobile. He is the original preceptor, and he is without a beginning, a middle and the end. His own *atman* is pervaded by the *brahman*. When *kali yuga* is almost over, his portion will be born in the house of Vishnuyasha, an eminent *brahmana* from the village of Shambala. He will possess the eight potencies and the eight qualities.[869] In his form of Kalki, he will descend on earth. He will use his greatness to destroy the strength of all those who are *mleccha*s, bandits and wicked in deeds and

---

[869] Compassion, forgiveness, cleanliness, lack of jealousy, altruism, lack of greed, purity and self-control are the eight potencies, and the eight qualities are the eight *siddhi*s.

thoughts. He will destroy them and establish everyone in their own *dharma*. After this, at the end of *kali yuga*, it will be as if one has woken up at the end of the night. The intelligence will be unblemished and pure in all countries, sparkling like crystal. At that time, all humans will change, and they will become the seeds, so that their offspring populate the new *krita yuga*. Their descendants will follow the principles of *krita yuga*. In this connection, the following is stated. "When Chandra, Surya, Tishya and Brihaspati are in the same *rashi*, that is when *krita yuga* will commence."[870] O supreme sage! I have thus described to you the royal lineages of the past, the present and the future. From the birth of Parikshit to the instatement of Nanda, it should be known that there are one thousand and fifty years.'

'Among the *saptarshi*s, two are first seen to rise in the eastern sky.[871] If a straight line is drawn between them, in the night, a *nakshatra* is seen at the midpoint. Those two *rishi*s will be associated with that *nakshatra* for one hundred human years. O supreme *brahmana*! When Parikshit was born, they were in Magha *nakshatra*. Since then, *kali yuga*, which lasts for twelve hundred years, has started. When the illustrious Vishnu's portion, born in Vasudeva's[872] house, returned to heaven, *kali yuga* started then. As long as his lotus feet touched the earth, till then, *kali yuga* was incapable of embracing the earth. When the eternal Vishnu's portion returned to heaven, Dharma's son, Yudhishthira, gave up the kingdom, along with his younger brothers. Pandava noticed that the portents were perverse. When Krishna left, Parikshit was instated on

[870] Tishya is another name for the *nakshatra* Pushya, which is in Karkataka (Cancer). Therefore, the sun, the moon and Jupiter will be in Cancer.

[871] In the constellation of the Big Dipper (part of Ursa Major), these are Pulaha and Kratu. Pulaha is Merak and Kratu is Dubhe.

[872] Krishna's father.

the throne. When those two great *rishi*s proceed from Magha
to Purvashadha, starting with Nanda's dynasty, *kali yuga*
will become more powerful. But it started from the day that
Krishna left for heaven. O *brahmana*! Now that *kali yuga* has
arrived, hear about its duration. *Kali yuga* will last for three
hundred and sixty thousand human years, that is, twelve
hundred divine years. O supreme *brahmana*! From one *yuga* to
another *yuga*, thousands of *brahmana*s, *kshatriya*s, *vaishya*s,
*shudra*s and great-souled ones have come and gone. There are
many names, many numbers and many families. Because there
will be repetition, I have not described all of them properly.
There are however two, Devapi from Puru's lineage and Maru
from Ikshvaku's lineage. They possess the strength of great
yoga and reside in Kalapagrama.[873] They are waiting for *krita*
yuga, so that they can start new lines of *kshatriya*s. They are
there, to carry forward the seed of Manu's lineage. In this way,
progressively, Manu's sons have enjoyed the earth during the
three *yuga*s of *krita*, *treta* and *dvapara*. O sage! Some remain
in *kali yuga*, as seeds. That is the way Devapi and Maru remain
even today. I have thus described to you the lineages of the
kings. Even in one hundred years, I am incapable of stating
everything.'

'There have been other kings on earth. Their bodies have
always been blinded by delusion and a sense of mine. "How
will this earth continue to remain mine? How will it continue to
belong to my sons and my lineage?" Afflicted by such thoughts,
all such kings have come and gone. There were those who came
before them. There were those who came after them. There
will be others in the future and there will still be others who
will follow these. On beholding these kings, who are unable
to conquer their *atman*s, the earth laughs, like flowers smiling

[873] The text says Puru instead of Maru. We have corrected it.

in the autumn. O Maitreya! In this connection, the earth sang some *shloka*s. Listen to me. Sage Asita repeated them to Janaka, who held aloft the standard of *dharma*. The earth said, "Despite possessing intelligence, how can these Indras among men be so deluded? Why do they place so much of trust on what they perceive to be *dharma*? Without having conquered their own *atman*s first, they seek to conquer their ministers, their servants and their citizens and wish to be victorious over their enemies. They think, in due course, they will conquer the earth, with all its oceans. With their minds attached in this way, they fail to see that death is not far away. For a person who has conquered his *atman*, bringing the earth, girdled by the ocean, under subjugation is nothing at all. The fruit of conquering one's own *atman* is emancipation. These foolish kings wish to conquer me. Giving me up, their ancestors had to leave. Without having obtained me, their fathers departed. For my sake, they have conflicts with fathers, sons and brothers. With a sense of 'mine' pervading the intelligence, excessive delusion has been generated in them. 'This entire earth is eternally mine. There is no one else it belongs to.' Any evil-minded king who thought in this way has suffered and is dead. Anyone who has glanced at me with a mind enveloped by 'mine' has had to give me up and has come under the subjugation of death. That being the case, why do they have this sense of 'mine'? Why do they seek to exercise their power over me? 'This is mine. Quickly give it up.' There are kings who send such messages to their enemies through messengers. Whenever I hear foolish kings utter such words, I laugh at them and am filled with compassion." O Maitreya! These are the *shloka*s that the earth was heard to sing. The sense of ownership dissolves away, like snow faced with heat. I have thus told you everything about Manu's lineage. Kings who are descended from Vishnu's portions are engaged in the task of preservation. If a man progressively and

faithfully listens to this recounting of Manu's lineage, all his
sins are destroyed, and his *atman* becomes unblemished. He
obtains unmatched wealth, grain and prosperity and his senses
remain unimpeded. The praised lineages of the sun and the
moon have had kings like Ikshvaku, Jahnu, Mandhata, Sagara,
Raghu, Yayati, Nahusha and others. They were immensely
strong and immensely valiant, possessing infinite stores of
riches. But they were conquered by the destroyer, who was
stronger, and these lords among men are only tales now. If
a man listens to everything about these lineages, he obtains
faith and learning. Having obtained this wisdom, a man no
longer has a sense of ownership about sons, wives, homes,
fields, objects and other things. There were foremost men who
tormented themselves through austerities, holding their arms
up for many years. Strong and very energetic, they performed
many excellent sacrifices. But in the course of time, they too
are nothing but tales. The unrestricted Prithu travelled in all
the worlds, conquering arrays of enemies. But he has been
struck down by the wind of time and has been destroyed, like
cotton from the *shalmali* tree, when it is dispersed. Kartyavirya
enjoyed all the *dvipa*s and conquered the enemy ranks. But he is
only a subject for tales now, discussed and debated. Raghava's
arrows destroyed Dashanana and his prosperity illuminated all
the directions. It is nothing now, instantly reduced to ashes
by the destroyer's frown. There was the body of a *chakravarti*
named Mandhata on earth. He is nothing more than a tale.
Hearing all this, how can evil-minded people not be virtuous
and still possess a sense of ownership? Bhagiratha, Sagara,
Kakutstha, Dashanana, Raghava, Lakshmana, Yudhisthira
and others existed. That is true, not false. Where are they now?
We don't know. O *brahmana*! I have told you about kings who
exist now and those who will exist in the future. They are fierce
in their valour. There are others who have not been named.

What happened to the earlier ones will happen to them too. Knowing this, no learned man should ever entertain a sense of "mine". Sons, daughters, wives, fields and other things exist only as long as the body exists.'

This ends Part IV.

Part V

Chapter 5(1): 87 shlokas	*Chapter 5(21): 32 shlokas*
Chapter 5(2): 21 shlokas	*Chapter 5(22): 18 shlokas*
Chapter 5(3): 29 shlokas	*Chapter 5(23): 47 shlokas*
Chapter 5(4): 17 shlokas	*Chapter 5(24): 21 shlokas*
Chapter 5(5): 23 shlokas	*Chapter 5(25): 19 shlokas*
Chapter 5(6): 51 shlokas	*Chapter 5(26): 12 shlokas*
Chapter 5(7): 83 shlokas	*Chapter 5(27): 32 shlokas*
Chapter 5(8): 13 shlokas	*Chapter 5(28): 28 shlokas*
Chapter 5(9): 38 shlokas	*Chapter 5(29): 35 shlokas*
Chapter 5(10): 49 shlokas	*Chapter 5(30): 80 shlokas*
Chapter 5(11): 25 shlokas	*Chapter 5(31): 20 shlokas*
Chapter 5(12): 26 shlokas	*Chapter 5(32): 30 shlokas*
Chapter 5(13): 62 shlokas	*Chapter 5(33): 53 shlokas*
Chapter 5(14): 14 shlokas	*Chapter 5(34): 44 shlokas*
Chapter 5(15): 24 shlokas	*Chapter 5(35): 38 shlokas*
Chapter 5(16): 28 shlokas	*Chapter 5(36): 24 shlokas*
Chapter 5(17): 33 shlokas	*Chapter 5(37): 75 shlokas*
Chapter 5(18): 58 shlokas	*Chapter 5(38): 94 shlokas*
Chapter 5(19): 29 shlokas	
Chapter 5(20): 105 shlokas	*Total in Part V: 1,517 shlokas*

Chapter 5(1) (Kamsa's Story)

Maitreya said, 'You have spoken about all the lineages of the kings in detail. You have also described the extension and conduct of those lineages. O *brahmarshi*! I wish to hear in detail the truth about how Vishnu's portion descended in the lineage of the Yadus. What were the deeds undertaken by the illustrious Purushottama when he descended in his portion? O sage! Please tell me that.'

Shri Parashara replied, 'O Maitreya! Now hear what you have asked me about. Part of Vishnu's portion descended, and his deeds were for the welfare of the world. O great sage! Earlier, Vasudeva married the immensely fortunate Devaki, Devaka's daughter, and she was like a goddess. On the occasion of Vasudeva and Devaki's union, Kamsa, the descendant of the Bhoja lineage, drove their chariot since he acted as charioteer. At that time, a loud voice lovingly addressed Kamsa from the sky. Rumbling like thunder, it uttered the following words. "O foolish one! Along with her husband, she is on your chariot, and you are driving them along. Her eighth child will rob you of your life." Hearing this, the immensely strong Kamsa unsheathed his sword. When he got ready to slay Devaki, Vasudeva spoke to him. "O immensely fortunate one! O unblemished one! You should not kill Devaki. I will surrender all the children that are born out of her womb to you." O supreme among *brahmanas*! Kamsa agreed. Honouring the pledge, he did not kill Vasudeva or Devaki.'

'At that time, the earth was suffering excessively from the burden. The earth went to the assembly of the residents of heaven on Meru. The earth prostrated herself before Brahma and all the other gods. In piteous tones, she told them everything about the reason for her grief. The earth said, "For gold, the *guru* is Agni. For cattle, the supreme *guru* is Surya. My *guru*,

and the *guru* of all the *guru*s, is Narayana. He is the lord of
the Prajapatis. He existed before Brahma and before everyone
else. *Kala, kashtha* and *nimesha* are in his *atman*. He is time.
He is disembodied and unmanifest. All the excellent gods are
his portion. The Adityas, the Maruts, the Sadhyas, the Rudras,
the Vasus, the Ashvins, the fires, the ancestors, the creators of
the worlds, Atri and all the others are forms of the great-souled
Vishnu, who is immeasurable. *Yaksha*s, *rakshasa*s, *daitya*s,
*pishacha*s, *uraga*s, *danava*s, *gandharva*s and *apsara*s are forms
of the great-souled Vishnu. Vishnu pervades every object in
the universe—planets, *nakshatra*s and stars, colourful in the
firmament, Agni, water, wind, I and every place. He has many
forms. Night and day, like waves in the oceans, those forms
are obstructed by other forms and cause obstructions to other
forms. Right now, the *daitya*s, with Kalanemi at the forefront,
have descended in the world of the mortals and are causing
obstructions to subjects, night and day. Vishnu killed Kalanemi.
Killed by the powerful Vishnu, the great *asura* has been born as
Kamsa, Ugrasena's son. There are other fierce *asura*s: Arishta,
Dhenuka, Keshin, Pralamba, Naraka, Sundra and Bana, Bali's
son. There are other immensely valiant ones. Those evil-souled
ones have been born in the homes of kings. I am incapable
of enumerating them. There are many *akshouhini*s.[874] Those
*asura*s have divine forms. Those immensely valiant Indras
among *daitya*s are insolent. They are on me, and I am incapable
of bearing the burden. O lords among immortals! I am afflicted
and suffering. I am informing you that they are terrifying me.
O immensely fortunate ones! Please do something to reduce
my burden. Otherwise, completely distracted, I will have to go
to Rasatala." Hearing the earth's words, urged by all the lords

[874] An *akshouhini* is an army and consists of 21,870 chariots,
21,870 elephants, 65,610 horses and 109,350 infantry men. Here, it
simply means a large number.

among the gods, Brahma spoke, explaining how her burden
might be reduced. Brahma said, "O residents of heaven!
What the earth has said is entirely true. I, Bhava,[875] and all
of you have Narayana in our *atman*s. Depending on whether
we possess a greater or lesser degree of his powers, we cause
obstructions to each other, or are obstructed. Therefore, let us
go to the northern shores of the ocean of milk. There, we will
worship Hari and tell him everything. He is in all atmans, and
the universe is in him. For everyone's sake and for the sake of
the world, he will descend in his portion of *sattva* and establish
dharma on earth." Having said this, along with the gods, the
grandfather departed.'

'They controlled themselves and praised the one who has
Garuda on his banner. Brahma said, "Though you have no
names, you have been spoken about in *para vidya* and *apara
vidya*.[876] O lord! In that way, your forms are both *murta* and
amurta.[877] You are the two *brahman*s, *para-brahma* and *shabda
brahma*.[878] You are smaller than the smallest. You are larger
than the largest. You are in every *atman*. You know everything.
You are *shabda-brahma*. You are *para-brahma*. The *brahman*
is you. You are *Rig Veda*, *Yajur Veda*, *Sama Veda* and *Atharva
Veda*. You are *shiksha*, *kalpa*, *nirukta*, *chhanda*, *jyotisha* and
vyakarana. O lord! You are Itihasa and Purana. O Adhokshaja!
You are *mimamsa*, *nyayashastra* and *dharmashastra*.[879] You
are words that reflect on the *paramatman* and the *jivatman*
and the qualities of body and matter. You are the one who is

[875] Shiva.
[876] *Para vidya* is transcendental/higher knowledge, *apara vidya* is
textual/lower knowledge.
[877] Respectively, disembodied and embodied.
[878] *Para-brahma* is the supreme *brahman*. *Shabda-brahma* is the
brahman, as described in texts.
[879] *Mimamsa darshana* (the philosophical school on critical
investigation), texts on policy and texts on *dharma* respectively.

beyond this, since *adhyatma*[880] is about your form. You are not manifest. You cannot be determined. You cannot be thought of. You do not possess names or complexions. Your pure form is without hands and feet. You are eternal and beyond the supreme. You hear, but not with ears. You see, but not with eyes. You do not have a form. You have many forms. You move, but without hands and feet. You are the one who knows everything. But everyone cannot know you. Those who possess supreme *nivritti* and *jnana* see you as smaller than the smallest. They see that everything is your form. Such a persevering person sees your resplendent form. Your form is pre-eminent. You have no form other than that of the *paramatman*. You are the nave of the universe. You are the earth's protector. You are inside all beings. You are everything that has been and will be. You are smaller than the smallest. You are the Purusha who is beyond Prakriti. You are one, but grant four illustrious forms as the fire,[881] so as to bestow illumination and prosperity on the world. You are the eyes of the universe. You are infinite in form. In three strides, you covered everything.[882] Agni is one, but is kindled in many kinds of ways. Though intrinsically it is without modification, it is subject to differences and modification. Like that, though your form is one, you are inside everything and have an infinite number of forms. You are the lord who sees everything. You have an extreme and supreme state. A person who sees that possesses the insight of *jnana* and is a *sura*.[883] There is no truth other than your own form. You are the past and the future. You are the

---

[880] The word *adhyatma* has many nuances. Stated simply, it is knowledge about the *atman*.

[881] *Garhapatya*, *ahavaniya* and *dakshinatya* and the fire of devotion (alternatively, the fire inside beings).

[882] A reference to the Vamana (dwarf) incarnation.

[883] *Sura* is usually translated as god, but also means a learned person.

paratman. The manifest and the unmanifest are your forms.
The collective and the individual are your own forms. You
know everything. You understand everything. You are every
kind of capacity, knowledge, strength and prosperity. You are
not subject to increase and decrease. You are independent and
not under anyone else's subjugation. You are not affected by
exhaustion, lassitude, fear, anger, avarice and other things.
You are supreme and without blemish. You are the supreme
objective. You do not require a foundation. Your progress
is without any decay. You are the supreme lord. You are the
supreme foundation and refuge. All refuges are in your *atman*.
You are imperishable. You are beyond all envelopes. You are
thought of as one who does not require any support. You are
the reservoir of all great powers. O Purushottama! I bow down
before you. When you assume a body, this is only for the sake
of saving *dharma*, not because there is any other reason, or
because of a lack of reason. You are beyond notions of reason
and lack of reason." Using his mental powers, the illustrious
one, who is without origin, heard these words of praise. He
is the one who makes the universe manifest itself. Pleased, he
spoke to Brahma. The illustrious one said, "O Brahma! Tell
me what you and the *deva*s desire. Tell me everything. You
will certainly be successful." Brahma saw Hari, with his divine
and universal form. Along with the *deva*s, he again prostrated
himself and uttered words of praise. Brahma said, "I bow down
before you. I prostrate myself before you. You are the one with
one thousand forms. You are the one with one thousand arms.
You are the one with many faces and feet. I bow down before
you. O immeasurable one! I prostrate myself before the one
who is the cause of the creation, preservation and destruction
of the universe. You are subtler than the most subtle. You
are larger than the greatest. You are more revered than the
most respected. You are Pradhana, *buddhi* and the senses.
You are the foremost principle. You are the *paramatman*. O

illustrious one! Be pleased. O divinity! This earth is bound
by the mountains. The great *asura*s have been born on earth
and are making her suffer. You are the supreme essence. The
earth has come before you for refuge, so that her burden can be
eased. There are others here: Vritra's enemy,[884] Nasatya, Dasra,
Varuna, the Rudras, the Vasus, the Suryas,[885] the winds, Agni
and all the others. All the gods are here. O lord of the gods!
O lord of everything! We will do whatever you command us
to do. O one without any taints! We are always ready to obey
you." In this way, the illustrious Parameshvara was praised.
O great sage! He plucked out one of his white hairs and one
of his black hairs and said, "O leaders of the gods! These two
hairs will descend on earth and remove the earth's burden. O
gods! All of you should use your portions to descend on earth.
Have a battle with the intoxicated and great *asura*s, who have
already been born there. Through this means, all the *daitya*s
will be exterminated from the face of the earth. Do not doubt
this. They will be crushed through my glances. Leave now.
Vasudeva's wife is Devaki, and she is like a goddess. O gods!
My hair will be born as her eighth conception. Descending on
earth, he will slay Kamsa, who is Kalanemi in his new form."
Saying this, Hari vanished. O great sage! When he disappeared,
the gods prostrated themselves before him and want to the
summit of Meru, so as to descend on the face of the earth.'

'The illustrious sage, Narada, told Kamsa that the one who
holds up the earth would be born as Devaki's eighth child.
Hearing this from Narada, Kamsa became angry. He imprisoned
Devaki and Vasudeva in their house. O *brahmana*! Vasudeva
had made a pledge to Kamsa earlier. Following this, Vasudeva
handed over his sons to him. It is said that these six children
used to be the sons of Hiranyakashipu. Instructed by Vishnu,

---

[884] Indra.
[885] In the plural.

one by one, they were introduced into the womb by Yoganidra.
Yoganidra is Vishnu's great *maya*, which causes delusion and
leads to ignorance in the entire universe. The illustrious Hari
spoke to her. The illustrious one said, "O Yoganidra! Follow
my command. Those six have sought refuge in Patala. One by
one, bring them and convey them to Devaki's womb. When
they have been killed by Kamsa, the seventh conception will
be a portion of the one known as Shesha, who is a part of
my portion. Vasudeva's other wife, Rohini, is in Gokula. O
goddess! Before the time of delivery has appeared, you will
transfer this fetus to her womb. People will say that Devaki's
seventh conception has miscarried, because she was imprisoned
and because she was scared of the king of Bhoja. Since that
child will drag the earth, the world will know the brave one as
Samkarshana. He will be like the summit of a white mountain.
O auspicious one! After that, I will be conceived in Devaki's
womb. Without any delay, you must also be conceived in
Yashoda's womb. I will be born during the rainy season, in
the month of Nabhas,[886] at night, on the eighth lunar day in
krishna paksha. You will be born on the ninth lunar day. O
unblemished one! Through my powers, Vasudeva will convey
me to Yashoda's birth and you to Devaki's bed. O goddess!
Kamsa will hurl you against a slab of stone. But as he hurls you
up, you will remain suspended in the air. Out of respect towards
me, Shakra, the one with one hundred eyes,[887] will bow down
before you. He will bow down, lower his head and accept you
as his sister. After killing Shumbha, Nishumbha and thousands
of other *daitya*s, you will ornament the earth in many places.[888]
You are Bhuti, Sannati, Kshanti, Kanti, Dyou, Prithivi, Dhriti,

[886] Shravana.

[887] Indra is usually described as one with one thousand eyes.

[888] This can simply be understood as temples to Durga but is
interpreted as the Shakti *pitha*s.

Lajja, Pushti, Rusha and everything else.[889] There will be those
who will worship you as Durga, Vedagarbha, Ambika, Bhadra,
Bhadrakali, Kshemada and Bhagyada. If they do this in the
morning and in the afternoon, with their heads bowed down,
through my favours, they will obtain everything that they wish
for. If men worship you with liquor, flesh, gifts and food, you
will be pleased and bestow everything that they desire on them.
O Bhadra! Through my favours, there is no doubt that they
will be devoted to you. O goddess! This will happen. Now go
and do as you have been told."'

Chapter 5(2) (Praise of Devaki)

Shri Parashara said, 'Jagaddhatri did as the lord of the gods
had asked her to. She placed those six fetuses and took the
seventh one away, to Rohini's womb. For the welfare of the
three worlds, Hari then entered Devaki's womb. As she had
been asked to do by Parameshthi, on the same day, Yoganidra
entered Yashoda's womb. O *brahmana*! In heaven, all the
planets were in excellent places. When Vishnu's portion came
to earth, the seasons turned pleasant. Because of her excessive
energy, no one was able to look at Devaki then. On seeing
her resplendent form, the mind was agitated. Unseen by men
and women, night and day, a large number of *deva*s praised
her, with the radiant Vishnu inside her body. *Deva*s said, "You
are Prakriti. You are supreme and subtle. In earlier times, you
bore Brahma in your womb.[890] O auspicious one! You are the
goddess of speech. You are the nurse of the universe. You hold

[889] Respectively prosperity, humility, forbearance, beauty, heaven,
earth, patience, modesty, nourishment and adornment.

[890] As Prakriti.

the *Veda*s in your womb. Your womb is the form from which creation proceeds. O eternal one! You are creation. You are the seed of everything. You are the sacrifice. You are the three.[891] The fruits originate in you. You are the offerings of *ghee*. You are the *arani*, with the fire inside you. You are Aditi, who gave birth to *deva*s. You are Diti, who gave birth to *daitya*s. You are the morning twilight, with the day in your womb. You are the source of *jnana*. You are humility. You are the one who conveys us to the supreme. You are good policy. You are modesty. You are the one who bestows assurance. You are the source of desire. You are wishes. You are satisfaction, with contentment in your womb. You are intellect and the source of understanding. You are fortitude and hold patience in your womb. You have the planets, *nakshatra*s and stars inside you. You are the cause behind heaven and everything else. O goddess! These, and many thousands of others, are your powers. O Jagaddhatri! All those are inside your womb now. O auspicious one! The oceans, mountains, rivers, *dvipa*s, forest, habitations, ornaments, villages, market towns, excellent hamlets and indeed, the entire earth, are there. All the fires and waters and all the winds are there. The giant *uraga*s, *yaksha*s, *rakshasa*s, *preta*s and *guhyaka*s are there. Planets, *nakshatra*s and hundreds of colourful *vimana*s are there. All space and everything that exists in the firmament is there. O auspicious one! Bhuloka, Bhuvarloka, Svarloka, Maharloka, Janaloka, Tapoloka, Brahmaloka and the entire Brahmanda is there. O reknowned one! *Deva*s, *daitya*s, *gandharva*s, *charana*s, giant *uraga*s, *yaksha*s, *rakshasa*s, *preta*s, *guhyaka*s, humans, animals and all creatures are inside you. The one who goes everywhere, the one who creates everything, is inside you. His form, deeds and true nature cannot be discerned or grasped. All measurements are in him. That Vishnu is in your womb.

---

[891] The three *Veda*s.

You are Svaha. You are Svadha. You are knowledge. You are the radiance in the firmament. To save all the worlds, you have descended on the face of the earth. O goddess! Be pleased. The entire universe is your portion. O auspicious one! Lovingly bear the lord. He is the one who holds up the entire universe."'

Chapter 5(3) (Krishna's Birth)

Shri Parashara said, 'Holding the lord of the gods inside her, she was praised in this fashion. Pundarikaksha, the cause responsible for saving the universe, was inside her womb. Devaki was like the morning *sandhya*. The one who makes the entire lotus of the universe bloom was like the rising Bhanu. The great-souled one arrived. On the day of his birth, all the directions sparkled in great joy. It was as if the moon's beams had spread throughout the world. The virtuous were extremely content and the fierce winds were pacified. When Janardana was born, the rivers flowed serenely. The oceans used their own sounds to play agreeable music. The lords of the *gandharva*s sang and large numbers of *apsara*s danced. From the firmament, *deva*s showered down flowers on earth. When Janardana was born, the blazing fires turned mild. O *brahmana*! The clouds rumbled gently and showered down flowers. Janardana, the foundation of everything, was born at midnight. His complexion was like the petals of a blossoming blue lotus. He was four-armed, with the *srivatsa* mark on his chest.[892] Witnessing his birth, Anakadundubhi praised him. O supreme among *brahmana*s! The eloquent and immensely intelligent one was pleased that his wishes had been fulfilled, but also told him about his fear of

---

[892] Vishnu/Krishna bears the *srivatsa* mark (or curl) on his chest. This is the place where Shri/Lakshmi resides.

Kamsa. Vasudeva said, "O lord of the gods! O one who holds
the conch shell, the *chakra* and the mace! You have been born.
O divinity! But please show me your favours and withdraw this
divine form. Otherwise, if Kamsa gets to know that you have
descended in my house, he will kill me today itself." Devaki
added, "O one who is infinite in form! O one whose form is the
universe! All the worlds are within your radiant form. O lord of
the gods! In your *maya*, you have assumed this form of an infant.
O one who is in every *atman*! Please show us your favours and
withdraw this four-armed form. Otherwise, Kamsa, Diti's son,
will get to know that you have descended." The illustrious one
replied, "Earlier, desiring a son, you prayed to me. O goddess!
Today, I have been born and have made those prayers successful.
I have been born from your womb." O supreme among sages!
Saying this, the illustrious one was silent. In the night, Vasudeva
took him and went out. Because of the delusion created by
Yoganidra, all the guards and gatekeepers of Mathura were
asleep. As Anakadundubhi proceeded in the night, there was a
torrential downpour of rain from the clouds. However, Shesha
held up his hoods and covered Anakadundubhi. Yamuna was
extremely deep and full of many whirlpools. But as Vasudeva
carried Vishnu across, the water extended only up to his thighs.
He saw Nanda and the other seniors among the *gopas*,[893] who
had arrived on the banks of the Yamuna to pay their taxes to
Kamsa. O Maitreya! At that time, Yashoda had given birth to
a daughter, Yoganidra. Because of Yoganidra, Yashoda and
everyone else was deluded and asleep. Vasudeva placed his son
there, on Yashoda's bed. The immensely radiant one took up
the daughter and swiftly returned. When Yashoda woke up,
she saw the son who had been born and was delighted. His
complexion was as dark as the petals of a blue lotus. Taking the

---

[893] *Gopas* are cowherds. Nanda and the *gopas* had come to
Mathura to pay their taxes to Kamsa. They lived in Gokula.

daughter, Vasudeva returned to his own house and placing her on Devaki's bed, remained as he had been before. The guards heard the sound of the infant crying and suddenly woke up. O *brahmana*! They informed Kamsa that Devaki had given birth. Kamsa swiftly went there and seized the daughter. In a choking voice, Devaki tried to restrain him. "Let her be. Please release her." However, he flung her against a slab of stone. But she rose up into the air and remained suspended there, assuming a giant eight-armed form that wielded weapons. She laughed loudly at Kamsa and angrily spoke to him. "O Kamsa! What is the point of flinging me away? The one who will kill you has been born. He is the one who exists in all *deva*s. He is the one who killed you earlier. If you want to ensure your welfare, quickly try to counter him." Saying this, the goddess, who was adorned in divine garlands and ornaments, left through the air, praised by the *siddha*s, while the king of the Bhojas only looked on.'

Chapter 5(4) (Kamsa's Order)

Shri Parashara said, 'Kamsa was anxious in his mind and spoke to all the giant *asura*s. He summoned Pralamba, Keshin and other chief bulls among the *asura*s. Kamsa said, "O Pralamba! O Mahabahu! O Keshin! O Dhenuka! O Putana! O Arishta and all the others! Listen to my words. The evil-souled ones are making efforts to kill me. They have been scorched by my valour. They aren't brave and I don't care about them. Indra is limited in prowess. What can Hara do? Hari looks for weaknesses to kill *asura*s. What can he do? There is nothing that Adityas or Vasus, limited in valour, can do. There is no need to speak about the Agnis or the other immortals. All of them have been defeated by the strength of my arms. Have I not seen the lord of the immortals flee from a battle with me? He ran

away, with many arrows on his back, not on his chest. What
happened when Shakra tried to stop the showering of rain in my
kingdom? Did my arrows not splinter the clouds and release the
desired rain? What about the kings on earth, who are scared of
the strength of my arms? With the exception of Jarasandha, my
senior,[894] all of them bowed down before me. O bulls among
the *daitya*s! I have no respect for the immortals. O brave ones!
I laugh at the efforts they make. O Indras among the *daitya*s!
Nevertheless, it is also true that these wicked ones are making
great efforts to harm me. We must therefore act against these
evil-souled ones. There are famous ones on earth who perform
sacrifices. To injure *deva*s, we must therefore kill them all. The
daughter who was born from Devaki's womb told me that my
death has already been born. Hence, we must make great efforts
to kill all children on the surface of the earth. Whenever a child
displays excessive strength, he must be killed." Issuing this
command to the *asura*s, Kamsa entered his house. He released
Vasudeva and Devaki from imprisonment. Kamsa said, "I have
killed your children in vain. There seems to be someone else who
has now been born for my destruction. But there is no point in
lamenting. Any children that the two of you have from now on
will be innocent. Their lifespans will not be cut short." Assuring
them, Kamsa released them. O best among *brahmana*s! Worried
about himself, he entered the inner quarters of his house.'

Chapter 5(5) (Return to Gokula and Putana)

Shri Parashara said, 'Released Vasudeva went to Nanda's
cart.[895] He saw that Nanda was delighted at a son having

---

[894] Jarasandha was Kamsa's father-in-law.

[895] The *gopa*s had come there temporarily, so there was a place
where all the carts were camped.

been born to him. Vasudeva lovingly told him, "This is good fortune. You are fortunate that a son has now been born to you in your old age. All of you have paid your yearly taxes to the king. Once the task for which one has come has been accomplished, extremely wealthy people should no longer remain there. The task for which you had come is over. Why are you still here? O Nanda! You should quickly return to your own Gokula. I also have a son, born through Rohini. You should protect him, like your own son." Thus addressed, the *gopas*, with Nandagopa at the forefront, departed. With the taxes having been paid, those immensely strong ones placed their vessels on their carts.'

'Putana killed children. While they resided in Gokula, she arrived there in the night. She took up the sleeping Krishna and offered him her breast. Whenever Putana offered a child her breast in the night, at that very instant, the child's limbs suffered, and he died. Krishna firmly kneaded her breast with his hands. Full of rage, he seized it and drank from it, sucking out her breath of life. With the bonds of her sinews severed, she emitted a loud roar. The extremely dreadful Putana fell down on the ground, dying. Hearing her roar, the terrified residents of Vraja woke up.[896] They saw Putana brought down on the ground, with Krishna in her arms. O supreme *brahmana*! Scared, Yashoda gathered Krishna up. To remove all taints from the child, she fanned him with a cow's tail. Nandagopa gathered some cow dung and placed it on his head. He gave Krishna a *raksha*[897] and uttered these words. Nandagopa said, "Through the powers of this, let Hari protect you from all creatures. The universe evolved from a lotus that sprouted

[896] Vraja is the area around Vrindavana and Gokula was a specific habitation within it. There were many forests in Vraja. Vrindavana was one of these forests.

[897] In this context, *raksha* means an amulet, over which, *mantras* have been pronounced. The cow dung was powdered.

from his navel. In his form as *varaha*, he held the earth on
the tips of his tusks and raised her up from the water. May
that divinity, Keshava, protect you. In his form as Nrisimha,
he used the tips of his nails to tear about the enemy's chest. Let
that Janardana protect you in every way. Let Vamana always
protect you. In an instant, the one with the sparkling weapons
covered the three worlds in three of his strides. Let Govinda
protect your head. Let Keshava protect your neck. Let Vishnu
protect your anus and stomach. Let Janardana protect your
thighs and feet. Narayana is without decay and his prosperity
is unimpeded. Let him protect your face, arms, hands, mind
and all your senses. He holds the Sharnga bow, chakra and
mace in his hands. From the sound of his conch shell, let
pretas, *kushmanda*s and *rakshasa*s who intend to harm you
be conveyed to their destruction. Let Vaikuntha protect you
in all the directions. Let Madhusudana protect you in all the
sub-directions. Let Hrishikesha protect you in the sky. Let
Mahidhara[898] protect you on earth." In this way, Nandagopa
pronounced benedictions over the child. The child was put
back to sleep, on his bed under a cart. The *gopa*s saw Putana's
gigantic body. Even though she was dead, they were amazed
and filled with great dread.'

Chapter 5(6) (Departure for Vrindavana)

Shri Parashara said, 'On one occasion, Madhusudana was
sleeping under a cart. Desiring milk from a breast, he cried
and kicked his feet upwards. As a result of the blow of his feet,
the cart was overturned. Shattered, the pots and vessels fell
down and were strewn around in all directions. O *brahmana*!

[898] One who holds up the earth, the same as Dharanidhara.

At this, *gopa*s and *gopi*s[899] raised sounds of lamentation.
They arrived there and saw that the child was sleeping on his
back. The *gopa*s asked, "Who did this? Who overturned the
cart?" The children who were there replied, "The infant has
overturned it. We saw him cry, fling his feet and overturn the
cart. He has overturned the cart. There is no one else who
has done this." At this, the *gopa*s were surprised yet again.
Extremely astounded, Nandagopa picked up the infant.
Yashoda used curds, flowers, fruits and *akshata*[900] to worship
the cart and the broken vessels and jars that had been on the
cart. Vasudeva sent Garga to Gokula. Unknown to the *gopa*s,
he performed the *samskara*s for those two. The immensely
intelligent Garga, supreme among intelligent ones, gave the
elder the name of Rama and the younger the name of Krishna.
Within a short period of time, they started to crawl around
and move. O *brahmana*! They crawled on their hands and
knees and moved around everywhere. As they moved around
here and there, their limbs were covered with dry cow dung
and ashes. Yashoda and Rohini were unable to restrain them.
They played in the cow pens. They got into the pens meant for
calves and amused themselves by tugging at the tails of calves.
Yashoda was unable to prevent those children from wandering
around. They did not stay in one place. They were very playful
and amused themselves. On one occasion, she angrily spoke to
Krishna, unblemished in his deeds. She tied a rope around his
stomach and tied it to a mortar. She said, "You are extremely
playful and are always trying to move around. If you can, move
now." Having said this, she focused on her household tasks.
When she had left, he eagerly tugged at the mortar. The lotus-

[899] Female *gopa*s.
[900] This can mean grain of any kind. But it is specifically used for
threshed and winnowed rice that has not been dehusked.

eyed one dragged it to between two twin *arjuna* trees.[901] As he
dragged it in between the two trees, the mortar got diagonally
stuck there. When he continued to tug, those two twin *arjuna*
trees, with lofty branches, were brought down. Hearing the
shattering sound, the people of Vraja hurried there. They saw
those two giant trees. The child was in between them, with a
rope firmly tied around his stomach. There were the beginnings
of newly formed white teeth and he was laughing. Since a rope
had been tied around his stomach, he came to be known as
Damodara.[902] All the elders among the gopas, with Nandagopa
at the forefront, consulted among themselves. They were
anxious and scared at these evil portents. "We should not
remain at this spot any longer. We should leave for another
forest. Many evil portents are witnessed here, and they signify
destruction. There was Putana's destruction and the calamity
over the cart. There was no storm and yet those two trees have
fallen down. Without any delay, we should leave this place and
go to Vrindavana. We should go to a place where evil portents,
caused by taints in the ground, do not exist." Thus, all the
residents of Vraja made up their mind to leave. They told their
respective families, "Hurry. Let us leave without delay." In a
short while, they departed, with their carts and wealth of cattle.
The leaders of the herds, those who looked after the calves and
the residents of Vraja were in separate sections. They threw
away the residual household articles. O *brahmana*! Within a
short space of time, the place where the Vraja had been was
only frequented by crows and vultures.'

'The illustrious Krishna, unblemished in his deeds, had
mentally thought of Vrindavana as an auspicious spot where
the cattle would get what they wanted. O supreme among

___

[901] *Arjuna* is a tall tree (teak). *Yamala* means twin. Since these twin
arjuna trees grew next to each other, they are known as *yamalarjuna*.
[902] *Dama* (rope) + *udara* (stomach).

brahmanas! In that place, whether it was the summer or the monsoon, new grass sprouted in every direction. Hence, all of them left Vraja, went to Vrindavana and started to live there. Along the boundaries of the habitation, the carts were set up in the form of a half moon. Rama and Damodara were surrounded by children who tended to calves. They lived in the same place and indulged in childish pastimes. They stuck feathers of peacocks and bunches of wildflowers in their hair. They made flutes used by *gopa*s and fashioned musical instruments out of leaves. Sporting *kakapaksha*s, they resembled Kumara, the son of Pavaka.[903] They laughed, amused themselves and wandered around in that large forest. Sometimes, as they played, they carried each other on their backs. Like the other sons of *gopa*s, they took the calves out to graze. Time passed in that large settlement, and they attained the age of seven years. Those who tend to the entire universe were tending to calves. Monsoon arrived and there were many large clouds in the sky. Torrential rain poured down and made the directions merge into one. The earth was covered with newly sprouted grass and became colourful with *shakragopa* insects.[904] It was as if it was adorned with emeralds and rubies. In every direction, the waters of the rivers flooded the banks and didn't follow the usual course, like the mind of an indisciplined person who has just obtained some wealth. The moon did not shine, its sparkle hidden behind thick clouds. This was just like the rational words of a virtuous person being overwhelmed by the excessive words of a fool. Like an unworthy person lacking in discrimination honoured

[903] Literally, this means crow's wing. It is an expression used when the head is shaved and sidelocks are left. Even if the head is not shaved, *kakapaksha* means a young boy's sidelocks. Kumara is Skanda/Kartikeya. After a fashion, Kumara was Pavaka's (Agni's) son.

[904] A reddish insect, sometimes identified with a firefly. Also known as *indragopa*.

by a king, Shakra's bow[905] was in the sky, but without its string.
There were radiant white cranes on the clouds, resembling an
exceedingly wonderful and noble person, surrounded by those
who are wicked in conduct. Like the friendship a supreme man
has with an evil one, the extremely fickle lighning was not tied
in a bond of friendship with the sky but moved around. The
paths could no longer be seen clearly, there were shrouded
with grass and crops. It was as if words full of meaning cannot
be uttered by the dumb. At the time, the great forest was
full of maddened peacocks and cuckoos.[906] Roaming around
with the *gopala*s and the cows,[907] Krishna and Rama happily
enjoyed themselves. Sometimes, the two of them sang beautiful
songs. Sometimes, they wandered around and took shelter
under the trees, as protection against the cold. Sometimes,
they adorned themselves with garlands made out of *kadamba*
flowers. Sometimes, the garlands were made out the feathers
of peacocks. Sometimes, they smeared themselves with many
kinds of minerals from the mountains. Sometimes, when they
wished to sleep, they lay themselves down on beds made out
of leaves and slept. When the clouds thundered, they became
anxious and uttered words of lamentation. At other times, they
praised the other *gopa*s and made them sing. They fashioned
flutes and imitated the calls of the peacocks. In this way, they
found pleasure in many kinds of ways. Content in their minds,
they played in the forest in this way. In the evening, like the
other *gopa*s and surrounded by the cows, those two extremely
strong ones returned to Vraja and just like mortals, played with
the *gopa*s on equal terms. In this way, the immensely radiant
Rama and Krishna resided there.'

[905] A rainbow.
[906] The word *saranga* can also mean spotted deer, or even
elephant. In conjunction with peacocks, cuckoos seems right.
[907] Cowherds.

Chapter 5(7) (Subjugation of Kaliya)

Shri Parashara said, 'On one occasion, Krishna went to Vrindavana without Rama.[908] He roamed around, surrounded by the gopas. With garlands made out of wildflowers, he was resplendent. He went to the Kalindi,[909] full of turbulent waves. As the foam struck to the banks, she seemed to be smiling in every direction. But within the river, he saw an extremely terrible pool that belonged to Kaliya naga. It was extremely horrible and was polluted by fire and poison. As the poisonous fire spread, it scorched the large trees along the banks. The wind hurled the spray up and if a bird happened to touch this, it was burnt. It was extremely fierce in this way. It was like a second mouth of death. The illustrious Madhusudana saw this and thought. "The evil-souled Kaliya resides here, and poison is his weapon. Earlier, when the wicked one had been defeated by me, he had left for the ocean. He is the one who has polluted the entire Yamuna, as she heads towards the ocean. When they are thirsty, men cannot drink this water. Nor can our wealth of cattle. Therefore, it is my task to chastise the king of the nagas. In this place, the residents of Vraja should be able to roam around freely, without fear. It is for this reason that I have incarnated myself in this world. It is my task to punish evil-souled ones who resort to contrary paths. I will climb onto the branches of that kadamba tree, which is not very far away. From above, I will leap into the pool which belongs to the one who feeds on wind."[910] Having thought in this way, he firmly girded his loins. With great force, he leapt into the pool that belonged to the king of the nagas. When he descended there,

[908] That is, he went to the forest without Balarama.
[909] Kalindi is another name for Yamuna.
[910] A serpent is believed to feed on wind. The text uses the word anilashana, something that feeds on the wind. This means serpent.

the waters of that great lake were agitated and drenched even
the large trees that were some distance away. The water was
hot and polluted from the evil and poisonous flames and thus
hurled up, immediately scorched the large trees in the groves
and made them blaze. Those flames enveloped the directions.
Using his arms, Krishna slapped on the waters of the *naga*'s
lake. Hearing that sound, the king of the *naga*s quickly arrived.
Because of his rage, his eyes turned coppery-red. His mouths
were full of the blazing poison. He was surrounded by many
other *uraga*s that were full of great poison. There were hundreds
of wives of the *naga*s, adorned with beautiful necklaces. As
those lovely ones moved, their earrings trembled because of
the movements. Krishna entered that circle of serpents and the
serpents bound him in their coils. Their mouths were foul with
poisonous flames, and they bit Krishna. The *gopa*s saw him fall
down there, suffering from the coils of the serpents. Suffering in
their grief and shrieking and lamenting, they rushed to Vraja.'

'The *gopa*s said, "In his confusion, Krishna has got
submerged in Kaliya's lake. The king of the *naga*s will devour
him. Go there and see." Hearing this, it was as if the *gopa*s
were struck by words that were like a bolt of lightning. With
the *gopi*s, with Yashoda leading the way, they rushed to the
lake. "Alas! What is this? Alas!" The people and the *gopi*s
were distracted. They were just as confused as Yashoda was,
and as they hurried, their steps faltered. Eager to see Krishna,
Nandagopa and the other *gopa*s and Rama, extraordinary
in his valour, quickly rushed to the Yamuna. They saw him,
under the subjugation of the king of the serpents. Since he was
encircled in the serpent's coils, Krishna's efforts were futile.
Looking at his son's face, Nandagopa became immobile. O
supreme among sages! The immensely fortunate Yashoda was
also exactly in that state. Seeing this, the other *gopi*s were
afflicted by grief and wept. Because of their love for Keshava
and because their minds were afflicted by fear, they spoke. The

*gopi*s said, "Along with Yashoda, all of us will enter this giant
lake of the king of the *naga*s. It is not appropriate for us to
return to Vraja. What is the day without the sun? What is the
night without the moon? What are cows without a bull? What
is Vraja without Krishna? Without Krishna, we are deprived,
and we will not go to Gokula. Like a lake that is without water,
it is no longer agreeable and does not deserve to be frequented.
When Hari, whose dark complexion is as beautiful as that of
a blue lotus, is not present, it will be amazing for a person to
find his mother's house agreeable. His eyes are as clear and
sparkling as the petals of a blossoming lotus. Without seeing
Hari, how can you miserable ones remain in the settlement?[911]
Our only wish is to hear his exceedingly sweet conversation.
Without Pundarikaksha, we will not return to Nanda's
Gokula. Look. Even now, though he is engulfed in the coils
of the king of the serpents, he is smiling." The chief gopis
continued to look towards Krishna's face. Hearing the terrified
lamentations of the *gopi*s, Rohini's immensely strong son
looked at the miserable *gopa*s with unruffled eyes. He saw that
Nanda's glance was fixed on his son and that he was suffering
greatly. Without being aware of Krishna's greatness, Yashoda
was senseless. He told Krishna, "O lord of the gods! Why are
you behaving like a human? O Ananta! Do you not know your
own self? You are the nave of the universe. You are the one
who supports the spokes. You are the creator, preserver and
destroyer of the three worlds. The three are in you.[912] Indra,
the Rudras, Agni, the Vasus, the Adityas, the Maruts and the
Ashvins meditate on you. Though you cannot be thought of,
all the *yogi*s meditate on you. O Jagannatha! To reduce the
burden of the universe, you wished to take an incarnation. As
part of your portion, I, your elder brother, have also descended

---

[911] This is probably addressed to the *gopa*s.
[912] Either the three worlds or the three *Veda*s.

in the world of the mortals. O illustrious one! To serve you, the
gods have also resorted to human pastimes. This is the mystery
of your pastimes, but all of them are with you. Earlier, the
divine women have also taken birth in Gokula. O eternal one!
To indulge in your pastimes, you descended last. O Krishna!
Both of us have assumed *avataras* here and the *gopas* are our
kin. The *gopis* are suffering. Why are you indifferent towards
your relatives? You have exhibited human nature. You have
exhibited childish fickleness. O Krishna! Now chastise this
evil-souled one who uses poison as a weapon." When he was
reminded in this way, there was a gentle smile on Krishna's
lips.'

'He slapped his arms and freed his body from the serpent's
coils. Using both his hands, he made the serpent's middle hood
bend down. When the head was lowered down, the valiant one
climbed up and danced on the hood. The blows from Krishna's
feet wounded the hood. Whenever he tried to raise his head, it
was forced to bend down. As a result of Krishna's kicks, the
naga was confused and completely lost his senses. As a result of
those fierce blows, he vomited a lot of blood. The head and the
neck were lowered, and blood flowed from the mouth. Seeing
this piteous state, his wives spoke to Madhusudana. The *naga*'s
wives said, "O lord of the gods! You have been discovered.
You are the excellent and you know everything. You are the
supreme light. You are unthinkable and Parameshavara is only
one of your portions. The gods are incapable of praising you.
You are the lord who has not been born from anyone else.
How can women describe your own nature? The entire earth,
sky, water, fire and wind are part of the cosmic egg and that
is only a small portion of you. You are eternal and *yogis* have
not been able to determine your nature. You are the supreme
objective, smaller than the smallest and larger than the largest.
We prostrate ourselves before you. At birth, there is no creator
other than you. At death, there is no destroyer other than you.

There is no one else who is the preserver. We always bow down before you. You do not possess the slightest bit of rage. You are the one who preserves and protects. There must be a reason behind this chastisement of Kaliya. Please listen to our words. Even wicked, foolish and inferior species must show compassion towards women. O supreme among those who forgive! He is distressed. You should forgive him. You are the foundation of the entire universe. He is one with a hood, limited in strength. Because of the blows from your feet, he will give up his life within half a *muhurta*. *Pannaga*s are limited in energy, and you are the refuge of the world. Love and enmity must be with equals. You are the one without decay. O lord of the universe! He is suffering. Therefore, please show him your favours. The *naga* will give up his life. Please grant us our husband's life. O lord of the world! O Jagannatha! O one who was there before all the great beings! This *naga* will give up his life. Please grant us our husband's life. O lord of the gods! You are the one who is known through Vedanta. You are the one who destroys wicked *daitya*s. This *naga* will give up his life. Please grant us our husband's life." The *pannaga*'s body was exhausted. When they said this, Kaliya spoke in faltering words. "O lord of the gods! Show me your favours. O protector! You naturally possess the eight kinds of prosperity[913] and are supreme. Since you have no one who can surpass you, how can I possibly praise you? You are supreme. You are greater than the greatest. Your *atman* is supreme. Since you are greater than the greatest, how can I possibly praise you? You are supreme. You existed before the supreme one.[914] You are the supreme truth. You are the *paramatman*. Since you are greater than the supreme, how can I possibly praise you? Since Brahma, the

---

[913] Compassion, forgiveness, cleanliness, lack of jealousy, altruism, lack of greed, purity and self-control.

[914] That is, Brahma.

Rudras, Chandra, Indra, the Maruts, the Ashvins, the Vasus
and the Adityas originate from you. How can I possibly praise
you? You have a single form, and your subtle portions pervade
the entire universe. One can only imagine portions of your
form. How can I possibly praise you? Even Brahma and the
lords of the gods do not comprehend the supreme truth about
your forms as cause and effect. How can I possibly praise you?
Brahma and the others worship you with fragrances, flowers
and unguents from Nandana and other celestial gardens.
How can I possibly worship you? The king of *deva*s always
worships your form as an *avatara*. But he does not know your
supreme form. How can I possibly worship you? *Yogi*s who
have withdrawn their eyes from all the material objects that
encompass us worship you through their meditations. How
can I possibly worship you? *Yogi*s worship you, with only your
form in their hearts and using their sentiments as offerings of
flowers. How can I possibly worship you? O lord of the gods!
I do not even know how to start your worship or hymns of
praise. The minds of those who are capable are driven towards
compassion. Please show me your favours. O Keshava! Snakes
are cruel as a species, and I have been born as one. O Achutya!
Since I have been born with that nature, there is no crime that I
have committed. You are the one who creates everything. You
are the one who destroys the world. I have been created as
this species, with the form and nature. You are behind that
creation. O lord! You have created me in a certain kind of
form. Everything that I have done is virtuous according to my
own nature. O lord of the gods! Had I acted contrary to your
words, it would have been proper for the rod of chastisement
to be imposed on me. O master of the universe! Nevertheless,
since you have brought the rod of chastisement down on
me, this is something to be proud about. In truth, this is not
punishment for me, but a boon. O Achyuta! I have been robbed
of my valour. I have been deprived of my poison. I have been

chastised. Grant me my life. Command me about what I should do." The illustrious one replied, "O serpent! You should never reside here, in the waters of the Yamuna. With your sons and family, go to the waters of the ocean. O serpent! When he sees the mark of my feet on your head in the ocean, Garuda, the enemy of the *pannaga*s, will not strike you." Having said this, the illustrious Hari released the king of the serpents. Bowing down before Krishna, he left for the store of waters. While all the creatures looked on, along with his servants, sons, relatives and all his wives, he left his own lake.'

'When the serpent had departed, the *gopa*s embraced Govinda, as if he had returned from the world of the dead. They sprinkled his head with tears that flowed from their eyes. The minds of others were astounded at Krishna's unblemished deeds. Happy to see that the waters of the river were now pure, the *gopa*s were happy and praised him. The *gopi*s sang about his conduct and virtuous deeds. Praised by the *gopa*s, Krishna reached Vraja.'

Chapter 5(8) (Death of Dhenuka)

Shri Parashara said, 'Together, Bala and Keshava started to tend to the cows again. Roaming around in the forest, they reached a beautiful grove of palm trees. In that divine grove of palm trees, there was a *danava* named Dhenuka, in the form of a donkey. It always fed on the flesh of deer. That grove of palm trees was full of fruit. On seeing this, the *gopa*s wished to gather some fruit and spoke these words. The *gopa*s said, "O Rama! O Krishna! This bit of land is always protected by Dhenuka. It is full of ripe fruit. Behold. The fragrance is spreading in all directions. If it so pleases you, we wish to bring down some fruit." Hearing the words of the *gopa* boys,

Samkarshana thought it was worth bringing down some
fruit. He told Krishna, "Let us bring those fruit down." The
extremely indomitable one heard the sound of the palm fruit
falling down. Diti's son, the evil-souled donkey, arrived, full
of rage. It struck the powerful Bala in the chest with its hind
legs. But he[915] seized it by those legs and whirled it around in
the sky. When it had lost its life, he powerfully flung it on the
top of a large tree. As it fell down on top of the palm tree, the
donkey brought down many fruits on the ground, like a strong
wind acting against clouds. It had other relatives who were
*daitya*s, in the form of donkeys. When they arrived, Krishna
and Balabhadra playfully flung them on the tops of palm trees.
O Maitreya! In a short while, the earth was ornamented with
ripe palm fruit. It looked even more resplendent because of the
bodies of the *daitya*s, in the form of donkeys. O *brahmana*!
Thereafter, cattle no longer faced any obstructions in that
grove of palm trees. They happily grazed on the fresh grass in a
spot where they had been unable to graze earlier.'

Chapter 5(9) (Death of Pralamba)

S hri Parashara said, 'The *daitya* and his younger brothers
were brought down and all the *gopa* boys and *gopi*s found
that the grove of palm trees was beautiful and calm. Vasudeva's
two sons were filled with joy. Having killed Dhenuka *daitya*,
they went to the forest of Bhandira.[916] They sought out the
trees and played and sang. Those two great-souled ones were
radiant, like young bulls with budding horns. They herded the
cows. When these ventured too far away, they called them

---

[915] Balarama.

[916] *Bhandira* is the Indian fig tree.

back by their names. They carried ropes for tethering on their shoulders. They were adorned with garlands of wildflowers. They were attired in garments that had the complexion of gold and collyrium.[917] They were like the weapon of the great Indra.[918] They were like white and dark clouds.[919] Like ordinary people, they wandered around and played. The protectors of all the worlds, the protectors of creatures, had come to earth. Therefore, they followed the *dharma* of humans and respected human qualities. They wandered around and played in the forest in accordance with the attributes of that species. Those two extremely strong ones swung from swings, wrestled, exercised and flung huge rocks around.'

'There was an *asura* known by the name of Pralamba. While they were amusing themselves, he arrived there, wishing to seize them. He disguised himself in the garb of a *gopa*. Without any hesitation, he entered amidst those humans. Pralamba, supreme among *danava*s, assumed a human form. He thought that he would quickly find a weakness in them. His wish was to kill Krishna and Rohini's son. There is a children's game known as *harina kridana*.[920] In this game, all of them played in pairs, leaping up and jumping down. Govinda played with Shridama and Bala with Pralamba. A cowherd played with another cowherd and jumped over him. Krishna defeated his opponent and Rohini's son defeated his. Thus, those on Krishna's side were victorious and defeated the other side. They carried each other. Those defeated carried the victorious ones, on their shoulders, up to the *bhandira* tree and returned.

[917] That is, they were yellow and blue. Krishna was attired in yellow and Balarama in blue.

[918] Because of those colours, they resembled the rainbow.

[919] Balarama was fair and Krishna was dark.

[920] Literally, playing like deer. This is like leapfrog, where one person jumps over another person's back. The defeated child has to carry the victorious child.

The *danava* swiftly bore Samkarshana on his shoulders. It
was as if a cloud was carrying the moon away in the sky.
However, the supreme *danava* found it impossible to bear
the load of Rohini's son. Therefore, he increased in size and
assumed a gigantic form, like a cloud during the rainy season.
Samkarshana saw his form, which was like that of a scorched
mountain. Unblemished garlands and ornaments hung around
his neck and there was a diadem on his head.[921] He was fierce,
and his eyes were like the wheels of a cart. As he moved his
feet, the earth trembled. Though he was being borne away,
Rohini's son was not frightened in his mind. He addressed
Krishna in these words. Balarama said, "O Krishna! Look at
this *daitya*, who assumed the disguise of a cowherd. O Krishna!
His fierce form is like a mountain, and I am being abducted by
him. O slayer of Madhu! What should I do now? Please tell
me. This evil-souled one is proceeding at a fast pace." With a
smile on his lips, Govinda spoke to Rama. He knew about the
greatness of Rohini's son and about the extent of his strength
and valour. Shri Krishna replied, "Why are you resorting to
a human sentiment that has become manifest in you? You
are the *atman* of everything. You are more mysterious than
everything mysterious. Your *atman* is mysterious. O seed of
the entire universe! O elder brother! O cause behind all causes!
Remember. When the entire universe is reduced to a single
ocean of water, the *atman* alone exists. Do you not know that
you and I are that and the reason for us being born on earth?
We have descended in the world of the mortals to remove
the earth's burden. Your head is the firmament. Your hair
constitutes the waters. Your feet are the earth. Your mouth is
the fire. Your mind is the moon. Your breathing is the wind.
Your four arms are the directions. You are without decay. You
possess one thousand faces. You are the illustrious and great-

[921] This is Pralamba's description.

souled one, with one thousand hands, one thousand feet and one thousand different bodies. You are the source of the one thousand who have been born from the lotus.[922] The sages sing about your one thousand forms. You possess the divine form, no one else. *Deva*s worship your infinite *avatara*s. Do you not know that it is into you that the universe is dissolved? O one who is infinite in form! The earth is held up by you and thus, the world nurtures mobile and immobile objects. In your form of time, you are the one who has created *krita yuga* and the other differences. In an instant, you devour the universe. The waters are swallowed by the Vadava fire and received by the Himalayas in the form of ice. Coming into contact with Bhanu's rays, they become water again. O lord of the *kalpa*s! Like that, at the time of dissolution, you are the one who withdraws the entire universe. You are the one who creates the universe again. You, and I, are the *atman* of the universe. We alone are its cause. For the universe, for the welfare of the universe, we are established as separate entities. Remember your immeasurable *atman*. Resort to your *atman* and slay the *danava*. However, do what is good for our relatives using human attributes alone." O *brahmana*! Reminded by the extremely great-souled Krishna in this way, Bala laughed and used his strength to make Pralamba suffer. His eyes red with rage, he struck him on the head with his fist. Because of these blows, his eyes popped out of their sockets. His brains came out and he vomited blood from his mouth. The noble *daitya* died and fell down on the ground. On seeing that Pralamba had been killed by Bala, whose deeds are extraordinary, the *gopa*s were delighted. They applauded him in words of praise. When the *daitya* Pralamba was brought down, Rama was praised by the *gopa*s and along with Krishna, he returned to Gokula again.'

[922] One thousand Brahmas.

Chapter 5(10) (Stopping Indra's Worship)

Shri Parashara said, 'While Rama and Keshava amused themselves in Vraja, the monsoon season passed. Autumn arrived and lotuses bloomed. Like a householder who possesses a sense of "mine" and is attached to a son and a wife, in their watery shelters, *saphari* fish[923] suffered excessively from the heat. Like *yogi*s who have ascertained that *samsara* has no substance, the peacocks in the forest were no longer maddened and became silent. Like householders who have acquired *vijnana*, clouds, which had released all their water, assumed a sparkling appearance and left the sky. Like the hearts of embodied creatures scorched by the fire of "mine", the autumn sun swiftly dried up whatever water was left in lakes. Like the minds of those who have achieved union with the sparkling *atman*, the autumn waters were united with white waterlilies. Like a *yogi* who has assumed a body in a virtuous family, the moon was radiant in the firmament, amidst sparkling stars. Like wise men who are freed from "mine" and attachment to a wife and sons, the waterbodies gradually withdrew from their banks. Like bad *yogi*s who could not cross the final hurdle and faced hardships, subsequently attempting *yoga* again, swans returned to lakes they had formerly abandoned. Like a mendicant who has practiced great *yoga* and stills his *atman*, the ocean was tranquil and withdrew its waves. Like the mind of an extremely intelligent person, who has seen Vishnu everywhere, the waters everywhere were clear. Like the minds of *yogi*s who have used the fire of *yoga* to scorch all hardships, with all clouds having been dispelled, the autumn sky was clear. Like great discrimination eliminates all misery

---

[923] A small silvery fish.

caused by *ahamkara*, the lord of the stars[924] alleviated the heat
caused by the sun's rays. Like senses withdraw from the objects
of the senses, autumn took away clouds from the sky, water
from the earth and mud from the water. Like the practice of
puraka, *rechaka* and *kumbhaka* every day, the water in the
lakes seemed to be practicing *pranayama*.[925] This was the time
when *nakshatra*s sparkled in the clear sky and this season
arrived in Vraja.'

'Krishna saw that the residents of Vraja were making
great preparations for Indra's festival. He saw that the
*gopa*s were eager and anxious to undertake these festivities.
Curious, the immensely intelligent one addressed the elders
in these words. Krishna said, "Who is this Shakra? His name
is bringing you this delight." When he asked with great
affection, Nandagopa replied. Nandagopa said, "Shatakratu,
the king of the gods, is the lord of water and the clouds.
Urged by him, the clouds shower down juices in the form of
rain. We and other embodied beings nourish ourselves on
the resultant grain. Since we sustain ourselves on that food,
we satisfy the *deva*s. Thus nourished, these cows have calves
and yield milk. Everyone is nourished and content because of
this and everyone prospers. When it is seen that the clouds
are full of rain, it is seen that the land does not lack in crops
or grass and people do not suffer from hunger. Parjanya uses
the sun's rays to drink up the water in the ground, as if it is
milk, and then showers it down on the ground again. This
is for the sustenance of all the worlds. Therefore, when it is
the rainy season, all the kings, we and all humans on earth

[924] The moon.
[925] *Puraka*, *rechaka* and *kumbhaka* are respectively inhalation,
retention and exhalation of air, while inhaling, retaining and exhaling
air. The comparison is with the water being filled, remaining constant
and then declining.

are delighted and worship the lord of the gods through a
sacrifice." Damodara heard Nandagopa's words about
the reason behind Shakra's worship. To enrage Indra of
the gods, he spoke these words. "We are not farmers. Nor
do we earn our living through trading. O father! Since we
are those who roam around in the forest, the cows are our
deities. There are four kinds of learning: *anvikshiki*, *trayi*,
varta and *dandaniti*.[926] Of these, hear about *varta* from me.
O immensely fortunate one! Specifically, for knowledge
about *varta*, there are three kinds of means of subsistence,
agriculture, trading and animal husbandry as the third.
Tilling the land is the means of subsistence for those who are
farmers. Trading is the means of subsistence for those who
are merchants. For us, cattle represent the supreme means
of subsistence. These are the three methods of earning a
living. Whatever be the mode that one is engaged with, that
should constitute the greatest divinity. That is what should
be venerated and worshipped. This is the means to ensure
welfare. If a man obtains fruits from one source but worships
another, then in this world and in the next world, he does
not obtain what is good for him. We should worship what is
known as our boundaries. Beyond the tilled land, there are
boundaries. Beyond the boundaries, there are forests. Beyond
the forests, there are all the mountains and those are our
supreme objective. We are not bound by doors and walls,
nor by houses and fields. We happily wander around the
entire earth, wherever our wheels take us. It has been heard
that the mountains in this forest can assume any form that
they want. Resorting to those forms, they roam around on

---

[926] *Anvikshiki* is the science of inquiry (the meaning changed
over time and varied according to the context), *trayi* stands for the
three *Veda*s, *varta* is livelihood and *dandaniti* is punishment and good
policy (broadly governance and jurisprudence).

their own summits. If they wish to bind down the residents of the forest, those mountains assume the forms of lions and other animals and kill them. Therefore, we should perform a *giriyajna* and a *goyajna*.[927] Since our divinities are cattle and mountains, what do we have to do with the great Indra? *Brahmana*s utter *mantra*s and perform sacrifices. Farmers use their ploughs to perform sacrifices. Since we depend on mountains and forests, we should perform sacrifices to mountains and cattle. Let all kinds of offerings be tendered to Mount Govardhana as worship. Let us follow the norms and kill and offer in worship sacrificial animals. Let milk and milk products be taken from all the settlements of cowherds. There is no need to think about this. Let *brahmana*s and others who so wish be fed. After the worship has been completed and oblations have been offered, let *dvija*s be fed. Let herds of cattle be taken there,[928] with autumn flowers decorating their heads. O *gopa*s! This is my view. If this appeals to you, act accordingly. If you act accordingly, the cattle, the mountain and I will be pleased." Hearing these words, Nanda and the other residents of Vraja applauded these words. The faces of the *gopa*s bloomed with joy and they said, "O child! What you have said is appropriate. Therefore, let all of us prepare for the *giriyajna*."[929] Thus, the residents of Vraja performed a sacrifice to the mountain. They offered curd, *payasam*, flesh and other offerings to the mountain. They fed hundreds and thousands of *dvija*s. The cows were worshipped and made

[927] Respectively, a sacrifice to the mountain and a sacrifice to cows.

[928] To the mountain.

[929] Though not explicitly stated, this is presumably Nanda speaking.

to perform *pradakshina*[930]around the mountain. The bulls
bellowed, like clouds full of rain. O *brahmana*! Krishna
embodied himself on the summit of the mountain and said,
"I am the mountain." He ate all the different kinds of food
that the *gopa*s brought. Along with the *gopa*s, in the form of
Krishna, he climbed to the summit of the mountain. Having
ascended, he worshipped his own second form.[931] When the
sacrifice was over, this form vanished. Having obtained their
boons, the *gopa*s returned to their own settlement again.'

Chapter 5(11) (Holding up Govardhana)

Shri Parashara said, 'O Maitreya! When his sacrifice was
stopped, Shakra became extremely angry. He spoke
to the category of clouds that are known by the name of
samvartaka.[932] "O clouds! Listen to the words that I speak.
Without thinking about it, swiftly act in accordance with my
commands. Nandagopa is extremely evil-minded and the other
*gopa*s have helped him. Depending on Krishna's strength, he
has broken the agreement about my sacrifice. Act according

[930] The word used is *pradakshina*, which is much more specific
than a mere act of circling. This circling or circumambulation has
to be done in a specific way, so that the right side (*dakshina*) always
faces what is being circled. If one is undertaking a tour of pilgrimage,
this must begin with the south, then move to the west, then the north
and finally the east. The right side, so to speak, then always faces the
centre of the earth, or the object being worshipped.

[931] This statement makes it clear. In the form of Krishna, he
remained with the *gopa*s. However, he created a second form that
appeared on the summit of the mountain and accepted the offerings.
It is this second form that vanished.

[932] These are clouds that appear at the time of universal
destruction.

to my instructions. Shower down rain and make the cows
suffer. They are the supreme reason behind the *gopa*s being
able to manage a means of sustenance. I will myself be astride
the elephant that resembles the summit of a mountain. I will
help you and the winds will also be invoked to aid the rain."
Having instructed them in this way, he released the clouds.
O *brahmana*! To destroy the cows, they showered down an
extremely terrible downpour of wind and rain. O sage! As a
result of the great downpour that encompassed everything, in
an instant, the earth, the directions and the sky appeared as one
torrent. The dense clouds thundered, as if terrified and lashed
by the flashes of lightning. They poured down in torrents.
Trembling because of the wind and the rain, the cows fell down.
With their heads and faces pointed in abnormal directions, all
of them lost their lives. O great sage! Other cows stood there,
sheltering the calves under their bodies. Because of the shower
of rain, other cows were separated from their calves. The faces
of the calves were miserable. Because of the wind, their heads
quivered. Suffering, they seemed to be uttering the muffled
sounds, "Save us! O Krishna! Save us!" In this way, Gokula,
with all the cattle, *gopa*s and *gopi*s, suffered greatly.'

'O Maitreya! Hari saw that they were suffering greatly and
thought. "Since his sacrifice has been stopped, the great Indra
has done this. Therefore, I must now save this entire cowherd
settlement. I will use my valour to uproot this mountain from
its base. Like a large umbrella, I will hold up the flat part of
the mountain above the cowherd settlement." Having made up
his mind about this, Krishna playfully used one of his hands
to uproot Mount Govardhana. Uprooting the mountain and
holding it up, Shouri smilingly told the *gopa*s, "To counter
the rain, quickly enter the space under this. There is no wind
here. Find an appropriate spot here and rest. Enter here, there
is no reason to be afraid. There is no need to be scared that the
mountain will fall down." Thus addressed, along with their

wealth of cattle, the gopas entered, placing their vessels on their carts. So did the gopis, who had suffered on account of the rain. Krishna held up the mountain, completely steady. Delighted and amazed, the residents of Vraja looked on. The gopas and gopis were happy and over-joyed and their eyes dilated in love. As Krishna held the mountain up, they praised his conduct. For seven nights, the large clouds showered down on Nanda's Gokula. O brahmana! Wishing to destroy the gopas, Indra urged the clouds. Thus, the great mountain was held up and Gokula saved. The wealth of cattle was saved. When the pledge made by Bala's slayer[933] was falsified, he restrained the clouds. The sky became bereft of clouds and the words of Indra of the gods were nullified. Emerging happily, they returned to their own places in Gokula. While all the residents of Vraja looked on with wonder on their faces, Krishna released the great mountain of Govardhana and placed it back in its own place.'

Chapter 5(12) (Indra's Conversation with Krishna)

Shri Parashara said, 'Mount Govardhana was held up and Gokula was saved. After this, the chastiser of Paka wished to see Krishna. Astride his giant elephant, Airavata, the slayer of enemies, the lord of the gods, came to see Krishna at Mount Govardhana. The immensely valiant one had assumed the form of a gopa and was herding cows. The protector of the entire universe was surrounded by gopa boys. O brahmana! Though others couldn't see him, he saw Garuda.[934] Using his wings, the leader of birds cast shade over Hari's head. Shakra

---

[933] Indra killed a demon named Bala.
[934] Indra saw Garuda, who remained invisible to others.

descended from the Indra among elephants and approached
Madhusudana. His eyes widened in affection. He smiled and
spoke. Indra said, "O Krishna! Listen to the reason why I
have come here, to you. O Krishna! O mighty-armed one!
You should not think otherwise. You are the supreme lord
who holds everything up. You have incarnated yourself on
earth so as to remove the earth's burden. Since my sacrifice
was stopped, I desired to destroy Gokula. I instructed the
giant clouds to implement this calamity. To save the cattle
who were tormented, you uprooted the great mountain. I am
satisfied at your extraordinary and valiant deed. O Krishna! I
now think that the objective of the gods will be accomplished.
You managed to hold up that excellent mountain on a single
hand. O Krishna! The cows have urged me to approach you.
You saved them. You are the cause behind all the causes. O
Krishna! Hence, urged by the words of the cows, I will instate
you as Upendra. As the Indra of the cows, you will become
Govinda."[935] He brought the bell that was on the elephant
Airavata. He filled it with sacred water and performed the
consecration.[936] As soon as Krishna's consecration was done,
milk flowed from the udders of the cows and immediately
moistened the earth. Urged by the words of the cows, Shachi's
consort consecrated Upendra Janardana. Happy, he again
addressed Krishna in affectionate words. "I have done this
because of the words of the cows. But listen to something else.
O immensely fortunate one! I am telling you this because I
want the earth's burden to be removed. O one who holds up
the earth! O tiger among men! My portion has been born on

[935] The usual etymology of Govinda is someone who knows cows
(*go*) or obtains delight from cows. Upendra is Indra's younger brother.
Vishnu is Upendra because as the offspring of Aditi, he was born after
Indra.

[936] By sprinkling water on the head.

earth under the name of Arjuna. You should always protect me.
In removing the burden, that valiant one will be your friend.
O Madhusudana! Please protect him as you protect your own
self." The illustrious one replied, "I know that your portion,
Partha, has been born in the lineage of Bharata. As long as I am
on earth, I will protect him. O Shakra! O scorcher of enemies!
O Indra of the gods! As long as I am on earth, no one will
be able to defeat Arjuna in battles. There is a mighty-armed
daitya named Kamsa. There are others like the *asura* Arishta,
Keshi, Kuvalayapida, Naraka and others. O Indra of the gods!
When they have been killed, there will be a great battle. O one
with a thousand eyes! Know that the burden of the earth will
be removed there. Go. You should not lament on account of
your son. No enemy of Arjuna's will be able to stand in front
of me. For Arjuna's sake, in the course of the Bharata battle, I
will protect the others, Yudhishthira being the foremost, and
return them unharmed to Kunti." Thus addressed, the king of
the gods embraced Janardana. He mounted Airavata elephant
again and returned to heaven. With the cows and the cowherds,
Krishna again returned to Vraja, with his path purified by the
glances of the *gopis*.'

Chapter 5(13) (Rasa Lila)

Shri Parashara said, 'When Shakra left, the delighted
cowherds affectionately spoke to Krishna, whose deeds
were unblemished. They had seen Krishna hold up Mount
Govardhana. Delighted, they spoke. They said, "O immensely
fortunate one! You have saved us and the cows from this great
fear, through this feat of unmatched holding up the mountain, as
if in childish sport. The state of being a cowherd is condemned.
O son! But your feat is divine. How is this possible? In the

water, you subjugated Kaliya. Dhenuka was brought down. You held up Govardhana. Our minds are scared.[937] This is the truth. We swear on Hari's feet that this is the truth. O infinitely valiant one! When we witness your valour, we do not think that you are human. O Keshava! We from Vraja, along with our wives and our sons, love you. But these feats are impossible for even the gods to accomplish. Since your birth amongst us, you have performed these auspicious, but extremely valiant, deeds in your childhood. O Krishna! When we think about them, our minds are filled with doubts. Whether you are a *deva*, a *danava*, a *yaksha* or a *gandharva*, since you are our relative, we bow down before you. What is the need to think?" Out of his affection, when he was addressed by the *gopa*s in this way, the immensely intelligent Krishna was silent for a while. But he pretended to be angry and spoke to them. The illustrious one replied, "O *gopa*s! If you are not ashamed of your relationship with me and if you think that I should be praised, what is the need to think about this? If you love me and if you think that I should be praised, then your intelligence should be such that you behave towards me as you would towards kin. I am not a *deva*, a *gandharva*, a *yaksha* or a *danava*. I have been born as your kin. There is no need to think of me in any other way." They heard Hari's words and were silent and left for the forest. O immensely fortunate one! The *gopa*s realized that he loved them, though he had pretended to be angry.'

'Krishna saw the sparkling sky and the beams of the autumn moon.[938] The night lotuses bloomed and made the directions fragrant. The buzzing of clusters of bees made the region of the forest pleasant. On seeing this, he made up his mind to find pleasure with the *gopi*s. Without Rama, he sang

[937] At these superhuman exploits.
[938] There is abruptness in this. Time has elapsed since the conversation.

songs that women loved, in sweet, soft and measured tones.
Hearing the notes of the lovely song, the *gopi*s abandoned
their homes and swiftly came to the place where Madhusudana
was. A *gopi* followed his melody and sang slowly. Another
one listened attentively. Yet another remembered him in her
mind. A *gopi* exclaimed "O Krishna! O Krishna!" and was
embarrassed. Another one was blind with love and went to his
side, without any sense of shame. Another one saw her senior
standing outside the house.[939] She closed her eyes and immersed
herself completely in Govinda. With her mind immersed in
him, all stores of good merits were exhausted, and all sins
and great miseries were destroyed. She obtained unblemished
bliss. Another *gopi* thought of the origin of the universe, whose
nature is the supreme *brahman*. Consequently, as she sighed,
she obtained emancipation. With the autumn moon, the night
was charming. Surrounded by the *gopi*s, Govinda was eager to
start the dance of *rasa*. The groups of *gopi*s were completely
engrossed in what Krishna was doing and in his form. When
Krishna went to another spot, they roamed around Vrindavana
in groups. With their hearts fixed on Krishna, they spoke to each
other. One said, "I am Krishna. Look at my elegant gait." A
second said, "I am Krishna! Listen to me singing." A third said,
"I am Krishna! O wicked Kaliya! Remain here." Saying this,
she slapped her arms and imitated all of Krishna's pastimes. A
fourth said, "O *gopa*s! Stay here. Do not be scared. Enough of
this fear on account of the rain. I have held Govardhana up."
A fifth addressed the cows and said, "Roam around as you
please. I have flung Dhenuka[940] away." Saying this, she imitated
Krishna's pastimes. In this fashion, the *gopi*s eagerly imitated
Krishna's deeds in many kinds of ways and wandered around

[939] Therefore, she couldn't leave the house and go to Krishna.
[940] With no distinction being drawn between Krishna and
Balarama.

the beautiful region of Vrindavana. Looking at the ground, one *gopi*'s face resembled a blooming lotus and the body hair stood up all over her limbs. She told another beautiful *gopi*, "Behold. Look at the ground. As Krishna proceeded on his pastimes, the marks of the standard, *vajra*, goad and lotus on his feet have left their imprints. Which maiden has accumulated sufficient good merits to be with him and take part in acts of desire? Here, the footprints are deep. There, they are shallow.[941] Damodara has certainly stopped to gather some flowers here. Only the tips of the great-souled one's feet can be seen in the marks. Who, adorned with flowers, sat down with him here? In another birth, she must have worshipped Vishnu with all her *atman*. Behold. Having honoured her with bunches of flowers here, Nandagopa's son has followed another path. Someone else has followed him here, moving slowly because of her heavy hips. Attempting to move fast, she has only left marks of the tips of her toes. There is another who has gone with him like a friend, hand in hand. There footmarks can be seen, mingled together. However, the deceiver has dishonoured her[942] and only touched her with his hand. Losing all hope, her footmarks can be seen to slow down and return. He must have told this one that he will return to her presence soon. Her footmarks are seen to be as swift as those of Krishna's. Since he has entered the dense forest, in this part, Krishna's footprints can no longer be seen. Like the beams of the moon, they have vanished and can no longer be seen." When they were unable to see Krishna, the *gopis* returned in despair.'

'They went to the banks of the Yamuna and sang about his conduct. Krishna's deeds were unblemished, and he was the protector of the three worlds. The *gopis* would then see

[941] It can be inferred that where the footmarks were deep, Krishna might have carried the maiden.

[942] Obviously another *gopi*.

him approach, his lotus face blooming. A *gopi* saw Govinda
approach and was extremely happy. Another exclaimed,
"Krishna! Krishna! Krishna!" Another knitted her eyebrows
and looked at Hari. With eyes that were like bees, she drank
the nectar from his lotus face. Another saw Govinda and closed
her eyes. Immersed in *yoga*, she meditated on him. With some,
Madhava had charming conversations. He assured some with
sidelong glances and others, by touching them with his hands.
Happy in his mind, Hari lovingly amused himself with the
*gopi*s. Extensive in his conduct, the *rasa* dance was performed
in groups. The *rasa* dance was supposed to be performed in a
circle. But the *gopi*s did not stick to this agreement and each
one sought his permission to be next to him. Their minds were
fickle, and they did not stick to one particular spot. Therefore,
Hari took each of the *gopi*s by the mind and completed the
circle for the *rasa* dance. Touched by his hand, they closed
their eyes. Thus, the circle was completed.[943] As the *rasa* dance
commenced, there were lovely sounds from the movements
in the bangles. These were progressively mixed with poems
and songs about the autumn. Krishna sang about the autumn
moon, the moon beams and the ponds full of lotuses. However,
the *gopi*s repeatedly only sang about Krishna's name. A *gopi*
became exhausted from dancing round and round and her
moving bangles wore her out. She placed her hands, which were
like creepers, on the shoulders of Madhu's slayer. Another *gopi*
was skilled in singing, praising and artifices. She embraced him
with her graceful arms and lovingly kissed him. Hari's desired
arms touched a *gopi*'s cheeks. Just as rain from a cloud leads to
crops growing, the resultant drops of sweat made her body hair
stand up. Krishna sang the songs of *rasa* and as the pitch of his
voice rose, they exclaimed "O Krishna! Well done, Krishna!" in

[943] Since they closed their eyes, each took her neighbour's hand to
be that of Krishna's.

a pitch that was double his. When he advanced, they followed him. When he moved in a circle, they proceeded ahead of him. The *gopis* proceeded ahead of Hari and followed him. At that time, Madhusudana amused himself with the *gopis*. Even if he was away for an instant, it seemed like crores of years. The *gopis* could not be restrained by their fathers, husbands or brothers. Full of desire, they amused themselves with Krishna during the nights. Though he was a youth, Madhusudana was wise and showed them respect, amusing himself with them.[944] Immeasurable in his *atman*, he spent the nights with them. The lord pervaded them and their husbands. He was the lord who was in all beings. His own form was in their *atmans*. Like the wind, he pervaded everything and was established in everything. Space, fire, earth, water and wind are in all beings. Just like that, he was in everything. He pervaded everything and was established in everything.'

Chapter 5(14) (Slaying of Arishta)

Shri Parashara said, 'There was an occasion in the evening when Janardana was engaged in *rasa*. The insolent Arishta arrived in the settlement, causing terror. His form was that of a bull and he resembled a monsoon cloud full of water. His horns were sharp, and his eyes were like the sun. He kicked the ground with the tips of his hooves and tore it up. He repeatedly licked his lips with his tongue and bit them. Full of rage, he raised up his tail. The muscles of his shoulder were tough. His hump was large and fierce. His size was unsurpassed. His hind quarters were smeared with urine and excrement. He caused

[944] The text uses the word *kishora*, which means less than fifteen years of age.

great anxiety among the cows. Loose skin hung down from
his neck. As a result of butting against trees, his face was
marked. This was a *daitya* in the form of a bull and he made
the cows have miscarriages. This fierce one oppressed ascetics
as he wandered around the forest. On seeing the one with the
terrible eyes advance, the *gopa*s and *gopi*s were afflicted by
fear. They shriekied, "O Krishna! O Krishna!" Keshava roared
like a lion and slapped the palms of his hands. Hearing that
sound, he rushed in Damodara's direction. With the tips of
his horns pointed towards Krishna's side, his eyes were fixed
on him. The evil-souled *danava*, in the form of a bull, rushed
towards Krishna. The immensely strong Krishna saw that the
daitya, in the form of a bull, was advancing. He did not move
from his spot but ignored him. He seemed to smile, in sport.
When he was about to reach, without moving, Madhusudana
seized him by the tips of his horns, like a crocodile seizes. He
then struck him in the sides with his knees. Seized by the horns,
all his insolence and strength disappeared. He seized Arishta's
throat and wrung it, as if it was a wet garment. He uprooted
one of the horns and struck him with that. Vomiting blood
from his mouth, the great *daitya* died. When the *daitya* was
killed, the *gopa*s praised Janardana, just as in ancient times, the
large number of gods had praised the one with one thousand
eyes when Jambha[945] had been slain.'

Chapter 5(15) (Kamsa's Preparations)

Shri Parashara said, 'The bull Arishta was killed. Dhenuka was
brought down. Pralamba was conveyed to his destruction.
Mount Govardhana was held up. Kaliya *naga* was subjugated.

---

[945] Demon killed by Indra.

The two lofty trees were shattered. Putana was killed. The cart was overturned. In due order, Narada told Kamsa everything that had happened. He also described the details about how Devaki and Yashoda's infants had been exchanged. Kamsa heard everything from Narada, who possessed divine vision. The evil-minded one became angry towards Vasudeva.[946] Because of his excessive rage, he censured him in an assembly of Yadavas. Having reprimanded the Yadavas, he thought about what should be done. "Bala and Krishna are still extremely young. They must be killed by me before they become extremely strong. When they become full-grown, it will be impossible to kill them. This Chanura is extremely valiant and Mushtika is extremely strong. Using them, I will have those two evil-minded ones killing in a wrestling match. Let a great festival of the bow be organized and let those two be brought from Vraja. I will then make efforts so that they are destroyed. Shvaphalka's brave son, Akrura, is a bull among Yadus. So as to fetch them here, I will send him to Gokula. The terrible Keshin roams around in Vrindavana. He is extremely strong, and he will certainly kill those two. Or, if they happen to come to my presence, my elephant, Kuvalayapida, will kill those two *gopas*, Vasudeva's sons." The evil-souled Kamsa reflected in this way and made up his mind to kill Rama and Janardana. He addressed the brave Akrura in these words. Kamsa said, "O Danapati![947] To cause me pleasure, act in accordance with my words. Ascend a chariot and leave this place. Go to Nanda's Gokula. Born from Vishnu's portions to bring about my destruction, two of Vasudeva's sons are there. The two wicked ones are growing. On the fourteenth lunar day, a great festival of the bow will take place here. For the sake of a wrestling match, bring the two of them here. Chanura

---

[946] Krishna's father.

[947] Akrura was generous in giving gifts and was known as Danapati.

and Mushtika are my wrestlers, and they are skilled in wrestling.
Let all the worlds witness a wrestling match between the two
sides. Let the elephant Kuvalayapida be urged by its keeper.[948]
Let it kill Vasudeva's wicked sons, who are still children. When
they have been killed, I will kill Vasudeva and the evil-minded
Nandagopa. I will also kill my father, the extremely evil-minded
Ugrasena. The wicked gopas desire to kill me. After this, I will
seize all their wealth of cattle and other riches. O Danapati!
With your exception, it is my view that all these Yadavas are
wicked.[949] I will make efforts to progressively kill them. After
this, without any Yadavas, the entire kingdom will be bereft of
thorns. O brave one! Therefore, out of affection towards me,
make efforts to go. Address words to the gopas so that they
quickly supply me with ghee and curd made from the milk of
buffaloes." O brahmana! When he was instructed in this way,
Akrura, the great devotee,[950] was delighted, because he would
quickly be able to see Krishna, the next day. He agreed to what
the king had said and swiftly mounted a beautiful chariot.
Madhupriya emerged from the city of Mathura.'[951]

[948] Mahamatra, which means superintendent of elephants, trainer
and keeper, mahout.

[949] The word Yadava is used both in a narrow sense and in a broad
sense, more often the latter. By using the word Yadava here, Kamsa
probably means the ones descended from the Devaka side of the family.
Through Devaki, this was Krishna's family. In a broad sense, Kamsa
was also a Yadava. But he was descended from Ugrasena, Devaka's
brother. Vasudeva (Krishna's father) was descended from Shurasena.

[950] Devotee of Krishna's.

[951] With the word Madhupriya used for Akrura, one has to
speculate about what it means. Madhupriya means someone who loves
madhu. The word madhu has multiple meanings: sweet, honey, liquor,
spring. But it probably does mean that Akrura loved to drink. This is
the sense in which it is used when the name Madhupriya is used for
Balarama. However, interpretations take this to mean that Akrura was
loved by the family of the Madhus, that is, the side Krishna belonged to.

Chapter 5(16) (Slaying of Keshin)

Shri Parashara said, 'Keshin was fierce in his valour. Kamsa's messenger urged him. Desiring to kill Krishna, he reached Vrindavana. He struck the ground with his hooves and tore it up. He shook his manes and dispelled the clouds. He displayed his valour and travelled along the paths of the sun and the moon.[952] In this way, the approached the *gopa*s. The *daitya* was in the form of a horse. Terrified and anxious at the sound of his neighing, the cowherds and *gopi*s sought refuge with Govinda. "Save us! Save us!" Govinda heard their words. He addressed them in a deep voice that rumbled like clouds full of rain. "O cowherds! Enough of this fright. Because of Keshi, why are you afflicted by fear? You have been born as *gopa*s. This one makes a lot of his neighing, but there is little substance in him. This *daitya*'s strength is only on the outside. Like a wicked horse, he should be reined in. O wicked one! Come here. I am Krishna. Just as the wielder of Pinaka knocked out Pusha's teeth,[953] I will knock out all the teeth from your mouth." Having said this, Govinda slapped his arms and advanced in front of Keshin. With a gaping mouth, the *daitya* also rushed towards him. Janardana enlarged his arm and thrust it into the mouth of Keshin, the evil horse. When Krishna's arm entered Keshin's mouth, his teeth were knocked out and resembled white clouds that had been scattered away. O *brahmana*! Krishna's enlarged arm entered Keshin's body and became the cause of his destruction, like an ailment that has been neglected.[954] His lips were torn apart, and he vomited a lot of blood mixed with froth. His pupils dilated and the sinews of the mouth were loosened. He sank down

---

[952] That is, he travelled through the sky.

[953] At the time of Daksha's sacrifice, Virabhadra knocked out Pusha's teeth.

[954] And has not been treated.

on the ground on his knees and released urine and excrement.
His limbs were drenched in sweat. He was exhausted and was
incapable of making any more efforts. Like a gigantic hole, the
asura's mouth was stretched open by Krishna's arm. He fell
down, like a tree torn into two by a bolt of lightning. Torn
into two parts, Keshin's body shone. Each part had two feet,
one ear, one eye, one nostril and a bit of the back and the tip
of the tail. When Keshin was killed by Krishna, the cowherds
were delighted and surrounded him. His body showed no signs
of exhaustion. Completely at ease, he stood there, laughing.
The *gopa*s and *gopi*s were astounded that Keshin had been
killed. They praised Pundarikaksha in charming words that
were full of love. O *brahmana*! Seated on a cloud, Narada
swiftly arrived there. Seeing that Keshin was dead, his mind
was filled with great joy. Narada said, "This is wonderful. O
Jagannatha! O Achyuta! Your pastimes are wonderful. You
have killed Keshin, who caused suffering to the residents of
heaven. You were eager to bring about his death in a great
encounter between a man and a horse. I have come here from
heaven, to witness an event, the likes of which have never
been seen before. O Madhusudana! In this incarnation, you
have performed deeds that have amazed me, but this one has
given me great satisfaction. O Krishna! Shakra and *deva*s were
terrified of this horse. Looking up at the clouds, he used to
shake his net of manes and neigh. O Janardana! You have now
killed the evil-souled Keshin. Therefore, you will be famous
in the world as Keshava.[955] O slayer of Keshin! May you be
fortunate. I will leave and meet you again day after tomorrow,
when you have an encounter with Kamsa. O one who holds up
the earth! You will bring down Ugrasena's son, Kamsa, and his
followers, and remove the burden of the earth. O Janardana! I

---

[955] The usual etymology of Keshava is someone with long/
handsome hair.

will witness many battles between you and the kings on earth, which you will bring about. I will leave now. O Govinda! You have accomplished a great task for *deva*s. You know all that. May you be fortunate. I will leave now." When Narada left, Krishna was not at all surprised. Along with the *gopa*s, he entered the settlement of cowherds and was the only one whom the eyes of the *gopi*s drank in.'

Chapter 5(17) (Akrura's Arrival)

Shri Parashara said, 'Akrura was eager to meet Krishna. On a chariot that could travel fast, he emerged and left for Nanda's Gokula. Akrura thought, "There is no one more blessed than me. The one who holds the *chakra* has used one of his portions to incarnate himself and I will see him. Today, my birth will be successful. My night has become an excellent morning. On waking up, I will today see the face of Vishnu, whose eyes are like the petals of lotuses. Even if men remember him in their fancies, all their sins are destroyed. I will see the lotus eyed Vishnu's face, from which, all the *Veda*s and *Vedanga*s emerged. I will see the illustrious one's face, which is the supreme refuge amongst all refuges. He is the being embodied in sacrifices. He is Purusha Purushottama. It is to him that all sacrifices are offered. He is the one who holds everything up. I will see the lord of the universe. By performing one hundred sacrifices to him, Indra became the king of the immortals. He has neither a beginning nor an end. I will see that infinite Keshava. Brahma, Indra, Rudra, the Ashvins, the Vasus, the Adityas and the large number of Maruts do not know his true nature. That Hari will be directly in front of me. He is in the *atman* of everything. He knows everything. He is everything. He is established in all beings. He cannot be thought of. He is the one who does not decay. He pervades everything. He will speak to me. Assuming the form of a fish, a tortoise, a boar, a horse and a lion,[956] he ensured the preservation of the universe. The one without origin will have a conversation with me today. To perform a task, that lord of the universe has now taken birth in Vraja and is there. To accomplish a task that only his heart knows, the lord of the universe, the one who does not decay, has voluntarily assumed a body and is acting like a human now. He is stationed as Ananta, holding up the earth on his head. He has descended for the sake of the world, and he will speak to me, Akrura. A father, a son, a well-wisher, a brother, a mother and a relative are relationships because of his *maya*. Enough of these. I bow down to the one who is embodied in the universe. I bow down to him. If he enters and spreads through a person's heart, he can cross over all this ignorance. All this is a consequence of his *yoga* and *maya*. I bow down to the immeasurable one whose *atman* is knowledge. For those who perform sacrifices, he is the being embodied in sacrifices.[957] He is the Vasudeva for the Satvatas.[958] Those who know *Vedanta* speak of him as Vishnu. I bow down to him. He is the refuge of the universe. He holds it up and it is established in him. He is the existence and the non-existence.[959] He is truth. May I be conveyed to that amiable one. If one remembers him, one becomes a recipient of everything that is beneficial. He is the supreme being. I always seek refuge with Hari." His mind full of devotion in this way, he thought of Vishnu. Akrura reached Gokula when the sun was still shining.'

[956] Respectively, Matsya, Kumara, Varaha, Hayagriva and Narasimha *avatara*s.

[957] Known as Yajnapurusha.

[958] Meaning, devotees.

[959] Alternatively, cause and effect.

'He saw Krishna there, engaged in the task of milking the cows. He was amidst the calves and his complexion was like that of a blooming blue lotus. His eyes were like the petals of a blossoming lotus and the *shrivatsa* mark was on his chest. His arms were elongated. His chest was broad, and his nose was raised. An enchanting smile played on his lips and decorated his lotus face. With his feet firmly placed on the ground, the nails on his toes were raised and red. He was radiant in his yellow garments and decorated with wildflowers. His complexion was like that of blue sapphire and resembling the moon, there were white lotuses on his head. O *brahmana*! He saw Balabhadra, the descendant of the Yadu lineage, near him. He was as fair as a swan, the moon or the *kunda* flower,[960] and was attired in blue garments. He was tall and his arms were long. His face was like a blooming lotus. He seemed to be like another Mount Kailasa, surrounded by garlands of clouds. O sage! When the immensely intelligent Akrura saw them both, his face turned as radiant as a blossoming lotus and the body hair on his limbs stood up. "This is the supreme refuge.[961] This is the supreme destination. The illustrious Vasudeva is present here, in two different forms. On having seen the creator of the universe in these two lofty forms, my eyes have attained success. Through the favours of the illustrious one, will my limbs come into contact with his limbs? Will I be embarked on that path of success? The prosperous Ananta is infinite in his forms. Will he touch me today with his lotus hands? Supreme men obtain success by being touched with his fingers. All their sins are destroyed. His hand holds the terrible and fierce *chakra*, which seems to have a liquid garland from the fire, the lightning and the sun. That *chakra* is used to slay the lords among the *daitya*s and wipe away the collyrium from the eyes of the *daitya* women.

---

[960] A type of jasmine.
[961] These are Akrura's thoughts.

This is the hand into which Bali sprinkled water and obtained agreeable objects of pleasure under the earth.[962] Earlier, in this way, Shakra became the lord of the immortals and obtained the status of being lord of the gods for the duration of one *manvantara*. However, it is possible that he may not show me any respect. Kamsa has held me, and I have been tainted because of association with that evil one. Even though I have caused no harm, shame on a person like me, who is shunned by those who are virtuous. All *jnana* is in his *atman*. He is a mass of *sattva*. He is pervasive and is never tainted. He is never manifest. Even if he is not known, he is present in the hearts of all men in this world. He is the lord of all lords. Therefore, bending down in devotion, I will go to him. Vishnu is without a beginning, without a middle and with an end. He is without birth. He has been incarnated as Purushottama's portion."'

Chapter 5(18) (Departure of Krishna and Balarama)

Shri Parashara said, 'Thinking in this way, the Yadava approached Govinda. Lowering his head down at Hari's feet, he said, "I am Akrura." His[963] hand was marked with the signs of a standard, a *vajra* and a lotus. Using this, he touched him. He lovingly pulled him towards himself and firmly embraced him. Bala and Keshava welcomed him in this way. They happily took him with them and entered their own house. Along with them, Akrura was welcomed in many kinds

---

[962] This is a reference to the Vamana *avatara* when Bali treated Vishnu like a guest. Though Bali lost the three worlds, he obtained the nether regions as a boon.

[963] Krishna's.

of ways. As is appropriate, he was offered food that he ate. After that, he told them everything: how Anakadundubhi had been reprimanded by Kamsa, how the evil-souled *danava* had treated the goddess Devaki, how the evil-souled Kamsa had behaved towards Ugrasena and the purpose for which Kamsa had sent him. Devaki's illustrious son heard everything in detail. He said, "O Danapati! I know all this. O immensely fortunate one! I will do whatever is held to be the best. It should not be thought that it will be otherwise. Know that Kamsa has already been killed by me. With you, Rama and I will go to Mathura tomorrow. With many types of gifts, the elders among the *gopa*s will also go. O brave one! Let the night pass. You should not worry. Within three nights, I will kill Kamsa and his followers." After instructing the *gopa*s about Akrura,[964] Keshava and Balabhadra went to Nandagopa's house and slept there.'

'When the sparkling day dawned, along with Akrura, the immensely radiant Rama and Krishna got ready to leave for the city of Mathura. Seeing this, the large number of *gopi*s shed tears. The bangles slipped from their hands. Extremely miserable, they sighed and spoke to each other. "If Govinda goes to Mathura, how will he return to Gokula? He will use his ears to drink in the sweet conversation of city women. The women of the city will enmesh him in their graceful and amorous words. How will his mind be attracted towards the *gopi*s of the village? Hari is the essence of this entire cowherd settlement and destiny has taken him away. Evil-souled and wicked fate has struck at the *gopa* women. The women of the city smile and utter words that are deep in sentiments. Their gait is languorous and graceful. They cast enchanting sidelong glances. Hari is from the village, and he will be bound up in their amorous bonds. How can he possibly return to our side

---

[964] Instructing them to take care of Akrura.

again? This Keshava will ascend a chariot and go to Mathura.
Our hopes have been destroyed by the cruel Akrura.[965] Does
the cruel one not know that these people are supremely in love
with him? Hari is the delight of our eyes, and he is taking our
Hari away. Extremely cruel, Govinda is leaving with Rama.
He has ascended the chariot. Restrain him quickly. Why are
you saying that it is not proper for us to speak in the presence
of our elders? When we are being scorched by the fire of
separation, what are the elders doing? With Nandagopa as
the foremost, the gopas have got ready to leave. No one is
making any efforts to restrain Govinda. For the women who
live in Mathura, night has yielded to an excellent morning
today. With eyes that are like arrays of bees, they will drink
in Achyuta's lotus face. As Krishna proceeds, those who have
an obstructed view of him along the route are blessed. Their
minds will be pleased, and their body hair will stand up in
delight. For the eyes of the citizens of the city of Mathura,
there will be a great festival. Today, they will be able to look at
Govinda's face. What dreams have those extremely fortunate
ones seen? With dilated eyes and without any obstruction, they
will be able to see Adhokshaja. Alas! The creator's heart is
merciless. After having shown the gopis a great treasure, he has
plucked out their eyes today. Since Hari is leaving, his love for
us has diminished. That is the reason the bangles have quickly
slipped off our hands. Akrura's heart is cruel. He is driving the
horses swiftly. Who will not feel compassion for such miserable
women? The dust raised by the wheels of Krishna's chariot
can be seen, though Hari has gone far away. Now even that
dust cannot be seen." Extremely miserable, the large number
of gopis looked on in this way. Along with Rama, Keshava left
the region of Vraja.'

---

[965] Since krura means cruel, there is a pun. Akrura means a person
who is not cruel.

'Travelling on a chariot yoked to swift horses, he reached the banks of the Yamuna. Rama, Akrura and Janardana reached the spot when it was midday. Akrura told Krishna, "Until I complete the required water-rites in the waters of Kalindi,[966] remain here." They agreed. O *brahmana*! Offering prayers to the supreme *brahman*, the immensely intelligent one entered the waters of the Yamuna. He bathed and performed his ablutions. He saw Balabhadra there, with one thousand hoods raised up.[967] His eyes were as large as the petals of a full-blown lotus, and he wore a garland made out of *kunda* flowers. He was surrounded by a large number of Vasuki's offspring, giant serpents who survive on air. They praised him. He was adorned in a garland of fragrant wildflowers. He was clad in blue garments and his beautiful form was excellent. He wore excellent earrings. Intoxicated, he was submerged in the water. He saw Krishna seated on his lap, with a complexion that was as dark as the clouds. His large eyes were coppery-red. His limbs were large, and he was four-armed. He was ornamented with the *chakra* and other weapons. He was attired in yellow garments and was adorned with colourful garlands. He was as colourful as a cloud tinged with a garland of lightning and Shakra's bow.[968] The *shrivatsa* mark was on his chest and his resplendent armlets and diadem were excellent. He saw Krishna, who is unblemished in deeds, adorned with lotuses. Sanandana[969] and other unblemished sages, those who have obtained success in *yoga*, were there, thinking of him with their eyes fixed on the tips of their noses.[970] Recognized Bala and Krishna, Akrura was

[966] Kalindi is another name for Yamuna.

[967] Balarama was in the form of Ananta and Krishna was lying down on Ananta.

[968] That is, a rainbow.

[969] That is, Sananda. As a group, this means Sanaka, Sananda, Sanatana and Sanatkumara.

[970] They were meditating on Krishna.

astounded. He thought, "How did they come here so fast?" He was about to speak, but Janardana paralyzed his power of speech. He emerged from the water and approached the chariot again. There, he saw both of them seated in the chariot. As earlier, Rama and Krishna were there in human form. He went and immersed himself in the water again. He again saw them being praised by gandharvas, sages, siddhas and giant uragas. At this, Danapati understood the true meaning of this. He praised the lord Achyuta, who is full of every kind of vijnana. Akrura said, "I bow down to the one who only exists in the form of consciousness. He is the paramatman, whose greatness is unthinkable. He pervades everything in a single form and in many forms. I bow down to you. You exist in everything. Your potencies cannot be thought of. I bow down to the one who is beyond vijnana. O Lord! You are beyond Prakriti. You alone exist in five forms: the atman of the elements, the atman of the senses, the atman of Pradhana, the atman[971] and the paramatman. Be pleased. You are in every atman. Among everything that perishes, you are the lord who is imperishable. You are thought of and praised as Brahma, Vishnu, Shiva and other names. Your own nature has many different forms that cannot be described. Your atman and your purpose cannot be described. Your designations cannot be described. I bow down before the supreme lord. O protector! Your names, types and other things are only conceptions. They don't exist. You are the supreme brahman. You are eternal and without transformation. You are without birth. However, though you are in everything, in the absence of some kind of conception, the objective cannot be accomplished. Hence, all the names are yours and you are worshipped under the names of Krishna, Achyuta, Ananta and Vishnu. You are in everything. You are without beginning. You are thought of as all the divinities and

[971] Meaning the jivatman.

the entire universe. You are the universe. You are the *atman* of the universe. You are devoid of any transformations and differences. Other than you, there is nothing in anything. You are Brahma, Pashupati, Aryama, Vidhatri, Dhatri, the lord of the gods, the wind god, the fire god, lord of the waters, the lord of wealth and the destroyer. You are one. However, you differentiate your powers in different forms throughout the universe. You create the universe. O Lord of lords! Surya's rays are your form. The universe is full of your qualities. You are without birth. But you exist in this visible universe. Your form is supreme existence. You are spoken of as the one without decay. Your *atman* is in *jnana*. You are cause and effect. I prostrate myself before you. Oum! I bow down to Vasudeva. I bow down to Samkarshana. I bow down to Pradyumna. I bow down to Aniruddha."'

Chapter 5(19) (Entry into Mathura)

Shri Parashara said, 'Inside the water, the Yadava praised Vishnu in this way. In his mind, he thought of incense and flowers and worshipped the lord of everything. Discarding all material objects, he immersed his mind in him. Immersed in the *brahman*, he remained there and meditated for a very long time.'

'Having decided that he had become successful in his objective, the immensely intelligent one emerged from the waters of the Yamuna and went to the chariot again. He saw Rama and Krishna there, stationed as they had been earlier. Noticing from his eyes that Akrura was amazed, Krishna spoke to him. Shri Krishna said, "O Akrura! In the waters of the Yamuna, you must have seen something wonderful. It can be ascertained from your wide-open eyes that you have been

amazed." Akrura replied, "O Achyuta! Inside the water, I saw
an extraordinary form. Now I see that figure in embodied
form in front of me. This universe is the great-souled one's
wonderful form. O Krishna! I am associated with you, who is
that extraordinary wonder. O Madhusudana! But what of all
this? We will go to Mathura, and I am scared of Kamsa. Shame
on a life where one has to subsist on scraps given by others."
Having said this, he urged the horses, which were as fleet as
the wind. In the evening, Akrura reached the city of Mathura.
Beholding Mathura, the Yadava spoke to Rama and Krishna.
Akrura said, "O immensely valiant ones! I alone will enter on
the chariot. The two of you proceed on foot. The two of you
should not go to Vasudeva's house. Because of you, that aged
person has been expelled by Kamsa." Having said this, Akrura
entered the city of Mathura.'

'Rama and Krishna entered and reached the royal road.
The men and the women looked at them with delighted eyes.
Like two young elephants that were maddened, those two brave
ones proceeded playfully. As they wandered around, they saw
a man who dyed clothes and washed them. They asked him for
beautiful and excellent garments. He was Kamsa's washerman,
and it wasn't surprising that because of those favours, he was
rude. He laughed at Rama and Keshava and used many words
to abuse them. At this, Krishna became angry. He used a blow of
his palm to strike the washerman, whose head fell down on the
ground. Having killed him, they took yellow and blue garments
from him. Full of joy, Krishna and Rama went to the house of
a garland-maker. The garland-maker was amazed, and his eyes
widened in surprise. O Maitreya! He thought, "Which noble
lineage have these two been born in?" He saw them attired in
those excellent yellow and blue garments and thought that they
were two *devas* who had come to earth. With faces that were
like blossoming lotuses, they asked him for flowers. With his
hands stretched out, he prostrated his head down on the ground.

The one who earned his living from making garlands said, "O supreme protectors! Be pleased. It is my good fortune that you have come to my house. I will worship you." With a cheerful face, he gave them the flowers they asked for. He tempted them by offering them more beautiful flowers. The garland-maker bowed down repeatedly before those two excellent men. He gave them beautiful and fragrant flowers that did not decay. Pleased, Krishna bestowed a boon on the garland-maker. "O fortunate one! Shri, who seeks refuge with me, will never desert you. O amiable one! Your strength will never diminish. Nor will your wealth ever diminish. As long as days exist, your sons and grandsons will enjoy extensive objects of pleasure. At the time of death, through my favours, you will remember me and obtain the celestial world. O fortunate one! Your mind will always turn towards *dharma*. The children born from your sons will have long lifespans. Your descendants will not suffer from calamities or taints. O immensely fortunate one! Your descendants will last as long as the sun exists." O best among sages! Having said this, worshipped by the garland-maker and with Baladeva as his companion, Krishna emerged from his house.'

Chapter 5(20) (Kamsa's Death)

Shri Parashara said, 'Along that royal road, Krishna saw a *kubja*[972] advancing, with a vessel full of unguents in her hand. She was in the bloom of youth. Playfully, Krishna asked her, "Who are these unguents for? Where are you taking them?

[972] *Kubja* means a woman who is hunch-backed, with a crooked back. The word also means a female servant, but here, the first meaning is intended.

O one with eyes like a blue lotus! Tell me truthfully." When she was addressed affectionately, she was attracted towards Hari. She spoke lovingly and sweetly to him, while glancing at Bala. "O beloved! How can you not know? I have been engaged by Kamsa. I am engaged in the task of preparing unguents and am known as Naikavakra.[973] Unguents crushed by others do not please Kamsa. Because of his favours, I have also obtained a great deal of wealth." Shri Krishna said, "O one with a beautiful face! Kings deserved these excellent fragrances. Please give us similar unguents for our bodies." Hearing this, Kubja lovingly said, "Let it be taken." She gave both of them appropriate unguents for their limbs. Those two bulls among men smeared their limbs with those unguents and were as resplendent as a white and a dark cloud, decorated with Indra's bow. Shouri was conversant with techniques of conversation. While talking, he placed two of his fingers under her chin and raised it up. Keshava pressed down on her feet and straightened her body. When she became upright, she turned into a beautiful woman. She became full of love and desire. With enchanting and graceful words, she caught hold of Govinda's garments and said, "Come to my house." Thus addressed, Shouri looked at Rama's face. Hari smiled and told the unblemished Naikavakra, "I will indeed come to your house." Then he let her go. He looked at Rama's face and laughed.'

'Their limbs were smeared with unguents, and they were clad in blue and yellow garments. Adorned with colourful garlands, they went to the place where the bow was kept. They asked the guards about where the jewel among bows was kept. When they were told, Krishna grasped the bow and powerfully strung it. When it was powerfully bent for stringing, that bow snapped. There was an extremely large sound that filled all

---

[973] One who is crooked in more than one place on the body.

of Mathura. When the bow was broken, the guards censured them. However, they quickly killed the guards and soldiers and left the place where the bow had been kept.'

'Kamsa heard the account about Akrura's return and he was also told about how the bow had been shattered. He spoke to Chanura and Mushtika. Kamsa said, "Those two cowherd boys have arrived. They will rob me of my life. In my presence, you should kill them in a wrestling match. O immensely strong ones! If you destroy them in a wrestling match, you will satisfy me. I will give you everything that you ask for. It cannot but be otherwise. They wish to harm me, and they must be killed, through fair means or foul. When they have been killed, the kingdom will generally become mine." Having instructed the wrestlers, he summoned the elephant keeper and addressed him in a loud voice. "Let Kuvalayapida, the crazy elephant, be placed at the gate of the wrestling arena. When those two cowherd boys arrive at the arena for the wrestling match, they must be killed." Having instructed him in this way, he checked to see that all arrangements had been made for the viewing galleries. With his death imminent, Kamsa waited for the sun to rise.'

'All the citizens and other people assembled and sat in the common viewing galleries. Along with their servants, the lords of the earth were seated in the royal galleries. The wrestlers and referees approached the wrestling arena prepared by Kamsa. Kamsa himself was seated in a lofty gallery. Galleries had been constructed for the women from the inner quarters, the courtesans and other women from the city. Nandagopa and the other gopas were in other galleries. Akrura and Vasudeva were in galleries that were towards the end. Devaki, who loved her son, was amidst the women from the city. Even if it happened to be the time of death, she wished to see her son's face. The trumpets were sounded. Chanura boasted a lot, while Mushtika slapped his arms. There were people who lamented. Those two brave ones, Balabhadra and Janardana, children who were attired as *gopa*s, easily entered the arena. The *mahamatra* urged Kuvalayapida and it rushed forward to kill the two *gopa* children. O supreme *brahmana*! Great lamentations arose in the middle of the arena. Baladeva looked at his younger brother and addressed him in these words. "O immensely fortunate one! This elephant has been dispatched by the enemy. It deserves to be killed." O *brahmana*! Thus addressed by his elder brother, Baladeva, Madhava, the destroyer of enemy heroes, roared like a lion. The destroyer of Keshin seized the elephant's trunk with his hand. Though the elephant was Airavata's equal in strength, Shouri whirled it around. The lord of the entire universe then played with it like a child. For a very long time, Krishna played with it, leaping on its tusks and slipping between its feet. He then used his right hand to uproot its left tusk. He then struck the elephant's driver with this and shattered his head into one hundred pieces. At the same time, Balabhadra uprooted its right tusk and used it to angrily strike down the elephant keepers who were by the side. With increasing force, Rohini's extremely strong son used his left foot to angrily kick the elephant on its head. As a result of Balabhadra's pastimes, it fell down and died, like a mountain that has been struck by the *vajra* of the one with one thousand eyes. Kuvalayapida had been urged on by the elephant keepers but was killed. With musth and blood from the elephant covering their limbs and wielding the elephant's tusks as excellent weapons, Balabhadra and Janardana entered that extremely large arena, like two lions playfully entering a herd of deer and proudly looking at them.'

'Immediately, there were loud lamentations in that large arena. Surprised, some people exclaimed, "This is Krishna. This is Balabhadra. This is the one who killed the terrible Putana, who was the slayer of children. This is the one who overturned the cart and shattered the twin *arjuna* trees. This is the child who climbed atop Kaliya *naga* and struck his inner organs. This is the one who held up Govardhana, the giant mountain, for seven nights. This is Achyuta, the great-souled one. As if playing, he killed Arishta, Dhenuka and Keshi, all wicked in conduct. Look at him. This is his elder brother, the mighty-armed Baladeva, who is advancing in front of him. He is advancing playfully, delighting the minds of the women. The wise people who know about the truth of the Puranas have spoken about him. 'Gopala will be born in the Yadava lineage and will save those who are submerged. Vishnu is in all beings and his birth has taken place from Vishnu's portion. He has been incarnated on earth from his portion. He will certainly remove the earth's burden.'" At that moment, this is the way the citizens described Rama and Krishna. Because of her love, milk started to flow from Devaki's breasts. On seeing his sons, it was as if Vasudeva was witnessing a great festival. Because of his delight, the old age deserted his body. The women from the royal inner quarters and the large number of women from the city looked on with wide open eyes. They could not stop looking at them. They said, "O friends! Look at Krishna's face. His eyes are extremely red. As a result of the exertions of fighting with the elephant, there are some beads of sweat. Look. His face resembles a blooming autumn lotus, with drops of water clinging to it. Your birth has now been enjoyed. Your vision has obtained success. He is the refuge of the universe. The *shrivatsa* mark is on his broad chest. Look at the child who has vanquished even those who cannot be destroyed. Look at this child. O beautiful one! Look at his arms, capable of crushing an enemy's chest. Can you not see the one whose form is as white as milk or a white lotus? This is Balabhadra. Clad in blue garments, he has arrived here. O friend! Look at him. Mushtika and Chanura may be there. But look at Balabhadra and Hari. They seem to be laughing and playing. O friend! Look. Hari is advancing to wrestle with Chanura. Are there

no aged ones here who will seek to free him? Hari's body is
delicate, and he is only approaching youth. That great *asura*
has a developed body that is as tough as the *vajra*. These two
extremely delicate ones are about to approach youth and have
arrived in this arena. Diti's son[974] and Chanura are foremost
among wrestlers. They are extremely terrible. In this great
wrestling match, the referees have caused a transgression of
the rules. Though a child is fighting with a strong person, the
referees, who are in the middle, have chosen to ignore it."
While the women of the city were speaking in this way, causing
great delight among the people, the illustrious Hari girded up
his loins. Balabhadra playfully slapped his arms, and it was a
great wonder that the earth did not shatter at each of his steps.'

'The extremely valiant Krishna fought with Chanura.
Mushtika, the accomplished *daitya*, fought with Baladeva. Hari
was Chanura's equal and there was a great encounter between
them. They shook each other and hurled each other down.
They struck each other with their fists, bringing down blows
as firm as the *vajra*. They elbowed and kicked each other. It
was an extremely great encounter. The clash was extremely
terrible and was conducted without the use of weapons. In
the presence of that assembly, they displayed their respective
strength and energy. The more Chanura fought with Hari, the
more he lost his energy and there were no relatives to cheer him
on. Krishna, who pervades the universe, fought with him, as
if he was toying with him. From his lofty perch, like a maned
lion, Kamsa watched the fight between Chanura and Krishna
and saw that his representative was becoming exhausted and
losing his strength, while that of Krishna was increasing. He
became angry. Filled with rage and despair, he angrily stopped
the trumpets from blaring. In that instant, the drums and
the playing of musical instruments stopped. However, many

[974] Mushtika.

trumpets of the gods were sounded from the sky. Remaining
invisible, *devas* praised him in their joy. "O Govinda! Victory
to you. O Keshava! Slay the *danava* Chanura." Madhusudana
made Chanura suffer for a long time. He then made efforts to
kill him. He raised him up and whirled him around. Having
whirled the *daitya* wrestler around one hundred times, the
slayer of enemies dashed him down on the ground and he lost
his life while he was still suspended in the air. Flung down on
the ground, Chanura's body shattered into one hundred pieces.
Because of the great flow of blood, the earth was covered in
mire. At that time, just as Hari had fought with Chanura, the
immensely strong Baladeva fought with Mushtika. He struck
him on the head with his fists and struck him on the chest
with his knees. He flung him down on the ground and crushed
him, making him lose his life. There was an immensely strong
king of wrestlers named Toshalaka. Striking him with his left
fist, Krishna brought him down on the ground. Chanura was
killed. The wrestler Mushtika was brought down. Toshalaka
was conveyed to his destruction. At this, all the wrestlers fled.
Krishna and Samkarshana jumped around in the arena. They
were delighted and dragged *gopas*, who were of the same ages
as they were, to the arena.'

'Kamsa's eyes became red with rage, and he spoke to
his men. "Use force to evict these *gopas* from the assembly.
Quickly seize and bind the wicked Nanda. Vasudeva must be
punished, like someone who is not aged.[975] Let him be killed.
Do the same with the *gopas* who are boasting with Krishna.
Seize their cattle and whatever riches they possess." As he was
commanding this, Madhusudana laughed. He leapt onto the
gallery where Kamsa was seated. He powerfully seized him
by the hair, so that his crown was dislodged and fell down
on the ground. He felled Kamsa down on the ground and

[975] An aged person should not be killed.

pinned him there with his own body. The weight of the entire
universe was in Krishna and when that weight descended on
him, the king, Ugrasena's son, lost his life. The immensely
strong Madhusudana seized Kamsa's dead body by the hair
and dragged it to the middle of the arena. The body was great
in weight and a great weight had fallen on it. In addition, the
great-souled one had dragged Kamsa's body with great force.
Therefore, the body was disfigured. As Krishna was dragging
Kamsa, his brother, Sunama, arrived there, full of rage.
However, playfully, Balabhadra brought him down. At this,
there was a tumultuous roar everywhere in that circular arena,
on seeing that Krishna had contemptuously killed the lord of
Mathura.'

'Krishna, with the immensely strong Baladeva as his aide,
quickly touched the feet of Vasudeva and Devaki. Vasudeva
and Devaki raised Janardana up. Remembering the words
that had been spoken at the time of his birth, they stood there,
bowing down before him. Shri Vasudeva said, "O lord! Show
your favours to those who are suffering. You are the one who
bestows boons on *deva*s. O Keshava! In that way, you have
saved us through your favours. Having been worshipped, the
illustrious one has taken an *avatara* in my house, for the sake
of slaying those who are wicked in conduct. Our lineage has
been sanctified. You are inside all beings. You are stationed
within all beings. It is the truth that everything, the past and the
future, flow from you. You are worshipped through sacrifices.
You cannot be thought of. O Achyuta! You are in all *deva*s.
You are the sacrifice. You are the one who performs the
sacrifice. You are the supreme lord. O Janardana! The entire
universe has originated from you. But since you have been
born as Devaki's son, the love causes this mental confusion
and mortification. You are the creator of all beings. You are
without a beginning and without an end. How can a human
tongue like mine address you as a son? O Jagannatha! This

entire universe has originated in you. Barring your *maya*, how can someone like you have been born from us? Everything in the universe, mobile and immobile, is established in you. How can someone like that lie down in a human womb or lap? O supreme lord! Be pleased. Save the universe. You have taken an incarnation and are not actually my son. O lord of the universe! O Purshottama! In truth, you confuse everyone, beginning with Brahma and ending with a tree. Why are you deluding me? With my eyes confused by *maya*, I thought of you as a son. O lord! Extremely scared of Kamsa and because of that fear, I conveyed you to Gokula. O lord! Because of that fear, I dared not rear you in my home. Rudra, the Maruts, the Asvhins, Shatakratu and the Sadhyas cannot witness your deeds. You are Vishnu. You are the lord. You have come to us for the welfare of the universe. Earlier, we were filled with great confusion."'

Chapter 5(21) (Return of Sandipani's Son)

Shri Parashara said, 'After witnessing the deeds of the illustrious one, *vijnana* was generated in Devaki and Vasudeva. Realizing this, to confound all the Yadus, Hari extended his Vaishnavi *maya* again.[976] He said, "O mother! O father! I and Samkarshana have been eager to see you for a very long time, but we were scared of Kamsa. Among virtuous sons, that part of the life that is spent without worshipping the mother and the father is futile. O father! If an embodied person who is born worships his *guru*, *devas*, *dvijas*, the mother and the father, his birth is successful. O father! Therefore,

---

[976] He wanted them to continue to think of him as the son of Devaki and Vasudeva.

pardon all the transgressions we have committed. Because of
Kamsa's valour and power, we were under the subjugation of
the enemy." Having said this, in due order, he bowed down
before the elders among the Yadus. He worshipped them in the
appropriate way and honoured the citizens.'

'Kamsa was lying down dead on the ground and Kamsa's
wives surrounded him. Overwhelmed by grief and misery, his
mothers lamented.[977] Hari also lamented at what he had been
forced to do and he comforted them in many ways. His own eyes
were full of tears, and he reassured them. Madhusudana freed
Ugrasena from his bondage. With his son dead, he instated him
in his own kingdom.[978] Having been instated in the kingdom
by Krishna, the lion among the Yadus performed the funeral
rites for his son and all the others who had been killed. When
the funeral rites had been performed, Hari approached the
throne and said, "O lord! Without any hesitation, instruct us
about the tasks we should perform. Because of Yayati's curse,
this lineage does not deserve this kingdom.[979] But you have
obtained it. With me as your servant, you can command devas,
not to speak of kings." Having told him this, the illustrious
Keshava, who was acting like a human,[980] remembered Vayu.
When Vayu instantly arrived, he spoke to him. "O Vayu! Go
to Indra. Tell him, 'O Vasava! Enough of your pride. Give
Ugrasena your assembly hall, known as Sudharma. Krishna has
said that the king deserves this excellent jewel. The assembly
hall known as Sudharma is appropriate for the Yadus.'" Thus
addressed, Vayu went and told Shachi's consort everything.

[977] Kamsa's mother was Padmavati, but Ugrasena had more than
one wife.

[978] Own kingdom because Ugrasena had originally been the king
before Kamsa ousted him.

[979] Yayati had cursed his sons, of whom Yadu was one, that they
would not be kings.

[980] Otherwise, Krishna could have performed the task himself.

Purandara gave Vayu the assembly hall known as Sudharma. Seeking refuge in Govinda's arms, the bulls among the Yadus enjoyed the divine assembly hall, decorated with excellent jewels, brought by Vayu.'

'Baladeva and Janardana knew every kind of *vijnana*. They knew every kind of *jnana*. But since those two valiant ones were known as two excellent members of the Yadu lineage, they wished to preserve the progression from preceptor to disciple. Sandipani from Kashi then resided in the city of Avanti.[981] For the sake of knowledge, those two children went to him and had there *upanayana* performed there. He happily taught Samkarshana and Janardana the *Veda*s. They became his disciples and behaved as one should towards a preceptor. Thus, those two brave ones demonstrated proper conduct to all the people. They studied the collected texts of *dhanurveda*, along with all its mysteries. O *brahmana*! This was extraordinary. They accomplished all this in sixty-four days and nights. This superhuman feat was impossible. Therefore, Sandipani thought that the sun god and the moon god had come to him. As soon as it was mentioned, they learned all the four *Veda*s, along with the *Vedanga*s, the sacred texts and everything about all the weapons. They then asked, "Please tell us. What shall we offer as a *guru*'s *dakshina*?" The immensely intelligent one witnessed that deed, which was beyond the senses. He asked for his son, who had died in Prabhasa, in the salty ocean. Taking their weapons, the two of them went there. The great ocean, with *arghya* in its hand, said, "I have not abducted Sandipani's son. O slayer of *asura*s! A *daitya* named Panchanjana, in the form of a conch shell, has seized the child. He is in my waters now." Thus addressed, Krishna entered the waters and killed Panchajana. He gathered the bones, and an excellent conch shell was created

[981] Ujjayini/Ujjain.

from this.[982] Its blare reduces the strength of the *daitya*s, destroys *adharma* and enhances the energy of *deva*s. Filling everything with the sound of Panchajanya, Hari went to Yama's city. With Baladeva's strength, he defeated Vaivasvata Yama. The child was undergoing hardships and he got him back, with a body just like it used to be earlier.[983] Along with Bala, Krishna, supreme among strong ones, returned the son to his father. They returned again to Mathura, protected by Ugrasena. Rama and Janardana delighted the men and women who were there.'

Chapter 5(22) (Jarasandha's Attack)

Shri Parashara said, 'O Maitreya! The immensely strong Kamsa had married two of Jarasandha's daughters, Asti and Prapti. The immensely strong and powerful lord of Magadha, Jarasandha, was filled with rage when their husband was killed. He arrived with a contingent, so as to kill Hari and the Yadavas. Arriving in Mathura, the lord of Magadha laid siege. He was surrounded by twenty-three *akshouhini*s of soldiers. Emerging with a small contingent, the powerful Rama and Janardana fought with those powerful soldiers. O supreme sage! Rama and Krishna made up their minds to invoke their ancient weapons. O *brahmana*! After this, Hari's Sharnga bow, the two quivers filled with inexhaustible arrows and the Koumadaki mace arrived through the sky. Through the sky, the plough arrived in Balabhadra's hands. O *brahmana*! The club Sunanda also arrived as soon as it was desired. In the battle, the lord of Magadha and his soldiers were defeated.

[982] Krishna's conch shell, known as Panchajanya.
[983] The child was undergoing hardships in hell. Krishna asked that the son be restored, with a body just like the one before death.

The brave Rama and Janardana entered the city again. O
great sage! Though the extremely wicked Jarasandha had
been defeated, he had escaped with his life. Therefore, Krishna
thought he had not been truly defeated. O supreme *brahmana*!
With his forces, Jarasandha arrived again and attacked. Rama
and Krishna defeated him again. Extremely indomitable, the
king of Magadha fought eighteen battles against the Yadus,
led by Krishna. In each battle, he was defeated by the Yadavas.
Though Jarasandha possessed a larger force, a smaller force
made him flee. That the Yadava force was able to counter
many was because of the proximity and greatness of Vishnu's
portion, the wielder of the *chakra*. The lord of the universe was
playfully observing the *dharma* and conduct of humans. But he
released many kinds of weapons against the enemy. He is the
one who creates and destroys the universe in his mind. He did
not have to do much to strike against the enemy. However,
he was observing the *dharma* of humans. This meant alliances
with the stronger and fighting against those who were weaker.
This meant exhibiting *sama*, *dana* and *bheda*,[984] bringing down
the staff on some occasions and fleeing on others. The lord
of the universe playfully undertakes what he wishes. Thus, he
followed efforts made by those with human bodies.'

Chapter 5(23) (Kalayavana and Muchukunda)

Shri Parashara said, 'O *brahmana*! In an assembly of the
Yadus in the settlement of cowherds, Shyala[985] called

---

[984] The traditional four means are *sama* (conciliation or
negotiation), *dana* (bribery), *danda* (punishment) and *bheda* (dissension).
[985] We have taken this as a proper name. But *shyala* also means
brother-in-law and could refer to Gargya's brother-in-law.

a *brahmana* named Gargya a eunuch. All the Yadavas who
were present laughed. Therefore, filled with anger, he went to
Dakshinapatha. Desiring a son who would cause fear among the
Yadus, he tormented himself through austerities. He worshipped
Mahadeva and only ate iron powder. In the twelfth year, Hara
was pleased and granted him a boon. The lord of the Yavanas
had no son. He had intercourse with his wife and a son who
was as black as a bee was born.[986] He was named Kalayavana,
and his chest was as hard as the tip of the *vajra*. Instating him
in his own kingdom, the lord of the Yavanas left for the forest.
He was maddened by his valour and pride. He asked Narada
about the most powerful kings on earth and Narada told him
about the Yadavas. He surrounded himself with one thousand
crores of *mleccha*s and with elephants, horses and chariots,
made great efforts. O Maitreya! He constantly thought about
the Yadavas every day and becoming intolerant towards them,
left for the city of Mathura. Krishna thought, "On seeing that
the Yadava forces have been reduced by Yavana in a battle,
Magadha will advance against us. Or, after destroying the
diminished forces of Magadha, Kalayavana will become strong
and will advance to kill us. The Yadus confront two calamities.
Therefore, I will construct an invincible fortress for the Yadus,
a place from which even the women will be able to fight, not to
speak of the bulls among the Vrishnis. It will be a place where
wicked enemies will not be able to advance much against
the Yadavas, even if I am intoxicated, distracted, sleeping or
am residing somewhere else." Having thought this, Govinda
sought twelve *yojana*s from the great ocean and constructed
the city of Dvaraka there. There were large gardens and large
ramparts there. It was adorned with hundreds of lakes. There
were mansions, houses and barriers and it resembled Indra's

[986] Gargya had intercourse with the wife of the king of the
Yavanas. Kalayavana is derived from black (*kala*) Yavana.

Amaravati. Janardana brought the people who resided in Mathura there. When Kalayavana's arrival was imminent, he himself went to Mathura.'

'When the soldiers arrived and set up camp outside Mathura, without any weapons, Govinda went out and Yavana saw him. The king came to know that this was Vasudeva, whom even great *yogi*s cannot obtain in their minds. With his arms as weapons,[987] he followed him. Followed by him, Krishna entered a large cave. The immensely valiant Muchukunda, lord of men, was sleeping there. Yavana also entered and saw the king lying down on a bed. Thinking that this was Krishna, the extremely evil-minded one kicked him with his foot. King Muchukunda woke up and saw Yavana. O Maitreya! As soon as he glanced at him, the blazing fire resulting from the rage instantly reduced Yavana to ashes. Having taken part in a battle between the gods and the *asura*s, he had defeated giant *asura*s and had not slept for a very long time. Therefore, he had asked the gods for a boon that he might be able to sleep. The gods had said, "When you are asleep, if anyone wakes you up, the fire that is generated from your body will instantly reduce that person to ashes."[988] Having thus burnt the wicked one, he saw Madhusudana.'

'He asked, "Who are you?" He replied, "I have been born in the lunar dynasty. I am Vasudeva's son, born in the Yadu lineage." Hearing this, Muchukunda remembered the words of the aged Gargya.[989] Remembering everything, he prostrated himself before Hari, the lord of everything and said, "I know that you have been born as Vishnu's portion. You are the supreme lord. Earlier, Gargya had said that Hari's birth

[987] Kalayavana did not carry any other weapons.

[988] Knowing about Muchukunda's boon, Krishna had set a trap for Kalayavana.

[989] The aged Gargya, Vriddha Gargya, is different from Gargya.

would occur in the Yadu lineage, at the end of *dvapara*, in the twenty-eighth *mahayuga*. There is no doubt that you are he and have arrived for the welfare of mortals. I am no longer able to tolerate your extremely great energy." He continued in words that rumbled deeply, like clouds full of rain. "Because of the pressure of your feet, the earth bends down. In the great battle between the gods and the *asura*s, the extremely great *daitya* soldiers are unable to withstand your energy. I can't stand it either. For a being who has descended into *samsara*, you are the supreme refuge. O one who destroys the afflictions of those who seek refuge! Be pleased. Take away everything inauspicious in me. You are the being who is the oceans, the mountains, the rivers, the forests, the earth, the sky, wind, water, fire and the mind. You are intelligence, the one known as Prakriti, the breath of life and Purusha. You are beyond Purusha. You pervade everything. You are beyond birth and transformations. You are devoid of sound and other objects of the senses. You do not suffer from old age. You have no birth. You cannot be measured. You are devoid of decay. You do not increase or decrease. You are the *brahman*, without a beginning and an end. The immortals, the ancestors, the *yaksha*s, the *gandharva*s, the *kinnara*s, the *siddha*s and the *apsara*s originate from you. Humans, large animals, birds, reptiles and small animals originate from you. So do the large trees, the past and the future, everything mobile and immobile, everything embodied and disembodied, gross and subtle. You are everything. You are the creator of the universe. Without you, there is nothing. O illustrious one! I have been whirled around in this cycle of *samsara*. I have suffered from the three kinds of hardship[990] and they have never ceased. Happiness and unhappiness have been like mirages, mistaken to be

---

[990] The three kinds of hardship relate to *adhidaivika* (destiny), *adhibhoutika* (nature) and *adhyatmika* (one's own nature).

waterbodies. O protector! O lord! Whatever I have accepted
has only led to torment—the kingdom, the earth, the army,
the treasury, allies, sons, wives, servants, people and sound
and other objects of the senses. O one without decay! O lord
of the gods! I accepted them, thinking that they would lead to
happiness. However, they have eventually caused me torment.
O protector! Even the large number of *deva*s, who had gone
to the world of *deva*s, desired to obtain my assistance. What
is eternal? Where is *nivritti*?[991] Everything in the universe
is the result of your powers. O supreme lord! Without
worshipping you, how can there be *nivritti*? Foolish ones
who are confounded by your *maya* obtain birth, death, old
age and the like. Having faced torments, they subsequently see
the king of the dead.[992] In extremely terrible hells, men suffer
miseries, as a consequence of what they themselves have done.
They do not know your true nature. Confounded by your
maya, I have been addicted to material objects and *ahamkara*.
O Parameshvara! Therefore, I have been whirled around in
this fathomless pit of 'mine'. Thus, without any shore, I seek
refuge with you now. You are immeasurable. You are the
supreme destination and there is nothing else. I am exhausted
and tormented from whirling around in *samsara*. O refuge! I
desire to obtain *nirvana*.'"

Chapter 5(24) (Krishna Returns and Balarama Leaves)

Shri Parashara said, 'The intelligent Muchukunda praised
him in this way. Hari is the lord of all beings and has no

[991] *Nivritti* is detachment from fruits and renunciation of action.
[992] Yama.

beginning and no end. He spoke. The illustrious one said,
"O lord of men! Go to the divine worlds that you desire.
Through my favours, your supreme prosperity will increase
and will be unimpeded. You will enjoy divine and great objects
of pleasure. After this, you will take birth in a great lineage.
However, through my favours, you will remember your past
lives and will obtain emancipation." Thus addressed, the king
prostrated himself before Achyuta, the lord of the universe. He
emerged through the mouth of the cave and saw that men had
become short. The king realized that *kali yuga* was imminent.
To torment himself through austerities, he went to Nara and
Narayana's place in Gandhamadana.'

'Having slain the enemy, Krishna seized his forces,
resplendent with elephants, horses and chariots, and arrived in
Mathura. Having brought them to Dvaravati, he offered them
to Ugrasena. The lineage of the Yadus became strong and no
longer worried about being defeated.'

'O Maitreya! Now that all conflicts had been pacified,
Baladeva was eager to meet his kin and went to Nanda's
Gokula. As was the case earlier, the *gopa*s and *gopi*s greeted
the conqueror of enemies affectionately and showed him a
great deal of respect. He embraced some and in turn, was
embraced by some. He laughed with some *gopa*s and *gopi*s
who were his equals. The *gopa*s addressed the wielder of the
plough in many pleasant words. Some *gopi*s were delighted
and full of affection. But there were others who were full of
anger. The *gopi*s asked, "Is Krishna, who loves the women
of the city, happy? He is fickle in his love. He laughs at our
attempts, but rarely at those of the women of the city. He
makes them possess greater fortune, while affection towards
us is of short duration. Does Krishna remember that we
followed him and sang with him? Will he come here at least
once, to see his mother? What is the point of conversing in

this way? Let us talk about other things. He will exist without us, and we will have to exist without him. For his sake, we abandoned our fathers, mothers, brothers, husbands, relatives and pledges. But he is ungrateful. Nevertheless, does Krishna ever speak about coming here? O Rama! Please do not utter a falsehood. Damodara Govinda's mind is attached to the women of the city. It is evident that, despite our love, we will find it extremely difficult to see him." With their minds attached to Hari, in melodious voices, they invited him and repeatedly addressed him as Krishna and Damodara. Krishna had delivered a message in extremely sweet voice, and it was full of deep love, devoid of pride. Comforting the *gopis*, Rama delivered this in a sweet and amiable voice. As used to be the case earlier, Rama laughed with them and conversed with all the residents of Vraja.'

Chapter 5(25) (Balarama and the Yamuna)

S hri Parashara said, 'With the *gopas*, the great-souled one roamed around in the forest. He was Shesha, who holds up the earth. But he was disguised in the form of a human. For the sake of the earth, he had performed extensive deeds. So as to enable him to enjoy himself, Varuna spoke to Varuni. "This immensely energetic one always desires liquor. O auspicious one! For the sake of Ananta's enjoyment, please go." Thus addressed, Varuni went near him. She went to the forest of Vrindavana and positioned herself in a hole in a *kadamba* tree. While wandering around, Baladeva, the noble one with the excellent face, inhaled the wonderful smell of liquor and experienced the delight that he had earlier had from liquor. O Maitreya! The wielder of the plough suddenly saw a stream of liquor descending from the *kadamba* tree and was filled with great delight. He was happy. Along with the *gopa*s and *gopi*s, who were accomplished in singing and the playing of musical instruments, he drank, while they sang. Because of the excessive heat and exhaustion, there were beads of sweat, resembling sparkling pearls, on him. Agitated, he said, "O Yamuna! Come here. I wish to have a bath." The river ignored the words of an intoxicated person and showed disrespect. Since she did not come there, the wielder of the plough became angry and seized his plough. Intoxicated because of the liquor, he seized her with the tip of his plough and said, "O evil one! You did not come. Since you did not come, according to your wishes, go elsewhere." Dragged by him, the river suddenly gave up her course and flooded the forest where Baladeva had dragged her. With scared and agitated eyes, she assumed a body and told Rama, "O one who has a club as his weapon! Please be pleased. Free me." Hearing her excellent words, the one with the plough as a weapon replied, "O river! If you know about my valour and strength, I will bring down my plough on you and divide you into one thousand flows." Thus addressed, the river was scared and placated him. Bala released Yamuna at the spot where the ground had been flooded. The great-souled one bathed there and obtained a handsome form. Lakshmi gave him blue garments that had the complexion of the ocean, a beautiful blue lotus to adorn himself, earrings and a garland made of lotuses that did not decay, given by Varuna. He adorned himself with the blue lotus and the beautiful earrings. Attired in blue garments and adorned in garlands, the auspicious one was handsome and resplendent. Thus adorned, Rama enjoyed himself in Vraja. After two months, he returned to the city of Dvaraka. King Raivata had a daughter named Revati. Bala married her, and Nishita and Ulmuka were born through her.'

Chapter 5(26) (Marriage with Rukmini)

Shri Parashara said, 'In the kingdom of Vidarbha, Bhishmaka was the king in Kundina.[993] His son was Rukmi, and his daughter was Rukmini, beautiful of face. Krishna desired Rukmini. The one with the beautiful smiles also desired him. However, because of his hatred, Rukmi did not wish that she should be bestowed on the one who holds the *chakra*. Urged by Jarasandha and Rukmi, Bhishmaka, extensive in his valour, bestowed Rukmini on Shishupala. All the kings, with Jarasandha as the foremost, wished to do what was agreeable to Shishupala and went to Bhishmaka's city for the marriage. To witness the marriage of the king of Chedi,[994] surrounded by the Yadus, Krishna and Balabhadra also went to Kundina. Though Rama and the other relatives opposed it, on the day before the marriage, Hari abducted the beautiful maiden. At this, the prosperous Poundraka, Dantavakra, Viduratha, Shishupala, Jarasandha, Shalva and other kings became angry and made great efforts to kill Hari. However, they were defeated by Rama and the assembled bulls among the Yadus. "I will not enter Kundina without killing Keshava in a battle." Having taken this pledge, Rukmi rushed against Krishna, so as to kill him. The one with the *chakra* toyed with him and slew his forces, consisting of elephants, horses, infantry and chariots. He defeated him and flung him down on the ground. Having vanquished Rukmi, following the norms of the *rakshasa* form of marriage, Madhusudana married Rukmini.[995] The valiant

[993] Kundina was the capital of Vidarbha, identified with Kaundinyapura in Amaravati division.

[994] That is, Shishupala.

[995] There were eight forms of marriage: *brahma, daiva, arsha, prajapatya, asura, gandharva, rakshasa* and *paishacha*. In the *rakshasa* form, the groom defeats the bride's kin, abducts her and marries her.

Pradyumna, Madana's portion, was born through her. The valiant one was abducted by Shambara but killed Shambara.'

Chapter 5(27) (Slaying of Shambara)

Shri Maitreya asked, 'O sage! How was the valiant Pradyumna abducted by Shambara? How did the immensely valiant Pradyumna kill him? How could he kill someone who had abducted him earlier? O *guru*! I wish to hear everything about this in detail.'

Shri Parashara replied, 'O sage! "This one will kill me." Thinking this, on the sixth day after birth, Kalashambara[996] abducted Pradyumna from the delivery chamber. Having abducted him, he flung him into the extremely terrible salty ocean, full of turbulent waves and whirlpools and the abode of fierce crocodiles and extremely terrible *makaras*. As he fell there, a fish swallowed the infant. Despite the blazing digestive fire inside the stomach, he did not die. O *brahmana*! Along with other fish, this fish was caught by those who captured fish. They killed it and offered it to Shambara, the noble *asura*. His wife, named Mayavati, was the mistress of the entire household. The unblemished one supervised everything that the cooks did. When the stomach of the fish was sliced open, she saw an extremely beautiful child, resembling new sprouts on Manmatha's tree, after it has been burnt.[997] Curious, the slender-limbed one asked, "Who is this? How did he enter here?" Narada replied, "Vishnu is the one who causes the creation and destruction of the entire universe, and this is his son. Shambara abducted him from the

---

[996] The same as Shambara.
[997] This is an allusion to Manmatha, the god of love, who had been burnt down by Shiva.

delivery chamber and flung him into the ocean. Swallowed by a fish, he has now come under your subjugation in your house. O one with the excellent eyebrows! This is a jewel among men. Rear him without any hesitation." Addressed in this way by Narada, she reared the child. Right from his childhood, she was confounded by his beauty and felt a great deal of love for him. O great sage! When the immensely intelligent one was adorned with the bloom of youth, the one with the gait of an elephant desired him. Mayavati taught the great-souled one all her *maya*. She was blind with love for Pradyumna, and her heart and eyes were immersed in him. When she wished to unite with him, Krishna's lotus-eyed one replied to her. "Casting aside maternal behaviour, why are you acting in this perverse way?" She told him, "You are not my son. You are Vishnu's son and you have been abducted by Kalashambara. He flung you into the ocean. I obtained you from the stomach of a fish. Your mother is crying for you. However, your beloved, who loves you a lot, is here." Hearing this, Pradyumna challenged Shambara to a fight. The immensely strong one's mind was full of rage, and he fought. Yadava slew all the *daitya* soldiers. After crossing seven forms of *maya*, he fought using the eighth kind of *maya*.[998] Using this *maya*, he killed the *daitya* Kalashambara. Taking her with him, he went to his father's city. With Mayavati, he descended in the inner quarters.[999] On seeing him, Krishna's women were delighted, but did not know what to do. The unblemished Rukmini's eyes were fixed on him with affection, and she spoke

[998] The word *maya* should be interpreted as power, with a hierarchy or layer in these. The first seven powers/layers were known to Shambara and were taught by Mayavati to Pradyumna. When Shambara used these against Pradyumna, he could counter them. The eighth or higher form of *maya* was Vaishnavi *maya*, known to Pradyumna, but not to Shambara.

[999] They descended because they travelled through the sky and arrived in the inner quarters.

lovingly. "You are in the bloom of youth and a mother with a son like you is blessed. Were my son Pradyumna alive, he would have been of the same age. O child! Since your mother has been adorned by you, she is fortunate. Who is she? Or, because of my affection towards you is evidently like that towards a son, perhaps you are another one of Hari's sons. O son! That seems to be apparent from your form." At that time, Narada arrived, along with Krishna.'

'Delighted, he[1000] spoke to the Queen Rukmini, who was roaming around in the inner quarters. "O one with the excellent eyebrows! This is indeed your son. After having been abducted by Shambara, he has returned. When he was still an infant, he was abducted from your delivery chamber. This virtuous Mayavati is his wife. She is not Shambara's wife. Listen to the reason for this. When Manmatha was destroyed, she[1001] waited for him to be born again. Using a form made out of *maya*, she confounded Shambara with her form. In the course of marriage and enjoyment with the *daitya*, this auspicious one with the intoxicating eyes only showed him the form made out of *maya*. Kama has again been born as your son and this is his beloved Rati. You should not harbor any doubts. This is your beautiful daughter-in-law." After this, Rukmini and Keshava were filled with joy. The entire city uttered words of praise. On seeing that Rukmini had got back and was united with her son, who had been destroyed a long time ago, all the people in Dvaravati were astounded.'

Chapter 5(28) (Rukmi's Death)

Shri Parashara said, 'Rukmini gave birth to the sons Charudeshna, Sudeshna, the valiant Charudeha, Sushena,

[1000] Krishna.
[1001] Manmatha's wife, Rati.

Charugupta, Bhadracharu, Charuvinda, Sucharu and Charu, supreme among strong ones. She also had a daughter, Charumati. Krishna had seven other beautiful wives: Kalindi; Mitravinda; Satya, the daughter of Nagnajit;[1002] Queen Jambavati; Rohini, the daughter of the king of Madra, desirable in form and full of good qualities and who was always good in conduct; Satyabhama, the daughter of Satrajit; and Lakshmana, who had a beautiful smile. The wielder of the *chakra* had sixteen thousand other wives. In a *svayamvara*, Rukmi's auspicious daughter chose the immensely valiant Pradyumna, Hari's son, and married him. These two had an extremely strong and valiant son, Aniruddha. This scorcher of enemies was valiant but was captured in a battle.[1003] For him, Keshava accepted Rukmi's granddaughter. Though Rukmi sought to rival the wielder of the *chakra*, he bestowed her on his daughter's son. O *brahmana*! On the occasion of the marriage, along with Hari, Rama and the other Yadavas went to Rukmi's city, known by the name of Bhojakata.[1004] To pronounce benedictions, all the other kings also went there.'

'When marriage of Pradyumna's great-souled son was over,[1005] the kings, with the king of Kalinga as the foremost,

[1002] Therefore, also known as Nagnajiti. The names of Krishna's principal wives vary from text to text. But the number is usually eight.

[1003] Aniruddha was captured by Bana. Aniruddha means someone who cannot be stopped or captured. Thus, the text has a pun with the word captured. Rukmi was Rukmini's brother. Aniruddha was the son of Pradyumna, the son of Krishna and Rukmini. Pradyumna's wife was Mayavati, Rukmi's daughter. Thus, Aniruddha was Rukmi's daughter's son. Aniruddha was married to Usha, Bana's daughter. But he was also married to Rochana, Rukmi's granddaughter.

[1004] Rukmi had pledged that he would not enter Kundina without killing Krishna but was instead defeated by Krishna. Therefore, instead of Kundina, he started to live in Bhojakata.

[1005] There is a typo in the text. It says Pradyumna's marriage but means Pradyumni's (Pradyumna's son) marriage.

addressed Rukmi in these words. Kalinga and the others said,
"The wielder of the plough is not skilled in playing with the
dice. But he has great addiction towards it. Therefore, we will
defeat the immensely strong Bala in a match with the dice."
Rukmi, who was full of pride and strength, agreed to what
the kings had said. In an assembly hall, he started a match
with the dice against Rama. When the stake was one thousand
nishkas,[1006] Rukmi defeated Bala. On the second stake, Rukmi
won another one thousand. Rukmi, who possessed excellent
knowledge about playing with the dice, put up a stake of
ten thousand nishkas and defeated Balabhadra again. O
brahmana! At this, the foolish lord of Kalinga behaved like
a dog. He displayed all his teeth and laughed at Bala. Puffed
up with pride, Rukmi said, "Bala is ignorant and has been
defeated by me in playing with the dice. Though he is blind
with addiction for playing with the dice, he does not know
anything about dice." The wielder of the plough saw that the
king of Kalinga was exhibiting his teeth. He heard Rukmi's
wicked words and became angry. Full of rage, he put up a stake
of one crore nishkas. Accepting the wager, Rukmi rolled the
dice. Having won, Baladeva loudly proclaimed, "This has been
won by me." However, Rukmi uttered false words and said,
"O Bala! It is mine. It is true that you had mentioned the stake.
But I had not accepted it. In that case, if you have won, how is
it that I have not won?" An invisible voice that rumbled deeply
was heard in the sky and this voice from the sky loudly said,
"According to dharma, Bala has won and Rukumi has uttered
a falsehood. Even though words have not been spoken, there
are things that are accepted through deeds."[1007] This increased
the great-souled Baladeva's rage. Bala stood up and his eyes

[1006] A nishka is a coin made out of gold.
[1007] Since Rukmi rolled the dice.

were red with anger. Using the *ashtapada*,[1008] the immensely
strong one killed Rukmi. The king of Kalinga was trembling,
and Bala forcibly seized him. In rage, he broke the teeth that
he had exhibited while he was laughing. Bala dragged the great
pillar that was made out molten gold. Using that, the extremely
angry Bala killed the kings who were on the other side. O
brahmana! Bala was angry with that entire assembly of kings
and as all of them were scared and started to run away, there
were sounds of lamentation. Madhusudana saw that Bala had
killed Rukmi. O Maitreya! However, because he was scared
of Rukmini and Bala, he did not utter a single word.[1009] O
supreme among *brahmana*s! Now, Aniruddha's wedding was
over, Keshava took him and the Yadus with him and returned
to Dvaraka.'

Chapter 5(29) (Naraka's Death)

Shri Parashara said, 'O Maitreya! While Krishna was in
Dvaravati, Shakra, the lord of the three worlds, came there
seated astride the crazy Airavata. He entered Dvaraka and
approached Hari. He told him what the *daitya* Naraka had done.
"O Madhusudana! O protector! Though you are established
in the form of a human, you have pacified all the miseries
of *deva*s. To remove the afflictions of the ascetics, you have
killed Arishta, Dhenuka, Keshi and all the others who caused
harm. You have conveyed all the others, those who caused
calamities in the world Kamsa, Kuvalayapida and Putana,

[1008] *Ashtapada* is the board used for playing with dice. It has eight
(*ashta*) squares along each side.
[1009] Whether he approved of the action or disapproved, he would
have offended one or the other.

the slayer of children, to their destruction. The three worlds
have been saved through your chastisement and intelligence.
The residents of heaven have obtained their shares offered at
sacrifices and have been satisfied. O Janardana! However, there
is a reason why I have come to you now. Hearing this, please
do whatever is necessary to act and counteract. The earth has
a son named Naraka and he is the lord of Pragjyotishapura.
O slayer of enemies! He causes suffering to all beings. O
Janardana! Having slain *deva*s, *siddha*s, *asura*s and kings,
that *asura* has imprisoned their daughters in his house. He has
seized the umbrella, from which water flows, from Prachetas.
He has taken away Maniparvata, the summit of Mandara. My
mother[1010] had two divine earrings. *Amrita* flowed from them.
Having taken these away from Aditi, the *asura* now desires the
elephant, Airavata. O Govinda! I have described his wicked
conduct to you. You should yourself think about what needs
to be done to counter him." Hearing this, Devaki's illustrious
son smiled. Arising from his excellent seat, he clasped Vasava
by the hand.'

'Having thought about it, he ascended Garuda, who
travelled through the sky. Making Satyabhama also mount, he
went to the city of Pragjyotishapura. While the residents of
Dvaraka watched, Shakra mounted the elephant Airavata and
went to the abode of the gods. Krishna also left. O supreme
among *brahmana*s! For one hundred *yojana*s on every side,
Pragyotishapura was surrounded by terrible nooses. They
were sharp as razors and had been fashioned by Mura.[1011]
Hurling Sudarshana *chakra*, Hari severed those nooses. When
Mura arose, Keshava killed him. The fire that emerged from
the sharp edges of Hari's *chakra* burnt down seven thousand

[1010] That is, Aditi.
[1011] Mura is an *asura*. Hence, Krishna is Murari, Mura's enemy
(*ari*).

of Mura's sons, as if they were moths. O *brahmana*! Having killed Mura, Hayagriva and Panchajana, the intelligent one hurried and attacked Pragjyotishapura.[1012] There was a great battle there, between Naraka and his large army and Krishna. Govinda killed thousands of *daitya*s. The powerful Bhouma Naraka[1013] unleashed showers of *shastra*s and *astra*s.[1014] The wielder of the *chakra* hurled his *chakra* and sliced the *daitya* into two. When Naraka was killed with the *chakra*, the earth took Aditi's earrings and approached. She addressed Jagannatha in these words. The earth said, "O protector! When you raised me up in your form as a boar, this son was born to me as a result of that touch with you. You are the one who gave him to me, and you are the one who has brought him down. Please accept these earrings and protect his offspring. O lord! O one with the excellent face! O illustrious one! It is for the sake of reducing my burden that you have used your portion to arrive in this world. Please show me your favours. You are the creator, the re-creator,[1015] the destroyer and the undecaying origin. You are the power. The universe is your form. O Achyuta! How can I praise you? O illustrious one! You are the one who pervades. You are that which is pervaded. You are the act, the doer and the task that is performed. How can I praise you? You are in the *atman*s of all beings. All beings originate from your *atman*. You are the *paramatman*. Since there is no way to praise you, why should one even attempt it?

[1012] Hayagriva and Panchajana do not belong here. Panchajana has already been killed by Krishna and Hayagriva was killed by Vishnu. But it is true that these two have already been killed.

[1013] The earth is Bhumi. Therefore, Naraka is known as Bhouma.

[1014] The text uses both *astra* and *shastra*. These are both weapons and the words are often used synonymously. However, an *astra* is a weapon that is hurled or released, while a *shastra* is held in the hand.

[1015] Referring to the primary creation and the secondary cycles of creation.

O one who is in the *atman*s of all creatures! Be pleased. Please pardon all the sins committed by Naraka. My son has been brought down." The illustrious one, the origin of all beings, agreed to what the earth had said. O supreme among sages! He took all the jewels from Naraka's residence. O great sage! In the place where maidens were kept, the infinitely valiant one saw sixteen thousand and one hundred maidens. He also saw six thousand elephants, each with four sharp tusks and twenty-one million horses from Kamboja. Using Naraka's servants, Govinda immediately sent the maidens, the horses and the elephants to the city of Dvaraka. Hari saw Varuna's umbrella and Maniparvata and placed these on top of Garuda, the lord of birds. With Satyabhama as his companion, Krishna himself ascended and went to the abode of the gods to return Aditi's earrings.'

Chapter 5(30) (The *Parijata* Tree)

Shri Parashara said, 'Garuda easily carried Varuna's umbrella, Maniparvata and Hrishikesha and his wife. Having reached at the gate of heaven, Hari blew on his conch shell. So as to worship Janardana, all *deva*s arrived, with *arghya* in their hands. Having been worshipped by *deva*s, Krishna entered the residence of the mother of *deva*s, which was like the summit of a white mountain, and saw Aditi. Along with Shakra, he bowed down before her. Janardana told her about Naraka's destruction and gave her the two excellent earrings.'

'Aditi, the mother of the universe was pleased. With an undisturbed mind, she praised Hari, the creator of the universe. Aditi said, "O Pundarikaksha! O one who grants devotees freedom from fear! I bow down before you. You are the eternal *atman*. You are in the *atman*s of all beings. Your *atman* is in

everything. You are the creator of beings. Your essence is in
prana, the mind, intelligence and the senses. Your *atman* is in
the *guna*s. You are beyond the three *guna*s. You are devoid
of the opposite pair of sentiments. You are pure *sattva* and
are established in all hearts. You are devoid of conceptions of
white, long and every other similar trait. You are not touched
by birth and similar things. You are devoid of a state where one
dreams. O Achyuta! You are *sandhya*, night, day, earth, sky,
wind, water, fire, mind, intelligence and the elements. You are
the cause behind creation, preservation and destruction. You
are the lord of all doers. Your forms are spoken of as Brahma,
Vishnu and Shiva. O Lord! You are embodied in everything:
*deva*s, *daitya*s, *yaksha*s, *rakshasa*s, *siddha*s, *pannaga*s,
*kushmanda*s, *pishacha*s, *gandharva*s, humans, wild animals,
sacrificial animals, birds, reptiles, trees, shrubs, creepers and
every kind of grass. You are gross, medium and subtle. You are
subtler than the most subtle. You are in everything that has a
body and in differences between bodies. Your *maya* confounds
the ignorant, who do not know about the supreme meaning.
Those fools are constrained because they do not possess *vijnana*
about the *atman* and take something else to be the *atman*. It is
because of this that a sense of ownership results among men.
In general, there is a feeling of 'I' and 'mine'. O protector!
In the midst of the afflictions of *samsara*, this is what your
maya does. O protector! Devoted to their own *dharma*, men
who worship you transcend all this and free themselves from
maya. Brahma and all the other *deva*s, humans and animals
are submerged in the great whirlpool of Vishnu's *maya*. They
are surrounded by the blinding darkness of confusion. They
worship you, hoping for their desires to end. O illustrious one!
These men are bound by your *maya*. For the sake of destroying
the enemy, I too worshipped you, desiring a son. Since it was
driven by *maya*, it was not for the sake of emancipation. This
is like asking for a loincloth as covering from a tree that grants

all objects of desire. Even for those who have performed good deeds, such transgressions result from their own taints. O one without decay! Be pleased. You are the one who confounds the entire universe with your *maya*. O origin and lord of beings! O origin of *jnana*! Destroy our ignorance. I bow down before the one who has the *chakra* in his hand. I bow down before the one who has the Sharnga bow in his hand. I bow down before the one who has Nanda in his hand.[1016] O Vishnu! I bow down before the one who has the conch shell in his hand. I have seen your form, adorned with the gross signs. I do not know your supreme truth. O Parameshvara! Show me your favours." Thus praised by Aditi, Vishnu smile and spoke to the one from whom the gods had resulted. "O goddess! You are our mother. Be pleased. Be the one who bestows boons." Aditi replied, "Let it be as you wish. O tiger among men! In the world of the mortals, all the gods and *asura*s will find it impossible to vanquish you." At that time, along with Shakra's consort, Krishna's wife, Satyabhama, bowed down before Aditi and repeatedly requested her to be pleased. Aditi said, "O one with the excellent eyebrows! Through my favours, you will not suffer from old age or disfigurement. O one with the unblemished limbs! You will enjoy ever-lasting youth." With Aditi's permission, the king of *deva*s showed a great deal of respect and worshipped Janardana in the proper way.'

'O excellent one! After this, along with Satyabhama, Krishna saw all the excellent celestial gardens and lakes, Nandana and the others. Taking Satyabhama to be human, Shachi did not give her the *parijata* flowers, but used those flowers to ornament herself. Jagannatha Keshava, the slayer of Keshi, saw the *parijata* tree. It had bunches of excellent and extremely fragrant blossoms. It was adorned with new copper-coloured sprouts and always caused delight. It was

---

[1016] Meaning Nandaka, Vishnu's sword.

adorned with tender sprouts. When these were crushed, *amrita* resulted. The bark was made out of molten gold. Seeing that excellent king among trees, they were extremely happy and content. O supreme among *brahmana*s! On seeing this, Satyabhama spoke to Govinda. "O Krishna! Why don't we take this tree to Dvaraka? You say that you love Satya[1017] a lot. If those words are true, please take it there, for the pleasure-garden in my house. You have said that you do not desire Jambavati or Rukmini as much as you desire me. O Krishna! If the words spoken by you are true, do what will bring me pleasure. O Govinda! If the words uttered by you are true and not deceitful, let this *parijata* become an ornament in my house. With a bunch of *parijata* flowers in my braid of hair, I wish to become radiant and beautiful amidst my co-wives. Hence, I desire it." Thus addressed, Hari laughed and placed the *parijata* tree on Garuda. The guards in the grove spoke to him. "O Govinda! Shachi is the queen of the king of *deva*s. You should not take away the *parijata* tree. When the ocean was churned for *amrita*, it arose and was accepted by *deva*s, so as to provide ornaments for Shachi. It originated in that way and was given to the king of *deva*s. O extremely fortunate one! Queen Shachi was curious about it and *deva*s gave it to her. You cannot take it and go to your house unharmed. This will slight the one towards whose face the king of *deva*s looks. You want it because of your folly. Who can take it to his house and expect to remain unharmed? O Krishna! Indra of the gods will certainly cause you discomfort. O Achyuta! Enough of this. Shakra will raise the *vajra* in his hand and all the immortals will follow him, leading to a conflict with all *deva*s. The learned do not praise a deed that leads to a bitter end." Addressed in such words, Satyabhama became extremely angry and said, "Who is Shachi? Who is Shakra, lord of the gods? Who does *parijata*

[1017] That is, Satyabhama. There is a pun on the word *satya* (true).

belong to? This *parijata* tree is the common property of all the worlds. When the tree arose out of the water, while churning for *amrita*, why should Vasava have taken it? O guards of the grove! Liquor, the moon and Shri are the common property of all the worlds.[1018] It is the same with *parijata* tree. If Shachi does not let it go, because she is extremely proud of the strength of her husband's arms, quickly go and tell Puloma's daughter my words." Proud of the words Aditi had spoken about her husband, Satyabhama said, "Satya is taking this unblemished tree away. If you love your husband and if he is obedient to you, act so as to prevent my husband from taking this tree away. I know that your husband, Shakra, is the lord of the gods. Yet, as a mere woman, I will take the *parijata* tree away." Thus addressed, the guards went and told Shachi what had been said. Hearing this, Shachi goaded her husband, the lord of the gods. O supreme among *brahmana*s! For the sake of the *parijata* tree, Indra, surrounded by all the soldiers of the gods, started to fight with Hari. The gods wielded weapons like clubs, swords, bludgeons, spears and other excellent weapons. Shakra was amidst the gods, with the *vajra* in his hand. Govinda saw that Shakra was astride the king of elephants and that all the gods had presented themselves for the battle. He blew on his conch shell and filled the directions with that sound. He shot sharp arrows, numbering thousands and tens of thousands. The sky and the directions were seen to be covered by hundreds of arrows. On seeing this, the gods released many kinds of *shastra*s and *astra*s. Madhusudana, the lord of the universe, toyed with them. With a single weapon, he sliced each of the weapons released by the gods into one thousand fragments. The destroyer of *uraga*s[1019] roamed around. He seized the noose of

---

[1018] These also arose as a result of the churning of the ocean.
[1019] Garuda.

the king of the waters[1020] and tore it to bits, as he does the body
of a young serpent. Devaki's illustrious son hurled a mace and
fragmented the staff hurled by Yama, making it fall down on
the ground. Using his *chakra*, the lord shattered the palanquin
of the lord of wealth[1021] into bits as small as sesamum seeds.
With Shouri's glance, the sun god and the moon god were
deprived of their energy. The sharp arrows drove Agni and the
Vasus away in different directions. The *chakra* severed the tips
of Rudra's trident and made it fall down on the ground. Like
bits of cotton from a *shalmali* tree dispersed in the air, arrows
shot from the Sharnga bow dispatched Sadhyas, Vishvadevas,
Maruts and *gandharva*s. The bird Garuda roamed around. He
used his mouth, wings and claws to mangle the bodies and
eat them. Like two clouds showering down rain, Indra of the
gods and Madhusudana showered down thousands of arrows
on each other. In that place, a battle raged between Airavata
and Garuda. Along with all the gods, Shakra fought with
Janardana. When all the *shastra*s and *astra*s were shattered,
Vasava quickly seized his *vajra* and Krishna his Sudarshana
chakra. O supreme among *brahmana*s! On seeing that the
king of the gods and Janardana had picked up the *vajra* and
chakra, great sounds of lamentation arose everywhere in the
three worlds. When Indra hurled the *vajra*, the illustrious Hari
seized it. Without releasing his *chakra*, he told Shakra, "Wait!
Wait!" The *vajra* belonging to Indra of the gods was lost. His
mount was mangled by Garuda. As he proceeded to run away,
Satyabhama addressed him in these words. Satyabhama said,
"O brave one! O lord of the three worlds! It is not proper that
Shachi's husband should run away in this manner. For your
enjoyment, Shachi will present you with a garland of *parijata*
flowers. What kind of a kingdom of the gods is this? You can

[1020] Varuna.
[1021] Kubera.

no longer see Shachi lovingly approach you with resplendent *parijata* flowers, as used to be the case earlier. O Shakra! Enough of trying. You should not be ashamed. Let this *parijata* tree be taken away. Let the miseries of the gods go away. When she saw me come to her house, because of her pride about her husband, Shachi did not honour me and show me sufficient respect. Since I am a woman, my mind gets drawn to trifling matters. O Shakra! Proud of my own husband, I picked a fight with you. Enough of *parijata*. Why should one take away what belongs to another? Because of beauty and fame, and because of her husband, which woman does not become proud?" O *brahmana*! Thus addressed, the king of *deva*s returned. He said, "O angry friend! Enough of admonishments on a friend. He is the cause behind the creation, preservation and creation of everything and I am not ashamed of being defeated by him. The universe is his form. He is without a beginning, and everything merges into him. He is without a beginning and without a middle. Without him, none of the beings would have originated. He is the cause behind creation, preservation and destruction. O queen! Having been routed by him, how can I be ashamed? The earth and all its groves are his form. The small and the extremely subtle are his form. He is known only by those who know everything that is to be known. He is not known by anyone else. He is the lord without birth. He is the one who has not been created. He is eternal. If he so wishes, the original lord can take the entire universe away. Who is capable of defeating him?"'

Chapter 5(31) (Krishna's Marriages)

Shri Parashara said, 'The illustrious Keshava was praised in this way by the king of *deva*s. O supreme among *brahmana*s!

He smiled and addressed Indra in words that were full of deep meaning. Shri Krishna said, "You are Indra, king of *devas*. O lord of the universe! We are mortals. You should pardon any transgressions that have been committed by me. Let this *parijata* tree be taken away to its proper spot. O Shakra! I seized it because of Satya's words. Take back the *vajra*, which you had hurled towards me. O Shakra! This is your weapon, used to shatter enemies." Indra replied, "O lord! Why are you confounding me by telling me that you are mortal? We know that you are the illustrious one, but we do not know your subtle form. O protector! You are who you are, established as one who is engaged in saving the world. O Madhusudana! You act so as to remove the stakes of the universe. O Krishna! Let this *parijata* be taken away to the city of Dvaravati. As long as you are in the world of the mortals, it will remain on earth. O Krishna! You are the lord of *devas*. O Jagannatha! O Vishnu! O mighty-armed one! O one who has the conch shell, *chakra* and mace in his hand! Please pardon my transgressions." Addressed in this way by Indra of the gods, Hari returned to earth, surrounded and praised by *siddhas*, *gandharvas* and celestial *rishis*. O *brahmana*! Arriving above Dvaraka,[1022] he blew on his conch shell, generating delight among the residents of Dvaraka. Along with Satyabhama, he descended from Garuda and placed the giant *parijata* tree in the pleasure-garden. People who approached it could remember their past lives. For a distance of three *yojanas* around it, the ground was rendered fragrant because of the scent of its flowers. When the Yadavas came to see the tree and looked at their own faces after that, they realized they were bound in human bodies.[1023] The immensely intelligent Krishna divided the servants, elephants, horses and wealth among his relatives and gave them those.

[1022] He was in the air, astride Garuda.
[1023] They remembered their divine origins.

When an auspicious occasion presented itself, Janardana
married all the maidens who had been abducted by Naraka and
whom he had brought back. O great sage! Govinda married
all the maidens abducted by Naraka at the same time. He
followed *dharma* and accepted their hands separately, in the
proper way. There were more than sixteen thousand and one
hundred women. The illustrious Madhusudana simultaneously
assumed that many forms. However, each maiden thought that
Madhusudana was with her alone. "He has accepted only my
hand." O Maitreya! O *brahmana*! Hari resides everywhere and
the universe is his form. Keshava, the creator of the universe,
spent the nights in each of their homes.'[1024]

Chapter 5(32) (Usha and Aniruddha)

Shri Parashara said, 'I have already told you about Hari's
sons born through Rukmini, Pradyumna and the others.
Satyabhama gave birth to Bhanu, Bhoumerika and others.
Through Rohini, Hari's sons are said to be Diptimat,
Tamrapaksha and others. Samba and others, strong in arms,
were born through Jambavati. Nagnajiti had Bhadravinda had
other extremely strong sons. Among Shaibya's sons through
Hari, Sangramjit was the foremost.[1025] Vrika and others were
the sons of Madri.[1026] Among Lakshmana's sons, the chief was
Gatravat. Shruta and others were the sons of Kalindi. The
wielder of the *chakra* had other sons through other wives. He

---

[1024] Assuming that many simultaneous forms.

[1025] Since Mitravinda was descended from King Shibi, she was
also known as Shaibya.

[1026] Madri means Rohini, the daughter of the king of Madra.

had eighty-one thousand and one hundred sons.[1027] Among all these, Pradyumna, Rukmini's son, was the eldest. Aniruddha was Pradyumna's son and Aniruddha's son was Vajra. O supreme among *brahmana*s! The immensely strong Aniruddha was captured in an encounter and married Usha, Bana's daughter and Bali's granddaughter. Because of this, there was a terrible and great battle between Hari and Shankara. The wielder of the *chakra* cut off Bana's one thousand arms.'

Maitreya asked, 'O *brahmana*! For the sake of Usha, how did a battle occur between Hara and Krishna? How did Hari destroy Bana's arms? O immensely fortunate one! You should tell me everything about this. I am extremely curious to hear about this account concerning Hari.'

Shri Parashara replied, 'O *brahmana*! Usha, Bana's daughter, saw Parvati sport with Shambhu and felt an urge that she should also do something like that. Gouri, who knows about the minds of everyone, spoke to the beautiful one. "Enough of this repentance. You will also amuse yourself with your husband." Thus addressed, she thought, "Who will be my husband and when?"[1028] Parvati spoke to her again. Parvati said, "O princess! On the twelfth day of *shukla paksha* in the month of Vaishakha, the person who overpowers you in your dreams will become your husband." As the goddess had spoken, on that particular day, a person appeared to Usha in her dreams, and she fell in love with him. However, when she awoke and was eager, she could not see that man. O Maitreya! Without any sense of shame, in front of her friend, she

---

[1027] The text is such that the number can be interpreted in different ways. Krishna had eight main wives and 16,100 minor ones. With each wife, he had ten sons and one daughter. That is the standard account. Therefore, there were eighty main sons, through the eight main wives. Collectively, there were 161,080 sons. In any event, the text varies from the standard account.

[1028] Usha didn't speak. Parvati knew her thoughts.

exclaimed, "Where has he gone?" Bana had a minister named
Kumbhanda and his daughter, Chitralekha, was her friend.
She asked, "Who are you speaking about?" At first, since she
was ashamed, she did not tell her friend. However, having
gained her trust, she[1029] heard everything that she said. When
she had got to know everything, she again told her everything
the goddess had spoken and said, "Quickly devise a means
so that the task can be accomplished." Chitralekha replied,
"One cannot speak about, or obtain, something that is not
known. O friend! Nevertheless, for your sake, I will think of
some means. Wait for a period of seven or eight days." Having
said this, she went inside and thought of a means. Chitralekha
drew pictures of the foremost *devas*, *daityas*, *gandharvas*
and humans and showed them to her. She looked away from
gandharvas, *uragas*, gods and *asuras* and fixed her glances on
humans, especially Andhakas and Vrishnis. Seeing Krishna and
Rama, the one with the excellent eyebrows became bashful.
O *brahmana*! When her glance fell on Pradyumna, she turned
away in shame. O *brahmana*! However, as soon as her glance
fell on her beloved, Pradyumna's son, her eyes were full of
desire, and she cast aside all shame. She exclaimed, "This is
he. This is he." Chitralekha possessed the powers of being able
to trave through *yoga*. She spoke to Usha, Bana's daughter.
Chitralekha said, "This is Krishna's grandson, known by the
name of Aniruddha. He is famous and handsome to behold.
Through the favours of the goddess, he will be your husband.
If you obtain him as a husband, you will obtain everything.
The city of Dvaraka is protected by Krishna and is difficult
to enter. O friend! Nevertheless, I will make efforts to bring
your husband to you. You should not speak about this secret
to anyone. I will return in a short while. Till then, tolerate this

[1029] Chitralekha.

separation from me." Having comforted Usha, the friend went
to Dvaravati.'

Chapter 5(33) (Encounter between Shiva and Krishna)

S hri Parashara said, 'O Maitreya! Bana prostrated himself
before the three-eyed one and said, "O divinity! Without
any battles, I am disgusted with my one thousand arms. Will
there be any battle where my arms can taste success? Without a
battle, what purpose do my heavy arms serve?" Shri Shankara
replied, "O Bana! Your standard, with the peacock, will break,
something that has never happened before. When that occurs,
you will face a battle that will delight those who eat flesh."
Happy, he bowed down to Shambhu, the bestower of boons,
and returned to his house. He saw that his standard had broken
down and was filled with great delight. Meanwhile, using her
knowledge and strength of yoga, Chitralekha, the supreme
apsara, brought Aniruddha there, where the maidens resided
in the middle of the inner quarters. There, he pleasured himself
with Usha. The guards got to know and went and told the king
of the *daitya*s. The great-souled one commanded his servants
and soldiers. However, using a terrible iron club, the slayer of
enemy heroes killed them. When they were slain, Bana himself
arrived there on his chariot, ready to kill him. But though
he fought to the best of his capacity, he was defeated by the
valiant Yadu. Thereafter, urged by his minister, he continued
to fight using *maya*. Using *mantra*s, he invoked *pannagastra*[1030]
and bound the descendant of the Yadu lineage.'

[1030] A weapon named after serpents (*pannaga*). This resulted in
bonds made out of serpents.

'There was speculation among the Yadus in Dvaravati. "Where has Aniruddha gone?" Narada told them that Bana had captured him. The Yadavas had already heard that a woman accomplished in knowledge had taken him away to Shonitapura. Therefore, the Yadavas believed this. As soon as Hari remembered Garuda, he arrived. With Bala and Pradyumna, he mounted and went to Bana's city. At the entry to the city, there was a fight between the great-souled ones and the *pramatha*s.[1031] Destroying them, Hari was conveyed near Bana's city. For the sake of protecting Bana, the great Maheshvara *jvara*,[1032] possessing three feet and three heads, fought with the wielder of the Sharnga bow. As soon as those ashes touched Krishna's limbs, he experienced a great scorching. Baladeva also experienced this and closed his eyes in exhaustion. Thus, he fought with the divinity who wields the Sharnga bow. Vaishnava *jvara*[1033] swiftly expelled him from Krishna's body. He was struck by blows from Narayana's arms. He was agitated and suffered. Seeing this, the god, the grandfather, exclaimed, "Please pardon him." "Let him be pardoned." Saying this, the illustrious Madhusudana dissolved Vaishnava *jvara* within his own body. The *jvara* said, "Men who remember the fight between you[1034] and me will be freed from fever." Saying this, the *jvara* went away. After this, the illustrious one defeated the five fires and conveyed them to their destruction.[1035] As if he was playing, Vishnu crushed the army of the *danava*s. After this, the entire *daitya* army, Shankara and Kartikeya united with Bali's son to fight against Shouri. There was an extremely terrible

---

[1031] Literally, those who strike, Shiva's companions.

[1032] Shiva's fever, fever caused by Shiva.

[1033] Vishnu's fever, fever caused by Vishnu.

[1034] Maheshvara *jvara*.

[1035] The five fires (*agnis*) were fighting on Shiva's side. Depending on the context, there are different names for these five sacred fires.

clash between Hari and Shankara. All the worlds were agitated
and suffered from the many kinds of *shastra*s and *astra*s. As
the great encounter raged there, the gods thought, "It is certain
that the destruction of the entire universe has arrived." Using
jrimbhakastra,[1036] Govinda made Shankara yawn. After this, in
every direction, the *daitya*s and the *pramatha*s were destroyed.
Overwhelmed by the yawning, Hara sat down on his chariot.
He was incapable of fighting with Krishna, whose deeds are
unblemished. Guha's[1037] mount was mangled by Garuda, he
himself suffered because of Pradyumna's weapon. Krishna's
humkara[1038] destroyed Guha's javelin and bow. Shankara was
destroyed because of the yawning. The wielder of the Sharnga
bow vanquished Guha and conveyed the *daitya* and *pramatha*
soldiers to their destruction.'

'At this, Bana arrived there, so as to fight with the forces of
Krishna and Krishna's son.[1039] He was astride a giant chariot,
with the horses controlled by Nandi. The immensely valiant
Balabhadra fought with many of Bana's soldiers. Without
deviating from *dharma*, he pierced them with radiant arrows,
and they fled. Bana saw that Bala was dragging his forces by the
tip of the plough and swiftly striking them with a club and that
they were devastated by the arrows of the wielder of the *chakra*.
Thereafter, there was an extremely terrible clash between
Krishna and Bana. They shot blazing arrows at each other,
piercing the bodies and the armour. Krishna used his arrows
to slice down the arrows shot by Bana. Bana pierced Keshava.
The wielder of the *chakra* pierced Bana. O *brahmana*! Wishing
to defeat each other, Bana and Krishna released weapons at

[1036] A weapon that causes yawning.
[1037] Kartikeya's.
[1038] *Humkara* means to utter the sound 'hum', a sound believed to
possess special powers.
[1039] Pradyumna.

each other. They exhibited their dexterity and injured each
other. All the extensive *shastra*s and *astra*s were severed and
destroyed. But neither one gave up. After this, Hari made up
his mind to kill Bana with the *chakra*. It was full of energy
and was as resplendent as one hundred suns. Hari, who used
his *chakra* to slay *daitya*s, picked up his Sudarshana *chakra*.
So as to destroy Bana, Madhu's enemy was about to release
the *chakra*. However, Kotari, the knowledge of the *daitya*s,
appeared in front of Hari.[1040] She was naked. When Hari saw
that she was in front of him, he closed his eyes. So as to slice of
the arms of Bana, his enemy, he released Sudarshana. Released
by Achyuta, one by one, it sliced off Bana's arms. The *chakra*
swiftly severed the *asura*'s arms, which had released torrents of
*shastra*s. Thereafter, it returned to Madhusudana's hand, and
he wished to release it again, to destroy Bana.'

'However, realizing this, Umapati,[1041] the destroyer of
Tripura, appeared before Govinda and spoke to him. He
saw that the terrible Bana's arms had been severed and that
blood was flowing from them. Shankara said, "O Krishna! O
Jagannatha! O Krishna! I know that you are Purushottama.
You are the supreme lord, the *paramatman*. You are without
a beginning and without an end. You are Hari. You are
supreme. In your pastimes, you yourself assume embodied
forms as *deva*s, humans and inferior species. The signs of your
movements are seen in all beings. Please show me your favours.
O lord! I have granted Bana freedom from fear. You should
not falsify the words that I have uttered. He has been insolent
because he sought refuge with me. O one without decay! It is
not his fault. I am the one who conferred a boon on the *daitya*.
You should pardon me." Thus addressed, Govinda spoke to

[1040] Kotari, or Kotavi, is one of Durga's names, in her naked form.
The word means a naked woman.
[1041] Uma's consort, Shiva, who destroyed the city of Tripura.

Umapati, the one who has the trident in his hand. His face was
amiable, and he had lost all intolerance towards the *asura*. The
illustrious one said, "O Shankara! Since you have granted him
a boon, let Bana remain alive. Out of deference to your words,
I am withdrawing my *chakra*. You granting him freedom from
all kinds of fear is like me granting him freedom from fear. O
Shankara! You should not look on me as different from you.
You, I and the entire universe with *devas*, *asuras* and humans,
are identical. A person should know that there is no difference
between you and me. Men who are confounded by ignorance
see us as distinct." Saying this, Krishna went to the spot where
Pradyumna's son was. The wind generated by Garuda destroyed
the bonds the hooded ones had created. He made Aniruddha
and his wife sit on Garuda. With Rama and Krishna's son,
Damodara arrived in the city of Dvaraka. Surrounded by his
sons and grandsons, Janardana was delighted. O *brahmana*!
As they will, *devas* can always come to earth.'

Chapter 5(34) (Burning of Kashi)

Maitreya asked, 'Shouri assumed a radiant human form
and performed great deeds. Playfully, he defeated
Shakra, Sharva and all the gods. To carry out divine tasks,
what other great deeds did Hari perform? Please tell me. I have
great curiosity.'

Shri Parashara replied, 'O *brahmana rishi*! I will tell
you. Listen lovingly. For instance, in his incarnation as a
man, Krishna burnt down Varanasi. There was Poundraka
Vasudeva.[1042] People who were confounded by their ignorance

[1042] King Poundraka, who pretended to be Vasudeva/Krishna,
called himself Vasudeva and sported all of Vasudeva's signs and
symbols.

said, "Vasudeva has been incarnated on earth. This is he." He
thought that he was Vasudeva and that he had assumed an
avatara on earth. With his entire memory destroyed, he sported
all of Vishnu's symbols. O extremely great-souled one! He
sent a messenger to Krishna. "Give up the *chakra* and other
symbols. Those truly belong to me. O foolish one! Give up
everything that is spoken of as belonging to Vasudeva. If you
wish to ensure your life, come and prostrate yourself before
me." Addressed in this way, Janardana laughed and spoke
to the messenger. "I will unleash my own sign, the *chakra*,
towards you. O messenger! Go and convey these words of
mine to Poundraka. I know that your words are driven by
good intentions. Therefore, let us act accordingly. I will take
my symbols and come to your city. There is no doubt that I
will unleash my own sign, the *chakra*, towards you. Since you
have commanded me, I will indeed follow your instructions
and come. Without any delay, I will act accordingly and come
tomorrow. O king! I will certainly seek refuge with you. I will
truly act so that there is no reason to fear you." Having been
told this, the messenger left. As soon as Hari remembered him,
Garuda arrived and astride Garuda, he swiftly left for the city.'

'The lord of Kashi heard about Keshava's efforts.[1043] With
all his soldiers and companions, he arrived, so as to provide
support along the flanks. Poundraka Vasudeva surrounded
himself with a large army, including the army of the king of
Kashi, and advanced against Keshava. Hari saw him from a
distance, seated on his chariot. He held a *chakra*, a mace and
the Sharnga bow in his hands. He also had a lotus in his hand.

[1043] Poundraka was not the king of Kashi. He was the king of
Vanga and Pundra, in what is West Bengal and Bangladesh now.
His capital, Mahasthangarh, is in the village of Mahasthan in Bogra
district of Bangladesh. At the time of this incident, he was visiting his
friend, the king of Kashi.

He was garlanded and dressed in yellow garments. Suprana adorned his standard. Hari saw that his chest bore the *shrivatsa* mark.[1044] He had a diadem and earrings and was adorned with many kinds of jewels. On seeing this, the one the Garuda on his standard laughed in a deep voice.'

'O *brahmana*! He fought with that army, consisting of elephants and horses and full of swords, double-edged swords, clubs, spears, javelins and bows. In an instant, piercing arrows that shattered the enemy were released from the Sharnga bow. That entire army was destroyed and brought down through these and the mace and the *chakra*. Janardana also conveyed the arm of the king of Kashi to its destruction. He then spoke to the foolish Poundraka, who was sporting his own signs. The illustrious one said, "O Poundraka! Through the mouth of the messenger, you had asked me to let go of my signs. That is exactly what I will do now. I am releasing my *chakra*. I am throwing away my mace. I have commanded Garuda. Let him climb atop your standard." Saying this, he released his own *chakra*, which destroyed his *chakra*. His mace uprooted his mace. His Garuda shattered his Garuda on his standard. At this, lamentations arose among the people. Seeing that his friend was in trouble, the lord of Kashi fought with Vasudeva. The arrows released from the Sharnga bow severed his head and flung it inside the city of Kashi, causing great wonder among the people. In this way, Shouri killed Poundraka and the king of Kashi and his followers. He returned to Dvaravati again and amused himself, as the immortals do in heaven.'

'The people saw the head of the king of Kashi fall down inside the city and exclaimed, "What is this? Who has done this?" They were astounded. Learning that he had been killed by Vasudeva, his son,[1045] assisted by the priests, satisfied Shankara.

[1044] All these were imitations.

[1045] The son of the king of Kashi.

Shankara was propitiated in the great *kshetra* of Avimukta[1046]
and told the son of the king, "Ask for a boon." He said, "O
illustrious one! O Maheshvara! Through your favours, for the
sake of slaying Krishna, my father's killer, let a *kritya* arise."
Thus addressed, he agreed that it would be this way. From a
spot beyond the *dakshinagni*, from the place where the fire was
kept, a giant *kritya* arose. She was like a destructive fire. Her
terrible and cruel mouth blazed. Her disheveled hair was in
flames. Angry, she exclaimed, "Krishna! Krishna!" and rushed
towards Dvaravati. O sage! All the people saw the terrible one,
with malformed eyes, and were terrified. They went and sought
shelter with Madhusudana, the refuge of the universe. "The
son of the king of Kashi has worshipped the one with the bull
on his banner. O one who wields the *chakra*! A giant *kritya*
has arisen and is advancing towards you. Slay the fierce *kritya*.
Her matted hair is blazing like flames." At that time, his mind
was fixed on playing on the dice. However, he playfully hurled
his *chakra*. It was extremely terrible and emitted flames, dense
with garlands of fire. Vishnu's Sudarshana *chakra* swiftly
followed the *kritya*. Devastated and tormented by the *chakra*,
Maheshvari *kritya* started to run away speedily. However,
just as fast, it started to follow her. O supreme among sages!
The *kritya* quickly entered Varanasi, her power having been
countered by Vishnu's *chakra*. The entire force of Kashi and
the army of *pramatha*s advanced against the *chakra*, with all
kinds of *shastra*s and *astra*s. The army unleashed many kinds
of *shastra*s and *astra*s. However, it easily consumed all these.
Having destroyed all these, it went to the city of Varanasi. There
were large numbers of servants, citizens, horses, elephants
and humans there. There were innumerable settlements and
treasuries that even the gods could not glance at. The flames
engulfed all the houses, ramparts and quadrangles. Swiftly, the

---

[1046] Avimukta is another name for Varanasi.

chakra burnt down the city and everything in it. It was fierce and its intolerance did not diminish. It wished to achieve what was difficult to do. Dazzling in its brilliance, the *chakra* then returned to Vishnu's hand.'

Chapter 5(35) (An Incident Involving Samba)

Maitreya said, 'O *brahmana*! I wish to hear about the intelligent Balabhadra again, about his valour. You should describe that to me. O illustrious one! I have already heard about his dragging the Yamuna and other deeds. O immensely fortunate one! Tell me everything else that Bala did.'

Shri Parashara replied, 'O Maitreya! Hear about Rama's deeds. He is infinite and immeasurable. He is Shesha, who holds up the earth. The brave Samba, Jambavati's son, forcibly abducted Duryodhana's daughter at the time when her *svayamvara* had been arranged. This enraged the immensely valiant Karna, Duryodhana and others and Bhishma, Drona and others. They defeated him in battle and bound him up. O Maitreya! Hearing this, all the Yadavas were angry at Duryodhana and the others , along with Krishna, made great efforts so that they might be killed. However, his words slurring because of his intoxication, Bala restrained them and said, "Because of my words, the Kouravas will release him." Baladeva saw the city of Nagasahvya.[1047] He didn't enter the city but remained in a grove that was outside the city. Having learnt that Bala had arrived, Duryodhana and the kings offered Rama a cow, *arghya* and water. Having accepted all these in the proper way, he told the Kouravas, "It is Ugrasena's command

[1047] Nagasahvya is another name for Hastinapura, as is Gajasahvya. All these expressions mean 'the city of the elephant'.

that Samba should be quickly released." O *brahmanas*! O
supreme among *brahmanas*! Hearing his words, Karna,
Duryodhana, Bhishma, Drona and Bahlika and the other
kings became angry. All the Kouravas glanced towards the one
who wielded the plough as a weapon, belonging to the Yadu
lineage, which did not deserve a kingdom. The Kouravas said,
"O Bala! What are these words that you have spoken? How
can a Yadava command one who has been born in the Kuru
lineage? If Ugrasena is capable of commanding the Kouravas,
then enough of these white umbrellas and other ornaments that
are appropriate for kings.[1048] O Bala! Therefore, depart. Samba
has committed a wicked deed. We will not release him because
of your or Ugrasena's command. Since we deserve respect, the
Kukuras and Andhakas used to bow down to us earlier. But
that is not being observed now. How is it that a master is being
commanded by servants? Because we treated you as equals and
sat down on the same seat to eat, you have become full of
insolence. But it is not your fault. Good policy does not please
those who should be ignored. O Bala! The person you have
spoken about should be honoured by us and treated lovingly.
But your lineage is not behaving in a similarly appropriate
way towards our lineage." Having said this, the Kurus did not
release Hari's son. Having made up their minds, they quickly
entered Gajasahvya.'

'The insult led to his becoming wrathful. Intoxicated,
the one who used the plough as a weapon raised his terrible
plough and whirled it around. The one who used the plough
as his weapon raised the plough and struck the earth with it
side. As the great-souled one struck with the side, the earth
was shattered. He slapped his chest, and the sound filled all
the directions. His eyes turned extremely coppery-red and as
he spoke, his forehead was furrowed in a frown. "These evil-

[1048] Possessed by Ugrasena because we will take them away.

souled Kouravas have no substance. But they are intoxicated
by their strength and wish to establish their supremacy over us.
This is indeed due to destiny. Ugrasena's instructions cannot be
disregarded and dishonoured. His commands are followed by
Shachi's consort, along with the gods. Ugrasena is always present
in Sudharma, the assembly hall of Shachi's consort. Shame on
these men. They are content with a king's seat, leftovers of
hundreds before them.[1049] The wives of his servants use clumps
of flowers from the *parijata* tree. However, they do not regard
him as a lord of the earth. Let Ugrasena, the protector of all the
kings, remain where he is. Today, I will go to his city only after
removing all the Kouravas from earth—Karna, Duryodhana,
Drona, Bhishma, Bahlika, Duhshasana, Bhuri, Bhurishrava,
Somadatta, Shala, Bhima, Arjuna, Yudhishthira, the twins
and all the other Kouravas. I will slay them and destroy their
horses, chariots and elephants. Taking the brave Samba and his
wife with me, I will go to the city of Dvaraka and see Ugrasena
and the other relatives. Alternatively, along with the Kurus and
all the Kouravas,[1050] I will swiftly hurl the city of Nagasahvya
into the Bhagirathi." The one who used the club as a weapon
said this and his eyes were red with intoxication. He turned the
face of the plough downwards and placing the tip on the walls
of Hastinapura, started to heave. The city of Hastinapura was
violently whirled around. On seeing this, the hearts of all the
Kouravas were agitated and they screamed. The Kouravas said,
"O Rama! O mighty-armed one! Please forgive us. O Rama!
You should pardon us. O one with the plough as a weapon!
Please be pacified and restrain your rage. O Bala! We are

[1049] There have been hundreds of ordinary kings earlier. Therefore,
the throne is like a leftover. However, Ugrasena has the *parijata* tree in
his garden and even the wives of his servants can use those flowers.

[1050] Kouravas means descendants of the Kurus. Hence, both terms
have been used, though they are really synonymous.

suffering because of your strength. Samba and his wife will be freed. We have been guilty of not knowing about your powers. Please forgive us." O bull among sages! Along with Samba and his wife, the Kouravas quickly emerged from their own city. Bhisma, Drona, Kripa and the others prostrated themselves before him and spoke pleasant words. Bala, supreme among strong ones, said, "I have pardoned you." O *brahmana*! Even today, the signs of the city being whirled around are evident. Such were Rama's powers. He possessed all the signs of strength and valour. The Kouravas honoured Samba, along with Bala, and sent him and his wife, with the riches given at the time of a marriage.'

Chapter 5(36) (Slaying of Dvivida)

Shri Parashara said, 'O Maitreya! Listen. Hear about the other things that Bala, full of strength, did. Naraka, Indra among the *asura*s, was opposed to the side of the *deva*s. The bull among *vanara*s, named Dvivida, was immensely valiant and was his friend. This strong one was bound in enmity against the gods. He thought, "Urged by the king of the gods, Krishna has killed Naraka. Therefore, I will act against all the *deva*s." Accordingly, he destroyed sacrifices and devastated the mortal world. Confounded by his ignorance, he destroyed sacrifices. He violated the rules of the virtuous and destroyed embodied beings. He burnt down sacrifices, countries, cities, villages and the intervening places. Sometimes, he hurled down mountains and crushed villages. He uprooted mountains and flung them into the waters of the oceans. He stood in the midst of oceans and agitated the oceans. O *brahmana*! Thus agitated, the ocean violated the shoreline. The great force flooded the shores, the villages and the cities. He could assume any form

at will and assumed giant forms. In these proud forms, the
vanara[1051] wandered around, plundering all the crops and
crushing everything. In this way, the evil-souled one distorted
the entire universe. O Maitreya! Deprived of self-studies and
vashatkara, the brahmanas were extremely miserable.'

'On one occasion, the one with the plough as his weapon
was drinking in the grove of Raivata. The immensely fortunate
Revati and other beautiful women were with him. As they
sang, amidst those charming women, he was like a crown.
The supreme one from the Yadu lineage pleasured himself,
like Kubera on Mandara. The vanara arrived there. Seizing
the plough and the club, he stood in front of him and started
to mimic him. Facing the women, the monkey[1052] laughed. He
hurled the vessels filled with liquor away with his hand. Full of
rage, the wielder of the plough reprimanded him. Nevertheless,
ignoring him, he[1053] continued to make a chattering sound. At
this, Bala stood up and angrily seized his club. The supreme
among monkeys seized the terrible summit of a mountain and
hurled it. However, as it was flung, the best among Yadavas
shattered it into one thousand fragments with his club and it
fell down on the ground. As the club was brought down, the
monkey avoided it and using his hand, struck Bala on the chest
with force, strength and rage. At this, Bala became angry and
struck him on the head with his fist. With a little bit of life left in
him, Dvivida fell down, vomiting blood. As his body fell down,
the summit of the mountain was shattered into a hundred
fragments. O Maitreya! It was as if it had been struck by the
vajra of the wielder of the vajra. From above, devas showered

[1051] Etymologically, vanara means similar to man (nara). The
word is translated as monkey/ape. But we have decided to leave it as
vanara here.
[1052] The word used here is kapi.
[1053] Dvivida.

down flowers on Rama. They praised him and applauded his
great deed. "This wicked monkey took the side of the *daitya*s
and caused harm. O brave one! He made the universe suffer.
It is good fortune that he has come to his end." Saying this,
along with the *guhyaka*s, the delighted *deva*s left for heaven.
In this way, there are many deeds that the intelligent Baladeva
performed. They cannot be enumerated. He is Shesha, who
holds up the earth.'

Chapter 5(37) (Destruction of Yadavas)

Shri Parashara said, 'In this way, with Baladeva as his
aide, Krishna killed *daitya*s. For the sake of the world, he
destroyed wicked kings. Along with Phalguna,[1054] the illustrious
lord reduced the burden of the earth and destroyed all the
*akshouhini*s. He assumed an *avatara*. To reduce the earth's
burden, he killed all the kings. Using the curse invoked by
*brahmana*s, he then destroyed his own lineage. O sage! Krishna
abandoned Dvaraka and gave up his human form, which was
Vishnu's portion. He again entered his own abode.'

Maitreya asked, 'How did he used a curse to exterminate
his own lineage? How did Janardana give up his human body?'

Shri Parashara replied, 'In the great *tirtha* of Pindaraka,
some young Yadu men met Vishvamitra, Kanva and the great
sage, Narada. They were insolent because of their youth
and were goaded by future events. They dressed up Samba,
Jambavati's son, as a woman. They approached the sages,
prostrated themselves and spoke confidently. "This woman
desires a son. What will she deliver? Please tell us." Those
*brahmana*s possessed divine knowledge and could not be

[1054] Arjuna.

deceived by the young men. The angry sages said, "She will deliver a club which will exterminate the entire lineage of Yadavas. Thereafter, all the Yadava lineages will be removed from earth." Addressed in this way, the young men told Ugrasena all that had happened. A club came out of Samba's stomach and Ugrasena had the club crushed to a powder. The powdered bits were flung into the ocean and some *eraka* grass was generated from this. O *brahmana*! However, when the iron club was powdered, a small fragment remained. It could not be powdered, and it was in the shape of a miniature club. When this was flung into the ocean, it was swallowed by a fish. The fish was caught in a net. A hunter named Jara[1055] eagerly killed the fish and took the piece out from its stomach. The illustrious Madhusudana knew the supreme purport of everything. However, he did not wish to act and counter what had been ordained by destiny.'

'Vayu, a messenger sent by *deva*s came and prostrated himself before Keshava. He spoke to him in secret and said, "O illustrious one! I am a messenger sent by the gods, the Vasus, the Ashvins, the Maruts, the Adityas, the Rudras, the Sadhyas and the others. O lord! Hear the message sent by Shakra to you. O illustrious one! More than one hundred years have passed since you incarnated yourself, urged by the gods, to reduce the burden. You have descended and have slayed *daitya*s and others who were wicked in conduct. The earth's burden has been reduced. Along with you, their protector, let the gods return to the abode of the gods.[1056] O Jagannatha! You have spent more than one hundred years here. If it pleases you, please return to heaven now. That is what *deva*s want. But if you still wish to remain here, as your followers, until such time, we, *deva*s, will also have to remain

---

[1055] *Jara* means old age.

[1056] Portions of the gods had also incarnated themselves on earth.

as humans." The illustrious one replied, "O messenger! I
know everything that you have told me. However, I have
started the destruction of the Yadavas. If the Yadavas are
not exterminated, they will constitute a grave burden for the
earth. I have taken an *avatara* to ensure that. I will quickly
ensure their destruction, within seven nights. Dvaraka was
retrieved from the ocean, and I will submerge it in the ocean
again. Having destroyed the Yadavas, I will proceed to the
abode of the gods. With Samkarshana as my companion, I
will give up this human body. The immortals, and Indra of
the gods, should take it as if I have already gone there. For
the sake of reducing the earth's burden, Jarasandha and the
others have been killed. However, the young Yadus constitute
an even greater burden and must be removed. I must reduce
this extremely great burden on earth. After this, I will do what
they have asked and go to the world of the immortals. Please
tell them that." Thus addressed by Vasudeva, the messenger
of the gods prostrated himself before him. O Maitreya! He
went to heaven and presented himself before the king of
the *devas*.'

'Night and day, the illustrious one witnessed evil portents
in heaven, in the sky and on earth, signifying the destruction
of the city of Dvaraka. Seeing this, he told the Yadavas,
"Behold these extremely terrible and great omens. To pacify
these, without any delay, we should go to Prabhasa." Thus
addressed by Krishna, Uddhava, the great devotee and
supreme Yadava, prostrated himself before Hari and asked,
"O illustrious one! What should I do now? Instruct me. O
illustrious one! I think that you will destroy this entire lineage.
O Achyuta! I can see portents that indicate the destruction
of the lineage." The illustrious one replied, "Through my
favours, you will have a divine power of movement. Go to the
sacred hermitage of Badari, on Mount Gandhamadana. This
is Nara and Narayana's region and is the most sacred spot on

earth. With your mind in me, through my favours, you will obtain success there. When I have destroyed the lineage, I will go to heaven. After it has been abandoned by me, the ocean will flood Dvaraka. My house alone will be spared from the terror of the flood. To ensure their welfare, I will gather my devotees there." Thus addressed and permitted by Keshava, Uddhava prostrated himself before him and swiftly went to the hermitage, Nara and Narayana's region. O *brahmana*! All the Yadavas mounted chariots that could travel fast. With Krishna, Rama and the others, they left for Prabhasa. Having reached Prabhasa, urged by Vasudeva, the Kukuras and Andhakas indulged in a great bout of drinking. As they drank, there was a clash between them. The serious arguments led to a fire of dissension that brought destruction.'

Maitreya asked, 'O best among *brahmana*s! Since each drank on his own, why was there a conflict? You should explain this to me.'

Shri Parashara replied, 'Sweet food that is given is no longer sweet if one debates over it. Sweet and harsh words were exchanged, and this led to quarrels and conflicts. They attacked each other, their eyes red with rage. Using the strength of divine weapons, they killed each other. When the weapons were exhausted, they seized the *eraka* reeds that were nearby. As soon as they seized the *eraka* reeds, these were seen to turn as hard as the *vajra*. With these, they struck extremely terrible blows and killed each other. O *brahmana*! Pradyumna, Samba, Kritavarma, Satyaki, Aniruddha, Prithu, Viprithu, Charuvarma, Charuka, Akrura and others struck each other with *eraka* grass that was like the *vajra* and killed each other. Hari tried to restrain them. But the Yadavas thought that Keshava had come to help them and continued to kill each other. At this, Krishna also became angry and seized a fistful of *eraka*. In his hands, this turned into an iron club. Acting like an assassin, he killed all the Yadavas who were left.

Others violently attacked and killed each other. O *brahmana*!
While Daruka looked on, Jaitra, the chariot of the wielder of
the *chakra*, was swiftly dragged into the middle of the ocean.
The *chakra*, mace, Sharnga bow, the quivers, the conch shell
and the sword circumambulated him and left along the path
of the sun. O great sage! In an instant, with the exception of
the mighty-armed Krishna and Daruka, all the Yadavas were
destroyed. As they roamed around, they saw Rama seated
near the root of a tree. They saw a giant *uraga* emerge from
his mouth. The giant serpent emerged from his mouth. Then,
worshipped by *siddha*s and *uraga*s, the serpent left for the
ocean. With an offering of *arghya*, the ocean presented himself
before him. Worshipped by the excellent serpents, he entered
the water. Witnessing Bala's departure, Keshava spoke to
Daruka. "Tell Vasudeva and Ugrasena everything—Baladeva's
departure and the destruction of the Yadavas. Seated in *yoga*
here, I will give up my body. Tell the residents of Dvaraka and
Ahuka that the ocean will flood the entire city. Therefore, all
of you wait for Arjuna to arrive. Do not remain in Dvaraka but
leave with Pandava. You should go wherever Kourava[1057] goes.
Go to Kounteya Arjuna and tell him my words. "These are my
relatives. To the best of your capacity, protect them." With
the people of Dvaravati, along with Arjuna, you will leave and
Vajra[1058] will become the king of the Yadus. Thus addressed,
Daruka repeatedly prostrated himself before Krishna. After
having performed *pradakshina* several times, he left, as he had
been instructed.'

'He first went to Dvarka. The immensely intelligent one
then brought Arjuna and made Vajra the king. The illustrious
Govinda Vasudeva, the supporter of all beings, merged his
atman into the supreme *atman* of the *brahman*. O immensely

[1057] As a descendant of Kuru, Arjuna was also Kourava.
[1058] Aniruddha's son.

fortunate one! He withdrew from Prapancha and merged
his *atman* into the *paramatman*. Immersed in the *turiya*
state,[1059] Purushottama lay down in the water. He honoured
the words of the *brahmana*s and showed respect to the words
of Durvasa.[1060] O excellent one! He seated himself in *yoga*,
placing one foot on the other knee. The hunter named Jara
arrived there. He held an arrow, the head made out of the last
bit of the iron club. He noticed the foot, which was in the form
of a deer.[1061] O supreme among *brahmana*s! He pierced the
sole with the spike. Having gone closer, he saw a four-armed
man. He prostrated himself and repeatedly said, "Please show
me your favours. Taking you to be a deer, I have done this
in my ignorance. Please pardon me. Since I am already being
consumed by my crime, you should pardon me and save me."
The illustrious one replied, "You should not have the slightest
bit of fear. O hunter! Through my favours, go to heaven, the
place for the gods." As soon as he spoke these words, a *vimana*
arrived. Through his favours, the hunter mounted it and left for
heaven. When he had left, the illustrious one united his *atman*
with the *atman*.[1062] He merged himself into the *brahman*—the
undecaying, unthinkable and sparkling essence of Vasudeva.
He is without birth and without death. Vishnu is immeasurable
and is in all *atman*s. Giving up his human body and the three
kinds of *guna*s.'

[1059] A living being has four states: waking, dreaming, sleeping and
turiya. *Turiya* is the fourth state, when one perceives union between
the human soul *atman* and the *brahman*. *Panchatva* is the fifth state,
beyond *turiya*.

[1060] That is, he honoured their curses.

[1061] Meaning a deer's ear.

[1062] The *jivatman* with the *paramatman*.

Chapter 5(38) (Start of *Kali Yuga*)

Shri Parashara said, 'Arjuna searched for the bodies of Krishna and Rama and performed the funeral rites. One by one, he did it for the others too. There were said to be eight main queens, Rukmini as the foremost. Embracing Hari's body, they entered the fire. O excellent one! Revati embraced Rama's body and entered the blazing fire, which turned cool as soon as it touched her. Hearing about this, Ugrasena, Anakadundubhi, Devaki and Rohini also entered the fire. Following the norms, Arjuna performed the funeral rites. Taking all the people, Vajra and thousands of Krishna's wives,[1063] he left Dvaravati. Protecting the people and Vajra, Kounteya proceeded slowly. O Maitreya! Krishna had brought the Sudharma assembly hall to the world of the mortals. It left for heaven, along with the *parijata* tree. On the day when Hari left earth and went to heaven, that is the day when the dark and strong *kali yuga* descended. The giant ocean flooded the empty city of Dvaraka. However, the ocean did not flood Vasudeva's house. O *brahmana*! The illustrious Keshava is always present there. Therefore, the giant ocean has not crossed that boundary, not even today. It is great and extremely sacred. It destroys every kind of sin. If one sees the place where Vishnu resided, one is freed from sins.'

'O supreme sage! The land of Panchanada has a lot of grain and wealth.[1064] Partha made arrangements for all the people to reside there. Partha, a single archer, was conveying all the women, their husbands having been killed. On seeing this, bandits, wicked in their deeds, became greedy. Avarice

---

[1063] Only the eight main ones immolated themselves.
[1064] The land of the five (*pancha*) rivers (*nada*), Punjab. The five rivers are Shatadru, Vipasha, Iravati, Chandrabhaga and Vitasta.

overwhelmed the minds of the evildoers. The *abhira*s were extremely difficult to subdue and they consulted each other.[1065] "Arjuna is a single archer. The husbands of the women have been killed. How can he cross us and take them away? Shame on our strength. Having killed Bhishma, Drona, Jayadratha, Karna and others, he is full of pride. He does not know about the strength of those who reside in villages. Holding a bow in his hand, the evil-minded one shows disrespect towards all other men, especially those who have staffs in their hands. Are our arms not strong?" Without sticks and stones as weapons, thousands of them attacked the people whose protectors had been killed. Kounteya reprimanded them. He laughed and spoke to the *abhira*s. Arjuna said, "O those who are ignorant of *dharma*! If you do not wish to die, withdraw." O Maitreya! Ignoring his words, they seized the wealth, the women and Vishvaksena's wives from him. At this, Arjuna started to string the divine Gandiva bow, which had never been destroyed in battle. However, the valiant one was unable to do this. When he managed to string it with a great deal of difficulty, it became loose again. Though he thought about them, Pandava could not remember the weapons. Intolerant in his mind, Partha tried to shoot the arrows towards the enemy. However, the wielder of Gandiva was unable to pierce the enemy. The inexhaustible arrows that the fire god had given him[1066] were destroyed. As he fought with the cowherds, Arjuna was defeated and exhausted. Kounteya thought, "Krishna was the strength when all the kings were slain through my torrent of arrows." As Pandu's son looked on, those excellent women were abducted by the *abhira*s. Others fled wherever they wished. O sage! When the arrows were exhausted, Dhananjaya struck the bandits with

---

[1065] *Abhira*s are cowherds. But here, they are being equated with bandits (*dasyus*) and later, with *mleccha*s.

[1066] At the time of the burning of the Khandava forest.

the end of his bow. But they only laughed at these blows. O
excellent sage! As Partha looked on, the *mlecchas* seized the
excellent Vrishni and Andhaka women and left in different
directions. Jishnu was extremely miserable and exclaimed,
"This is a great sorrow. Alas! It is misery that the illustrious
one has abandoned me." He wept. "The bow, the weapons,
the chariot, the horses—all of these have been destroyed in an
instant, like donations given to a person who is not learned.
Destiny is indeed strong. Without the great-souled one, I am no
longer capable. I have been defeated by those who are inferior.
These are the same arms. This is the same fist. This is the
same spot. I am the same Arjuna. But without the sacred one,
everything is without substance. It is certain that my nature as
Arjuna and Bhima's nature as Bhima were determined by him.
Without him, I, a supreme charioteer, have been defeated by
*abhira*s." Having said this, Jishnu went to the excellent city of
Indraprastha and instated Vajra, the descendant of the Yadava
lineage, as the king there.'[1067]

'After this, Phalguna saw Vyasa, who was residing in a
forest. Having met the immensely fortunate one, he humbly
greeted him. As he bent down at his feet, the sage scrutinized
him for a long time and asked him in these words. "Why is there
such a shadow over you now? Have you followed dust created
by goats? Have you killed a *brahmana*? Are you miserable
because your desire has been shattered? What deviation has
led to this present shadow? Were your offspring refused when
they asked for something? Have you got attached to a woman
one should not have intercourse with? Is that the reason you
have lost your radiance? Have you eaten sweets alone, without
having given them to *brahmana*s first? O Arjuna! Did you take
away wealth from someone who was distressed? O Arjuna!
Has the ray of the sun or the force of the wind touched you?

[1067] Parikshit was the king in Hastinapura.

Have you been struck by evil glances? How else can you be
deprived of your prosperity? Have you touched water with
nails in it? Have you been sprinkled by water from a pot?[1068]
Why is there this great shadow on you? In a battle, have you
been defeated by a person who is inferior?" Partha sighed and
said, "O illustrious one! Listen." He told Vyasa about how he
had been defeated. Arjuna said, "He was our strength. He was
our energy. He was our valour. He was our prowess. He was
our prosperity and our shade. Hari has forsaken us and has
departed. O sage! Though we were inferior, in his greatness,
the lord smiled at us before he spoke. With him gone, we are
deprived and are like grass. Purushottama was the essence
behind my weapons, arrows and Gandiva. He has now given
up his body and has left. It was because Govinda looked on
us that our prosperity, victory and improvement resulted. But
that illustrious one has abandoned us and has left. Bhishma,
Drona, the king of Anga,[1069] Duryodhana and others were
consumed because of his powers. But that Krishna has now
left the earth. It seems to me that the earth is like a lady who
has lost her youth, her beauty and her shade. O father![1070] As
a result of being separated from the wielder of the *chakra*, I
am not the only one who is suffering. Because of his powers,
Bhishma and the others were like moths before a fire. Without
Krishna, I have now been defeated by cowherds. It is because
of his powers that Gandiva was famous in the three worlds.
Without him, I have been chastised by *abhira*s wielding sticks.
O great sage! I was conveying thousands of women who were
without protectors. But bandits, using sticks as weapons, have

---

[1068] There are injunctions on water that can be used for bathing.
It should not be from a pot, and it should not be water in which there
are parings of clipped nails.

[1069] Karna.

[1070] The word used is *tata*.

taken them away. O Krishna![1071] Using sticks as weapons, *abhira*s have subjugated my strength and have taken away all of Krishna's excellent riches, brought by me. It shouldn't be surprising that I am faded. It is extraordinary that I am still alive. O grandfather! I am without shame. My limbs have been smeared by the mud of being dishonoured by those who are inferior."'

'Vyasa replied, "O Partha! Enough of being ashamed. You should not grieve. Know that for all creatures, the working of time is like this. O Pandava! Time is responsible for creatures existing and not existing. O Arjuna! Understanding that time is the root of everything, act so as to steady your mind. Rivers, oceans, all the mountains, the entire earth, *deva*s, humans, animals, trees and reptiles have all been created by time. It is time that will again lead to their destruction. When you understand that everything is because of time, you will obtain peace. O Dhananjaya! Krishna's greatness is exactly as you have described it. The illustrious and lotus-eyed Krishna has a form as time. He assumed an *avatara* to reduce the earth's burden. In earlier times, suffering from the burden, the earth went to an assembly of *deva*s. Janardana, whose form is time, incarnated himself for that purpose. That task has been accomplished. All the kings have been killed. O Partha! The entire lineage of Vrishnis and Andhakas has been destroyed. No other task was left for the lord on the surface of the earth. Having accomplished what needed to be done, as he willed, the illustrious one has departed. The lord of the gods originates creation. He is the one who sustains preservation. He is also capable of destroying, as he has done now. O Partha! Therefore, you should not lament at your being vanquished. When the time is right, men will exhibit praiseworthy valour. You could single-handedly kill Bhishma, Drona, Karna and the

[1071] Vedavyasa's name is Krishna Dvaipayana.

others in battle. O Arjuna! Did their defeat not have a cause in
time? Their defeat was because of the powers of Vishnu. That
is also the truth about your defeat by bandits. He is origin and
preservation. The divinity, the lord of the gods, enters other
bodies. Established there, in the end, the lord of the universe
is the one who brings about the destruction of all beings. O
Kounteya! At the time of your rise, Janardana was your aide.
At the time of your end, Keshava glanced favourably towards
your adversaries. Who would have believed that you would
kill all the Kouravas, including Gangeya?[1072] Who would have
believed that the killer of the Kouravas would be defeated by
*abhira*s? You should not grieve that the women have been
seized by bandits and *abhira*s. O Arjuna! In this connection, I
will tell you about an account. O Partha! In ancient times, the
brahmana Ashtavakra remained submerged in water for many
years, praising the eternal *brahman*. When large numbers of
*asura*s were defeated, there was a great festival on the slopes of
Meru. Hundreds and thousands of celestial women, Rambha,
Tilottama and others, were going there and saw him. O
Pandava! They praised and worshipped the great-souled one.
The sage was immersed in water up to his neck and he had
a burden of matted hair. As he was engaged in uttering the
*stotra*s, they humbly prostrated themselves before him. O best
among Kouravas! All of them praised that senior *brahmana*.
Ashtavakra said, 'O immensely fortunate ones! I am pleased
with you. I will grant you everything that you wish for, even
if it is very difficult to obtain.' Rambha, Tilottama and other
divine *apsara*s replied. 'O *brahmana*! If you are pleased, that is
sufficient. What else do we need?' Others said, 'O *brahmana*! O
illustrious one! O Indra among *brahmana*s! If you are pleased,
we wish to obtain Purushottama as a husband.' From inside the
water, the sage replied that it would indeed be that way. As he

---

[1072] Gangeya is Ganga's son, Bhishma.

arose from the water, they saw his disfigured form, crooked in eight parts.[1073] On seeing him, some concealed their smiles. But others laughed out aloud. O descendant of the Kuru lineage! Enraged, the sage cursed them. 'You laughed at me and showed me disrespect because of my form. Because of what you have done, I will curse you. Because of my favours, you will obtain Purushottama as your husband. However, all of you will suffer because of my curse. You will fall into the hands of bandits.' When they heard what the sage had said, they placated him and he said, 'You will again return to the world of Indra of the gods.' Thus, because of Ashtavakra, those divine women obtained the wielder of the *chakra* as a husband and because of the sage's curse, they fell into the hands of bandits. O Pandava! You should not have the slightest bit of grief on this account. Everything is taken away by the one who is the lord of everything. O Pandava! Your imminent destruction has also been decided by him. That is the reason your strength, energy, valour and greatness have been taken away. For those who are born, death is inevitable. Every fall leads to a rise. Union ends in separation. Any accumulation is destroyed. Understanding this, the learned do not grieve. Nor are they delighted. There are others, like the learned, who seek to learn from these events. O best among men! Knowing this, along with your brothers, give up everything. Go and perform austerities in the forest. Go and tell Dharmaraja these words of mine. O brave one! Day after tomorrow, along with your brothers, act towards the appropriate objective." Thus addressed, Arjuna went and told the Parthas and the twins everything that he had seen and everything that he had experienced.[1074] All of them

[1073] Ashtavakra was born crooked (*vakra*) in eight (*ashta*) parts of his body.

[1074] The text has the word Parthas in the plural. It means both Yudhishthira and Bhima.

heard Vyasa's words, as narrated by Arjuna. Handing over the kingdom to Parikshit, the sons of Pandu went to the forest. O Maitreya! I have thus told you in detail how Vasudeva was born in the Yadu lineage and about everything that he did. A person who hears about Krishna's conduct is freed from all sins and goes to Vishnu's world.'

This ends Part V.

Part VI

Chapter 6(1) (Dissolution and *Kali Yuga*)

Maitreya asked, 'O great sage! In detail, you have described *sarga*, *vamsha*, the duration of *manvantaras* and *vamshanucharita*. I now wish to hear about withdrawal. O great sage! At the end of a *kalpa*, what is described as the great *pralaya*?'

Shri Parashara replied, 'O Maitreya! From me, hear accurately about withdrawal. At the end of a *kalpa*, there is *prakrita pralaya*.[1075] A day and night for the ancestors is a month for the residents of heaven. O supreme among *brahmanas*!

[1075] *Prakrita pralaya* happens at the end of a *kalpa* and *maha pralaya* happens at the end of Brahma's life.

491

There are four *yuga*s: *krita*, *treta*, *dvapara* and *kali*. There are one thousand divine *mahayuga*s in each of Brahma's days, but the number is actually twelve thousand.[1076] Each of the four *yuga*s has a corresponding nature. O Maitreya! *Krita yuga* is said to be the first and *kali yuga* the last. In the first *krita yuga*, Brahma embarks on his task of creation. In the last *kali yuga*, he embarks on the task of withdrawal.'

Maitreya said, 'O illustrious one! You should describe in detail the nature of *kali yuga* to me. *Dharma*, which possesses four feet, is submerged then.'

Shri Parashara replied, 'O Maitreya! You wish to hear about the nature of *kali yuga*. O great sage! Hear in detail about what has now arrived. In *kali yuga*, men do not follow the conduct appropriate for *varna*s and *ashrama*s. They see no reason to undertake the *dharma* of the *Rig*, *Sama* and *Yajur Veda*s. In *kali yuga*, marriages and the relationship between a *guru* and a disciple are not in accordance with *dharma*. The norms for a husband and wife are not followed. Nor are they followed for offering oblations to *deva*s through the fire. In *kali yuga*, regardless of the lineage into which he has been born, a powerful man becomes everyone's lord. He is deemed worthy of being bestowed excellent maidens from every *varna*. In *kali yuga*, a *dvija* will be consecrated by whatever means possible. O Maitreya! In *kali yuga*, an act of *prayashchitta* will just be that.[1077] O *brahmana*! In *kali yuga*, anything that is spoken will become a sacred text. In *kali yuga*, everything will be a divinity, and everyone will practice every *ashrama*. In *kali yuga*, fasting, donations of wealth and austerities will be performed as one wishes. Merely undertaking it will become an act of *dharma*. In *kali yuga*, even with a little bit of wealth a man will become supreme and insolent. Women will be proud

[1076] Because the *sandhyamsha*s are added.
[1077] It will only be the act and will not lead to any results.

of their beauty only on the basis of their hair. Gold, jewels, gems and garments will be destroyed. Therefore, in *kali yuga*, hair will be the only ornament for women. Women will desert husbands who do not possess riches. In *kali yuga*, women will choose husbands only on the basis of their wealth. A person who gives away a lot will always become the lord of men. A relationship will be decided on the basis of this lordship and will not be based on nobility of birth. The mind will turn towards material objects and the objective will be to seize any accumulation of material objects. In *kali yuga*, the objective will be *artha* and enjoyment. In *kali yuga*, women will be *svairinis*[1078] and will desire pleasure. Men will desire to obtain wealth, even if it is acquired through illegitimate means. Selfishness will be seen to predominate. Even if requested by a well-wisher, a person will not wish to part with even a quarter of a *pana*.[1079] In *kali yuga*, all men will think of themselves as equal to *brahmana*s. Cows will be honoured only because of the connection that they yield milk. In general, people will suffer from the fear of drought. They will be afflicted by hunger and fear. Everyone's eyes will therefore always be directed towards the sky. Men will be like ascetics, with tubers, roots and fruits as food. Extremely miserable because of lack of rain, they will kill themselves. They will have no protectors and will always suffer on account of famine. In *kali yuga*, the happiness and pleasures of humans will be impeded. They will eat without bathing, without offering oblations into the fire and without honouring gods and guests. When *kali*

[1078] *Svairini*s are loose women who have sex with anyone they want, but only with those from the same *varna*. *Kamini*s are loose women who have sex with anyone they want, irrespective of *varna*. *Pumshchali*s have no sense of discrimination and are almost like harlots. Here, the word *svarini* is used in the broader sense of being loose in morals.

[1079] *Pana* is a small coin, sometimes equated with eighty cowries.

yuga arrives, no one will offer *pinda* or perform water-rites. In *kali yuga*, women will be greedy and short in stature. They will be addicted to eating a lot. They will have many offspring but will be limited in fortune. Women will scratch their heads with both their hands. They will censure the commands of seniors and husbands and pay no heed to them. In *kali yuga*, women will be devoted to nurturing themselves. They will be inferior and will not clean their bodies. They will be harsh and false in speech. They will be wicked in conduct and will wish to associate with those who are evil in conduct. The women of the family will attach themselves to wicked men. Without observing the vows, boys will try to acquire the *Veda*s. Householders will not think of offering oblations or donating. Those in *vanaprastha* will survive on food obtained from villagers. Those who are mendicants will be tied by bonds of friendship and affection. Kings will not protect, but will seize, levying taxes and interest. When *kali yuga* arrives, they will steal the wealth of people. Anyone who possesses excellent horses, chariots and elephants will become a king. In *kali yuga*, anyone who is inferior in strength will become a servant. *Vaishya*s will abandon their own work of agriculture and trade. They will earn a living through artisanship, the work of *shudra*s. Inferior *shudra*s will exhibit the signs of being mendicants and earn subsistence through alms. They will regard resorting to the conduct of *pashanda*s[1080] as good behaviour. People will suffer a lot on account of famine and taxes. Miserable, they will leave for regions where inferior grain, like wheat and barley, can be grown. The path of the *Veda*s will be destroyed, and people will follow the path of *pashanda*s. With *adharma* increasing, lifespans will be limited. Because of terrible austerities that are not in accordance with the sacred texts and because of the sins of kings, men will die

[1080] Heretics.

when they are children. Women will give birth at the age of five, six or seven years. In *kali yuga*, men will have children when they are eight, nine or ten years old. At the age of twelve years, the hair will turn grey. In *kali yuga*, no one will live for more than twenty years of age. In *kali yuga*, wisdom will be limited and since hearts will be wicked, all outwardly signs will be pointless. Here and there, men will be destroyed within a very short period. O Maitreya! Wherever a decline in *dharma* is noticed, the discriminating will understand that to be a sign of an increase in *kali*. O Maitreya! Wherever there is an increase in *pashanda*s, great-souled ones will understand that to be a sign of an increase in *kali*. Wherever there is a decline in the number of people who follow the path of the *Veda*s, the discriminating will understand that to be a sign of an increase in *kali*. O Maitreya! Wherever men who follow *dharma* begin to suffer, the learned will understand that to be the importance of *kali*. Wherever Purushottama, the lord of sacrifices, is not worshipped by men through sacrifices, this should be known as a sign of *kali*'s strength. Wherever people do not like the words of the *Veda*s, but like *pashanda*s instead, the wise and the discriminating understand that to be a sign of an increase in the importance of *kali*. O Maitreya! The lord Vishnu is the lord of the universe and is the creator of everything. Made to deviate by *pashanda*s, people will not worship him. O *brahmana*! Made to deviate by *pashanda*s, people will say, "Who are *deva*s? Who are *dvija*s? What are the *Veda*s? What is the need for purification with water?" Parjanya will only shower down a little bit of rain. The crops will yield limited results. O *brahmana*! When *kali yuga* arrives, all fruits will be limited in substance. Garments will generally be made out of hemp. All large trees will come to resemble the *shami* tree. In *kali yuga*, all *varna*s will generally be like *shudra*s. Grains will generally be fragmented. Milk will generally be that obtained from goats. When *kali yuga* arrives, unguents will

be made out of *ushira*.[1081] O supreme among sages! Men will
hold the father-in-law and the mother-in-law to be superior
to parents and well-wishers will become a beautiful wife, a
brother-in-law and the like. Men will say, "Whose mother?
Whose father? Men have to follow *karma*." Saying this, men
will be devoted to their fathers-in-law. Men will repeatedly be
overwhelmed by taints, in thoughts, words and deeds. Limited
in intelligence, they will perform wicked deeds every day.
Men will be limited in substance. They will be impure and
shameless. When it is *kali yuga*, there will be such miseries
everywhere. There will be no studies, *vashatkara*, *svadha* and
svaha. *Dharma* will be rare and only a few people will be left.
However, with a little bit of effort, men will become excellent
and will achieve what people obtained through austerities in
krita yuga.'[1082]

Chapter 6(2) (Devotion to Vishnu)

Shri Parashara said, 'O Maitreya! O immensely fortunate
one! In this connection, hear what the immensely intelligent
Vyasa told me. On one occasion, there was a discussion
amongst the sages, auspicious in speech, about the time when
a little bit of *dharma* bestows extremely great fruits and
happiness. To clear their doubts, they went to the great sage,
Vedavyasa. O Maitreya! The bulls among sages asked him
about their doubt. O *brahmana*! They saw the sage, my son,
the immensely fortunate Vedavyasa, immersed in the waters
of Jahnavi, having only half finished his bath. The *maharshis*

[1081] A fragrant root.
[1082] Unlike *krita yuga*, a little bit of effort will ensure *dharma* in
kali yuga.

waited for the bathing to be over. They remained on the banks
of that great rivers, seeking refuge amidst a clump of trees.
As he repeatedly immersed himself in the waters of Jahnavi,
they heard my son say, "O *shudra*! *Kali yuga* is virtuous, it is
praiseworthy." As the sages heard these words, he immersed
himself in the waters of the river again. As he arose again, he
exclaimed, "O *shudra*! This is good. This is praiseworthy. You
are blessed." The great sage immersed himself again and said,
"O woman! You are to be praised. You are blessed. Who is
more fortunate than you?" In this way, he finished his bath.
As is proper, the sages observed the norms and approached my
immensely fortunate son. He honoured them and gave them
seats. When they were seated, Satyavati's son asked, "Why
have you come here?" They replied, "We have come here to
ask you about a doubt. But that can wait. Please tell us about
something else. You said *kali yuga* is praiseworthy and that
a *shudra* and a woman are to be praised. O illustrious one!
You repeatedly addressed them as being fortunate. O great
sage! If this is not a secret, we wish to hear everything about
this. After you have told us about this, we will ask you about
our need." Addressed by the sage in this way, Vyasa smiled
and spoke to them. "O best among sages! Hear about why
I repeatedly said praiseworthy. What can be accomplished in
ten years in *krita yuga*, one year in *treta yuga* and one month
in *dvapara yuga*, can be accomplished in a day and a night
in *kali yuga*. O *brahmanas*! I mean the fruits of austerities,
brahmacharya and *japa*. Since a man can obtain all that, I
said *kali yuga* is to be praised. What is obtained in *krita yuga*
through *dhyana*, in *tretya yuga* through performing sacrifices
and in *dvapara yuga* through worship, is obtained in *kali yuga*
through chanting Keshava's name. In *kali yuga*, a man obtains
excellent *dharma* through a little bit of effort. O ones who
know about *dharma*! That is the reason I am satisfied with
kali yuga. Formerly, *dvijas* received the *Vedas* after observing

vows. They achieved *dharma* by following the norms and
performing sacrifices. Since they were not performed with due
control, reciting accounts, being fed and the performance of
sacrifices by those known as *brahmana*s was futile and led to
their downfall. Since these tasks were not performed properly,
there were taints in everything. Though food, drink and other
things were obtained by *brahmana*s, they did not obtain what
they desired through this. In everything that they did, they
were under the control of others. Therefore, the *brahmana*s
conquered their own worlds only after great hardships. The
*shudra*s were more blessed. They served *dvija*s, adhered to
their rights of *paka yajna* and conquered their own worlds.
They did not face distinctions about what should be eaten and
what should not be eaten, what should be drunk and what
should not be drunk. O tigers among sages! Since they had
no such rules, they were praiseworthy. If a man does not act
against his own *dharma*, he always obtains riches. Following
the norms, he must then perform sacrifices and donate these to
worthy recipients. O best among *brahmana*s! There are great
difficulties in earning wealth, preserving it and employing it
in the appropriate way. For men, all of these are known to
be mysterious. O best among *brahmana*s! After going through
these kinds of difficulties, men duly conquer their own worlds,
those of Prajapati and others. O *brahmana*s! However, in
thoughts, words and deeds, a woman only has to serve her
husband. Through this alone, she obtains auspicious worlds
that are equal to his. Unlike men, she does not have to go
through great hardships. Hence, I spoke of a woman as the
third one[1083] to be praised. O *brahmana*s! After this, tell me
about the reason why you have come. Ask me what you wish,
and I will answer clearly." The *rishi*s said, "O great sage! You
have already accurately answered the question we intended to

[1083] After *kali yuga* and *shudra*.

ask you." At this, Krishna Dvaipayana laughed. The eyes of
the ascetics who had come dilated in wonder and he spoke to
them. "Through my divine insight, I knew about the question
you intended to ask. In that connection, I uttered the words,
'Praiseworthy! Praiseworthy!' In *kali yuga*, *dharma* can be
achieved with a little bit of effort. Through his own qualities, a
man can cleanse every kind of sin. O best among *brahmanas*!
Shudras obtain this through serving *dvijas*, women by serving
their husbands. That is the reason for my view that these three
are the most blessed. In *krita yuga* and the others, *dvijas* achieve
dharma through a great deal of effort. O ones who know
about *dharma*! O *brahmanas*! I have thus told you what you
intended, without your having to ask me. What else should I
do?" The *brahmanas* repeatedly worshipped and praised Vyasa
and returned to wherever they had come from. Because of what
Vyasa said, they became certain. O immensely fortunate one! I
have also spoken to you about this mystery. Though *kali yuga*
is extremely evil, it possesses this great quality. I will now tell
you about the withdrawal of the universe and *prakrita pralaya*.
You asked me about that.'

Chapter 6(3) (*Parardha* and *Pralaya*)

Shri Parashara said, 'For all creatures, there are three
kinds of withdrawal, *naimittika*, *prakritika* and *atyantika*
pralaya. The withdrawal at the end of a *kalpa* is Brahma or
naimittika, the one that leads to *moksha* is said to be *atyantika*
and *prakrita* occurs at the end of two *parardhas*.'[1084]

[1084] *Naimittika pralaya* occurs at the end of Brahma's day,
prakrita/prakritika at the end of Brahma's lifespan and *atyantika* is
individual, when a being attains *moksha* and is freed from *samsara*.

Maitreya said, 'O illustrious one! Please tell me about the measurement of a *parardha*. Double that is known as *prakrita* withdrawal.'

Shri Parashara replied, 'O *brahmana*! Following the decimal system of enumeration, a *parardha* is known as the eighteenth position.[1085] O *brahmana*! *Prakrita pralaya* occurs after two *parardha*s. At that time, everything that is manifest is withdrawn into the unmaniufest origin. The smallest unit of measurement is *matra* or *nimesha*, the twinkling of the human eye. Fifteen *nimesha*s are said to make up a *kashtha* and thirty *kashtha*s make up one *kala*. Fifteen *kala*s make up one *nadika*. O supreme among *brahmana*s! In a vessel that is six and a half *pala*s[1086] in weight, with sides measuring four *angula*s, a hole that is four *angula*s in length is made and a golden *wire* four *angula*s long and one *masha* in weight is inserted into it. The time taken for this to be submerged in water is one *nadika*. In Magadha, the measurement is for water to pass through a *prastha*.[1087] O supreme among *brahmana*s! Two *nadika*s make up one *muhurta*. Thirty *muhurta*s make up a day and night.[1088] There are thirty days in a month. Twelve months make up a year and this is equivalent to a day and night in heaven. Three hundred and sixty human years amount to one year for those who are enemies of *asura*s. Twelve thousand

---

[1085] Ten followed by eighteen zeros, ten to the power eighteen.

[1086] A *pala* is a measure of weight, but its stated weight varies across sources. Thirty grams is a rough indication. *Angula* is the length of a finger. *Masha* is just short of one gram. This entire *shloka* is very cryptic and impossible to understand. Therefore, we have expanded the translation, so as to make the meaning clear.

[1087] A *prastha* is thirty-two *pala*s. Instead of six-and-a-half *pala*s, the vessel has a weight of thirty-two *pala*s.

[1088] Therefore, a *muhurta* is forty-eight minutes and a *nadika* is twenty-four minutes.

divine years are said to amount to a set of the four *yugas*.[1089]
One thousand *mahayugas* amount to one of Brahma's days. O
great sage! This is a *kalpa* and within this, there are fourteen
Manus. O Maitreya! At the end of this, Brahma's *naimittika
pralaya* occurs. O Maitreya! Its nature is terrible. Listen to my
words. I will tell you about *prakrita pralaya* later. At the end
of one thousand *mahayugas*, the earth is almost destroyed. For
one hundred years, a terrible drought occurs. O best among
sages! Almost every being on earth that has limited energy and
substance suffers a great deal and is destroyed. The illustrious
and undecaying Vishnu assumes the form of Rudra. He makes
all the subjects, headed for destruction, a part of his own self.
O supreme sage! The illustrious Vishnu is stationed in the form
of the sun, with seven rays, and drinks up all the water. O
Maitreya! After having drunk up all the water in the creatures
and beings, he conveys the entire surface of the earth to
destruction. The oceans, the rivers, the mountains, the springs
in the mountains and all the water in the nether regions is
conveyed to destruction. There is a lack of water. Having drunk
up the water, seven suns and their rays are generated through
his powers. Those seven blazing suns heat from above and
below. O *brahmana*! They scorch the three worlds and nether
regions. O *brahmana*! The blazing and resplendent suns scorch
the three worlds. Nothing liquid is left in the mountains, rivers
and oceans. O *brahmana*! Everywhere in the three worlds, the
trees and water are scorched. The earth assumes the form of
the back of a tortoise. Rudra, the destroyer of the creation of
beings, assumes the form of a fire, the fire of destruction. Using
the breath of the serpent Shesha, he burns the nether regions
from below. The great blaze scorches all the nether regions and
reaching the earth, burns down everything on the surface of the
earth. There are extremely terrible garlands of fire everywhere

[1089] That is, a *mahayuga*.

in *bhuvarloka* and *svarloka*. Giant storms swirl around. All
the three worlds come to resemble a frying pan. Surrounded
by whirling flames, all the residents, mobile and immobile,
lose their strength. O great sage! Suffering from the heat, the
residents of the two worlds, who possess the right, seek refuge
in Maharloka. But there too, beings are scorched by the great
heat. Surrounded by this grief, seeking to save themselves from
the calamity, they go to Janaloka. O supreme among sages!
Having scorched the entire universe in his form of Rudra,
from the breath that is expelled from his mouth, Janardana
creates clouds. They resemble elephants born in excellent
lineages and thunder, tinged with lightning. These dense and
terrible *samvartaka* clouds[1090] cover the sky. Some are as dark
as blue lotuses, others have the complexion of Kumuda.[1091]
Some clouds have the complexion of smoke, other clouds are
yellow. Some have the complexion of donkeys, others have the
complexion of the juice of lac. Some are like lapis lazuli, others
are like blue sapphire. Some have hues like the conch shell or
the moon. Others are like *jati* and *kunda* flowers.[1092] Some
have complexions like the *indragopa* insect,[1093] others have
the complexion of red arsenic. Others have the complexion
of yellow pigeons. Some have the complexion of lotus petals,
other clouds rise up atop other clouds. Some have the forms of
excellent cities, others are like mountains. Some clouds have
the complexion of the turrets of mansions, others have the
complexion of barren ground. They are gigantic in form and
with their loud roars, they fill up the firmament. O *brahmana*!
Extremely dense, they shower down and pacify that extremely

[1090] Clouds of destruction.
[1091] The name of a gigantic elephant that guards the southern
direction. But *kumuda* is also a waterlily.
[1092] Both are types of white jasmine.
[1093] A reddish insect, sometimes identified with a firefly.

terrible fire that has spread everywhere in the three worlds.
When the fire has been extinguished, the clouds shower down,
night and day, for one hundred years. O supreme among sages!
They shower and flood the entire universe. O supreme among
*brahmana*s! The torrential downpour floods and deluges
bhuloka and *bhuvarloka*, and all that is above. The worlds are
enveloped in darkness and everything mobile and immobile
is destroyed. The giant clouds shower down for more than
one hundred years. O supreme among sages! All this happens
to whatever is not eternal at the end of a *kalpa*, because of
paramatman Vasudeva's greatness.'

Chapter 6(4) (*Prakritika Pralaya*)

Shri Parashara said, 'O great sage! The water approaches
the place of the *saptarshi*s[1094] and everything in the three
worlds becomes a single ocean of water. O Maitreya! After
more than one hundred years have passed, the wind generated
from Vishnu's breathing dispels those clouds. The unthinkable
and illustrious creator of all beings has all the beings in him.
He is the origin but is without a beginning. He drinks up all
the wind in the firmament. The lord lies down on that single
ocean of water, resting on Shesha. Hari is the creator of
everything. Assuming the form of the *brahman*, the illustrious
one lies down. Sanaka and the other *siddha*s who have gone to
Janaloka praise him. Those who desire *moksha* and have gone
to Brahmaloka think about him. In his own divine *maya*, he
lies down in *yoganidra*.[1095] Madhusudana, known as Vasudeva,
thinks about himself. O Maitreya! This withdrawal is known

[1094] The Great Dipper, part of Ursa Major.
[1095] Asleep, immersed in *yoga*.

as *naimittika*. This is because Hari, in his form of the *brahman*, lies down as *nimitta*.[1096] When the one who is the *atman* of everything is awake, the universe moves. When Achyuta lies down in his bed of *maya*, everything shuts down. One thousand *mahayuga*s are one day for the one who originated from the lotus.[1097] When the entire universe is reduced to a single ocean of water, it is said to be night for him. When he wakes up at the end of the night, Aja[1098] creates again. As has been told to you earlier, it is Vishnu who assumes the form of Brahma to do all this. O *brahmana*! This *pralaya*, the withdrawal at the end of a *kalpa*, is known as *naimittika*.[1099] I have told you about this. Hear about *prakrita pralaya* next. O sage! Through lack of rain and other associated things, everything in the nether regions and in all the worlds is completely destroyed. Mahat and the other specific transformations are destroyed. This withdrawal is brought about when Krishna so desires it. First, water devours smell and the other attributes of the earth. When smell is taken away, the earth is ready for dissolution. When the subtle attribute of smell vanishes, the earth merges into water. The forceful water is everywhere and emits a loud roar. It fills everything, exists everywhere and roams around. Everything, right up to Lokaloka,[1100] is enveloped in waves of water. The attribute of water is drunk up by fire. When taste, the attribute of water, is destroyed, the water is severely scorched and is also destroyed. With taste, the attribute of water, destroyed, merges into fire. The energy of fire surrounds water from every direction. That fire pervades every direction and water

---

[1096] Thus, the expression *naimittika*, *nimitta* means cause.

[1097] Brahma.

[1098] The one without birth, Brahma.

[1099] This is secondary dissolution, at the end of one of Brahma's days. *Prakrita pralaya* occurs at the time of primary dissolution.

[1100] The mountain that separates the region illuminated by the sun from the region not illuminated by the sun.

is withdrawn. Fire gradually fills up everything in the universe. The rays are everywhere, above, below and diagonal. Form is the subtle attribute of fire, giving it luster, but fire is drunk up by wind. When that is destroyed, everything is filled up by wind. The subtle attribute of fire is form and fire loses its form. When fire has been pacified, the great wind starts to blow. The entire world is without light, since all that energy is inside wind. It is withdrawn inside wind, which was its origin. The wind blows in the ten directions, above, below and diagonal. Space devours touch, the subtle attribute of wind. Wind is pacified and space remains, without any cover. It has no form, taste, touch or smell and is without any embodied form. It is not manifest but fills everything. The subtle attribute of space is sound, and this circles everything. Everything is enveloped by space, with its subtle attribute of sound. The attribute of sound is next devoured by *ahamkara*.[1101] The senses exist simultaneously with *ahamkara*. However, since *ahamkara* is based on pride[1102] it is said that *ahamkara* has a *tamas* characteristic. *Mahabuddhi*,[1103] with its attribute of intelligence, devours *ahamkara*. This great space exists inside and outside the universe. In this way, *Mahabuddhi* and the seven *prakriti*s are progressively drawn into each other.[1104] Everything is enveloped in darkness and merges into the cosmic egg, which is in the water. The seven *dvipa*s, ending in the oceans, and the seven worlds, along with the mountains, are surrounded by water, which is drunk up by fire. Fire merges into wind and wind finds its disssolution

---

[1101] The text uses the word *bhutadi* (origin of the elements), meaning *ahamkara*.

[1102] *Abhimana*.

[1103] The great intellect.

[1104] This is the essence of *samkhya* philosophy and the seven *prakriti*s presumably mean the five elements, the mind and *ahamkara*. This use of the word *prakriti* is not to be confused with the subsequent Prakriti.

in space. Space is devoured by *ahamkara* and *ahamkara* is
devoured by *Mahat*.[1105] O *brahmana*! Prakriti devours Mahat
and everything else. O great sage! Prakriti is that in which all
the *gunas*[1106] are in balance. Nothing is excessive or deficient.
Prakriti is said to be the cause. Pradhana[1107] is the supreme
cause beyond this. Prakriti is everywhere, sometimes manifest
and sometimes unmanifest. O Maitreya! The manifest part of
Prakriti merges into the unmanifest part. After this, there is a
single pure *akshara*[1108] that pervades everything. O Maitreya!
A portion of the *paramatman* exists within all beings. When
everything is destroyed, all conceptions of names and categories
are also destroyed. What exists is only consciousness. This
knowledge about the *paramatman* is *jnana*. This is the *brahman*,
the supreme abode. This is the *paramatman*, the supreme lord.
This is Vishnu, who exists everywhere. On obtaining him, no
one returns. I have told you that Prakriti has both a manifest
part and an unmanifest part. Both Purusha and Prakriti merge
into the *paramatman*. The *paramatman* is Parameshvara, the
foundation of everything. In the *Veda*s and Vedanta, he is
chanted about, using the name of Vishnu. There are two kinds
of rites in the *Veda*s, with *nivritti* and *pravritti*.[1109] In both of
these, Purusha is worshipped in all his forms through sacrifices.
Using the paths of the *Rig Veda*, the *Yajur Veda* and the *Sama
Veda*, he is worshipped through *pravritti*. He is the lord of
the sacrifice. He is Purusha. He is the being in the sacrifice.
He is Purushottama. He is also worshipped through the path
of *jnana*. His *atman* is *jnana*. He is the embodiment of *jnana*.

[1105] *Mahat* is another word for *Mahabuddhi*.
[1106] *Sattva*, *rajas* and *tamas*.
[1107] Purusha, also referred to in these sections as the unmanifest
part of Prakriti.
[1108] The one without destruction, the *paramatman*.
[1109] *Nivritti* is detachment from fruits and renunciation of action.
Pravritti is action with a desire for the fruits.

When this path of *yoga* and *nivritti* is used, Vishnu confers the fruits of emancipation. There are things that are spoken about through *hrasva*, *dirgha* and *pluta* vowels and there are things that are beyond speech.[1110] The undecaying Vishnu is all of these. Purushottama is manifest and he is unmanifest. He is the *paramatman*. He is the *atman* of the universe. Hari assumes the form of the universe. It is into him that the manifest and unmanifest forms of Prakriti dissolve. O Maitreya! Purusha also merges into the undifferentiated *atman*. O Maitreya! I have spoken to you about a period of time that lasts for two *parardha*s. When Prakriti is manifest, this is spoken about as the Lord Vishnu's day. O great sage! When Prakriti merges into Purusha, that duration of time is his night. However, for the *paramatman*, there is no real night or day. O *brahmana*! For the lord, such expressions are only used to articulate matters. O Maitreya! I have thus spoken to you about *prakrita laya*. O *brahmana*! Now hear about *atyantika* withdrawal.'

Chapter 6(5) (*Atyantika Pralaya*)

Shri Parashara said, 'O Maitreya! After learning about the three kinds of torment, *adhyatmika* and the others,[1111] a learned man obtains *jnana*, develops non-attachment and proceeds to *atyantika* dissolution. There are two kinds of *adhyatmika* suffering, physical and mental. The physical suffering can of many types. Listen. Pain in the head, cold, fever,

---

[1110] *Hrasva* or short vowels are pronounced over one *matra* (a prosodial or syllabic instant), *dirgha* or long vowels over two *matra*s and *pluta* or elongated vowels over three *matra*s.

[1111] Relating to *adhidaivika* (destiny), *adhibhoutika* (nature) and *adhyatmika* (one's own nature).

rheumatism, fistula, enlargement of the spleen, piles, swelling, asthma, nausea, disease of the eyes, diarrhea, leprosy, those that are described as diseases of the limbs and many others—these result from tortments of the body. You should now hear about mental torments. O best among *brahmanas*! There are many kinds of torments of the mind—desire, anger, fear, hatred, greed, confusion, grief, sorrow, jealousy, dishonour, envy and malice. O best among *brahmanas*! These are the different kinds of mental torments and there is more than one. These different kinds of torments are said to be of the *adhyatmika* type. Men suffer from *adhibhoutika* torments on account of animals, birds, other men, *pishacha*s, *uraga*s, *rakshasa*s and reptiles. O foremost among supreme *brahmanas*! *Adhidaivika* torments are said to be because of cold, heat, wind, rain, water and lightning.'

'O supreme among sages! Due to conception, birth, old age, ignorance, death and hell, there are thousands of different kinds of hardships. In the womb, the delicate being is surrounded by a lot of excrement. Engulfed in this, its back, neck and joints in the bones are broken. The mother eats food that is excessively pungent, bitter, sharp, hot and salty and makes it suffer a lot. Confined in this way, it suffers a lot of pain. It is not lord of its own self and cannot stretch or contract its limbs. Lying down in the great mire of urine and excrement, it suffers in every possible way. It is breathless but is conscious and remembers hundreds of births. Because of the bondage of its own *karma*, it suffers from this great misery in the womb. When the infant is born, its face is smeared with urine, blood, excrement and semen. The joints in its body suffer from the wind known as *prajapatya*. When it is born, those strong winds make it face downwards. Suffering, it emerges from the mother's womb with a great deal of difficulty. When it is touched by the wind outside, it suffers from a great loss of consciousness. O supreme among sages!

When it is born, all its *vijnana* is destroyed. Its limbs seem to be pierced by thorns. It seems to be sliced with saws. It falls down on the ground, like an insect from a wound full of pus. It isn't capable of scratching itself or turning around. Someone else is its master. It is only through the desires of others that it can be bathed and obtain drink and food. When it lies down on a dirty bed, it is bitten by insects and gnats. Though it is bitten by them, it is incapable of repulsing them. There are many kinds of hardship at the time of birth and there are other kinds of miseries after birth. When he becomes a child, he faces *adhibhoutika* suffering. Enveloped by the darkness of ignorance, a man is foolish inside. He does not know, "Where have I come from? Who am I? Where will I go? What is my *atman*? Why am I fettered in these bonds? What is the reason? Or is there no reason? What should be done? What should not be done? What should be spoken? What should not be spoken? What is *dharma*? What is *adharma*? What constitutes it and how? What is duty? What is not duty? What is good? What is bad?" In this way, he is foolish, like an animal, because of the great power of ignorance. Addicted to the penis and the stomach, men suffer from pain. Ignorance is due to the sentiment of *tamas*. O *brahmana*! Though there is an inclination to undertake tasks, because of ignorance about what should be done, *karma* suffers. Learned ones have said that when *karma* suffers, one goes to hell. Therefore, those who are ignorant suffer pain in this world and in the world hereafter. A man's body is devastated by old age and the body turns flaccid. The teeth decay and are dislodged. The sinews and nerves are covered by wrinkles. The pupils are fixed towards the sky. Hair sticks out of the nostrils. The body trembles. All the creature's bones stick out. The joints of the bones in the back are bent. Since the digestive fire no longer functions, he eats little. He can only move a little. He can move, rise, lie down, sit or exert himself with a great deal of effort. Sight and hearing weaken. He exudes saliva that smears his face. Unable to control anything, he looks forward to dying. He is incapable of feeling anything that happens at that moment. He cannot remember anything. He has to make tremendous efforts to speak even a little. Because of problems with breathing, he remains awake in the night. When he is aged, others have to make him get up, or lie down. He is dishonoured by his own servants, sons and wives. All purity becomes lax, but he still retains his desire for pleasures and eating. His family members laugh at him, and his relatives no longer feel any attachment towards him. He feels and remembers everything that he has done, as if they have been done in some other birth. Remembering and tormented, he heaves deep sighs. These are the miseries he suffers in old age. Now hear about the miseries he faces at the time of death. His neck, hands and legs become loose. The man keeps trembling terribly. Because of these miseries and under the control of others, he sighs repeatedly. He repeatedly tries to find strength in his knowledge. Extremely anxious because of a sense of ownership, he wonders, "What will happen to my gold, grain, sons, wives, servants and home?" Major ailments strike at his inner organs, like terrible saws. Fierce arrows of such fears pierce his mind. The pupils of his eyes roll, and he repeatedly flings his hand and feet around. His throat and palate turn dry, and he cries out in distress. The *udana* breath makes him suffer and chokes his throat. He is enveloped in a great heat, and he is afflicted by hunger and thirst. He leaves the body with great difficulty and is oppressed by Yama's servants. With great difficulty, he assumes another body in which he undergoes pain. Men face many other terrible sufferings at the time of death. When men die, they go to *naraka*. Hear about this. Yama's servants seize him with nooses and strike him with rods. The sight of Yama is terrible. The path that takes one to Yama is also terrible. O *brahmana*! It is strewn with

terrible mire, sand, fires, machines and weapons. The pain in
each *naraka* is impossible to tolerate. Saws and black crucibles
are used to scorch. They are struck with battle-axes. They are
buried in pits in the ground. They are impaled on spikes and
forced to enter the mouths of tigers. Vultures devour them and
they are fed to wolves. They are boiled in oil and smeared with
corrosive mud. They are hurled down from above and catapults
are used to fling them away. Because of the sins, there are many
hardships in hell. O *brahmana*! The number of miseries in
naraka cannot be counted. O best among *brahmana*s! It is not
that miseries are faced only in hell. Because of the fear of falling
down, there is no respite in heaven either. He is conceived in a
womb again and takes birth again. He finds himself in a womb
again. Having been born, he dies again. Sometimes, he dies as
soon as he is born. Sometimes, he dies in childhood or youth.
Sometimes, he dies when he is middle-aged or old. As long
as he is alive, he is overwhelmed by many kinds of miseries.
He is just like cotton seeds in filaments that are being woven.
Men always face miseries in earning and preserving wealth
and when that wealth is destroyed. O Maitreya! Anything
that men find pleasing has the seed of misery. It is this seed
that gives rise to the tree of unhappiness. Men endeavor to
find a lot of happiness in wives, sons, friends, prosperity,
homes, fields, wealth and other things. However, these bring
unhappiness. Tormented by the grief of *samsara*, the senses
are scorched. Without the tree that yields emancipation, how
can men possibly obtain happiness?'

'Thus, three kinds of misery are caused by the sense of
"mine". They make one suffer in the womb, at the time of
birth and old age. Though they may be seen to exhibit the signs
of delight, they actually cause misery. It is held that the only
medication is *atyantika* dissolution into the illustrious one.
Therefore, a learned man must make efforts to achieve this. O
great sage! The means of obtaining him are said to be *jnana* and

karma. Jnana is said to be of two types, from the *agama* texts and from discrimination.[1112] The *agama* texts are full of *shabda-brahma. Para-brahma* is achieved through discrimination.[1113] Ignorance is like a blinding darkness, the *jnana* that results from the sense of discrimination is like a lamp. O *brahmana rishi*! *Jnana* that results from a sense of discrimination is like the sun. O supreme sage! Manu has spoken about the meaning of the *Vedas*. That should be remembered. In this connection, I will state it. Listen to my words. There are two *brahman*s that should be known, *shabda-brahma* and *para-brahma*. If one is conversant with *shabda-brahma*, one achieves *para-brahma*. The *Atharva Veda* has said that both kinds of learning must be understood. The achievement of *para-brahma* is without decay, *Rig Veda* and the others lead to the other one. Those who desire emancipation should comprehend the supreme refuge of the *brahman*. He is not manifest. He is without old age. He cannot be thought of. He is without birth. He is without decay. He cannot be indicated. He has no form. He has no hands or feet. He is not associated with anything else. He is the worthy one. He goes everywhere. He is eternal. He is the cause behind the origin of beings. Everything that deserves to be pervaded is pervaded by him. All the learned ones look on him that way. He is the one who is spoken about in the words of the *shruti* texts. He is subtle. He is Vishnu's supreme destination. The *paramatman*'s nature is spoken of as Bhagavat. The word Bhagavat is used for the original *atman*, who is without decay. Anyone who listens to this and comprehends its true meaning, knows the truth. This is the supreme *jnana* that should be known, it is the essence of the three.[1114] O *brahmana*! The *brahman* cannot be

---

[1112] *Viveka.*

[1113] *Shabda-brahma* is the ritualistic elements of the *Vedas*, the *karmakanda. Para-brahma* is the *paramatman.*

[1114] The three *Vedas.*

perceived through any words. The word Bhagavat is only used for acts of worship. The supreme *brahman* cannot be described through words. He is only a great and pure power. O Maitreya! The word Bhagavat means the cause behind all causes. The "bha" indicates the one who nurtures and supports.[1115] O sage! The "ga" indicates the one who is the creator and leader, the one who causes movement.[1116] "Bhaga" signifies the six attributes of all lordship, valour, fame, prosperity, *jnana* and non-attachment.[1117] "Va" signifies that all beings reside in him and he resides in the *atman*s of all beings.[1118] The one without decay is the lord of all beings. O Maitreya! Such is the great word Bhagavat. Vasudeva is the supreme *brahman* and there is no one else. This word is hence speficially used for the one who is the object of worship. However, without that context of worship, the word is also used in a general sense. If a person knows about the origin and dissolution of beings and about their progress, if he can distinguish between learning and ignorance, the word Bhagavat is also applied to him.[1119] When the word Bhagavat is used, this means all *jnana*, powers, strength, prosperity, valour and energy exist, with inferior qualities being absent. The *paramatman* resides in all beings. As the *atman* who resides in all beings, he is known as Vasudeva. In ancient times, Keshidhvaja was asked by Khandikya Janaka about the true meaning of the word Vasudeva, and this is exactly what he told him.[1120] "The Lord Vasudeva is the one who resides in all beings and he is inside all beings. He is the

[1115] The root verb means to nourish.

[1116] The root verb means to go.

[1117] *Bhaga* means excellent/glorious.

[1118] The root verb means to reside.

[1119] That is, the word Bhagavat is used for Vishnu, but it is also used for a wise person.

[1120] Both Keshidhvaja and Khandikya were born in the Janaka dynasty, as will become clear later.

creator and the arranger of the universe." O sage! Though he
assumes all the forms in Prakriti, he is beyond the taints of
transformations and *gunas*. He is beyond all coverings and is
the universal *atman*. He is inside everything in the universe.
He possesses all the auspicious qualities. With a little bit of
his powers, he creates all the categories of beings. To bring
about the success of everything in the universe, depending on
his wishes, he assumes different forms. There are no limits to
his great energy, strength and prosperity. Through his own
energy and powers, he is a reservoir of every kind of quality.
He is greater than the greatest. He is the lord of all those who
are supreme. When one reaches him, there is no hardship.
In his individual and collective forms, he is Ishvara.[1121] He
is not manifest. He manifests himself in his own forms. His
own form is evident. He is the lord of everything. His eyes are
everywhere. He knows everything. He possesses all the powers.
He is known as Parameshvara.[1122] He is said to be without any
taints. He is pure and supreme. He sparkles in his single form.
He can be comprehended, one can see him and one can go
to him, through *jnana*. Everything else that is spoken about is
ignorance.'

Chapter 6(6) (Keshidhvaja and Khandikya)

Shri Parashara said, 'Through studies and self-control,
Purushottama can be seen. It is read that either is a method
for attaining the *brahman*. Self-studies can lead to *yoga* and
that, in turn, perfects self-studying. The reverse also happens.
The *parmatman* becomes evident through excellence in self-

[1121] The lord.
[1122] The supreme lord.

studies and *yoga*. Self-studying is one eye, while *yoga* is the other. One is incapable of seeing the *brahman* with eyes made out of flesh.'

Maitreya said, 'O illustrious one! I wish to know about *yoga*. Please tell me. Knowing that, I can see Parameshvara, who holds up everything.'

Shri Parashara replied, 'In ancient times, Keshidhvaja spoke about *yoga* to the great-souled Khandikya Janaka.[1123] I will tell you about this.'

Maitreya asked, 'O *brahmana*! Who was Khandikya and who was Keshidvaja? In connection with *yoga*, how did the conversation between them take place?'

Shri Parashara replied, 'Dharmadhvaja, of the Janaka lineage, had two sons, Mitadhvaja and Kritadhvaja. Kritadhvaja was a king who was always interested in *adhyatma* and Kritadhvaja had a son who was known as King Keshidhvaja. Mitadhvaja's son was Khandikya Janaka. Khanidkya, lord of the earth, followed the path of *karma*. Keshidhvaja was accomplished in knowledge about the *atman*. These two wished to defeat each other and Keshidhvaja drove Khandikya away from his kingdom. With limited means and driven away from his kingdom, with his priest and ministers, he roamed around in forts and mountains. Since he still sought refuge in ignorance, he undertook many sacrifices. He wished to obtain knowledge about the *brahman* and free himself from ignorance, which is death.'

'On one occasion, the supreme among those who know about *yoga*[1124] was engaged in a sacrifice and in a desolate forest,

[1123] In the Janaka dynasty, Dharmadhvaja had two sons, Kritadhvaja and Mitadhvaja. Kritadhvaja's son was Keshidhvaja, while Mitadhvaja's son was Khandikya. These details are given in the Bhagavata Purana.

[1124] That is, Keshidhvaja.

a fierce tiger killed his cow, the one needed for *dharma*.[1125]
Hearing that the cow had been killed by a tiger, the king asked
the officiating priests about the recommended *prayashchitta*.
They answered, "We don't know. Please ask Kasheru." When
asked, Kasheru told him, "O Indra among kings! I do not
know. Please ask Bhargava Shunaka. He knows." O sage!
When he went and asked him, listen to what he heard in reply.
"Like Kasheru, I don't know the answer. With the exception
of your enemy, Khandikya, whom you have defeated, there
is no one on earth who will be able to answer." O sage! He
responded, "O best among sages! I will go and ask my enemy.
If he does not kill me, I will go and ask him everything about
prayashchitta and perform the great sacrifice he tells me about.
Perhaps I will accomplish complete *yoga* then." Saying this,
the king attired himself in black antelope skin and ascended his
chariot. He went to the forest where the immensely intelligent
Khandikya was. Khandikya saw that his enemy was arriving.
His eyes turned coppery-red in rage. He strung his bow and
spoke to him. Khanikya said, "Wearing armour of black
antelope skin, you think that you cannot be killed. I will kill
you. Wearing black antelope skin, you think that I will not
strike you. O foolish one! But think about the deer who used
to have the black antelope skins on their backs. You and I have
struck them with fierce arrows. In that way, I will kill you. You
will not escape with your life. O evil-minded one! You are an
assassin. You are an enemy who has stolen my kingdom from
me." Keshidhvaja replied, "O Khandikya! I have come here
to ask you about a doubt, not to kill you. Therefore, restrain
your rage and do not think about releasing your arrow." At
this, the immensely intelligent Khandikya consulted with all his
ministers and priests. All the ministers said, "Your enemy has
come under your subjugation and should be killed. When he

[1125] The cow yielded products required for the sacrifice.

has been killed, the entire earth will come under your control." Khandikya replied, "When he has been killed, there is no doubt that the entire earth will come under my control. However, even though the entire earth becomes mine, he will conquer the world hereafter. On the other hand, if I do not kill him, he will have the earth and I will conquer those worlds. I do not think the earth is superior to conquering those worlds. The conquest of the world hereafter is for eternity. The conquest of the earth is for a limited period. Therefore, I will not kill him. I will answer what he asks me." Therefore, Khandikya Janaka approached his enemy and said, "Ask everything that you want, and I will answer what you ask." O *brahmana*! He told him everything that had happened, about the killing of the cow required for *dharma*. Having told him, he asked him about the *prayashchitta* that should be undertaken. O *brahmana*! Accordingly, he told him everything about the recommended *prayashchitta* for a situation like this.'

'Learning about this, he took his leave of the great-souled one. He went to the sacrificial grounds and performed all the rituals. Having performed all the rituals in the due order, he had his *avabhritha* bath. Having done all this, the king thought. "I have worshipped all the *brahmana*s. I have honoured all the officiating priests. I have given all those who seek whatever they wish for. Depending on what they deserve, I have done everything for everyone. Nevertheless, why do I feel that all the rituals have not been completed?" The great king thought in this way and remembered. "I have not given Khandikya the *dakshina* due to a *guru*." Ascending his chariot again, the king departed. O Maitreya! He went to the thick and impenetrable place where Khandikya was. Seeing that he had arrived again, Khandikya raised up his weapon. Seeing that he had made up his mind to kill him, the king spoke to him again. "O Khandikya! I have not come here to harm you. Do not be angry. I have come to you because I have not given the required donation to my *guru*. Following your instructions, I have properly completed the entire sacrifice. I now wish to give something to you. Please ask for the *dakshina* due to a *guru*." The king consulted with his ministers again. "As a *guru*, what should I ask for?" The ministers asked him to ask for the entire kingdom. Someone who doesn't have soldiers should always ask for the kingdom from the enemy. The immensely intelligent king, Khandikya, laughed and spoke to them. "I will be lord of the earth for a limited period of time. Why should I ask for that? It is true that you are accomplished ministers in the pursuit of *artha*. But there is no one here who is accomplished in the pursuit of the supreme objective." Having said this, the king went to Keshidhvaja and asked, "Is it certain that you will give a *dakshina* to your *guru*?" When he agreed, Khandikya told him, "You are accomplished in the supreme objective. You possess *vijnana* about the *atman*. If you wish to give me, your *guru*, something, tell me about the *karma* that pacifies hardships. That alone will be sufficient."'

Chapter 6(7) (The Path of *Yoga*)

'Keshidhvaja asked, "Why did you not ask for the kingdom, bereft of all thorns? The mind of *kshatriyas* is such that there is nothing that is loved as much as the obtaining of a kingdom."'

'Khandikya replied, "O Keshidhvaja! Listen to the reason why I did not ask for that. There are many taints associated with a kingdom and only the ignorant crave it. For *kshatriyas*, the *dharma* is that one should protect subjects and follow *dharma* in fighting, one should kill those who are against one's own kingdom. Since you have taken it away from someone who was incapable, no taint is attached to you. I was bound in ignorance, and you conquered someone from the bond of ignorance. My selfish desire for the kingdom originated from greed towards something that only yields limited pleasure. The taints due to others do not constrain proper *dharma*. It is the view of the virtuous that this is *dharma* only for *kshatra-bandhu*s.[1126] One should not crave. Since that would have been based on ignorance, I did not ask you for the kingdom. Only those who are ignorant crave after a kingdom. Their minds are overwhelmed by a sense of 'mine'. They are insolent because of a great sense of *ahamkara*. I am not like them."'

Shri Parashara continued, 'Delighted, King Keshidhvaja praised these words. Happy, he told Khandikya Janaka, "Listen to my words."'

'Keshidhava said, "I am overcome by the ignorance of 'I'. I wish to undertake works to overcome death. I rule over the kingdom and undertake many kinds of sacrifices. However, all these pleasures reduce my store of good merits. Therefore, it is good fortune that your mind has turned towards the prosperity of discrimination. O descendant of the lineage! Therefore, hear about the true nature of ignorance. The intellect takes what is not the *atman* to be the *atman*. Hence, the mind takes what is not one's own to be 'mine'. In the tree that is *samsara*, there are two seeds of ignorance.[1127] The body is made out of the five elements. However, the one occupying the body is enveloped by delusion. With his mind fixed on 'I' and 'mine', he acts in a perverse way. Space, wind, fire, water and earth are distinct from the *atman*. That being the case, who will take the body to be 'I'? The body is for enjoying objects of pleasure, homes, fields and the like. Since the *atman* is not the body, which wise person will have a sense of 'mine' in these? That apart, sons and grandsons are generated by the body. Since the *atman* is not the

---

[1126] Inferior *kshatriyas*.
[1127] Implying 'I' and 'mine'.

body, which learned person will have a sense of ownership in
these? A man undertakes every task for the enjoyment of the
body. However, a man is bound by these, and the subsequent
consequence is the adoption of another body. This is like a
house made out of clay that is plastered with mud and water.
The body is like that, made out of mud and water.[1128] All
objects of pleasure are based on the five elements. The body
is made out of the five elements. Since that is the case, why
does a man pursue objects of pleasure? Following the trail of
samsara, one has thousands of births. He proceeds, exhausted
by delusion. He does not waver, pursuing the dust of desire.
Warm water washes away the dust from grain. Like that, for
a traveler along the path of samsara, jnana pacifies delusion
and exhaustion. When delusion and exhaustion are pacified, a
man finds serenity within his own self. Everything else is great
bondage. Therefore, he desires supreme nirvana. The atman is
full of nirvana and is full of unblemished jnana. This misery and
ignorance are the nature of Prakriti, not of the atman. Water
has no link with fire. O king! However, when water is in a
vessel and placed above a fire, it boils and makes a sound. That
is its nature. In that way, associated with Prakriti, the atman is
tainted by ahamkara. Therefore, though it is without decay, it
serves the inferior dharma of nature. That is the reason I told
you about the seed of ignorance. To destroy hardships, there is
nothing other than yoga."'

'Khandiyka said, "O immensely fortunate one! O supreme
among those who know about yoga. Please tell me about yoga.
Among the descendants of Nimi, you are the one who knows
the meaning of the texts of yoga."'

'Keshidhvaja replied, "O Khandikya! Listen to my words
about the nature of yoga. When a sage achieves this, he dissolves
into the brahman and does not return again. For humans, the

[1128] Alluding to food and drink.

mind is a cause of both bondage and liberation. Attached to material objects, it is the cause for bondage. Not attached to material objects, the mind leads to liberation. A sage who possesses *vijnana* about the *atman* withdraws from material objects. Thinking about emancipation, he immerses himself in the supreme lord, the *brahman*. Sense about the *atman* conveys the sage to meditating about the *brahman*. This is like a magnet attracting a lump of iron. One is then incapable of being attracted towards perverse tasks. Having made efforts to control oneself, the specific nature of the mind is such that it seeks union with the *brahman*. This is said to be *yoga*. Such is the great and specific attribute of those who follow this *dharma*. This is said to be the *yogi* who desires liberation and engages in *yoga*. At first, the *yogi* is spoken of as *yoga-yuj*, someone who has united himself through *yoga*. When he accomplishes *samadhi*, he attains the supreme *brahman*. If his mind does not suffer from inner taints, after several former births, he achieves emancipation. By using the fire of *yoga* to burn down the accumulated store of *karma*, in that birth itself, the *yogi* soon accomplishes *samadhi* and achieves emancipation. The *yogi* makes himself worthy by following *brahmacharya*, non-violence and truthfulness and avoiding theft and desire. He perfects himself through self-control, self-studying, purity, contentment and austerities and focuses his mind on the supreme *brahman*. These are respectively described as the five kinds of *yama* and the five kinds of *niyama*. These yield specific fruits that are desired, but for the sake of emancipation, one should not have desires. Observing these qualities, he should be seated in *bhadrasana*[1129] or any of the other postures. The practitioner must restrain himself and follow what has been described as *yama* and *niyama*. He must practice so as to bring the wind known as *prana* under his control. This is known as *pranayama*

[1129] Any posture fit for meditation.

and it can be with a *bija* or without a *bija*.[1130] The *prana* and *apana* breath are alternatively stopped, constituting two steps. There is a third step of suspending both.[1131] O supreme among *brahmanas*![1132] This is the gross form of *alambana*.[1133] Through practice, the yogi is said to seek *alambana* in Ananta. A person practicing yoga restrains his eyes and other sense organs from sound and the other objects of the senses. Devoted to *pratyahara*, he uses his mind to direct them. Through this, the fickle mind is fixed on the supreme. A *yogi* who practices *yoga* must certainly bring his senses under control. *Pranayama* is for controlling the breath of life and *pratyahara* is for controlling the senses. When both are controlled, he will obtain an auspicious refuge."'

'Khandikya said, "O immensely fortunate one! Please tell me about this excellent refuge for the mind, using which as a foundation, the roots of all taints and blemishes are destroyed."'

'Keshidhvaja replied, "O lord of the earth! The mind's refuge is the *brahman* and he has two kinds of forms, embodied and disembodied. Either can be *para* or *apara*.[1134] O lord of the earth! There are three kinds of conceptions in the universe. Hear about them. There is the appellation of Brahma and there is the attribute of *karma*. Both exist. It is the same conception of Brahma. When defined by *karma*, Brahma is *apara*. When not defined by *karma*, Brahma's conception is *para*. When both are thought of together, that

---

[1130] *Bija* is a mystic *akshara* from a *mantra*. When *yoga* has such an object of meditation, it is *sabija*. When meditation is on the *atman*, without any other object, it is *nirbija*.

[1131] *Rechaka*, *puraka* and *kumbhaka*.

[1132] Since this is being addressed to Khandikya, this is an inconsistency.

[1133] Literally, seeking support, interpreted as *japa*.

[1134] *Para* is *nirguna*, without attributes. *Apara* is *saguna*, with attributes. Both embodied and disembodied forms can be *saguna* or *nirguna*.

is a third kind of conception. Sanandana and the others had one particular conception of Brahma. However, *deva*s and others, mobile and immobile objects, based their conception of him on *karma*. Hiranyagarbha and the other conceptions of Brahma encompass both *karma* and its lack. Any conception is based on how much right to comprehend one possesses. Until all specific knowledge about *karma* is extinguished, men possess differential vision and perceive the universe as one and the supreme as another. When distinctions end, one experiences true knowledge. This is *jnana* about the *brahman*, and he cannot be described through words. This is described as Vishnu's supreme and excellent form. This is the *paramatman*. His own form can be seen in various modifications in the universe. O king! But a *yoga-yuj* is incapable of thinking about this. He thinks of Hari's gross form, which can be perceived in the universe—Hiranyagarbha, the illustrious Vasudeva, Prajapati, the Maruts, the Vasus, the Rudras, the Bhaskaras, the stars, the planets, *gandharva*s, *yaksha*s, all the others born as *deva*s, humans, animals, mountains, oceans, rivers, all the other beings, all the causes of beings, Pradhana and other descriptions, conscious and insentient, with one foot, bipeds and with many feet. O lord of the earth! All these are Hari's forms, with the three kinds of conceptions. Everything in the universe and every mobile and immobile object in the world is the supreme *brahman*'s own nature, pervaded by Vishnu's potency. Vishnu's potency can be *para* and when it is described as *kshetrajna*, it is *apara*. There is a third kind of potency, and it is characterized by ignorance and *karma*. O king! The potency of *kshetrajna* acts and goes everywhere. It constantly suffers from all the torments of *samsara*. O lord of the earth! When the potency known as *kshetrajna* withdraws, it is seen that all beings can cross over.[1135] For those without life, it exists

---

[1135] Beyond *samsara*.

in a small measure. For those with life, but immobile, a little
bit more. Reptiles possess more of this potency and birds even
more. Wild animals possess more of this potency and domestic
animals even more. Humans possess more of the supreme
being's potency than domestic animals and this gives them
the power. O king! Purusha's potency is seen to progressively
increase in *nagas*, *gandharvas*, *yakshas*, *devas* and Shakra. It
is more in Prajapati than in *devas* and more in Hiranyagarbha
than in Prajapati. O lord of the earth! All these innumerable
forms are his forms. They are all suffused with his potency, just
as space pervades everything. O king! All of them are based
on his energy. However, other than this modification of Hari
through his universal form, he has another great form too. O
lord of men! In his own pastimes, he makes all these potencies
act in *devas*, inferior species and men and makes them act. This
is for the welfare of the universe. *Karma* is not the motive. The
tasks of the immeasurable one pervade but they do not affect his
atman. O king! The one with the universal form possesses this
other form and a *yoga-yuj* should think of this, for the sake of
purifying himself and destroying all his sins. Aided by the wind,
the flames of a fire rise and burn down dry wood. Like that,
inside the heart, Vishnu destroys all sins for *yogis*. Therefore,
one must fix one's mind on the reservoir of all potencies. One
should understand that this state is pure *dharana*. This is an
auspicious state for the mind, fixing one's *atman* on the one
who goes everywhere. O king! In this way, beyond the three
kinds of thoughts,[1136] the *yogi* proceeds towards emancipation.
O tiger among men! Because of their *karma*, there are others
whose minds are fixed on all that is impure, *devas* and the
others, and this makes them act. Without any desire, when
one seeks refuge in the embodied form of the illustrious one in

---

[1136] The three kinds of hardships, *adhidaivika* and the others, or
the three periods of time, the past, the present and the future.

every way, this is said to be *dharana*, since the mind holds it.[1137]
O lord of men! Hari's form cannot be seen or thought of. But
there is an embodied form the mind can think of and use for
dharana. Hear about it. His face is pleasant. His beautiful eyes
are like the petals of lotuses. His cheeks are excellent, and his
forehead is broad and resplendent. His eyes are symmetric and
are adorned with beautiful earrings. His neck is like a conch
shell, and he wears the *shrivatsa* mark on his broad chest.
There are three lines on his stomach and the navel is deep.
Vishnu possesses eight, or four, long arms. His thighs and legs
are firm, and his feet are well-formed, resembling excellent
lotuses. He[1138] should think of this form, full of the *brahman*,
adorned in sparkling and yellow garments. He is adorned with
a diadem, armlets and bracelets. He holds the Sharnga bow,
conch shell, mace, sword, *chakra* and a string of *aksha* beads.[1139]
Adorned with jewels, a hand is in the *varada mudra*.[1140] When
the *yogi*'s mind is completely immersed in this contemplation,
he approaches *samadhi*. O king! This *dharana* becomes fixed,
whether the *yogi* is walking, standing or performing whatever
task he wills. When this contemplation does not go away, the
yogi can think of himself as having become a *siddha*. A learned
person can then contemplate on the illustrious one's serene
form, without the conch shell, mace, *chakra* and Sharnga
bow, holding only the string of *aksha* beads. As this *dharana*
becomes firmer, he can remember the conception without
ornaments like the diadem, armlets and bracelets. Thereafter,
a learned person's mind can contemplate only a single form

[1137] The root word for *dharana* is *dhri*, to hold.

[1138] The *yogi*.

[1139] The seed of a plant, used for making rosaries.

[1140] A *mudra* is a symbolic and mystical positioning of the fingers
and the thumb. The *varada mudra* is a *mudra* of bestowing boons and
one of the hands is in this *mudra*, the palm pointing downwards.

of the divinity and meditate only on that form. O king! That
meditation on a single form, without desiring to think of
anything else, is accomplished through six steps.[1141] The next
step is *dhyana*. When *dhyana* has been perfected such that one
can perceive his nature without any other conception being
required, that is spoken of as *samadhi*. O lord of the earth!
He then achieves *vijnana* and obtains the supreme *brahman*.
All other conceptions dwindle away, and he comprehends the
atman. *Jnana* is the instrument and *kshetrajna* is the one who
uses this instrument. When the objective is emancipation, one
withdraws from all other tasks that need to be accomplished.
He imbibes the sentiment that there is no difference between
the *paramatman* and the *jivatman*. All such differentiation
is because of the lack of *jnana*. When one accomplishes the
end objective of destroying all sense of differentiation, which
virtuous person will distinguish between the *jivatman* and the
brahman? O Khandikya! You asked me about *yoga*, and I have
explained it to you, briefly and in detail. What else can I do for
you?"

'Khandikya replied, "Having explained the virtuous nature
of *yoga*, you have done everything for me. Because of your
instructions, all the blemishes in my mind have been destroyed. I
have spoken about 'mine' and it does not exist. O Indra among
men! Those who know what is to be known can but state it in any
other way. Conduct based on notions of 'I' and 'mine' are based
on ignorance. The supreme truth cannot be perceived through
conversation or words. You have done everything beneficial for
me. Therefore, leave. O Keshidhvaja! You have told me about
union with the undecaying one, the source of emancipation."'

Shri Parashara continued, 'King Keshidhvaja was
appropriately worshipped by Khandikya, and he honoured

[1141] *Yama* (restraint), *niyama* (rituals), *asana* (posture), *pranayama*
(breathing), *pratyahara* (withdrawal) and *dharana* (retention).

him back. O *brahmana*! He returned to his own city. Khandikya instated his own son as the king. To accomplish *yoga*, he left for the forest and immersed his mind in Govinda. His mind was single-mindedly fixed on the one known as Vishnu and he possessed the qualities, *yama* and the others. Thus purified, the king was absorbed into the *brahman*. In pursuit of emancipation, Keshidhvaja also turned away from his own tasks. Though he engaged with material objects and *karma*, he was not attached to them. Objects of pleasure do not bring benefit. Therefore, he focuses on destroying his sins and blemishes. O *brahmana*! When all his accumulated fruits were exhausted, he obtained success.'

Chapter 6(8) (Conclusion of the Dialogue)

Shri Parashara said, 'I have thus properly spoke to you about the third kind of withdrawal. This is *atyantika pralaya* when one is emancipated and merges into the eternal *brahman*. I have spoken to you about *sarga*, *pratisarga*, *vamsha*, *manvantara* and *vamshanucharita* and about Vishnu Purana, which destroys every kind of sin. It is special among all the sacred texts and achieves the *purushartha*s. O Maitreya! I have narrated this imperishable account to you, and you have faithfully heard it. Is there anything else you want me to tell you? Please tell me.'

Maitreya replied, 'O illustrious one! O sage! You have told me everything that I asked you about. I have faithfully heard it and there is nothing else for me to ask. All my doubts have been dispelled and my mind has been cleansed of blemishes. Through your favours, I have learnt about creation, preservation and destruction. I have learnt about the three types of accumulation of potencies and the three kinds of *gurus*. I have learnt everything about the three kinds of conceptions. O *brahmana!* Through your favours, I have got to know about this and about everything else. There is no difference between Vishnu and this entire universe. O great sage! Through your favours, I have accomplished my objective and all my doubts have been dispelled. You have told me about the *dharma* of the *varna*s and I have got to know everything about *dharma*. I obtained knowledge about *pravritti*, *nivritti* and every kind of *karma*. O supreme among *brahmana*s! Please show me your favours. There is nothing else for me to ask. O *guru*! Please pardon me if this recital has caused you any exhaustion. In particular, the virtuous draw no distinction between a son and a disciple.'

Shri Parashara said, 'The Purana I have narrated is in conformity with the *Veda*s. If one hears it, all taints and the accumulation of sins are destroyed. I have told you everything about *sarga*, *pratisarga*, *vamsha*, *manvantara* and *vamshanucharita*. *Deva*s, *daitya*s, *gandharva*s, *uraga*s, *rakshasa*s, *yaksha*s, *vidyadhara*s, *siddha*s and *apsara*s are spoken about here. Sages, cleansed in their souls and full of austerities, are described. The four *varna*s and the conduct of special men are narrated. There is a description of sacred regions on earth, sacred rivers and oceans, mountains and the extremely sacred account of the intelligent. There is a description of the *dharma* for the *varna*s and the entire *dharma* of the *Veda*s and the sacred texts. If one remembers this, one is instantly cleansed of all sins. The undecaying one is the cause behind the creation, preservation and destruction of the universe. The illustrious Hari is spoken about. He is in all beings and is in the *atman*s of all beings. Even if a man involuntarily chants his name, he is instantly freed from all sins. When his excellent name is faithfully chanted, all sins run away, like deer at the sight of a lion. O Maitreya! It purifies and cleanses all sins. Men suffer from the fierce blemishes of *kali yuga* and the afflictions of *naraka*. Even if his name is remembered only once, these are destroyed. O *brahmana*! O supreme among *brahmana*s! He is everything. He knows everything. Though he is without a form, his own form is in everything—Hiranyagarbha, Indra of the *deva*s, Rudras, Adityas, Ashvins, Agnis, Vasus, Sadhyas, Vishvadevas, *asura*s, *yaksha*s, *rakshasa*s, *uraga*s, *siddha*s, *daitya*s, *gandharva*s, *danava*s, *apsara*s, stars, *nakshatra*s, all the planets, *saptarshi*s, lords, lords of the lords, *brahmana*s and other humans, wild animals, domestic animals, reptiles, birds, *palasha* and other large trees, forests, fires, oceans, rivers, nether regions, fires of the gods, sound and everything else in *brahmanda*. He pervades everything, from Meru to the smallest atom. The illustrious Vishnu, destroyer of sins, has been described here. O supreme among sages! From hearing this, a man obtains the fruits obtained through the *avabhritha* bath after a horse sacrifice, or fasting and bathing in Prayaga, Pushkara, Kurukshetra and the ocean. Hearing this, a man obtains all those fruits. O *brahmana*! A man obtains fruits by offering excellent oblations at *agnihotra* sacrifices over several years. Those great fruits are obtained by listening to this only once. A man obtains fruits by bathing in the waters of Yamuna on *dvadashi* in *shukla paksha* in the month of Jyeshtha and seeing Hari in Mathura. O *brahmana rishi*! If one fixes one's mind on Keshava and properly meditates on this Purana and hears it, all those fruits are obtained. O supreme among sages! If a man controls himself, fasts and bathes in the waters of the Yamuna on *dvadashi* in *shukla paksha* in the month of Jyeshtha when Mula *nakshatra* is in the ascendant, and if he properly worships Achyuta in Mathura, he obtains the fruits of a completed horse sacrifice. Beholding the prosperity of their own descendant, the fathers and the grandfathers then exclaim, "Indeed, those in our lineage who bathe in the waters of Kalindi and fasting, worship Govinda in Mathura, in *shukla paksha* in the month of Jyeshtha when Mula *nakshatra* is in the ascendant, they obtain great prosperity and save everyone born in our lineage. Those who properly worship Janardana in *shukla paksha* in the month of Jyeshtha when Mula *nakshatra* is in the ascendant are fortunate in our lineage. They offer us *pinda* in Yamuna." At that time, if a person controls himself and worships Krishna properly, offering *pinda* to the ancestors in the waters of the Yamuna, he obtains auspicious fruits and makes his ancestors cross over. However, those auspicious fruits are also obtained if one hears a chapter of this Purana. For those who are sacred of *samsara*, hearing this is an excellent means of salvation. This is extremely sacred. Among everything that should be heard, this should be heard the most. For men, it dispels nightmares and destroys everything that is wicked. It is most auspicious amongst everything that is auspicious. It bestows sons and wealth. In ancient times, the *rishi* spoke about this to the one who orginated from the lotus.[1142] Brahma narrated it to Ribhu, Ribhu narrated it to Priyavrata and Priyavrata narrated it to Bhaguri. Bhaguri narrated it to Tambhamitra, who narrated it to Dadhichi. Dadhichi narrated it to Sarasvata and Sarasvata narrated it to Bhrigu. Bhrigu narrated it to Purukutsa and Purukutsa narrated it to Narmada. Narmada narrated it to the *naga*s Dhritarashtra and Apurana. O *brahmana*! They repeated it to Vasuki, the king of the *naga*s. Vasuki narrated it to Vatsa and Vatsa to Ashvatara. Ashvatara narrated it to Kambala and Kambala narrated it to his son, Elapatra. When the sage Vedashira went to Patala, he obtained it and gave all of it to Pramati. Pramati narrated it to the intelligent Jatukarna. Jatukarna narrated it to others who were auspicious in deeds. Through the boon bestowed by Pulastya, I obtained this *smriti* text. O Maitreya! I have accurately narrated it to you. At the end of *kali yuga*, you will narrate it to Shinika and others. This is extremely secret and destroys the sins of *kali yuga*. If a man

---

[1142] The *rishi* Narayana communicated it to Brahma.

listens to it faithfully, he is cleansed of all sins. There are fruits obtained from bathing in all the *tirtha*s and praising all the immortals. There are also extremely rare and auspicious fruits obtained from donating a *kapila* cow. If a man listens to this every day, he obtains all those fruits. There is no doubt that all these fruits are obtained by listening to the ten chapters.[1143] Achyuta is everything. He pervades everything. He is the refuge and support of the entire universe. He is *jnana*. He is everything there is to be known. He is without a beginning and without an end. If a man fixes his mind and listens to everything that is said about him here, there is no doubt that he obtains benefit greater than that obtained by all the immortals. The illustrious one is the *guru* of all mobile and immobile objects. He is without a beginning, a middle and an end. He is the lord of the creation, preservation and destruction of the entire universe. He is *jnana* about the *brahman*, and he is described here. He is everything. He is the sacred and unblemished Purusha. Therefore, if a person reads it, or listens to it, he obtains the fruits obtained from performing a completed horse sacrifice. He obtains success by obtaining Hari, the lord of the three worlds. A person whose mind is fixed on him does not go to *naraka* or to heaven. These are impediments to the mind. If the mind is submerged on him, Brahma's world is insignificant. When a man's mind is fixed on him and on emancipation, why should the unblemished one bestow anything that causes an impurity in the intelligence? If a person chants Achyuta's name, it is not extraordinary that he should achieve this *pralaya*. Those who know about sacrifices worship the lord of sacrifices through the *karma* of sacrifices. Those who have *jnana* meditate on him, greater than the supreme, the one who is full of the *brahman*. A person who thinks about him does not die. Nor is he born. He does not experience increase or decrease. He does

---

[1143] This is an obvious inconsistency.

not suffer. Therefore, shouldn't the virtuous serve Hari? In the form of the ancestors, he receives *kavya*. In the form of the gods, the lord enjoys the oblations of *havya*. The illustrious one, without a beginning and without an end, is addressed through "*svaha*" and "*svadha*". He is the abode of all Brahma's powers. Those who try to measure cannot measure him. When Hari enters through the earts, his powers destroy all sins. He has no end. He has no origin. He has no increase. He is devoid of any consequences. He is an entity who possesses no decay or transformation. I prostrate myself before Purushottama, the supreme lord of everything. He is pure. But because of the *guna*s, he appears in many impure forms and differences are seen in his embodied forms. He is the truth behind every kind of *jnana*. He is the one who creates all the powers. I prostrate myself before Purusha, who is always without any decay. He is absolute but encompasses *jnana*, *pravritti* and *niyama*. He is the being who is accomplished in bestowing objects of pleasure. He assumes the three *guna*s. He does not experience any modification but is the cause behind the origin of the world. I worship the one who is his own form. I worship the one who is always without old age. He pervades space, wind, fire, earth and water. He is the one who bestows enjoyment of sound and the other objects of the senses. He is the Purusha, who assumes the form of every instrument and agent. He manifests himself as gross and subtle. I prostrate myself before him. In this way, the one without origin has diverse forms. He is beyond Prakriti. He is the eternal *paramatman*. Hari is without birth and without old age and the like. May the illustrious one instruct all men about achieving success.'

This ends Part VI.

This concludes the Vishnu Purana.